Microsoft® Office 365™
WORD 2016

INTERMEDIATE

Misty E. Vermaat

CENGAGE
Learning®

CENGAGE
Learning®

Microsoft Word 2016: Intermediate
Misty E. Vermaat

SVP, GM Skills & Global Product Management: Dawn Gerrain

Product Director: Kathleen McMahon

Senior Product Team Manager: Lauren Murphy

Product Team Manager: Andrea Topping

Senior Director, Development: Marah Bellegarde

Product Development Manager: Leigh Hefferon

Managing Content Developer: Emma F. Newsom

Developmental Editor: Lyn Markowicz

Product Assistant: Erica Chapman

Manuscript Quality Assurance:
Jeffrey Schwartz, John Freitas,
Serge Palladino, Susan Pedicini,
Danielle Shaw

Senior Production Director: Wendy Troeger

Production Director: Patty Stephan

Senior Content Project Manager: Matthew Hutchinson

Manufacturing Planner: Julio Esperas

Designer: Diana Graham

Text Design: Joel Sadagursky

Cover Template Designer: Diana Graham

Cover image(s): Piotr Zajc/Shutterstock.com; Mrs. Opossum/Shutterstock.com

Compositor: Lumina Datamatics

Vice President, Marketing: Brian Joyner

Marketing Director: Michele McTighe

Marketing Manager: Stephanie Albracht

For product information and technology assistance, contact us at
Cengage Learning Customer & Sales Support, 1-800-354-9706

For permission to use material from this text or product, submit all requests online at **www.cengage.com/permissions.**
Further permissions questions can be e-mailed to **permissionrequest@cengage.com**

Library of Congress Control Number: 2016933288

ISBN: 978-1-305-87100-7

Cengage Learning
20 Channel Center Street
Boston, MA 02210
USA

Cengage Learning is a leading provider of customized learning solutions with employees residing in nearly 40 different countries and sales in more than 125 countries around the world. Find your local representative at **www.cengage.com.**

Cengage Learning products are represented in Canada by Nelson Education, Ltd.

To learn more about Cengage Learning, visit **www.cengage.com**
Purchase any of our products at your local college store or at our preferred online store **www.cengagebrain.com**

Printed in the United States of America
Print Number: 02   Print Year: 2017

Microsoft® Office 365™ WORD 2016

INTERMEDIATE

Contents

Productivity Apps for School and Work
Introduction to OneNote 2016 — PA 2
Introduction to Sway — PA 6
Introduction to Office Mix — PA 10
Introduction to Microsoft Edge — PA 14

Microsoft **Office 2016 and Windows 10**

Office 2016 and Windows 10: Essential Concepts and Skills

Objectives — **OFF 1**
Roadmap — OFF 1
Introduction to the Windows 10 Operating System — **OFF 2**
Using a Touch Screen and a Mouse — OFF 3
Scrolling — OFF 4
Keyboard Shortcuts — OFF 5
Starting Windows — OFF 5
To Sign In to an Account — OFF 6
The Windows Desktop — OFF 7
Introduction to Microsoft Office 2016 — **OFF 7**
Microsoft Office 2016 Apps — OFF 7
Microsoft Office 2016 Suites — OFF 8
Running and Using an App — **OFF 9**
Word — OFF 9
To Run an App Using the Start Menu and
 Create a Blank Document — OFF 9
To Maximize a Window — OFF 11
Word Document Window, Ribbon, and
 Elements Common to Office Apps — OFF 12
To Display a Different Tab on the Ribbon — OFF 16
To Collapse and Expand the Ribbon
 and Use Full Screen Mode — OFF 17
To Use a Shortcut Menu to Relocate
 the Quick Access Toolbar — OFF 19
To Customize the Quick Access Toolbar — OFF 20
To Enter Text in a Document — OFF 21
Document Properties — **OFF 22**
To Change Document Properties — OFF 22
Printing, Saving, and Organizing Files — **OFF 23**
Printing a Document — OFF 23
To Print a Document — OFF 23
Organizing Files and Folders — OFF 25

To Create a Folder — OFF 26
Folder Windows — OFF 27
To Create a Folder within a Folder — OFF 28
To Expand a Folder, Scroll through
 Folder Contents, and Collapse a Folder — OFF 28
To Switch from One App to Another — OFF 29
To Save a File in a Folder — OFF 30
Navigating in Dialog Boxes — OFF 33
To Minimize and Restore a Window — OFF 33
To Save a File on OneDrive — OFF 34
To Sign Out of a Microsoft Account — OFF 36
Screen Resolution — **OFF 37**
To Change the Screen Resolution — OFF 38
To Exit an App with One Document Open — OFF 40
To Copy a Folder to OneDrive — OFF 40
To Unlink a OneDrive Account — OFF 42
Additional Common Features of Office Apps — **OFF 44**
To Run an App Using the Search Box — OFF 44
To Open an Existing File — OFF 45
To Create a New Document
 from the Backstage View — OFF 45
To Enter Text in a Document — OFF 47
To Save a File in a Folder — OFF 47
To Close a File Using the Backstage View — OFF 47
To Open a Recent File Using the Backstage View — OFF 48
To Create a New Blank Document
 from File Explorer — OFF 48
To Run an App from File Explorer
 and Open a File — OFF 49
To Enter Text in a Document — OFF 50
To Save an Existing Office File
 with the Same File Name — OFF 50
To Save a File with a New File Name — OFF 50
To Exit an Office App — OFF 51
Renaming, Moving, and Deleting Files — **OFF 51**
To Rename a File — OFF 51
To Move a File — OFF 52
To Delete a File — OFF 53
Microsoft Office and Windows Help — **OFF 53**
To Open the Help Window in an Office App — OFF 54
Moving and Resizing Windows — OFF 54
To Move a Window by Dragging — OFF 54
To Resize a Window by Dragging — OFF 55

Using Office Help   OFF 56
To Obtain Help Using the Search Text Box   OFF 56
Obtaining Help while Working in an Office App   OFF 57
To Obtain Help Using the Tell Me Box   OFF 58
Using the Windows Search Box   OFF 59
To Use the Windows Search Box   OFF 59
Summary   **OFF 59**
Apply Your Knowledge   **OFF 61**
Extend Your Knowledge   **OFF 61**
Expand Your World   **OFF 62**
In the Labs   **OFF 63**

Microsoft **Office 365 & Word 2016**

MODULE ONE

Creating, Formatting, and Editing a Word Document with a Picture

Objectives   **WD 1**
Introduction   **WD 1**
Project — Flyer with a Picture   **WD 1**
To Run Word and Specify Settings   WD 3
Entering Text   **WD 3**
To Type Text   WD 4
To Display Formatting Marks   WD 5
To Insert a Blank Line   WD 5
To Zoom Page Width   WD 6
Wordwrap   WD 7
To Wordwrap Text as You Type   WD 7
Spelling and Grammar Check   WD 8
To Check Spelling and Grammar as You Type   WD 8
To Enter More Text   WD 9
Navigating a Document   WD 10
Formatting Paragraphs and Characters   **WD 11**
Font, Font Sizes, and Themes   WD 12
To Center a Paragraph   WD 13
To Center Another Paragraph   WD 13
Formatting Single versus Multiple Paragraphs
    and Characters   WD 14
To Select a Line   WD 14
To Change the Font Size of Selected Text   WD 15
To Change the Font of Selected Text   WD 16
To Change the Case of Selected Text   WD 17
To Apply a Text Effect to Selected Text   WD 18
To Shade a Paragraph   WD 19
To Select Multiple Lines   WD 20
To Change the Font Size of Selected Text   WD 20
To Bullet a List of Paragraphs   WD 21
To Undo and Redo an Action   WD 22
To Italicize Text   WD 23
To Color Text   WD 24
To Use the Mini Toolbar to Format Text   WD 25
To Select a Group of Words   WD 26
To Underline Text   WD 27
To Bold Text   WD 27
To Zoom One Page   WD 28
To Change Theme Colors   WD 29
To Zoom Page Width   WD 30
Selecting Text   WD 30
**Inserting and Formatting a Picture in a Word
    Document**   **WD 31**
To Center Another Paragraph   WD 31

To Insert a Picture   WD 31
To Zoom the Document   WD 33
To Resize a Graphic   WD 34
To Zoom 100%   WD 35
To Apply a Picture Style   WD 36
To Apply Picture Effects   WD 37
Enhancing the Page   **WD 38**
To Add a Page Border   WD 39
To Zoom One Page   WD 40
To Change Spacing before and after Paragraphs   WD 40
To Center Page Contents Vertically   WD 41
To Change Document Properties   WD 42
To Save the Document and Exit Word   WD 42
Correcting Errors and Revising a Document   **WD 42**
Types of Changes Made to Documents   WD 43
To Run Word, Open a Document, and Specify
    Settings   WD 43
To Insert Text in an Existing Document   WD 43
To Delete Text   WD 44
To Move Text   WD 44
To Save and Print the Document   WD 45
To Switch to Read Mode   WD 46
To Switch to Print Layout View   WD 46
Summary   **WD 47**
Apply Your Knowledge   **WD 48**
Extend Your Knowledge   **WD 50**
Expand Your World   **WD 51**
In the Labs   **WD 52**

MODULE TWO

Creating a Research Paper with References and Sources

Objectives   **WD 57**
Introduction   **WD 57**
Project — Research Paper   **WD 57**
MLA Documentation Style   WD 58
Changing Document Settings   **WD 60**
To Run Word and Specify Settings   WD 60
Styles   WD 60
To Modify a Style   WD 61
Adjusting Line and Paragraph Spacing   WD 62
To Change Line Spacing   WD 62
To Remove Space after a Paragraph   WD 63
To Update a Style to Match a Selection   WD 64
Creating a Header   **WD 64**
To Switch to the Header   WD 65
To Right-Align a Paragraph   WD 66
To Enter Text   WD 66
To Insert a Page Number   WD 66
To Close the Header   WD 68
Typing the Research Paper Text   **WD 68**
To Enter Name and Course Information   WD 69
To Click and Type   WD 70
Keyboard Shortcuts   WD 71
To Format Text Using a Keyboard Shortcut   WD 71
To Display the Rulers   WD 72
To First-Line Indent Paragraphs   WD 72
To AutoCorrect as You Type   WD 74
To Use the AutoCorrect Options Button   WD 75
To Create an AutoCorrect Entry   WD 75
The AutoCorrect Dialog Box   WD 77
To Enter More Text   WD 77

Citations WD 78
To Change the Bibliography Style WD 78
To Insert a Citation and Create Its Source WD 79
To Enter More Text WD 81
Footnotes WD 82
To Insert a Footnote Reference Mark WD 82
To Enter Footnote Text WD 83
To Insert a Citation Placeholder WD 83
Footnote Text Style WD 84
To Modify a Style Using a Shortcut Menu WD 84
To Edit a Source WD 86
To Edit a Citation WD 88
Working with Footnotes and Endnotes WD 89
To Enter More Text WD 90
To Count Words WD 90
Automatic Page Breaks WD 91
To Enter More Text and Insert a Citation
Placeholder WD 91
To Hide and Show White Space WD 92
To Edit a Source WD 93
To Enter More Text WD 94
Creating an Alphabetical Works Cited Page **WD 95**
To Page Break Manually WD 95
To Apply a Style WD 96
To Center Text WD 96
To Create a Bibliographical List WD 96
To Format Paragraphs with a Hanging Indent WD 98
Proofreading and Revising the Research Paper **WD 98**
To Modify a Source WD 99
To Update a Field WD 99
To Convert a Field to Regular Text WD 100
To Go to a Page WD 101
Copying, Cutting, and Pasting WD 101
To Copy and Paste WD 102
To Display the Paste Options Menu WD 103
To Find Text WD 103
To Replace Text WD 104
Find and Replace Dialog Box WD 105
To Find and Insert a Synonym WD 105
To Check Spelling and Grammar at Once WD 106
The Main and Custom Dictionaries WD 107
To Look Up Information WD 108
To Zoom Multiple Pages WD 109
To Change Read Mode Color WD 110
To Save and Print the Document and Exit Word WD 111
Summary **WD 111**
Apply Your Knowledge **WD 112**
Extend Your Knowledge **WD 113**
Expand Your World **WD 115**
In the Labs **WD 116**

MODULE THREE
Creating a Business Letter with a Letterhead and Table
Objectives **WD 121**
Introduction **WD 121**
**Project — Business Letter with a Letterhead
and Table** **WD 121**
To Run Word and Change Word Settings WD 123
To Change Margin Settings WD 123

Creating a Letterhead **WD 124**
To Insert a Shape WD 125
Floating versus Inline Objects WD 127
To Change an Object's Position WD 127
To Change an Object's Text Wrapping WD 128
To Apply a Shape Style WD 129
To Add Text to a Shape WD 129
To Use the 'Increase Font Size' Button WD 130
To Bold Selected Text WD 131
To Change the Document Theme WD 131
To Insert an Online Picture WD 131
To Resize a Graphic to a Percent
of the Original Size WD 133
To Change the Color of a Graphic WD 134
To Set a Transparent Color in a Graphic WD 135
To Adjust the Brightness and
Contrast of a Graphic WD 136
To Change the Border Color on a Graphic WD 137
To Change an Object's Text Wrapping WD 137
To Move a Graphic WD 138
To Copy a Graphic WD 138
To Use Paste Options WD 139
To Move a Graphic WD 139
To Flip a Graphic WD 140
To Format and Enter Text WD 140
To Insert a Symbol from the Symbol Dialog Box WD 141
To Insert a Symbol from the Insert a Symbol
Gallery WD 142
To Enter Text WD 143
To Bottom Border a Paragraph WD 143
To Clear Formatting WD 144
AutoFormat As You Type WD 145
To Convert a Hyperlink to Regular Text WD 146
Creating a Business Letter **WD 147**
To Save a Document with a New File Name WD 147
To Apply a Style WD 147
Using Tab Stops to Align Text WD 149
To Display the Ruler WD 149
To Set Custom Tab Stops WD 149
To Insert the Current Date in a Document WD 151
To Enter the Inside Address and Salutation WD 152
To Create a Building Block WD 152
To Modify a Building Block WD 153
To Insert a Building Block WD 154
Building Blocks versus AutoCorrect WD 155
To Insert a Nonbreaking Space WD 155
To Enter Text WD 156
Tables WD 157
To Insert an Empty Table WD 157
To Enter Data in a Table WD 158
To Enter More Data in a Table WD 159
To Apply a Table Style WD 160
To Resize Table Columns to Fit Table Contents WD 161
To Select a Column WD 162
Selecting Table Contents WD 163
To Align Data in Cells WD 163
To Center a Table WD 164
To Insert a Row in a Table WD 165
To Insert a Column in a Table WD 167
To Merge Cells WD 167
To Split Table Cells WD 168

To Split a Table WD 168
To Change the Font of Text in a Table Row WD 168
Deleting Table Data WD 169
To Add More Text WD 169
To Bullet a List as You Type WD 169
To Enter More Text and then Save and Print
   the Letter WD 171
Addressing and Printing Envelopes
   and Mailing Labels **WD 171**
To Address and Print an Envelope WD 171
Envelopes and Labels WD 172
Summary **WD 173**
Apply Your Knowledge **WD 174**
Extend Your Knowledge **WD 175**
Expand Your World **WD 177**
In the Labs **WD 178**

MODULE FOUR

Creating a Document with a Title Page, Lists, Tables, and a Watermark

Objectives **WD 185**
Introduction **WD 185**
Project — Sales Proposal **WD 186**
To Run Word and Change Word Settings WD 186
To Change Theme Colors WD 188
Creating a Title Page **WD 188**
To Format Characters WD 188
To Border a Paragraph WD 189
To Shade a Paragraph and Change Font Color WD 190
To Border Another Paragraph WD 191
To Change Spacing after a Paragraph WD 192
To Change Left and Right Paragraph Indent WD 192
To Clear Formatting WD 193
SmartArt Graphics WD 194
To Insert a SmartArt Graphic WD 195
To Delete Shapes from a SmartArt Graphic WD 196
To Add Text to Shapes in a SmartArt Graphic WD 197
To Add Shapes to a SmartArt Graphic WD 197
To Change Colors of a SmartArt Graphic WD 198
To Apply a SmartArt Style WD 199
To Modify Character Spacing and Format
   Characters Using the Font Dialog Box WD 200
To Zoom One Page, Change Spacing before
   and after a Paragraph, and Set
   Zoom Level WD 201
Inserting an Existing Document
   in an Open Document **WD 203**
To Save an Open Document with a New
   File Name WD 203
Sections WD 203
To Insert a Next Page Section Break WD 203
To Delete a Section Break WD 205
To Clear Formatting WD 205
To Insert a Word Document in
   an Open Document WD 205
To Print Specific Pages in a Document WD 207
To Delete a Page Break WD 209
To Apply Heading Styles WD 209
To Change Spacing before and after
   a Paragraph WD 210
To Update a Style to Match a Selection WD 210
Creating Headers and Footers **WD 211**

To Insert a Formatted Header Different
   from the Previous Header WD 211
To Insert a Formatted Footer WD 213
To Format Page Numbers to Start
   at a Different Number WD 213
Editing and Formatting Lists **WD 215**
To Sort Paragraphs WD 215
To Apply a Style Using the Mini Toolbar WD 216
To Use the Format Painter Button WD 216
To Customize Bullets in a List WD 217
To Create a Multilevel Numbered List WD 219
Editing and Formatting Tables **WD 222**
To Show Gridlines WD 222
To Change Column Width WD 223
To Change Row Height WD 224
To Align Data in Cells WD 225
To Shade a Table Cell WD 226
To Sort a Table WD 227
To Select Nonadjacent Items WD 228
To Shade Selected Cells WD 229
To Change Cell Spacing WD 229
To Change Column Width WD 230
To Page Break Manually WD 231
To Delete a Column WD 231
To Split Cells WD 232
To Move Cell Contents WD 233
To Move a Cell Boundary WD 233
To Distribute Columns WD 234
To Distribute Rows WD 235
To Insert a Column WD 235
To Merge Cells and Enter Text WD 235
To Display Text in a Cell Vertically WD 236
To Change Column Width WD 237
To Remove Cell Shading WD 237
To Hide Gridlines WD 238
To Border a Table WD 238
To Sum Columns in a Table WD 239
To Delete a Blank Paragraph WD 240
Creating a Watermark **WD 240**
To Zoom Multiple Pages WD 241
To Create a Watermark WD 241
To Change Theme Fonts WD 242
To Check Spelling, Save, Print, and Exit Word WD 243
Summary **WD 243**
Apply Your Knowledge **WD 244**
Extend Your Knowledge **WD 246**
Expand Your World **WD 247**
In the Labs **WD 248**

MODULE FIVE

Using a Template to Create a Resume and Sharing a Finished Document

Objectives **WD 257**
Introduction **WD 257**
Project — Resume **WD 257**
To Run Word and Change Word Settings WD 259
Using a Template to Create a Resume **WD 259**
To Create a New Document from
   an Online Template WD 259
To Open a Document Created from a
   Template WD 262
Resume Template WD 262

To Change Theme Colors WD 263
To Set Custom Margins WD 263
To View Gridlines WD 264
To Modify a Content Control and
    Replace Its Placeholder Text WD 265
To Replace Placeholder Text in More
    Content Controls WD 266
To Delete a Content Control WD 266
To Move Table Rows WD 267
To Modify Text in a Content Control WD 269
To Copy and Paste Items in a Table Cell WD 269
To Replace Placeholder Text in a
    Content Control WD 271
To Use AutoComplete WD 271
To Enter More Text WD 272
To Enter a Line Break WD 272
To Replace Placeholder Text in Content Controls WD 273
To Delete Text WD 273
To Replace Placeholder Text in Content
    Controls WD 274
To Indent a Paragraph WD 274
To Replace Placeholder Text in Content Controls WD 275
To Copy and Paste a Table Item WD 275
To Delete Rows and Edit Text WD 277
To Customize Theme Fonts WD 278
To Create a Style WD 279
To Apply a Style WD 280
To Reveal Formatting WD 280
To Modify a Style Using the Styles Dialog Box WD 281
Sharing a Document with Others **WD 282**
To Insert a Building Block Using
    the Building Blocks Organizer WD 282
To Edit Properties of Building Block Elements WD 284
To Save a Word Document as a PDF File and
    View the PDF File in Adobe Reader WD 285
To Open a PDF File from Word WD 287
To Save a Word Document as an XPS Document WD 288
To Run the Compatibility Checker WD 289
To Save a Word 2016 Document
    in an Earlier Word Format WD 289
File Types WD 291
To Save a Word 2016 Document as a
    Different File Type WD 292
To Invite Others to View or Edit a Document WD 293
To Get a Sharing Link WD 295
To Remove a Watermark WD 296
To Send a Document Using Email WD 296
To Use the Document Inspector WD 297
To Customize How Word Opens
    Email Attachments WD 297
Creating a Webpage from a Word Document **WD 298**
To Save a Word Document as a Webpage WD 298
To Set a Default Save Location WD 300
To Format Text as a Hyperlink WD 300
To Edit a Hyperlink WD 301
To Change the Style Set WD 301
To Test a Webpage in a Browser WD 302
Summary **WD 304**
Apply Your Knowledge **WD 305**
Extend Your Knowledge **WD 306**
Expand Your World **WD 307**
In the Labs **WD 308**

MODULE SIX
Generating Form Letters, Mailing
Labels, and a Directory
Objectives **WD 313**
Introduction **WD 313**
Project — Form Letters, Mailing Labels,
    and a Directory **WD 313**
To Run Word and Change Word Settings WD 314
Identifying the Main Document for Form Letters **WD 316**
To Identify the Main Document for the Form
    Letter Using the Mail Merge Task Pane WD 316
To Start a Mail Merge from an Existing
    Document WD 319
To Change the User Name and Initials WD 319
To Change Theme Colors WD 319
To Enter and Format the Sender Information WD 319
To Change a Picture and Format It WD 320
To Shade Cells and a Shape WD 321
To Change Margin Settings WD 322
To Specify the Position of a Graphic WD 323
To Create a Folder while Saving WD 324
Creating a Data Source **WD 325**
To Create a New Data Source WD 326
To Enter More Records WD 330
To Save a Data Source when Prompted by Word WD 331
Editing Records in the Data Source WD 332
Using an Existing Data Source WD 332
Composing the Main Document
    for the Form Letters **WD 333**
To Display the Next Step in the
    Mail Merge Wizard WD 333
To Enter the Date WD 334
Merge Fields WD 334
To Insert the AddressBlock Merge Field WD 335
To Edit the AddressBlock Merge Field WD 336
To View Merged Data in the Main Document WD 337
To Insert the GreetingLine Merge Field WD 337
To Edit the GreetingLine Merge Field WD 338
To View Merge Fields in the Main Document WD 338
To Begin Typing the Body of the Form Letter WD 338
To Insert a Merge Field in the Main Document WD 339
To Enter More Text and Merge Fields in the
    Main Document WD 340
IF Fields WD 340
To Insert an IF Field in the Main Document WD 341
To Enter the Remaining Text in the
    Main Document WD 342
To Highlight Merge Fields WD 343
To Display a Field Code WD 343
To Print Field Codes in the Main Document WD 344
Opening a Main Document WD 345
Merging the Data Source with the Main Document to
    Generate Form Letters **WD 345**
To Preview the Merged Letters
    Using the Mail Merge Task Pane WD 345
To Check for Errors WD 346
To Merge the Form Letters to a New Document
    Using the Mail Merge Task Pane WD 346
Correcting Merge Field Errors in
    Merged Documents WD 348
To Merge the Form Letters to a Printer WD 348
To Select Records to Merge WD 348

To Merge the Form Letters to a New Document
   Using the Ribbon | WD 350
To Remove a Merge Condition | WD 351
To Sort the Data Records in a Data Source | WD 352
To Find and Display Data | WD 353
Displaying Data Source Records in the
   Main Document | WD 353
Addressing Mailing Labels and Envelopes | **WD 353**
To Address and Print Mailing Labels Using
   an Existing Data Source | WD 354
To Address and Print Envelopes | WD 360
Merging All Data Records to a Directory | **WD 360**
To Change Page Orientation | WD 361
To Merge to a Directory | WD 362
To Merge to a New Document | WD 364
To Convert Text to a Table | WD 364
To Modify and Format a Table | WD 366
To Sort a Table by Multiple Columns | WD 366
Summary | **WD 367**
Apply Your Knowledge | **WD 368**
Extend Your Knowledge | **WD 370**
Expand Your World | **WD 371**
In the Labs | **WD 372**

MODULE SEVEN

Creating a Newsletter with a Pull-Quote and Graphics

Objectives | **WD 377**
Introduction | **WD 377**
Project — Newsletter | **WD 378**
Desktop Publishing Terminology | WD 378
To Run Word and Change Word Settings | WD 380
To Change Spacing above and below
   Paragraphs and Margin Settings | WD 380
To Change Theme Colors | WD 381
Creating the Nameplate | **WD 381**
To Insert WordArt | WD 381
To Resize WordArt | WD 382
To Change the Font and Font Size of
   WordArt Text | WD 383
To Change an Object's Text Wrapping | WD 383
To Change the WordArt Fill Color | WD 384
To Change the WordArt Shape | WD 387
To Set Custom Tab Stops
   Using the Tabs Dialog Box | WD 387
To Enter Text | WD 389
To Border One Edge of a Paragraph | WD 389
To Insert a Picture | WD 390
To Change the Color of a Graphic | WD 391
To Crop a Graphic | WD 392
To Change an Object's Text Wrapping and Size | WD 393
To Move a Graphic | WD 393
To Use the Selection Task Pane | WD 393
To Rotate a Graphic | WD 394
**Formatting the First Page of the
   Body of the Newsletter** | **WD 395**
To Clear Formatting | WD 395
To Format Text as a Heading Style, Modify a
   Heading Style, and Adjust Spacing
   before and after the Paragraph | WD 396
Columns | WD 396
To Insert a Continuous Section Break | WD 397

To Change the Number of Columns | WD 397
To Justify a Paragraph | WD 398
To Insert a File in a Column
   of the Newsletter | WD 399
To Increase Column Width and Place
   a Vertical Rule between Columns | WD 401
To Hyphenate a Document | WD 402
To Format a Character as a Drop Cap | WD 403
To Format the Drop Cap | WD 404
To Insert a Next Page Section Break | WD 404
To Enter Text | WD 405
To Insert a Column Break | WD 405
To Insert a File in a Column of the Newsletter | WD 406
Creating a Pull-Quote | **WD 406**
To Insert a Text Box | WD 407
To Split the Window | WD 408
To Arrange All Open Word Documents
   on the Screen | WD 409
To Copy and Paste Using Split Windows | WD 409
To Remove a Split Window | WD 410
To Format Text in the Text Box | WD 410
To Resize a Text Box | WD 410
To Apply a Shape Style to a Text Box | WD 411
To Position a Text Box | WD 411
Formatting the Second Page of the Newsletter | **WD 412**
To Change Column Formatting | WD 412
To Set Custom Tab Stops Using the Tabs
   Dialog Box | WD 414
To Format and Enter Text and Add a Border | WD 415
To Enter Text | WD 415
To Balance Columns | WD 416
Modifying and Formatting a SmartArt
   Graphic | WD 417
To Open a Document from Word | WD 417
To Change the Layout of a SmartArt Graphic | WD 417
To Add a Shape to a SmartArt Graphic | WD 418
To Add Text to a SmartArt Graphic
   through the Text Pane | WD 419
To Format SmartArt Graphic Text | WD 419
To Modify Theme Effects | WD 419
To Save Customized Themes | WD 419
Copying and Pasting | WD 420
To Copy a SmartArt Graphic Using
   the Office Clipboard | WD 420
To Switch from One Open Document
   to Another | WD 420
To Paste from the Office Clipboard | WD 421
To Format a Graphic as Floating | WD 422
To Format and Position the SmartArt Graphic | WD 422
To Layer the SmartArt Graphic in Front of Text | WD 422
To Edit Wrap Points in an Object | WD 423
Finishing the Newsletter | **WD 424**
To Adjust Headings, Turn Off Formatting
   Marks, and Zoom Multiple Pages | WD 424
To Add an Art Page Border | WD 425
To Save, Print, and Exit Word | WD 426
Summary | **WD 426**
Apply Your Knowledge | **WD 427**
Extend Your Knowledge | **WD 428**
Expand Your World | **WD 429**
In the Labs | **WD 429**

Index | **IND 1**

Productivity Apps for School and Work

Corinne Hoisington

OneNote
Sway
Office Mix
Edge

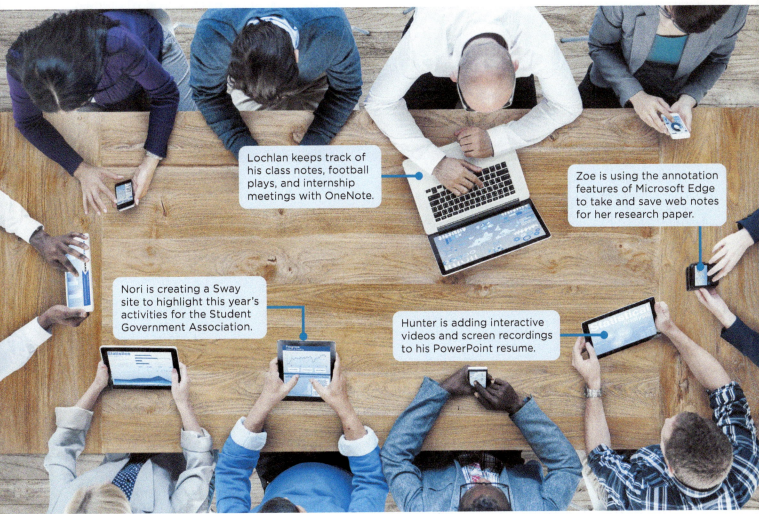

Lochlan keeps track of his class notes, football plays, and internship meetings with OneNote.

Zoe is using the annotation features of Microsoft Edge to take and save web notes for her research paper.

Nori is creating a Sway site to highlight this year's activities for the Student Government Association.

Hunter is adding interactive videos and screen recordings to his PowerPoint resume.

© Rawpixel/Shutterstock.com

Being computer literate no longer means mastery of only Word, Excel, PowerPoint, Outlook, and Access. To become technology power users, Hunter, Nori, Zoe, and Lochlan are exploring Microsoft OneNote, Sway, Mix, and Edge in Office 2016 and Windows 10.

In this Module

Introduction to OneNote 2016 2
Introduction to Sway 6
Introduction to Office Mix 10
Introduction to Microsoft Edge............. 14

Learn to use productivity apps!
Links to companion **Sways**, featuring **videos** with hands-on instructions, are located on www.cengagebrain.com.

Introduction to OneNote 2016

notebook | section tab | To Do tag | screen clipping | note | template | Microsoft OneNote Mobile app | sync | drawing canvas | inked handwriting | Ink to Text

Bottom Line
- OneNote is a note-taking app for your academic and professional life.
- Use OneNote to get organized by gathering your ideas, sketches, webpages, photos, videos, and notes in one place.

As you glance around any classroom, you invariably see paper notebooks and notepads on each desk. Because deciphering and sharing handwritten notes can be a challenge, Microsoft OneNote 2016 replaces physical notebooks, binders, and paper notes with a searchable, digital notebook. OneNote captures your ideas and schoolwork on any device so you can stay organized, share notes, and work with others on projects. Whether you are a student taking class notes as shown in **Figure 1** or an employee taking notes in company meetings, OneNote is the one place to keep notes for all of your projects.

Figure 1: OneNote 2016 notebook

Each **notebook** is divided into sections, also called **section tabs**, by subject or topic.

Use **To Do tags**, icons that help you keep track of your assignments and other tasks.

Type on a page to add a **note**, a small window that contains text or other types of information.

Personalize a page with a **template**, or stationery.

Write or draw directly on the page using drawing tools.

Pages can include pictures such as **screen clippings**, images from any part of a computer screen.

Attach files and enter equations so you have everything you need in one place.

Creating a OneNote Notebook

OneNote is divided into sections similar to those in a spiral-bound notebook. Each OneNote notebook contains sections, pages, and other notebooks. You can use One-Note for school, business, and personal projects. Store information for each type of project in different notebooks to keep your tasks separate, or use any other organization that suits you. OneNote is flexible enough to adapt to the way you want to work.

When you create a notebook, it contains a blank page with a plain white background by default, though you can use templates, or stationery, to apply designs in categories such as Academic, Business, Decorative, and Planners. Start typing or use the buttons on the Insert tab to insert notes, which are small resizable windows that can contain text, equations, tables, on-screen writing, images, audio and video recordings, to-do lists, file attachments, and file printouts. Add as many notes as you need to each page.

Learn to use OneNote!
Links to companion **Sways**, featuring **videos** with hands-on instructions, are located on www.cengagebrain.com.

Syncing a Notebook to the Cloud

OneNote saves your notes every time you make a change in a notebook. To make sure you can access your notebooks with a laptop, tablet, or smartphone wherever you are, OneNote uses cloud-based storage, such as OneDrive or SharePoint. **Microsoft OneNote Mobile app**, a lightweight version of OneNote 2016 shown in **Figure 2**, is available for free in the Windows Store, Google Play for Android devices, and the AppStore for iOS devices.

If you have a Microsoft account, OneNote saves your notes on OneDrive automatically for all your mobile devices and computers, which is called **syncing**. For example, you can use OneNote to take notes on your laptop during class, and then open OneNote on your phone to study later. To use a notebook stored on your computer with your OneNote Mobile app, move the notebook to OneDrive. You can quickly share notebook content with other people using OneDrive.

Figure 2: Microsoft OneNote Mobile app

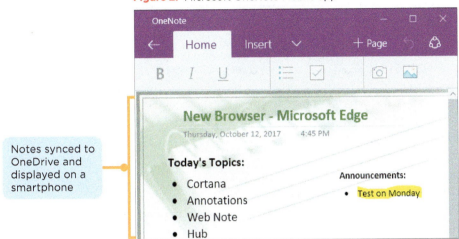

Notes synced to OneDrive and displayed on a smartphone

Taking Notes

Use OneNote pages to organize your notes by class and topic or lecture. Beyond simple typed notes, OneNote stores drawings, converts handwriting to searchable text and mathematical sketches to equations, and records audio and video.

OneNote includes drawing tools that let you sketch freehand drawings such as biological cell diagrams and financial supply-and-demand charts. As shown in **Figure 3**, the Draw tab on the ribbon provides these drawing tools along with shapes so you can insert diagrams and other illustrations to represent your ideas. When you draw on a page, OneNote creates a **drawing canvas**, which is a container for shapes and lines.

On the Job Now

OneNote is ideal for taking notes during meetings, whether you are recording minutes, documenting a discussion, sketching product diagrams, or listing follow-up items. Use a meeting template to add pages with content appropriate for meetings.

Figure 3: Tools on the Draw tab

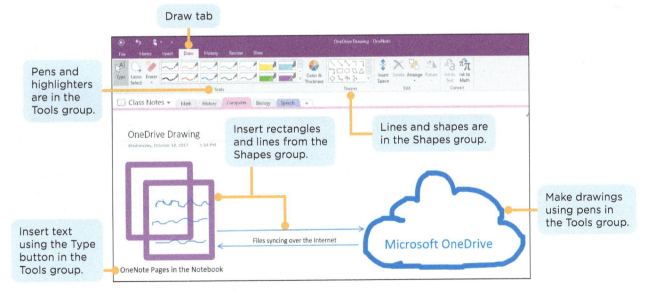

Draw tab

Pens and highlighters are in the Tools group.

Insert rectangles and lines from the Shapes group.

Lines and shapes are in the Shapes group.

Make drawings using pens in the Tools group.

Insert text using the Type button in the Tools group.

Converting Handwriting to Text

When you use a pen tool to write on a notebook page, the text you enter is called **inked handwriting**. OneNote can convert inked handwriting to typed text when you use the **Ink to Text** button in the Convert group on the Draw tab, as shown in **Figure 4**. After OneNote converts the handwriting to text, you can use the Search box to find terms in the converted text or any other note in your notebooks.

Figure 4: Converting handwriting to text

Ink to Text button

Writing inserted with a fingertip

Handwriting converted to searchable text

Recording a Lecture

If your computer or mobile device has a microphone or camera, OneNote can record the audio or video from a lecture or business meeting as shown in **Figure 5**. When you record a lecture (with your instructor's permission), you can follow along, take regular notes at your own pace, and review the video recording later. You can control the start, pause, and stop motions of the recording when you play back the recording of your notes.

Figure 5: Video inserted in a notebook

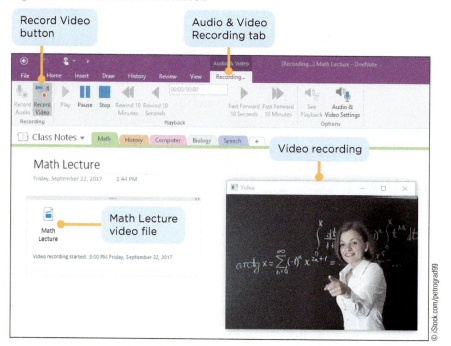

Record Video button

Audio & Video Recording tab

Video recording

Math Lecture video file

© iStock.com/petrograd99

Try This Now

Learn to use OneNote!
Links to companion **Sways**, featuring **videos** with hands-on instructions, are located on www.cengagebrain.com.

1: Taking Notes for a Week

As a student, you can get organized by using OneNote to take detailed notes in your classes. Perform the following tasks:

a. Create a new OneNote notebook on your Microsoft OneDrive account (the default location for new notebooks). Name the notebook with your first name followed by "Notes," as in **Caleb Notes**.

b. Create four section tabs, each with a different class name.

c. Take detailed notes in those classes for one week. Be sure to include notes, drawings, and other types of content.

d. Sync your notes with your OneDrive. Submit your assignment in the format specified by your instructor.

2: Using OneNote to Organize a Research Paper

You have a research paper due on the topic of three habits of successful students. Use OneNote to organize your research. Perform the following tasks:

a. Create a new OneNote notebook on your Microsoft OneDrive account. Name the notebook **Success Research**.

b. Create three section tabs with the following names:

- **Take Detailed Notes**
- **Be Respectful in Class**
- **Come to Class Prepared**

c. On the web, research the topics and find three sources for each section. Copy a sentence from each source and paste the sentence into the appropriate section. When you paste the sentence, OneNote inserts it in a note with a link to the source.

d. Sync your notes with your OneDrive. Submit your assignment in the format specified by your instructor.

3: Planning Your Career

Note: This activity requires a webcam or built-in video camera on any type of device.

Consider an occupation that interests you. Using OneNote, examine the responsibilities, education requirements, potential salary, and employment outlook of a specific career. Perform the following tasks:

a. Create a new OneNote notebook on your Microsoft OneDrive account. Name the notebook with your first name followed by a career title, such as **Kara - App Developer**.

b. Create four section tabs with the names **Responsibilities, Education Requirements, Median Salary**, and **Employment Outlook**.

c. Research the responsibilities of your career path. Using OneNote, record a short video (approximately 30 seconds) of yourself explaining the responsibilities of your career path. Place the video in the Responsibilities section.

d. On the web, research the educational requirements for your career path and find two appropriate sources. Copy a paragraph from each source and paste them into the appropriate section. When you paste a paragraph, OneNote inserts it in a note with a link to the source.

e. Research the median salary for a single year for this career. Create a mathematical equation in the Median Salary section that multiplies the amount of the median salary times 20 years to calculate how much you will possibly earn.

f. For the Employment Outlook section, research the outlook for your career path. Take at least four notes about what you find when researching the topic.

g. Sync your notes with your OneDrive. Submit your assignment in the format specified by your instructor.

Introduction to Sway

Sway site | responsive design | Storyline | card | Creative Commons license | animation emphasis effects | Docs.com

Bottom Line
- Drag photos, videos, and files from your computer and content from Facebook and Twitter directly to your Sway presentation.
- Run Sway in a web browser or as an app on your smartphone, and save presentations as webpages.

Expressing your ideas in a presentation typically means creating PowerPoint slides or a Word document. Microsoft Sway gives you another way to engage an audience. Sway is a free Microsoft tool available at Sway.com or as an app in Office 365. Using Sway, you can combine text, images, videos, and social media in a website called a **Sway site** that you can share and display on any device. To get started, you create a digital story on a web-based canvas without borders, slides, cells, or page breaks. A Sway site organizes the text, images, and video into a **responsive design**, which means your content adapts perfectly to any screen size as shown in **Figure 6**. You store a Sway site in the cloud on OneDrive using a free Microsoft account.

Figure 6: Sway site with responsive design

You can display a Sway presentation in a web browser.

Sway uses responsive design to make sure pages fit perfectly on any device.

The Market for Commercial Drones

Medical Defibrillator

- Ambulance drone can help heart attack victims in under 2 minutes with

© iStock.com/marinello, © iStock.com/marekuliasz

Learn to use Sway!
Links to companion **Sways**, featuring **videos** with hands-on instructions, are located on www.cengagebrain.com.

Creating a Sway Presentation

You can use Sway to build a digital flyer, a club newsletter, a vacation blog, an informational site, a digital art portfolio, or a new product rollout. After you select your topic and sign into Sway with your Microsoft account, a **Storyline** opens, providing tools and a work area for composing your digital story. See **Figure 7**. Each story can include text, images, and videos. You create a Sway by adding text and media content into a Storyline section, or **card**. To add pictures, videos, or documents, select a card in the left pane and then select the Insert Content button. The first card in a Sway presentation contains a title and background image.

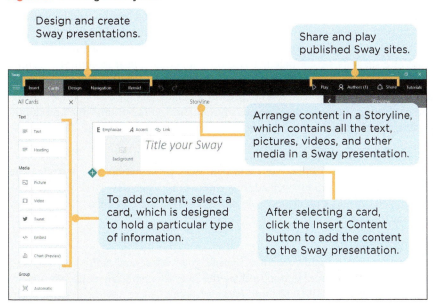

Design and create Sway presentations.

Share and play published Sway sites.

Arrange content in a Storyline, which contains all the text, pictures, videos, and other media in a Sway presentation.

To add content, select a card, which is designed to hold a particular type of information.

After selecting a card, click the Insert Content button to add the content to the Sway presentation.

Adding Content to Build a Story

As you work, Sway searches the Internet to help you find relevant images, videos, tweets, and other content from online sources such as Bing, YouTube, Twitter, and Facebook. You can drag content from the search results right into the Storyline. In addition, you can upload your own images and videos directly in the presentation. For example, if you are creating a Sway presentation about the market for commercial drones, Sway suggests content to incorporate into the presentation by displaying it in the left pane as search results. The search results include drone images tagged with a **Creative Commons license** at online sources as shown in **Figure 8**. A Creative Commons license is a public copyright license that allows the free distribution of an otherwise copyrighted work. In addition, you can specify the source of the media. For example, you can add your own Facebook or OneNote pictures and videos in Sway without leaving the app.

On the Job Now

If you have a Microsoft Word document containing an outline of your business content, drag the outline into Sway to create a card for each topic.

Figure 8: Images in Sway search results

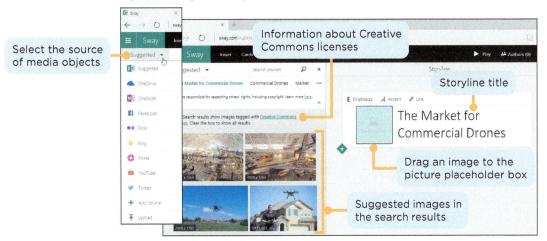

Select the source of media objects

Information about Creative Commons licenses

Storyline title

The Market for Commercial Drones

Drag an image to the picture placeholder box

Suggested images in the search results

Designing a Sway

Sway professionally designs your Storyline content by resizing background images and fonts to fit your display, and by floating text, animating media, embedding video, and removing images as a page scrolls out of view. Sway also evaluates the images in your Storyline and suggests a color palette based on colors that appear in your photos. Use the Design button to display tools including color palettes, font choices, **animation emphasis effects**, and style templates to provide a personality for a Sway presentation. Instead of creating your own design, you can click the Remix button, which randomly selects unique designs for your Sway site.

Publishing a Sway

Use the Play button to display your finished Sway presentation as a website. The Address bar includes a unique web address where others can view your Sway site. As the author, you can edit a published Sway site by clicking the Edit button (pencil icon) on the Sway toolbar.

Sharing a Sway

When you are ready to share your Sway website, you have several options as shown in **Figure 9**. Use the Share slider button to share the Sway site publically or keep it private. If you add the Sway site to the Microsoft **Docs.com** public gallery, anyone worldwide can use Bing, Google, or other search engines to find, view, and share your Sway site. You can also share your Sway site using Facebook, Twitter, Google+, Yammer, and other social media sites. Link your presentation to any webpage or email the link to your audience. Sway can also generate a code for embedding the link within another webpage.

Figure 9: Sharing a Sway site

Share button

Drag the slider button to Just me to keep the Sway site private

Post the Sway site on Docs.com

Options differ depending on your Microsoft account

Send friends a link to the Sway site

Try This Now

Learn to use Sway!
Links to companion **Sways**, featuring **videos** with hands-on instructions, are located on www.cengagebrain.com.

1: Creating a Sway Resume

Sway is a digital storytelling app. Create a Sway resume to share the skills, job experiences, and achievements you have that match the requirements of a future job interest. Perform the following tasks:

    a. Create a new presentation in Sway to use as a digital resume. Title the Sway Storyline with your full name and then select a background image.

    b. Create three separate sections titled **Academic Background, Work Experience**, and **Skills**, and insert text, a picture, and a paragraph or bulleted points in each section. Be sure to include your own picture.

    c. Add a fourth section that includes a video about your school that you find online.

    d. Customize the design of your presentation.

    e. Submit your assignment link in the format specified by your instructor.

2: Creating an Online Sway Newsletter

Newsletters are designed to capture the attention of their target audience. Using Sway, create a newsletter for a club, organization, or your favorite music group. Perform the following tasks:

    a. Create a new presentation in Sway to use as a digital newsletter for a club, organization, or your favorite music group. Provide a title for the Sway Storyline and select an appropriate background image.

    b. Select three separate sections with appropriate titles, such as Upcoming Events. In each section, insert text, a picture, and a paragraph or bulleted points.

    c. Add a fourth section that includes a video about your selected topic.

    d. Customize the design of your presentation.

    e. Submit your assignment link in the format specified by your instructor.

3: Creating and Sharing a Technology Presentation

To place a Sway presentation in the hands of your entire audience, you can share a link to the Sway presentation. Create a Sway presentation on a new technology and share it with your class. Perform the following tasks:

    a. Create a new presentation in Sway about a cutting-edge technology topic. Provide a title for the Sway Storyline and select a background image.

    b. Create four separate sections about your topic, and include text, a picture, and a paragraph in each section.

    c. Add a fifth section that includes a video about your topic.

    d. Customize the design of your presentation.

    e. Share the link to your Sway with your classmates and submit your assignment link in the format specified by your instructor.

Introduction to Office Mix

add-in | clip | slide recording | Slide Notes | screen recording | free-response quiz

To enliven business meetings and lectures, Microsoft adds a new dimension to presentations with a powerful toolset called Office Mix, a free add-in for PowerPoint. (An **add-in** is software that works with an installed app to extend its features.) Using Office Mix, you can record yourself on video, capture still and moving images on your desktop, and insert interactive elements such as quizzes and live webpages directly into PowerPoint slides. When you post the finished presentation to OneDrive, Office Mix provides a link you can share with friends and colleagues. Anyone with an Internet connection and a web browser can watch a published Office Mix presentation, such as the one in **Figure 10**, on a computer or mobile device.

Figure 10: Office Mix presentation

Adding Office Mix to PowerPoint

To get started, you create an Office Mix account at the website mix.office.com using an email address or a Facebook or Google account. Next, you download and install the Office Mix add-in (see **Figure 11**). Office Mix appears as a new tab named Mix on the PowerPoint ribbon in versions of Office 2013 and Office 2016 running on personal computers (PCs).

Figure 11: Getting started with Office Mix

Capturing Video Clips

A **clip** is a short segment of audio, such as music, or video. After finishing the content on a PowerPoint slide, you can use Office Mix to add a video clip to animate or illustrate the content. Office Mix creates video clips in two ways: by recording live action on a webcam and by capturing screen images and movements. If your computer has a webcam, you can record yourself and annotate the slide to create a **slide recording** as shown in **Figure 12**.

On the Job Now

Companies are using Office Mix to train employees about new products, to explain benefit packages to new workers, and to educate interns about office procedures.

Figure 12: Making a slide recording

Record your voice; also record video if your computer has a camera.

Use the Slide Notes button to display notes for your narration.

For best results, look directly at your webcam while recording video.

Choose a video and audio device to record images and sound.

Use inking tools to write and draw on the slide as you record.

When you are making a slide recording, you can record your spoken narration at the same time. The **Slide Notes** feature works like a teleprompter to help you focus on your presentation content instead of memorizing your narration. Use the Inking tools to make annotations or add highlighting using different pen types and colors. After finishing a recording, edit the video in PowerPoint to trim the length or set playback options.

The second way to create a video is to capture on-screen images and actions with or without a voiceover. This method is ideal if you want to show how to use your favorite website or demonstrate an app such as OneNote. To share your screen with an audience, select the part of the screen you want to show in the video. Office Mix captures everything that happens in that area to create a **screen recording**, as shown in **Figure 13**. Office Mix inserts the screen recording as a video in the slide.

On the Job Now

To make your video recordings accessible to people with hearing impairments, use the Office Mix closed-captioning tools. You can also use closed captions to supplement audio that is difficult to understand and to provide an aid for those learning to read.

Figure 13: Making a screen recording

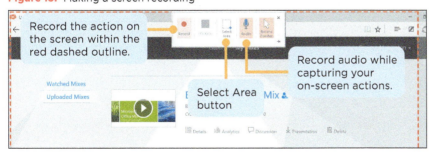

Record the action on the screen within the red dashed outline.

Record audio while capturing your on-screen actions.

Select Area button

Inserting Quizzes, Live Webpages, and Apps

To enhance and assess audience understanding, make your slides interactive by adding quizzes, live webpages, and apps. Quizzes give immediate feedback to the user as shown in **Figure 14**. Office Mix supports several quiz formats, including a **free-response quiz** similar to a short answer quiz, and true/false, multiple-choice, and multiple-response formats.

Figure 14: Creating an interactive quiz

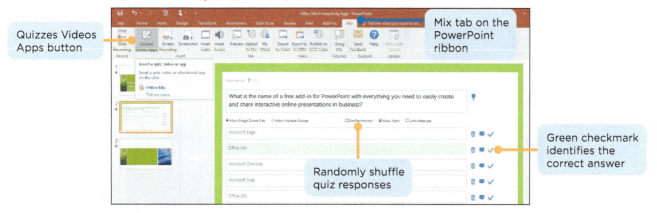

Sharing an Office Mix Presentation

When you complete your work with Office Mix, upload the presentation to your personal Office Mix dashboard as shown in **Figure 15**. Users of PCs, Macs, iOS devices, and Android devices can access and play Office Mix presentations. The Office Mix dashboard displays built-in analytics that include the quiz results and how much time viewers spent on each slide. You can play completed Office Mix presentations online or download them as movies.

Figure 15: Sharing an Office Mix presentation

Try This Now

1: Creating an Office Mix Tutorial for OneNote

Note: This activity requires a microphone on your computer.

Office Mix makes it easy to record screens and their contents. Create PowerPoint slides with an Office Mix screen recording to show OneNote 2016 features. Perform the following tasks:

    a. Create a PowerPoint presentation with the Ion Boardroom template. Create an opening slide with the title **My Favorite OneNote Features** and enter your name in the subtitle.

    b. Create three additional slides, each titled with a new feature of OneNote. Open OneNote and use the Mix tab in PowerPoint to capture three separate screen recordings that teach your favorite features.

    c. Add a fifth slide that quizzes the user with a multiple-choice question about OneNote and includes four responses. Be sure to insert a checkmark indicating the correct response.

    d. Upload the completed presentation to your Office Mix dashboard and share the link with your instructor.

    e. Submit your assignment link in the format specified by your instructor.

2: Teaching Augmented Reality with Office Mix

Note: This activity requires a webcam or built-in video camera on your computer.

A local elementary school has asked you to teach augmented reality to its students using Office Mix. Perform the following tasks:

    a. Research augmented reality using your favorite online search tools.

    b. Create a PowerPoint presentation with the Frame template. Create an opening slide with the title **Augmented Reality** and enter your name in the subtitle.

    c. Create a slide with four bullets summarizing your research of augmented reality. Create a 20-second slide recording of yourself providing a quick overview of augmented reality.

    d. Create another slide with a 30-second screen recording of a video about augmented reality from a site such as YouTube or another video-sharing site.

    e. Add a final slide that quizzes the user with a true/false question about augmented reality. Be sure to insert a checkmark indicating the correct response.

    f. Upload the completed presentation to your Office Mix dashboard and share the link with your instructor.

    g. Submit your assignment link in the format specified by your instructor.

3: Marketing a Travel Destination with Office Mix

Note: This activity requires a webcam or built-in video camera on your computer.

To convince your audience to travel to a particular city, create a slide presentation marketing any city in the world using a slide recording, screen recording, and a quiz. Perform the following tasks:

    a. Create a PowerPoint presentation with any template. Create an opening slide with the title of the city you are marketing as a travel destination and your name in the subtitle.

    b. Create a slide with four bullets about the featured city. Create a 30-second slide recording of yourself explaining why this city is the perfect vacation destination.

    c. Create another slide with a 20-second screen recording of a travel video about the city from a site such as YouTube or another video-sharing site.

    d. Add a final slide that quizzes the user with a multiple-choice question about the featured city with five responses. Be sure to include a checkmark indicating the correct response.

    e. Upload the completed presentation to your Office Mix dashboard and share your link with your instructor.

    f. Submit your assignment link in the format specified by your instructor.

Introduction to Microsoft Edge

Reading view | Hub | Cortana | Web Note | Inking | sandbox

Bottom Line

- Microsoft Edge is the name of the new web browser built into Windows 10.
- Microsoft Edge allows you to search the web faster, take web notes, read webpages without distractions, and get instant assistance from Cortana.

Microsoft Edge is the default web browser developed for the Windows 10 operating system as a replacement for Internet Explorer. Unlike its predecessor, Edge lets you write on webpages, read webpages without advertisements and other distractions, and search for information using a virtual personal assistant. The Edge interface is clean and basic, as shown in **Figure 16**, meaning you can pay more attention to the webpage content.

Figure 16: Microsoft Edge tools

Learn to use Edge!

Links to companion **Sways**, featuring **videos** with hands-on instructions, are located on www.cengagebrain.com.

On the Job Now

Businesses started adopting Internet Explorer more than 20 years ago simply to view webpages. Today, Microsoft Edge has a different purpose: to promote interaction with the web and share its contents with colleagues.

Browsing the Web with Microsoft Edge

One of the fastest browsers available, Edge allows you to type search text directly in the Address bar. As you view the resulting webpage, you can switch to **Reading view**, which is available for most news and research sites, to eliminate distracting advertisements. For example, if you are catching up on technology news online, the webpage might be difficult to read due to a busy layout cluttered with ads. Switch to Reading view to refresh the page and remove the original page formatting, ads, and menu sidebars to read the article distraction-free.

Consider the **Hub** in Microsoft Edge as providing one-stop access to all the things you collect on the web, such as your favorite websites, reading list, surfing history, and downloaded files.

Locating Information with Cortana

Cortana, the Windows 10 virtual assistant, plays an important role in Microsoft Edge. After you turn on Cortana, it appears as an animated circle in the Address bar when you might need assistance, as shown in the restaurant website in **Figure 17**. When you click the Cortana icon, a pane slides in from the right of the browser window to display detailed information about the restaurant, including maps and reviews. Cortana can also assist you in defining words, finding the weather, suggesting coupons for shopping, updating stock market information, and calculating math.

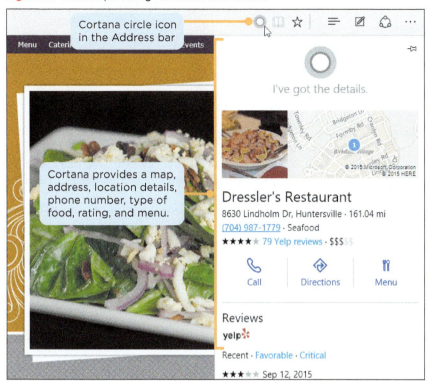

Annotating Webpages

One of the most impressive Microsoft Edge features are the **Web Note** tools, which you use to write on a webpage or to highlight text. When you click the Make a Web Note button, an **Inking** toolbar appears, as shown in **Figure 18**, that provides writing and drawing tools. These tools include an eraser, a pen, and a highlighter with different colors. You can also insert a typed note and copy a screen image (called a screen clipping). You can draw with a pointing device, fingertip, or stylus using different pen colors. Whether you add notes to a recipe, annotate sources for a research paper, or select a product while shopping online, the Web Note tools can enhance your productivity. After you complete your notes, click the Save button to save the annotations to OneNote, your Favorites list, or your Reading list. You can share the inked page with others using the Share Web Note button.

On the Job Now

To enhance security, Microsoft Edge runs in a partial sandbox, an arrangement that prevents attackers from gaining control of your computer. Browsing within the **sandbox** protects computer resources and information from hackers.

Figure 18: Web Note tools in Microsoft Edge

Try This Now

Learn to use Edge!
Links to companion **Sways**, featuring **videos** with hands-on instructions, are located on www.cengagebrain.com.

1: Using Cortana in Microsoft Edge

Note: This activity requires using Microsoft Edge on a Windows 10 computer.

Cortana can assist you in finding information on a webpage in Microsoft Edge. Perform the following tasks:

a. Create a Word document using the Word Screen Clipping tool to capture the following screenshots.

- Screenshot A—Using Microsoft Edge, open a webpage with a technology news article. Right-click a term in the article and ask Cortana to define it.
- Screenshot B—Using Microsoft Edge, open the website of a fancy restaurant in a city near you. Make sure the Cortana circle icon is displayed in the Address bar. (If it's not displayed, find a different restaurant website.) Click the Cortana circle icon to display a pane with information about the restaurant.
- Screenshot C—Using Microsoft Edge, type **10 USD to Euros** in the Address bar without pressing the Enter key. Cortana converts the U.S. dollars to Euros.
- Screenshot D—Using Microsoft Edge, type **Apple stock** in the Address bar without pressing the Enter key. Cortana displays the current stock quote.

b. Submit your assignment in the format specified by your instructor.

2: Viewing Online News with Reading View

Note: This activity requires using Microsoft Edge on a Windows 10 computer.

Reading view in Microsoft Edge can make a webpage less cluttered with ads and other distractions. Perform the following tasks:

a. Create a Word document using the Word Screen Clipping tool to capture the following screenshots.

- Screenshot A—Using Microsoft Edge, open the website **mashable.com**. Open a technology article. Click the Reading view button to display an ad-free page that uses only basic text formatting.
- Screenshot B—Using Microsoft Edge, open the website **bbc.com**. Open any news article. Click the Reading view button to display an ad-free page that uses only basic text formatting.
- Screenshot C—Make three types of annotations (Pen, Highlighter, and Add a typed note) on the BBC article page displayed in Reading view.

b. Submit your assignment in the format specified by your instructor.

3: Inking with Microsoft Edge

Note: This activity requires using Microsoft Edge on a Windows 10 computer.

Microsoft Edge provides many annotation options to record your ideas. Perform the following tasks:

a. Open the website **wolframalpha.com** in the Microsoft Edge browser. Wolfram Alpha is a well-respected academic search engine. Type **US$100 1965 dollars in 2015** in the Wolfram Alpha search text box and press the Enter key.

b. Click the Make a Web Note button to display the Web Note tools. Using the Pen tool, draw a circle around the result on the webpage. Save the page to OneNote.

c. In the Wolfram Alpha search text box, type the name of the city closest to where you live and press the Enter key. Using the Highlighter tool, highlight at least three interesting results. Add a note and then type a sentence about what you learned about this city. Save the page to OneNote. Share your OneNote notebook with your instructor.

d. Submit your assignment link in the format specified by your instructor.

Office 2016 and Windows 10: Essential Concepts and Skills

Objectives

You will have mastered the material in this module when you can:

- Use a touch screen
- Perform basic mouse operations
- Start Windows and sign in to an account
- Identify the objects on the Windows 10 desktop
- Identify the apps in and versions of Microsoft Office 2016
- Run an app
- Identify the components of the Microsoft Office ribbon

- Create folders
- Save files
- Change screen resolution
- Perform basic tasks in Microsoft Office apps
- Manage files
- Use Microsoft Office Help and Windows Help

This introductory module uses Word 2016 to cover features and functions common to Office 2016 apps, as well as the basics of Windows 10.

Roadmap

In this module, you will learn how to perform basic tasks in Windows and Word. The following roadmap identifies general activities you will perform as you progress through this module:

1. SIGN IN to an account.
2. USE WINDOWS.
3. USE features in Word that are common across Office APPS.
4. FILE and folder MANAGEMENT.
5. SWITCH between APPS.
6. SAVE and manage FILES.

7. **CHANGE SCREEN RESOLUTION**.

8. **EXIT APPS**.

9. **USE ADDITIONAL** Office **APPS FEATURES**.

10. **USE** Office and Windows **HELP**.

At the beginning of the step instructions throughout each module, you will see an abbreviated form of this roadmap. The abbreviated roadmap uses colors to indicate module progress: gray means the module is beyond that activity, blue means the task being shown is covered in that activity, and black means that activity is yet to be covered. For example, the following abbreviated roadmap indicates the module would be showing a task in the USE APPS activity.

1 SIGN IN | 2 USE WINDOWS | **3 USE APPS** | 4 FILE MANAGEMENT | 5 SWITCH APPS | 6 SAVE FILES

7 CHANGE SCREEN RESOLUTION | 8 EXIT APPS | 9 USE ADDITIONAL APP FEATURES | 10 USE HELP

Use the abbreviated roadmap as a progress guide while you read or step through the instructions in this module.

Introduction to the Windows 10 Operating System

Windows 10 is the newest version of Microsoft Windows, which is a popular and widely used operating system (Figure 1). An **operating system (OS)** is a set of programs that coordinate all the activities among computer or mobile device hardware.

Figure 1

The Windows operating system simplifies the process of working with documents and apps by organizing the manner in which you interact with the computer. Windows is used to run apps. An application, or **app**, consists of programs designed to make users more productive and/or assist them with personal tasks, such as word processing or browsing the web.

Using a Touch Screen and a Mouse

Windows users who have computers or devices with touch screen capability can interact with the screen using gestures. A **gesture** is a motion you make on a touch screen with the tip of one or more fingers or your hand. Touch screens are convenient because they do not require a separate device for input. Table 1 presents common ways to interact with a touch screen.

If you are using your finger on a touch screen and are having difficulty completing the steps in this module, consider using a stylus. Many people find it easier to be precise with a stylus than with a finger. In addition, with a stylus you see the pointer. If you still are having trouble completing the steps with a stylus, try using a mouse.

Table 1 Touch Screen Gestures

Motion	Description	Common Uses	Equivalent Mouse Operation
Tap	Quickly touch and release one finger one time.	Activate a link (built-in connection). Press a button. Run a program or an app.	Click
Double-tap	Quickly touch and release one finger two times.	Run a program or an app. Zoom in (show a smaller area on the screen, so that contents appear larger) at the location of the double-tap.	Double-click
Press and hold	Press and hold one finger to cause an action to occur, or until an action occurs.	Display a shortcut menu (immediate access to allowable actions). Activate a mode enabling you to move an item with one finger to a new location.	Right-click
Drag, or slide	Press and hold one finger on an object and then move the finger to the new location.	Move an item around the screen. Scroll.	Drag
Swipe	Press and hold one finger and then move the finger horizontally or vertically on the screen.	Select an object. Swipe from edge to display a bar such as the Action Center, Apps bar, and Navigation bar (all discussed later).	Drag
Stretch	Move two fingers apart.	Zoom in (show a smaller area on the screen, so that contents appear larger).	None
Pinch	Move two fingers together.	Zoom out (show a larger area on the screen, so that contents appear smaller).	None

© 2015 Cengage Learning

Will the screen look different if you are using a touch screen?
The Windows and Microsoft Office interface varies slightly if you are using a touch screen. For this reason, you might notice that your Windows or Word screens looks slightly different from the screens in this book.

CONSIDER THIS

Windows users who do not have touch screen capabilities typically work with a mouse that has at least two buttons. For a right-handed user, the left button usually is

BTW
Pointer
If you are using a touch screen, the pointer may not appear on the screen as you perform touch gestures. The pointer will reappear when you begin using the mouse.

the primary mouse button, and the right mouse button is the secondary mouse button. Left-handed people, however, can reverse the function of these buttons.

Table 2 explains how to perform a variety of mouse operations. Some apps also use keys in combination with the mouse to perform certain actions. For example, when you hold down the CTRL key while rolling the mouse wheel, text on the screen may become larger or smaller based on the direction you roll the wheel. The function of the mouse buttons and the wheel varies depending on the app.

Table 2 Mouse Operations			
Operation	**Mouse Action**	**Example***	**Equivalent Touch Gesture**
Point	Move the mouse until the pointer on the desktop is positioned on the item of choice.	Position the pointer on the screen.	None
Click	Press and release the primary mouse button, which usually is the left mouse button.	Select or deselect items on the screen or run an app or app feature.	Tap
Right-click	Press and release the secondary mouse button, which usually is the right mouse button.	Display a shortcut menu.	Press and hold
Double-click	Quickly press and release the primary mouse button twice without moving the mouse.	Run an app or app feature.	Double-tap
Triple-click	Quickly press and release the primary mouse button three times without moving the mouse.	Select a paragraph.	Triple-tap
Drag	Point to an item, hold down the primary mouse button, move the item to the desired location on the screen, and then release the mouse button.	Move an object from one location to another or draw pictures.	Drag or slide
Right-drag	Point to an item, hold down the right mouse button, move the item to the desired location on the screen, and then release the right mouse button.	Display a shortcut menu after moving an object from one location to another.	Press and hold, then drag
Rotate wheel	Roll the wheel forward or backward.	Scroll vertically (up and down).	Swipe
Free-spin wheel	Whirl the wheel forward or backward so that it spins freely on its own.	Scroll through many pages in seconds.	Swipe
Press wheel	Press the wheel button while moving the mouse.	Scroll continuously.	None
Tilt wheel	Press the wheel toward the right or left.	Scroll horizontally (left and right).	None
Press thumb button	Press the button on the side of the mouse with your thumb.	Move forward or backward through webpages and/or control media, games, etc.	None

*Note: The examples presented in this column are discussed as they are demonstrated in this module.

Figure 2

Scrolling

A **scroll bar** is a horizontal or vertical bar that appears when the contents of an area may not be visible completely on the screen (Figure 2). A scroll bar contains **scroll arrows** and a **scroll box** that enable you to view areas that currently cannot be seen on the screen. Clicking the up and down scroll arrows moves the screen content up or down one line. You also can click above or below the scroll box to move up or down a section, or drag the scroll box up or down to move to a specific location.

Keyboard Shortcuts

In many cases, you can use the keyboard instead of the mouse to accomplish a task. To perform tasks using the keyboard, you press one or more keyboard keys, sometimes identified as a **keyboard shortcut**. Some keyboard shortcuts consist of a single key, such as the F1 key. For example, to obtain help in many apps, you can press the F1 key. Other keyboard shortcuts consist of multiple keys, in which case a plus sign separates the key names, such as CTRL+ESC. This notation means to press and hold down the first key listed, press one or more additional keys, and then release all keys. For example, to display the Start menu, press CTRL+ESC, that is, hold down the CTRL key, press the ESC key, and then release both keys.

Starting Windows

It is not unusual for multiple people to use the same computer in a work, educational, recreational, or home setting. Windows enables each user to establish a **user account**, which identifies to Windows the resources, such as apps and storage locations, a user can access when working with the computer.

Each user account has a user name and may have a password and an icon, as well. A **user name** is a unique combination of letters or numbers that identifies a specific user to Windows. A **password** is a private combination of letters, numbers, and special characters associated with the user name that allows access to a user's account resources. An icon is a small image that represents an object; thus, a **user icon** is a picture associated with a user name.

When you turn on a computer, Windows starts and displays a **lock screen** consisting of the time and date (Figure 3). To unlock the screen, click the lock screen. Depending on your computer's settings, Windows may or may not display a sign-in screen that shows the user names and user icons for users who have accounts on the computer. This **sign-in screen** enables you to sign in to your user account and makes the computer available for use. Clicking the user icon begins the process of signing in, also called logging on, to your user account.

BTW

Minimize Wrist Injury
Computer users frequently switch between the keyboard and the mouse during a word processing session; such switching strains the wrist. To help prevent wrist injury, minimize switching. For instance, if your fingers already are on the keyboard, use keyboard keys to scroll. If your hand already is on the mouse, use the mouse to scroll. If your hand is on the touch screen, use touch gestures to scroll.

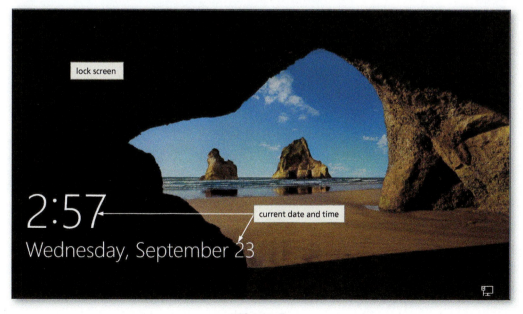

Figure 3

At the bottom of the sign-in screen is the 'Connect to Internet' button, 'Ease of access' button, and a Shut down button. Clicking the 'Connect to Internet' button displays a list of each network connection and its status. You also can connect to or disconnect from a network. Clicking the 'Ease of access' button displays the Ease of access menu, which provides tools to optimize a computer to accommodate the needs of mobility, hearing, and vision impaired users. Clicking the Shut down button displays a menu containing commands related to putting the computer or mobile device in a low-power state, shutting it down, and restarting the computer or mobile device. The commands available on your computer or mobile device may differ.

- The Sleep command saves your work, turns off the computer fans and hard drive, and places the computer in a lower-power state. To wake the computer from sleep mode, press the power button or lift a laptop's cover, and sign in to your account.
- The Shut down command exits running apps, shuts down Windows, and then turns off the computer.
- The Restart command exits running apps, shuts down Windows, and then restarts Windows.

1 SIGN IN | 2 USE WINDOWS | 3 USE APPS | 4 FILE MANAGEMENT | 5 SWITCH APPS | 6 SAVE FILES
7 CHANGE SCREEN RESOLUTION | 8 EXIT APPS | 9 USE ADDITIONAL APP FEATURES | 10 USE HELP

To Sign In to an Account

The following steps, which use SCSeries as the user name, sign in to an account based on a typical Windows installation. *Why? After starting Windows, you might be required to sign in to an account to access the computer or mobile device's resources.* You may need to ask your instructor how to sign in to your account.

1

- Click the lock screen (shown in Figure 3) to display a sign-in screen.

- Click the user icon (for SCSeries, in this case) on the sign-in screen, which depending on settings, either will display a second sign-in screen that contains a Password text box (Figure 4) or will display the Windows desktop (Figure 5).

Figure 4

Q&A

Why do I not see a user icon?
Your computer may require you to type a user name instead of clicking an icon.

What is a text box?
A text box is a rectangular box in which you type text.

Why does my screen not show a Password text box?
Your account does not require a password.

- If Windows displays a sign-in screen with a Password text box, type your password in the text box.

2

- Click the Submit button (shown in Figure 4) to sign in to your account and display the Windows desktop (Figure 5).

Q&A

Why does my desktop look different from the one in Figure 5?
The Windows desktop is customizable, and your school or employer may have modified the desktop to meet its needs. Also, your screen resolution, which affects the size of the elements on the screen, may differ from the screen resolution used in this book. Later in this module, you learn how to change screen resolution.

How do I type if my tablet has no keyboard?
You can use your fingers to press keys on a keyboard that appears on the screen, called an on-screen keyboard, or you can purchase a separate physical keyboard that attaches to or wirelessly communicates with the tablet.

Figure 5

The Windows Desktop

The Windows 10 desktop (shown in Figure 5) and the objects on the desktop emulate a work area in an office. Think of the Windows desktop as an electronic version of the top of your desk. You can perform tasks such as placing objects on the desktop, moving the objects around the desktop, and removing items from the desktop.

When you run an app in Windows 10, it appears on the desktop. Some icons also may be displayed on the desktop. For instance, the icon for the **Recycle Bin**, the location of files that have been deleted, appears on the desktop by default. A **file** is a named unit of storage. Files can contain text, images, audio, and video. You can customize your desktop so that icons representing programs and files you use often appear on your desktop.

Introduction to Microsoft Office 2016

Microsoft Office 2016 is the newest version of Microsoft Office, offering features that provide users with better functionality and easier ways to work with the various files they create. This version of Office also is designed to work more optimally on mobile devices and online.

Microsoft Office 2016 Apps

Microsoft Office 2016 includes a wide variety of apps, such as Word, PowerPoint, Excel, Access, Outlook, Publisher, and OneNote:

- **Microsoft Word 2016**, or Word, is a full-featured word processing app that allows you to create professional-looking documents and revise them easily.

- **Microsoft PowerPoint 2016**, or PowerPoint, is a complete presentation app that enables you to produce professional-looking presentations and then deliver them to an audience.
- **Microsoft Excel 2016**, or Excel, is a powerful spreadsheet app that allows you to organize data, complete calculations, make decisions, graph data, develop professional-looking reports, publish organized data to the web, and access real-time data from websites.
- **Microsoft Access 2016**, or Access, is a database management system that enables you to create a database; add, change, and delete data in the database; ask questions concerning the data in the database; and create forms and reports using the data in the database.
- **Microsoft Outlook 2016**, or Outlook, is a communications and scheduling app that allows you to manage email accounts, calendars, contacts, and access to other Internet content.
- **Microsoft Publisher 2016**, or Publisher, is a desktop publishing app that helps you create professional-quality publications and marketing materials that can be shared easily.
- **Microsoft OneNote 2016**, or OneNote, is a note taking app that allows you to store and share information in notebooks with other people.

Microsoft Office 2016 Suites

A **suite** is a collection of individual apps available together as a unit. Microsoft offers a variety of Office suites, including a stand-alone desktop app, Microsoft Office 365, and Microsoft Office Online. **Microsoft Office 365**, or Office 365, provides plans that allow organizations to use Office in a mobile setting while also being able to communicate and share files, depending upon the type of plan selected by the organization. **Microsoft Office Online** includes apps that allow you to edit and share files on the web using the familiar Office interface.

During the Office 365 installation, you select a plan, and depending on your plan, you receive different apps and services. Office Online apps do not require a local installation and can be accessed through OneDrive and your browser. **OneDrive** is a cloud storage service that provides storage and other services, such as Office Online, to computer and mobile device users.

CONSIDER THIS

How do you sign up for a OneDrive account?

- Use your browser to navigate to onedrive.live.com.
- Create a Microsoft account by clicking the Sign up button and then entering your information to create the account.
- Sign in to OneDrive using your new account or use it in Word to save your files on OneDrive.

Apps in a suite, such as Microsoft Office, typically use a similar interface and share features. Once you are comfortable working with the elements and the interface and performing tasks in one app, the similarity can help you apply the knowledge and skills you have learned to another app(s) in the suite. For example, the process for saving a file in Word is the same in PowerPoint, Excel, and some of the other Office apps. While briefly showing how to use Word, this module illustrates some of the common functions across the Office apps and identifies the characteristics unique to Word.

Running and Using an App

To use an app, you must instruct the operating system to run the app. Windows provides many different ways to run an app, one of which is presented in this section (other ways to run an app are presented throughout this module). After an app is running, you can use it to perform a variety of tasks. The following pages use Word to discuss some elements of the Office interface and to perform tasks that are common to other Office apps.

Word

Word is a full-featured word processing app that allows you to create many types of personal and business documents, including flyers, letters, memos, resumes, reports, fax cover sheets, mailing labels, and newsletters. Word also provides tools that enable you to create webpages and save these webpages directly on a web server. Word has many features designed to simplify the production of documents and add visual appeal. Using Word, you easily can change the shape, size, and color of text. You also can include borders, shading, tables, images, pictures, charts, and web addresses in documents.

To Run an App Using the Start Menu and Create a Blank Document

1 SIGN IN | **2 USE WINDOWS** | 3 USE APPS | 4 FILE MANAGEMENT | 5 SWITCH APPS | 6 SAVE FILES
7 CHANGE SCREEN RESOLUTION | 8 EXIT APPS | 9 USE ADDITIONAL APP FEATURES | 10 USE HELP

Across the bottom of the Windows 10 desktop is the taskbar. The taskbar contains the **Start button**, which you use to access apps, files, folders, and settings. A **folder** is a named location on a storage medium that usually contains related documents.

Clicking the Start button displays the Start menu. The **Start menu** allows you to access programs, folders, and files on the computer or mobile device and contains commands that allow you to start programs, store and search for documents, customize the computer or mobile device, and sign out of a user account or shut down the computer or mobile device. A **menu** is a list of related items, including folders, programs, and commands. Each **command** on a menu performs a specific action, such as saving a file or obtaining help. *Why? When you install an app, for example, the app's name will be added to the All apps list on the Start menu.*

The following steps, which assume Windows is running, use the Start menu to run Word and create a blank document based on a typical installation. You may need to ask your instructor how to run Word on your computer. Although the steps illustrate running the Word app, the steps to run any Office app are similar.

- Click the Start button on the Windows 10 taskbar to display the Start menu (Figure 6).

Figure 6

2

- Click All apps at the bottom of the left pane of the Start menu to display a list of apps installed on the computer or mobile device. If necessary, scroll to display the app you wish to run, Word 2016, in this case (Figure 7).

Figure 7

3

- If the app you wish to run is located in a folder, click or scroll to and then click the folder in the All apps list to display a list of the folder's contents.

- Click, or scroll to and then click the app name (Word 2016, in this case) in the list to run the selected app (Figure 8).

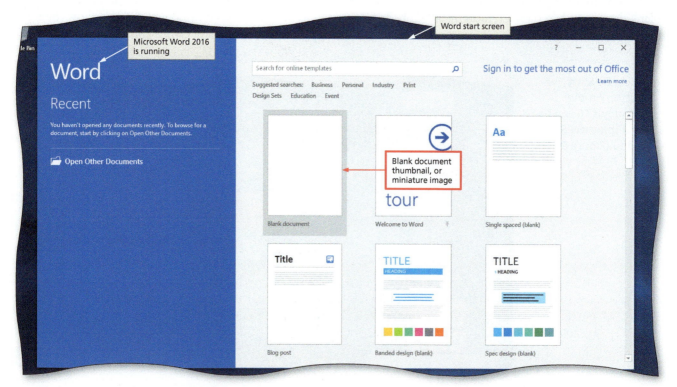

Figure 8

4

- Click the Blank document thumbnail on the Word start screen to create a blank Word document in the Word window (Figure 9).

Q&A What happens when you run an app?

Some apps provide a means for you to create a blank document, as shown in Figure 8; others immediately display a blank document in an app window, such as the Word window shown in Figure 9. A **window** is a rectangular area that displays data and information. The top of a window has a **title bar**, which is a horizontal space that contains the window's name.

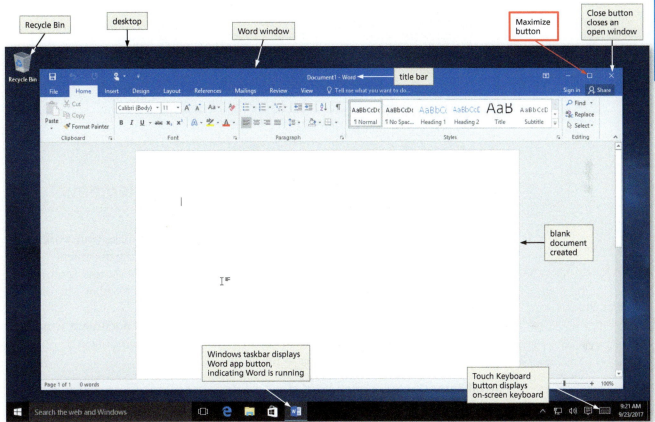

Figure 9

Other Ways

1. Type app name in search box, click app name in results list
2. Double-click file created in app you want to run

1 SIGN IN | **2 USE WINDOWS** | 3 USE APPS | 4 FILE MANAGEMENT | 5 SWITCH APPS | 6 SAVE FILES

7 CHANGE SCREEN RESOLUTION | 8 EXIT APPS | 9 USE ADDITIONAL APP FEATURES | 10 USE HELP

To Maximize a Window

Sometimes content is not visible completely in a window. One method of displaying the entire contents of a window is to **maximize** it, or enlarge the window so that it fills the entire screen. The following step maximizes the Word window; however, any Office app's window can be maximized using this step. *Why? A maximized window provides the most space available for using the app.*

- If the Word window is not maximized already, click the Maximize button (shown in Figure 9) next to the Close button on the Word window's title bar to maximize the window (Figure 10).

Q&A

What happened to the Maximize button?
It changed to a Restore Down button, which you can use to return a window to its size and location before you maximized it.

How do I know whether a window is maximized?
A window is maximized if it fills the entire display area and the Restore Down button is displayed on the title bar.

Figure 10

Other Ways

1. Double-click title bar

2. Drag title bar to top of screen

Word Document Window, Ribbon, and Elements Common to Office Apps

The Word window consists of a variety of components to make your work more efficient and documents more professional. These include the document window, ribbon, Tell Me box, mini toolbar, shortcut menus, Quick Access Toolbar, and Microsoft Account area. Most of these components are common to other Microsoft Office apps; others are unique to Word.

You view a portion of a document on the screen through a **document window** (Figure 11). The default (preset) view is **Print Layout view**, which shows the document on a mock sheet of paper in the document window.

Scroll Bars   You use a scroll bar to display different portions of a document in the document window. At the right edge of the document window is a vertical scroll bar. If a document is too wide to fit in the document window, a horizontal scroll bar also appears at the bottom of the document window. On a scroll bar, the position of the scroll box reflects the location of the portion of the document that is displayed in the document window.

Status Bar   The **status bar**, located at the bottom of the document window above the Windows taskbar, presents information about the document, the progress of current tasks, and the status of certain commands and keys; it also provides controls for viewing the document. As you type text or perform certain tasks, various indicators and buttons may appear on the status bar.

The left side of the status bar in Figure 11 shows the current page followed by the total number of pages in the document, the number of words in the document, and an icon to check spelling and grammar. The right side of the status bar includes buttons and controls you can use to change the view of a document and adjust the size of the displayed document.

Ribbon   The ribbon, located near the top of the window below the title bar, is the control center in Word and other Office apps (Figure 12). The ribbon provides easy, central access to the tasks you perform while creating a document. The ribbon consists

BTW

Touch Keyboard
To display the on-screen touch keyboard, click the Touch Keyboard button on the Windows taskbar (shown in Figure 9). When finished using the touch keyboard, click the X button on the touch keyboard to close the keyboard.

courtesy of opendipart.org

Figure 11

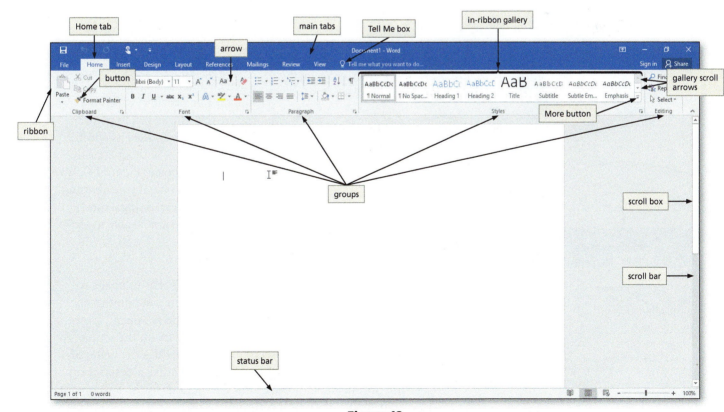

Figure 12

of tabs, groups, and commands. Each **tab** contains a collection of groups, and each **group** contains related commands. When you run an Office app, such as Word, it initially displays several main tabs, also called default or top-level tabs. All Office apps have a Home tab, which contains the more frequently used commands.

Figure 13

In addition to the main tabs, the Office apps display **tool tabs**, also called contextual tabs (Figure 13), when you perform certain tasks or work with objects such as pictures or tables. If you insert a picture in a Word document, for example, the Picture Tools tab and its related subordinate Format tab appear, collectively referred to as the Picture Tools Format tab. When you are finished working with the picture, the Picture Tools Format tab disappears from the ribbon. Word and other Office apps determine when tool tabs should appear and disappear based on tasks you perform. Some tool tabs, such as the Table Tools tab, have more than one related subordinate tab.

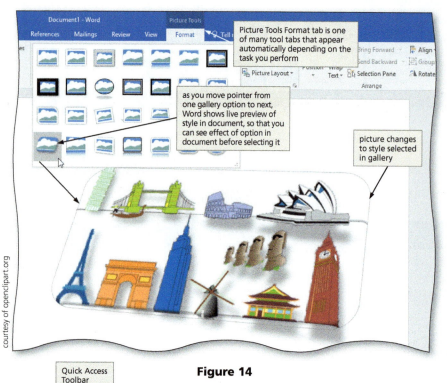

Figure 14

Items on the ribbon include buttons, boxes, and galleries (shown in Figure 12). A **gallery** is a set of choices, often graphical, arranged in a grid or in a list. You can scroll through choices in an in-ribbon gallery by clicking the gallery's scroll arrows. Or, you can click a gallery's More button to view more gallery options on the screen at a time.

Some buttons and boxes have arrows that, when clicked, also display a gallery; others always cause a gallery to be displayed when clicked. Most galleries support **live preview**, which is a feature that allows you to point to a gallery choice and see its effect in the document — without actually selecting the choice (Figure 14). Live preview works only if you are using a mouse; if you are using a touch screen, you will not be able to view live previews.

Figure 15

Some commands on the ribbon display an image to help you remember their function. When you point to a command on the ribbon, all or part of the command glows in a shade of gray, and a ScreenTip appears on the screen. A **ScreenTip** is an on-screen note that provides the name of the command, available keyboard shortcut(s), a description of the command, and sometimes instructions for how to obtain help about the command (Figure 15).

courtesy of openclipart.org

Some groups on the ribbon have a small arrow in the lower-right corner, called a **Dialog Box Launcher**, that when clicked, displays a dialog box or a task pane with additional options for the group (Figure 16). When presented with a dialog box, you make selections and must close the dialog box before returning to the document. A **task pane**, in contrast to a dialog box, is a window that can remain open and visible while you work in the document.

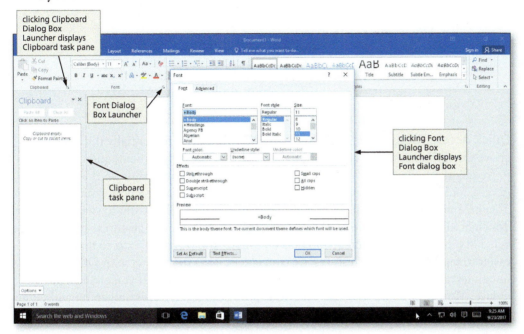

Figure 16

Tell Me Box The **Tell Me box**, which appears to the right of the tabs on the ribbon, is a type of search box that helps you to perform specific tasks in an Office app (Figure 17). As you type in the Tell Me box, the word-wheeling feature displays search results that are refined as you type. For example, if you want to center text in a document, you can type "center" in the Tell Me box and then select the appropriate command. The Tell Me box also lists the last five commands accessed from the box.

Figure 17

Mini Toolbar The **mini toolbar**, which appears automatically based on tasks you perform, contains commands related to changing the appearance of text in a document (Figure 18). If you do not use the mini toolbar, it disappears from the screen. The buttons, arrows, and boxes on the mini toolbar vary, depending on whether you are using Touch mode versus Mouse mode. If you right-click an item in the document window, Word displays both the mini toolbar and a shortcut menu, which is discussed in a later section in this module.

All commands on the mini toolbar also exist on the ribbon. The purpose of the mini toolbar is to minimize hand or mouse movement.

BTW

Turning Off the Mini Toolbar

If you do not want the mini toolbar to appear, click File on the ribbon to open the Backstage view, click the Options tab in the Backstage view, if necessary, click General (Options dialog box), remove the check mark from the 'Show Mini Toolbar on selection' check box, and then click the OK button.

Figure 18

courtesy of openclipart.org

Quick Access Toolbar   The **Quick Access Toolbar**, located initially (by default) above the ribbon at the left edge of the title bar, provides convenient, one-click access to frequently used commands (shown in Figure 15). The commands on the Quick Access Toolbar always are available, regardless of the task you are performing. The Touch/Mouse Mode button on the Quick Access Toolbar allows you to switch between Touch mode and Mouse mode. If you primarily are using touch gestures, Touch mode will add more space between commands on menus and on the ribbon so that they are easier to tap. While touch gestures are convenient ways to interact with Office apps, not all features are supported when you are using Touch mode. If you are using a mouse, Mouse mode will not add the extra space between buttons and commands. The Quick Access Toolbar is discussed in more depth later in the module.

KeyTips   If you prefer using the keyboard instead of the mouse, you can press the ALT key on the keyboard to display **KeyTips**, or keyboard code icons, for certain commands (Figure 19). To select a command using the keyboard, press the letter or number displayed in the KeyTip, which may cause additional KeyTips related to the selected command to appear. To remove KeyTips from the screen, press the ALT key or the ESC key until all KeyTips disappear, or click anywhere in the app window.

Figure 19

Microsoft Account Area   In this area, you can use the Sign in link to sign in to your Microsoft account. Once signed in, you will see your account information, as well as a picture if you have included one in your Microsoft account.

To Display a Different Tab on the Ribbon

1 SIGN IN | 2 USE WINDOWS | 3 USE APPS | 4 FILE MANAGEMENT | 5 SWITCH APPS | 6 SAVE FILES
7 CHANGE SCREEN RESOLUTION | 8 EXIT APPS | 9 USE ADDITIONAL APP FEATURES | 10 USE HELP

When you run Word, the ribbon displays nine main tabs: File, Home, Insert, Design, Layout, References, Mailings, Review, and View. The tab currently displayed is called the **active tab**.

The following step displays the Insert tab, that is, makes it the active tab. *Why? When working with an Office app, you may need to switch tabs to access other options for working with a document.*

1
- Click Insert on the ribbon to display the Insert tab (Figure 20).

 Experiment
- Click the other tabs on the ribbon to view their contents. When you are finished, click Insert on the ribbon to redisplay the Insert tab.

Figure 20

Other Ways

1. Press ALT, press letter corresponding to tab to display   2. Press ALT, press LEFT ARROW or RIGHT ARROW until desired tab is displayed

To Collapse and Expand the Ribbon and Use Full Screen Mode

1 SIGN IN | 2 USE WINDOWS | 3 USE APPS | 4 FILE MANAGEMENT | 5 SWITCH APPS | 6 SAVE FILES
7 CHANGE SCREEN RESOLUTION | 8 EXIT APPS | 9 USE ADDITIONAL APP FEATURES | 10 USE HELP

To display more of a document or other item in the window of an Office app, some users prefer to collapse the ribbon, which hides the groups on the ribbon and displays only the main tabs, or to use **Full Screen mode**, which hides all the commands and just displays the document. Each time you run an Office app, such as Word, the ribbon appears the same way it did the last time you used that Office app. The modules in this book, however, begin with the ribbon appearing as it did at the initial installation of Office or Word.

The following steps collapse, expand, and restore the ribbon in Word and then switch to Full Screen mode. *Why? If you need more space on the screen to work with your document, you may consider collapsing the ribbon or switching to Full Screen mode to gain additional workspace.*

1
- Click the 'Collapse the Ribbon' button on the ribbon (shown in Figure 20) to collapse the ribbon (Figure 21).

Q&A What happened to the 'Collapse the Ribbon' button?
The 'Pin the ribbon' button replaces the 'Collapse the Ribbon' button when the ribbon is collapsed. You will see the 'Pin the ribbon' button only when you expand a ribbon by clicking a tab.

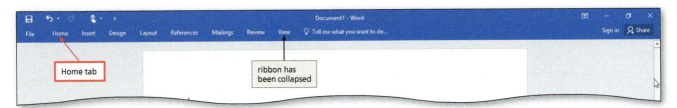

Figure 21

2

● Click Home on the ribbon to expand the Home tab (Figure 22).

Q&A | Why would I click the Home tab?
If you want to use a command on a collapsed ribbon, click the main tab to display the groups for that tab. After you select a command on the ribbon and resume working in the document, the groups will be collapsed once again. If you decide not to use a command on the ribbon, you can collapse the groups by clicking the same main tab or clicking in the app window.

Experiment

● Click Home on the ribbon to collapse the groups again. Click Home on the ribbon to expand the Home tab.

Figure 22

3

● Click the 'Pin the ribbon' button on the expanded Home tab to restore the ribbon.

● Click the 'Ribbon Display Options' button to display the Ribbon Display Options menu (Figure 23).

Figure 23

4

- Click Auto-hide Ribbon to use Full Screen mode, which hides all the commands from the screen (Figure 24).

- Click the ellipsis to display the ribbon temporarily.

- Click the 'Ribbon Display Options' button to display the Ribbon Display Options menu (shown in Figure 23).

- Click 'Show Tabs and Commands' on the Ribbon Display Options menu to exit Full Screen mode.

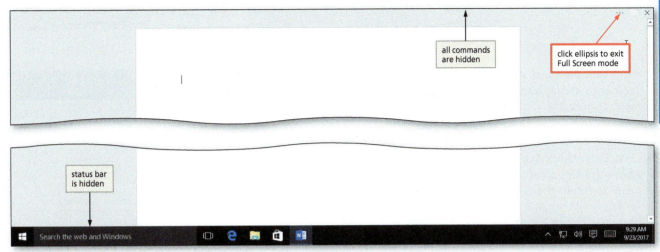

Figure 24

Other Ways

1. Double-click a main tab on the ribbon
2. Press CTRL+F1

To Use a Shortcut Menu to Relocate the Quick Access Toolbar

1 SIGN IN | 2 USE WINDOWS | **3 USE APPS** | 4 FILE MANAGEMENT | 5 SWITCH APPS | 6 SAVE FILES
7 CHANGE SCREEN RESOLUTION | 8 EXIT APPS | 9 USE ADDITIONAL APP FEATURES | 10 USE HELP

When you right-click certain areas of the Word and other Office app windows, a shortcut menu will appear. A **shortcut menu** is a list of frequently used commands that relate to an object. *Why? You can use shortcut menus to access common commands quickly.* When you right-click the status bar, for example, a shortcut menu appears with commands related to the status bar. When you right-click the Quick Access Toolbar, a shortcut menu appears with commands related to the Quick Access Toolbar. The following steps use a shortcut menu to move the Quick Access Toolbar, which by default is located on the title bar.

1

- Right-click the Quick Access Toolbar to display a shortcut menu that presents a list of commands related to the Quick Access Toolbar (Figure 25).

Figure 25

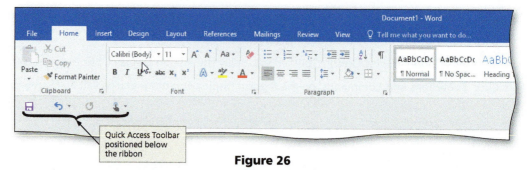

2

- Click 'Show Quick Access Toolbar Below the Ribbon' on the shortcut menu to display the Quick Access Toolbar below the ribbon (Figure 26).

Quick Access Toolbar positioned below the ribbon

Figure 26

3

- Right-click the Quick Access Toolbar to display a shortcut menu (Figure 27).

Quick Access Toolbar

shortcut menu

'Show Quick Access Toolbar Above the Ribbon' command

4

- Click 'Show Quick Access Toolbar Above the Ribbon' on the shortcut menu to return the Quick Access Toolbar to its original position (shown in Figure 25).

Figure 27

Other Ways

1. Click 'Customize Quick Access Toolbar' button on Quick Access Toolbar, click 'Show Below the Ribbon' or 'Show Above the Ribbon'

To Customize the Quick Access Toolbar

1 SIGN IN | 2 USE WINDOWS | **3 USE APPS** | 4 FILE MANAGEMENT | 5 SWITCH APPS | 6 SAVE FILES
7 CHANGE SCREEN RESOLUTION | 8 EXIT APPS | 9 USE ADDITIONAL APP FEATURES | 10 USE HELP

The Quick Access Toolbar provides easy access to some of the more frequently used commands in the Office apps. By default, the Quick Access Toolbar contains buttons for the Save, Undo, and Redo commands. If your computer or mobile device has a touch screen, the Quick Access Toolbar also might display the Touch/ Mouse Mode button. You can customize the Quick Access Toolbar by changing its location in the window, as shown in the previous steps, and by adding more buttons to reflect commands you would like to access easily. The following steps add the Quick Print button to the Quick Access Toolbar in the Word window. *Why? Adding the Quick Print button to the Quick Access Toolbar speeds up the process of printing.*

'Customize Quick Access Toolbar' button

Customize Quick Access Toolbar menu

1

- Click the 'Customize Quick Access Toolbar' button to display the Customize Quick Access Toolbar menu (Figure 28).

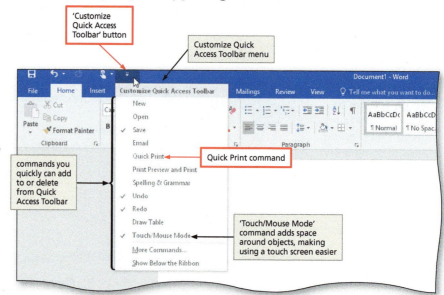

Q&A

Which commands are listed on the Customize Quick Access Toolbar menu?

It lists commands that commonly are added to the Quick Access Toolbar.

commands you quickly can add to or delete from Quick Access Toolbar

Quick Print command

'Touch/Mouse Mode' command adds space around objects, making using a touch screen easier

Figure 28

②

- If it is not selected already, click Quick Print on the Customize Quick Access Toolbar menu to add the Quick Print button to the Quick Access Toolbar (Figure 29).

Q&A How would I remove a button from the Quick Access Toolbar?
You would right-click the button you wish to remove and then click 'Remove from Quick Access Toolbar' on the shortcut menu or click the 'Customize Quick Access Toolbar' button on the Quick Access Toolbar and then click the button name in the Customize Quick Access Toolbar menu to remove the check mark.

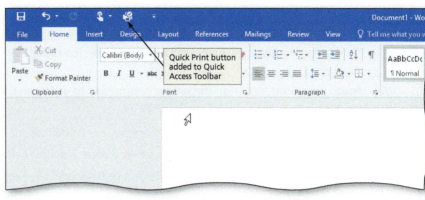

Figure 29

To Enter Text in a Document

1 SIGN IN | 2 USE WINDOWS | **3 USE APPS** | 4 FILE MANAGEMENT | 5 SWITCH APPS | 6 SAVE FILES
7 CHANGE SCREEN RESOLUTION | 8 EXIT APPS | 9 USE ADDITIONAL APP FEATURES | 10 USE HELP

The first step in creating a document is to enter its text by typing on the keyboard. By default, Word positions text at the left margin as you type. The following steps type this first line of a flyer. *Why? To begin creating a flyer, for example, you type the headline in the document window.*

①

- Type **VISIT NATIONAL MONUMENTS** as the text (Figure 30).

Q&A What is the blinking vertical bar to the right of the text?
The blinking bar is the insertion point, which indicates where text, graphics, and other items will be inserted in the document. As you type, the insertion point moves to the right, and when you reach the end of a line, it moves down to the beginning of the next line.

What if I make an error while typing?
You can press the BACKSPACE key until you have deleted the text in error and then retype the text correctly.

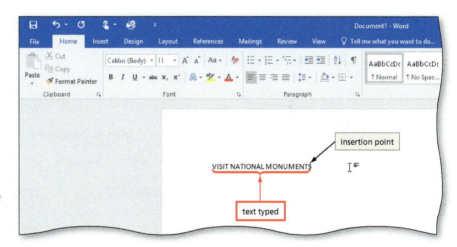

Figure 30

②

- Press the ENTER key to move the insertion point to the beginning of the next line (Figure 31).

Q&A Why did blank space appear between the entered text and the insertion point?
Each time you press the ENTER key, Word creates a new paragraph and inserts blank space between the two paragraphs. Depending on your settings, Word may or may not insert a blank space between the two paragraphs.

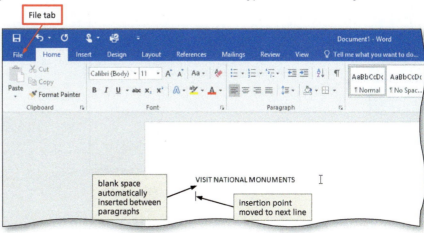

Figure 31

Document Properties

You can organize and identify your files by using **document properties**, which are the details about a file, such as the project author, title, and subject. For example, a class name or document topic can describe the file's purpose or content.

CONSIDER THIS

Why would you want to assign document properties to a document?
Document properties are valuable for a variety of reasons:

- Users can save time locating a particular file because they can view a file's document properties without opening the file.
- By creating consistent properties for files having similar content, users can better organize their files.
- Some organizations require users to add document properties so that other employees can view details about these files.

To Change Document Properties

1 SIGN IN | 2 USE WINDOWS | 3 USE APPS | **4 FILE MANAGEMENT** | 5 SWITCH APPS | 6 SAVE FILES
7 CHANGE SCREEN RESOLUTION | 8 EXIT APPS | 9 USE ADDITIONAL APP FEATURES | 10 USE HELP

You can change the document properties while working with the file in an Office app. When you save the file, the Office app (Word, in this case) will save the document properties with the file. The following steps change document properties. *Why? Adding document properties will help you identify characteristics of the file without opening it.*

1

- Click File on the ribbon (shown in Figure 31) to open the Backstage view and then, if necessary, click the Info tab in the Backstage view to display the Info gallery.

Q&A

What is the purpose of the File tab on the ribbon, and what is the Backstage view?
The File tab opens the Backstage view for each Office app, including Word. The **Backstage view** contains a set of commands that enable you to manage documents and provides data about the documents.

What is the purpose of the Info gallery in the Backstage view?
The Info tab, which is selected by default when you click File on the ribbon, displays the Info gallery, where you can protect a document, inspect a document, and manage versions of a document, as well as view all the file properties, such as when the file was created.

- Click to the right of the Comments property in the Properties list and then type **CIS 101 Assignment** in the Comments text box (Figure 32).

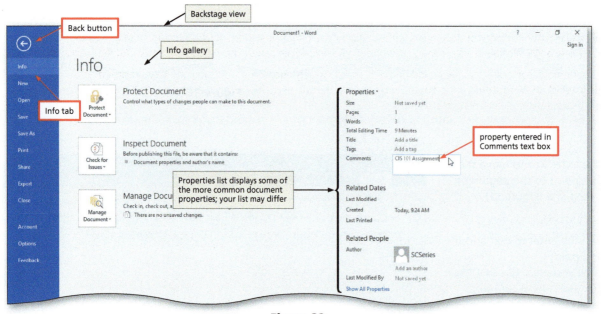

Figure 32

2

- Click the Back button in the upper-left corner of the Backstage view to return to the document window.

Printing, Saving, and Organizing Files

While you are creating a document, the computer or mobile device stores it in memory. When you save a document, the computer or mobile device places it on a storage medium, such as a hard disk, solid state drive (SSD), USB flash drive, or optical disc. The storage medium can be permanent in your computer, may be portable where you remove it from your computer, or may be on a web server you access through a network or the Internet.

A saved document is referred to as a file. A **file name** is the name assigned to a file when it is saved. When saving files, you should organize them so that you easily can find them later. Windows provides tools to help you organize files.

> **BTW**
>
> **File Type**
> Depending on your Windows settings, the file type .docx may be displayed immediately to the right of the file name after you save the file. The file type .docx is a Word 2016 document.

Printing a Document

After creating a document, you may want to print it. Printing a document enables you to distribute it to others in a form that can be read or viewed but typically not edited.

CONSIDER THIS

What is the best method for distributing a document?

The traditional method of distributing a document uses a printer to produce a hard copy. A **hard copy** or **printout** is information that exists on a physical medium, such as paper. Hard copies can be useful for the following reasons:

• Some people prefer proofreading a hard copy of a document rather than viewing it on the screen to check for errors and readability.

• Hard copies can serve as a backup reference if your storage medium is lost or becomes corrupted and you need to recreate the document.

Instead of distributing a hard copy of a document, users can distribute the document as an electronic image that mirrors the original document's appearance. The electronic image of the document can be sent as an email attachment, posted on a website, or copied to a portable storage medium, such as a USB flash drive. Two popular electronic image formats, sometimes called fixed formats, are PDF by Adobe Systems and XPS by Microsoft. In Word, you can create electronic image files through the Save As dialog box and the Export, Share, and Print tabs in the Backstage view. Electronic images of documents, such as PDF and XPS, can be useful for the following reasons:

• Users can view electronic images of documents without the software that created the original document (e.g., Word). For example, to view a PDF file use a program called Adobe Reader, which can be downloaded free from Adobe's website.

• Sending electronic documents saves paper and printer supplies. Society encourages users to contribute to **green computing**, which involves reducing the electricity consumed and environmental waste generated when using computers, mobile devices, and related technologies.

To Print a Document

1 SIGN IN | 2 USE WINDOWS | 3 USE APPS | **4 FILE MANAGEMENT** | **5 SWITCH APPS** | **6 SAVE FILES**
7 CHANGE SCREEN RESOLUTION | **8 EXIT APPS** | **9 USE ADDITIONAL APP FEATURES** | **10 USE HELP**

With the document opened, you may want to print it. *Why? Because you want to see how the text will appear on paper; you want to print a hard copy on a printer.* The following steps print a hard copy of the contents of the document.

- Click File on the ribbon to open the Backstage view.
- Click the Print tab in the Backstage view to display the Print gallery (Figure 33).

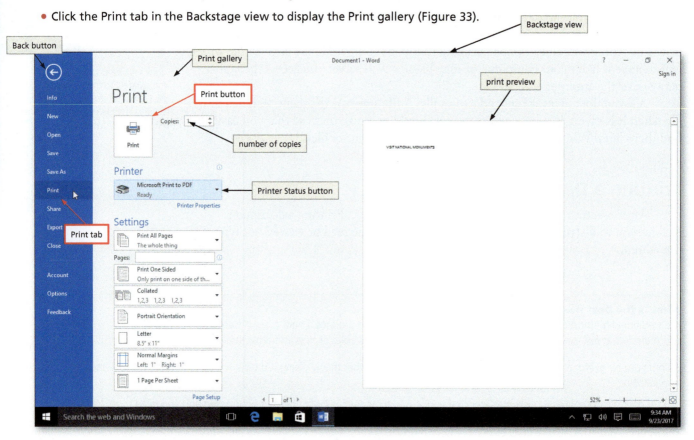

Figure 33

Q&A How can I print multiple copies of my document?
Increase the number in the Copies box in the Print gallery.

What if I decide not to print the document at this time?
Click the Back button in the upper-left corner of the Backstage view to return to the document window.

- Verify that the selected printer will print a hard copy of the document. If necessary, click the Printer Status button to display a list of available printer options and then click the desired printer to change the currently selected printer.

- Click the Print button in the Print gallery to print the document on the currently selected printer.

- When the printer stops, retrieve the hard copy (Figure 34).

Q&A What if I want to print an electronic image of a document instead of a hard copy?
You would click the Printer Status button in the Print gallery and then select the desired electronic image option, such as Microsoft XPS Document Writer, which would create an XPS file.

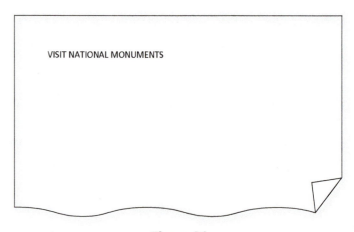

VISIT NATIONAL MONUMENTS

Figure 34

Other Ways

1. Press CTRL+P

Organizing Files and Folders

A file contains data. This data can range from a research paper to an accounting spreadsheet to an electronic math quiz. You should organize and store files in folders to avoid misplacing a file and to help you find a file quickly.

If you are taking an introductory computer class (CIS 101, for example), you may want to design a series of folders for the different subjects covered in the class. To accomplish this, you can arrange the folders in a hierarchy for the class, as shown in Figure 35. The hierarchy contains three levels. The first level contains the storage medium, such as a hard drive. The second level contains the class folder (CIS 101, in this case), and the third level contains seven folders, one each for a different Office app that will be covered in the class (Word, PowerPoint, Excel, Access, Outlook, Publisher, and OneNote).

Figure 35

When the hierarchy in Figure 35 is created, the storage medium is said to contain the CIS 101 folder, and the CIS 101 folder is said to contain the separate Office folders (i.e., Word, PowerPoint, Excel, etc.). In addition, this hierarchy easily can be expanded to include folders from other classes taken during additional semesters.

The vertical and horizontal lines in Figure 35 form a pathway that allows you to navigate to a drive or folder on a computer or network. A **path** consists of a drive letter (preceded by a drive name when necessary) and colon, to identify the storage device, and one or more folder names. A hard drive typically has a drive letter of C. Each drive or folder in the hierarchy has a corresponding path.

By default, Windows saves documents in the Documents folder, music in the Music folder, photos in the Pictures folder, videos in the Videos folder, and downloads in the Downloads folder.

The following pages illustrate the steps to organize the folders for this class and save a file in a folder:

1. Create the folder identifying your class.

2. Create the Word folder in the folder identifying your class.

3. Save a file in the Word folder.

4. Verify the location of the saved file.

To Create a Folder

When you create a folder, such as the CIS 101 folder shown in Figure 35, you must name the folder. A folder name should describe the folder and its contents. A folder name can contain spaces and any uppercase or lowercase characters, except a backslash (\), slash (/), colon (:), asterisk (*), question mark (?), quotation marks ("), less than symbol (<), greater than symbol (>), or vertical bar (|). Folder names cannot be CON, AUX, COM1, COM2, COM3, COM4, LPT1, LPT2, LPT3, PRN, or NUL. The same rules for naming folders also apply to naming files.

The following steps create a class folder (CIS 101, in this case) in the Documents folder. *Why? When storing files, you should organize the files so that it will be easier to find them later.*

1

- Click the File Explorer button on the taskbar to run File Explorer.

- If necessary, double-click This PC in the navigation pane to expand the contents of your computer.

- Click the Documents folder in the navigation pane to display the contents of the Documents folder in the file list (Figure 36).

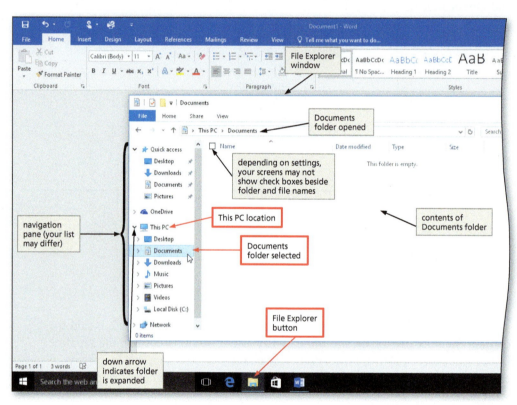

Figure 36

2

- Click the New folder button on the Quick Access Toolbar to create a new folder with the name, New folder, selected in a text box (Figure 37).

Q&A Why is the folder icon displayed differently on my computer or mobile device?
Windows might be configured to display contents differently on your computer or mobile device.

Figure 37

3

- Type **CIS 101** (or your class code) in the text box as the new folder name.

  If requested by your instructor, add your last name to the end of the folder name.

- Press the ENTER key to change the folder name from New folder to a folder name identifying your class (Figure 38).

Q&A

What happens when I press the ENTER key?

The class folder (CIS 101, in this case) is displayed in the file list, which contains the folder name, date modified, type, and size.

Figure 38

Other Ways

1. Press CTRL+SHIFT+N

2. Click the New folder button (Home tab | New group)

Folder Windows

The File Explorer window (shown in Figure 38) is called a folder window. Recall that a folder is a specific named location on a storage medium that contains related files. Most users rely on **folder windows** for finding, viewing, and managing information on their computers. Folder windows have common design elements, including the following (shown in Figure 38).

- The **address bar** provides quick navigation options. The arrows on the address bar allow you to visit different locations on the computer or mobile device.

- The buttons to the left of the address bar allow you to navigate the contents of the navigation pane and view recent pages.

- The **Previous Locations arrow** displays the locations you have visited.

- The **Refresh button** on the right side of the address bar refreshes the contents of the folder list.

- The **Search box** contains the dimmed words, Search Documents. You can type a term in the search box for a list of files, folders, shortcuts, and elements containing that term within the location you are searching.

- The **ribbon** contains four tabs used to accomplish various tasks on the computer or mobile device related to organizing and managing the contents of the open window. This ribbon works similarly to the ribbon in the Office apps.
- The **navigation pane** on the left contains the Quick access area, the OneDrive area, the This PC area, and the Network area.
- The **Quick access area** shows locations you access frequently. By default, this list contains links only to your Desktop, Downloads, Documents, and Pictures.

To Create a Folder within a Folder

With the class folder created, you can create folders that will store the files you create using Word. The following step creates a Word folder in the CIS 101 folder (or the folder identifying your class). *Why? To be able to organize your files, you should create a folder structure.*

- Double-click the icon or folder name for the CIS 101 folder (or the folder identifying your class) in the file list to open the folder.
- Click the New folder button on the Quick Access Toolbar to create a new folder with the name, New folder, selected in a text box folder.
- Type **Word** in the text box as the new folder name.
- Press the ENTER key to rename the folder (Figure 39).

Figure 39

Other Ways
1. Press CTRL+SHIFT+N	2. Click the New folder button (Home tab | New group)

To Expand a Folder, Scroll through Folder Contents, and Collapse a Folder

Folder windows display the hierarchy of items and the contents of drives and folders in the file list. You might want to expand a folder in the navigation pane to view its contents, scroll through its contents, and collapse it when you are finished viewing its contents. *Why? When a folder is expanded, you can see all the folders it contains. By contrast, a collapsed folder hides the folders it contains.* The following steps expand, scroll through, and then collapse the folder identifying your class (CIS 101, in this case).

- Double-click the Documents folder in the This PC area of the navigation pane, which expands the folder to display its contents and displays a black down arrow to the left of the Documents folder icon (Figure 40).

Figure 40

- Double-click the CIS 101 folder, which expands the folder to display its contents and displays a black down arrow to the left of the folder icon (Figure 41).

Experiment

- Drag the scroll box down or click the down scroll arrow on the vertical scroll bar to display additional folders at the bottom of the navigation pane. Drag the scroll box up or click the scroll bar above the scroll box to move the scroll box to the top of the navigation pane. Drag the scroll box down the scroll bar until the scroll box is halfway down the scroll bar.

Figure 41

- Double-click the folder identifying your class (CIS 101, in this case) to collapse the folder (Figure 42).

Q&A Why are some folders indented below others?
A folder contains the indented folders below it.

Figure 42

Other Ways

1. Point to display arrows in navigation pane, click arrow to expand or collapse

2. Select folder to expand or collapse using arrow keys, press RIGHT ARROW to expand; press LEFT ARROW to collapse

To Switch from One App to Another

The next step is to save the Word file containing the headline you typed earlier. Word, however, currently is not the active window. You can use the Word app button on the taskbar and live preview to switch to Word and then save the document in the Word document window.

Why? *By clicking the appropriate app button on the taskbar, you can switch to the running app you want to use.* The following steps switch to the Word window; however, the steps are the same for any active Office app currently displayed as a button on the taskbar.

- Point to the Word app button on the taskbar to see a live preview of the open document(s) or the window title(s) of the open document(s), depending on your computer's configuration (Figure 43).

Q&A What if I am using a touch screen?
Live preview will not work if you are using a touch screen. If you are using a touch screen and do not have a mouse, proceed to Step 2.

Figure 43

- Click the Word app button or the live preview to make the app associated with the app button the active window (Figure 44).

Q&A What if multiple documents are open in an app?
Click the desired live preview to switch to the window you want to use.

Figure 44

Other Ways

1. Press ALT+TAB until app you wish to display is selected

To Save a File in a Folder

1 SIGN IN | 2 USE WINDOWS | 3 USE APPS | 4 FILE MANAGEMENT | 5 SWITCH APPS | **6 SAVE FILES**
7 CHANGE SCREEN RESOLUTION | 8 EXIT APPS | 9 USE ADDITIONAL APP FEATURES | 10 USE HELP

With the Word folder created, you can save the Word document shown in the document window in the Word folder. *Why? Without saving a file, you may lose all the work you have completed and will be unable to reuse or share it with others later.* The following steps save a file in the Word folder contained in your class folder (CIS 101, in this case) using the file name, National Monuments.

- Click the Save button (shown in Figure 44) on the Quick Access Toolbar, which depending on settings, will display either the Save As gallery in the Backstage view (Figure 45) or the Save As dialog box (Figure 46).

Q&A What if the Save As gallery is not displayed in the Backstage view?
Click the Save As tab to display the Save As gallery.

How do I close the Backstage view?
Click the Back button in the upper-left corner of the Backstage view to return to the Word window.

Figure 45

2

• If your screen displays the Backstage view, click This PC, if necessary, to display options in the right pane related to saving on your computer or mobile device; if your screen already displays the Save As dialog box, proceed to Step 3.

Q&A What if I wanted to save on OneDrive instead?
You would click OneDrive. Saving on OneDrive is discussed in a later section in this module.

• Click the Browse button in the left pane to display the Save As dialog box (Figure 46).

navigation pane (your list may differ)

Save As dialog box

depending on settings, your screens may not display this folder while you are working in Word

first few words from document are displayed as default file name and are selected in File name box

default file type is Word Document

details pane shows file properties

Figure 46

Q&A Why does a file name already appear in the File name box?
Word automatically suggests a file name the first time you save a document. The file name normally consists of the first few words contained in the document. Because the suggested file name is selected, you do not need to delete it; as soon as you begin typing, the new file name replaces the selected text.

3

• Type **National Monuments** in the File name box (Save As dialog box) to change the file name. Do not press the ENTER key after typing the file name because you do not want to close the dialog box at this time (Figure 47).

Q&A What characters can I use in a file name?
The only invalid characters are the backslash (\), slash (/), colon (:), asterisk (*), question mark (?), quotation mark ("), less than symbol (<), greater than symbol (>), and vertical bar (|).

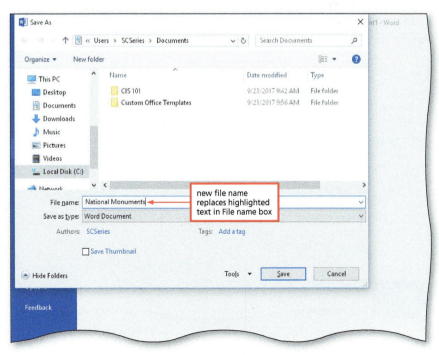

new file name replaces highlighted text in File name box

Figure 47

4

- Navigate to the desired save location (in this case, the Word folder in the CIS 101 folder [or your class folder] in the Documents folder) by performing the tasks in Steps 4a and 4b.

4a

- If the Documents folder is not displayed in the navigation pane, drag the scroll bar in the navigation pane until Documents appears.

- If the Documents folder is not expanded in the navigation pane, double-click Documents to display its folders in the navigation pane.

- If your class folder (CIS 101, in this case) is not expanded, double-click the CIS 101 folder to select the folder and display its contents in the navigation pane (Figure 48).

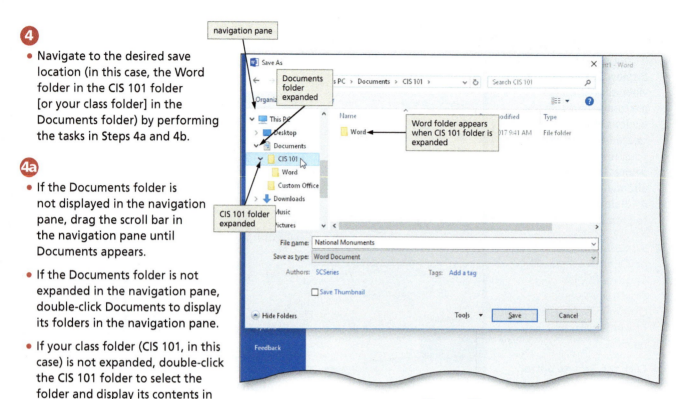

Figure 48

Q&A   What if I do not want to save in a folder?

Although storing files in folders is an effective technique for organizing files, some users prefer not to store files in folders. If you prefer not to save this file in a folder, select the storage device on which you wish to save the file and then proceed to Step 5.

4b

- Click the Word folder in the navigation pane to select it as the new save location and display its contents in the file list (Figure 49).

Figure 49

⑤

- Click the Save button (Save As dialog box) to save the document in the selected folder in the selected location with the entered file name (Figure 50).

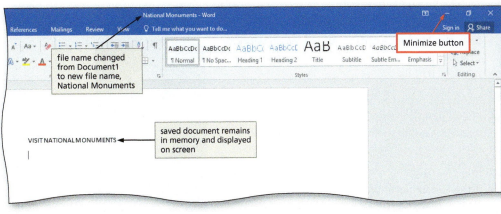

Figure 50

Q&A How do I know that the file is saved?
While an Office app such as Word is saving a file, it briefly displays a message on the status bar indicating the amount of the file saved. In addition, the file name appears on the title bar.

Other Ways

1. Click File on ribbon, click Save As tab in Backstage view, click This PC, click Browse button, type file name (Save As dialog box), navigate to desired save location, click Save button
2. Press F12, type file name (Save As dialog box), navigate to desired save location, click Save button

---

How often should you save a document?

It is important to save a document frequently for the following reasons:

- The document in memory might be lost if the computer is turned off or you lose electrical power while an app is running.

- If you run out of time before completing a project, you may finish it at a future time without starting over.

Navigating in Dialog Boxes

Navigating is the process of finding a location on a storage device. While saving the National Monuments file, for example, Steps 4a and 4b navigated to the Word folder located in the CIS 101 folder in the Documents folder. When performing certain functions in Windows apps, such as saving a file, opening a file, or inserting a picture in an existing document, you most likely will have to navigate to the location where you want to save the file or to the folder containing the file you want to open or insert. Most dialog boxes in Windows apps requiring navigation follow a similar procedure; that is, the way you navigate to a folder in one dialog box, such as the Save As dialog box, is similar to how you might navigate in another dialog box, such as the Open dialog box. If you chose to navigate to a specific location in a dialog box, you would follow the instructions in Steps 4a and 4b.

To Minimize and Restore a Window

1 SIGN IN | **2 USE WINDOWS** | 3 USE APPS | 4 FILE MANAGEMENT | 5 SWITCH APPS | 6 SAVE FILES
7 CHANGE SCREEN RESOLUTION | 8 EXIT APPS | 9 USE ADDITIONAL APP FEATURES | 10 USE HELP

Before continuing, you can verify that the Word file was saved properly. To do this, you will minimize the Word window and then open the CIS 101 window so that you can verify the file is stored in the CIS 101 folder on the hard drive. A **minimized window** is an open window that is hidden from view but can be displayed quickly by clicking the window's button on the taskbar.

In the following example, Word is used to illustrate minimizing and restoring windows; however, you would follow the same steps regardless of the Office app you are using. *Why? Before closing an app, you should make sure your file saved correctly so that you can find it later.*

The following steps minimize the Word window, verify that the file is saved, and then restore the minimized window.

- Click the Minimize button on the Word window title bar (shown in Figure 50) to minimize the window (Figure 51).

Q&A

Is the minimized window still available?
The minimized window, Word in this case, remains available but no longer is the active window. It is minimized as a button on the taskbar.

- If the File Explorer window is not open on the screen, click the File Explorer button on the taskbar to make the File Explorer window the active window.

Figure 51

- Double-click the Word folder in the file list to select the folder and display its contents (Figure 52).

Q&A

Why does the File Explorer button on the taskbar change?
A selected app button indicates that the app is active on the screen. When the button is not selected, the app is running but not active.

- After viewing the contents of the selected folder, click the Word app button on the taskbar to restore the minimized window (as shown in Figure 50).

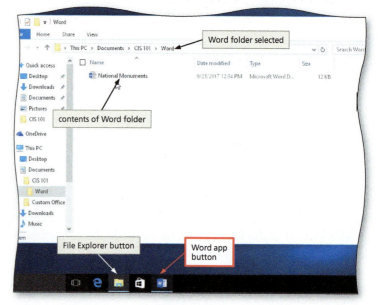

Figure 52

Other Ways

1. Right-click title bar, click Minimize on shortcut menu, click taskbar button in taskbar button area
2. Press WINDOWS+M, press WINDOWS+SHIFT+M
3. Click Word app button on taskbar to minimize window. Click Word app button again to restore window.

To Save a File on OneDrive

One of the features of Office is the capability to save files on OneDrive so that you can use the files on multiple computers or mobile devices without having to use an external storage device, such as a USB flash drive. Storing files on OneDrive also enables you to share files more efficiently with others, such as when using Office Online and Office 365.

In the following example, Word is used to save a file on OneDrive. *Why? Storing files on OneDrive provides more portability options than are available from storing files in the Documents folder.*

You can save files directly on OneDrive from within an Office app. The following steps save the current Word file on OneDrive. These steps require that you have a Microsoft account and an Internet connection.

1

- Click File on the ribbon to open the Backstage view.

- Click the Save As tab in the Backstage view to display the Save As gallery.

- Click OneDrive in the left pane to display OneDrive saving options or a Sign In button, if you are not signed in already to your Microsoft account (Figure 53).

Figure 53

2

- If your screen displays a Sign In button (shown in Figure 53), click it to display the Sign in dialog box (Figure 54).

Q&A What if the Sign In button does not appear?
If you already are signed into your Microsoft account, the Sign In button will not be displayed. In this case, proceed to Step 3.

- Follow the instructions on the screen to sign in to your Microsoft account.

Figure 54

3

- If necessary, in the Backstage view, click OneDrive in the left pane in the Save As gallery to select OneDrive as the save location.

- Click the Documents, or similar, folder in the right pane to display the Save As dialog box (Figure 55).

Q&A Why does the path in the OneDrive address bar in the Save As dialog box contain various letters and numbers?
The letters and numbers in the address bar uniquely identify the location of your OneDrive files and folders.

Figure 55

4

- Click the Save button (Save As dialog box) to save the file on OneDrive.

To Sign Out of a Microsoft Account

If you are using a public computer or otherwise wish to sign out of your Microsoft account, you should sign out of the account from the Accounts gallery in the Backstage view. Signing out of the account is the safest way to make sure that nobody else can access online files or settings stored in your Microsoft account. *Why? For security reasons, you should sign out of your Microsoft account when you are finished using a public or shared computer. Staying signed in to your Microsoft account might enable others to access your files.*

The following steps sign out of a Microsoft account from Word. You would use the same steps in any Office app. If you do not wish to sign out of your Microsoft account, read these steps without performing them.

1 Click File on the ribbon to open the Backstage view.

2 Click the Account tab to display the Account gallery (Figure 56).

3 Click the Sign out link, which displays the Remove Account dialog box. If a Can't remove Windows accounts dialog box appears instead of the Remove Account dialog box, click the OK button and skip the remaining steps.

    Q&A Why does a Can't remove Windows accounts dialog box appear?
    If you signed in to Windows using your Microsoft account, then you also must sign out from Windows, rather than signing out from within Word. When you are finished using Windows, be sure to sign out at that time.

4 Click the Yes button (Remove Account dialog box) to sign out of your Microsoft account on this computer or mobile device.

    Q&A Should I sign out of Windows after removing my Microsoft account?
    When you are finished using the computer, you should sign out of Windows for maximum security.

5 Click the Back button in the upper-left corner of the Backstage view to return to the document.

Figure 56

Screen Resolution

Screen resolution indicates the number of pixels (dots) that the computer uses to display the letters, numbers, graphics, and background you see on the screen. When you increase the screen resolution, Windows displays more information on the screen, but the information decreases in size. The reverse also is true: as you decrease the screen resolution, Windows displays less information on the screen, but the information increases in size.

Screen resolution usually is stated as the product of two numbers, such as 1366 × 768 (pronounced "thirteen sixty-six by seven sixty-eight"). A 1366 × 768 screen resolution results in a display of 1366 distinct pixels on each of 768 lines, or about 1,050,624 pixels. Changing the screen resolution affects how the ribbon appears in Office apps and some Windows dialog boxes. Figure 57, for example, shows the Word ribbon at screen resolutions of 1366 × 768 and 1024 × 768. All of the same commands are available regardless of screen resolution. The app (Word, in this case), however, makes changes to the groups and the buttons within the groups to accommodate the various screen resolutions. The result is that certain commands may need to be accessed differently depending on the resolution chosen. A command that is visible on the ribbon and available by clicking a button at one resolution may not be visible and may need to be accessed using its Dialog Box Launcher at a different resolution.

Figure 57 (a) Ribbon at 1366 × 768 Resolution

Figure 57 (b) Ribbon at 1024 × 768 Resolution

Comparing the two ribbons in Figure 57, notice the changes in content and layout of the groups and galleries. In some cases, the content of a group is the same in each resolution, but the layout of the group differs. For example, the same gallery and buttons appear in the Styles groups in the two resolutions, but the layouts differ. In other cases, the content and layout are the same across the resolution, but the level of detail differs with the resolution.

To Change the Screen Resolution

If you are using a computer to step through the modules in this book and you want your screen to match the figures, you may need to change your screen's resolution. *Why? The figures in this book use a screen resolution of 1366 × 768.* The following steps change the screen resolution to 1366 × 768. Your computer already may be set to 1366 × 768. Keep in mind that many computer labs prevent users from changing the screen resolution; in that case, read the following steps for illustration purposes.

- Click the Show desktop button, which is located at the far-right edge of the taskbar, to display the Windows desktop.

- Right-click an empty area on the Windows desktop to display a shortcut menu that contains a list of commands related to the desktop (Figure 58).

Q&A

Why does my shortcut menu display different commands?
Depending on your computer's hardware and configuration, different commands might appear on the shortcut menu.

Figure 58

2

- Click Display settings on the shortcut menu to open the Settings app window. If necessary, scroll to display the 'Advanced display settings' link (Figure 59).

Figure 59

- Click 'Advanced display settings' in the Settings app window to display the advanced display settings.

- If necessary, scroll to display the Resolution box (Figure 60).

Figure 60

- Click the Resolution box to display a list of available screen resolutions (Figure 61).

- If necessary, scroll to and then click **1366 × 768** to select the screen resolution.

Q&A What if my computer does not support the 1366 × 768 resolution?
Some computers do not support the 1366 × 768 resolution. In this case, select a resolution that is close to the 1366 × 768 resolution.

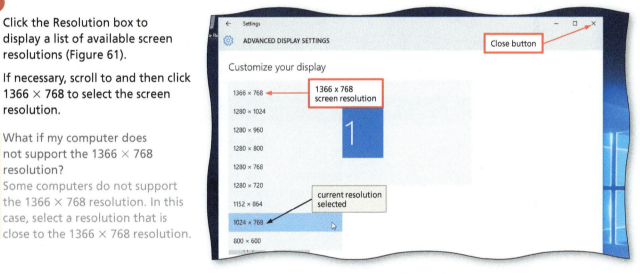

Figure 61

- Click the Apply button (Advanced Display Settings window), shown in Figure 60, to change the screen resolution and a confirmation message (Figure 62).

- Click the Keep changes button to accept the new screen resolution.

- Click the Close button (shown in Figure 61) to close the Settings app window.

Figure 62

Other Ways

1. Click Start button, click Settings, click System, click Display, click 'Advanced display settings,' select desired resolution in Resolution box, click Apply button, click Keep changes button

2. Type **screen resolution** in search box, click 'Change the screen resolution,' select desired resolution in Resolution box, click Apply button, click Keep changes button

To Exit an App with One Document Open

1 SIGN IN | 2 USE WINDOWS | 3 USE APPS | 4 FILE MANAGEMENT | 5 SWITCH APPS | 6 SAVE FILES
7 CHANGE SCREEN RESOLUTION | **8 EXIT APPS** | **9 USE ADDITIONAL APP FEATURES** | **10 USE HELP**

When you exit an Office app, such as Word, if you have made changes to a file since the last time the file was saved, the app displays a dialog box asking if you want to save the changes you made to the file before it closes the app window. *Why? The dialog box contains three buttons with these resulting actions: the Save button saves the changes and then exits the app, the Don't Save button exits the app without saving changes, and the Cancel button closes the dialog box and redisplays the file without saving the changes.*

If no changes have been made to an open document since the last time the file was saved, the app will close the window without displaying a dialog box.

The following steps exit Word. You would follow similar steps in other Office apps.

- If necessary, click the Word app button on the taskbar to display the Word window on the desktop (Figure 63).

Figure 63

- Click the Close button on the right side of the Word window title bar to close the document and exit Word. If a Microsoft Word dialog box appears, click the Save button to save any changes made to the document since the last save.

Q&A   What if I have more than one document open in Word?
You could click the Close button for each open document. When you click the last open document's Close button, you also exit Word. As an alternative that is more efficient, you could right-click the Word app button on the taskbar and then click 'Close all windows' on the shortcut menu to close all open documents and exit Word.

Other Ways

1. Right-click the Word app button on Windows taskbar, click 'Close all windows' on shortcut menu
2. Press ALT + F4

To Copy a Folder to OneDrive

1 SIGN IN | 2 USE WINDOWS | 3 USE APPS | **4 FILE MANAGEMENT** | 5 SWITCH APPS | 6 SAVE FILES
7 CHANGE SCREEN RESOLUTION | 8 EXIT APPS | **9 USE ADDITIONAL APP FEATURES** | **10 USE HELP**

To back up your files or easily make them available on another computer or mobile device, you can copy them to OneDrive. The following steps copy your CIS 101 folder to OneDrive. If you do not have access to a OneDrive account, read the following steps without performing them. *Why? It often is good practice to have a backup of your files so that they are available in case something happens to your original copies.*

- Click the File Explorer button on the taskbar to make the folder window the active window.

- Navigate to the CIS 101 folder (or your class folder) in the Documents folder.

- Click Documents in the This PC area of the navigation pane to display the CIS 101 folder in the file list.

Q&A What if my CIS 101 folder is stored in a different location? Use the navigation pane to navigate to the location of your CIS 101 folder. The CIS 101 folder should be displayed in the file list once you have located it.

- Click the CIS 101 folder in the file list to select it (Figure 64).

Figure 64

2

- Click Home on the ribbon to display the Home tab.

- Click the Copy to button (Home tab | Organize group) to display the Copy to menu (Figure 65).

Figure 65

- Click Choose location on the Copy to menu to display the Copy Items dialog box.

- Click OneDrive (Copy Items dialog box) to select it (Figure 66).

Figure 66

- Click the Copy button (Copy Items dialog box) to copy the selected folder to OneDrive.

- Click OneDrive in the navigation pane to verify the CIS 101 folder displays in the file list (Figure 67).

Q&A Why does a Microsoft OneDrive dialog box appear when I click OneDrive in the navigation pane?
If you are not currently signed in to Windows using a Microsoft account, you will manually need to sign in to a Microsoft account to save files to OneDrive. Follow the instructions on the screen to sign in to your Microsoft account.

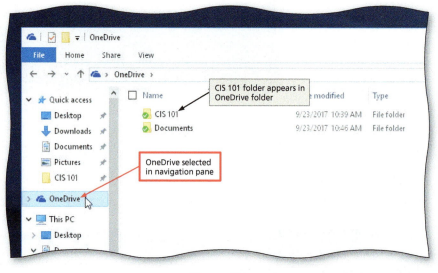

Figure 67

Other Ways

1. In File Explorer, select folder to copy, click Copy button (Home tab | Clipboard group), display contents of OneDrive in file list, click Paste button (Home tab | Clipboard group)

2. In File Explorer, select folder to copy, press CTRL+C, display contents of OneDrive in file list, press CTRL+V

1 SIGN IN | 2 USE WINDOWS | 3 USE APPS | **4 FILE MANAGEMENT** | 5 SWITCH APPS | 6 SAVE FILES
7 CHANGE SCREEN RESOLUTION | 8 EXIT APPS | **9 USE ADDITIONAL APP FEATURES** | 10 USE HELP

To Unlink a OneDrive Account

If you are using a public computer and are not signed in to Windows with a Microsoft account, you should unlink your OneDrive account so that other users cannot access it. *Why? If you do not unlink your OneDrive account, other people accessing the same user account on the computer will be able to view, remove, and add to files stored in your OneDrive account.*

The following steps unlink your OneDrive account. If you do not wish to sign out of your Microsoft account, read these steps without performing them.

- Click the 'Show hidden icons' button on the Windows taskbar to show a menu of hidden icons (Figure 68).

Figure 68

- Right click the OneDrive icon (shown in Figure 68) to display a shortcut menu (Figure 69).

Figure 69

3

- Click Settings on the shortcut menu to display the Microsoft OneDrive dialog box (Figure 70).

- If necessary, click the Settings tab. (Some versions require you click an Account tab instead.)

- Click the Unlink OneDrive button (Microsoft OneDrive dialog box) to unlink the OneDrive account.

- When the Microsoft OneDrive dialog box appears with a Welcome to OneDrive message, click the Close button.

- Minimize the File Explorer window.

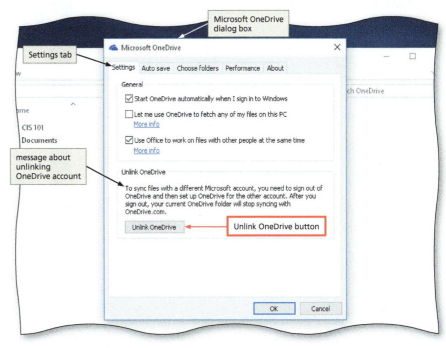

Figure 70

Break Point: If you wish to take a break, this is a good place to do so. To resume at a later time, continue to follow the steps from this location forward.

Additional Common Features of Office Apps

The previous section used Word to illustrate common features of Office and some basic elements unique to Word. The following sections continue to use Word present additional common features of Office.

In the following pages, you will learn how to do the following:

1. Run Word using the search box.

2. Open a document in Word.

3. Close the document.

4. Reopen the document just closed.

5. Create a blank Word document from Windows Explorer and then open the file.

6. Save a document with a new file name.

To Run an App Using the Search Box

1 SIGN IN | **2 USE WINDOWS** | 3 USE APPS | 4 FILE MANAGEMENT | 5 SWITCH APPS | 6 SAVE FILES
7 CHANGE SCREEN RESOLUTION | 8 EXIT APPS | **9 USE ADDITIONAL APP FEATURES** | 10 USE HELP

The following steps, which assume Windows is running, use the search box to run Word based on a typical installation; however, you would follow similar steps to run any app. *Why? Some people prefer to use the search box to locate and run an app, as opposed to searching through a list of all apps on the Start menu.* You may need to ask your instructor how to run Word on your computer.

- Type `Word 2016` as the search text in the search box and watch the search results appear in the search results (Figure 71).

Q&A
Do I need to type the complete app name or use correct capitalization?
No, you need to type just enough characters of the app name for it to appear in the search results. For example, you may be able to type Word or word, instead of Word 2016.

What if the search does not locate the Word app on my computer?
You may need to adjust the Windows search settings. Search for the word, index; click 'Indexing Options Control panel'; click the Modify button (Indexing Options dialog box); expand the Local Disk, if necessary; place a check mark beside all Program Files entries; and then click the OK button. It may take a few minutes for the index to rebuild. If it still does not work, you may need to click the Advanced button (Indexing Options dialog box) and then click the Rebuild button (Advanced Options dialog box).

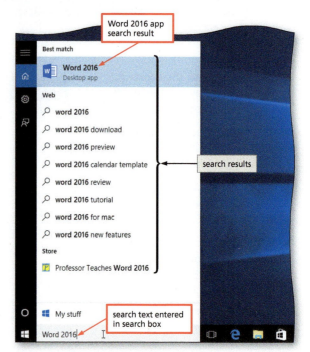

Figure 71

2

- Click the app name, Word 2016 in this case, in the search results to run Word and display the Word start screen.

- Click the Blank document thumbnail on the Word start screen (shown earlier in this module in Figure 8) to create a blank document and display it in the Word window. If the Word window is not maximized, click the Maximize button on its title bar to maximize the window.

To Open an Existing File

As discussed earlier, the Backstage view contains a set of commands that enable you to manage documents and data about the documents. *Why? From the Backstage view in Word, for example, you can create, open, print, and save documents. You also can share documents, manage versions, set permissions, and modify document properties. In other Office apps, the Backstage view may contain features specific to those apps.* The following steps open a saved file, specifically the National Monuments file, that recently was saved.

- Click File on the ribbon to open the Backstage view and then click the Open tab in the Backstage view to display the Open gallery in the Backstage view.

- Click This PC to display recent folders accessed on your computer.

- Click the Browse button to display the Open dialog box.

- If necessary, navigate to the location of the file to open (Word folder in the CIS 101 folder).

- Click the file to open, National Monuments in this case, to select the file (Figure 72).

- Click the Open button (Open dialog box) to open the file (shown earlier in the module in Figure 50). If necessary, click the Enable Content button.

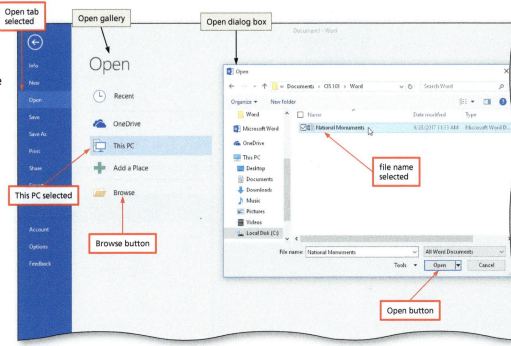

Figure 72

Q&A Why did a Security Warning appear?
The Security Warning appears when you open an Office file that might contain harmful content. The files you create in this module are not harmful, but you should be cautious when opening files from other people.

Other Ways

1. Press CTRL+O

2. Navigate to file in File Explorer window, double-click file name

To Create a New Document
from the Backstage View

You can open multiple documents in an Office program, such as Word, so that you can work on the documents at the same time. The following steps create a file, a blank document in this case, from the Backstage view. *Why? You want to create a new document while keeping the current document open.*

- Click File on the ribbon to open the Backstage view.

- Click the New tab in the Backstage view to display the New gallery (Figure 73).

Q&A Can I create documents through the Backstage view in other Office apps? Yes. If the Office app has a New tab in the Backstage view, the New gallery displays various options for creating a new file.

Figure 73

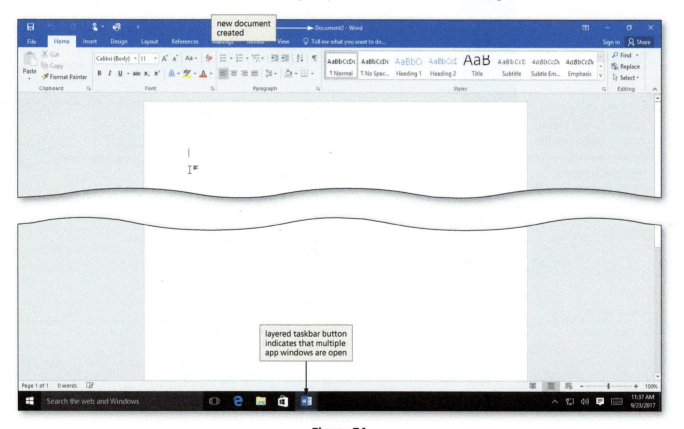

2

- Click the Blank document thumbnail in the New gallery to create a new document (Figure 74).

Figure 74

Other Ways

1. Press CTRL+N

To Enter Text in a Document

The following step enters the first line of text in a document.

1 Type **List of Special Rates for National Monuments** and then press the ENTER key (Figure 75).

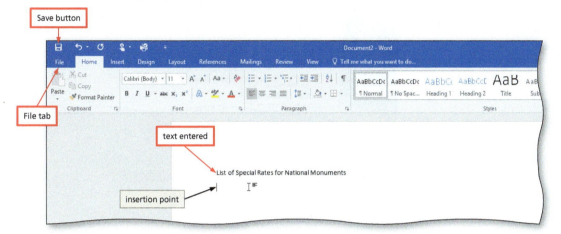

Figure 75

To Save a File in a Folder

The following steps save the second document in the Word folder in the class folder (CIS 101, in this case) in the Documents folder using the file name, Special Rates.

1 Click the Save button on the Quick Access Toolbar, which depending on settings, will display either the Save As gallery in the Backstage view or the Save As dialog box.

2 If your screen displays the Backstage view, click This PC, if necessary, to display options in the right pane related to saving on your computer; if your screen already displays the Save As dialog box, proceed to Step 4.

3 Click the Browse button in the left pane to display the Save As dialog box.

4 If necessary, type **Special Rates** in the File name box (Save As dialog box) to change the file name. Do not press the ENTER key after typing the file name because you do not want to close the dialog box at this time.

5 If necessary, navigate to the desired save location (in this case, the Word folder in the CIS 101 folder [or your class folder] in the Documents folder). For specific instructions, perform the tasks in Steps 4a and 4b in the previous section in this module titled To Save a File in a Folder.

6 Click the Save button (Save As dialog box) to save the document in the selected folder on the selected drive with the entered file name.

To Close a File Using the Backstage View

1 SIGN IN | 2 USE WINDOWS | 3 USE APPS | 4 FILE MANAGEMENT | 5 SWITCH APPS | 6 SAVE FILES
7 CHANGE SCREEN RESOLUTION | 8 EXIT APPS | 9 USE ADDITIONAL APP FEATURES | 10 USE HELP

Sometimes, you may want to close an Office file, such as a Word document, entirely and start over with a new file. You also may want to close a file when you are done working with it. ***Why?*** *You should close a file when you are done working with it so that you do not make inadvertent changes to it.* The following steps close the current active Word file, that is, the Special Rates document, without exiting Word.

①

- Click File on the ribbon to open the Backstage view (Figure 76).

②

- Click Close in the Backstage view to close the open file (Special Rates, in this case) without exiting the active app (Word).

Q&A

What if Word displays a dialog box about saving?

Click the Save button if you want to save the changes, click the Don't Save button if you want to ignore the changes since the last time you saved, and click the Cancel button if you do not want to close the document.

Can I use the Backstage view to close an open file in other Office apps, such as PowerPoint and Excel?
Yes.

Figure 76

Other Ways

1. Press CTRL+F4

To Open a Recent File Using the Backstage View

1 SIGN IN | 2 USE WINDOWS | 3 USE APPS | 4 FILE MANAGEMENT | 5 SWITCH APPS | 6 SAVE FILES
7 CHANGE SCREEN RESOLUTION | 8 EXIT APPS | 9 USE ADDITIONAL APP FEATURES | 10 USE HELP

You sometimes need to open a file that you recently modified. *Why? You may have more changes to make, such as adding more content or correcting errors.* The Backstage view allows you to access recent files easily. The following steps reopen the Special Rates file just closed.

①

- Click File on the ribbon to open the Backstage view.

- Click the Open tab in the Backstage view to display the Open gallery (Figure 77).

②

- Click the desired file name in the Recent list, Special Rates in this case, to open the file.

Figure 77

Other Ways

1. Click File on ribbon, click Open tab in Backstage view, click This PC, click Browse button, navigate to file (Open dialog box), click Open button

To Create a New Blank Document from File Explorer

1 SIGN IN | 2 USE WINDOWS | 3 USE APPS | 4 FILE MANAGEMENT | 5 SWITCH APPS | 6 SAVE FILES
7 CHANGE SCREEN RESOLUTION | 8 EXIT APPS | 9 USE ADDITIONAL APP FEATURES | 10 USE HELP

File Explorer provides a means to create a blank Office document without running an Office app. The following steps use File Explorer to create a blank Word document. *Why? Sometimes you might need to create a blank document and then return to it later for editing.*

1

- Click the File Explorer button on the taskbar to make the folder window the active window.

- If necessary, double-click the Documents folder in the navigation pane to expand the Documents folder.

- If necessary, double-click your class folder (CIS 101, in this case) in the navigation pane to expand the folder.

- Click the Word folder in the navigation pane to display its contents in the file list.

- With the Word folder selected, right-click an open area in the file list to display a shortcut menu.

- Point to New on the shortcut menu to display the New submenu (Figure 78).

Figure 78

2

- Click 'Microsoft Word Document' on the New submenu to display an icon and text box for a new file in the current folder window with the file name, New Microsoft Word Document, selected (Figure 79).

Figure 79

3

- Type **Recommended Travel Agents** in the text box and then press the ENTER key to assign a new file name to the new file in the current folder (Figure 80).

Figure 80

To Run an App from File Explorer and Open a File

1 SIGN IN | 2 USE WINDOWS | 3 USE APPS | 4 FILE MANAGEMENT | 5 SWITCH APPS | 6 SAVE FILES
7 CHANGE SCREEN RESOLUTION | 8 EXIT APPS | 9 USE ADDITIONAL APP FEATURES | 10 USE HELP

Previously in this module, you learned how to run Word using the Start menu and the search box. The following steps, which assume Windows is running, use File Explorer to run Word based on a typical installation. *Why? When you open an existing file from File Explorer, the app in which the file was created runs and then opens the selected file.* You may need to ask your instructor how to run Word for your computer.

- If necessary, display the file to open in the folder window in File Explorer.

- Right-click the file icon or file name you want to open (Recommended Travel Agents, in this case) to display a shortcut menu (Figure 81).

- Click Open on the shortcut menu to open the selected file in the app used to create the file, Word in this case (shown in Figure 82).

Figure 81

- If the window is not maximized, click the Maximize button on the title bar to maximize the window.

Other Ways

1. Double-click the file name in the file list

To Enter Text in a Document

The following step enters a line of text in the blank Word document.

1 Type **List of Recommended Travel Agents** and then press the ENTER key (shown in Figure 82).

To Save an Existing Office File with the Same File Name

1 SIGN IN | 2 USE WINDOWS | 3 USE APPS | 4 FILE MANAGEMENT | 5 SWITCH APPS | 6 SAVE FILES
7 CHANGE SCREEN RESOLUTION | 8 EXIT APPS | 9 USE ADDITIONAL APP FEATURES | 10 USE HELP

Saving frequently cannot be overemphasized. **Why?** *You have made modifications to the file (document) since you created it. Thus, you should save again. You should continue saving files frequently so that you do not lose the changes you have made since the time you last saved the file.* You can use the same file name, such as Recommended Travel Agents, to save the changes made to the document. The following step saves a file again with the same file name.

1

- Click the Save button on the Quick Access Toolbar to overwrite the previously saved file (Recommended Travel Agents, in this case) in the Word folder (Figure 82).

Figure 82

Other Ways

1. Press CTRL+S   2. Press SHIFT+F12

To Save a File with a New File Name

You might want to save a file with a different file name or to a different location. For example, you might start a homework assignment with a data file and then save it with a final file name for submission to your instructor, saving it to a location designated by your instructor. The following steps save a file with a different file name.

1 Click the File tab to open the Backstage view. Click the Save As tab to display the Save As gallery.

2 If necessary, click This PC to display options in the right pane related to saving on your computer. Click the Browse button in the left pane to display the Save As dialog box.

3 Type **Travel Agents** in the File name box (Save As dialog box) to change the file name. Do not press the ENTER key after typing the file name because you do not want to close the dialog box at this time.

4 If necessary, navigate to the desired save location (in this case, the Word folder in the CIS 101 folder [or your class folder] in the Documents folder). For specific instructions, perform the tasks in Steps 4a and 4b in the previous section titled To Save a File in a Folder.

5 Click the Save button (Save As dialog box) to save the document in the selected folder on the selected drive with the entered file name.

To Exit an Office App

You are finished using Word. The following steps exit Word.

1 Because you have multiple Word documents open, right-click the Word app button on the taskbar and then click 'Close all windows' on the shortcut menu to close all open documents and exit Word.

2 If a dialog box appears, click the Save button to save any changes made to the file since the last save.

Renaming, Moving, and Deleting Files

Earlier in this module, you learned how to organize files in folders, which is part of a process known as **file management**. The following sections cover additional file management topics including renaming, moving, and deleting files.

To Rename a File

1 SIGN IN | 2 USE WINDOWS | 3 USE APPS | **4 FILE MANAGEMENT** | 5 SWITCH APPS | 6 SAVE FILES
7 CHANGE SCREEN RESOLUTION | 8 EXIT APPS | 9 USE ADDITIONAL APP FEATURES | **10 USE HELP**

You may want to change the name of, or rename, a file or a folder. ***Why?*** *You may want to distinguish a file in one folder or drive from a copy of a similar file, or you may decide to rename a file to better identify its contents.* The following steps change the name of the National Monuments file in the Word folder to National Monuments Flyer.

1

- If necessary, click the File Explorer button on the taskbar to make the folder window the active window.

- Navigate to the location of the file to be renamed (in this case, the Word folder in the CIS 101 [or your class folder] folder in the Documents folder) to display the file(s) it contains in the file list.

- Click the file to be renamed, the National Monuments icon or file name in the file list in this case, to select it.

- Right-click the selected file to display a shortcut menu that presents a list of commands related to files (Figure 83).

Figure 83

2

- Click Rename on the shortcut menu to place the current file name in a text box.

- Type **National Monuments Flyer** in the text box and then press the ENTER key (Figure 84).

Q&A Are any risks involved in renaming files that are located on a hard drive?

If you inadvertently rename a file that is associated with certain apps, the apps may not be able to find the file and, therefore, may not run properly. Always use caution when renaming files.

Can I rename a file when it is open?

No, a file must be closed to change the file name.

Figure 84

Other Ways

1. Select file, press F2, type new file name, press ENTER

2. Select file, click Rename (Home tab | Organize group), type new file name, press ENTER

To Move a File

1 SIGN IN | 2 USE WINDOWS | 3 USE APPS | **4 FILE MANAGEMENT** | 5 SWITCH APPS | 6 SAVE FILES
7 CHANGE SCREEN RESOLUTION | 8 EXIT APPS | 9 USE ADDITIONAL APP FEATURES | **10 USE HELP**

Why? At some time, you may want to move a file from one folder, called the source folder, to another, called the destination folder. When you move a file, it no longer appears in the original folder. If the destination and the source folders are on the same media, you can move a file by dragging it. If the folders are on different media, you will need to right-drag the file and then click Move here on the shortcut menu. The following step moves the Recommended Travel Agents file from the Word folder to the CIS 101 folder.

1

- If necessary, in File Explorer, navigate to the location of the file to be moved (in this case, the Word folder in the CIS 101 folder [or your class folder] in the Documents folder).

- If necessary, click the Word folder in the navigation pane to display the files it contains in the right pane.

- Drag the file to be moved, the Recommended Travel Agents file in the right pane in this case, to the CIS 101 folder in the navigation pane (Figure 85).

Experiment

- Click the CIS 101 folder in the navigation pane to verify that the file was moved.

Figure 85

Other Ways

1. Right-click file to move, click Cut on shortcut menu, right-click destination folder, click Paste on shortcut menu

2. Select file to move, press CTRL+X, select destination folder, press CTRL+V

Essential Concepts and Skills   **Office 2016 and Windows 10 Module**   **OFF** 53

1 SIGN IN | 2 USE WINDOWS | 3 USE APPS | **4 FILE MANAGEMENT** | 5 SWITCH APPS | 6 SAVE FILES
7 CHANGE SCREEN RESOLUTION | 8 EXIT APPS | 9 USE ADDITIONAL APP FEATURES | 10 USE HELP

To Delete a File

A final task you may want to perform is to delete a file. Exercise extreme caution when deleting a file or files. When you delete a file from a hard drive, the deleted file is stored in the Recycle Bin where you can recover it until you empty the Recycle Bin. If you delete a file from removable media, such as a USB flash drive, the file is deleted permanently. The next steps delete the Recommended Travel Agents file from the CIS 101 folder. *Why? When a file no longer is needed, you can delete it to conserve space on your storage location.*

- If necessary, in File Explorer, navigate to the location of the file to be deleted (in this case, the CIS 101 folder [or your class folder] in the Documents folder).

- Click the file to be deleted, the Recommended Travel Agents icon or file name in the right pane in this case, to select the file.

- Right-click the selected file to display a shortcut menu (Figure 86).

2

- Click Delete on the shortcut menu to delete the file.

- If a dialog box appears, click the Yes button to delete the file.

Figure 86

Q&A Can I use this same technique to delete a folder?

Yes. Right-click the folder and then click Delete on the shortcut menu. When you delete a folder, all of the files and folders contained in the folder you are deleting, together with any files and folders on lower hierarchical levels, are deleted as well. For example, if you delete the CIS 101 folder, you will delete all folders and files inside the CIS 101 folder.

Other Ways

1. Select file, press DELETE

Microsoft Office and Windows Help

At any time while you are using one of the Office apps, such as Word, you can use Office Help to display information about all topics associated with the app. Help in other Office apps operates in a similar fashion.

In Office, Help is presented in a window that has browser-style navigation buttons. Each Office app has its own Help home page, which is the starting Help page that is displayed in the Help window. If your computer is connected to the Internet, the contents of the Help page reflect both the local help files installed on the computer and material from Microsoft's website.

To Open the Help Window in an Office App

1 SIGN IN | 2 USE WINDOWS | 3 USE APPS | 4 FILE MANAGEMENT | 5 SWITCH APPS | 6 SAVE FILES

7 CHANGE SCREEN RESOLUTION | 8 EXIT APPS | 9 USE ADDITIONAL APP FEATURES | 10 USE HELP

The following step opens the Word Help window. *Why? You might not understand how certain commands or operations work in Word, so you can obtain the necessary information using help.*

- Run Word.

- Click the Blank document thumbnail to display a blank document.

- Press F1 to open the Word Help window (Figure 87).

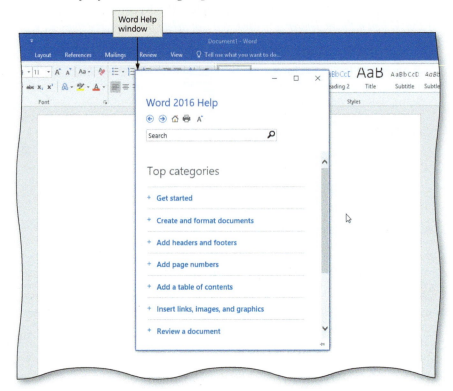

Figure 87

Moving and Resizing Windows

At times, it is useful, or even necessary, to have more than one window open and visible on the screen at the same time. You can resize and move these open windows so that you can view different areas of and elements in the window. In the case of the Help window, for example, it could be covering document text in the Word window that you need to see.

To Move a Window by Dragging

1 SIGN IN | 2 USE WINDOWS | 3 USE APPS | 4 FILE MANAGEMENT | 5 SWITCH APPS | 6 SAVE FILES

7 CHANGE SCREEN RESOLUTION | 8 EXIT APPS | 9 USE ADDITIONAL APP FEATURES | 10 USE HELP

You can move any open window that is not maximized to another location on the desktop by dragging the title bar of the window. *Why? You might want to have a better view of what is behind the window or just want to move the window so that you can see it better.* The following step drags the Word Help window to the upper-left corner of the desktop.

- Drag the window title bar (the Word Help window title bar, in this case) so that the window moves to the upper-left corner of the desktop, as shown in Figure 88.

Figure 88

To Resize a Window by Dragging

1 SIGN IN | **2 USE WINDOWS** | 3 USE APPS | 4 FILE MANAGEMENT | 5 SWITCH APPS | 6 SAVE FILES
7 CHANGE SCREEN RESOLUTION | 8 EXIT APPS | 9 USE ADDITIONAL APP FEATURES | 10 USE HELP

A method used to change the size of the window is to drag the window borders. The following step changes the size of the Word Help window by dragging its borders. *Why? Sometimes, information is not visible completely in a window, and you want to increase the size of the window.*

- Point to the lower-right corner of the window (the Word Help window, in this case) until the pointer changes to a two-headed arrow.

- Drag the bottom border downward to display more of the active window (Figure 89).

Q&A

Can I drag other borders on the window to enlarge or shrink the window?
Yes, you can drag the left, right, and top borders and any window corner to resize a window.

Will Windows remember the new size of the window after I close it?
Yes. When you reopen the window, Windows will display it at the same size it was when you closed it.

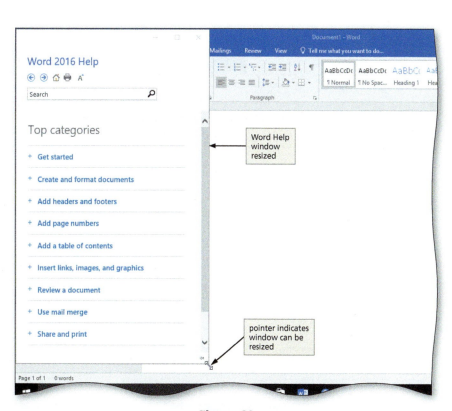

Figure 89

Using Office Help

Once an Office app's Help window is open, several methods exist for navigating Help. You can search for help by using any of the three following methods from the Help window:

1. Enter search text in the Search text box.
2. Click the links in the Help window.
3. Use the Table of Contents.

To Obtain Help Using the Search Text Box

1 SIGN IN | 2 USE WINDOWS | 3 USE APPS | 4 FILE MANAGEMENT | 5 SWITCH APPS | 6 SAVE FILES
7 CHANGE SCREEN RESOLUTION | 8 EXIT APPS | 9 USE ADDITIONAL APP FEATURES | 10 USE HELP

Assume for the following example that you want to know more about fonts. The following steps use the Search text box to obtain useful information about fonts by entering the word, fonts, as search text. *Why? You may not know the exact help topic you are looking to find, so using keywords can help narrow your search.*

- Type **fonts** in the Search text box at the top of the Word Help window to enter the search text.

- Press the ENTER key to display the search results (Figure 90).

Q&A

Why do my search results differ?
If you do not have an Internet connection, your results will reflect only the content of the Help files on your computer. When searching for help online, results also can change as content is added, deleted, and updated on the online Help webpages maintained by Microsoft.

Why were my search results not very helpful?
When initiating a search, be sure to check the spelling of the search text; also, keep your search specific to return the most accurate results.

Figure 90

- Click the 'Change the font color (text color)', or a similar, link to display the Help information associated with the selected topic (Figure 91).

Figure 91

- Click the Home button in the Help window to clear the search results and redisplay the Help home page (Figure 92).

- Click the Close button in the Word 2016 Help window to close the window.

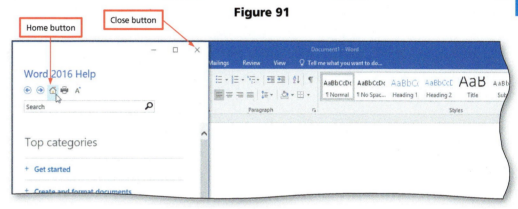

Figure 92

Obtaining Help while Working in an Office App

Help in the Office apps, such as Word, provides you with the ability to obtain help directly, without opening the Help window and initiating a search. For example, you may be unsure about how a particular command works, or you may be presented with a dialog box that you are not sure how to use.

Figure 93 shows one option for obtaining help while working in an Office app. If you want to learn more about a command, point to its button and wait for the ScreenTip to appear. If the Help icon and 'Tell me more' link appear in the ScreenTip, click the 'Tell me more' link or press the F1 key while pointing to the button to open the Help window associated with that command.

BTW

Customizing the Ribbon

In addition to customizing the Quick Access Toolbar, you can add items to and remove items from the ribbon. To customize the ribbon, click File on the ribbon to open the Backstage view, click the Options tab in the Backstage view, and then click Customize Ribbon in the left pane of the Options dialog box. More information about customizing the ribbon is presented in a later module.

Figure 93

Figure 94 shows a dialog box that contains a Help button. Clicking the Help button or pressing the F1 key while the dialog box is displayed opens a Help window. The Help window contains help about that dialog box, if available. If no help file is available for that particular dialog box, then the main Help window opens.

As mentioned previously, the Tell Me box is available in most Office apps and can perform a variety of functions. One of these functions is to provide easy access to commands by typing a description of the command.

Figure 94

To Obtain Help Using the Tell Me Box

1 SIGN IN | 2 USE WINDOWS | 3 USE APPS | 4 FILE MANAGEMENT | 5 SWITCH APPS | 6 SAVE FILES
7 CHANGE SCREEN RESOLUTION | 8 EXIT APPS | 9 USE ADDITIONAL APP FEATURES | 10 USE HELP

If you are having trouble finding a command in an Office app, you can use the Tell Me box to search for the function you are trying to perform. As you type, the Tell Me box will suggest commands that match the search text you are entering. **Why?** *You can use the Tell Me box to access commands quickly that you otherwise may be unable to find on the ribbon.* The following steps find information about margins.

1

- Type **margins** in the Tell Me box and watch the search results appear.

- Point to Adjust Margins to display a submenu displaying the various margin settings (Figure 95).

- Click an empty area of the document window to close the search results.

2

- Exit Microsoft Word.

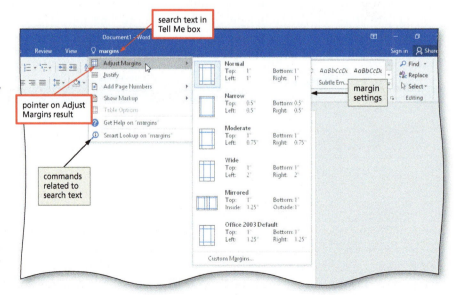

Figure 95

Using the Windows Search Box

One of the more powerful Windows features is the Windows search box. The search box is a central location from where you can type search text and quickly access related Windows commands or web search results. In addition, **Cortana** is a new search tool in Windows that you can access using the search box. It can act as a personal assistant by performing functions such as providing ideas; searching for apps, files, and folders; and setting reminders. In addition to typing search text in the search box, you also can use your computer or mobile device's microphone to give verbal commands.

To Use the Windows Search Box

1 SIGN IN | 2 USE WINDOWS | 3 USE APPS | 4 FILE MANAGEMENT | 5 SWITCH APPS | 6 SAVE FILES
7 CHANGE SCREEN RESOLUTION | 8 EXIT APPS | 9 USE ADDITIONAL APP FEATURES | 10 USE HELP

The following step uses the Windows search box to search for a Windows command. *Why? Using the search box to locate apps, settings, folders, and files can be faster than navigating windows and dialog boxes to search for the desired content.*

- Type **notification** in the search box to display the search results. The search results include related Windows settings, Windows Store apps, and web search results (Figure 96).

- Click an empty area of the desktop to close the search results.

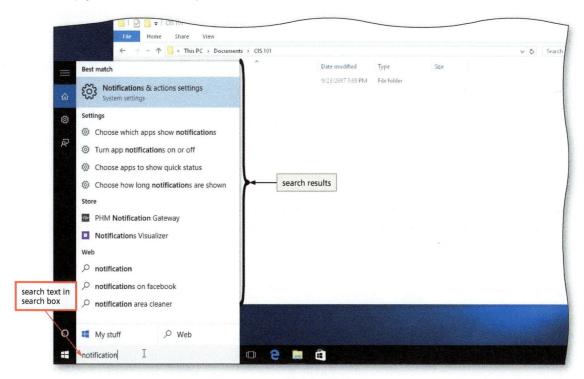

Figure 96

Summary

In this module, you learned how to use the Windows interface, several touch screen and mouse operations, and file and folder management. You also learned some basic features of Word and discovered the common elements that exist among Microsoft Office apps. Topics covered included signing in, using Windows, using apps, file management, switching between apps, saving files, changing screen resolution, exiting apps, using additional app features, and using Help.

CONSIDER THIS: PLAN AHEAD

What guidelines should you follow to plan your projects?

The process of communicating specific information is a learned, rational skill. Computers and software, especially Microsoft Office 2016, can help you develop ideas and present detailed information to a particular audience and minimize much of the laborious work of drafting and revising projects. No matter what method you use to plan a project, it is beneficial to follow some specific guidelines from the onset to arrive at a final product that is informative, relevant, and effective. Use some aspects of these guidelines every time you undertake a project, and others as needed in specific instances.

1. Determine the project's purpose.

   a) Clearly define why you are undertaking this assignment.

   b) Begin to draft ideas of how best to communicate information by handwriting ideas on paper; composing directly on a laptop, tablet, or mobile device; or developing a strategy that fits your particular thinking and writing style.

2. Analyze your audience.

   a) Learn about the people who will read, analyze, or view your work.

   b) Determine their interests and needs so that you can present the information they need to know and omit the information they already possess.

   c) Form a mental picture of these people or find photos of people who fit this profile so that you can develop a project with the audience in mind.

3. Gather possible content.

   a) Locate existing information that may reside in spreadsheets, databases, or other files.

   b) Conduct a web search to find relevant websites.

   c) Read pamphlets, magazine and newspaper articles, and books to gain insights of how others have approached your topic.

   d) Conduct personal interviews to obtain perspectives not available by any other means.

   e) Consider video and audio clips as potential sources for material that might complement or support the factual data you uncover.

4. Determine what content to present to your audience.

   a) Write three or four major ideas you want an audience member to remember after reading or viewing your project.

   b) Envision your project's endpoint, the key fact you wish to emphasize, so that all project elements lead to this final element.

   c) Determine relevant time factors, such as the length of time to develop the project, how long readers will spend reviewing your project, or the amount of time allocated for your speaking engagement.

   d) Decide whether a graph, photo, or artistic element can express or enhance a particular concept.

   e) Be mindful of the order in which you plan to present the content, and place the most important material at the top or bottom of the page, because readers and audience members generally remember the first and last pieces of information they see and hear.

CONSIDER THIS

How should you submit solutions to questions in the assignments identified with a 🌟 symbol?

Every assignment in this book contains one or more questions with a 🌟 symbol. These questions require you to think beyond the assigned file. Present your solutions to the question in the format required by your instructor. Possible formats may include one or more of these options: write the answer; create a document that contains the answer; present your answer to the class; discuss your answer in a group; record the answer as audio or video using a webcam, smartphone, or portable media player; or post answers on a blog, wiki, or website.

Apply Your Knowledge

Reinforce the skills and apply the concepts you learned in this module.

Creating a Folder and a Document

Instructions: You will create a Word Assignments folder and then create a Word document and save it in the folder.

Perform the following tasks:

1. Open the File Explorer window and then double-click to open the Documents folder.

2. Click the New folder button on the Quick Access Toolbar to display a new folder icon and text box for the folder name.

3. Type **Word Assignments** in the text box to name the folder. Press the ENTER key to create the folder in the Documents folder.

4. Run Word and create a new blank document.

5. Type **Contact Information** and then press then ENTER key to enter a line of text (Figure 97).

Figure 97

6. If requested by your instructor, enter your name, phone number, and email address in the Word document.

7. Click the Save button on the Quick Access Toolbar. Navigate to the Word Assignments folder in the Documents folder and then save the document using the file name, Apply 1 Document.

8. If your Quick Access Toolbar does not show the Quick Print button, add the Quick Print button to the Quick Access Toolbar. Print the document using the Quick Print button on the Quick Access Toolbar. When you are finished printing, remove the Quick Print button from the Quick Access Toolbar.

9. Submit the printout to your instructor.

10. Exit Word.

11. ✸ What other commands might you find useful to include on the Quick Access Toolbar?

Extend Your Knowledge

Extend the skills you learned in this module and experiment with new skills. You will use Help to complete the assignment.

Continued >

Extend Your Knowledge *continued*

Using Help

Instructions: Use Word Help to perform the following tasks.

Perform the following tasks:

1. Run Word.

2. Press F1 to open the Word Help window (shown in Figure 87).

3. Search Word Help to answer the following questions.

    a. What are three new features of Word 2016?

    b. What type of training is available through Word Help for Word 2016?

    c. What are the steps to customize the ribbon?

    d. What is the purpose of the Office Clipboard?

    e. What is the purpose of Read mode?

    f. Why would you use mail merge?

    g. How do you insert pictures?

    h. How do you change the size of text?

    i. What are the steps to zoom in and out of a document?

    j. What is the purpose of the Insights pane? How do you display it?

4. Type the answers from your searches in a new blank Word document. Save the document with a new file name and then submit it in the format specified by your instructor.

5. If requested by your instructor, enter your name in the Word document.

6. Exit Word.

7. ✳ What search text did you use to perform the searches above? Did it take multiple attempts to search and locate the exact information for which you were searching?

Expand Your World

Create a solution that uses cloud or web technologies by learning and investigating on your own from general guidance.

Creating Folders on OneDrive and Using the Word Online App

Instructions: You will create the folders shown in Figure 98 on OneDrive. Then, you will use the Word Online app to create a small file and save it in a folder on OneDrive.

Perform the following tasks:

1. Sign in to OneDrive in your browser.

2. Use the New button to create the folder structure shown in Figure 98.

Figure 98

3. In the Upcoming Events folder, use the New button to create a Word document with the file name, Expand 1 Task List, that contains the text, Prepare agenda for Tuesday's meeting.

4. If requested by your instructor, add your name to the Word document.

5. Save the document in the Upcoming Events folder and then exit the app.

6. Submit the assignment in the format specified by your instructor.

7. ✳ Based on your current knowledge of OneDrive, do you think you will use it? What about the Word Online app?

In the Labs

Design, create, modify, and/or use files following the guidelines, concepts, and skills presented in this module. Labs 1 and 2, which increase in difficulty, require you to create solutions based on what you learned in the module; Lab 3 requires you to apply your creative thinking and problem-solving skills to design and implement a solution.

Lab 1: **Creating Folders for a Bookstore**

Problem: Your friend works for a local bookstore. He would like to organize his files in relation to the types of books available in the store. He has seven main categories: fiction, biography, children, humor, social science, nonfiction, and medical. You are to create a folder structure similar to Figure 99.

Figure 99

Perform the following tasks:

1. Click the File Explorer button on the taskbar and display the contents of the Documents folder.

2. In the Documents folder, create the main folder and name it Book Categories.

3. Navigate to the Book Categories folder.

4. Within the Book Categories folder, create a folder for each of the following: Fiction, Biography, Children, Humor, Social Science, Nonfiction, and Medical.

5. Within the Fiction folder, create two additional folders, one for Science Fiction and the second for Western.

6. If requested by your instructor, add another folder using your last name as the folder name.

7. Submit the assignment in the format specified by your instructor.

8. ✳ Think about how you use your computer for various tasks (consider personal, professional, and academic reasons). What folders do you think will be required on your computer to store the files you save?

Lab 2: **Creating Word Documents and Saving Them in Appropriate Folders**

Problem: You are taking a class that requires you to complete three Word modules. You will save the work completed in each module in a different folder (Figure 100).

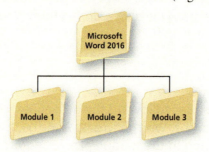

Figure 100

Perform the following tasks:

1. Create the folders shown in Figure 100.

2. Create a Word document containing the text, Module 1 Notes.

3. In the Backstage view, click Save As and then click This PC.

4. Click the Browse button to display the Save As dialog box. Click Documents to open the Documents folder. Navigate to the Module 1 folder and then save the file in the Word folder using the file name, Lab 2 Module 1 Notes.

5. Create another Word document containing the text, Module 2 Notes, and then save it in the Module 2 folder using the file name, Lab 2 Module 2 Notes.

6. Create a third Word document containing the text, Module 3 Notes, and then save it in the Module 3 folder using the file name, Lab 2 Module 3 Notes.

7. If requested by your instructor, add your name to each of the three Word documents.

8. Submit the assignment in the format specified by your instructor.

9. ✳ Based on your current knowledge of Windows and Word, how will you organize folders for assignments in this class? Why?

Lab 3: **Consider This: Your Turn**

Performing Research about Malware

Problem: You have just installed a new computer with the Windows operating system. Because you want to be sure that it is protected from the threat of malware, you decide to research malware, malware protection, and removing malware.

Perform the following tasks:

Part 1:   Research the following three topics: malware, malware protection, and removing malware. Use the concepts and techniques presented in this module to use the search box to find information regarding these topics. Create a Word document that contains steps to safeguard a computer properly from malware, ways to prevent malware, as well as the different ways to remove malware or a virus should your computer become infected. Submit your assignment and the answers to the following critical thinking questions in the format specified by your instructor.

Part 2: ✳ You made several decisions while searching for this assignment. What decisions did you make? What was the rationale behind these decisions? How did you locate the required information about malware?

1 Creating, Formatting, and Editing a Word Document with a Picture

Objectives

You will have mastered the material in this module when you can:

- Enter text in a Word document
- Check spelling as you type
- Format paragraphs
- Format text
- Undo and redo commands or actions
- Change theme colors

- Insert digital pictures in a Word document
- Resize pictures
- Format pictures
- Add a page border
- Adjust spacing
- Correct errors and revise a document

Introduction

To advertise a sale, promote a business, publicize an event, or convey a message to the community, you may want to create a flyer and hand it out in person or post it in a public location. Libraries, schools, community organizations, grocery stores, coffee shops, and other places often provide bulletin boards or windows for flyers. You also see flyers posted on webpages, on social media, or in email messages.

Flyers announce personal items for sale or rent (car, boat, apartment); events, such as garage or block sales; services being offered (animal care, housecleaning, lessons, tours); membership, sponsorship, or donation requests (club, community organization, charity); and other messages, such as a lost or found pet.

Project — Flyer with a Picture

Individuals and businesses create flyers to gain public attention. Flyers, which usually are a single page in length, are an inexpensive means of reaching the community. Many flyers, however, go unnoticed because they are designed poorly.

The project in this module follows general guidelines and uses Word to create the flyer shown in Figure 1–1. This colorful, eye-catching flyer announces surfing lessons. The picture of the surfer riding a wave, taken with a digital camera, entices passersby or viewers to stop and look at the flyer. The headline on the flyer is large and colorful to draw attention into the text. The body copy below the picture briefly describes what is included in the lessons, along with a bulleted list that concisely highlights important information. The signature line of the flyer calls attention to the contact phone number. The word, expert, and the signature line are in a different color so that they stand apart from the rest of the text on the flyer. Finally, the graphical page border nicely frames and complements the contents of the flyer.

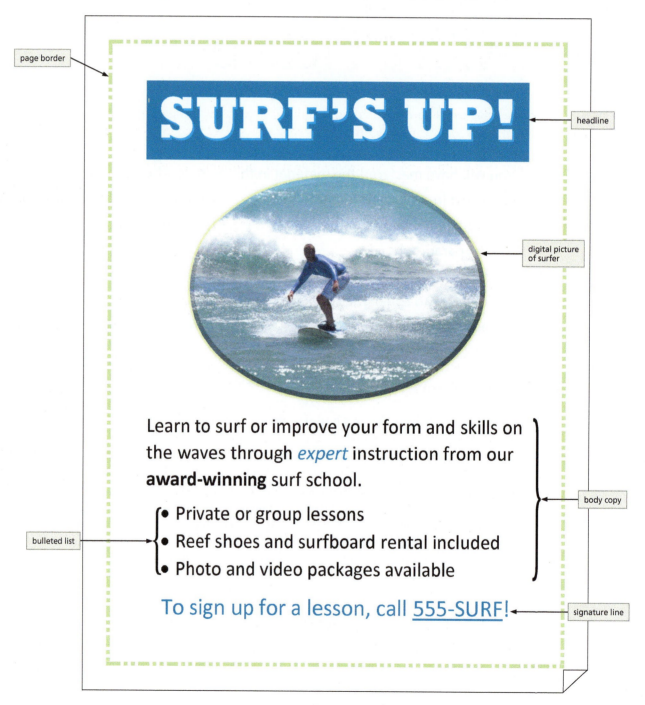

Figure 1–1

In this module, you will learn how to create the flyer shown in Figure 1–1. The following roadmap identifies general activities you will perform as you progress through this module:

1. **ENTER TEXT** in a new document.

2. **FORMAT** the **TEXT** in the flyer.

3. **INSERT** a **PICTURE**, called Surfer, in the flyer.

4. **FORMAT** the **PICTURE** in the flyer.

5. **ENHANCE** the **PAGE** with a border and spacing.

6. **CORRECT** errors **AND REVISE** text in the flyer.

To Run Word and Specify Settings

If you are using a computer to step through the project in this module and you want your screens to match the figures in this book, you should change your screen's resolution to 1366 × 768. For information about how to change a computer's resolution, refer to the Office and Windows module at the beginning of this book.

1 Run Word and create a blank document in the Word window.

2 If the Word window is not maximized, click the Maximize button on its title bar to maximize the window.

3 If the Print Layout button on the status bar is not selected (shown in Figure 1–2), click it so that your screen is in Print Layout view.

Q&A What is Print Layout view?
The default (preset) view in Word is **Print Layout view**, which shows the document on a mock sheet of paper in the document window.

4 If Normal (Home tab | Styles group) is not selected in the Styles gallery (shown in Figure 1–2), click it so that your document uses the Normal style.

Q&A What is the Normal style?
When you create a document, Word formats the text using a particular style. The default style in Word is called the **Normal style**, which is discussed later in this book.

What if rulers appear on my screen?
Click View on the ribbon to display the View tab and then remove the check mark from the View Ruler check box (View tab | Show group).

Entering Text

The first step in creating a document is to enter its text. With the projects in this book, you enter text by typing on the keyboard. By default, Word positions text you type at the left margin. In a later section of this module, you will learn how to format, or change the appearance of, the entered text.

For an introduction to Office and instructions about how to perform basic tasks in Office apps, read the Office and Windows module at the beginning of this book, where you can learn how to run an application, use the ribbon, save a file, open a file, print a file, exit an application, use Help, and much more.

For an introduction to Windows and instructions about how to perform basic Windows tasks, read the Office and Windows module at the beginning of this book, where you can learn how to resize windows, change screen resolution, create folders, move and rename files, use Windows Help, and much more.

BTW
The Word Window
The modules in this book begin with the Word window appearing as it did at the initial installation of the software. Your Word window may look different depending on your screen resolution and other Word settings.

To Type Text

To begin creating the flyer in this module, type the headline in the document window. **Why?** *The headline is the first line of text in the Surf Flyer.* The following steps type the first line of text in the document.

- Type **Surf's Up!** as the headline (Figure 1–2).

Figure 1–2

 What if I make an error while typing?
You can press the BACKSPACE key until you have deleted the text in error and then retype the text correctly.

What is the purpose of the 'Spelling and Grammar Check' icon on the status bar?
The **'Spelling and Grammar Check' icon** displays either a check mark to indicate the entered text contains no spelling or grammar errors, or an X to indicate that it found potential errors. Word flags potential errors in the document with a red, green, or blue wavy underline. Later in this module, you will learn how to fix flagged errors.

2

- Press the ENTER key to move the insertion point to the beginning of the next line (Figure 1–3).

Why did blank space appear between the headline and the insertion point?
Each time you press the ENTER key, Word creates a new paragraph and inserts blank space between the two paragraphs. Later in this module, you will learn how to increase and decrease the spacing between paragraphs.

Figure 1–3

How do you use the touch keyboard with a touch screen?

To display the on-screen touch keyboard, tap the Touch Keyboard button on the Windows taskbar as shown in the Office and Windows module at the beginning of this book. When finished using the touch keyboard, tap the X button on the touch keyboard to close the keyboard.

To Display Formatting Marks

1 ENTER TEXT | 2 FORMAT TEXT | 3 INSERT PICTURE
4 FORMAT PICTURE | 5 ENHANCE PAGE | 6 CORRECT & REVISE

You may find it helpful to display formatting marks while working in a document. *Why? Formatting marks indicate where in a document you pressed the* ENTER *key,* SPACEBAR, *and other nonprinting characters.* A **formatting mark** is a character that Word displays on the screen but is not visible on a printed document. For example, the paragraph mark (¶) is a formatting mark that indicates where you pressed the ENTER key. A raised dot (·) shows where you pressed the SPACEBAR. Formatting marks are discussed as they appear on the screen.

Depending on settings made during previous Word sessions, your Word screen already may display formatting marks (Figure 1–4). The following step displays formatting marks, if they do not show already on the screen.

- If the Home tab is not the active tab, click Home on the ribbon to display the Home tab.
- If it is not selected already, click the 'Show/Hide ¶' button (Home tab | Paragraph group) to display formatting marks on the screen (Figure 1–4).

Q&A What if I do not want formatting marks to show on the screen?

You can hide them by clicking the 'Show/Hide ¶' button (Home tab | Paragraph group) again. It is recommended that you display formatting marks so that you visually can identify when you press the ENTER key, SPACEBAR, and other keys associated with nonprinting characters. Most of the document windows presented in this book, therefore, show formatting marks.

'Show/Hide ¶' button selected

Home tab is active tab

Paragraph group

Surf's-Up!¶

paragraph mark at end of line indicates ENTER key has been pressed

paragraph mark at end of document

Figure 1–4

Other Ways

1. Press CTRL+SHIFT+*

To Insert a Blank Line

1 ENTER TEXT | 2 FORMAT TEXT | 3 INSERT PICTURE
4 FORMAT PICTURE | 5 ENHANCE PAGE | 6 CORRECT & REVISE

In the flyer, the digital picture of the surfer appears between the headline and body copy. You will not insert this picture, however, until after you enter and format all text. *Why? Although you can format text and insert pictures in any order, for illustration purposes, this module formats all text first before inserting the picture. Thus, you leave a blank line in the document as a placeholder for the picture.*

To enter a blank line in a document, press the ENTER key without typing any text on the line. The following step inserts one blank line below the headline.

• Press the ENTER key to insert a blank line in the document (Figure 1–5).

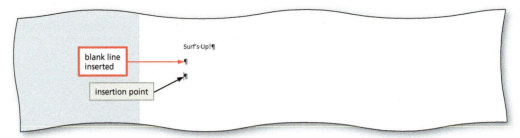

Figure 1–5

To Zoom Page Width

1 ENTER TEXT | **2 FORMAT TEXT** | **3 INSERT PICTURE**
4 FORMAT PICTURE | **5 ENHANCE PAGE** | **6 CORRECT & REVISE**

The next step in creating this flyer is to enlarge the contents that appear on the screen. ***Why? You would like the text on the screen to be larger so that it is easier to read.*** The document currently displays at 100% (shown in Figure 1–6). With Word, you can zoom page width, which zooms (enlarges or shrinks) the mock sheet of paper on the screen so that it is the width of the Word window. The following steps zoom page width.

• Click View on the ribbon to display the View tab (Figure 1–6).

Q&A | Why did the groups on the ribbon change?

When you switch from one tab to another on the ribbon, the groups on the ribbon change to show commands related to the selected tab.

Figure 1–6

• Click the Page Width button (View tab | Zoom group) to display the page the same width as the document window (Figure 1–7).

Q&A | If I change the zoom, will the document print differently?

Changing the zoom has no effect on the printed document.

Figure 1–7

Q&A What are the other predefined zoom options?
Through the View tab | Zoom group or the Zoom dialog box (Zoom button in Zoom group), you can zoom to one page (an entire single page appears in the document window), many pages (multiple pages appear at once in the document window), page width, text width, and a variety of set percentages. Whereas page width zoom places the edges of the page at the edges of the document window, text width zoom places the document contents at the edges of the document window.

Other Ways

1. Click Zoom button (View tab | Zoom group), click Page width (Zoom dialog box), click OK button

Wordwrap

Wordwrap allows you to type words in a paragraph continually without pressing the ENTER key at the end of each line. As you type, if a word extends beyond the right margin, Word also automatically positions that word on the next line along with the insertion point.

Word creates a new paragraph each time you press the ENTER key. Thus, as you type text in the document window, do not press the ENTER key when the insertion point reaches the right margin. Instead, press the ENTER key only in these circumstances:

1. To insert a blank line(s) in a document (as shown in previous steps)
2. To begin a new paragraph
3. To terminate a short line of text and advance to the next line
4. To respond to questions or prompts in Word dialog boxes, task panes, and other on-screen objects

BTW

Zooming
If text is too small for you to read on the screen, you can zoom the document by dragging the Zoom slider on the status bar or by clicking the Zoom Out or Zoom In buttons on the status bar. Changing the zoom has no effect on the printed document.

1 ENTER TEXT | 2 FORMAT TEXT | 3 INSERT PICTURE
4 FORMAT PICTURE | 5 ENHANCE PAGE | 6 CORRECT & REVISE

To Wordwrap Text as You Type

The next step in creating the flyer is to type the body copy. ***Why?*** *In many flyers, the body copy text appears below the headline.* The following steps illustrate how the body copy text wordwraps as you enter it in the document, which means you will not have to press the ENTER key at the end of the line.

 1

- Type the first sentence of the body copy: **Learn to surf or improve your form and skills on the waves through expert instruction from our award-winning surf school.**

Q&A Why does my document wrap on different words?
The printer connected to a computer is one factor that can control where wordwrap occurs for each line in a document. Thus, it is possible that the same document could wordwrap differently if printed on different printers.

2

- Press the ENTER key to position the insertion point on the next line in the document (Figure 1–8).

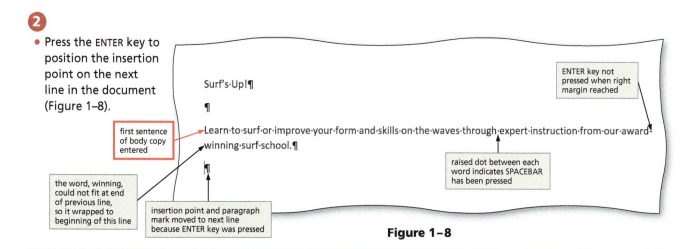

Surf's·Up!¶

¶

first sentence of body copy entered

Learn·to·surf·or·improve·your·form·and·skills·on·the·waves·through·expert·instruction·from·our·award-winning·surf·school.¶

¶

ENTER key not pressed when right margin reached

raised dot between each word indicates SPACEBAR has been pressed

the word, winning, could not fit at end of previous line, so it wrapped to beginning of this line

insertion point and paragraph mark moved to next line because ENTER key was pressed

Figure 1–8

Spelling and Grammar Check

As you type text in a document, Word checks your typing for possible spelling and grammar errors. If all of the words you have typed are in Word's dictionary and your grammar is correct, as mentioned earlier, the Spelling and Grammar Check icon on the status bar displays a check mark. Otherwise, the icon shows an X. In this case, Word flags the potential error(s) in the document window with a red, green, or blue wavy underline.

BTW

Automatic Spelling Correction

As you type, Word automatically corrects some misspelled words. For example, if you type recieve, Word automatically corrects the misspelling and displays the word, receive, when you press the SPACEBAR or type a punctuation mark. To see a complete list of automatically corrected words, click File on the ribbon to open the Backstage view, click the Options tab in the Backstage view, click Proofing in the left pane (Word Options dialog box), click the AutoCorrect Options button, and then scroll through the list near the bottom of the dialog box.

- A red wavy underline means the flagged text is not in Word's dictionary (because it is a proper name or misspelled).
- A green wavy underline indicates the text may be incorrect grammatically.
- A blue wavy underline indicates the text may contain a contextual spelling error, such as the misuse of homophones (words that are pronounced the same but that have different spellings or meanings, such as one and won).

Although you can check the entire document for spelling and grammar errors at once, you also can check flagged errors as they appear on the screen.

A flagged word is not necessarily misspelled. For example, many names, abbreviations, and specialized terms are not in Word's main dictionary. In these cases, you can instruct Word to ignore the flagged word. As you type, Word also detects duplicate words while checking for spelling errors. For example, if your document contains the phrase, to the the store, Word places a red wavy underline below the second occurrence of the word, the.

1 ENTER TEXT | 2 FORMAT TEXT | 3 INSERT PICTURE
4 FORMAT PICTURE | 5 ENHANCE PAGE | 6 CORRECT & REVISE

To Check Spelling and Grammar as You Type

In the following steps, the word, group, has been misspelled intentionally as goup. *Why? These steps illustrate Word's check spelling as you type feature. If you are completing this project on a computer, your flyer may contain different or no misspelled words, depending on the accuracy of your typing.*

- Type **Private or goup** and then press the SPACEBAR, so that a red wavy line appears below the misspelled word (Figure 1–9).

Q&A
What if Word does not flag my spelling and grammar errors with wavy underlines?
To verify that the check spelling and grammar as you type features are enabled, click File on the ribbon to open the Backstage view and then click the Options tab in the Backstage view. When the Word Options dialog box is displayed, click Proofing in the left pane and then ensure the 'Check spelling as you type' and 'Mark grammar errors as you type' check boxes contain check marks. Also ensure the 'Hide spelling errors in this document only' and 'Hide grammar errors in this document only' check boxes do not contain check marks. Click the OK button to close the Word Options dialog box.

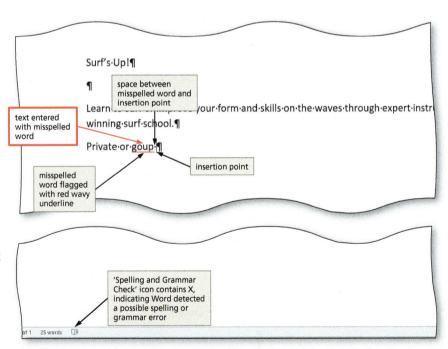

Figure 1–9

2

- Right-click the flagged word (goup, in this case) to display a shortcut menu that presents a list of suggested spelling corrections for the flagged word (Figure 1–10).

Q&A

What if, when I right-click the misspelled word, my desired correction is not in the list on the shortcut menu?
You can click outside the shortcut menu to close the shortcut menu and then retype the correct word.

What if a flagged word actually is, for example, a proper name and spelled correctly?
Right-click it and then click Ignore All on the shortcut menu to instruct Word not to flag future occurrences of the same word in this document.

Figure 1–10

3

- Click group on the shortcut menu to replace the misspelled word in the document with a correctly spelled word (Figure 1–11).

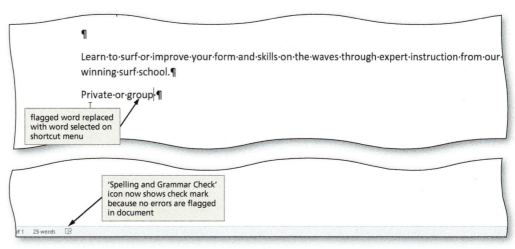

Figure 1–11

Other Ways

1. Click 'Spelling and Grammar Check' icon on status bar, click desired word in Spelling pane, click Change button, click OK button

To Enter More Text

In the flyer, the text yet to be entered includes the remainder of the body copy, which will be formatted as a bulleted list, and the signature line. The following steps enter the remainder of text in the flyer.

1 Press the END key to move the insertion point to the end of the current line.

2 Type **lessons** and then press the ENTER key.

3 Type `Photo and video packages available` and then press the ENTER key.

4 Type `Reef shoes and surfboard rental included` and then press the ENTER key.

5 Type the signature line in the flyer (Figure 1–12): `To sign up for a lesson, call 555-SURF!`
If requested by your instructor, enter your phone number instead of 555-SURF in the signature line.

Surf's·Up!¶

¶

Learn·to·surf·or·improve·your·form·and·skills·on·the·waves·through·expert·instructi... winning·surf·school.¶

three paragraphs of body copy that will be formatted as a bulleted list entered → Private·or·group·lessons¶

Photo·and·video·packages·available¶

Reef·shoes·and·surfboard·rental·included¶

signature line entered → To·sign·up·for·a·lesson,·call·555-SURF!¶

Figure 1–12

6 Save the flyer on your hard drive, OneDrive, or other storage location using Surf Flyer as the file name.

Q&A Why should I save the flyer at this time?
You have performed many tasks while creating this flyer and do not want to risk losing work completed thus far. For information about how to save, refer to the Office and Windows module at the beginning of this book.

How should you organize text in a flyer?
The text in a flyer typically is organized into three areas: headline, body copy, and signature line.

- The **headline** is the first line of text on the flyer. It conveys the product or service being offered (such as a car for sale, lessons, or sightseeing tours) or the benefit that will be gained (such as a convenience, better performance, greater security, higher earnings, or more comfort), or it can contain a message (such as a lost or found pet).

- The **body copy** consists of text between the headline and the signature line. This text highlights the key points of the message in as few words as possible. It should be easy to read and follow. While emphasizing the positive, the body copy must be realistic, truthful, and believable.

- The **signature line**, which is the last line of text on the flyer, contains contact information or identifies a call to action.

Navigating a Document

You view only a portion of a document on the screen through the document window. At some point when you type text or insert graphics, Word probably will **scroll** the top or bottom portion of the document off the screen. Although you cannot see the text and graphics once they scroll off the screen, they remain in the document.

You can use touch gestures, the keyboard, or a mouse to scroll to a different location in a document and/or move the insertion point around a document. If you are using a touch screen, simply use your finger to slide the document up or down to display a different location in the document and then tap to move the insertion point to a new location. When you use the keyboard, the insertion point automatically moves when you press the desired keys. For example, the previous steps used the END key to move the insertion point to the end of the current line. Table 1–1 outlines various techniques to navigate a document using the keyboard.

Table 1–1 Moving the Insertion Point with the Keyboard			
Insertion Point Direction	**Key(s) to Press**	**Insertion Point Direction**	**Key(s) to Press**
Left one character	LEFT ARROW	Up one paragraph	CTRL+UP ARROW
Right one character	RIGHT ARROW	Down one paragraph	CTRL+DOWN ARROW
Left one word	CTRL+LEFT ARROW	Up one screen	PAGE UP
Right one word	CTRL+RIGHT ARROW	Down one screen	PAGE DOWN
Up one line	UP ARROW	To top of document window	ALT+CTRL+PAGE UP
Down one line	DOWN ARROW	To bottom of document window	ALT+CTRL+PAGE DOWN
To end of line	END	To beginning of document	CTRL+HOME
To beginning of line	HOME	To end of document	CTRL+END

© 2015 Cengage Learning

With the mouse, you can use the scroll arrows or the scroll box on the scroll bar to display a different portion of the document in the document window and then click the mouse to move the insertion point to that location. Table 1–2 explains various techniques for using the scroll bar to scroll vertically with the mouse.

Table 1–2 Using the Scroll Bar to Scroll Vertically with the Mouse			
Scroll Direction	**Mouse Action**	**Scroll Direction**	**Mouse Action**
Up	Drag the scroll box upward.	Down one screen	Click anywhere below the scroll box on the vertical scroll bar.
Down	Drag the scroll box downward.	Up one line	Click the scroll arrow at the top of the vertical scroll bar.
Up one screen	Click anywhere above the scroll box on the vertical scroll bar.	Down one line	Click the scroll arrow at the bottom of the vertical scroll bar.

© 2015 Cengage Learning

Formatting Paragraphs and Characters

With the text for the flyer entered, the next step is to **format**, or change the appearance of, its text. A paragraph encompasses the text from the first character in the paragraph up to and including its paragraph mark (¶). **Paragraph formatting** is the process of changing the appearance of a paragraph. For example, you can center or add bullets to a paragraph. Characters include letters, numbers, punctuation marks, and symbols. **Character formatting** is the process of changing the way characters appear on the screen and in print. You use character formatting to emphasize certain words and improve readability of a document. For example, you can color, italicize, or underline characters. Often, you apply both paragraph and character formatting to the same text. For example, you may center a paragraph (paragraph formatting) and underline some of the characters in the same paragraph (character formatting).

Although you can format paragraphs and characters before you type, many Word users enter text first and then format the existing text. Figure 1–13a shows the flyer in this module before formatting its paragraphs and characters. Figure 1–13b shows the flyer after formatting. As you can see from the two figures, a document that is formatted is easier to read and looks more professional. The following sections discuss how to format the flyer so that it looks like Figure 1–13b.

BTW
Minimize Wrist Injury
Computer users frequently switch among the keyboard, the mouse, and touch gestures during a word processing session; such switching strains the wrist. To help prevent wrist injury, minimize switching. For instance, if your hand already is on the mouse, use the mouse to scroll. If your fingers already are on the keyboard, use keyboard keys to scroll. If your fingertips already are on the screen, use your finger to slide the document to a new location.

Figure 1–13a Unformatted Flyer

Figure 1–13b Formatted Flyer

Figure 1–13

Font, Font Sizes, and Themes

Characters that appear on the screen are a specific shape and size. The **font**, or typeface, defines the appearance and shape of the letters, numbers, and special characters. In Word, the default font usually is Calibri (shown in Figure 1–14). You can leave characters in the default font or change them to a different font. **Font size** specifies the size of the characters and is determined by a measurement system called points. A single **point** is about 1/72 of one inch in height. The default font size in Word typically is 11 (Figure 1–14). Thus, a character with a font size of 11 is about 11/72 or a little less than 1/6 of one inch in height. You can increase or decrease the font size of characters in a document.

A document **theme** is a set of unified formats for fonts, colors, and graphics. Word includes a variety of document themes to assist you with coordinating these visual elements in a document. The default theme fonts are Calibri Light for headings and Calibri for body text. By changing the document theme, you quickly can give your document a new look. You also can define your own document themes.

CONSIDER THIS

How do I know which formats to use in a flyer?
In a flyer, consider the following formatting suggestions.

- **Increase the font size of characters.** Flyers usually are posted on a bulletin board or in a window. Thus, the font size should be as large as possible so that passersby easily can read the flyer. To give the headline more impact, its font size should be larger than the font size of the text in the body copy. If possible, make the font size of the signature line larger than the body copy but smaller than the headline.

- **Change the font of characters.** Use fonts that are easy to read. Try to use only two different fonts in a flyer; for example, use one for the headline and the other for all other text. Too many fonts can make the flyer visually confusing.

- **Change the paragraph alignment.** The default alignment for paragraphs in a document is **left-aligned**, that is, flush at the left margin of the document with uneven right edges. Consider changing the alignment of some of the paragraphs to add interest and variety to the flyer.

- **Highlight key paragraphs with bullets.** A bulleted paragraph is a paragraph that begins with a dot or other symbol. Use bulleted paragraphs to highlight important points in a flyer.

- **Emphasize important words.** To call attention to certain words or lines, you can underline them, italicize them, or bold them. Use these formats sparingly, however, because overuse will minimize their effect and make the flyer look too busy.

- **Use color.** Use colors that complement each other and convey the meaning of the flyer. Vary colors in terms of hue and brightness. Headline colors, for example, can be bold and bright. Signature lines should stand out more than body copy but less than headlines. Keep in mind that too many colors can detract from the flyer and make it difficult to read.

To Center a Paragraph

The headline in the flyer currently is left-aligned (shown in Figure 1–14). *Why? Word, by default, left-aligns text, unless you specifically change the alignment.* You want the headline to be **centered**, that is, positioned horizontally between the left and right margins on the page. Recall that Word considers a single short line of text, such as the one-word headline, a paragraph. Thus, you will center the paragraph containing the headline. The following steps center a paragraph.

- Click Home on the ribbon to display the Home tab.
- Click somewhere in the paragraph to be centered (in this case, the headline) to position the insertion point in the paragraph to be centered (Figure 1–14).

Figure 1–14

- Click the Center button (Home tab | Paragraph group) to center the paragraph containing the insertion point (Figure 1–15).

Q&A What if I want to return the paragraph to left-aligned?
You would click the Center button again or click the Align Left button (Home tab | Paragraph group).

Figure 1–15

Other Ways

1. Right-click paragraph (or if using touch, tap 'Show Context Menu' button on mini toolbar), click Paragraph on shortcut menu, click Indents and Spacing tab (Paragraph dialog box), click Alignment arrow, click Centered, click OK button

2. Click Paragraph Settings Dialog Box Launcher (Home tab or Layout tab | Paragraph group), click Indents and Spacing tab (Paragraph dialog box), click Alignment arrow, click Centered, click OK button

3. Press CTRL+E

To Center Another Paragraph

In the flyer, the signature line is to be centered to match the paragraph alignment of the headline. The following steps center the signature line.

1. Click somewhere in the paragraph to be centered (in this case, the signature line) to position the insertion point in the paragraph to be formatted.

2. Click the Center button (Home tab | Paragraph group) to center the paragraph containing the insertion point (shown in Figure 1–16).

BTW
File Type
Depending on your Windows settings, the file type .docx may be displayed on the title bar immediately to the right of the file name after you save the file. The file type .docx identifies a Word 2016 document.

BTW
The Ribbon and Screen Resolution
Word may change how the groups and buttons within the groups appear on the ribbon, depending on the computer or mobile device's screen resolution. Thus, your ribbon may look different from the ones in this book if you are using a screen resolution other than 1366 × 768.

Formatting Single versus Multiple Paragraphs and Characters

As shown in the previous sections, to format a single paragraph, simply position the insertion point in the paragraph to make it the current paragraph and then format the paragraph. Similarly, to format a single word, position the insertion point in the word to make it the current word, and then format the word.

To format multiple paragraphs or words, however, you first must select the paragraphs or words you want to format and then format the selection.

To Select a Line

The default font size of 11 point is too small for a headline in a flyer. To increase the font size of the characters in the headline, you first must select the line of text containing the headline. *Why? If you increase the font size of text without selecting any text, Word will increase the font size only of the word containing the insertion point.* The following step selects a line.

1

- Move the pointer to the left of the line to be selected (in this case, the headline) until the pointer changes to a right-pointing block arrow (Figure 1–16).

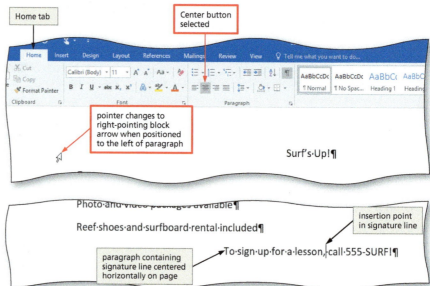

Figure 1–16

2

- While the pointer is a right-pointing block arrow, click the mouse button to select the entire line to the right of the pointer (Figure 1–17).

Q&A
What if I am using a touch screen?
You would double-tap to the left of the line to be selected to select the line.

Why is the selected text shaded gray?
If your screen normally displays dark letters on a light background, which is the default setting in Word, then selected text is displayed with a light shading color, such as gray, on the dark letters. Note that the selection that appears on the text does not print.

Figure 1–17

Other Ways

1. Drag pointer through line

2. With insertion point at beginning of desired line, press CRTL+SHIFT+DOWN ARROW

To Change the Font Size of Selected Text

The next step is to increase the font size of the characters in the selected headline. ***Why?*** *You would like the headline to be as large as possible and still fit on a single line, which in this case is 72 point.* The following steps increase the font size of the headline from 11 to 72 point.

1

- With the text selected, click the Font Size arrow (Home tab | Font group) to display the Font Size gallery (Figure 1–18).

Q&A

What is the Font Size arrow?
The Font Size arrow is the arrow to the right of the Font Size box, which is the text box that displays the current font size.

Why are the font sizes in my Font Size gallery different from those in Figure 1–18?
Font sizes may vary depending on the current font and your printer driver.

What happened to the mini toolbar?
The mini toolbar disappears if you do not use it. These steps use the Font Size arrow on the Home tab instead of the Font Size arrow on the mini toolbar.

Figure 1–18

2

- Point to 72 in the Font Size gallery to display a live preview of the selected text at the selected point size (Figure 1–19).

Q&A

What is live preview?
Recall from the Office and Windows module at the beginning of this book that live preview is a feature that allows you to point to a gallery choice and see its effect in the document — without actually selecting the choice.

Can I use live preview on a touch screen?
Live preview is not available on a touch screen.

Figure 1–19

 Experiment

- Point to various font sizes in the Font Size gallery and watch the font size of the selected text change in the document window.

3

- Click 72 in the Font Size gallery to increase the font size of the selected text.

Other Ways

1. Click Font Size arrow on mini toolbar, click desired font size in Font Size gallery	2. Right-click selected text (or, if using touch, tap 'Show Context Menu' button on mini toolbar), click Font on shortcut menu, click Font tab (Font dialog box), select desired font size in Size list, click OK button	3. Click Font Dialog Box Launcher, (Home tab | Font group) click Font tab (Font dialog box), select desired font size in Size list, click OK button	4. Press CTRL+D, click Font tab (Font dialog box), select desired font size in Size list, click OK button

To Change the Font of Selected Text

The default theme font for headings is Calibri Light and for all other text, called body text in Word, is Calibri. Many other fonts are available, however, so that you can add variety to documents.

The following steps change the font of the headline from Calibri to Rockwell Extra Bold. *Why? To draw more attention to the headline, you change its font so that it differs from the font of other text in the flyer.*

1

- With the text selected, click the Font arrow (Home tab | Font group) to display the Font gallery (Figure 1–20).

Q&A

Will the fonts in my Font gallery be the same as those in Figure 1–20?
Your list of available fonts may differ, depending on the type of printer you are using and other settings.

What if the text no longer is selected?
Follow the steps described earlier to select a line.

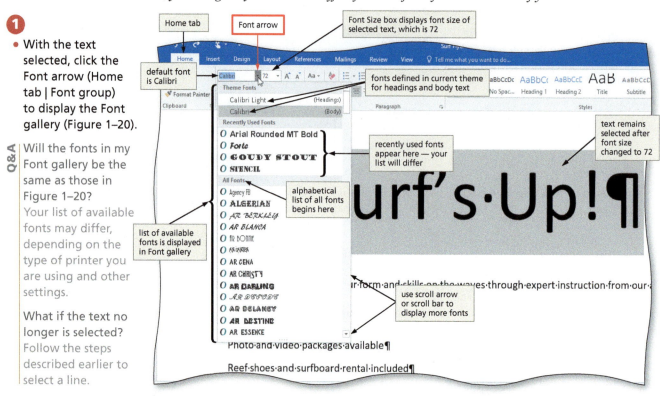

Figure 1–20

2

- If necessary, scroll through the Font gallery to display Rockwell Extra Bold (or a similar font).
- Point to 'Rockwell Extra Bold' (or a similar font) to display a live preview of the selected text in the selected font (Figure 1–21).

Experiment

- Point to various fonts in the Font gallery and watch the font of the selected text change in the document window.

Figure 1–21

• Click 'Rockwell Extra Bold' (or a similar font) in the Font gallery to change the font of the selected text.

Q&A If the font I want to use appears in the Recently Used Fonts list in the Font gallery, could I click it there instead?
Yes.

Other Ways

1. Click Font arrow on mini toolbar, click desired font in Font gallery

2. Right-click selected text (or, if using touch, tap 'Show Context Menu' button on mini toolbar), click Font on shortcut menu, click Font tab (Font dialog box), select desired font in Font list, click OK button

3. Click Font Dialog Box Launcher (Home tab | Font group), click Font tab (Font dialog box), select desired font in Font list, click OK button

4. Press CTRL+D, click Font tab (Font dialog box), select desired font in Font list, click OK button

---

To Change the Case of Selected Text

1 ENTER TEXT | **2 FORMAT TEXT** | 3 INSERT PICTURE

4 FORMAT PICTURE | 5 ENHANCE PAGE | 6 CORRECT & REVISE

The headline currently shows the first letter in each word capitalized, which sometimes is referred to as initial cap. The following steps change the headline to uppercase. *Why? To draw more attention to the headline, you would like the entire line of text to be capitalized, or in uppercase letters.*

1

• With the text selected, click the Change Case button (Home tab | Font group) to display the Change Case gallery (Figure 1–22).

Figure 1–22

2

• Click UPPERCASE in the Change Case gallery to change the case of the selected text (Figure 1–23).

Q&A What if a ruler appears on the screen or the pointer shape changes?
If you are using a mouse, depending on the position of your pointer and locations you click on the screen, a ruler may appear automatically or the pointer's shape may change. Simply move the mouse and the ruler should disappear and/or the pointer shape will change.

Figure 1–23

Other Ways

1. Right-click selected text (or, if using touch, tap 'Show Context Menu' button on mini toolbar), click Font on shortcut menu, click Font tab (Font dialog box), select All caps in Effects area, click OK button

2. Click Font Dialog Box Launcher (Home tab | Font group), click Font tab (Font dialog box), select All caps in Effects area, click OK button

3. Press SHIFT+F3 repeatedly until text is desired case

To Apply a Text Effect to Selected Text

Word provides many text effects to add interest and variety to text. The following steps apply a text effect to the headline. **Why?** *You would like the text in the headline to be even more noticeable.*

- With the text selected, click the 'Text Effects and Typography' button (Home tab | Font group) to display the Text Effects and Typography gallery (Figure 1–24).

Figure 1–24

- Point to 'Fill - White, Outline - Accent 2, Hard Shadow - Accent 2' (fourth text effect in third row) to display a live preview of the selected text with the selected text effect (Figure 1–25).

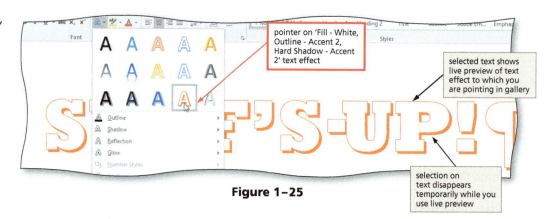

Figure 1–25

🔎 **Experiment**

- Point to various text effects in the Text Effects and Typography gallery and watch the text effects of the selected text change in the document window.

- Click 'Fill - White, Outline - Accent 2, Hard Shadow - Accent 2' to change the text effect of the selected text.

- Click anywhere in the document window to remove the selection from the selected text.

Other Ways

1. Right-click selected text (or, if using touch, tap 'Show Context Menu' button on mini toolbar), click Font on shortcut menu, click Font tab (Font dialog box), click Text Effects button, expand Text Fill or Text Outline section and then select the desired text effect(s) (Format Text Effects dialog box), click OK button, click OK button

2. Click Font Dialog Box Launcher (Home tab | Font group), click Font tab (Font dialog box), click Text Effects button, expand Text Fill or Text Outline section and then select desired text effect (Format Text Effects dialog box), click OK button, click OK button

To Shade a Paragraph

When you **shade** text, Word colors the rectangular area behind any text or graphics. If the text to shade is a paragraph, Word shades the area from the left margin to the right margin of the current paragraph. To shade a paragraph, place the insertion point in the paragraph. To shade any other text, you must first select the text to be shaded.

This flyer uses a shading color for the headline. ***Why?*** *To make the headline of the flyer more eye-catching, you shade it.* The following steps shade a paragraph.

1
- Click somewhere in the paragraph to be shaded (in this case, the headline) to position the insertion point in the paragraph to be formatted.

- Click the Shading arrow (Home tab | Paragraph group) to display the Shading gallery (Figure 1–26).

Figure 1–26

Q&A What if I click the Shading button by mistake?
Click the Shading arrow and proceed with Step 2. Note that if you are using a touch screen, you may not have a separate Shading button.

Why does my Shading gallery display different colors?
Your color scheme setting may display colors in a different order or may be different from Office, which is the default color scheme. To change the color scheme, click Design on the ribbon, click the Theme Colors button (Design tab | Document Formatting group), and then click Office in the Theme Colors gallery.

🔎 Experiment
- Point to various colors in the Shading gallery and watch the shading color of the current paragraph change.

2
- Click 'Orange, Accent 2, Darker 25%' (sixth color in fifth row) to shade the current paragraph (Figure 1–27).

Q&A What if I apply a dark shading color to dark text?
When the font color of text is Automatic, the color usually is black. If you select a dark shading color, Word automatically may change the text color to white so that the shaded text is easier to read.

Figure 1–27

Other Ways

1. Click Borders arrow (Home tab | Paragraph group), click Borders and Shading, click Shading tab (Borders and Shading dialog box), click Fill arrow, select desired color, click OK button

To Select Multiple Lines

The next formatting step for the flyer is to increase the font size of the characters between the headline and the signature line. **Why?** *You want this text to be easier to read from a distance.*

To change the font size of the characters in multiple lines, you first must select all the lines to be formatted. The following steps select multiple lines.

- Scroll, if necessary, so that all text below the headline is displayed on the screen.

- Move the pointer to the left of the first paragraph to be selected until the pointer changes to a right-pointing block arrow (Figure 1–28).

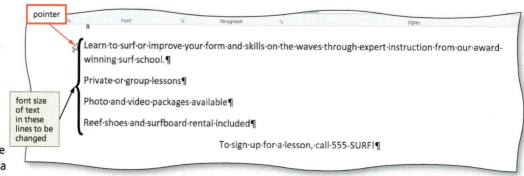

Figure 1–28

Q&A
What if I am using a touch screen?
You would tap to position the insertion point in the text to select.

2

- While the pointer is a right-pointing block arrow, drag downward to select all lines that will be formatted (Figure 1–29).

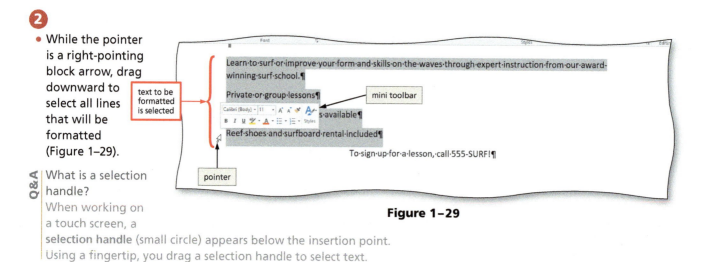

Figure 1–29

Q&A
What is a selection handle?
When working on a touch screen, a **selection handle** (small circle) appears below the insertion point. Using a fingertip, you drag a selection handle to select text.

Other Ways

1. With insertion point at beginning of desired line, press SHIFT+DOWN ARROW repeatedly until all lines are selected

---

BTW
Formatting Marks
With some fonts, the formatting marks will not be displayed properly on the screen. For example, the raised dot that signifies a blank space between words may be displayed behind a character instead of in the blank space, causing the characters to look incorrect.

To Change the Font Size of Selected Text

The characters between the headline and the signature line in the flyer currently are 11 point. To make them easier to read from a distance, this flyer uses a 24-point font size for these characters. The following steps change the font size of the selected text.

1 With the text selected, click the Font Size arrow (Home tab | Font group) to display the Font Size gallery.

2 Click 24 in the Font Size gallery to increase the font size of the selected text.

③ Click anywhere in the document window to remove the selection from the text.

④ If necessary, scroll so that you can see all the resized text on the screen (Figure 1–30).

Figure 1–30

To Bullet a List of Paragraphs

1 ENTER TEXT | **2 FORMAT TEXT** | 3 INSERT PICTURE
4 FORMAT PICTURE | 5 ENHANCE PAGE | 6 CORRECT & REVISE

A **bulleted list** is a series of paragraphs, each beginning with a bullet character. The next step is to format the three paragraphs about the lessons that are above the signature line in the flyer as a bulleted list.

To format a list of paragraphs with bullets, you first must select all the lines in the paragraphs. ***Why?*** *If you do not select all paragraphs, Word will place a bullet only in the paragraph containing the insertion point.* The following steps bullet a list of paragraphs.

①

- Move the pointer to the left of the first paragraph to be selected until the pointer changes to a right-pointing block arrow.

- Drag downward until all paragraphs that will be formatted with a bullet character are selected (Figure 1–31).

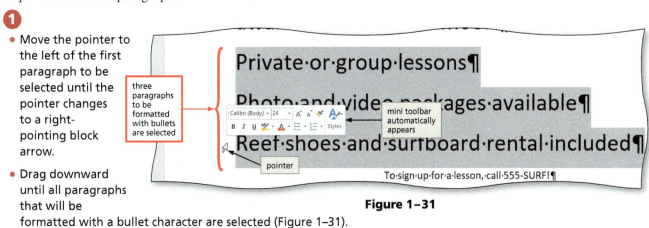

Figure 1–31

Q&A
What if I am using a touch screen?
Tap to position the insertion point in the text to select and then drag the selection handle(s) as necessary to select the text that will be formatted.

2

● Click the Bullets button (Home tab | Paragraph group) to place a bullet character at the beginning of each selected paragraph (Figure 1–32).

Q&A

Why does my screen display a Bullets gallery?
If you are using a touch screen, you may not have a separate Bullets button and Bullets arrow. In this case, select the desired bullet style in the Bullets gallery.

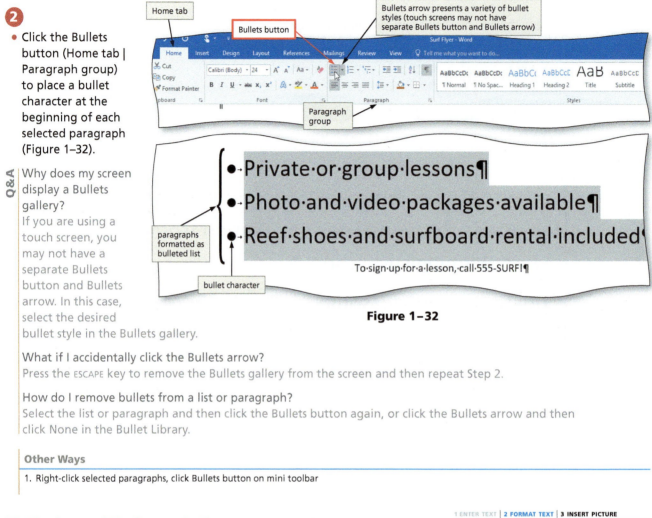

Figure 1–32

What if I accidentally click the Bullets arrow?
Press the ESCAPE key to remove the Bullets gallery from the screen and then repeat Step 2.

How do I remove bullets from a list or paragraph?
Select the list or paragraph and then click the Bullets button again, or click the Bullets arrow and then click None in the Bullet Library.

Other Ways

1. Right-click selected paragraphs, click Bullets button on mini toolbar

To Undo and Redo an Action

1 ENTER TEXT | **2 FORMAT TEXT** | 3 INSERT PICTURE
4 FORMAT PICTURE | 5 ENHANCE PAGE | 6 CORRECT & REVISE

Word provides a means of canceling your recent command(s) or action(s). For example, if you format text incorrectly, you can undo the format and try it again. When you point to the Undo button, Word displays the action you can undo as part of a ScreenTip.

If, after you undo an action, you decide you did not want to perform the undo, you can redo the undone action. Word does not allow you to undo or redo some actions, such as saving or printing a document. The following steps undo the bullet format just applied and then redo the bullet format. *Why? These steps illustrate the undo and redo actions.*

1

● Click the Undo button on the Quick Access Toolbar to reverse your most recent action (in this case, remove the bullets from the paragraphs) (Figure 1–33).

Figure 1–33

2

- Click the Redo button on the Quick Access Toolbar to reverse your most recent undo (in this case, place a bullet character on the paragraphs again) (shown in Figure 1–32).

Other Ways

1. Press CTRL+Z to undo; press CTRL+Y to redo

To Italicize Text

Italic text has a slanted appearance. The next step is to italicize the word, expert, in the flyer to further emphasize it. As with a single paragraph, if you want to format a single word, you do not need to select it. *Why?* *To format a single word, you simply position the insertion point somewhere in the word and apply the desired format.* The following step italicizes a word.

1

- Click somewhere in the word to be italicized (expert, in this case) to position the insertion point in the word to be formatted.

- Click the Italic button (Home tab | Font group) to italicize the word containing the insertion point (Figure 1–34).

Q&A
How would I remove an italic format?
You would click the Italic button a second time, or you immediately could click the Undo button on the Quick Access Toolbar or press CTRL+Z.

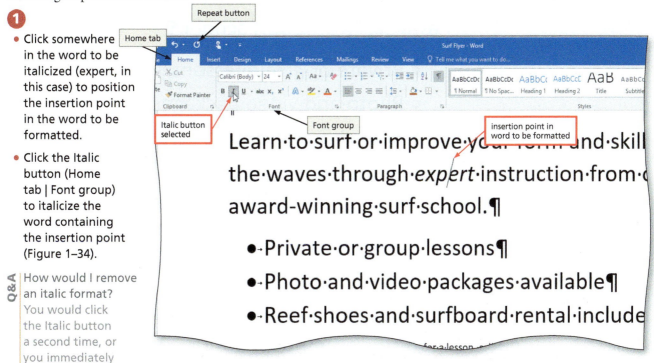

Figure 1–34

How can I tell what formatting has been applied to text?
The selected buttons and boxes on the Home tab show formatting characteristics of the location of the insertion point. With the insertion point in the word, expert, the Home tab shows these formats: 24-point Calibri italic font.

Why did the appearance of the Redo button change?
It changed to a Repeat button. When it is a Repeat button, you can click it to repeat your last action. For example, you can select different text and then click the Repeat button to apply (repeat) the italic format to the selected text.

Other Ways

1. Click Italic button on mini toolbar

2. Right-click selected text (or, if using touch, tap 'Show Context Menu' button on mini toolbar), click Font on shortcut menu, click Font tab (Font dialog box), click Italic in Font style list, click OK button

3. Click Font Dialog Box Launcher (Home tab | Font group), click Font tab (Font dialog box), click Italic in Font style list, click OK button

4. Press CTRL+I

To Color Text

The following steps change the color of the word, expert. *Why?* *To emphasize the word even more, you change its color.*

- With the insertion point in the word to format, click the Font Color arrow (Home tab | Font group) to display the Font Color gallery (Figure 1–35).

Q&A What if I click the Font Color button by mistake?
Click the Font Color arrow and then proceed with Step 2. Note that you may not have a separate Font Color button if you are using a touch screen.

Figure 1–35

 Experiment

- If you are using a mouse, point to various colors in the Font Color gallery and watch the color of the current word change.

2

- Click 'Orange, Accent 2, Darker 25%' (sixth color in fifth row) to change the color of the text (Figure 1–36).

Q&A How would I change the text color back to black?
You would position the insertion point in the word or select the text, click the Font Color arrow (Home tab | Font group) again, and then click Automatic in the Font Color gallery.

Figure 1–36

Other Ways

1. Click Font Color arrow on mini toolbar, click desired color

2. Right-click selected text (or, if using touch, tap 'Show Context Menu' button on mini toolbar), click Font on shortcut menu, click Font tab (Font dialog box), click Font color arrow, click desired color, click OK button

3. Click Font Dialog Box Launcher (Home tab | Font group), click Font tab (Font dialog box), click Font color arrow, click desired color, click OK button

To Use the Mini Toolbar to Format Text

Recall from the Office and Windows module at the beginning of this book that the mini toolbar automatically appears based on certain tasks you perform. ***Why?*** *Word places commonly used buttons and boxes on the mini toolbar for your convenience. If you do not use the mini toolbar, it disappears from the screen.* All commands on the mini toolbar also exist on the ribbon.

The following steps use the mini toolbar to change the color and font size of text in the signature line of the flyer.

1

- Move the pointer to the left of the line to be selected until the pointer changes to a right-pointing block arrow and then click to select the line and display the mini toolbar (Figure 1–37).

Q&A

What if I am using a touch screen?
Double-tap to the left of the line to be selected to select the line and then tap the selection

Figure 1–37

to display the mini toolbar. If you are using a touch screen, the buttons and boxes on the mini toolbar differ. For example, it contains a 'Show Context Menu' button at the far-right edge, which you tap to display a shortcut menu.

2

- Click the Font Size arrow on the mini toolbar to display the Font Size gallery.
- Point to 28 in the Font Size gallery to display a live preview of the selected font size (Figure 1–38).

3

- Click 28 in the Font Size gallery to increase the font size of the selected text.

Figure 1–38

4

- With the text still selected and the mini toolbar still displayed, click the Font Color arrow on the mini toolbar to display the Font Color gallery.
- Point to 'Orange, Accent 2, Darker 25%' (sixth color in the fifth row) to display a live preview of the selected font color (Figure 1–39).

Figure 1–39

5

- Click 'Orange, Accent 2, Darker 25%' to change the color of the selected text.
- Click anywhere in the document window to remove the selection from the text.

To Select a Group of Words

1 ENTER TEXT | **2 FORMAT TEXT** | 3 INSERT PICTURE
4 FORMAT PICTURE | 5 ENHANCE PAGE | 6 CORRECT & REVISE

To emphasize the contact phone number (555-SURF), this text is underlined in the flyer. Because the phone number is separated with a hyphen, Word considers it a group of words. To format a group of words, you first must select them. ***Why?*** *If you underline text without selecting any text first, Word will underline only the word containing the insertion point.* The following steps select a group of words.

1

- Position the pointer immediately to the left of the first character of the text to be selected, in this case, the 5 in 555 (Figure 1–40).

Q&A Why did the shape of the pointer change?
The pointer's shape is an I-beam when positioned in unselected text in the document window.

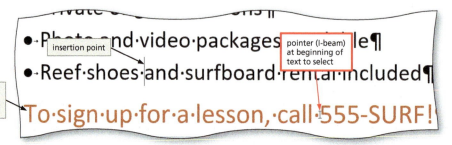

Figure 1–40

2

- Drag the pointer through the last character of the text to be selected, in this case, the F in the phone number (Figure 1–41).

Q&A Why did the pointer shape change again?
When the pointer is positioned in selected text, its shape is a left-pointing block arrow.

Figure 1–41

Other Ways

1. With insertion point at beginning of first word in group, press CTRL+SHIFT+RIGHT ARROW repeatedly until all words are selected

To Underline Text

Underlined text prints with an underscore (_) below each character. In the flyer, the contact phone number, 555-SURF, in the signature line is underlined. **Why?** *Underlines are used to emphasize or draw attention to specific text.* The following step formats selected text with an underline.

1

- With the text selected, click the Underline button (Home tab | Font group) to underline the selected text (Figure 1–42).

Figure 1–42

 What if my screen displays an Underline gallery?
If you are using a touch screen, you may not have a separate Underline button and Underline arrow. In this case, select the desired underline style in the Underline gallery.

If a button exists on the mini toolbar, can I click that instead of using the ribbon?
Yes.

How would I remove an underline?
You would click the Underline button a second time, or you immediately could click the Undo button on the Quick Access Toolbar.

Other Ways

1. Click Underline button on mini toolbar	2. Right-click text (or, if using touch, tap 'Show Context Menu' button on mini toolbar), click Font on shortcut menu, click Font tab (Font dialog box), click Underline style box arrow, click desired underline style, click OK button	3. Click Font Dialog Box Launcher (Home tab | Font group), click Font tab (Font dialog box), click Underline style arrow, click desired underline style, click OK button	4. Press CTRL+U

To Bold Text

Bold characters appear somewhat thicker and darker than those that are not bold. The following steps format the text, award-winning, in bold characters. **Why?** *To further emphasize this text, it is bold in the flyer.* Recall that if you want to format a single word, you simply position the insertion point in the word and then format the word. To format text that consists of more than one word, as you have learned previously, you select the text first.

1

- Select the text to be formatted (the text, award-winning, in this case); that is, position the pointer immediately to the left of the first character of the text to be selected and then drag the pointer through the last character of the text to be selected.

 What if I am using a touch screen?
Tap to position the insertion point in the text you want to select and then drag the selection handle(s) to select the text to be formatted.

- With the text selected, click the Bold button (Home tab | Font group) to bold the selected text (Figure 1–43).

Q&A How would I remove a bold format?

You would click the Bold button a second time, or you immediately could click the Undo button on the Quick Access Toolbar.

- Click anywhere in the document window to remove the selection from the screen.

Figure 1–43

Other Ways

1. Click Bold button on mini toolbar	2. Right-click selected text (or, if using touch, tap 'Show Context Menu' button on mini toolbar), click Font on shortcut menu, click Font tab (Font dialog box), click Bold in Font style list, click OK button	3. Click Font Dialog Box Launcher (Home tab | Font group), click Font tab (Font dialog box), click Bold in Font style list, click OK button	4. Press CTRL+B

To Zoom One Page

1 ENTER TEXT | 2 FORMAT TEXT | 3 INSERT PICTURE
4 FORMAT PICTURE | 5 ENHANCE PAGE | 6 CORRECT & REVISE

Earlier in this module, you changed the zoom to page width so that the text on the screen was larger and easier to read. In the next set of steps, you want to see the entire page (as a mock sheet of paper) on the screen at once. *Why? You want be able to see the effect of adjusting colors in the document as a whole.* The next step displays a single page in its entirety in the document window as large as possible.

- Click View on the ribbon to display the View tab.
- Click the One Page button (View tab | Zoom group) to display the entire page in the document window as large as possible (Figure 1–44).

Figure 1–44

Other Ways

1. Click Zoom button (View tab | Zoom group), click Whole page (Zoom dialog box), click OK button

What colors should I choose when creating documents?

When choosing color, associate the meaning of the color with your message:

- Red expresses danger, power, or energy and often is associated with sports or physical exertion.
- Brown represents simplicity, honesty, and dependability.
- Orange denotes success, victory, creativity, and enthusiasm.
- Yellow suggests sunshine, happiness, hope, liveliness, and intelligence.
- Green symbolizes growth, healthiness, harmony, and healing and often is associated with safety or money.
- Blue indicates integrity, trust, importance, confidence, and stability.
- Purple represents wealth, power, comfort, extravagance, magic, mystery, and spirituality.
- White stands for purity, goodness, cleanliness, precision, and perfection.
- Black suggests authority, strength, elegance, power, and prestige.
- Gray conveys neutrality and, thus, often is found in backgrounds and other effects.

To Change Theme Colors

1 ENTER TEXT | **2 FORMAT TEXT** | 3 INSERT PICTURE
4 FORMAT PICTURE | 5 ENHANCE PAGE | 6 CORRECT & REVISE

A **color scheme** in Word is a document theme that identifies complementary colors for text, background, accents, and links in a document. With more than 20 predefined color schemes, Word provides a simple way to coordinate colors in a document.

The default color scheme is called Office. In the flyer, you will change the color scheme. *Why? You want the colors in the flyer to represent integrity, trust, confidence, stability, healthiness, harmony, blooming, and safety, which are conveyed by shades of blues and greens. In Word, the Blue color scheme uses these colors.* The following steps change theme colors.

- Click Design on the ribbon to display the Design tab.

- Click the Theme Colors button (Design tab | Document Formatting group) to display the Theme Colors gallery.

- Point to Blue in the Theme Colors gallery to display a live preview of the selected theme color (Figure 1–45).

 Experiment

- Point to various color schemes in the Theme Colors gallery and watch the colors change in the document.

Figure 1–45

- Click Blue in the Theme Colors gallery to change the document theme colors.

Q&A | What if I want to return to the original color scheme?
You would click the Theme Colors button again and then click Office in the Theme Colors gallery.

To Zoom Page Width

Because the document contents are small when displayed on one page, the next steps zoom page width again.

1 Click View on the ribbon to display the View tab.

2 Click the Page Width button (View tab | Zoom group) to display the page the same width as the document window (shown earlier in the module in Figure 1–7).

3 Save the flyer again on the same storage location with the same file name.

Q&A Why should I save the flyer again?
You have made several modifications to the flyer since you last saved it; thus, you should save it again.

Selecting Text

In many of the previous steps, you have selected text. Table 1–3 summarizes the techniques used to select various items.

Table 1–3 Techniques for Selecting Text

Item to Select	Touch	Mouse	Keyboard (where applicable)
Block of text	Tap to position insertion point in text to select and then drag selection handle(s) to select text.	Click at beginning of selection, scroll to end of selection, position pointer at end of selection, hold down SHIFT key, and then click; or drag through the text.	
Character(s)	Tap to position insertion point in text to select and then drag selection handle(s) to select text.	Drag through character(s).	SHIFT+RIGHT ARROW or SHIFT+LEFT ARROW
Document		Move pointer to left of text until pointer changes to right-pointing block arrow and then triple-click.	CTRL+A
Graphic	Tap the graphic.	Click the graphic.	
Line	Double-tap to left of line to be selected.	Move pointer to left of line until pointer changes to right-pointing block arrow and then click.	HOME, then SHIFT+END or END, then SHIFT+HOME
Lines	Tap to position insertion point in text to select and then drag selection handle(s) to select text.	Move pointer to left of first line until pointer changes to right-pointing block arrow and then drag up or down.	HOME, then SHIFT+DOWN ARROW or END, then SHIFT+UP ARROW
Paragraph	Tap to position insertion point in text to select and then drag selection handle(s) to select text.	Triple-click paragraph; or move pointer to left of paragraph until pointer changes to right-pointing block arrow and then double-click.	CTRL+SHIFT+DOWN ARROW or CTRL+SHIFT+UP ARROW
Paragraphs	Tap to position insertion point in text to select and then drag selection handle(s) to select text.	Move pointer to left of paragraph until pointer changes to right-pointing block arrow, double-click, and then drag up or down.	CTRL+SHIFT+DOWN ARROW or CTRL+SHIFT+UP ARROW repeatedly
Sentence	Tap to position insertion point in text to select and then drag selection handle(s) to select text.	Press and hold down CTRL key and then click sentence.	
Word	Double-tap word.	Double-click word.	CTRL+SHIFT+RIGHT ARROW or CTRL+SHIFT+LEFT ARROW
Words	Tap to position insertion point in text to select and then drag selection handle(s) to select text.	Drag through words.	CTRL+SHIFT+RIGHT ARROW or CTRL+SHIFT+LEFT ARROW repeatedly

Inserting and Formatting a Picture in a Word Document

With the text formatted in the flyer, the next step is to insert a digital picture in the flyer and format the picture. Flyers usually contain a graphical image(s), such as a picture, to attract the attention of passersby. In the following sections, you will perform these tasks:

1. Insert a digital picture into the flyer.
2. Reduce the size of the picture.
3. Change the look of the picture.

How do I locate a graphic file to use in a document?

To use a graphic in a Word document, the image must be stored digitally in a file. Files containing graphics are available from a variety of sources:

• The web has images available, some of which are free, while others require a fee.

• You can take a picture with a digital camera or smartphone and **download** it, which is the process of copying the digital picture from the camera or phone to your computer.

• With a scanner, you can convert a printed picture, drawing, or diagram to a digital file.

If you receive a picture from a source other than yourself, do not use the file until you are certain it does not contain a virus. A **virus** is a computer program that can damage files and programs on your computer. Use an antivirus program to verify that any files you use are virus free.

To Center Another Paragraph

In the flyer, the digital picture of a surfer should be centered on the blank line below the headline. The blank paragraph below the headline currently is left-aligned. The following steps center this paragraph.

1 Click Home on the ribbon to display the Home tab.

2 Click somewhere in the paragraph to be centered (in this case, the blank line below the headline) to position the insertion point in the paragraph to be formatted.

3 Click the Center button (Home tab | Paragraph group) to center the paragraph containing the insertion point (shown in Figure 1–46).

To Insert a Picture

1 ENTER TEXT | 2 FORMAT TEXT | **3 INSERT PICTURE**

4 FORMAT PICTURE | 5 ENHANCE PAGE | 6 CORRECT & REVISE

The next step in creating the flyer is to insert a digital picture of a surfer in the flyer on the blank line below the headline. The picture, which was taken with a digital camera, is available on the Data Files. Please contact your instructor for information about accessing Data Files.

The following steps insert a picture, which, in this example, is located in the Module 01 folder in the Data Files folder. *Why? It is good practice to organize and store files in folders so that you easily can find the files at a later date.*

1

- If necessary, position the insertion point at the location where you want to insert the picture (in this case, on the centered blank paragraph below the headline).

- Click Insert on the ribbon to display the Insert tab (Figure 1–46).

Figure 1–46

2

- Click the From File button (Insert tab | Illustrations group) (shown in Figure 1–46) to display the Insert Picture dialog box (shown in Figure 1–47).

3

- Navigate to the desired picture location (in this case, the Module 01 folder in the Data Files folder). For a detailed example of this procedure, refer to Steps 4a and 4b in the To Save a File in a Folder section in the Office and Windows module at the beginning of this book.

- Click Surfing to select the file (Figure 1–47).

Figure 1–47

4

- Click the Insert button (Insert Picture dialog box) to insert the picture at the location of the insertion point in the document (Figure 1–48).

Q&A What are the symbols around the picture?

A selected graphic appears surrounded by a **selection rectangle**, which has small squares and circles, called **sizing handles**, at each corner and middle location.

What is the purpose of the Layout Options button?

When you click the Layout Options button, Word provides options for changing how the graphic is positioned with text in the document.

Figure 1–48

How do you know where to position a graphic on a flyer?

The content, size, shape, position, and format of a graphic should capture the interest of passersby, enticing them to stop and read the flyer. Often, the graphic is the center of attention and visually the largest element on a flyer. If you use colors in the graphical image, be sure they are part of the document's color scheme.

CONSIDER THIS

1 ENTER TEXT | 2 FORMAT TEXT | **3 INSERT PICTURE**
4 FORMAT PICTURE | 5 ENHANCE PAGE | 6 CORRECT & REVISE

To Zoom the Document

In the steps in the following sections, you will work with the picture just inserted. The next task is to adjust the zoom percentage. *Why? Currently, you can see only a small amount of text with the picture. Seeing more of the document at once helps you determine the appropriate size for the picture.* The following step zooms the document.

1

 Experiment

- Repeatedly click the Zoom Out and Zoom In buttons on the status bar and watch the size of the document change in the document window.

What if I am using a touch screen?
Repeatedly pinch (move two fingers together on the screen) and stretch (move two fingers apart on the screen) and watch the size of the document change in the document window.

- Click the Zoom Out or Zoom In button as many times as necessary until the Zoom button on the status bar displays 40% on its face (Figure 1–49).

Figure 1–49

Other Ways

1. Drag Zoom slider on status bar

2. Click Zoom level button on status bar, select desired zoom percent or type (Zoom dialog box), click OK button

3. Click Zoom button (View tab | Zoom group), select desired zoom percent or type (Zoom dialog box), click OK button

To Resize a Graphic

1 ENTER TEXT | 2 FORMAT TEXT | 3 INSERT PICTURE
4 FORMAT PICTURE | 5 ENHANCE PAGE | 6 CORRECT & REVISE

Resizing includes both increasing and reducing the size of a graphic. The next step is to resize the picture so that it is smaller in the flyer. **Why?** *You want the graphic and all the text on the flyer to fit on a single sheet of paper.* The following steps resize a selected graphic.

1

- Be sure the graphic still is selected.

 What if my graphic (picture) is not selected?
To select a graphic, click it.

- Point to the lower-left corner sizing handle on the picture so that the pointer shape changes to a two-headed arrow (Figure 1–50).

Figure 1–50

- Drag the sizing handle diagonally inward until the lower-left corner of the picture is positioned approximately as shown in Figure 1–51. Do not release the mouse button at this point.

 What if I am using a touch screen?
Drag a corner of the graphic, without lifting your finger, until the graphic is the desired size.

when using a mouse to drag a corner sizing handle, Word changes pointer to a crosshair shape

as you drag, Word resizes selected graphic to show how it will look at proposed size

flyer contents fit on a single page

Figure 1–51

- Release the mouse button to resize the graphic, which, in this case, should have a height of about 3.7" and a width of about 5.06".

 How can I see the height and width measurements?
Look in the Size group on the Picture Tools Format tab to see the height and width measurements of the currently selected graphic (shown in Figure 1–49).

What if the graphic is the wrong size?
Repeat Steps 1, 2, and 3, or enter the desired height and width values in the Shape Height and Shape Width boxes (Picture Tools Format tab | Size group).

What if I want to return a graphic to its original size and start again?
With the graphic selected, click the Size Dialog Box Launcher (Picture Tools Format tab | Size group), click the Size tab (Layout dialog box), click the Reset button, and then click the OK button.

Other Ways

1. Enter height and width of graphic in Shape Height and Shape Width boxes (Picture Tools Format tab | Size group)

2. Click Advanced Layout: Size Dialog Box Launcher (Picture Tools Format tab | Size group), click Size tab (Layout dialog box), enter desired height and width values in boxes, click OK button

1 ENTER TEXT | 2 FORMAT TEXT | 3 INSERT PICTURE
4 FORMAT PICTURE | 5 ENHANCE PAGE | 6 CORRECT & REVISE

To Zoom 100%

In the next series of steps, you will format the picture. Earlier in this module, you changed the zoom to 40% so that you could see more of the page while resizing the graphic. The following step zooms the screen to 100%. **Why?** *You want the contents of the image to be enlarged a bit, while still seeing some of the text in the document.*

- Click View on the ribbon to display the View tab.

- Click the 100% button (View tab | Zoom group) to display the page at 100% in the document window (Figure 1–52).

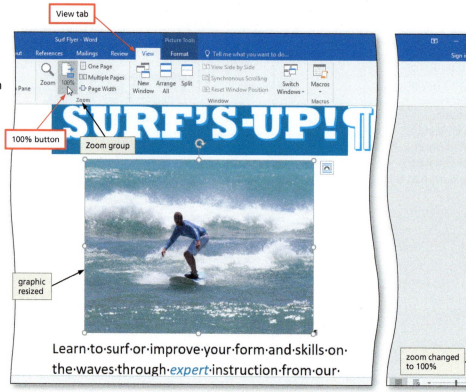

Figure 1–52

Other Ways

1. Click Zoom button (View tab | Zoom group), click 100% (Zoom dialog box), click OK button

To Apply a Picture Style

1 ENTER TEXT | 2 FORMAT TEXT | 3 INSERT PICTURE
4 FORMAT PICTURE | 5 ENHANCE PAGE | 6 CORRECT & REVISE

A **style** is a named group of formatting characteristics. Word provides more than 25 picture styles. *Why? Picture styles enable you easily to change a picture's look to a more visually appealing style, including a variety of shapes, angles, borders, and reflections.* The flyer in this module uses a style that applies an oval shape to the picture. The following steps apply a picture style to a picture.

- Ensure the graphic still is selected and then click Picture Tools Format on the ribbon to display the Picture Tools Format tab (Figure 1–53).

Q&A
What if my graphic (picture) is not selected?
To select a graphic, click it.

What is the white circle attached to top of the selected graphic?
It is called a rotate handle. When you drag a graphic's **rotate handle,** the graphic moves in either a clockwise or counterclockwise direction.

Figure 1–53

- Click the More button in the Picture Styles gallery (Picture Tools Format tab | Picture Styles group) (shown in Figure 1–53) to expand the gallery.

- Point to 'Soft Edge Oval' in the Picture Styles gallery to display a live preview of that style applied to the picture in the document (Figure 1–54).

 Experiment

- Point to various picture styles in the Picture Styles gallery and watch the style of the picture change in the document window.

- Click 'Soft Edge Oval' in the Picture Styles gallery (sixth style in third row) to apply the style to the selected picture.

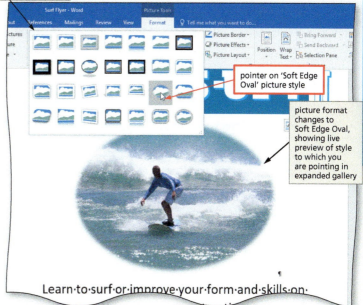

Figure 1–54

Other Ways

1. Right-click picture, click 'Picture Styles' on mini toolbar, select desired style

To Apply Picture Effects

1 ENTER TEXT | 2 FORMAT TEXT | 3 INSERT PICTURE
4 FORMAT PICTURE | 5 ENHANCE PAGE | 6 CORRECT & REVISE

Word provides a variety of picture effects, such as shadows, reflections, glow, soft edges, bevel, and 3-D rotation. The difference between the effects and the styles is that each effect has several options, providing you with more control over the exact look of the image.

In this flyer, the picture has a slight lime green glow effect and beveled edges. The following steps apply picture effects to the selected picture. ***Why?*** *Picture effects enable you to further customize a picture.*

- With the picture still selected, click the Picture Effects button (Picture Tools Format tab | Picture Styles group) to display the Picture Effects menu.

- Point to Glow on the Picture Effects menu to display the Glow gallery.

- Point to 'Lime, 5 pt glow, Accent color 6' in the Glow Variations area (rightmost glow in first row) to display a live preview of the selected glow effect applied to the picture in the document window (Figure 1–55).

 Experiment

- If you are using a mouse, point to various glow effects in the Glow gallery and watch the picture change in the document window.

Figure 1–55

2

- Click 'Lime, 5 pt glow, Accent color 6' in the Glow gallery to apply the selected picture effect.

Q&A What if I wanted to discard formatting applied to a picture?
You would click the Reset Picture button (Picture Tools Format tab | Adjust group). To reset formatting and size, you would click the Reset Picture arrow (Picture Tools Format tab | Adjust group) and then click 'Reset Picture & Size' on the Reset Picture menu.

3

- Click the Picture Effects button (Picture Tools Format tab | Picture Styles group) to display the Picture Effects menu again.

- Point to Bevel on the Picture Effects menu to display the Bevel gallery.

- Point to Angle in the Bevel area (first effect in second row) to display a live preview of the selected bevel effect applied to the picture in the document window (Figure 1–56).

 Experiment

- If you are using a mouse, point to various bevel effects in the Bevel gallery and watch the picture change in the document window.

Figure 1–56

4

- Click Angle in the Bevel gallery to apply the selected picture effect.

Other Ways
1. Right-click picture (or, if using touch, tap 'Show Context Menu' button on mini toolbar), click Format Object or Format Picture on shortcut menu, click Effects button (Format Picture task pane), select desired options, click Close button
2. Click Format Shape Dialog Box Launcher (Picture Tools Format tab | Picture Styles group), click Effects button (Format Picture task pane), select desired options, click Close button

Enhancing the Page

With the text and graphics entered and formatted, the next step is to look at the page as a whole and determine if it looks finished in its current state. As you review the page, answer these questions:

- Does it need a page border to frame its contents, or would a page border make it look too busy?

- Is the spacing between paragraphs and graphics on the page adequate? Do any sections of text or graphics look as if they are positioned too closely to the items above or below them?

- Does the flyer have too much space at the top or bottom? Should the contents be centered vertically?

You determine that a graphical, color-coordinated border would enhance the flyer. You also notice that the flyer would look better proportioned if it had a little more space above and below the picture. You also want to ensure that the contents are centered vertically. The following sections make these enhancements to the flyer.

To Add a Page Border

In Word, you can add a border around the perimeter of an entire page. The flyer in this module has a lime border. *Why? This border color complements the color of the flyer contents.* The following steps add a page border.

- Click Design on the ribbon to display the Design tab.

- Click the 'Borders and Shading' button (Design tab | Page Background group) to display the Borders and Shading dialog box (Figure 1–57).

Figure 1–57

- Scroll to, if necessary, and then click the sixth border style in the Style list (Borders and Shading dialog box) to select the style.

- Click the Color arrow to display a Color palette (Figure 1–58).

Figure 1–58

- Click 'Lime, Accent 6, Lighter 40%' (rightmost color in fourth row) in the Color palette to select the color for the page border.

- Click the Width arrow to display the Width list and then click 4 ½ pt to select the thickness of the page border (Figure 1–59).

- Click the OK button to add the border to the page (shown in Figure 1–60).

Q&A What if I wanted to remove the border?
You would click None in the Setting list in the Borders and Shading dialog box.

Figure 1–59

To Zoom One Page

The next steps zoom one page so that you can see the entire page on the screen at once.

1 Click View on the ribbon to display the View tab.

2 Click the One Page button (View tab | Zoom group) to display the entire page in the document window as large as possible.

To Change Spacing before and after Paragraphs

1 ENTER TEXT | 2 FORMAT TEXT | 3 INSERT PICTURE

4 FORMAT PICTURE | 5 ENHANCE PAGE | 6 CORRECT & REVISE

The default spacing above (before) a paragraph in Word is 0 points and below (after) is 8 points. In the flyer, you want to increase the spacing below the paragraph containing the headline and above the signature line. **Why?** *The flyer spacing will look more balanced with spacing increased above and below these paragraphs.* The following steps change the spacing above and below a paragraph.

- Position the insertion point in the paragraph to be adjusted, in this case, the paragraph containing the headline.

Q&A What happened to the Picture Tools Format tab?
When you click outside of a graphic or press a key to scroll through a document, Word deselects the graphic and removes the Picture Tools Format tab from the screen. That is, this tab appears only when a graphic is selected.

- Click Layout on the ribbon to display the Layout tab.

- Click the Spacing After up arrow (Layout tab | Paragraph group) so that 12 pt is displayed in the Spacing After box to increase the space below the current paragraph (Figure 1–60).

Figure 1–60

- Position the insertion point in the paragraph to be adjusted, in this case, the paragraph containing the signature line.

- Click the Spacing Before up arrow (Layout tab | Paragraph group) as many times as necessary so that 12 pt is displayed in the Spacing Before box to increase the space above the current paragraph (Figure 1–61).

- If the text flows to two pages, reduce the spacing above and below paragraphs as necessary.

Figure 1–61

Other Ways

1. Right-click paragraph (or, if using touch, tap 'Show Context Menu' button on mini toolbar), click Paragraph on shortcut menu, click Indents and Spacing tab (Paragraph dialog box), enter spacing before and after values, click OK button

2. Click Paragraph Settings Dialog Box Launcher (Home tab or Layout tab | Paragraph group), click Indents and Spacing tab (Paragraph dialog box), enter spacing before and after values, click OK button

To Center Page Contents Vertically

1 ENTER TEXT | 2 FORMAT TEXT | 3 INSERT PICTURE
4 FORMAT PICTURE | 5 ENHANCE PAGE | 6 CORRECT & REVISE

In Word, you can center the page contents vertically. *Why? This places the same amount of space at the top and bottom of the page.* The following steps center page contents vertically.

1

- If necessary, click Layout on the ribbon to display the Layout tab.

- Click the Page Setup Dialog Box Launcher (Layout tab | Page Setup group) to display the Page Setup dialog box.

- Click the Layout tab (Page Setup dialog box) to display the Layout sheet (Figure 1–62).

Figure 1–62

2

- Click the Vertical alignment arrow (Page Setup dialog box) to display the list of alignment options and then click Center in the list (Figure 1–63).

3

- Click the OK button to center the page contents vertically on the screen (shown in Figure 1–1 at the beginning of this module).

Q&A What if I wanted to change the alignment back?

You would select the Top vertical alignment from the Vertical alignment list in the Layout sheet (Page Setup dialog box).

Figure 1–63

TO CHANGE DOCUMENT PROPERTIES

Word helps you organize and identify your files by using **document properties**, which, as discussed in the Office and Windows module at the beginning of this book, are the details about a file, such as the project author, title, and subject. For example, a class name or document topic can describe the file's purpose or content.

The more common document properties are standard and automatically updated properties. **Standard properties** are associated with all Microsoft Office files and include author, title, and subject. **Automatically updated properties** include file system properties, such as the date you create or change a file, and statistics, such as the file size.

If you wanted to change document properties, you would follow these steps.

1. Click File on the ribbon to open the Backstage view and then, if necessary, click the Info tab in the Backstage view to display the Info gallery.

2. If the property you wish to change is displayed in the Properties list in the right pane of the Info gallery, try to click to the right of the property. If a text box appears to the right of the property, type the text for the property in the text box and then click the Back button in the upper-left corner of the Backstage view to return to the Word window. Skip the remaining steps.

3. If the property you wish to change is not displayed in the Properties list in the right pane of the Info gallery or you cannot change it in the Info gallery, click the Properties button in the right pane to display the Properties menu and then click Advanced Properties on the Properties menu to display the Properties dialog box. If necessary, click the Summary tab (Properties dialog box) to display the Summary sheet, fill in the appropriate text boxes, and then click the OK button.

Q&A

Why are some of the document properties in the dialog box already filled in?
The person who installed Office 2016 on your computer or network may have set or customized the properties.

BTW

Printing Document Properties

To print document properties, click File on the ribbon to open the Backstage view, click the Print tab in the Backstage view to display the Print gallery, click the first button in the Settings area to display a list of options specifying what you can print, click Document Info in the list to specify you want to print the document properties instead of the actual document, and then click the Print button in the Print gallery to print the document properties on the currently selected printer.

To Save the Document and Exit Word

Although you still need to make some edits to this document, you want to exit Word and resume working on the project at a later time. Thus, the following steps save the document and exit Word. For a detailed example of the procedure summarized below, refer to the Office and Windows module at the beginning of this book.

1 Save the flyer again on the same storage location with the same file name.

2 Close the open document and exit Word.

Break Point: If you wish to take a break, this is a good place to do so. To resume at a later time, continue following the steps from this location forward.

Correcting Errors and Revising a Document

After creating a document, you may need to change it. For example, the document may contain an error, or new circumstances may require you to add text to the document.

Types of Changes Made to Documents

The types of changes made to documents normally fall into one of the three following categories: additions, deletions, or modifications.

Additions Additional words, sentences, or paragraphs may be required in a document. Additions occur when you omit text from a document and want to insert it later. For example, you may want to add your email address to the flyer.

Deletions Sometimes, text in a document is incorrect or no longer is needed. For example, you may discover that the lessons no longer include reef shoes. In this case, you would delete the words, reef shoes, from the flyer.

Modifications If an error is made in a document or changes take place that affect the document, you might have to revise a word(s) in the text. For example, the phone number may change.

To Run Word, Open a Document, and Specify Settings

Once you have created and saved a document, you may need to retrieve it from storage. For example, you might want to revise the document or distribute it. Earlier in this module you saved the flyer using the file name, Surf Flyer. The following steps run Word, open this document, and specify settings. For a detailed example of the procedures summarized below for running Word or opening a document, refer to the Office and Windows module.

1 Run Word.

2 Open the document named Surf Flyer from the Recent list or use the Open dialog box to navigate to the location of the file and then open it in the Word window.

3 If the Word window is not maximized, click the Maximize button on its title bar to maximize the window.

4 Click View on the ribbon to display the View tab and then click the 100% button (View tab | Zoom group) to display the page at 100% in the document window.

BTW

Word Help
At any time while using Word, you can find answers to questions and display information about various topics through Word Help. Used properly, this form of assistance can increase your productivity and reduce your frustrations by minimizing the time you spend learning how to use Word. For instructions about Word Help and exercises that will help you gain confidence in using it, read the Office and Windows module at the beginning of this book.

1 ENTER TEXT | 2 FORMAT TEXT | 3 INSERT PICTURE
4 FORMAT PICTURE | 5 ENHANCE PAGE | **6 CORRECT & REVISE**

To Insert Text in an Existing Document

Word inserts text to the left of the insertion point. The text to the right of the insertion point moves to the right and downward to fit the new text. The following steps insert the word, today, to the left of the word, or, in the flyer. **Why?** *These steps illustrate the process of inserting text.*

1

- Scroll through the document and then click to the left of the location of text to be inserted (in this case, the o in or) to position the insertion point where text should be inserted (Figure 1–64).

Figure 1–64

2

- Type **today** and then press the SPACEBAR to insert the word to the left of the insertion point (Figure 1–65).

Q&A Why did the text move to the right as I typed?
In Word, the default typing mode is **insert mode**, which means as you type a character, Word moves all the characters to the right of the typed character one position to the right.

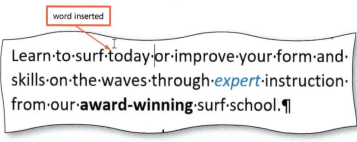

word inserted

Learn·to·surf·today·or·improve·your·form·and·
skills·on·the·waves·through·*expert*·instruction·
from·our·**award-winning**·surf·school.¶

Figure 1–65

To Delete Text

1 ENTER TEXT | 2 FORMAT TEXT | 3 INSERT PICTURE
4 FORMAT PICTURE | 5 ENHANCE PAGE | **6 CORRECT & REVISE**

It is not unusual to type incorrect characters or words in a document. As discussed earlier in this module, you can click the Undo button on the Quick Access Toolbar to undo a command or action immediately — this includes typing. Word also provides other methods of correcting typing errors.

To delete an incorrect character in a document, simply click next to the incorrect character and then press the BACKSPACE key to erase to the left of the insertion point, or press the DELETE key to erase to the right of the insertion point.

To delete a word or phrase, you first must select the word or phrase. The following steps select the word, today, which was just added in the previous steps, and then delete the selection. *Why? These steps illustrate the process of selecting a word and then deleting selected text.*

1

- Double-click the word to be selected (in this case, today) to select the word (Figure 1–66).

2

- Press the DELETE key to delete the selected text.

Q&A What if I am using a touch screen?
Tap the selected text to display the mini toolbar and then tap the Cut button on the mini toolbar to delete the selected text.

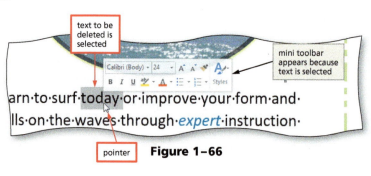

text to be deleted is selected

mini toolbar appears because text is selected

Calibri (Body) 24
B I U · A · Styles

arn·to·surf·today·or·improve·your·form·and·
lls·on·the·waves·through·*expert*·instruction·

pointer   **Figure 1–66**

Other Ways		
1. Right-click selected item, click Cut on shortcut menu	2. Select item, press BACKSPACE to delete to left of insertion point or press DELETE to delete to right of insertion point	3. Select item, press CTRL+X

To Move Text

1 ENTER TEXT | 2 FORMAT TEXT | 3 INSERT PICTURE
4 FORMAT PICTURE | 5 ENHANCE PAGE | **6 CORRECT & REVISE**

An efficient way to move text a short distance is drag-and-drop editing. With **drag-and-drop editing**, you select the item to be moved, drag the selected item to the new location, and then drop, or insert, it in the new location. Another technique for moving text is the cut-and-paste technique, which is discussed in the next module.

The following steps use drag-and-drop editing to move text. *Why? While proofreading the flyer, you realize that the body copy would read better if the last two bulleted paragraphs were reversed.*

- Position the pointer in the paragraph to be moved (in this case, the last bulleted item) and then triple-click to select the paragraph.

- With the pointer in the selected text, press and hold down the mouse button, which displays a small dotted box with the pointer (Figure 1–67).

Figure 1–67

- Drag the insertion point to the location where the selected text is to be moved, as shown in Figure 1–68.

Figure 1–68

- Release the mouse button to move the selected text to the location of the dotted insertion point (Figure 1–69).

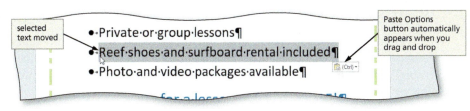

Figure 1–69

Q&A What if I accidentally drag text to the wrong location?
Click the Undo button on the Quick Access Toolbar and try again.

Can I use drag-and-drop editing to move any selected item?
Yes, you can select words, sentences, phrases, and graphics and then use drag-and-drop editing to move them.

What is the purpose of the Paste Options button?
If you click the Paste Options button, a menu appears that allows you to change the format of the item that was moved. The next module discusses the Paste Options menu.

- Click anywhere in the document window to remove the selection from the bulleted item.

Q&A What if I am using a touch screen?
If you have a stylus, you can follow Steps 1 through 3 using the stylus. If you are using your finger, you will need to use the cut-and-paste technique: tap to position the insertion point in the text to be moved and then drag the selection handles as necessary to select the text that you want to move; tap the selection to display the mini toolbar and then tap the Cut button on the mini toolbar to remove the text; tap to position the insertion point at the location where you want to move the text; display the Home tab and then tap the Paste button on the Home tab to place the text at the location of the insertion point. The next module discusses this procedure in more depth.

Other Ways

1. Click Cut button (Home tab | Clipboard group), click where text or object is to be pasted, click Paste button (Home tab | Clipboard group)

2. Right-click selected text, click Cut on mini toolbar or shortcut menu, right-click where text or object is to be pasted, click Paste on mini toolbar or 'Keep Source Formatting' on shortcut menu

3. Press CTRL+X, position insertion point where text or object is to be pasted, press CTRL+V

To Save and Print the Document

It is a good practice to save a document before printing it, in the event you experience difficulties printing. The following steps save and print the document. For a detailed example of the procedure summarized next for saving and printing a document, refer to the Office and Windows module at the beginning of this book.

BTW

Conserving Ink and Toner

If you want to conserve ink or toner, you can instruct Word to print draft quality documents by clicking File on the ribbon to open the Backstage view, clicking the Options tab in the Backstage view to display the Word Options dialog box, clicking Advanced in the left pane (Word Options dialog box), scrolling to the Print area in the right pane, placing a check mark in the 'Use draft quality' check box, and then clicking the OK button. Then, use the Backstage view to print the document as usual.

 1 Save the flyer again on the same storage location with the same file name.

2 If requested by your instructor, print the flyer.

Q&A | What if one or more of my borders do not print?
Click the Page Borders button (Design tab | Page Background group), click the Options button (Borders and Shading dialog box), click the Measure from arrow and click Text, change the four text boxes to 15 pt, and then click the OK button in each dialog box. Try printing the document again. If the borders still do not print, adjust the boxes in the dialog box to a number smaller than 15 point.

To Switch to Read Mode

1 ENTER TEXT | 2 FORMAT TEXT | 3 INSERT PICTURE
4 FORMAT PICTURE | 5 ENHANCE PAGE | 6 CORRECT & REVISE

Some users prefer reading a document on-screen instead of on paper. **Why?** *If you are not composing a document, you can switch to* **Read mode**, *which hides the ribbon and other writing tools so that more content fits on the screen. Read mode is intended to make it easier to read a document.* The following step switches from Print Layout view to Read mode.

1

• Click the Read Mode button on the status bar to switch to Read mode (Figure 1–70).

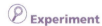 **Experiment**

• Click the arrows to advance forward and then move backward through the document.

Q&A | Besides reading, what can I do in Read mode?
You can zoom, copy text, highlight text, search, add comments, and more.

Figure 1–70

Other Ways

1. Click Read Mode button (View tab | Views group)

BTW

Distributing a Document

Instead of printing and distributing a hard copy of a document, you can distribute the document electronically. Options include sending the document via email; posting it on cloud storage (such as OneDrive) and sharing the file with others; posting it on social media, a blog, or other website; and sharing a link associated with an online location of the document. You also can create and share a PDF or XPS image of the document, so that users can view the file in Acrobat Reader or XPS Viewer instead of in Word.

To Switch to Print Layout View

1 ENTER TEXT | 2 FORMAT TEXT | 3 INSERT PICTURE
4 FORMAT PICTURE | 5 ENHANCE PAGE | 6 CORRECT & REVISE

The next steps switch back to Print Layout view. **Why?** *If you want to show the document on a mock sheet of paper in the document window, along with the ribbon and other writing tools, you should switch to Print Layout view.* The following step switches to Print Layout view.

- Click the Print Layout button on the status bar to switch to Print Layout view (Figure 1–71).

- Because the project now is complete, you can exit Word.

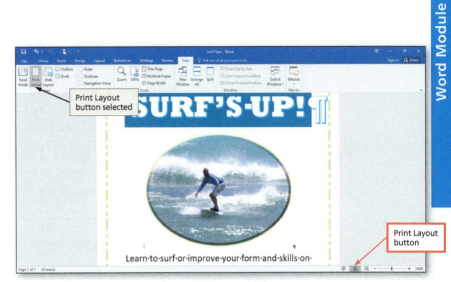

Figure 1–71

Other Ways

1. Click Print Layout button (View tab | Views group)   2. Click View on the ribbon, click Edit Document

Summary

In this module, you have learned how to enter text in a document, correct spelling errors as you type, format paragraphs and characters, insert and format a picture, add a page border, adjust paragraph and page spacing, and correct errors and revise a document.

What decisions will you need to make when creating your next flyer?

Use these guidelines as you complete the assignments in this module and create your own flyers outside of this class. .

1. Choose the text for the headline, body copy, and signature line — using as few words as possible to make a point.

2. Format various elements of the text.

    a) Select appropriate font sizes for text in the headline, body copy, and signature line.

    b) Select appropriate fonts for text in the headline, body copy, and signature line.

    c) Adjust paragraph alignment, as appropriate.

    d) Highlight key paragraphs with bullets.

    e) Emphasize important words.

    f) Use color to convey meaning and add appeal.

3. Find an eye-catching graphic(s) that conveys the overall message and meaning of the flyer.

4. Establish where to position and how to format the graphical image(s) so that the image grabs the attention of passersby and draws them into reading the flyer.

5. Determine whether the flyer needs enhancements, such as a graphical, color-coordinated border, or spacing adjustments to improve readability or overall appearance.

6. Correct errors and revise the document as necessary.

    a) Post the flyer on a wall and make sure all text and images are legible from a distance.

    b) Ask someone else to read the flyer and give you suggestions for improvements.

7. Determine the best method for distributing the document, such as printing, sending via email, or posting on the web or social media.

CONSIDER THIS: PLAN AHEAD

Apply Your Knowledge

Reinforce the skills and apply the concepts you learned in this module.

Modifying Text and Formatting a Document

Note: To complete this assignment, you will be required to use the Data Files. Please contact your instructor for information about accessing the Data Files.

Instructions: Run Word. Open the document, Apply 1–1 Graduation Flyer Unformatted, which is located in the Data Files. The flyer you open contains an unformatted flyer. You are to modify text, format paragraphs and characters, and insert a picture in the flyer to create the flyer shown in Figure 1–72.

Figure 1–72

Perform the following tasks:

1. Correct each spelling (red wavy underline) and grammar (green and blue wavy underlines) error by right-clicking the flagged text and then clicking the appropriate correction on the shortcut menu.

2. Delete the word, degree, in the sentence below the headline.

3. Insert the word, need, between the words, or directions (so that it reads: Questions or need directions?), in the second to last line of the flyer.

4. Change the word, on, to the word, by, in the last line so that the text reads: Please RSVP by May 18.

5. If requested by your instructor, change the phone number in the flyer to your phone number.

6. Center the headline and the last two paragraphs of the flyer.

7. Select the third, fourth, and fifth paragraphs of text in the flyer and add bullets to the selected paragraphs.

8. Change the theme colors to the Blue II color scheme.

9. Change the font and font size of the headline to 48-point Arial Rounded MT Bold, or a similar font. Change the case of the word, Celebrate, in the headline to uppercase letters. Apply the text effect called Fill - Dark Green, Accent 1, Outline - Background 1, Hard Shadow - Accent 1 to the entire headline. Change the font color of the headline text to Dark Green, Accent 5, Darker 25%.

10. Change the font size of the sentence below the headline, the bulleted list, and the last line of flyer to 26 point.

11. Use the mini toolbar to change the font size of the sentence below the bulleted list to 18 point.

12. Switch the last two bulleted paragraphs. That is, select the '125 Park Court in Condor' bullet and move it so that it is the second bulleted paragraph.

13. Select the words, open house, in the paragraph below the headline and italicize these words. Undo this change and then redo the change.

14. Select the text, Saturday, May 27, in the first bulleted paragraph and bold this text. Change the font color of this same text to Dark Red.

15. Underline the word, and, in the third bulleted paragraph.

16. Bold the text, Please RSVP by May 18., in the last line of the flyer. Shade this same text Dark Green, Accent 5, Darker 50%. If the font color does not automatically change to a lighter color, change its color to White, Background 1.

17. Change the zoom so that the entire page is visible in the document window.

18. Insert the picture of the graduate centered on the blank line below the headline. The picture is called Graduation and is available on the Data Files. Resize the picture so that it is approximately 2.9" × 2.89". Apply the Simple Frame, Black picture style to the inserted picture.

19. Change the spacing before the first bulleted paragraph to 12 points and the spacing after the last bulleted paragraph to 24 points.

20. The entire flyer should fit on a single page. If it flows to two pages, resize the picture or decrease spacing before and after paragraphs until the entire flyer text fits on a single page.

21. Change the zoom to text width, then page width, then 100% and notice the differences.

22. If requested by your instructor, enter the text, Graduation Open House, as the keywords in the document properties. Change the other document properties, as specified by your instructor.

23. Click File on the ribbon and then click Save As. Save the document using the file name, Apply 1–1 Graduation Flyer Formatted.

24. Print the document. Switch to Read Mode and browse pages through the document. Switch to Print Layout view.

25. Submit the revised document, shown in Figure 1–72, in the format specified by your instructor.

26. Exit Word.

27. ✳ If this flyer were announcing a victory parade instead of a graduation, which color scheme would you apply and why?

Extend Your Knowledge

Extend the skills you learned in this module and experiment with new skills. You may need to use Help to complete the assignment.

Modifying Text and Picture Formats and Adding Page Borders

Note: To complete this assignment, you will be required to use the Data Files. Please contact your instructor for information about accessing the Data Files.

add art page border

change border color and add shadow effect; change color saturation and color tone

use 'Increase Font Size' button to increase font size

change to picture bullets

change underline style and color

remove bullet

Figure 1–73

Instructions: Run Word. Open the document, Extend 1–1 Painting Lessons Flyer Draft, from the Data Files. You will enhance the look of the flyer shown in Figure 1–73. *Hint:* Remember, if you make a mistake while formatting the picture, you can reset it by using the Reset Picture button or Reset Picture arrow (Picture Tools Format tab | Adjust group).

Perform the following tasks:

1. Use Help to learn about the following: remove bullets, grow font, shrink font, art page borders, decorative underline(s), picture bullets, picture border shading, picture border color, shadow picture effects, and color saturation and tone.

2. Remove the bullet from the last paragraph of the flyer.

3. Select the text, Painting Lessons, and use the 'Increase Font Size' button (Home tab | Font group) to increase its font size.

4. Add an art page border to the flyer. If the border is not in color, add color to it if the border supports color.

5. Change the solid underline below the word, all, to a decorative underline. Change the color of the underline.

6. Change the style of the bullets to picture bullet(s). Adjust the hanging indent, if necessary, to align the text in the bulleted list.

7. Change the color of the picture border. Add a shadow picture effect to the picture.

8. Change the color saturation and color tone of the picture.

9. If requested by your instructor, change the name of the art studio (Bakersfield) to your last name.

10. Save the revised document with the file name, Extend 1–1 Painting Lessons Flyer Final, and then submit it in the format specified by your instructor.

11. ❂ In this assignment, you changed the bullets to picture bullets. Which bullet character did you select and why?

Expand Your World

Create a solution that uses cloud or web technologies by learning and investigating on your own from general guidance.

Using Word Online to Create a Flyer with a Picture

Note: To complete this assignment, you will be required to use the Data Files. Please contact your instructor for information about accessing the Data Files.

Instructions: You will use Word Online to prepare a flyer. The text for the unformatted flyer is shown in Figure 1–74. You will enter the text in Word Online and then use its tools to enhance the look of the flyer.

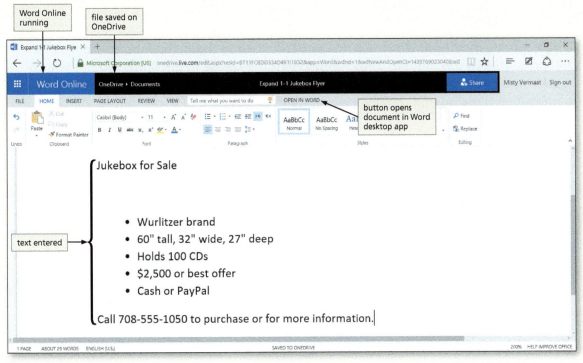

Figure 1–74

Perform the following tasks:

1. Run a browser. Search for the text, Word Online, using a search engine. Visit several websites to learn about Word Online. Navigate to the Office Online website. You will need to sign in to your OneDrive account.

2. Create a new blank Word document using Word Online. Name the document Expand 1–1 Jukebox Flyer.

3. Notice the differences between Word Online and the Word desktop app you used to create the project in this module.

4. Enter the text in the flyer, shown in Figure 1–74, checking spelling as you type.

5. Insert the picture called Jukebox, which is located in the Data Files.

Continued >

STUDENT ASSIGNMENTS

Expand Your World *continued*

6. Use the features available in Word Online, along with the concepts and techniques presented in this module, to format this flyer. Be sure to change the font and font size of text, center a paragraph(s), italicize text, color text, underline text, and apply a picture style. Resize the picture. Adjust spacing above and below paragraphs as necessary. The flyer should fit on a single page.

7. If requested by your instructor, replace the phone number in the flyer with your phone number.

8. Save the document again. Click the button to open the document in the Word desktop app. If necessary, sign in to your Microsoft account when prompted. Notice how the document appears in the Word desktop app.

9. Using either Word Online or the Word desktop app, submit the document in the format requested by your instructor. Exit Word Online. If necessary, sign out of your OneDrive account and your Microsoft account in Word.

10. ✳ What is Word Online? Which features that are covered in this module are not available in Word Online? Do you prefer using Word Online or the Word desktop app? Why?

In the Labs

Design, create, modify, and/or use a document following the guidelines, concepts, and skills presented in this module. Labs 1 and 2, which increase in difficulty, require you to create solutions based on what you learned in the module; Lab 3 requires you to apply your creative thinking and problem-solving skills to design and implement a solution.

Lab 1: **Creating a Flyer with a Picture**

Note: To complete this assignment, you will be required to use the Data Files. Please contact your instructor for information about accessing the Data Files.

Problem: Your boss asked you to prepare a flyer that advertises the company's commodity trading seminars. First, you prepare the unformatted flyer shown in Figure 1–75a, and then you format it so that it looks like Figure 1–75b. *Hint:* Remember, if you make a mistake while formatting the flyer, you can use the Undo button on the Quick Access Toolbar to undo your last action.

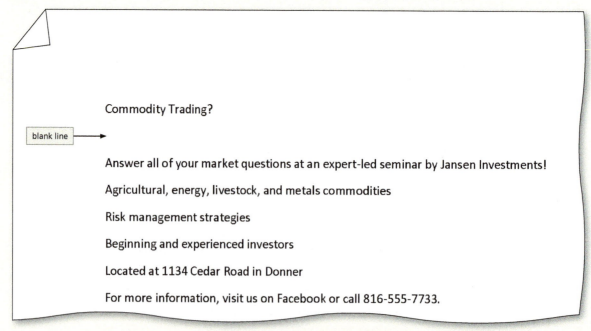

Commodity Trading?

blank line →

Answer all of your market questions at an expert-led seminar by Jansen Investments!

Agricultural, energy, livestock, and metals commodities

Risk management strategies

Beginning and experienced investors

Located at 1134 Cedar Road in Donner

For more information, visit us on Facebook or call 816-555-7733.

Figure 1–75a Unformatted Text

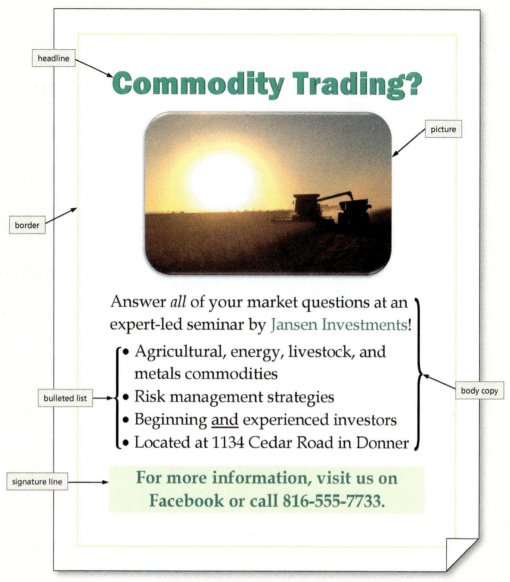

Figure 1–75b Formatted Document

Perform the following tasks:

1. Run Word. Display formatting marks on the screen.

2. Type the flyer text, unformatted, as shown in Figure 1–75a, inserting a blank line between the headline and the body copy. If Word flags any misspelled words as you type, check their spelling and correct them.

3. Save the document using the file name, Lab 1–1 Commodity Trading Flyer.

4. Center the headline and the signature line.

5. Change the theme colors to Green.

6. Change the font size of the headline to 48 point and the font to Franklin Gothic Heavy or a similar font. Apply the text effect called Fill - Dark Teal, Accent 4, Soft Bevel.

7. Change the font size of body copy between the headline and the signature line to 24 point.

8. Change the font size of the signature line to 26 point.

9. Change the font of the body copy and signature line to Book Antiqua.

Continued >

In the Labs *continued*

10. Bullet the four lines (paragraphs) of text above the signature line.

11. Italicize the word, all, in the paragraph above the bulleted list.

12. In the same paragraph, change the color of the words, Jansen Investments, to Dark Teal, Accent 4, Darker 25%.

13. Underline the word, and, in the third bulleted paragraph.

14. Bold the text in the signature line and change its color to Dark Teal, Accent 4, Darker 25%. Shade the paragraph containing the signature line in Lime, Accent 2, Lighter 80%.

15. Change the zoom so that the entire page is visible in the document window.

16. Insert the picture centered on a blank line below the headline. The picture is called Harvest, which is on the Data Files. Reduce the size of the picture to approximately 3.29" × 5.11".

17. Apply the Bevel Rectangle picture style to the inserted picture.

18. Change the spacing after the paragraph containing the headline to 0 pt. Change the spacing above (before) the paragraph below the picture to 12 pt. Change the spacing above (before) the signature line to 18 pt. The entire flyer should fit on a single page. If it flows to two pages, resize the picture or decrease spacing before and after paragraphs until the entire flyer text fits on a single page.

19. Add a ½-pt Lime, Accent 3, Lighter 40% page border, as shown in Figure 1–75b.

20. If requested by your instructor, change the street address in the flyer to your home street address.

21. Save the flyer again with the same file name. Submit the document, shown in Figure 1–75b, in the format specified by your instructor.

22. ✺ Why do you think this flyer used shades of green?

Lab 2: **Creating a Flyer with Multiple Pictures**

Note: To complete this assignment, you will be required to use the Data Files. Please contact your instructor for information about accessing the Data Files.

Problem: Your boss at Gingham Travel has asked you to prepare a flyer that promotes its business. You prepare the flyer shown in Figure 1–76. *Hint*: Remember, if you make a mistake while formatting the flyer, you can use the Undo button on the Quick Access Toolbar to undo your last action.

Perform the following tasks:
1. Run Word. Type the flyer text, unformatted. If Word flags any misspelled words as you type, check their spelling and correct them.

2. Save the document using the file name, Lab 1–2 Spring Break Flyer.

3. Change the theme colors to the Aspect color scheme.

4. Add bullets to the four paragraphs shown in the figure. Center all paragraphs, except the paragraphs containing the bulleted list.

5. Change the font size of both lines in the headline to 48 point. Change the font of the first line in the headline to Ravie, or a similar font, and the second line in the headline to Arial Rounded MT Bold, or a similar font. Apply this text effect to the first line in the headline: Fill - Dark Purple, Accent 1, Outline - Background 1, Hard Shadow - Accent 1. Shade the second line of the headline to the Dark Green, Accent 4 color, and change the font color to White, Background 1.

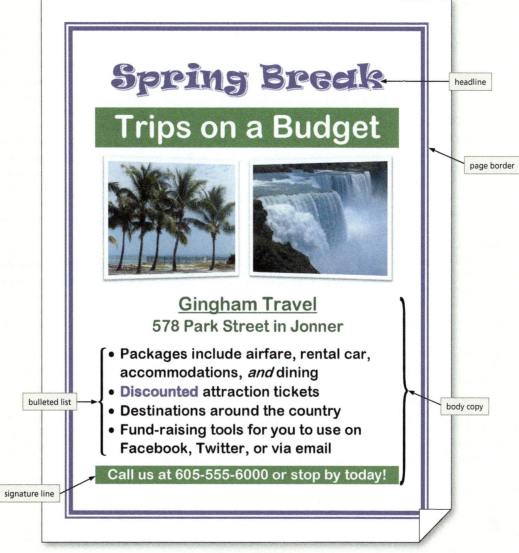

Figure 1–76

6. Change the font of all text below the headline to Arial Rounded MT Bold. Change the font size of the company name to 28 point, the company address to 24 point, and the bulleted list and signature line to 22 point.

7. Change the color of the company name and address to Dark Green, Accent 4, Darker 25%. Underline the company name.

8. Italicize the word, and, in the first bulleted paragraph.

9. Bold the word, Discounted, in the second bulleted paragraph. Change the color of this same word to Dark Purple, Accent 5.

10. Shade the signature line to the Dark Green, Accent 4 color, and change the font color to White, Background 1.

11. Change the zoom so that the entire page is visible in the document window.

12. Insert two pictures on the same blank line below the headline. The pictures are called Spring Break - Florida and Spring Break - New York, which are both in the Data Files.

Continued >

In the Labs *continued*

13. Resize the top picture so that it is approximately 2.4" × 3". Apply the Simple Frame, White picture style to both pictures. Apply the Perspective Right 3-D Rotation picture effect to the picture on the left and the Perspective Left 3-D Rotation to the picture on the right. Resize the pictures, if necessary, so that they fit on the same line. Add space as necessary between the two pictures.

14. Change the spacing before and after the paragraph containing the company name to 0 pt, the spacing after the company address to 12 pt, and the spacing before the signature line to 12 pt. The entire flyer should fit on a single page. If it flows to two pages, resize the pictures or decrease spacing before and after paragraphs until the entire flyer text fits on a single page.

15. Add the 6-point page border shown in Figure 1–76, using the color Dark Purple, Accent 5.

16. Center the page contents vertically.

17. If requested by your instructor, change the company name to your last name.

18. Save the flyer again with the same file name. Submit the document, shown in Figure 1–76, in the format specified by your instructor.

19. ✳ Why do you think this flyer used shades of purple and green?

Lab 3: **Consider This: Your Turn**

Design and Create an Antique Store Flyer

Note: To complete this assignment, you will be required to use the Data Files. Please contact your instructor for information about accessing the Data Files.

Problem: Your boss at Antiques Galore has asked you to prepare a flyer that promotes its business.

Perform the following tasks:

Part 1: The flyer should contain two digital pictures appropriately resized; the Data Files contains two pictures called Vintage Phone and Vintage Scale, or you can use your own digital pictures if they are appropriate for the topic of the flyer. The flyer should contain the headline, Antiques Galore, and this signature line: Questions? Call 312-555-2000 or find us on Facebook. The body copy consists of the following text, in any order: We sell all types of vintage items and also buy items individually or as an entire estate. Bring your items in for a free appraisal!; 1,200 square foot shop; Collectibles, costume jewelry, furniture, paintings, pottery, toys, and more!; Affordable items with new inventory daily; Located at 229 Center Street in Snow Hill; Open from 9:00 a.m. to 8:00 p.m. daily.

Use the concepts and techniques presented in this module to create and format this flyer. Be sure to check spelling and grammar. Submit your assignment and answers to the Part 2 critical thinking questions in the format specified by your instructor.

Part 2: ✳ You made several decisions while creating the flyer in this assignment: where to place text, how to format the text (i.e., font, font size, paragraph alignment, bulleted paragraphs, underlines, italics, bold, color, etc.), which graphics to use, where to position the graphics, how to format the graphics, and which page enhancements to add (i.e., borders and spacing). What was the rationale behind each of these decisions? When you proofread the document, what further revisions did you make and why? How would you recommend distributing this flyer?

2 | Creating a Research Paper with References and Sources

Objectives

You will have mastered the material in this module when you can:

- Describe the MLA documentation style for research papers
- Modify a style
- Change line and paragraph spacing in a document
- Use a header to number pages of a document
- Apply formatting using keyboard shortcuts
- Modify paragraph indentation

- Insert and edit citations and their sources
- Add a footnote to a document
- Insert a manual page break
- Create a bibliographical list of sources
- Cut, copy, and paste text
- Find text and replace text
- Find a synonym
- Check spelling and grammar at once
- Look up information

Introduction

In both academic and business environments, you will be asked to write reports. Business reports range from proposals to cost justifications to five-year plans to research findings. Academic reports focus mostly on research findings.

A **research paper** is a document you can use to communicate the results of research findings. To write a research paper, you learn about a particular topic from a variety of sources (research), organize your ideas from the research results, and then present relevant facts and/or opinions that support the topic. Your final research paper combines properly credited outside information along with personal insights. Thus, no two research papers — even if they are about the same topic — will or should be the same.

Project — Research Paper

When preparing a research paper, you should follow a standard documentation style that defines the rules for creating the paper and crediting sources. A variety of documentation styles exists, depending on the nature of the research paper. Each style

BTW

APA Appendix

If you are required to create a research paper that uses APA style instead of MLA style, you can visit www.cengagebrain.com for the steps required to create this module's research paper. Alternately, you can utilize any number of APA guidelines available in print or online, or ask your instructor.

requires the same basic information; the differences in styles relate to requirements for presenting the information. For example, one documentation style uses the term, bibliography, for the list of sources, whereas another uses the term, references, and yet a third prefers the term, works cited. Two popular documentation styles for research papers are the **Modern Language Association of America (MLA)** and **American Psychological Association (APA)** styles. This module uses the MLA documentation style because it is used in a wide range of disciplines.

The project in this module follows research paper guidelines and uses Word to create the short research paper shown in Figure 2–1. This paper, which discusses using headphones and earbuds safely, follows the MLA documentation style. Each page contains a page number. The first two pages present the name and course information (student name, instructor name, course name, and paper due date), paper title, an introduction with a thesis statement, details that support the thesis, and a conclusion. This section of the paper also includes references to research sources and a footnote. The third page contains a detailed, alphabetical list of the sources referenced in the research paper. All pages include a header at the upper-right edge of the page.

In this module, you will learn how to create the research paper shown in Figure 2–1. The following roadmap identifies general activities you will perform as you progress through this module:

1. CHANGE the DOCUMENT SETTINGS.
2. CREATE the HEADER for each page of the research paper.
3. TYPE the RESEARCH PAPER text WITH CITATIONS.
4. CREATE an ALPHABETICAL WORKS CITED page.
5. PROOFREAD AND REVISE the RESEARCH PAPER.

MLA Documentation Style

The research paper in this project follows the guidelines presented by the MLA. To follow the MLA documentation style, use a 12-point Times New Roman or similar font. Double-space text on all pages of the paper using one-inch top, bottom, left, and right margins. Indent the first word of each paragraph one-half inch from the left margin. At the right margin of each page, place a page number one-half inch from the top margin. On each page, precede the page number with your last name.

The MLA documentation style does not require a title page. Instead, place your name and course information in a block at the left margin beginning one inch from the top of the page. Center the title one double-spaced line below your name and course information.

BTW

APA Documentation Style

In the APA style, a separate title page is required instead of placing name and course information on the paper's first page. Double-space all pages of the paper with one-inch top, bottom, left, and right margins. Indent the first word of each paragraph one-half inch from the left margin. In the upper-right margin of each page, including the title page, place a running head that consists of the page number preceded by a brief summary of the paper title.

In the text of the paper, place author references in parentheses with the page number(s) of the referenced information. The MLA documentation style uses in-text **parenthetical references** instead of noting each source at the bottom of the page or at the end of the paper. In the MLA documentation style, notes are used only for optional content or bibliographic notes.

If used, content notes elaborate on points discussed in the paper, and bibliographic notes direct the reader to evaluations of statements in a source or provide a means for identifying multiple sources. Use a superscript (raised number) both to signal that a note exists and to sequence the notes (shown in Figure 2–1). Position notes at the bottom of the page as footnotes or at the end of the paper as endnotes. Indent the first line of each note one-half inch from the left margin. Place one space following the superscripted number before beginning the note text. Double-space the note text (shown in Figure 2–1).

Figure 2–1

The MLA documentation style uses the term, works cited, to refer to the bibliographic list of sources at the end of the paper. The **works cited** page alphabetically lists sources that are referenced directly in the paper. Place the list of sources on a separate numbered page. Center the title, Works Cited, one inch from the top margin. Double-space all lines. Begin the first line of each source at the left margin, indenting subsequent lines of the same source one-half inch from the left margin. List each source by the author's last name or, if the author's name is not available, by the title of the source.

Changing Document Settings

The MLA documentation style defines some global formats that apply to the entire research paper. Some of these formats are the default in Word. For example, the default left, right, top, and bottom margin settings in Word are one inch, which meets the MLA documentation style. You will modify, however, the font, font size, and line and paragraph spacing.

To Run Word and Specify Settings

If you are using a computer to step through the project in this module and you want your screens to match the figures in this book, you should change your screen's resolution to 1366 × 768. For information about how to change a computer's resolution, refer to the Office and Windows module at the beginning of this book.

1. Run Word and create a blank document in the Word window.

2. If the Word window is not maximized, click the Maximize button on its title bar to maximize the window.

3. If the Print Layout button on the status bar is not selected (shown in Figure 2–2), click it so that your screen is in Print Layout view.

4. If Normal (Home tab | Styles group) is not selected in the Styles gallery (shown in Figure 2–2), click it so that your document uses the Normal style.

5. Display the View tab. To display the page the same width as the document window, if necessary, click the Page Width button (View tab | Zoom group).

6. Display the Home tab. If the 'Show/Hide ¶' button (Home tab | Paragraph group) is not selected already, click it to display formatting marks on the screen.

Styles

When you create a document, Word formats the text using a particular style. A **style** is a named group of formatting characteristics, including font and font size. The default style in Word is called the **Normal style**, which most likely uses an 11-point Calibri font. If you do not specify a style for text you type, Word applies the Normal style to the text. In addition to the Normal style, Word has many other built-in, or predefined, styles that you can use to format text. Styles make it easy to apply many formats at once to text. You can modify existing styles and create your own styles. Styles are discussed as they are used in this book.

For an introduction to Office and instructions about how to perform basic tasks in Office apps, read the Office and Windows module at the beginning of this book, where you can learn how to run an application, use the ribbon, save a file, open a file, print a file, exit an application, use Help, and much more.

For an introduction to Windows and instructions about how to perform basic Windows tasks, read the Office and Windows module at the beginning of this book, where you can learn how to resize windows, change screen resolution, create folders, move and rename files, use Windows Help, and much more.

BTW
Style Formats
To see the formats assigned to a particular style in a document, click the Styles Dialog Box Launcher (Home tab | Styles group) and then click the Style Inspector button in the Styles task pane. Position the insertion point in the style in the document and then point to the Paragraph formatting or Text level formatting areas in the Style Inspector task pane to display a ScreenTip describing formats assigned to the location of the insertion point. You also can click the Reveal Formatting button in the Style Inspector task pane or press SHIFT+F1 to display the Reveal Formatting task pane.

To Modify a Style

The MLA documentation style requires that all text in the research paper use a 12-point Times New Roman or similar font. If you change the font and font size using buttons on the ribbon, you will need to make the change many times during the course of creating the paper. ***Why?*** *Word formats various areas of a document based on the Normal style, which uses an 11-point Calibri font. For example, body text, headers, and bibliographies all display text based on the Normal style.*

Thus, instead of changing the font and font size for various document elements, a more efficient technique is to change the Normal style for this document to use a 12-point Times New Roman font. ***Why?*** *By changing the Normal style, you ensure that all text in the document will use the format required by the MLA.* The following steps change the Normal style.

• Right-click Normal in the Styles gallery (Home tab | Styles group) to display a shortcut menu related to styles (Figure 2–2).

Figure 2–2

• Click Modify on the shortcut menu to display the Modify Style dialog box (Figure 2–3).

Figure 2–3

3

- Click the Font arrow (Modify Style dialog box) to display the Font list. Scroll to and then click Times New Roman in the list to change the font for the style being modified.
- Click the Font Size arrow (Modify Style dialog box) and then click 12 in the Font Size list to change the font size for the style being modified.
- Ensure that the 'Only in this document' option button is selected (Figure 2–4).

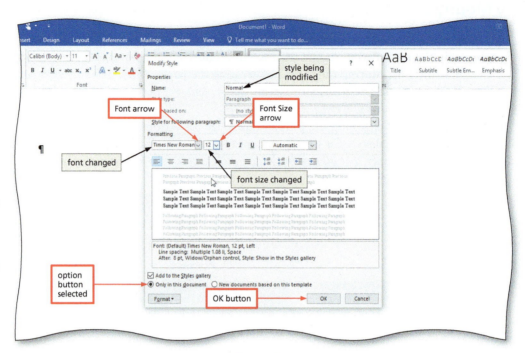

Figure 2–4

Q&A

Will all future documents use the new font and font size?

No, because the 'Only in this document' option button is selected. If you wanted all future documents to use a new setting, you would select the 'New documents based on this template' option button.

4

- Click the OK button (Modify Style dialog box) to update the Normal style to the specified settings.

Other Ways

1. Click Styles Dialog Box Launcher, click arrow next to style name, click Modify on menu, change settings (Modify Style dialog box), click OK button

2. Press ALT+CTRL+SHIFT+S, click arrow next to style name, click Modify on menu, change settings (Modify Style dialog box), click OK button

---

BTW

Line Spacing
If the top of a set of characters or a graphical image is chopped off, then line spacing may be set to Exactly. To remedy the problem, change line spacing to 1.0, 1.15, 1.5, 2.0, 2.5, 3.0, or At least (in the Paragraph dialog box), all of which accommodate the largest font or image.

Adjusting Line and Paragraph Spacing

Line spacing is the amount of vertical space between lines of text in a paragraph. **Paragraph spacing** is the amount of space above and below a paragraph. By default, the Normal style places 8 points of blank space after each paragraph and inserts a vertical space equal to 1.08 lines between each line of text. It also automatically adjusts line height to accommodate various font sizes and graphics.

The MLA documentation style requires that you double-space the entire research paper. That is, specifying a document use **double-space** means that the amount of vertical space between each line of text and above and below paragraphs should be equal to one blank line. The next sets of steps adjust line spacing and paragraph spacing according to the MLA documentation style.

To Change Line Spacing

1 CHANGE DOCUMENT SETTINGS | 2 CREATE HEADER | 3 TYPE RESEARCH PAPER WITH CITATIONS
4 CREATE ALPHABETICAL WORKS CITED | 5 PROOFREAD & REVISE RESEARCH PAPER

The following steps change the line spacing to 2.0 to double-space lines in a paragraph. *Why? The lines of the research paper should be double-spaced, according to the MLA documentation style.*

1

- Click the 'Line and Paragraph Spacing' button (Home tab | Paragraph group) to display the Line and Paragraph Spacing gallery (Figure 2–5).

Q&A What do the numbers in the Line and Paragraph Spacing gallery represent?

The options 1.0, 2.0, and 3.0 set line spacing to single, double, and triple, respectively. Similarly, the 1.15, 1.5, and 2.5 options set line spacing to 1.15, 1.5, and 2.5 lines. All of these options adjust line spacing automatically to accommodate the largest font or graphic on a line.

Figure 2–5

2

- Click 2.0 in the Line and Paragraph Spacing gallery to change the line spacing at the location of the insertion point.

Q&A Can I change the line spacing of existing text?

Yes. Select the text first and then change the line spacing as described in these steps.

Other Ways

1. Right-click paragraph (or, if using touch, tap 'Show Context Menu' on mini toolbar), click Paragraph on shortcut menu, or click Indents and Spacing tab (Paragraph dialog box), click Line spacing arrow, select desired spacing, click OK button

2. Click Paragraph Settings Dialog Box Launcher (Home tab or Layout tab | Paragraph group), click Indents and Spacing tab (Paragraph dialog box), click Line spacing arrow, select desired spacing, click OK button

3. Press CTRL+2 for double-spacing

To Remove Space after a Paragraph

1 CHANGE DOCUMENT SETTINGS | 2 CREATE HEADER | 3 TYPE RESEARCH PAPER WITH CITATIONS
4 CREATE ALPHABETICAL WORKS CITED | 5 PROOFREAD & REVISE RESEARCH PAPER

The following steps remove space after a paragraph. *Why? The research paper should not have additional blank space after each paragraph, according to the MLA documentation style.*

1

- Click the 'Line and Paragraph Spacing' button (Home tab | Paragraph group) to display the Line and Paragraph Spacing gallery (Figure 2–6).

Q&A Why does a check mark appear to the left of 2.0 in the gallery?

The check mark indicates the currently selected line spacing.

Figure 2–6

- Click 'Remove Space After Paragraph' in the Line and Paragraph Spacing gallery so that no blank space appears after paragraphs.

Q&A
Can I remove space after existing paragraphs?
Yes. Select the paragraphs first and then remove the space as described in these steps.

Other Ways

1. Adjust Spacing After arrows (Layout tab | Paragraph group) until 0 pt is displayed

2. Right-click paragraph (or, if using touch, tap 'Show Context Menu' on mini toolbar), click Paragraph on shortcut menu, click Indents and Spacing tab (Paragraph dialog box), adjust After arrows until 0 pt is displayed, click OK button

3. Click Paragraph Settings Dialog Box Launcher (Home tab or Layout tab | Paragraph group), click Indents and Spacing tab (Paragraph dialog box), adjust After arrows until 0 pt is displayed, click OK button

---

To Update a Style to Match a Selection

1 CHANGE DOCUMENT SETTINGS | 2 CREATE HEADER | 3 TYPE RESEARCH PAPER WITH CITATIONS
4 CREATE ALPHABETICAL WORKS CITED | 5 PROOFREAD & REVISE RESEARCH PAPER

To ensure that all paragraphs in the paper will be double-spaced and do not have space after the paragraphs, you want the Normal style to include the line and paragraph spacing changes made in the previous two sets of steps. The following steps update the Normal style. *Why? You can update a style to reflect the settings of the location of the insertion point or selected text. Because no text has been typed in the research paper yet, you do not need to select text prior to updating the Normal style.*

- Right-click Normal in the Styles gallery (Home tab | Styles group) to display a shortcut menu (Figure 2–7).

- Click 'Update Normal to Match Selection' on the shortcut menu to update the selected (or current) style to reflect the settings at the location of the insertion point.

Figure 2–7

Other Ways

1. Click Styles Dialog Box Launcher, click arrow next to style name, click 'Update Normal to Match Selection'

2. Press ALT+CTRL+SHIFT+S, click arrow next to style name in Styles pane, click 'Update Normal to Match Selection'

Creating a Header

BTW

The Ribbon and Screen Resolution
Word may change how the groups and buttons within the groups appear on the ribbon, depending on the computer or mobile device's screen resolution. Thus, your ribbon may look different from the ones in this book if you are using a screen resolution other than 1366 x 768.

A **header** is text and/or graphics that print at the top of each page in a document. Similarly, a **footer** is text and/or graphics that print at the bottom of every page. In Word, headers print in the top margin one-half inch from the top of every page, and footers print in the bottom margin one-half inch from the bottom of each page, which meets the MLA documentation style. In addition to text and graphics, headers and footers can include document information, such as the page number, current date, current time, and author's name.

In this research paper, you are to precede the page number with your last name placed one-half inch from the upper-right edge of each page. The procedures in the following sections enter your name and the page number in the header, as specified by the MLA documentation style.

To Switch to the Header

The following steps switch from editing the document text to editing the header. *Why? To enter text in the header, you instruct Word to edit the header.*

 1

- Click Insert on the ribbon to display the Insert tab.
- Click the 'Add a Header' button (Insert tab | Header & Footer group) to display the Add a Header gallery (Figure 2–8)

🔍 **Experiment**

- Click the down scroll arrow in the Add a Header gallery to see the available built-in headers.

Q&A Can I use a built-in header for this research paper?

None of the built-in headers adheres to the MLA documentation style; thus, you should enter your own header content instead of using a built-in header for this research paper.

How would I remove a header from a document?

You would click Remove Header in the Add a Header gallery. Similarly, to remove a footer, you would click Remove Footer in the Add a Footer gallery.

Figure 2–8

 2

- Click Edit Header in the Add a Header gallery to switch from the document text to the header, which allows you to edit the contents of the header (Figure 2–9).

Q&A How do I remove the Header & Footer Tools Design tab from the ribbon?

When you are finished editing the header, you will close it, which removes the Header & Footer Tools Design tab.

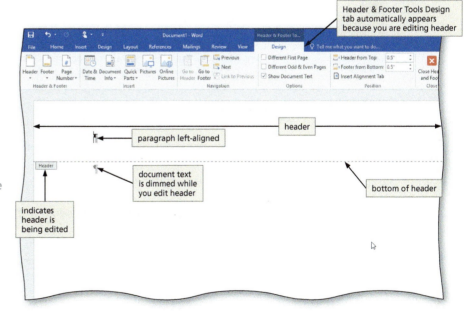

Figure 2–9

Other Ways

1. Double-click dimmed header

2. Right-click header in document, click Edit Header button that appears

To Right-Align a Paragraph

1 CHANGE DOCUMENT SETTINGS | **2 CREATE HEADER** | 3 TYPE RESEARCH PAPER WITH CITATIONS
4 CREATE ALPHABETICAL WORKS CITED | 5 PROOFREAD & REVISE RESEARCH PAPER

The paragraph in the header currently is left-aligned (shown in Figure 2–9). The following steps right-align this paragraph. ***Why?*** *Your last name and the page number should print **right-aligned**; that is, they should print at the right margin, according to the MLA documentation style.*

• Click Home on the ribbon to display the Home tab.

• Click the Align Right button (Home tab | Paragraph group) to right-align the current paragraph (Figure 2–10).

Q&A What if I wanted to return the paragraph to left-aligned?
You would click the Align Right button again, or click the Align Left button (Home tab | Paragraph group).

Figure 2–10

Other Ways

1. Right-click paragraph (or, if using touch, tap 'Show Context Menu' button on mini toolbar), click Paragraph on shortcut menu, click Indents and Spacing tab (Paragraph dialog box), click Alignment arrow, click Right, click OK button

2. Click Paragraph Settings Dialog Box Launcher (Home tab or Layout tab | Paragraph group), click Indents and Spacing tab (Paragraph dialog box), click Alignment arrow, click Right, click OK button

3. Press CTRL+R

BTW

Footers
If you wanted to create a footer, you would click the 'Add a Footer' button (Insert tab | Header & Footer group) and then select the desired built-in footer or click Edit Footer in the Add a Footer gallery to create a customized footer; or, you could double-click the dimmed footer.

To Enter Text

The following step enters the last name right-aligned in the header area.

1 Type **Carter** and then press the SPACEBAR to enter the last name in the header.

If requested by your instructor, enter your last name instead of Carter in the header.

To Insert a Page Number

1 CHANGE DOCUMENT SETTINGS | **2 CREATE HEADER** | 3 TYPE RESEARCH PAPER WITH CITATIONS
4 CREATE ALPHABETICAL WORKS CITED | 5 PROOFREAD & REVISE RESEARCH PAPER

The following steps insert a page number at the location of the insertion point. ***Why?*** *The MLA documentation style requires a page number following the last name in the header.*

- Click Header & Footer Tools Design on the ribbon to display the Header & Footer Tools Design tab.
- Click the 'Add Page Numbers' button (Header & Footer Tools Design tab | Header & Footer group) to display the Add Page Numbers menu.

Q&A Why does the button name in the step differ from the name on the face of the button in the figure?

The text that appears on the face of the button may vary, depending on screen resolution. The name that appears in the ScreenTip (when you point to the button), however, never changes. For this reason, this book uses the name that appears in the ScreenTip to identify buttons, boxes, and other on-screen elements.

- Point to Current Position on the Add Page Numbers menu to display the Current Position gallery (Figure 2–11).

 Experiment

- Click the down scroll arrow in the Current Position gallery to see the available page number formats.

Figure 2–11

- If necessary, scroll to the top of the Current Position gallery.
- Click Plain Number in the Current Position gallery to insert an unformatted page number at the location of the insertion point (Figure 2–12).

Figure 2–12

Other Ways

1. Click 'Add Page Numbers' button (Insert tab | Header & Footer group)

2. Click 'Explore Quick Parts' button (Insert tab | Text group or Header & Footer Tools Design tab | Insert group), click Field on Explore Quick Parts menu, select Page in Field names list (Field dialog box), select desired format in Format list, click OK button

To Close the Header

The next task is to switch back to the document text. *Why? You are finished entering text in the header.* The following step closes the header.

- Click the 'Close Header and Footer' button (Header & Footer Tools Design tab | Close group) (shown in Figure 2–12) to close the header and switch back to the document text (Figure 2–13).

Q&A

How do I make changes to existing header text? Switch to the header using the steps described previously in the section titled To Switch to the Header, edit the header as you would edit text in the document window, and then switch back to the document text.

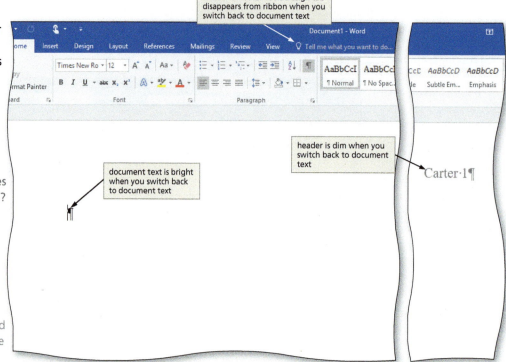

Header & Footer Tools Design tab disappears from ribbon when you switch back to document text

document text is bright when you switch back to document text

header is dim when you switch back to document text

Carter·1¶

Figure 2–13

Other Ways

1. Double-click dimmed document text

Typing the Research Paper Text

The text of the research paper in this module encompasses the first two pages of the paper. You will type the text of the research paper and then modify it later in the module, so that it matches Figure 2–1 shown at the beginning of this module.

CONSIDER THIS

What should you consider when writing the first draft of a research paper?
As you write the first draft of a research paper, be sure it includes the proper components, uses credible sources, and does not contain any plagiarized material.

- **Include an introduction, body, and conclusion.** The first paragraph of the paper introduces the topic and captures the reader's attention. The body, which follows the introduction, consists of several paragraphs that support the topic. The conclusion summarizes the main points in the body and restates the topic.

- **Evaluate sources for authority, currency, and accuracy.** Be especially wary of information obtained on the web. Any person, company, or organization can publish a webpage on the Internet. When considering the source, consider the following:

  - Authority: Does a reputable institution or group support the source? Is the information presented without bias? Are the author's credentials listed and verifiable?

  - Currency: Is the information up to date? Are dates of sources listed? What is the last date revised or updated?

  - Accuracy: Is the information free of errors? Is it verifiable? Are the sources clearly identified?

- **Acknowledge all sources of information; do not plagiarize.** Sources of research include books, magazines, newspapers, and the Internet. As you record facts and ideas, list details about the source: title, author, place of publication, publisher, date of publication, etc. When taking notes, be careful not to **plagiarize**. That is, do not use someone else's work and claim it to be your own. If you copy information directly, place it in quotation marks and identify its source. Not only is plagiarism unethical, but it is considered an academic crime that can have severe punishments, such as failing a course or being expelled from school.

When you summarize, paraphrase (rewrite information in your own words), present facts, give statistics, quote exact words, or show a map, chart, or other graphic, you must acknowledge the source. Information that commonly is known or accessible to the audience constitutes common knowledge and does not need to be acknowledged. If, however, you question whether certain information is common knowledge, you should document it — just to be safe.

To Enter Name and Course Information

As discussed earlier in this module, the MLA documentation style does not require a separate title page for research papers. Instead, place your name and course information in a block at the top of the page, below the header, at the left margin. The following steps enter the name and course information in the research paper.

BTW

Date Formats
The MLA style prefers the day-month-year (10 October 2017) or month-day-year (October 10, 2017) format.

1 Type **Oswald Carter** as the student name and then press the ENTER key.

2 Type **Ms. Ruiz** as the instructor name and then press the ENTER key.

3 Type **English 104** as the course name and then press the ENTER key.

4 Type **October 10, 2017** as the paper's due date and then press the ENTER key (Figure 2–14).

If requested by your instructor, enter your name and course information instead of the information shown above.

Q&A Why did the word, October, appear on the screen as I began typing the month name?
Word has an AutoComplete feature, where it predicts some words or phrases as you are typing and displays its prediction in a ScreenTip. If the AutoComplete prediction is correct, you can press the ENTER key (or, if using touch, tap the ScreenTip) to instruct Word to finish your typing with the word or phrase that appears in the ScreenTip.

Figure 2–14

To Click and Type

The next task is to enter the title of the research paper centered between the page margins. In Module 1, you used the Center button (Home tab | Paragraph group) to center text and graphics. As an alternative, if you are using a mouse, you can use Word's Click and Type feature to format and enter text, graphics, and other items. *Why? With **Click and Type**, you can double-click a blank area of the document window and Word automatically formats the item you type or insert according to the location where you double-clicked.* The following steps use Click and Type to center and then type the title of the research paper.

Experiment

- Move the pointer around the document below the entered name and course information and observe the various icons that appear with the I-beam.

- Position the pointer in the center of the document at the approximate location for the research paper title until a center icon appears below the I-beam (Figure 2–15).

Figure 2–15

Q&A

What are the other icons that appear in the Click and Type pointer?
A left-align icon appears to the right of the I-beam when the Click and Type pointer is in certain locations on the left side of the document window. A right-align icon appears to the left of the I-beam when the Click and Type pointer is in certain locations on the right side of the document window.

What if I am using a touch screen?
Tap the Center button (Home tab | Paragraph group) and then proceed to Step 3 because the Click and Type feature does not work with a touch screen.

- Double-click to center the paragraph mark and insertion point between the left and right margins.

3

- Type `Safely Using Headphones and Earbuds` as the paper title and then press the ENTER key to position the insertion point on the next line (Figure 2–16).

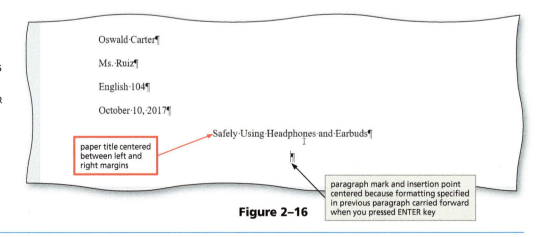

Figure 2–16

Keyboard Shortcuts

Word has many **keyboard shortcuts**, sometimes called shortcut keys or keyboard key combinations, for your convenience while typing. Table 2–1 lists the common keyboard shortcuts for formatting characters. Table 2–2 lists common keyboard shortcuts for formatting paragraphs.

Table 2–1 Keyboard Shortcuts for Formatting Characters

Character Formatting Task	Keyboard Shortcut	Character Formatting Task	Keyboard Shortcut
All capital letters	CTRL+SHIFT+A	Italic	CTRL+I
Bold	CTRL+B	Remove character formatting (plain text)	CTRL+SPACEBAR
Case of letters	SHIFT+F3	Small uppercase letters	CTRL+SHIFT+K
Decrease font size	CTRL+SHIFT+<	Subscript	CTRL+EQUAL SIGN
Decrease font size 1 point	CTRL+[	Superscript	CTRL+SHIFT+PLUS SIGN
Double-underline	CTRL+SHIFT+D	Underline	CTRL+U
Increase font size	CTRL+SHIFT+>	Underline words, not spaces	CTRL+SHIFT+W
Increase font size 1 point	CTRL+]		

© 2015 Cengage Learning

Table 2–2 Keyboard Shortcuts for Formatting Paragraphs

Paragraph Formatting	Keyboard Shortcut	Paragraph Formatting	Keyboard Shortcut
1.5 line spacing	CTRL+5	Justify paragraph	CTRL+J
Add/remove one line above paragraph	CTRL+0 (ZERO)	Left-align paragraph	CTRL+L
Center paragraph	CTRL+E	Remove hanging indent	CTRL+SHIFT+T
Decrease paragraph indent	CTRL+SHIFT+M	Remove paragraph formatting	CTRL+Q
Double-space lines	CTRL+2	Right-align paragraph	CTRL+R
Hanging indent	CTRL+T	Single-space lines	CTRL+1
Increase paragraph indent	CTRL+M		

© 2015 Cengage Learning

To Format Text Using a Keyboard Shortcut

The paragraphs below the paper title should be left-aligned, instead of centered. Thus, the next step is to left-align the paragraph below the paper title. When your fingers already are on the keyboard, you may prefer using keyboard shortcuts to format text as you type it.

The following step left-aligns a paragraph using the keyboard shortcut CTRL+L. (Recall from Module 1 that a notation such as CTRL+L means to press the letter L on the keyboard while holding down the CTRL key.)

1 Press CTRL+L to left-align the current paragraph, that is, the paragraph containing the insertion point (shown in Figure 2–17).

Q&A Why would I use a keyboard shortcut instead of the ribbon to format text?
Switching between the mouse and the keyboard takes time. If your hands are already on the keyboard, use a keyboard shortcut. If your hand is on the mouse, use the ribbon.

2 Save the research paper on your hard drive, OneDrive, or other storage location using the file name, Headphones and Earbuds Paper.

Q&A Why should I save the research paper at this time?
You have performed many tasks while creating this flyer and do not want to risk losing work completed thus far.

BTW

Keyboard Shortcuts
To print a complete list of keyboard shortcuts in Word, press F1 to display the Word Help window, type **keyboard shortcuts** in the Search box in the Word Help window, press the ENTER key, click the Keyboard shortcuts for Microsoft Word link, click the Print button in the Help window, and then click the Print button in the Print dialog box.

To Display the Rulers

According to the MLA documentation style, the first line of each paragraph in the research paper is to be indented one-half inch from the left margin. Although you can use a dialog box to indent paragraphs, Word provides a quicker way through the **horizontal ruler**. This ruler is displayed at the top edge of the document window just below the ribbon. Word also provides a **vertical ruler** that is displayed along the left edge of the Word window. The following step displays the rulers. ***Why?*** *You want to use the horizontal ruler to indent paragraphs.*

- If necessary, scroll the document so that the research paper title is at the top of the document window.
- Click View on the ribbon to display the View tab.
- If the rulers are not displayed, click the View Ruler check box (View tab | Show group) to place a check mark in the check box and display the horizontal and vertical rulers on the screen (Figure 2–17).

Q&A What tasks can I accomplish using the rulers?
You can use the rulers to indent paragraphs, set tab stops, change page margins, and adjust column widths.

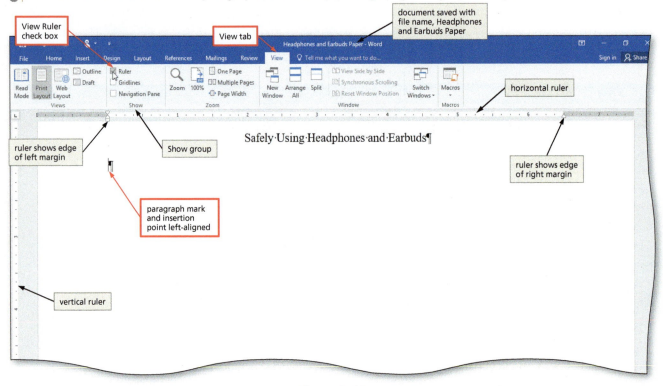

Figure 2–17

To First-Line Indent Paragraphs

If you are using a mouse, you can use the horizontal ruler, usually simply called the **ruler**, to indent just the first line of a paragraph, which is called a **first-line indent**. The left margin on the ruler contains two triangles above a square. The '**First Line Indent**' **marker** is the top triangle at the 0" mark on the ruler (shown in Figure 2–18). The bottom triangle is discussed later in this module. The small square at the 0" mark is the Left Indent marker. The **Left Indent marker** allows you to change the entire left margin, whereas the 'First Line Indent' marker indents only the first line of the paragraph.

The following steps first-line indent paragraphs in the research paper. ***Why?*** *The first line of each paragraph in the research paper is to be indented one-half inch from the left margin, according to the MLA documentation style.*

1

- With the insertion point on the paragraph mark below the research paper title, point to the 'First Line Indent' marker on the ruler (Figure 2–18).

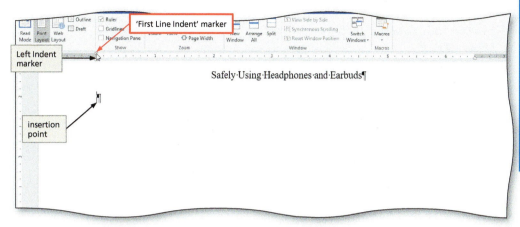

Figure 2–18

2

- Drag the 'First Line Indent' marker to the .5" mark on the ruler to display a vertical dotted line in the document window, which indicates the proposed indent location of the first line of the paragraph (Figure 2–19).

Figure 2–19

3

- Release the mouse button to place the 'First Line Indent' marker at the .5" mark on the ruler, or one-half inch from the left margin (Figure 2–20).

Q&A

What if I am using a touch screen?

If you are using a touch screen, you cannot drag the 'First Line Indent' marker and must follow these steps instead: tap the Paragraph Settings Dialog Box Launcher (Home tab or Layout tab | Paragraph group) to display the Paragraph dialog box, tap the Indents and Spacing tab (Paragraph dialog box), tap the Special arrow, tap First line, and then tap the OK button.

Figure 2–20

- Type **People often listen to sound from their computers or portable devices through headphones or earbuds.** and notice that Word automatically indents the first line of the paragraph by one-half inch (Figure 2–21).

Figure 2–21

Will I have to set a first-line indent for each paragraph in the paper?

No. Each time you press the ENTER key, paragraph formatting in the previous paragraph carries forward to the next paragraph. Thus, once you set the first-line indent, its format carries forward automatically to each subsequent paragraph you type.

Other Ways

1. Right-click paragraph (or, if using touch, tap 'Show Context Menu' button on mini toolbar), click Paragraph on shortcut menu, click Indents and Spacing tab (Paragraph dialog box), click Special arrow, click First line, click OK button

2. Click Paragraph Settings Dialog Box Launcher (Home tab or Layout tab | Paragraph group), click Indents and Spacing tab (Paragraph dialog box), click Special arrow, click First line, click OK button

To AutoCorrect as You Type

1 CHANGE DOCUMENT SETTINGS | 2 CREATE HEADER | **3 TYPE RESEARCH PAPER WITH CITATIONS**
4 CREATE ALPHABETICAL WORKS CITED | 5 PROOFREAD & REVISE RESEARCH PAPER

Word has predefined many commonly misspelled words, which it automatically corrects for you. ***Why?*** *As you type, you may make typing, spelling, capitalization, or grammar errors. Word's **AutoCorrect** feature automatically corrects these kinds of errors as you type them in the document. For example, if you type the characters, ahve, Word automatically changes it to the correct spelling, have, when you press the* SPACEBAR *or a punctuation mark key, such as a period or comma.*

The following steps intentionally misspell the word, the, as teh to illustrate the AutoCorrect feature.

- Press the SPACEBAR.
- Type the beginning of the next sentence, misspelling the word, the, as follows: **Headphones cover or are placed outside of teh** (Figure 2–22).

Figure 2–22

- Press the SPACEBAR and watch Word automatically correct the misspelled word.
- Type the rest of the sentence (Figure 2–23): **ear, whereas earbuds rest inside the ear canal.**

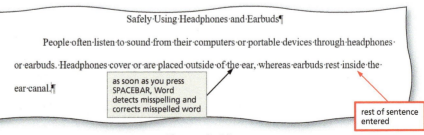

Figure 2–23

To Use the AutoCorrect Options Button

The following steps illustrate the AutoCorrect Options button and menu. ***Why?*** *If you are using a mouse, when you position the pointer on text that Word automatically corrected, a small blue box appears below the text. If you point to the small blue box, Word displays the AutoCorrect Options button. When you click the **AutoCorrect Options button**, Word displays a menu that allows you to undo a correction or change how Word handles future automatic corrections of this type.*

- Position the pointer in the text automatically corrected by Word (the word, the, in this case) to display a small blue box below the automatically corrected word (Figure 2–24).

Figure 2–24

- Point to the small blue box to display the AutoCorrect Options button.
- Click the AutoCorrect Options button to display the AutoCorrect Options menu (Figure 2–25).
- Press the ESC key to remove the AutoCorrect Options menu from the screen.

Q&A

Do I need to remove the AutoCorrect Options button from the screen?

No. When you move the pointer, the AutoCorrect Options button will disappear from the screen. If, for some reason, you wanted to remove the AutoCorrect Options button from the screen, you could press the ESC key a second time.

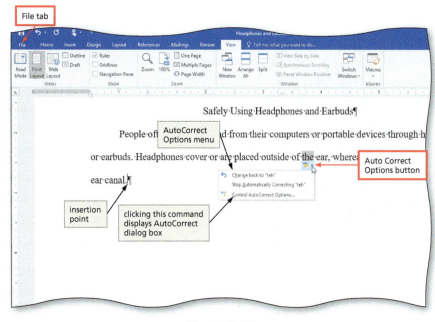

Figure 2–25

To Create an AutoCorrect Entry

The next steps create an AutoCorrect entry. ***Why?*** *In addition to the predefined list of AutoCorrect spelling, capitalization, and grammar errors, you can create your own AutoCorrect entries to add to the list. For example, if you tend to mistype the word computer as comptuer, you should create an AutoCorrect entry for it.*

1

- Click File on the ribbon (shown in Figure 2–25) to open the Backstage view (Figure 2–26).

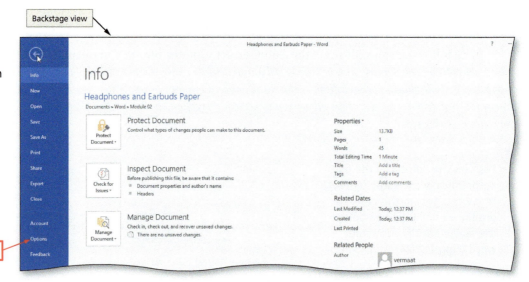

Backstage view

Options tab

Figure 2–26

2

- Click the Options tab in the Backstage view to display the Word Options dialog box.
- Click Proofing in the left pane (Word Options dialog box) to display proofing options in the right pane.
- Click the AutoCorrect Options button in the right pane to display the AutoCorrect dialog box.
- When Word displays the AutoCorrect dialog box, type **comptuer** in the Replace text box.
- Press the TAB key and then type **computer** in the With text box (Figure 2–27).

Word Options dialog box

right pane displays options related to command selected in left pane

Proofing command

AutoCorrect dialog box

AutoCorrect Options button

AutoCorrect tab

'Replace text as you type' check box

correct spelling entered in With text box

Exceptions button

left pane

misspelled word entered in Replace text box

alphabetical list of currently defined AutoCorrect entries

Add button

Delete button

OK button

Figure 2–27

Q&A How would I delete an existing AutoCorrect entry?
You would select the entry to be deleted in the list of defined entries in the AutoCorrect dialog box and then click the Delete button (AutoCorrect dialog box).

3

- Click the Add button (AutoCorrect dialog box) to add the entry alphabetically to the list of words to correct automatically as you type. (If your dialog box displays a Replace button instead, click it and then click the Yes button in the Microsoft Word dialog box to replace the previously defined entry.)
- Click the OK button (AutoCorrect dialog box) to close the dialog box.
- Click the OK button (Word Options dialog box) to close the dialog box.

The AutoCorrect Dialog Box

In addition to creating AutoCorrect entries for words you commonly misspell or mistype, you can create entries for abbreviations, codes, and so on. For example, you could create an AutoCorrect entry for asap, indicating that Word should replace this text with the phrase, as soon as possible.

If, for some reason, you do not want Word to correct automatically as you type, you can turn off the Replace text as you type feature by clicking the Options tab in the Backstage view, clicking Proofing in the left pane (Word Options dialog box), clicking the AutoCorrect Options button in the right pane (shown in Figure 2–27), removing the check mark from the 'Replace text as you type' check box, and then clicking the OK button in each open dialog box.

The AutoCorrect sheet in the AutoCorrect dialog box (Figure 2–27) contains other check boxes that correct capitalization errors if the check boxes are selected:

- If you type two capital letters in a row, such as TH, Word makes the second letter lowercase, Th.

- If you begin a sentence with a lowercase letter, Word capitalizes the first letter of the sentence.

- If you type the name of a day in lowercase letters, such as tuesday, Word capitalizes the first letter in the name of the day, Tuesday.

- If you leave the CAPS LOCK key on and begin a new sentence, such as after, Word corrects the typing, After, and turns off the CAPS LOCK key.

If you do not want Word to perform any of these corrections automatically, simply remove the check mark from the appropriate check box in the AutoCorrect dialog box.

Sometimes, you do not want Word to AutoCorrect a particular word or phrase. For example, you may use the code, WD., in your documents. Because Word automatically capitalizes the first letter of a sentence, the character you enter following the period will be capitalized (in the previous sentence, it would capitalize the letter i in the word, in). To allow the code, WD., to be entered into a document and still leave the AutoCorrect feature turned on, you would set an exception. To set an exception to an AutoCorrect rule, click the Options tab in the Backstage view, click Proofing in the left pane (Word Options dialog box), click the AutoCorrect Options button in the right pane, click the Exceptions button (Figure 2–27), click the appropriate tab in the AutoCorrect Exceptions dialog box, type the exception entry in the text box, click the Add button, click the Close button (AutoCorrect Exceptions dialog box), and then click the OK button in each of the remaining dialog boxes.

To Enter More Text

The next task is to continue typing text in the research paper up to the location of the in-text parenthetical reference. The following steps enter this text.

① With the insertion point positioned at the end of the first paragraph in the paper, as shown in Figure 2–25, press the SPACEBAR and then type these three sentences, intentionally misspelling the word sound as sould: `With these listening devices, only the individual wearing the device hears the sould. Using headphones or earbuds improperly can lead to permanent hearing loss. Items that may protect hearing include quality of these devices and volume levels.`

Q&A | Why is the word, sound, misspelled?
Later in this module, you will use Word's check spelling and grammar at once feature to check the entire document for errors.

BTW
Automatic Corrections
If you do not want to keep a change made automatically by Word and you immediately notice the automatic correction, you can undo the change by clicking the Undo button on the Quick Access Toolbar or pressing CTRL+Z. You also can undo a correction through the AutoCorrect Options button (Word Options dialog box) (shown in Figure 2–27).

BTW
Spacing after Punctuation
Because word processing documents use variable character fonts, it often is difficult to determine in a printed document how many times someone has pressed the SPACEBAR between sentences. Thus, the rule is to press the SPACEBAR only once after periods, colons, and other punctuation marks.

2 Press the ENTER key to start a new paragraph.

3 Type **The features of certain headphones and earbuds can help to prevent hearing loss. Higher-quality headphones and earbuds tend to produce a clearer sound, enabling wearers to listen at a lower volume** and then press the SPACEBAR (Figure 2–28).

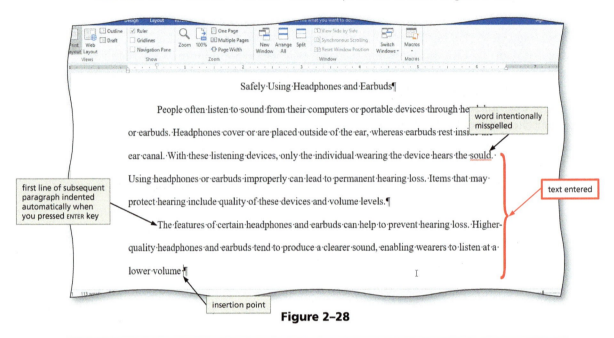

Figure 2–28

BTW

Word Help

At any time while using Word, you can find answers to questions and display information about various topics through Word Help. Used properly, this form of assistance can increase your productivity and reduce your frustrations by minimizing the time you spend learning how to use Word. For instructions about Word Help and exercises that will help you gain confidence in using it, read the Office and Windows module at the beginning of this book.

Citations

Both the MLA and APA guidelines suggest the use of in-text parenthetical references (placed at the end of a sentence), instead of footnoting each source of material in a paper. These parenthetical references, called citations in Word, guide the reader to the end of the paper for complete information about the source.

Word provides tools to assist you with inserting citations in a paper and later generating a list of sources from the citations. With a documentation style selected, Word automatically formats the citations and list of sources according to that style. The process for adding citations in Word is as follows:

1. Modify the documentation style, if necessary.
2. Insert a citation placeholder.
3. Enter the source information for the citation.

You can combine Steps 2 and 3, where you insert the citation placeholder and enter the source information at once. Or, you can insert the citation placeholder as you write and then enter the source information for the citation at a later time. While creating the research paper in this module, you will use both methods.

1 CHANGE DOCUMENT SETTINGS | 2 CREATE HEADER | **3 TYPE RESEARCH PAPER WITH CITATIONS**

4 CREATE ALPHABETICAL WORKS CITED | 5 PROOFREAD & REVISE RESEARCH PAPER

To Change the Bibliography Style

The first step in inserting a citation is to be sure the citations and sources will be formatted using the correct documentation style, called the bibliography style in Word. **Why?** *You want to ensure that Word is using the MLA documentation style for this paper.* The following steps change the specified documentation style.

1

- Click References on the ribbon to display the References tab.
- Click the Bibliography Style arrow (References tab | Citations & Bibliography group) to display the Bibliography Style gallery, which lists predefined documentation styles (Figure 2–29).

2

- Click 'MLA Seventh Edition' in the Bibliography Style gallery to change the documentation style to MLA.

Q&A

What if I am using a different edition of a documentation style shown in the Bibliography Style gallery?
Select the closest one and then, if necessary, perform necessary edits before submitting the paper.

Figure 2–29

What details are required for sources?

During your research, be sure to record essential publication information about each of your sources. Following is a sample list of types of required information for the MLA documentation style.

- Book: full name of author(s), complete title of book, edition (if available), volume (if available), publication city, publisher name, publication year, and publication medium

- Magazine: full name of author(s), complete title of article, magazine title, issue number (if available), date of magazine, page numbers of article, publication medium, and date viewed (if medium is a website)

- Website: full name of author(s), title of website, website publisher or sponsor (if none, write N.p.), publication date (if none, write n.d.), publication medium, and date viewed

CONSIDER THIS

To Insert a Citation and Create Its Source

1 CHANGE DOCUMENT SETTINGS | 2 CREATE HEADER | **3 TYPE RESEARCH PAPER WITH CITATIONS**
4 CREATE ALPHABETICAL WORKS CITED | 5 PROOFREAD & REVISE RESEARCH PAPER

With the documentation style selected, the next task is to insert a citation at the location of the insertion point and enter the source information for the citation. You can accomplish these steps at once by instructing Word to add a new source. The following steps add a new source for a magazine (periodical) article on the web. *Why? The material preceding the insertion point was summarized from an online magazine article.*

1

- With the insertion point at the location for the citation (as shown in Figure 2–28), click the Insert Citation button (References tab | Citations & Bibliography group) to display the Insert Citation menu (Figure 2–30).

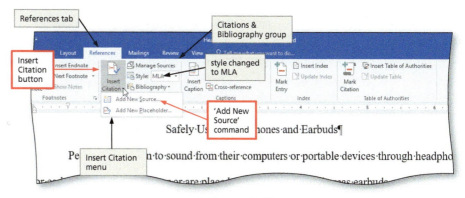

Figure 2–30

2

- Click 'Add New Source' on the Insert Citation menu to display the Create Source dialog box (Figure 2–31).

What are the Bibliography Fields in the Create Source dialog box?
A **field** is a placeholder for data whose contents can change. You enter data in some fields; Word supplies data for others. In this case, you enter the contents of the fields for a particular source, for example, the author name in the Author field.

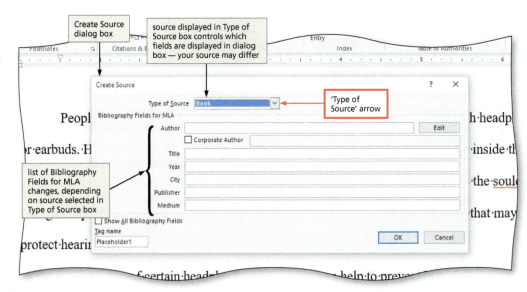

Figure 2–31

- Click the 'Type of Source' arrow and then click one of the source types in the list, so that you can see how the list of fields changes to reflect the type of source you selected.

3

- If necessary, click the 'Type of Source' arrow (Create Source dialog box) and then click 'Article in a Periodical', so that the list shows fields required for a magazine (periodical).

- Click the Author text box. Type **Tu, Mingzhu Lin** as the author.

- Click the Title text box. Type **Headphones and Earbuds** as the article title.

- Press the TAB key and then type **Technology and Trends Today** as the periodical title.

- Press the TAB key and then type **2017** as the year.

- Press the TAB key and then type **Aug.** as the month.

- Press the TAB key twice and then type **n. pag.** as the number of pages.

- Press the TAB key and then type **Web** as the medium (Figure 2–32).

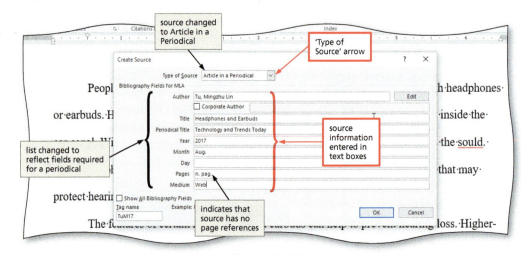

Figure 2–32

Why is the month abbreviated?
The MLA documentation style abbreviates all months, except May, June, and July, when they appear in a source.

What does the n. pag. entry mean in the Pages text box?
The MLA documentation style uses the abbreviation n. pag. for no pagination, which indicates the source has no page references. This is common for web sources.

4

- Place a check mark in the 'Show All Bibliography Fields' check box so that Word displays all fields available for the selected source, including the date viewed (accessed) fields.

- If necessary, scroll to the bottom of the Bibliography Fields list to display the date viewed (accessed) fields.

- Click the Year Accessed text box. Type **2017** as the year.

- Press the TAB key and then type **Oct.** as the month accessed.

- Press the TAB key and then type **3** as the day accessed (Figure 2–33).

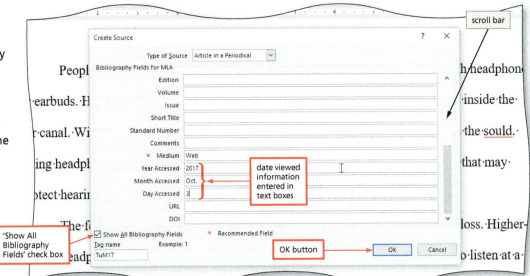

Figure 2–33

What if some of the text boxes disappear as I enter the fields?

With the 'Show All Bibliography Fields' check box selected, the dialog box may not be able to display all fields at the same time. In this case, some may scroll up off the screen.

5

- Click the OK button to close the dialog box, create the source, and insert the citation in the document at the location of the insertion point.
- Press the END key to move the insertion point to the end of the line, if necessary, which also deselects the citation.
- Press the PERIOD key to end the sentence (Figure 2–34).

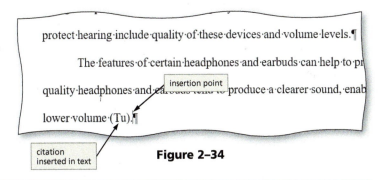

protect·hearing·include·quality·of·these·devices·and·volume·levels.¶

The·features·of·certain·headphones·and·earbuds·can·help·to·pr

quality·headphones·and·earbuds tend to produce·a·clearer·sound,·enab

lower·volume·(Tu).¶

citation inserted in text

Figure 2–34

To Enter More Text

The next task is to continue typing text in the research paper up to the location of the footnote. The following steps enter this text.

1 Press the SPACEBAR.

2 Type the next sentences (Figure 2–35): **Properly designed headphones**

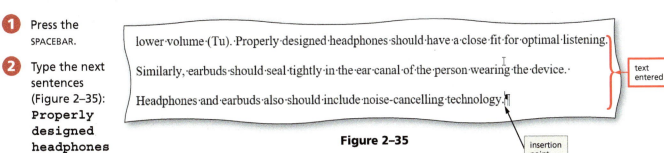

lower·volume·(Tu).·Properly·designed·headphones·should·have·a·close·fit·for·optimal·listening.

Similarly,·earbuds·should·seal·tightly·in·the·ear·canal·of·the·person·wearing·the·device.·

Headphones·and·earbuds·also·should·include·noise-cancelling·technology.¶

text entered

Figure 2–35

insertion point

```
should have a close fit for optimal listening. Similarly,
earbuds should seal tightly in the ear canal of the person
wearing the device. Headphones and earbuds also should
include noise-cancelling technology.
```

3 Save the research paper again on the same storage location with the same file name.

Q&A Why should I save the research paper again?
You have made several modifications to the research paper since you last saved it; thus, you should save it again.

Footnotes

BTW
Touch Screen Differences
The Office and Windows interfaces may vary if you are using a touch screen. For this reason, you might notice that the function or appearance of your touch screen differs slightly from this module's presentation.

As discussed earlier in this module, notes are optional in the MLA documentation style. If used, content notes elaborate on points discussed in the paper, and bibliographic notes direct the reader to evaluations of statements in a source or provide a means for identifying multiple sources. The MLA documentation style specifies that a superscript (raised number) be used for a **note reference mark** to signal that a note exists either at the bottom of the page as a **footnote** or at the end of the document as an **endnote**.

In Word, **note text** can be any length and format. Word automatically numbers notes sequentially by placing a note reference mark both in the body of the document and to the left of the note text. If you insert, rearrange, or remove notes, Word renumbers any subsequent note reference marks according to their new sequence in the document.

To Insert a Footnote Reference Mark

1 CHANGE DOCUMENT SETTINGS | 2 CREATE HEADER | **3 TYPE RESEARCH PAPER WITH CITATIONS**
4 CREATE ALPHABETICAL WORKS CITED | 5 PROOFREAD & REVISE RESEARCH PAPER

The following step inserts a footnote reference mark in the document at the location of the insertion point and at the location where the footnote text will be typed. ***Why?*** *You will insert a content note elaborating on noise-cancelling technology, which you want to position as a footnote.*

1

• With the insertion point positioned as shown in Figure 2–35, click the Insert Footnote button (References tab | Footnotes group) to display a note reference mark (a superscripted 1) in two places: (1) in the document window at the location of the insertion point and (2) at the bottom of the page where the footnote will be positioned, just below a separator line (Figure 2–36).

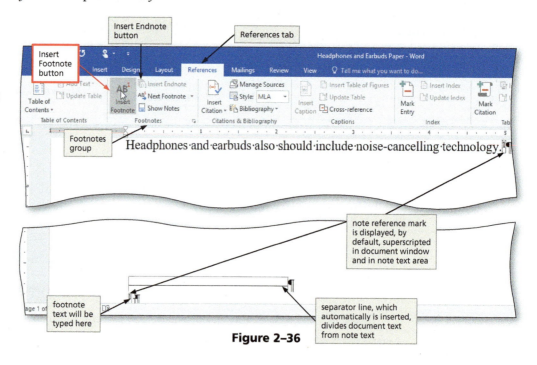

Figure 2–36

Q&A What if I wanted notes to be positioned as endnotes instead of as footnotes?
You would click the Insert Endnote button (References tab | Footnotes group), which places the separator line and the endnote text at the end of the document, instead of the bottom of the page containing the reference.

Other Ways

1. Press ALT+CTRL+F

To Enter Footnote Text

The following step types the footnote text to the right of the note reference mark below the separator line.

1 Type the footnote text up to the citation (shown in Figure 2–37): `Gupta and Padro state that effective noise-cancelling technology reduces the interference of sounds from the surrounding environment, reducing the volume level required by headphones and earbuds` and then press the SPACEBAR.

To Insert a Citation Placeholder

1 CHANGE DOCUMENT SETTINGS | 2 CREATE HEADER | **3 TYPE RESEARCH PAPER WITH CITATIONS**
4 CREATE ALPHABETICAL WORKS CITED | 5 PROOFREAD & REVISE RESEARCH PAPER

Earlier in this module, you inserted a citation and its source at once. In Word, you also can insert a citation without entering the source information. **Why?** *Sometimes, you may not have the source information readily available and would prefer to enter it at a later time.*

The following steps insert a citation placeholder in the footnote, so that you can enter the source information later.

1

• With the insertion point positioned as shown in Figure 2–37, click the Insert Citation button (References tab | Citations & Bibliography group) to display the Insert Citation menu (Figure 2–37).

Figure 2–37

2

- Click 'Add New Placeholder' on the Insert Citation menu to display the Placeholder Name dialog box.
- Type **Gupta** as the tag name for the source (Figure 2–38).

Q&A | What is a tag name?
A tag name is an identifier that links a citation to a source. Word automatically creates a tag name when you enter a source. When you create a citation placeholder, enter a meaningful tag name, which will appear in the citation placeholder until you edit the source.

Figure 2–38

3

- Click the OK button (Placeholder Name dialog box) to close the dialog box and insert the entered tag name in the citation placeholder in the document (shown in Figure 2–39).
- Press the PERIOD key to end the sentence.

Q&A | What if the citation is in the wrong location?
Click the citation to select it and then drag the citation tab (on the upper-left corner of the selected citation) to any location in the document.

Footnote Text Style

When you insert a footnote, Word formats it using the Footnote Text style, which does not adhere to the MLA documentation style. For example, notice in Figure 2–37 that the footnote text is single-spaced, left-aligned, and a smaller font size than the text in the research paper. According to the MLA documentation style, notes should be formatted like all other paragraphs in the paper.

You could change the paragraph formatting of the footnote text to first-line indent and double-spacing and then change the font size from 10 to 12 point. If you use this technique, however, you will need to change the format of the footnote text for each footnote you enter into the document.

A more efficient technique is to modify the format of the Footnote Text style so that every footnote you enter in the document will use the formats defined in this style.

To Modify a Style Using a Shortcut Menu

1 CHANGE DOCUMENT SETTINGS | 2 CREATE HEADER | **3 TYPE RESEARCH PAPER WITH CITATIONS**
4 CREATE ALPHABETICAL WORKS CITED | **5 PROOFREAD & REVISE RESEARCH PAPER**

The Footnote Text style specifies left-aligned single-spaced paragraphs with a 10-point font size for text. The following steps modify the Footnote Text style. ***Why?*** *To meet MLA documentation style, the footnotes should be double-spaced with a first-line indent and a 12-point font size for text.*

1

- Right-click the note text in the footnote to display a shortcut menu related to footnotes (Figure 2–39).

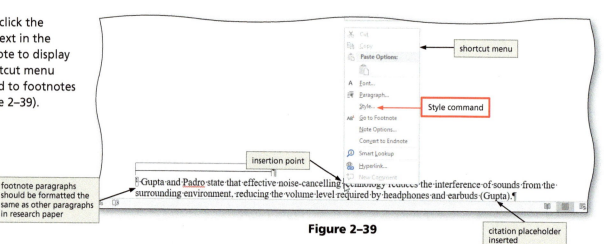

Figure 2–39

2

- Click Style on the shortcut menu to display the Style dialog box. If necessary, click the Category arrow, click All styles in the Category list, and then click Footnote Text in the Styles list to select the style to modify.

- Click the Modify button (Style dialog box) to display the Modify Style dialog box.

- Click the Font Size arrow (Modify Style dialog box) to display the Font Size list and then click 12 in the Font Size list to change the font size.

- Click the Double Space button to change the line spacing.

- Click the Format button to display the Format menu (Figure 2–40).

Figure 2–40

3

- Click Paragraph on the Format menu (Modify Style dialog box) to display the Paragraph dialog box.

- Click the Special arrow in the Indentation area (Paragraph dialog box) and then click First line (Figure 2–41).

Figure 2–41

4

- Click the OK button (Paragraph dialog box) to close the dialog box.

- Click the OK button (Modify Style dialog box) to close the dialog box.

- Click the Apply button (Style dialog box) to apply the style changes to the footnote text (Figure 2–42).

Q&A Will all footnotes use this modified style?
Yes. Any future footnotes entered in the document will use a 12-point font with the paragraphs first-line indented and double-spaced.

Figure 2–42

Other Ways

1. Click Styles Dialog Box Launcher (Home tab | Styles group), point to style name in list, click style name arrow, click Modify, change settings (Modify Style dialog box), click OK button

2. Click Styles Dialog Box Launcher (Home tab | Styles group), click Manage Styles button in task pane, select style name in list, click Modify button (Manage Styles dialog box), change settings (Modify Style dialog box), click OK button in each dialog box

To Edit a Source

1 CHANGE DOCUMENT SETTINGS | 2 CREATE HEADER | **3 TYPE RESEARCH PAPER WITH CITATIONS**
4 CREATE ALPHABETICAL WORKS CITED | 5 PROOFREAD & REVISE RESEARCH PAPER

When you typed the footnote text for this research paper, you inserted a citation placeholder for the source. The following steps edit a source. **_Why?_** _Assume you now have the source information and are ready to enter it._

1

- Click somewhere in the citation placeholder to be edited, in this case (Gupta), to select the citation placeholder.

- Click the Citation Options arrow to display the Citation Options menu (Figure 2–43).

Q&A What is the purpose of the tab to the left of the selected citation? If, for some reason, you wanted to move a citation to a different location in the document, you would select the citation and then drag the citation tab to the desired location.

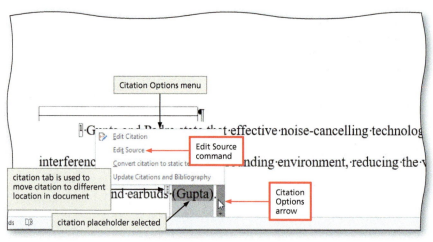

Figure 2–43

2

- Click Edit Source on the Citation Options menu to display the Edit Source dialog box.

- If necessary, click the 'Type of Source' arrow (Edit Source dialog box) and then click Book, so that the list shows fields required for a book.

- Because this source has two authors, click the Edit button to display the Edit Name dialog box, which assists you with entering multiple author names.

- Type **Gupta** as the first author's last name; press the TAB key and then type **Elena** as the first name; press the TAB key and then type **Maia** as the middle name (Figure 2–44).

Figure 2–44

Q&A What if I already know how to punctuate the author entry properly?
You can enter the name directly in the Author box.

3

- Click the Add button (Edit Name dialog box) to add the first author name to the Names list.

- Type **Padro** as the second author's last name; press the TAB key and then type **Adelbert** as the first name; press the TAB key and then type **Luis** as the middle name.

- Click the Add button (Edit Name dialog box) to add the second author name to the Names list (Figure 2–45).

Figure 2–45

- Click the OK button (Edit Name dialog box) to add the author names that appear in the Names list to the Author box in the Edit Source dialog box.

- Click the Title text box (Edit Source dialog box). Type **Hearing Protection Methods** as the book title.

- Press the TAB key and then type **2017** as the year.

- Press the TAB key and then type **Orlando** as the city.

- Press the TAB key and then type **Palm Press** as the publisher.

- Press the TAB key and then type **Print** as the medium (Figure 2–46).

Figure 2–46

- Click the OK button to close the dialog box, create the source, and update the citation to display both author last names (shown in Figure 2–47).

Other Ways

1. Click Manage Sources button (References tab | Citations & Bibliography group), click placeholder source in Current List, click Edit button (Source Manager dialog box)

To Edit a Citation

1 CHANGE DOCUMENT SETTINGS | 2 CREATE HEADER | **3 TYPE RESEARCH PAPER WITH CITATIONS**
4 CREATE ALPHABETICAL WORKS CITED | **5 PROOFREAD & REVISE RESEARCH PAPER**

In the MLA documentation style, if a source has page numbers, you should include them in the citation. Thus, Word provides a means to enter the page numbers to be displayed in the citation. Also, if you reference the author's name in the text, you should not list it again in the parenthetical citation. Instead, just list the page number(s) in the citation. To do this, you instruct Word to suppress author and title. **Why?** *If you suppress the author, Word automatically displays the title, so you need to suppress both the author and title if you want just the page number(s) to be displayed.* The following steps edit the citation, suppressing the author and title but displaying the page numbers.

1

- If necessary, click somewhere in the citation to be edited, in this case somewhere in (Gupta and Padro), which selects the citation and displays the Citation Options arrow.

- Click the Citation Options arrow to display the Citation Options menu (Figure 2–47).

Figure 2–47

2

- Click Edit Citation on the Citation Options menu to display the Edit Citation dialog box.

- Type **75–78** in the Pages text box (Edit Citation dialog box).

- Click the Author check box to place a check mark in it.

- Click the Title check box to place a check mark in it (Figure 2–48).

Figure 2–48

3

- Click the OK button to close the dialog box, remove the author names from the citation in the footnote, suppress the title from showing, and add page numbers to the citation.

- Press the END key to move the insertion point to the end of the line, which also deselects the citation (Figure 2–49).

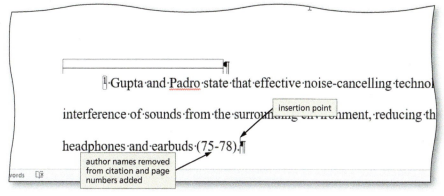

Figure 2–49

Working with Footnotes and Endnotes

You edit footnote text just as you edit any other text in the document. To delete or move a note reference mark, however, the insertion point must be in the document text (not in the footnote text).

To delete a note, select the note reference mark in the document text (not in the footnote text) by dragging through the note reference mark and then click the Cut button (Home tab | Clipboard group). Or, click immediately to the right of the note reference mark in the document text and then press the BACKSPACE key twice, or click immediately to the left of the note reference mark in the document text and then press the DELETE key twice.

To move a note to a different location in a document, select the note reference mark in the document text (not in the footnote text), click the Cut button (Home tab | Clipboard group), click the location where you want to move the note, and then click the Paste button (Home tab | Clipboard group). When you move or delete notes, Word automatically renumbers any remaining notes in the correct sequence.

If you are using a mouse and position the pointer on the note reference mark in the document text, the note text is displayed above the note reference mark as a ScreenTip. To remove the ScreenTip, move the pointer.

If, for some reason, you wanted to change the format of note reference marks in footnotes or endnotes (i.e., from 1, 2, 3 to A, B, C), you would click the Footnote & Endnote Dialog Box Launcher (References tab | Footnotes group) to display the Footnote and Endnote dialog box, click the Number format arrow (Footnote and Endnote dialog box), click the desired number format in the list, and then click the Apply button.

BTW

Footnote and Endnote Location
You can change the location of footnotes from the bottom of the page to the end of the text by clicking the Footnote & Endnote Dialog Box Launcher (References tab | Footnotes group), clicking the Footnotes arrow (Footnote and Endnote dialog box), and then clicking Below text. Similarly, clicking the Endnotes arrow (Footnote and Endnote dialog box) enables you to change the location of endnotes from the end of the document to the end of a section.

If, for some reason, you wanted to change a footnote number, you would click the Footnote & Endnote Dialog Box Launcher (References tab | Footnotes group) to display the Footnote and Endnote dialog box, enter the desired number in the Start at box, and then click the Apply button (Footnote and Endnote dialog box).

If, for some reason, you wanted to convert footnotes to endnotes, you would click the Footnote & Endnote Dialog Box Launcher (References tab | Footnotes group) to display the Footnote and Endnote dialog box, click the Convert button (Footnote and Endnote dialog box), select the 'Convert all footnotes to endnotes' option button (Convert Notes dialog box), click the OK button (Convert Notes dialog box), and then click the Close button (Footnote and Endnote dialog box).

To Enter More Text

The next task is to continue typing text in the body of the research paper. The following steps enter this text.

1 Position the insertion point after the note reference mark in the document and then press the ENTER key.

2 Type the first three sentences in the third paragraph of the research paper (shown in Figure 2–50): **The volume level of the sound that transmits from headphones or earbuds into the ear of a person wearing this type of device has been linked to hearing loss. The volume should be set low enough that other people nearby cannot hear the sound being transmitted. The quieter the sounds, the less possibility of hearing damage.**

To Count Words

1 CHANGE DOCUMENT SETTINGS | 2 CREATE HEADER | **3 TYPE RESEARCH PAPER WITH CITATIONS**

4 CREATE ALPHABETICAL WORKS CITED | 5 PROOFREAD & REVISE RESEARCH PAPER

Often when you write papers, you are required to compose the papers with a minimum number of words. The minimum requirement for the research paper in this module is 275 words. You can look on the status bar and see the total number of words thus far in a document. For example, Figure 2–50 shows the research paper has 231 words, but you are not sure if that count includes the words in your footnote. The following steps display the Word Count dialog box. **Why?** *You want to verify that the footnote text is included in the count.*

1

• Click the Word Count indicator on the status bar to display the Word Count dialog box.

• If necessary, place a check mark in the 'Include textboxes, footnotes and endnotes' check box (Word Count dialog box) (Figure 2–50).

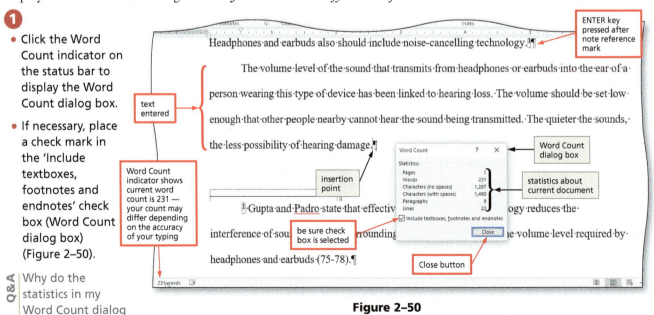

Figure 2–50

Q&A

Why do the statistics in my Word Count dialog box differ from those in Figure 2–50?
Depending on the accuracy of your typing, your statistics may differ.

2
- Click the Close button (Word Count dialog box) to close the dialog box.

Q&A Can I display statistics for just a section of the document?
Yes. Select the section and then click the Word Count indicator on the status bar to display statistics about the selected text.

Other Ways

1. Click Word Count button (Review tab | Proofing group)   2. Press CTRL+SHIFT+G

Automatic Page Breaks

As you type documents that exceed one page, Word automatically inserts page breaks, called **automatic page breaks** or **soft page breaks**, when it determines the text has filled one page according to paper size, margin settings, line spacing, and other settings. If you add text, delete text, or modify text on a page, Word recalculates the location of automatic page breaks and adjusts them accordingly.

Word performs page recalculation between the keystrokes, that is, in between the pauses in your typing. Thus, Word refers to the automatic page break task as **background repagination**. An automatic page break will occur in the next set of steps.

To Enter More Text and Insert a Citation Placeholder

The next task is to type the remainder of the third paragraph in the body of the research paper. The following steps enter this text and a citation placeholder at the end of the paragraph.

1 With the insertion point positioned at the end of the third sentence in the third paragraph, as shown in Figure 2–50, press the SPACEBAR.

2 Type the rest of the third paragraph: `Further, listening at a higher volume for extended periods of time could be unsafe. One expert suggests people should listen at only 30 percent maximum` and then press the SPACEBAR.

Q&A Why does the text move from the second page to the first page as I am typing?
Word, by default, will not allow the first line of a paragraph to be by itself at the bottom of a page (an **orphan**) or the last line of a paragraph to be by itself at the top of a page (a **widow**). As you type, Word adjusts the placement of the paragraph to avoid orphans and widows.

3 Click the Insert Citation button (References tab | Citations & Bibliography group) to display the Insert Citation menu. Click 'Add New Placeholder' on the Insert Citation menu to display the Placeholder Name dialog box.

4 Type `Chamberlain` as the tag name for the source.

5 Click the OK button (Placeholder Name dialog box) to close the dialog box and insert the tag name in the citation placeholder (shown in Figure 2–51).

6 Press the PERIOD key to end the sentence.

BTW
Page Break Locations
As you type, your page break may occur at different locations depending on Word settings and the type of printer connected to the computer.

To Hide and Show White Space

With the page break and header, it is difficult to see the entire third paragraph at once on the screen. With the screen in Print Layout view, you can hide white space, which is the space that is displayed at the top and bottom of pages (including headers and footers) and also the space between pages. The following steps hide white space, if your screen displays it, and then shows white space. *Why? You want to see as much of the third paragraph as possible at once, which spans the bottom of the first page and the top of the second page.*

1

• Position the pointer in the document window in the space between pages so that the pointer changes to a 'Hide White Space' button (Figure 2–51).

Q&A What if I am using a touch screen?
Proceed to step 2.

Figure 2–51

2

• Double-click while the pointer is a 'Hide White Space' button to hide white space.

Q&A What if I am using a touch screen?
Double-tap in the space between pages.

Does hiding white space have any effect on the printed document?
No.

3

• Position the pointer in the document window on the page break between pages so that the pointer changes to a 'Show White Space' button (Figure 2–52).

Figure 2–52

4

• Double-click while the pointer is a 'Show White Space' button to show white space.

Q&A What if I am using a touch screen?
Double-tap the page break.

Other Ways

1. Click File on ribbon, click Options tab in Backstage view, click Display in left pane (Word Options dialog box), remove or select check mark from 'Show white space between pages in Print Layout view' check box, click OK button

To Edit a Source

When you typed the third paragraph of the research paper, you inserted a citation placeholder, Chamberlain, for the source. You now have the source information, which is for a website, and are ready to enter it. The following steps edit the source for the Chamberlain citation placeholder.

1 Click somewhere in the citation placeholder to be edited, in this case (Chamberlain), to select the citation placeholder.

2 Click the Citation Options arrow to display the Citation Options menu.

3 Click Edit Source on the Citation Options menu to display the Edit Source dialog box.

4 If necessary, click the 'Type of Source' arrow (Edit Source dialog box); scroll to and then click Web site, so that the list shows fields required for a Web site.

5 Place a check mark in the 'Show All Bibliography Fields' check box to display more fields related to Web sites.

6 Click the Author text box. Type `Chamberlain, Megan Lynn` as the author.

7 Click the 'Name of Web Page' text box. Type `Understanding How Volume Levels Affect Hearing` as the webpage name.

8 Click the Production Company text box. Type `Course Technology` as the production company.

9 Click the Year Accessed text box. Type `2017` as the year accessed (Figure 2–53).

Figure 2–53

10 Press the TAB key and then type `Sept.` as the month accessed.

11 Press the TAB key and then type `16` as the day accessed.

12 Press the TAB key as many times as necessary to move the insertion point to the Medium text box and then type `Web` as the Medium.

Q&A Do I need to enter a web address (URL)?
The latest MLA documentation style update does not require the web address in the source.

13 Click the OK button to close the dialog box and create the source.

BTW

Organizing Files and Folders

You should organize and store files in folders so that you easily can find the files later. For example, if you are taking an introductory technology class called CIS 101, a good practice would be to save all Word files in a Word folder in a CIS 101 folder. For a discussion of folders and detailed examples of creating folders, refer to the Office and Windows module at the beginning of this book.

To Enter More Text

The next task is to type the last paragraph of text in the research paper. The following steps enter this text.

1 Press the END key to position the insertion point at the end of the third paragraph and then press the ENTER key.

2 Type the last paragraph of the research paper (Figure 2–54): `More and more people are using headphones and earbuds with their computers and portable devices. Using high-quality listening devices and lowering the volume can help to lessen potential hearing loss from the use of headphones and earbuds.`

3 Save the research paper again on the same storage location with the same file name.

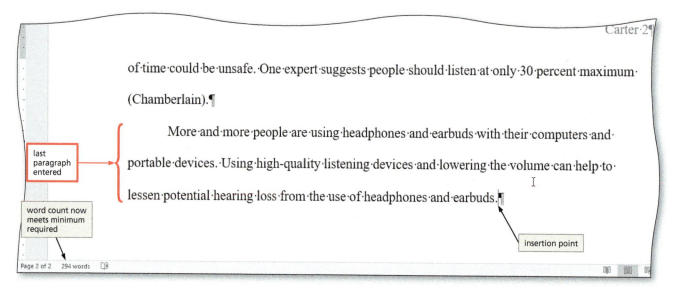

of·time·could·be·unsafe.·One·expert·suggests·people·should·listen·at·only·30·percent·maximum· (Chamberlain).¶

More·and·more·people·are·using·headphones·and·earbuds·with·their·computers·and· portable·devices.·Using·high-quality·listening·devices·and·lowering·the·volume·can·help·to· lessen·potential·hearing·loss·from·the·use·of·headphones·and·earbuds.¶

Carter·2¶

last paragraph entered

word count now meets minimum required

insertion point

Page 2 of 2   294 words

Figure 2–54

Break Point: If you wish to take a break, this is a good place to do so. You can exit Word now. To resume at a later time, run Word, open the file called Headphones and Earbuds Paper, and continue following the steps from this location forward. For a detailed example of exiting Word, running Word, and opening a file, refer to the Office and Windows module at the beginning of the book.

Creating an Alphabetical Works Cited Page

According to the MLA documentation style, the **works cited page** is a list of sources that are referenced directly in a research paper. You place the list on a separate numbered page with the title, Works Cited, centered one inch from the top margin. The works are to be alphabetized by the author's last name or, if the work has no author, by the work's title. The first line of each entry begins at the left margin. Indent subsequent lines of the same entry one-half inch from the left margin.

CONSIDER THIS

What is a bibliography?

A **bibliography** is an alphabetical list of sources referenced in a paper. Whereas the text of the research paper contains brief references to the source (the citations), the bibliography lists all publication information about the source. Documentation styles differ significantly in their guidelines for preparing a bibliography. Each style identifies formats for various sources, including books, magazines, pamphlets, newspapers, websites, television programs, paintings, maps, advertisements, letters, memos, and much more. You can find information about various styles and their guidelines in printed style guides and on the web.

1 CHANGE DOCUMENT SETTINGS | 2 CREATE HEADER | 3 TYPE RESEARCH PAPER WITH CITATIONS
4 CREATE ALPHABETICAL WORKS CITED | 5 PROOFREAD & REVISE RESEARCH PAPER

To Page Break Manually

The next step is to insert a manual page break following the body of the research paper. *Why? According to the MLA documentation style, the works cited are to be displayed on a separate numbered page.*

A **manual page break**, or **hard page break**, is one that you force into the document at a specific location. Word never moves or adjusts manual page breaks. Word, however, does adjust any automatic page breaks that follow a manual page break. Word inserts manual page breaks immediately above or to the left of the location of the insertion point. The following step inserts a manual page break after the text of the research paper.

1

- Verify that the insertion point is positioned at the end of the text of the research paper, as shown in Figure 2–54.

- Click Insert on the ribbon to display the Insert tab.

- Click the 'Insert a Page Break' button (Insert tab | Pages group) to insert a manual page break immediately to the left of the insertion point and position the insertion point immediately below the manual page break (Figure 2–55).

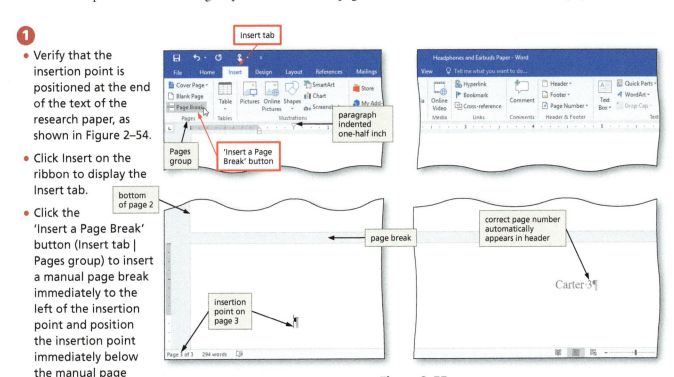

Figure 2–55

Other Ways

1. Press CTRL+ENTER

To Apply a Style

The works cited title is to be centered between the margins of the paper. If you simply issue the Center command, the title will not be centered properly. *Why? It will be to the right of the center point because earlier you set the first-line indent for paragraphs to one-half inch.*

To properly center the title of the works cited page, you could drag the 'First Line Indent' marker back to the left margin before centering the paragraph, or you could apply the Normal style to the location of the insertion point. Recall that you modified the Normal style for this document to 12-point Times New Roman with double-spaced, left-aligned paragraphs that have no space after the paragraphs.

To apply a style to a paragraph, first position the insertion point in the paragraph and then apply the style. The following step applies the modified Normal style to the location of the insertion point.

1

- Click Home on the ribbon to display the Home tab.

- With the insertion point on the paragraph mark at the top of page 3 (as shown in Figure 2–55) even if Normal is selected, click Normal in the Styles gallery (Home tab | Styles group) to apply the Normal style to the paragraph containing the insertion point (Figure 2–56).

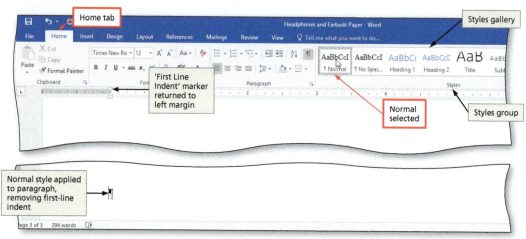

Figure 2–56

Other Ways

1. Click Styles Dialog Box Launcher (Home tab | Styles group), select desired style in Styles task pane

2. Press CTRL+SHIFT+S, click Style Name arrow in Apply Styles task pane, select desired style in list

To Center Text

The next task is to enter the title, Works Cited, centered between the margins of the paper. The following steps use a keyboard shortcut to format the title.

1 Press CTRL+E to center the paragraph mark.

2 Type **Works Cited** as the title.

3 Press the ENTER key.

4 Press CTRL+L to left-align the paragraph mark (shown in Figure 2–57).

To Create a Bibliographical List

While typing the research paper, you created several citations and their sources. The next task is to use Word to format the list of sources and alphabetize them in a **bibliographical list**. *Why? Word can create a bibliographical list with each element of the source placed in its correct position with proper punctuation, according to the specified style, saving you time looking up style guidelines. For example, in this research paper, the book source will list, in* *this order, the author name(s), book title, publisher city, publishing company name, and publication year with the correct punctuation between each element according to the MLA documentation style.* The following steps create an MLA-styled bibliographical list from the sources previously entered.

1

• Click References on the ribbon to display the References tab.

• With the insertion point positioned as shown in Figure 2–57, click the Bibliography button (References tab | Citations & Bibliography group) to display the Bibliography gallery (Figure 2–57).

Q&A Will I select the Works Cited option from the Bibliography gallery? No. The title it inserts is not formatted according to the MLA documentation style. Thus, you will use the Insert Bibliography command instead.

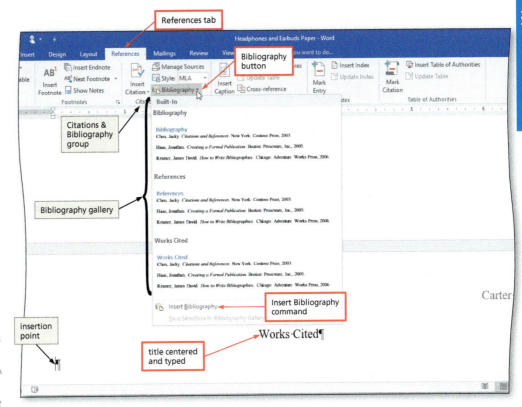

Figure 2–57

2

• Click Insert Bibliography in the Bibliography gallery to insert a list of sources at the location of the insertion point.

• If necessary, scroll to display the entire list of sources in the document window (Figure 2–58).

Q&A What is the n.d. in the first work? The MLA documentation style uses the abbreviation n.d. for no date (for example, no date appears on the webpage).

Carter 3¶

stands for no date

Works Cited¶

Hanging Indent marker

Chamberlain, Megan Lynn. *Understanding How Volume Levels Affect Hearing.* n.d. Course Technology. Web. 16 Sept. 2017.¶

second line in paragraphs indented one-half inch from left margin, called a hanging indent

Gupta, Elena Maia and Adelbert Luis Padro. *Hearing Protection Methods.* Orlando: Palm Press, 2017. Print.¶

Tu, Mingzhu Lin. "Headphones and Earbuds." *Technology and Trends Today* Aug. 2017: n. pag. Web. 3 Oct. 2017.¶

alphabetical list of sources automatically generated by Word

Figure 2–58

• Save the research paper again on the same storage location with the same file name.

TO FORMAT PARAGRAPHS WITH A HANGING INDENT

Notice in Figure 2–58 that the first line of each source entry begins at the left margin, and subsequent lines in the same paragraph are indented one-half inch from the left margin. In essence, the first line hangs to the left of the rest of the paragraph; thus, this type of paragraph formatting is called a **hanging indent**. The Bibliography style in Word automatically formats the works cited paragraphs with a hanging indent.

If you wanted to format paragraphs with a hanging indent, you would use one of the following techniques.

- With the insertion point in the paragraph to format, drag the **Hanging Indent marker** (the bottom triangle) on the ruler to the desired mark on the ruler (i.e., .5") to set the hanging indent at that location from the left margin.

or

- Right-click the paragraph to format (or, if using a touch screen, tap the 'Show Context Menu' button on the mini toolbar), click Paragraph on the shortcut menu, click the Indents and Spacing tab (Paragraph dialog box), click the Special arrow, click Hanging, and then click the OK button.

or

- Click the Paragraph Dialog Box Launcher (Home tab or Layout tab | Paragraph group), click the Indents and Spacing tab (Paragraph dialog box), click the Special arrow, click Hanging, and then click the OK button.

or

- With the insertion point in the paragraph to format, press CTRL+T.

Proofreading and Revising the Research Paper

As discussed in Module 1, once you complete a document, you might find it necessary to make changes to it. Before submitting a paper to be graded, you should proofread it. While **proofreading**, ensure all the source information is correct and look for grammatical, typographical, and spelling errors. Also ensure that transitions between sentences flow smoothly and the sentences themselves make sense.

To assist you with the proofreading effort, Word provides several tools. You can go to a page, copy text, find text, replace text, insert a synonym, check spelling and grammar, and look up information. The following pages discuss these tools.

CONSIDER THIS

What should you consider when proofreading and revising a paper?

As you proofread the paper, look for ways to improve it. Check all grammar, spelling, and punctuation. Be sure the text is logical and transitions are smooth. Where necessary, add text, delete text, reword text, and move text to different locations. Ask yourself these questions:

- Does the title suggest the topic?
- Is the thesis clear?
- Is the purpose of the paper clear?
- Does the paper have an introduction, body, and conclusion?
- Does each paragraph in the body relate to the thesis?
- Is the conclusion effective?
- Are sources acknowledged correctly?

To Modify a Source

While proofreading the paper, you notice an error in the magazine title; specifically, the word, and, should be removed. If you modify the contents of any source, the list of sources automatically updates. *Why? Word automatically updates the contents of fields, and the bibliography is a field.* The following steps delete a word from the title of the magazine article.

- Click the Manage Sources button (References tab | Citations & Bibliography group) to display the Source Manager dialog box.
- Click the source you wish to edit in the Current List, in this case the article by Tu, to select the source.
- Click the Edit button (Source Manager dialog box) to display the Edit Source dialog box.
- In the Periodical Title text box, delete the word, and, from the title (Figure 2–59).

Figure 2–59

- Click the OK button (Edit Source dialog box) to close the dialog box.
- If a Microsoft Word dialog box appears, click its Yes button to update all occurrences of the source.
- Click the Close button (Source Manager dialog box) to update the list of sources and close the dialog box.

To Update a Field

Depending on settings, the bibliography field may not automatically reflect the edited magazine title. Thus, the following steps update the bibliography field. *Why? Because the bibliography is a field, you may need to instruct Word to update its contents.*

1

- Right-click anywhere in the bibliography text to display a shortcut menu related to fields (Figure 2–60).

Q&A What if I am using a touch screen?
Press and hold anywhere in the bibliography text and then tap the 'Show Context Menu' button on the mini toolbar.

Figure 2–60

Why are all the words in the bibliography shaded gray?
By default, Word shades selected fields gray.

What if the bibliography field is not shaded gray?
Click File on the ribbon to open the Backstage view, click the Options tab in the Backstage view, click Advanced in the left pane (Word Options dialog box), scroll to the 'Show document content' area, click the Field shading arrow, click When selected, and then click the OK button.

2

- Click Update Field on the shortcut menu to update the selected field (Figure 2–61).

Q&A Can I update all fields in a document at once?
Yes. Select the entire document and then follow these steps.

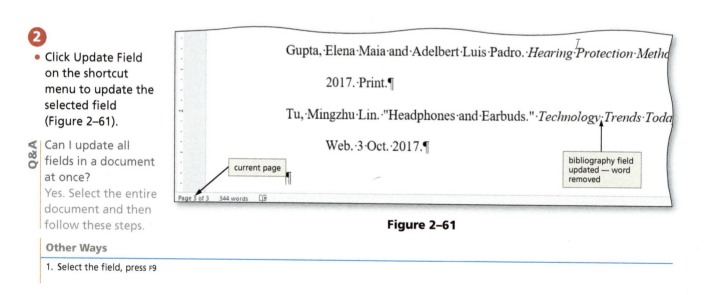

Figure 2–61

Other Ways

1. Select the field, press F9

TO CONVERT A FIELD TO REGULAR TEXT

If, for some reason, you wanted to convert a field, such as the bibliography field, to regular text, you would perform the following steps. Keep in mind, though, once you convert the field to regular text, it no longer is a field that can be updated.

1. Click somewhere in the field to select it, in this case, somewhere in the bibliography.

2. Press CTRL+SHIFT+F9 to convert the selected field to regular text.

To Go to a Page

The next task in revising the paper is to modify text on the second page of the document. *Why? You want to copy text from one location to another on the second page.* You could scroll to the desired location in the document, or you can use the Navigation Pane to browse through pages in a document. The following steps display the top of the second page in the document window and position the insertion point at the beginning of that page.

- Click View on the ribbon to display the View tab.

- Place a check mark in the 'Open the Navigation Pane' check box (View tab | Show group) to open the Navigation Pane on the left side of the Word window.

- If necessary, click the Pages tab in the Navigation Pane to display thumbnails of the pages in the document.

- Scroll to, if necessary, and then click the thumbnail of the second page to display the top of the selected page in the top of the document window (Figure 2–62).

Q&A

What is the Navigation Pane?
The Navigation Pane is a window that enables you to browse through headings in a document, browse through pages in a document, or search for text in a document.

Figure 2–62

- Click the Close button in the Navigation Pane to close the pane.

Other Ways
1. Click Find arrow (Home tab | Editing group), click Go To on Find menu, click Go To tab (Find and Replace dialog box), enter page number, click Go To button	2. Click Page Number indicator on status bar, click Pages tab in Navigation Pane, click thumbnail of desired page (Navigation Pane)	3. Press CTRL+G, enter page number (Find and Replace dialog box), click Go To button

Copying, Cutting, and Pasting

While proofreading the research paper, you decide it would read better if the word, volume, in the second sentence of the last paragraph also appeared after the word, maximum, in the last sentence of the previous paragraph. You could type the word at the desired location, but you decide to use the Office Clipboard. The **Office Clipboard** is a temporary storage area that holds up to 24 items (text or graphics) copied from any Office program. The Office Clipboard works with the copy, cut, and paste commands:

- **Copying** is the process of placing items on the Office Clipboard, leaving the item in the document.

- **Cutting** removes the item from the document before placing it on the Office Clipboard.

- **Pasting** is the process of copying an item from the Office Clipboard into the document at the location of the insertion point.

To Copy and Paste

In the research paper, you copy a word from one location to another. ***Why?*** *The sentence reads better with the word,* volume, *inserted after the word,* maximum. The following steps copy and paste a word.

- Select the item to be copied (the word, volume, in this case).
- Click Home on the ribbon to display the Home tab.
- Click the Copy button (Home tab | Clipboard group) to copy the selected item in the document to the Office Clipboard (Figure 2–63).

Figure 2–63

- Position the insertion point at the location where the item should be pasted (immediately following the space to the right of the word, maximum, in this case) (Figure 2–64).

Figure 2–64

- Click the Paste button (Home tab | Clipboard group) to paste the copied item in the document at the location of the insertion point (Figure 2–65).

Q&A

What if I click the Paste arrow by mistake?
Click the Paste arrow again to remove the Paste menu and repeat Step 3.

Figure 2–65

Other Ways

1. Click Copy on shortcut menu (or, if using touch, tap Copy on mini toolbar), right-click where item is to be pasted, click 'Keep Source Formatting' in Paste Options area on shortcut menu (or, if using touch, tap Paste on mini toolbar)

2. Select item, press CTRL+C, position insertion point at paste location, press CTRL+V

To Display the Paste Options Menu

1 CHANGE DOCUMENT SETTINGS | 2 CREATE HEADER | 3 TYPE RESEARCH PAPER WITH CITATIONS
4 CREATE ALPHABETICAL WORKS CITED | 5 PROOFREAD & REVISE RESEARCH PAPER

When you paste an item or move an item using drag-and-drop editing, which was discussed in the previous module, Word automatically displays a Paste Options button near the pasted or moved text (shown in Figure 2–65). **Why?** *The Paste Options button allows you to change the format of a pasted item. For example, you can instruct Word to format the pasted item the same way as where it was copied (the source) or format it the same way as where it is being pasted (the destination).* The following steps display the Paste Options menu.

①

- Click the Paste Options button to display the Paste Options menu (Figure 2–66).

Q&A What are the functions of the buttons on the Paste Options menu?

In general, the left button indicates the pasted item should look the same as it did in its original location (the source). The second button formats the pasted text to match the rest of the item where it was pasted (the destination). The third button removes all formatting from the pasted item. The 'Set Default Paste' command displays the Word Options dialog box. Keep in mind that the buttons shown on a Paste Options menu will vary, depending on the item being pasted.

Figure 2–66

②

- Click anywhere to remove the Paste Options menu from the window.

Other Ways

1. CTRL or ESC (to remove the Paste Options menu)

To Find Text

1 CHANGE DOCUMENT SETTINGS | 2 CREATE HEADER | 3 TYPE RESEARCH PAPER WITH CITATIONS
4 CREATE ALPHABETICAL WORKS CITED | 5 PROOFREAD & REVISE RESEARCH PAPER

While proofreading the paper, you would like to locate all occurrences of the word, portable. **Why?** *You are contemplating changing occurrences of this word to the word, mobile.* The following steps find all occurrences of specific text in a document.

①

- Click the Find button (Home tab | Editing group) to display the Navigation Pane.

Q&A What if I am using a touch screen?

Tap the Find button (Home tab | Editing group) and then tap Find on the menu.

- If necessary, click the Results tab in the Navigation Pane, which displays a Search box where you can type text for which you want to search (Figure 2–67).

Figure 2–67

• Type **portable** in the Navigation Pane Search box to display all occurrences of the typed text, called the search text, in the Navigation Pane and to highlight the occurrences of the search text in the document window (Figure 2–68).

Figure 2–68

Experiment

• Click both occurrences in the Navigation Pane and watch Word display the associated text in the document window.

Experiment

• Type various search text in the Navigation Pane Search box, and watch Word both list matches in the Navigation Pane and highlight matches in the document window.

• Click the Close button in the Navigation Pane to close the pane.

Other Ways
1. Click Find arrow (Home tab | Editing group), click Find on Find menu, enter search text in Navigation Pane	2. Click Page Number indicator on status bar, enter search text in Navigation Pane	3. Press CTRL+F, enter search text in Navigation Pane

To Replace Text

1 CHANGE DOCUMENT SETTINGS | 2 CREATE HEADER | 3 TYPE RESEARCH PAPER WITH CITATIONS
4 CREATE ALPHABETICAL WORKS CITED | 5 PROOFREAD & REVISE RESEARCH PAPER

You decide to change all occurrences of the word, portable, to the word, mobile. **Why?** *The term, mobile devices, is more commonly used than portable devices.* Word's find and replace feature locates each occurrence of a word or phrase and then replaces it with text you specify. The following steps find and replace text.

• Click the Replace button (Home tab | Editing group) to display the Replace sheet in the Find and Replace dialog box.

• If necessary, type **portable** in the Find what box (Find and Replace dialog box).

• Type **mobile** in the Replace with box (Figure 2–69).

Figure 2–69

2

- Click the Replace All button to instruct Word to replace all occurrences of the Find what text with the Replace with text (Figure 2–70). If Word displays a dialog box asking if you want to continue searching from the beginning of the document, click the Yes button.

Figure 2–70

Q&A Does Word search the entire document?

If the insertion point is at the beginning of the document, Word searches the entire document; otherwise, Word may search from the location of the insertion point to the end of the document and then display a dialog box asking if you want to continue searching from the beginning. You also can search a section of text by selecting the text before clicking the Replace or Replace All button.

3

- Click the OK button (Microsoft Word dialog box) to close the dialog box.
- Click the Close button (Find and Replace dialog box) to close the dialog box.

Other Ways

1. Press CTRL+H

Find and Replace Dialog Box

The Replace All button (Find and Replace dialog box) replaces all occurrences of the Find what text with the Replace with text. In some cases, you may want to replace only certain occurrences of a word or phrase, not all of them. To instruct Word to confirm each change, click the Find Next button (Find and Replace dialog box) (shown in Figure 2–70), instead of the Replace All button. When Word locates an occurrence of the text, it pauses and waits for you to click either the Replace button or the Find Next button. Clicking the Replace button changes the text; clicking the Find Next button instructs Word to disregard the replacement and look for the next occurrence of the Find what text.

If you accidentally replace the wrong text, you can undo a replacement by clicking the Undo button on the Quick Access Toolbar. If you used the Replace All button, Word undoes all replacements. If you used the Replace button, Word undoes only the most recent replacement.

BTW

Finding Formatting
To search for formatting or a special character, click the More button in the Find and Replace dialog box (shown in Figure 2–69). To find formatting, use the Format button in the Find dialog box. To find a special character, use the Special button.

To Find and Insert a Synonym

1 CHANGE DOCUMENT SETTINGS | 2 CREATE HEADER | 3 TYPE RESEARCH PAPER WITH CITATIONS
4 CREATE ALPHABETICAL WORKS CITED | **5 PROOFREAD & REVISE RESEARCH PAPER**

In this project, you would like a synonym for the word, lessen, in the last paragraph of the research paper. *Why? When writing, you may discover that you used the same word in multiple locations or that a word you used was not quite appropriate, which is the case here.* In these instances, you will want to look up a **synonym**, or a word similar in meaning, to the duplicate or inappropriate word. A **thesaurus** is a book of synonyms. Word provides synonyms and a thesaurus for your convenience. The following steps find a suitable synonym.

1

- Right-click the word for which you want to find a synonym (in this case, lessen) to display a shortcut menu.
- Point to Synonyms on the shortcut menu to display a list of synonyms for the word you right-clicked (Figure 2–71).

Q&A

What if I am using a touch screen? Press and hold the word for which you want a synonym, tap the 'Show Context Menu' button on the mini toolbar, and then tap Synonyms on the shortcut menu.

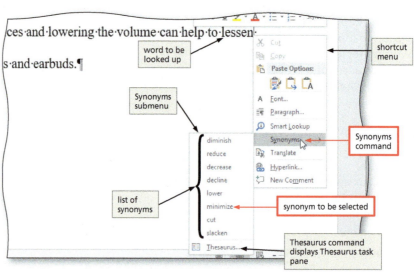

Figure 2–71

2

- Click the synonym you want (in this case, minimize) on the Synonyms submenu to replace the selected word in the document with the selected synonym (Figure 2–72).

Q&A

What if the synonyms list on the shortcut menu does not display a suitable word?
You can display the thesaurus in the Thesaurus task pane by clicking Thesaurus on the Synonyms submenu. The Thesaurus task pane displays a complete thesaurus, in which you can look up synonyms for various meanings of a word. You also can look up an antonym, or word with an opposite meaning.

Figure 2–72

Other Ways

1. Click Thesaurus button (Review tab | Proofing group)

2. Press SHIFT+F7

To Check Spelling and Grammar at Once

1 CHANGE DOCUMENT SETTINGS | 2 CREATE HEADER | 3 TYPE RESEARCH PAPER WITH CITATIONS
4 CREATE ALPHABETICAL WORKS CITED | 5 PROOFREAD & REVISE RESEARCH PAPER

As discussed in Module 1, Word checks spelling and grammar as you type and places a wavy underline below possible spelling or grammar errors. Module 1 illustrated how to check these flagged words immediately. The next steps check spelling and grammar at once. *Why? Some users prefer to wait and check their entire document for spelling and grammar errors at once.*

Note: In the following steps, the word, sound, has been misspelled intentionally as sould to illustrate the use of Word's check spelling and grammar at once feature. If you are completing this project on a computer or mobile device, your research paper may contain different misspelled words, depending on the accuracy of your typing.

1

- Press CTRL+HOME because you want the spelling and grammar check to begin from the top of the document.

- Click Review on the ribbon to display the Review tab.

- Click the 'Spelling & Grammar' button (Review tab | Proofing group) to begin the spelling and grammar check at the location of the insertion point, which, in this case, is at the beginning of the document.
- Click the desired word in the list of suggestions in the Spelling task pane (sound, in this case) (Figure 2–73).

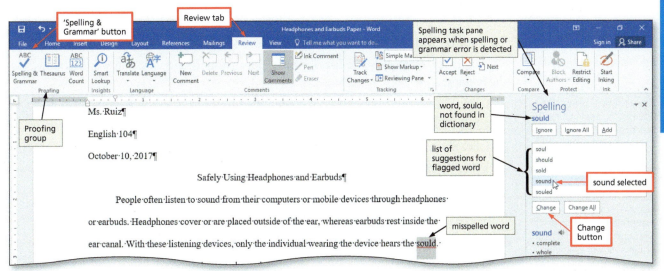

Figure 2–73

2

- With the word, sound, selected in the list of suggestions, click the Change button (Spelling task pane) to change the flagged word to the selected suggestion and then continue the spelling and grammar check until the next error is identified or the end of the document is reached (Figure 2–74).

3

- Because the flagged word is a proper noun and spelled correctly, click the Ignore All button (Spelling task pane) to ignore this and future occurrences of the flagged proper noun and then continue the spelling and grammar check until the next error is identified or the end of the document is reached.

Figure 2–74

4

- When the spelling and grammar check is finished and Word displays a dialog box, click its OK button.

Q&A Can I check spelling of just a section of a document?
Yes, select the text before starting the spelling and grammar check.

Other Ways

1. Click 'Spelling and Grammar Check' icon on status bar
2. Press F7

The Main and Custom Dictionaries

As shown in the previous steps, Word may flag a proper noun as an error because the proper noun is not in its main dictionary. You may want to add some proper nouns that you use repeatedly, such as a company name or employee names, to Word's dictionary. To prevent Word from flagging proper nouns as errors, you can add the proper nouns to the custom dictionary. To add a correctly spelled word to the custom dictionary, click the Add button (Spelling task pane) or right-click the flagged word

BTW
Readability Statistics
You can instruct Word to display readability statistics when it has finished a spelling and grammar check on a document. Three readability statistics presented are the percent of passive sentences, the Flesch Reading Ease score, and the Flesch-Kincaid Grade Level score. The Flesch Reading Ease score uses a 100-point scale to rate the ease with which a reader can understand the text in a document. A higher score means the document is easier to understand. The Flesch-Kincaid Grade Level score rates the text in a document on a U.S. school grade level. For example, a score of 10.0 indicates a student in the tenth grade can understand the material. To show readability statistics when the spelling check is complete, open the Backstage view, click the Options tab in the Backstage view, click Proofing in the left pane (Word Options dialog box), place a check mark in the 'Show readability statistics' check box, and then click the OK button. Readability statistics will be displayed the next time you check spelling and grammar at once in the document.

(or, if using touch, press and hold and then tap 'Show Context Menu' button on the mini toolbar) and then click 'Add to Dictionary' on the shortcut menu. Once you have added a word to the custom dictionary, Word no longer will flag it as an error.

TO VIEW OR MODIFY ENTRIES IN A CUSTOM DICTIONARY

To view or modify the list of words in a custom dictionary, you would follow these steps.

1. Click File on the ribbon and then click the Options tab in the Backstage view.
2. Click Proofing in the left pane (Word Options dialog box).
3. Click the Custom Dictionaries button.
4. When Word displays the Custom Dictionaries dialog box, if necessary, place a check mark next to the dictionary name to view or modify. Click the 'Edit Word List' button (Custom Dictionaries dialog box). (In this dialog box, you can add or delete entries to and from the selected custom dictionary.)
5. When finished viewing and/or modifying the list, click the OK button in the dialog box.
6. Click the OK button (Custom Dictionaries dialog box).
7. If the 'Suggest from main dictionary only' check box is selected in the Word Options dialog box, remove the check mark. Click the OK button (Word Options dialog box).

TO SET THE DEFAULT CUSTOM DICTIONARY

If you have multiple custom dictionaries, you can specify which one Word should use when checking spelling. To set the default custom dictionary, you would follow these steps.

1. Click File on the ribbon and then click the Options tab in the Backstage view.
2. Click Proofing in the left pane (Word Options dialog box).
3. Click the Custom Dictionaries button.
4. When the Custom Dictionaries dialog box is displayed, place a check mark next to the desired dictionary name. Click the Change Default button (Custom Dictionaries dialog box).
5. Click the OK button (Custom Dictionaries dialog box).
6. If the 'Suggest from main dictionary only' check box is selected in the Word Options dialog box, remove the check mark. Click the OK button (Word Options dialog box).

To Look Up Information

1 CHANGE DOCUMENT SETTINGS | 2 CREATE HEADER | 3 TYPE RESEARCH PAPER WITH CITATIONS
4 CREATE ALPHABETICAL WORKS CITED | 5 PROOFREAD & REVISE RESEARCH PAPER

If you are connected to the Internet, you can use the Insights task pane to search through various forms of reference information, including images, on the web and/or look up a definition of a word. The following steps use the Insights task pane to look up a definition of a word. *Why? Assume you want to see some images and know more about the word, headphones.*

1

- Position the insertion point in the word you want to look up (in this case, headphones).

- Click the Smart Lookup button (Review tab | Insights group) to open the Insights task pane (Figure 2–75).

Q&A | Why does my Insights task pane look different?
Depending on your settings, your Insights task pane may appear different from the figure shown here.

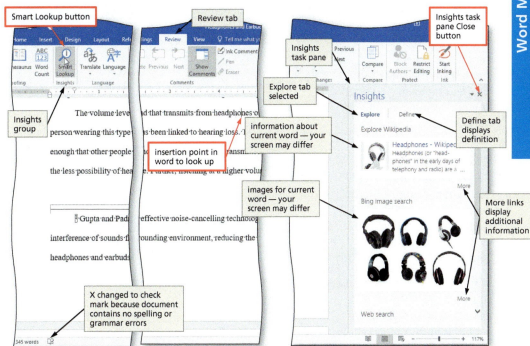

Figure 2–75

Experiment

- With the Explore tab selected in the Insights task pane, scroll through the information and images that appear in the Insights task pane. Click the Define tab in the Insights task pane to see a definition of the current word. Click the Explore tab to redisplay information from the web and images of the current word. Click one of the More links in the Insights task pane to view additional information. Click the Back button at the top of the Insights task pane to return to the previous display.

Q&A | Can I copy information from the Insights task pane into my document?
Yes, you can use the Copy and Paste commands. When using Word to insert material from the Insights task pane or any other online reference, however, be careful not to plagiarize.

2

- Click the Close button in the Insights task pane.

Q&A | Is the Research task pane from previous Word editions still available?
Yes. While holding down the ALT key, you can click the word you want to look up (such as headphones) to open the Research task pane and display a dictionary entry for the ALT+clicked word.

To Zoom Multiple Pages

1 CHANGE DOCUMENT SETTINGS | 2 CREATE HEADER | 3 TYPE RESEARCH PAPER WITH CITATIONS
4 CREATE ALPHABETICAL WORKS CITED | 5 PROOFREAD & REVISE RESEARCH PAPER

The next steps display multiple pages in the document window at once. ***Why?*** *You want to be able to see all pages in the research paper on the screen at the same time. You also hide formatting marks and the rulers so that the display is easier to view.*

1

- Click Home on the ribbon to display the Home tab.

- If the 'Show/Hide ¶' button (Home tab | Paragraph group) is selected, click it to hide formatting marks.

- Click View on the ribbon to display the View tab.

- If the rulers are displayed, click the View Ruler check box (View tab | Show group) to remove the check mark from the check box and remove the horizontal and vertical rulers from the screen.

- Click the Multiple Pages button (View tab | Zoom group) to display all three pages at once in the document window (Figure 2–76).

Q&A Why do the pages appear differently on my screen?
Depending on settings, Word may display all the pages as shown in Figure 2–76 or may show the pages differently.

Figure 2–76

- When finished, click the Page Width button (View tab | Zoom group) to return to the page width zoom.

To Change Read Mode Color

1 CHANGE DOCUMENT SETTINGS | 2 CREATE HEADER | 3 TYPE RESEARCH PAPER WITH CITATIONS
4 CREATE ALPHABETICAL WORKS CITED | **5 PROOFREAD & REVISE RESEARCH PAPER**

You would like to read the entire research paper using Read mode but would like to change the background color of the Read mode screen. *Why? You prefer a different background color for reading on the screen.* The following steps change the color of the screen in Read mode.

1

- Click the Read Mode button on the status bar to switch to Read mode.
- Click the View tab to display the View menu.
- Point to Page Color on the View menu to display the Page Color submenu (Figure 2–77).

Figure 2–77

2

• Click Inverse on the Page Color submenu to change the color of the Read mode screen to inverse (Figure 2–78).

3

• When finished, click the Print Layout button (shown in Figure 2–77) on the status bar to return to Print Layout view.

Figure 2–78

To Save and Print the Document and Exit Word

The following steps save and print the document and then exit Word. For a detailed example of the procedure summarized below, refer to the Office and Windows module at the beginning of this book.

1 Save the research paper again on the same storage location with the same file name.

2 If requested by your instructor, print the research paper.

3 Exit Word.

Summary

In this module, you have learned how to modify styles, adjust line and paragraph spacing, use headers to number pages, insert and edit citations and their sources, add footnotes, create a bibliographical list of sources, update a field, go to a page, copy and paste text, find and replace text, check spelling and grammar, and look up information.

What decisions will you need to make when creating your next research paper?
Use these guidelines as you complete the assignments in this module and create your own research papers outside of this class.

1. Select a topic.
    a) Spend time brainstorming ideas for a topic.
    b) Choose a topic you find interesting.
    c) For shorter papers, narrow the scope of the topic; for longer papers, broaden the scope.
    d) Identify a tentative thesis statement, which is a sentence describing the paper's subject matter.
2. Research the topic and take notes, being careful not to plagiarize.
3. Organize your notes into related concepts, identifying all main ideas and supporting details in an outline.
4. Write the first draft from the outline, referencing all sources of information and following the guidelines identified in the required documentation style.
5. Create the list of sources, using the formats specified in the required documentation style.
6. Proofread and revise the paper.

CONSIDER THIS: PLAN AHEAD

Apply Your Knowledge

Reinforce the skills and apply the concepts you learned in this module.

Revising Text and Paragraphs in a Document

Note: To complete this assignment, you will be required to use the Data Files. Please contact your instructor for information about accessing the Data Files.

Instructions: Run Word. Open the document, Apply 2-1 3-D Printers Paragraph Draft, which is located in the Data Files. The document you open contains a paragraph of text. You are to revise the document as follows: move a word, move another word and change the format of the moved word, change paragraph indentation, change line spacing, find all occurrences of a word, replace all occurrences of a word with another word, locate a synonym, and edit the header. The modified paragraph is shown in Figure 2–79.

Figure 2–79

Perform the following tasks:

1. Copy the text, printers, from the second sentence and paste it in the third sentence after the underlined word, liquid.

2. Select the underlined word, liquid, in the third sentence. Use drag-and-drop editing to move the selected word, liquid, so that it is before the word, polymer, in the last sentence. (If you are using a touch screen, use the cut and paste commands to move the word.) Click the Paste Options button that displays to the right of the moved word, liquid. Remove the underline format from the moved word by clicking 'Keep Text Only' on the Paste Options menu.

3. Display the ruler, if necessary. Use the ruler to indent the first line of the paragraph one-half inch. (If you are using a touch screen, use the Paragraph dialog box.)

4. Change the line spacing of the paragraph to double.

5. Use the Navigation Pane to find all occurrences of the word, printer. How many are there?

6. Use the Find and Replace dialog box to replace all occurrences of the word, 3D, with the word, 3-D. How many replacements were made?

7. Use the Navigation Pane to find the word, finished. Use Word's thesaurus to change the word, finished, to the word, complete. What other words are in the list of synonyms?

8. Switch to the header so that you can edit it. In the first line of the header, change the word, Draft, to the word, Modified, so that it reads: 3-D Printers Paragraph Modified.

9. In the second line of the header, insert a page number (a plain number with no formatting) one space after the word, Page.

10. Change the alignment of both lines of text in the header from left-aligned to right-aligned. Switch back to the document text.

11. If requested by your instructor, enter your first and last name on a separate line below the page number in the header.

12. Click File on the ribbon and then click Save As. Save the document using the file name, Apply 2-1 3-D Printers Paragraph Modified.

13. Submit the modified document, shown in Figure 2–79, in the format specified by your instructor.

14. Use the Insights task pane to look up the word prosthetics. Click the Explore tab in the Insights task pane. Which web articles appeared? What images appeared? Click the Define tab in the Insights task pane. Which dictionary was used?

15. ✺ Answer the questions posed in #5, #6, #7, and #14. How would you find and replace a special character, such as a paragraph mark?

Extend Your Knowledge

Extend the skills you learned in this module and experiment with new skills. You may need to use Help to complete the assignment.

Working with References and Proofing Tools

Note: To complete this assignment, you will be required to use the Data Files. Please contact your instructor for information about accessing the Data Files.

Instructions: Run Word. Open the document, Extend 2-1 Databases Paper Draft, from the Data Files. You will add another footnote to the paper, convert the footnotes to endnotes, modify the Endnote Text style, change the format of the note reference marks, use Word's readability statistics, translate the document to another language (Figure 2–80), and convert the document from MLA to APA documentation style.

Perform the following tasks:

1. Use Help to learn more about footers, footnotes and endnotes, readability statistics, bibliography styles, AutoCorrect, and Word's translation features.

2. Delete the footer from the document.

3. Insert a second footnote at an appropriate place in the research paper. Use the following footnote text: A data warehouse is a huge database that stores and manages the data required to analyze past and current transactions.

4. Change the location of the footnotes from bottom of page to below text. How did the placement of the footnotes change?

5. Convert the footnotes to endnotes. Where are the endnotes positioned?

6. Modify the Endnote Text style to 12-point Times New Roman font, double-spaced text with a hanging-line indent.

7. Change the format of the note reference marks to capital letters (A, B, etc.).

Continued >

Extend Your Knowledge continued

8. Add an AutoCorrect entry that replaces the word, buziness, with the word, business. Type the following sentence as the first sentence in the last paragraph of the paper, misspelling the word, business, as buziness to test the AutoCorrect entry: **Organizations often use a database to manage buziness or other functions.** Delete the AutoCorrect entry that replaces buziness with the word, business.

9. Display the Word Count dialog box. How many words, characters without spaces, characters with spaces, paragraphs, and lines are in the document? Be sure to include footnote and endnote text in the statistics.

10. Check spelling of the document, displaying readability statistics. What are the Flesch-Kincaid Grade Level and the Flesch Reading Ease score? Modify the paper to increase the reading ease score. How did you modify the paper? What are the new statistics?

11. If requested by your instructor, change the student name at the top of the paper to your name, including the last name in the header.

12. Save the revised document with the file name, Extend 2-1 Databases Paper Modified, and then submit it in the format specified by your instructor.

13. If you have an Internet connection, translate the research paper into a language of your choice using the Translate button (Review tab | Language group), as shown in Figure 2–80. Submit the translated document in the format specified by your instructor. Use the Mini Translator to hear how to pronounce three words in your paper.

14. Select the entire document and then change the documentation style from MLA to APA. Save the APA version of the document with a new file name. Compare the APA version to the MLA version. If you have a hard copy of each and your instructor requests it, circle the differences between the two documents.

15. ✻ Answer the questions posed in #4, #5, #9, and #10. Where did you insert the second footnote and why?

Figure 2–80

Expand Your World

Create a solution that uses cloud or web technologies by learning and investigating on your own from general guidance.

Using an Online Bibliography Tool to Create a List of Sources

Instructions: Assume you are using a computer or mobile device that does not have Word but has Internet access. To make use of time between classes, you use an online bibliography tool to create a list of sources that you can copy and paste into the Works Cited pages of a research paper that is due tomorrow.

Perform the following tasks:

1. Run a browser. Search for the text, online bibliography tool, using a search engine. Visit several of the online bibliography tools and determine which you would like to use to create a list of sources. Navigate to the desired online bibliography tool.

2. Use the online bibliography tool to enter list of sources shown below (Figure 2–81):

   Alverez, Juan and Tracy Marie Wilson. *Radon in the Home*. Chicago: Martin Publishing, 2017. Print.

   Buchalski, Leonard Adam. *Radon and Your Health*. Los Angeles: Coastal Works, 2017. Print.

   Johnson, Shantair Jada. "Radon Facts." *Environment Danger* Aug. 2017. Web. 31 Aug. 2017.

   Slobovnik, Vincent Alexander. *The Radon Guide*. Aug. 2017. Course Technology. Web. 18 Sept. 2017.

   Wakefield, Ginger Lynn and Bethany Olivia Ames. "Radon Removal Systems." *Living Well Today* Aug. 2017. Web. 3 Oct. 2017.

   Zhao, Shen Li. *Radon Testing Procedures*. Sept. 2017. Course Technology. Web. 8 Sept. 2017.

3. If requested by your instructor, replace the name in one of the sources above with your name.

4. Search for another source that discusses radon issues in the home. Add that source.

5. Copy and paste the list of sources into a Word document.

6. Save the document with the file name, Expand 2-1 Radon Issues Sources. Submit the document in the format specified by your instructor.

7. ✺ Which online bibliography tools did you evaluate? Which one did you select to use and why? Do you prefer using the online bibliography tool or Word to create sources? Why? What differences, if any, did you notice between the list of sources created with the online bibliography tool and the lists created when you use Word?

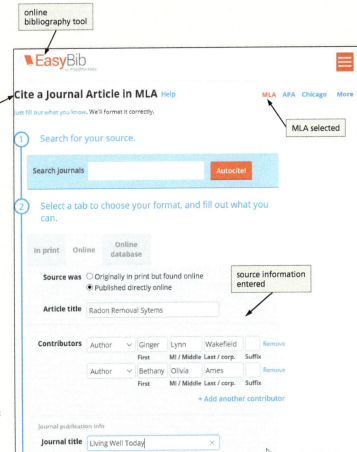

Figure 2–81

In the Labs

Design, create, modify, and/or use a document following the guidelines, concepts, and skills presented in this module. Labs 1 and 2, which increase in difficulty, require you to create solutions based on what you learned in the module; Lab 3 requires you to apply your creative thinking and problem-solving skills to design and implement a solution.

Lab 1: **Preparing a Short Research Paper**

Problem: You are a college student currently enrolled in an introductory English class. Your assignment is to prepare a short research paper (300–350 words) in any area of interest to you. The requirements are that the paper be presented according to the MLA documentation style and have three references. At least one of the three references must be from the web. You prepare the paper shown in Figure 2–82, which discusses wearable devices.

Perform the following tasks:

1. Run Word. If necessary, display formatting marks on the screen.

2. Modify the Normal style to the 12-point Times New Roman font.

3. Adjust line spacing to double.

4. Remove space below (after) paragraphs.

5. Update the Normal style to reflect the adjusted line and paragraph spacing.

6. Create a header to number pages.

7. Type the name and course information at the left margin. If requested by your instructor, use your name and course information instead of the information shown in Figure 2–82a. Center and type the title.

8. Set a first-line indent to one-half inch for paragraphs in the body of the research paper.

9. Type the research paper as shown in Figures 2–82a and 2–82b. Change the bibliography style to MLA. As you insert citations, enter their source information (shown in Figure 2–82c). Edit the citations so that they are displayed according to Figures 2–82a and 2–82b.

10. At the end of the research paper text, press the ENTER key and then insert a manual page break so that the Works Cited page begins on a new page. Enter and format the works cited title (Figure 2–82c). Use Word to insert the bibliographical list (bibliography).

11. Check the spelling and grammar of the paper at once.

12. Save the document using the file name, Lab 2–1 Wearable Devices Paper. Submit the document, shown in Figure 2–82, in the format specified by your instructor.

13. ✺ Read the paper in Print Layout view. Switch to Read mode and scroll through the pages. Do you prefer reading in Print Layout view or Read mode? Why? In Read mode, which of the page colors do you like best and why?

Hakimi 1

Farrah Iman Hakimi

Mr. Danshov

English 103

November 15, 2017

Wearable Devices

A wearable device or wearable is a small, mobile computing device designed to be worn

by a consumer. These devices often communicate with a mobile device or computer using

Bluetooth. Three popular types of wearable devices are activity trackers, smartwatches, and

smart glasses.

An activity tracker is a wearable device that monitors fitness-related activities such as

distance walked, heart rate, pulse, calories consumed, and sleep patterns. These devices typically

sync, usually wirelessly, with a web or mobile app on your computer or mobile device to extend

the capability of the wearable device (Pappas 32-41).

A smartwatch is a wearable device that, in addition to keeping time, can communicate

wirelessly with a smartphone to make and answer phone calls, read and send messages, access

the web, play music, work with apps such as fitness trackers and GPS, and more. Most include a

touch screen (Carter and Schmidt).

Smart glasses, also called smart eyewear, are wearable head-mounted eyeglass-type

devices that enable the user to view information or take photos and videos that are projected to a

miniature screen in the user's field of vision. For example, the device wearer could run an app

while wearing smart glasses that display flight status information when he or she walks into an

airport. Users control the device through voice commands or by touching controls on its frame.

Some smart glasses also include mobile apps, such as fitness trackers and GPS (Yazzie).

Figure 2–82a

Continued >

In the Labs *continued*

Hakimi 2

Activity trackers, smartwatches, and smart eyewear are available from a variety of

manufacturers. Before making a purchase, consumers should research costs and features of all

options to determine the device that best suits their requirements.

Figure 2–82b

Hakimi 3

Works Cited

Carter, Calvin J. and Karl Hans Schmidt. "Smartwatch Review." *Technology Trends* Aug. 2017:

n. pag. Web. 12 October 2017.

Pappas, Anastasia Maria. *Activity Trackers and Other Wearable Devices*. Dallas: Western Star

Publishing, 2017. Print.

Yazzie, Nina Tamaya. *Evaluating Today's Smart Glasses*. 25 Aug. 2017. Course Technology.

Web. 25 Sept. 2017.

Figure 2–82c

Lab 2: Preparing a Research Report with a Footnote

Problem: You are a college student enrolled in an introductory technology class. Your assignment is to prepare a short research paper (350–400 words) in any area of interest to you. The requirements are that the paper be presented according to the MLA documentation style, contain at least one note positioned as a footnote, and have three references. At least one of the three references must be from the web. You prepare a paper about two-step verification (Figure 2–83).

Perform the following tasks:

1. Run Word. Modify the Normal style to the 12-point Times New Roman font. Adjust line spacing to double and remove space below (after) paragraphs. Update the Normal style to include the adjusted line and paragraph spacing. Create a header to number pages. Type the name and course information at the left margin. If requested by your instructor, use your name and course information instead of the information shown in Figure 2–83a. Center and type the title. Set a first-line indent for paragraphs in the body of the research paper.

2. Type the research paper as shown in Figures 2–83a and 2–83b. Insert the footnote as shown in Figure 2–83a. Change the Footnote Text style to the format specified in the MLA documentation

Wagner 1

Bryan Wagner

Dr. Rosenberg

Technology 104

October 27, 2017

Two-Step Verification

In an attempt to protect personal data and information from online thieves, many organizations, such as financial institutions or universities, that store sensitive or confidential items use a two-step verification process. With two-step verification, a computer or mobile device uses two separate methods, one after the next, to verify the identity of a user.

ATMs (automated teller machines) usually require a two-step verification. Users first insert their ATM card into the ATM (Step 1) and then enter a PIN, or personal identification number, (Step 2) to access their bank account. If someone steals these cards, the thief must enter the user's PIN to access the account (Tanaka).

Another use of two-step verification requires a mobile phone and a computer or mobile device.[1] When users sign in to an account on a computer or mobile device, they enter a user name and password (Step 1). Next, they are prompted to enter another authentication code (Step 2), which is sent as a text or voice message or via an app on a smartphone. This second code generally is valid for a set time, sometimes only for a few minutes or hours. If users do not sign in during this time limit, they must repeat the process and request another verification code

---

[1] According to Moore and O'Sullivan, users should register an alternate mobile phone number, landline phone number, email address, or other form of contact beyond a mobile phone number so that they still can access their accounts even if they lose their mobile phone (54).

Figure 2–83a

Wagner 2

(Marcy). Microsoft and Google commonly use two-step verification when users sign in to these websites (Moore and O'Sullivan).

Some organizations use two separate methods to verify the identity of users. These two-step verification procedures are designed to protect users' sensitive and confidential items from online thieves.

Figure 2–83b

Continued >

In the Labs *continued*

style. Change the bibliography style to MLA. As you insert citations, use the following source information, entering it according to the MLA style:

a. Type of Source: Article
in a Periodical
Author: Hana Kei
Tanaka
Article Title: Safeguards
against Unauthorized
Access and Use
Periodical Title:
Technology Today
Year: 2017
Month: Sept.
Pages: no pages used
Medium: Web
Year Accessed: 2017
Month Accessed: Oct.
Day Accessed: 3

b. Type of Source: Web site
Author: Fredrick Lee
Marcy
Name of webpage:
Two-Step Verification
Year/Month/Date: none
given
Production Company:
Course Technology
Medium: Web
Year Accessed: 2017
Month Accessed: Sept.
Day Accessed: 18

c. Type of Source: Book
Author: Aaron Bradley
Moore and Brianna
Clare O'Sullivan
Title: Authentication
Techniques
Year: 2017
City: Detroit
Publisher: Great Lakes
Press
Medium: Print

3. At the end of the research paper text, press the ENTER key once and insert a manual page break so that the Works Cited page begins on a new page. Enter and format the works cited title. Use Word to insert the bibliographical list.

4. Check the spelling and grammar of the paper.

5. Save the document using the file name, Lab 2–2 Two-Step Verification Paper. Submit the document, shown in Figure 2–83, in the format specified by your instructor.

6. ✳ This paper uses web sources. What factors should you consider when selecting web sources?

Lab 3: **Consider This: Your Turn**

Create a Research Paper about Wireless Communications

Note: To complete this assignment, you will be required to use the Data Files. Please contact your instructor for information about accessing the Data Files.

Problem: As a student in an introductory computer class, your instructor has assigned a brief research paper that discusses wireless communications.

Perform the following tasks:

Part 1:   The source for the text in your research paper is in a file called Lab 2–3 Consider This Your Turn Wireless Communications Notes, which is located in the Data Files. If your instructor requests, use the Insights task pane to obtain information from another source and include that information as a note positioned as a footnote in the paper, along with entering its corresponding source information as appropriate. Add an AutoCorrect entry to correct a word you commonly mistype. If necessary, set the default dictionary. Add one of the source last names to the dictionary.

Using the concepts and techniques presented in this module, organize the notes in the text in the file on the Data Files, rewording as necessary, and then create and format this research paper according to the MLA documentation style. Be sure to check spelling and grammar of the finished paper. Submit your assignment and answers to the critical thinking questions in the format specified by your instructor.

Part 2: ✳ You made several decisions while creating the research paper in this assignment: how to organize the notes, where to place citations, how to format sources, and which source on the web to use for the footnote text (if requested by your instructor). What was the rationale behind each of these decisions? When you proofread the document, what further revisions did you make and why?

3 Creating a Business Letter with a Letterhead and Table

Objectives

You will have mastered the material in this module when you can:

- Change margins
- Insert and format a shape
- Change text wrapping
- Insert an online picture and format it
- Insert a symbol
- Add a border to a paragraph
- Clear formatting
- Convert a hyperlink to regular text

- Apply a style
- Set and use tab stops
- Insert the current date
- Create, modify, and insert a building block
- Insert a Word table, enter data in the table, and format the table
- Address and print an envelope

Introduction

In a business environment, people use documents to communicate with others. Business documents can include letters, memos, newsletters, proposals, and resumes. An effective business document clearly and concisely conveys its message and has a professional, organized appearance. You can use your own creative skills to design and compose business documents. Using Word, for example, you can develop the content and decide on the location of each item in a business document.

Project — Business Letter with a Letterhead and Table

At some time, you more than likely will prepare a business letter. Contents of business letters include requests, inquiries, confirmations, acknowledgements, recommendations, notifications, responses, thank you letters, invitations, offers, referrals, complaints, and more.

The project in this module follows generally accepted guidelines for writing letters and uses Word to create the business letter shown in Figure 3–1. This business

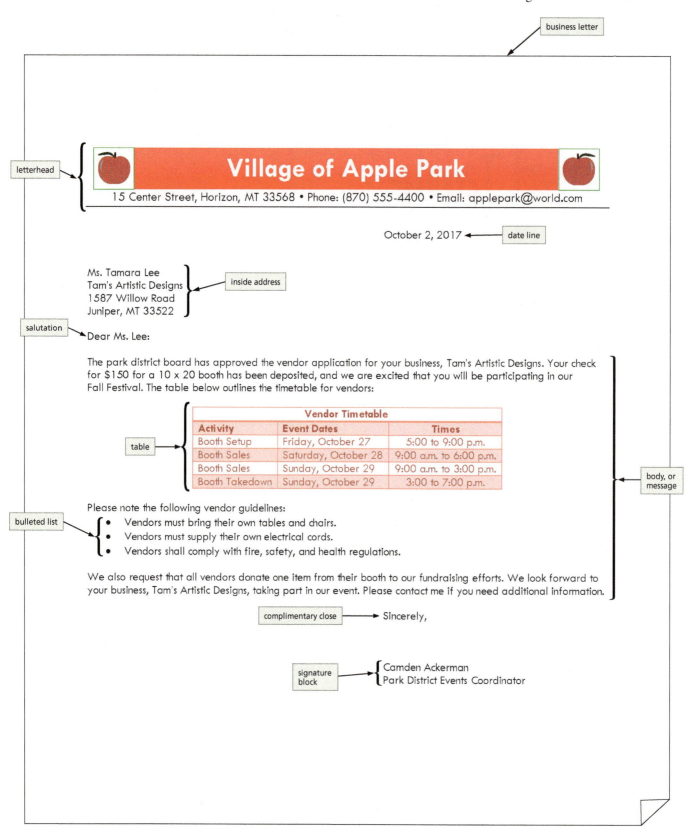

Figure 3–1

letter is a letter from the park district events coordinator at the Village of Apple Park that confirms a vendor application to participate in its community event. The letter includes a custom letterhead, as well as all essential business letter components: date line, inside address, salutation, body, complimentary close, and signature block. To easily present the vendor timetable during the event, the letter shows this information in a table. The vendor guidelines appear in a bulleted list.

In this module, you will learn how to create the letter shown in Figure 3–1. The following roadmap identifies general activities you will perform as you progress through this module:

1. CREATE AND FORMAT a LETTERHEAD WITH GRAPHICS.
2. SPECIFY the LETTER FORMATS according to business letter guidelines.
3. INSERT a TABLE in the letter.
4. FORMAT the TABLE in the letter.
5. INSERT a BULLETED LIST in the letter.
6. ADDRESS an ENVELOPE for the letter.

To Run Word and Change Word Settings

If you are using a computer to step through the project in this module and you want your screens to match the figures in this book, you should change your screen's resolution to 1366×768. For information about how to change a computer's resolution, refer to the Office and Windows module at the beginning of this book.

The following steps run Word, display formatting marks, and change the zoom to page width.

1 Run Word and create a blank document in the Word window. If necessary, maximize the Word window.

2 If the Print Layout button on the status bar is not selected (shown in Figure 3–2), click it so that your screen is in Print Layout view.

3 If the 'Show/Hide ¶' button (Home tab | Paragraph group) is not selected already, click it to display formatting marks on the screen.

4 To display the page the same width as the document window, if necessary, click the Page Width button (View tab | Zoom group).

For an introduction to Windows and instructions about how to perform basic Windows tasks, read the Office and Windows module at the beginning of this book, where you can learn how to resize windows, change screen resolution, create folders, move and rename files, use Windows Help, and much more.

For an introduction to Office and instructions about how to perform basic tasks in Office apps, read the Office and Windows module at the beginning of this book, where you can learn how to run an application, use the ribbon, save a file, open a file, print a file, exit an application, use Help, and much more.

1 CREATE & FORMAT LETTERHEAD WITH GRAPHICS | 2 SPECIFY LETTER FORMATS
3 INSERT TABLE | 4 FORMAT TABLE | 5 INSERT BULLETED LIST | 6 ADDRESS ENVELOPE

To Change Margin Settings

Word is preset to use standard 8.5-by-11-inch paper, with 1-inch top, bottom, left, and right margins. The business letter in this module uses .75-inch left and right margins and 1-inch top and bottom margins. *Why? You would like more text to fit from left to right on the page.*

When you change the default (preset) margin settings, the new margin settings affect every page in the document. If you wanted the margins to affect just a portion of the document, you would divide the document into sections (discussed in a later module), which enables you to specify different margin settings for each section. The following steps change margin settings.

1

- Display the Layout tab.

- Click the Adjust Margins button (Layout tab | Page Setup group) to display the Adjust Margins gallery (Figure 3–2).

2

- Click Moderate in the Adjust Margins gallery to change the margins to the specified settings.

What if the margin settings I want are not in the Adjust Margins gallery?
You can click Custom Margins in the Adjust Margins gallery and then enter your desired margin values in the top, bottom, left, and right boxes in the Page Setup dialog box.

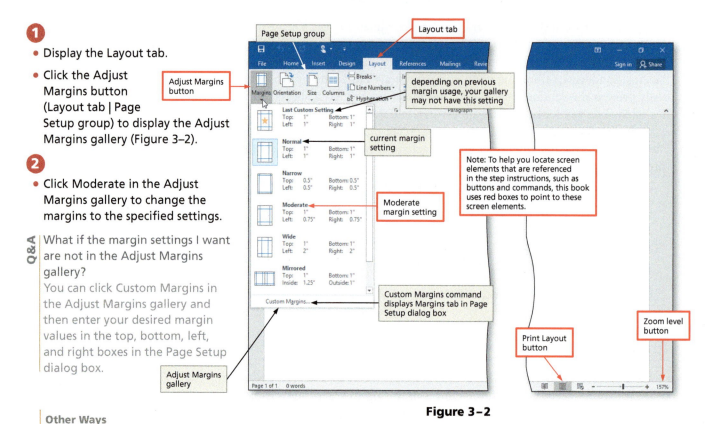

Figure 3–2

Other Ways

1. Position pointer on margin boundary on ruler; when pointer changes to two-headed arrow, drag margin boundary on ruler

Creating a Letterhead

The cost of preprinted letterhead can be high. An alternative is to create your own letterhead and save it in a file. When you want to create a letter at a later time, you can start by using the letterhead file. The following sections create a letterhead and then save it in a file for future use.

What is a letterhead?
A **letterhead** is the section of a letter that identifies an organization or individual. Often, the letterhead appears at the top of a letter. Although you can design and print a letterhead yourself, many businesses pay an outside firm to design and print their letterhead, usually on higher-quality paper. They then use the professionally preprinted paper for external business communications.

If you do not have preprinted letterhead paper, you can design a creative letterhead. It is important the letterhead appropriately represent the essence of the organization or individual (i.e., formal, technical, creative, etc.). That is, it should use text, graphics, formats, and colors that reflect the organization or individual. The letterhead should leave ample room for the contents of the letter.

When designing a letterhead, consider its contents, placement, and appearance.

- **Contents of letterhead.** A letterhead should contain these elements:
  - Complete legal name of the individual, group, or company
  - Complete mailing address: street address including building, room, suite number, or post office box, along with city, state, and postal code
  - Phone number(s) and fax number, if applicable
  - Email address

– Website address, if applicable

– Many letterheads also include a logo or other image; if an image is used, it should express the organization or individual's personality or goals

• **Placement of elements in the letterhead.** Many letterheads center their elements across the top of the page. Others align some or all of the elements with the left or right margins. Sometimes, the elements are split between the top and bottom of the page. For example, a name and logo may be at the top of the page with the address at the bottom of the page.

• **Appearance of letterhead elements.** Use fonts that are easy to read. Give the organization or individual name impact by making its font size larger than the rest of the text in the letterhead. For additional emphasis, consider formatting the name in bold, italic, or a different color. Choose colors that complement each other and convey the goals of the organization or individual.

When finished designing the letterhead, determine if a divider line would help to visually separate the letterhead from the remainder of the letter.

The letterhead for the letter in this module consists of the organization's name, appropriate graphics, postal address, phone number, and email address. The name and graphics are enclosed in a rectangular shape (shown in Figure 3–1), and the contact information is below the shape. You will follow these general steps to create the letterhead in this module:

1. Insert and format a shape.
2. Enter and format the organization name in the shape.
3. Insert, format, and position the images in the shape.
4. Enter the contact information below the shape.
5. Add a border below the contact information.

BTW

The Ribbon and Screen Resolution
Word may change how the groups and buttons within the groups appear on the ribbon, depending on the computer or mobile device's screen resolution. Thus, your ribbon may look different from the ones in this book if you are using a screen resolution other than 1366 x 768.

To Insert a Shape

1 CREATE & FORMAT LETTERHEAD WITH GRAPHICS | 2 SPECIFY LETTER FORMATS
3 INSERT TABLE | 4 FORMAT TABLE | 5 INSERT BULLETED LIST | 6 ADDRESS ENVELOPE

Word has a variety of predefined shapes, which are a type of drawing object, that you can insert in documents. A **drawing object** is a graphic that you create using Word. Examples of shape drawing objects include rectangles, circles, triangles, arrows, flowcharting symbols, stars, banners, and callouts. The following steps insert a rectangle shape in the letterhead. *Why? The organization's name is placed in a rectangle for emphasis and visual appeal.*

• Display the Insert tab.

• Click the 'Draw a Shape' button (Insert tab | Illustrations group) to display the Draw a Shape gallery (Figure 3–3).

Figure 3–3

- Click the Rectangle shape in the Rectangles area in the Draw a Shape gallery, which removes the gallery.

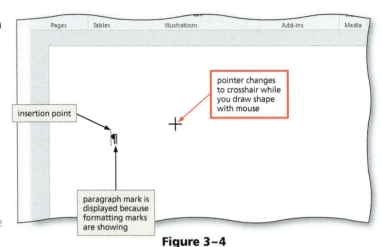

Q&A What if I am using a touch screen?
The shape is inserted in the document window. Skip Steps 3 and 4, and proceed to Step 5.

- Position the pointer (a crosshair) in the approximate location for the upper-left corner of the desired shape (Figure 3–4).

Q&A What is the purpose of the crosshair pointer?
You drag the crosshair pointer from the upper-left corner to the lower-right corner to form the desired location and size of the shape.

Figure 3–4

- Drag the mouse to the right and downward to form the boundaries of the shape, as shown in Figure 3–5. Do not release the mouse button.

Figure 3–5

- Release the mouse button so that Word draws the shape according to your drawing in the document window.

- Verify your shape is the same approximate height and width as the one in this project by reviewing, and if necessary changing, the values in the Shape Height box and Shape Width boxes (Drawing Tools Format tab | Size group) to 0.53" and 5.7" by typing each value in the respective box and then pressing the ENTER key (Figure 3–6).

Q&A What is the purpose of the rotate handle?
When you drag an object's **rotate handle**, which is the white circle on the top of the object, Word rotates the object in the direction you drag the mouse.

What if I wanted to delete a shape and start over?
With the shape selected, you would press the DELETE key.

Figure 3–6

Floating versus Inline Objects

When you insert an object in a document, Word inserts it as either an inline object or a floating object. An **inline object** is an object that is part of a paragraph. With inline objects, you change the location of the object by setting paragraph options, such as centered, right-aligned, and so on. For example, when you inserted the picture of the surfer in Module 1, Word inserted it as an inline object. A **floating object**, by contrast, is an object that can be positioned at a specific location in a document or in a layer over or behind text in a document. The shape you just inserted is a floating object. You have more flexibility with floating objects because you can position a floating object anywhere on the page.

In addition to changing an object from inline to floating and vice versa, Word provides several floating options, which (along with inline) are called text wrapping options because they affect how text wraps with or around the object. Table 3–1 presents the various text wrapping options.

Table 3–1 Text Wrapping Options

Text Wrapping Option	Object Type	How It Works
In Line with Text	Inline	Object positioned according to paragraph formatting; for example, if paragraph is centered, object will be centered with any text in the paragraph.
Square	Floating	Text wraps around object, with text forming a box around the object.
Tight	Floating	Text wraps around object, with text forming to shape of the object.
Through	Floating	Object appears at beginning, middle, or end of text. Moving object changes location of text.
Top and Bottom	Floating	Object appears above or below text. Moving object changes location of text.
Behind Text	Floating	Object appears behind text.
In Front of Text	Floating	Object appears in front of text and may cover the text.

To Change an Object's Position

**1 CREATE & FORMAT LETTERHEAD WITH GRAPHICS | 2 SPECIFY LETTER FORMATS
3 INSERT TABLE | 4 FORMAT TABLE | 5 INSERT BULLETED LIST | 6 ADDRESS ENVELOPE**

You can specify an object's vertical position on a page (top, middle, bottom) and its horizontal position (left, center, right). The following steps change the position of an object, specifically, the rectangle shape. *Why? You want the shape to be centered at the top of the page in the letterhead.*

1

- With the shape still selected, click the Position Object button (Drawing Tools Format tab | Arrange group) to display the Position Object gallery (Figure 3–7).

Q&A
What if the shape is not still selected? Click the shape to select it.

Figure 3–7

Experiment

- Point to various options in the Position Object gallery and watch the shape move to the selected position option.

2

- Click 'Position in Top Center with Square Text Wrapping' in the Position Object gallery so that the object does not cover the document and is centered at the top of the document.

Other Ways

1. Click Layout Options button attached to graphic (shown in Figure 3–8), click See more link in Layout Options gallery, click Horizontal Alignment arrow and select alignment (Layout dialog box), click Vertical Alignment arrow and select alignment, click OK button

2. Click Advanced Layout: Size Dialog Box Launcher (Drawing Tools Format tab | Size group), click Position tab (Layout dialog box), click Horizontal Alignment arrow and select alignment, click Vertical Alignment arrow and select alignment, click OK button

To Change an Object's Text Wrapping

1 CREATE & FORMAT LETTERHEAD WITH GRAPHICS | 2 SPECIFY LETTER FORMATS
3 INSERT TABLE | 4 FORMAT TABLE | 5 INSERT BULLETED LIST | 6 ADDRESS ENVELOPE

When you insert a shape in a Word document, the default text wrapping is In Front of Text, which means the object will cover any text behind it. The previous steps, which changed the shape's position, changed the text wrapping to Square. In the letterhead, you want the shape's text wrapping to be Top and Bottom. *Why? You want the letterhead above the contents of the letter when you type it, instead of covering the contents of the letter.* The following steps change an object's text wrapping.

1

- With the shape still selected, click the Layout Options button attached to the graphic to display the Layout Options gallery (Figure 3–8).

2

- Click 'Top and Bottom' in the Layout Options gallery so that the object does not cover the document text (shown in Figure 3–9).

Q&A

How can I tell that the text wrapping has changed?
Because the letter has no text, you need to look at the paragraph mark, which now is positioned below the shape instead of to its left.

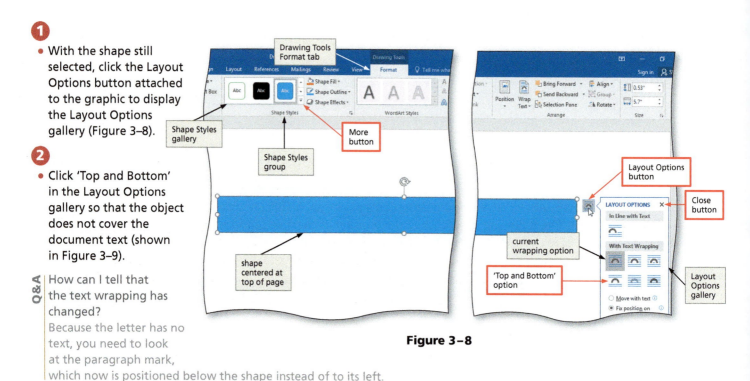

Figure 3–8

- Click the Close button in the Layout Options gallery to close the gallery.

Other Ways

1. Right-click object (or, if using touch, tap 'Show Context Menu' button on mini toolbar), point to Wrap Text on shortcut menu, click desired wrapping option

2. Click Wrap Text button (Drawing Tools Format tab | Arrange group), select desired wrapping option

To Apply a Shape Style

Why apply a shape style? *Word provides a Shape Styles gallery so that you easily can change the appearance of the shape.* The following steps apply a shape style to the rectangle shape.

- With the shape still selected, click the More button (shown in Figure 3–8) in the Shape Styles gallery (Drawing Tools Format tab | Shape Styles group) to expand the gallery.

Q&A
What if the shape no longer is selected?
Click the shape to select it.

- Point to 'Moderate Effect - Gray-50%, Accent 3' (fourth effect in fifth row) in the Shape Styles gallery to display a live preview of that style applied to the shape in the document (Figure 3–9).

 Experiment

- Point to various styles in the Shape Styles gallery and watch the style of the shape change in the document.

Figure 3–9

- Click 'Moderate Effect - Gray-50%, Accent 3' in the Shape Styles gallery to apply the selected style to the shape.

Other Ways
1. Right-click shape, click 'Shape Quick Styles' button on mini toolbar, select desired style	2. Click Format Shape Dialog Box Launcher (Drawing Tools Format tab | Shape Styles group), click 'Fill & Line' button (Format Shape task pane), expand Fill section, select desired colors, click Close button

To Add Text to a Shape

The following steps add text (the organization name) to a shape. *Why? In the letterhead for this module, the name is in the shape. Similarly, an individual could put his or her name in a shape on a letterhead in order to create personalized letterhead.*

- Right-click the shape to display a mini toolbar and/or shortcut menu (Figure 3–10).

Figure 3–10

2

- Click Add Text on the shortcut menu to place an insertion point in the shape.

Q&A What if I am using a touch screen?
Tap the Edit Text button on the mini toolbar.

Why do the buttons on my mini toolbar differ?
If you are using a mouse in Mouse mode, the buttons on your mini toolbar will differ from those that appear when you use a touch screen in Touch mode.

- If the insertion point and paragraph mark are not centered in the shape, click the Center button (Home tab | Paragraph group) to center them.

- Type **Village of Apple Park** as the name in the shape (Figure 3–11).

    If requested by your instructor, enter your name instead of the name shown in Figure 3–11.

text entered and centered

Village·of·Apple·Park¶

Figure 3–11

To Use the 'Increase Font Size' Button

1 CREATE & FORMAT LETTERHEAD WITH GRAPHICS | 2 SPECIFY LETTER FORMATS
3 INSERT TABLE | 4 FORMAT TABLE | 5 INSERT BULLETED LIST | 6 ADDRESS ENVELOPE

In previous modules, you used the Font Size arrow (Home tab | Font group) to change the font size of text. Word also provides an 'Increase Font Size' button (Home tab | Font group), which increases the font size of selected text each time you click the button. The following steps use the 'Increase Font Size' button to increase the font size of the name in the shape to 26 point. **Why?** *You want the name to be as large as possible in the shape.*

 1

- Drag through the text to be formatted (in this case, the name in the shape).

2

- If necessary, display the Home tab.

- Repeatedly click the 'Increase Font Size' button (Home tab | Font group) until the Font Size box displays 26 to increase the font size of the selected text (Figure 3–12).

Q&A What if I click the 'Increase Font Size' button (Home tab | Font group) too many times, causing the font size to be too big?
Click the 'Decrease Font Size' button (Home tab | Font group) until the desired font size is displayed.

Figure 3–12

Experiment

- Repeatedly click the 'Increase Font Size' and 'Decrease Font Size' buttons (Home tab | Font group) and watch the font size of the selected text change in the document window. When you are finished experimenting with these two buttons, set the font size to 26.

Other Ways

1. Press CTRL+SHIFT+>

To Bold Selected Text

To make the name stand out even more, bold it. The following steps bold the selected text.

1 With the text selected, click the Bold button (Home tab | Font group) to bold the selected text (shown in Figure 3–13).

2 Click anywhere in the text in the shape to remove the selection and place the insertion point in the shape.

To Change the Document Theme

1 CREATE & FORMAT LETTERHEAD WITH GRAPHICS | 2 SPECIFY LETTER FORMATS
3 INSERT TABLE | 4 FORMAT TABLE | 5 INSERT BULLETED LIST | 6 ADDRESS ENVELOPE

A **document theme** is a coordinated combination of colors, fonts, and effects. The current default document theme is Office, which uses Calibri and Calibri Light as its font and shades of grays and blues primarily. The following steps change the document theme to Circuit for the letter in this module. *Why? You want to use shades of reds and oranges in the letterhead because those colors are associated with energy, success, creativity, and enthusiasm.*

1

- Display the Design tab.

- Click the Themes button (Design tab | Document Formatting group) to display the Themes gallery.

- Point to Circuit in the Themes gallery to display a live preview of that theme applied to the document (Figure 3–13).

Figure 3–13

 Experiment

- Point to various themes in the Themes gallery and watch the color scheme and font set change in the document window.

2

- Click Circuit in the Themes gallery to change the document theme.

To Insert an Online Picture

1 CREATE & FORMAT LETTERHEAD WITH GRAPHICS | 2 SPECIFY LETTER FORMATS
3 INSERT TABLE | 4 FORMAT TABLE | 5 INSERT BULLETED LIST | 6 ADDRESS ENVELOPE

Files containing graphics are available from a variety of sources. In the Module 1 flyer, you inserted a digital picture taken with a camera. In this project, you insert a picture from the web. Microsoft Office applications can access a collection of royalty-free photos and animations.

The letterhead in this project contains a picture of an apple (shown in Figure 3–1). *Why? Because the name of the organization is Village of Apple Park, an apple is an appropriate image for this letterhead.* The following steps insert an online picture in the document.

1

- If necessary, click the paragraph mark below the shape to position the insertion point where you want to insert the picture.

- Display the Insert tab.

- Click the Online Pictures button (Insert tab | Illustrations group) to display the Insert Pictures dialog box.

- Type **apple** in the Search box (Insert Pictures dialog box) to specify the search text, which indicates the type of image you want to locate (Figure 3–14).

Figure 3–14

2

- Click the Search button to display a list of online pictures that matches the entered search text.

- Scroll through the list of pictures to locate the one shown in Figure 3–15, or a similar image.

Q&A Why is my list of pictures different from Figure 3–15? The online images are continually updated.

What is Creative Commons? **Creative Commons** is a nonprofit organization that provides several standard licensing options that owners of creative works may specify when granting permission for others to use their digital content, such as the online pictures that appear in the Bing Image Search. Be sure to follow an image's guidelines when using it in a document.

Figure 3–15

Q&A What if I cannot locate the image in Figure 3–15, and I would like to use that exact image?
The image is located in the Data Files. You can click the Cancel button and then click the From File button (Insert tab | Illustrations group), navigate to the file called apple-02.wmf in the Data Files, and then click the Insert button (Insert Picture dialog box).

③

- If necessary, click the 'Show all web results' button to display more images that match the search text.

- Click the desired picture to select it.

- Click the Insert button to insert the selected image in the document at the location of the insertion point. If necessary, scroll to display the image (picture) in the document window (Figure 3–16).

Figure 3–16

To Resize a Graphic to a Percent of the Original Size

1 CREATE & FORMAT LETTERHEAD WITH GRAPHICS | 2 SPECIFY LETTER FORMATS
3 INSERT TABLE | 4 FORMAT TABLE | 5 INSERT BULLETED LIST | 6 ADDRESS ENVELOPE

Instead of dragging a sizing handle to change the graphic's size, as you learned in Module 1, you can specify that the graphic be resized to a percent of its original size. In this module, the graphic is resized to 8 percent of its original size. **Why?** *The original size of the picture is too large for the letterhead.* The following steps resize a graphic to a percent of the original.

- With the graphic still selected, click the Advanced Layout: Size Dialog Box Launcher (Picture Tools Format tab | Size group) to display the Size sheet in the Layout dialog box.

Q&A What if the graphic is not selected or the Picture Tools Format tab is not on the ribbon?
Click the graphic to select it or double-click the graphic to make the Picture Tools Format tab the active tab.

- In the Scale area (Layout dialog box), double-click the current value in the Height box to select it.

- Type **8** in the Height box and then press the TAB key to display the same percent value in the Width box (Figure 3–17).

Figure 3–17

Q&A

Why did Word automatically fill in the value in the Width box?

When the 'Lock aspect ratio' check box (Layout dialog box) is selected, Word automatically maintains the size proportions of the graphic.

How do I know to use 8 percent for the resized graphic?

The larger graphic consumed too much room on the page. Try various percentages to determine the size that works best in the letterhead design.

3

- Click the OK button to close the dialog box and resize the selected graphic.
- If necessary, scroll to display the top of the document
- Verify that the Shape Height and Shape Width boxes (Picture Tools Format tab | Size group) display 0.53". If they do not, change their values to 0.53" (Figure 3–18).

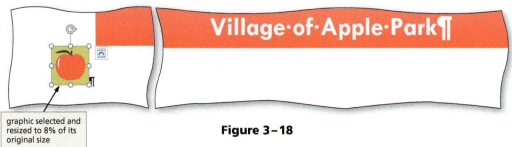

Figure 3–18

Other Ways

1. Click Layout Options button attached to graphic, click See more link in the Layout Options gallery, click Size tab (Layout dialog box), enter height and width values, click OK button

2. Right-click graphic, click 'Size and Position' on shortcut menu, enter height and width values (Layout dialog box), click OK button

---

1 CREATE & FORMAT LETTERHEAD WITH GRAPHICS | 2 SPECIFY LETTER FORMATS

3 INSERT TABLE | 4 FORMAT TABLE | 5 INSERT BULLETED LIST | 6 ADDRESS ENVELOPE

To Change the Color of a Graphic

In Word, you can change the color of a graphic. The apple image (graphic) currently is a bright red color. The following steps change the color of the graphic. *Why? Because the image in this project will be placed beside the rectangle shape, you prefer to use lighter colors.*

1

- With the graphic still selected (shown in Figure 3–18), click the Color button (Picture Tools Format tab | Adjust group) to display the Color gallery.
- Point to Washout in the Color gallery (fourth color in first row) to display a live preview of that color applied to the selected graphic in the document (Figure 3–19).

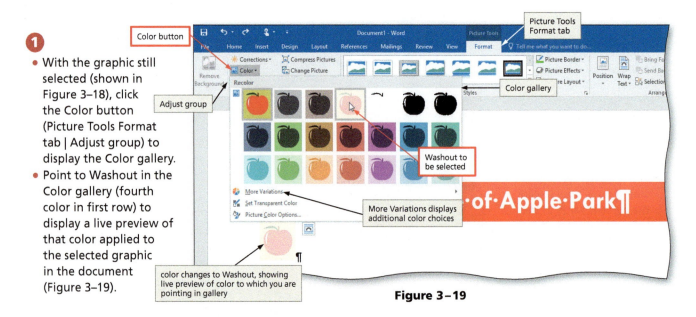

Figure 3–19

⌕ Experiment

- Point to various colors in the Color gallery and watch the color of the graphic change in the document.

②

- Click Washout in the Color gallery to change the color of the selected graphic.

Q&A How would I change a graphic back to its original colors?
With the graphic selected, you would click No Recolor, which is the upper-left color in the Color gallery.

Other Ways
1. Click Format Shape Dialog Box Launcher (Picture Tools Format tab | Picture Styles group), click Picture button (Format Picture task pane), expand Picture Color section, select desired options   2. Right-click graphic (or, if using touch, tap 'Show Context Menu' button on mini toolbar), click Format Picture on shortcut menu (or, if using touch, tap Format Object), click Picture button (Format Picture task pane), expand Picture Color section, select desired options

To Set a Transparent Color in a Graphic

1 CREATE & FORMAT LETTERHEAD WITH GRAPHICS | 2 SPECIFY LETTER FORMATS
3 INSERT TABLE | 4 FORMAT TABLE | 5 INSERT BULLETED LIST | 6 ADDRESS ENVELOPE

In Word, you can make one color in a graphic transparent; that is, you remove the color. You would make a color transparent if you wanted to remove part of a graphic or see text or colors behind a graphic. The following steps set the light green background around the apple in a transparent color. *Why? You prefer the light green color to be transparent.*

①

- With the graphic still selected, click the Color button (Picture Tools Format tab | Adjust group) to display the Color gallery (Figure 3–20).

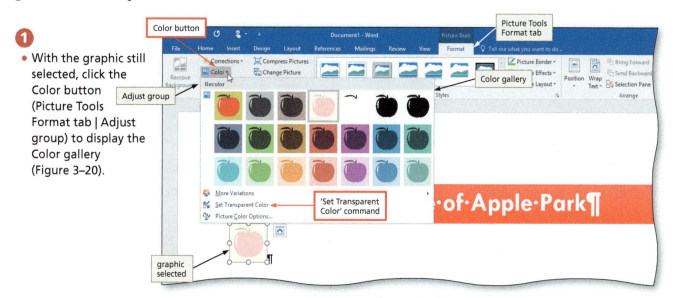

Figure 3–20

②

- Click 'Set Transparent Color' in the Color gallery to display a pen pointer in the document window.

Q&A What if I am using a touch screen?
You may need to use a stylus or mouse to perform these steps.

- Position the pen pointer in the graphic where you want to make the color transparent (Figure 3–21).

Q&A Can I make multiple colors in a graphic transparent?
No, you can make only one color transparent.

Figure 3–21

- Click the location in the graphic where you want the color to be transparent (Figure 3–22).

Q&A

What if I make the wrong color transparent? Click the Undo button on the Quick Access Toolbar, or press CTRL+Z, and then repeat these steps.

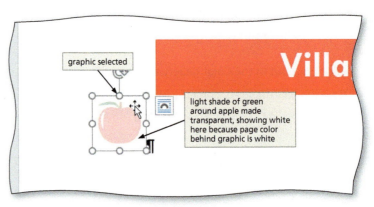

Figure 3–22

To Adjust the Brightness and Contrast of a Graphic

1 CREATE & FORMAT LETTERHEAD WITH GRAPHICS | 2 SPECIFY LETTER FORMATS

3 INSERT TABLE | 4 FORMAT TABLE | 5 INSERT BULLETED LIST | 6 ADDRESS ENVELOPE

In Word, you can adjust the brightness, or lightness, of a graphic and also the **contrast**, or the difference between the lightest and darkest areas of the graphic. The following steps decrease the brightness and contrast of the apple graphic, each by 20%. *Why? You want to darken the graphic slightly to increase its emphasis on the page and, at the same time, decrease the difference between the light and dark areas of the graphic.*

- If necessary, display the Picture Tools Format tab.
- With the graphic still selected (shown in Figure 3–22), click the Corrections button (Picture Tools Format tab | Adjust group) to display the Corrections gallery.
- Point to 'Brightness: -20% Contrast: -20%' (second image in second row) in the Corrections gallery to display a live preview of that correction applied to the graphic in the document (Figure 3–23).

 Experiment

- Point to various corrections in the Corrections gallery and watch the brightness and contrast of the graphic change in the document.

Figure 3–23

2

- Click 'Brightness: -20% Contrast: -20%' in the Corrections gallery to change the brightness and contrast of the selected graphic.

Other Ways

1. Click Format Shape Dialog Box Launcher (Picture Tools Format tab | Picture Styles group), click Picture button (Format Picture task pane), expand Picture Corrections section, select desired options

2. Right-click graphic (or, if using touch, tap 'Show Context Menu' button on mini toolbar), click Format Picture on shortcut menu (or, if using touch, tap Format Object on shortcut menu), click Picture button (Format Picture task pane), expand Picture Corrections section, select desired options

To Change the Border Color on a Graphic

The apple graphic currently has no border (outline). The following steps change the border color on the graphic. *Why? You would like the graphic to have a lime border so that it is in the same color family as the leaf on the apple.*

1

- Click the Picture Border arrow (Picture Tools Format tab | Picture Styles group) to display the Picture Border gallery.
- Point to 'Lime, Accent 1, Darker 25%' (fifth theme color in fifth row) in the Picture Border gallery to display a live preview of that border color around the picture (Figure 3–24).

Figure 3–24

Q&A What if I click the Picture Border button by mistake?
Click the Picture Border arrow and proceed with Step 2.

 Experiment

- Point to various colors in the Picture Border gallery and watch the border color on the graphic change in the document window.

2

- Click 'Lime, Accent 1, Darker 25%' in the Picture Border gallery to change the picture border color.

Q&A How would I remove a border from a graphic?
With the graphic selected, you would click No Outline in the Picture Border gallery.

Can I remove all formatting applied to a graphic and start over?
Yes. With the graphic selected, you would click the Reset Picture button (Picture Tools Format tab | Adjust group).

To Change an Object's Text Wrapping

The apple graphic is to be positioned to the left of the shape. By default, when you insert a picture, it is formatted as an inline graphic. Inline graphics cannot be moved to a precise location on a page. Recall that inline graphics are part of a paragraph and, thus, can be positioned according to paragraph formatting, such as centered or left-aligned. To move the graphic to the left of the shape, you format it as a

BTW
Touch Screen Differences
The Office and Windows interfaces may vary if you are using a touch screen. For this reason, you might notice that the function or appearance of your touch screen differs slightly from this module's presentation.

floating object with In Front of Text wrapping. The following steps change a graphic's text wrapping.

1 If necessary, click the graphic to select it.

2 Click the Layout Options button attached to the graphic to display the Layout Options gallery.

3 Click 'In Front of Text' in the Layout Options gallery so that you can position the object on top of any item in the document, in this case, on top of the rectangular shape.

4 Click the Close button to close the gallery.

To Move a Graphic

1 CREATE & FORMAT LETTERHEAD WITH GRAPHICS | 2 SPECIFY LETTER FORMATS
3 INSERT TABLE | 4 FORMAT TABLE | 5 INSERT BULLETED LIST | 6 ADDRESS ENVELOPE

The following steps move a graphic. **Why?** *In this letterhead, the first apple graphic is positioned to the left of the shape.*

1

- Position the pointer in the graphic so that the pointer has a four-headed arrow attached to it (Figure 3–25).

when pointer has four-headed arrow attached to it, you can drag floating graphic to any location in document

Figure 3–25

2

- Drag the graphic to the left of the shape, as shown in Figure 3–26.

Q&A What if I moved the graphic to the wrong location?
Repeat these steps. You can drag a floating graphic to any location in a document.

Why do green lines appear on my screen as I drag a graphic?
You have alignment guides set, which help you line up graphics. To set alignment guides, click the Align Objects button (Picture Tools Format tab | Arrange group) and then click 'Use Alignment Guides'.

graphic moved to left of the shape

Figure 3–26

To Copy a Graphic

In this project, the same apple graphic is to be placed to the right of the shape. Instead of performing the same steps to insert and format a second identical apple graphic, you can copy the graphic to the Office Clipboard, paste the graphic from the Office Clipboard, and then move the graphic to the desired location.

You use the same steps to copy a graphic as you used in Module 2 to copy text. The following steps copy a graphic.

1 If necessary, click the graphic to select it.

2 Display the Home tab.

3 Click the Copy button, shown in Figure 3–27 (Home tab | Clipboard group), to copy the selected item to the Office Clipboard.

1 CREATE & FORMAT LETTERHEAD WITH GRAPHICS | 2 SPECIFY LETTER FORMATS
3 INSERT TABLE | 4 FORMAT TABLE | 5 INSERT BULLETED LIST | 6 ADDRESS ENVELOPE

To Use Paste Options

The following steps paste a graphic using the Paste Options gallery. *Why? Recall from Module 2 that you can specify the format of a pasted item using Paste Options.*

1

• Click the Paste arrow (Home tab | Clipboard group) to display the Paste gallery.

Q&A What if I accidentally click the Paste button?
Click the Paste Options button below the graphic pasted in the document to display a Paste Options gallery.

• Point to the 'Keep Source Formatting' button in the Paste gallery to display a live preview of that paste option (Figure 3–27).

⊙ Experiment

• Point to the two buttons in the Paste gallery and watch the appearance of the pasted graphic change.

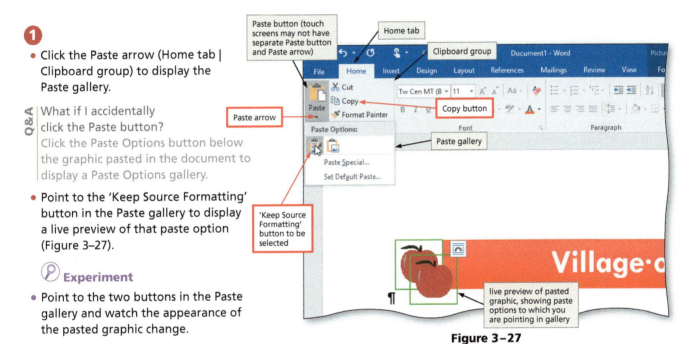

Figure 3–27

Q&A What do the buttons in the Paste gallery mean?
The 'Keep Source Formatting' button indicates the pasted graphic should have the same formats as it did in its original location. The Picture button removes some formatting from the graphic.

Why are these paste buttons different from the ones in Module 2?
The buttons that appear in the Paste gallery differ depending on the item you are pasting. Use live preview to see how the pasted object will look in the document.

2

• Click the 'Keep Source Formatting' button in the Paste gallery to paste the object using the same formatting as the original.

To Move a Graphic

The next step is to move the second apple graphic so that it is positioned to the right of the rectangle shape. The following steps move a graphic.

1 If you are using a mouse, position the pointer in the graphic so that the pointer has a four-headed arrow attached to it.

2 Drag the graphic to the location shown in Figure 3–28.

To Flip a Graphic

The following steps flip a graphic horizontally. *Why? In this letterhead, you want the leaves on the apple graphics to point toward the edge of the paper.*

- If necessary, display the Picture Tools Format tab.
- With the graphic still selected, click the Rotate Objects button (Picture Tools Format tab | Arrange group) to display the Rotate Objects gallery (Figure 3–28).

🔍 **Experiment**

- Point to the various rotate options in the Rotate Options gallery and watch the picture rotate in the document window.

- Click Flip Horizontal in the Rotate Options gallery, so that Word flips the graphic to display its mirror image (shown in Figure 3–29).

Figure 3–28

Q&A Can I flip a graphic vertically?
Yes, you would click Flip Vertical in the Rotate Options gallery. You also can rotate a graphic clockwise or counterclockwise by clicking 'Rotate Right 90°' and 'Rotate Left 90°', respectively, in the Rotate Options gallery.

- Save the letterhead on your hard drive, OneDrive, or other storage location using the file name, Apple Park Letterhead.

Q&A Why should I save the letterhead at this time?
You have performed many tasks while creating this letterhead and do not want to risk losing work completed thus far.

To Format and Enter Text

The contact information for the letterhead in this project is located on the line below the shape containing the name. The following steps format and then enter the mailing address in the letterhead.

1 Position the insertion point on the line below the shape containing the name.

2 If necessary, display the Home tab. Click the Center button (Home tab | Paragraph group) to center the paragraph.

3 Click the 'Increase Font Size' button (Home tab | Font group) to increase the font size to 12 point.

4 Type **15 Center Street, Horizon, MT 33568** and then press the SPACEBAR (shown in Figure 3–29).

To Insert a Symbol from the Symbol Dialog Box

Word provides a method of inserting dots and other symbols, such as letters in the Greek alphabet and mathematical characters, that are not on the keyboard. The following steps insert a dot symbol, sometimes called a bullet symbol, in the letterhead. ***Why?*** *You want a visual separator between the mailing address and phone number in the letterhead and also between the phone number and email address.*

- If necessary, position the insertion point as shown in Figure 3–29.
- Display the Insert tab.
- Click the 'Insert a Symbol' button (Insert tab | Symbols group) to display the Insert a Symbol gallery (Figure 3–29).

Q&A What if the symbol I want to insert already appears in the Insert a Symbol gallery?
You can click any symbol shown in the Insert a Symbol gallery to insert it in the document.

Figure 3–29

- Click More Symbols in the Insert a Symbol gallery to display the Symbol dialog box.
- If the font in the Font box is not (normal text), click the Font arrow (Symbol dialog box) and then scroll to and click (normal text) to select this font.
- If the subset in the Subset box is not General Punctuation, click the Subset arrow and then scroll and click General Punctuation to select this subset.
- In the list of symbols, if necessary, scroll to the dot symbol shown in Figure 3–30 and then click the symbol to select it.
- Click the Insert button (Symbol dialog box) to place the selected symbol in the document to the left of the insertion point (Figure 3–30).

Figure 3–30

 Why is the Symbol dialog box still open?
The Symbol dialog box remains open, allowing you to insert additional symbols.

3

- Click the Close button (Symbol dialog box) to close the dialog box.

To Insert a Symbol from the Insert a Symbol Gallery

1 CREATE & FORMAT LETTERHEAD WITH GRAPHICS | 2 SPECIFY LETTER FORMATS
3 INSERT TABLE | 4 FORMAT TABLE | 5 INSERT BULLETED LIST | 6 ADDRESS ENVELOPE

In the letterhead, another dot symbol separates the phone number from the email address. The following steps use the Insert a Symbol gallery to insert a dot symbol between the phone number and email address. *Why? Once you insert a symbol using the Symbol dialog box, Word adds that symbol to the Insert a Symbol gallery so that it is more readily available.*

1

- Press the SPACEBAR, type **Phone: (870) 555-4400** and then press the SPACEBAR.

2

- Click the 'Insert a Symbol' button (Insert tab | Symbols group) to display the Insert a Symbol gallery (Figure 3–31).

Figure 3–31

Q&A | Why is the dot symbol now in the Insert a Symbol gallery?
When you insert a symbol from the Symbol dialog box, Word automatically adds the symbol to the Insert a Symbol gallery.

3

- Click the dot symbol in the Insert a Symbol gallery to insert the symbol at the location of the insertion point (shown in Figure 3–32).

To Enter Text

The following steps enter the email address in the letterhead.

1 Press the SPACEBAR.

2 Type **Email: applepark@world.com** to finish the text in the letterhead (Figure 3–32).

Figure 3–32

BTW

Inserting Special Characters
In addition to symbols, you can insert a variety of special characters, including dashes, hyphens, spaces, apostrophes, and quotation marks. Click the Special Characters tab in the Symbol dialog box (shown in Figure 3–30), click the desired character in the Character list, click the Insert button, and then click the Close button (Symbol dialog box).

To Bottom Border a Paragraph

1 CREATE & FORMAT LETTERHEAD WITH GRAPHICS | 2 SPECIFY LETTER FORMATS

3 INSERT TABLE | 4 FORMAT TABLE | 5 INSERT BULLETED LIST | 6 ADDRESS ENVELOPE

In Word, you can draw a solid line, called a **border**, at any edge of a paragraph. That is, borders may be added above or below a paragraph, to the left or right of a paragraph, or in any combination of these sides.

The letterhead in this project has a border that extends from the left margin to the right margin immediately below the mailing address, phone, and email address information. *Why? The horizontal line separates the letterhead from the rest of the letter.* The following steps add a bottom border to a paragraph.

1

- Display the Home tab.

- With the insertion point in the paragraph to border, click the Borders arrow (Home tab | Paragraph group) to display the Borders gallery (Figure 3–33).

Figure 3–33

● Click Bottom Border in the Borders gallery to place a border below the paragraph containing the insertion point (Figure 3–34).

Figure 3–34

Q&A

If the face of the Borders button displays the border icon I want to use, can I click the Borders button instead of using the Borders arrow?
Yes.

How would I remove an existing border from a paragraph?
If, for some reason, you wanted to remove a border from a paragraph, you would position the insertion point in the paragraph, click the Borders arrow (Home tab | Paragraph group), and then click No Border in the Borders gallery.

Other Ways

1. Click 'Borders and Shading' button (Design tab | Page Background group), click Borders tab (Borders and Shading dialog box), select desired border options, click OK button

To Clear Formatting

1 CREATE & FORMAT LETTERHEAD WITH GRAPHICS | 2 SPECIFY LETTER FORMATS
3 INSERT TABLE | 4 FORMAT TABLE | 5 INSERT BULLETED LIST | 6 ADDRESS ENVELOPE

The next step is to position the insertion point below the letterhead, so that you can type the contents of the letter. When you press the ENTER key at the end of a paragraph containing a border, Word moves the border forward to the next paragraph. The paragraph also retains all current settings, such as the center format. Instead, you want the paragraph and characters on the new line to use the Normal style: black font with no border.

Word uses the term, **clear formatting**, to refer to returning the formats to the Normal style. The following steps clear formatting at the location of the insertion point. ***Why?*** *You do not want to retain the current formatting in the new paragraph.*

● With the insertion point between the email address and paragraph mark at the end of the contact information line (as shown in Figure 3–34), press the ENTER key to move the insertion point and paragraph to the next line (Figure 3–35).

Figure 3–35

2

- Click the 'Clear All Formatting' button (Home tab | Font group) to apply the Normal style to the location of the insertion point (Figure 3–36).

Figure 3–36

Other Ways

1. Click More button in Styles gallery (Home tab | Styles group), click Clear Formatting

2. Click Styles Dialog Box Launcher (Home tab | Styles group), click Clear All in Styles task pane

3. Select text, press CTRL+SPACEBAR, press CTRL+Q

AutoFormat As You Type

As you type text in a document, Word automatically formats some of it for you. For example, when you press the ENTER key or SPACEBAR after typing an email address or web address, Word automatically formats the address as a hyperlink, that is, in a different color and underlined. In Figure 3–35, for example, Word formatted the email address as a hyperlink because you pressed the ENTER key at the end of the line. Table 3–2 outlines commonly used AutoFormat As You Type options and their results.

Table 3–2 Commonly Used AutoFormat As You Type Options

Typed Text	AutoFormat As You Type Feature	Example
Quotation marks or apostrophes	Changes straight quotation marks or apostrophes to curly ones	"the" becomes "the"
Text, a space, one hyphen, one or no spaces, text, space	Changes the hyphen to an en dash	ages 20-45 becomes ages 20–45
Text, two hyphens, text, space	Changes the two hyphens to an em dash	Two types--yellow and red becomes Two types—yellow and red
Web or email address followed by SPACEBAR or ENTER key	Formats web or email address as a hyperlink	www.cengagebrain.com becomes www.cengagebrain.com
Number followed by a period, hyphen, right parenthesis, or greater than sign and then a space or tab followed by text	Creates a numbered list	1. Word 2. PowerPoint becomes 1. Word 2. PowerPoint
Asterisk, hyphen, or greater than sign and then a space or tab followed by text	Creates a bulleted list	* Home tab * Insert tab becomes • Home tab • Insert tab
Fraction and then a space or hyphen	Condenses the fraction entry so that it consumes one space instead of three	1/2 becomes ½
Ordinal and then a space or hyphen	Makes part of the ordinal a superscript	3rd becomes 3rd

To Convert a Hyperlink to Regular Text

The email address in the letterhead should be formatted as regular text; that is, it should not be a different color or underlined. *Why? Hyperlinks are useful only in online documents, and this letter will be printed instead of distributed electronically.* The following steps remove a hyperlink format.

- Right-click the hyperlink (in this case, the email address) to display a shortcut menu (or, if using a touch screen, press and hold the hyperlink and then tap the 'Show Context Menu' button on the mini toolbar) (Figure 3–37).

Figure 3–37

- Click Remove Hyperlink on the shortcut menu to remove the hyperlink format from the text.
- Position the insertion point on the paragraph mark below the border because you are finished with the letterhead (Figure 3–38).

Q&A

Could I have used the AutoCorrect Options button instead of the Remove Hyperlink command?
Yes. Alternatively, you could have pointed to the small blue box at the beginning of the hyperlink, clicked the AutoCorrect Options button, and then clicked Undo Hyperlink on the AutoCorrect Options menu.

Figure 3–38

- Save the letterhead again on the same storage location with the same file name.

Other Ways

1. With insertion point in hyperlink, click 'Add a Hyperlink' button (Insert tab | Links group), click Remove Link button

Break Point: If you wish to take a break, this is a good place to do so. You can exit Word now. To resume at a later time, run Word, open the file called Apple Park Letterhead, and continue following the steps from this location forward.

Creating a Business Letter

With the letterhead for the business letter complete, the next task is to create the remainder of the content in the letter. The following sections use Word to create a business letter that contains a table and a bulleted list.

What should you consider when writing a business letter?

A finished business letter should look like a symmetrically framed picture with evenly spaced margins, all balanced below an attractive letterhead. The letter should be well written, properly formatted, logically organized, and use visuals where appropriate. The content of a letter should contain proper grammar, correct spelling, logically constructed sentences, flowing paragraphs, and sound ideas.

Be sure to include all essential elements, use proper spacing and formats, and determine which letter style to use.

- **Include all essential letter elements.** All business letters contain the same basic elements, including the date line, inside address, message, and signature block (shown in Figure 3–1 at the beginning of this module). If a business letter does not use a letterhead, then the top of the letter should include return address information in a heading.

- **Use proper spacing and formats for the contents of the letter below the letterhead.** Use a font that is easy to read, in a size between 8 and 12 point. Add emphasis with bold, italic, and bullets where appropriate, and use tables to present numeric information. Paragraphs should be single-spaced, with double-spacing between paragraphs.

- **Determine which letter style to use.** You can follow many different styles when creating business letters. A letter style specifies guidelines for the alignment and spacing of elements in the business letter.

If possible, keep the length of a business letter to one page. Be sure to proofread the finished letter carefully.

To Save a Document with a New File Name

The current open file has the name Apple Park Letterhead, which is the name of the organization letterhead. Because you want the letterhead file to remain intact so that you can reuse it, you save the document with a new file name. The following step saves a document with a new file name. For a detailed example of the procedure summarized below, refer to the Office and Windows module at the beginning of this book.

 Save the letter on your hard drive, OneDrive, or other storage location using a new file name, Lee Vendor Letter.

To Apply a Style

1 CREATE & FORMAT LETTERHEAD WITH GRAPHICS | **2 SPECIFY LETTER FORMATS**
3 INSERT TABLE | 4 FORMAT TABLE | 5 INSERT BULLETED LIST | 6 ADDRESS ENVELOPE

Recall that the Normal style in Word places 8 points of blank space after each paragraph and inserts a vertical space equal to 1.08 lines between each line of text. You will need to modify the spacing used for the paragraphs in the business letter. **Why?** *Business letters should use single spacing for paragraphs and double spacing between paragraphs.*

Word has many built-in, or predefined, styles that you can use to format text. The No Spacing style, for example, defines line spacing as single and does not insert any additional blank space between lines when you press the ENTER key. To apply a style to a paragraph, you first position the insertion point in the paragraph. The following step applies the No Spacing style to a paragraph.

1

- With the insertion point positioned in the paragraph to be formatted, click No Spacing in the Styles gallery (Home tab | Styles group) to apply the selected style to the current paragraph (Figure 3–39).

Q&A

Will this style be used in the rest of the document?

Yes. The paragraph formatting, which includes the style, will carry forward to subsequent paragraphs each time you press the ENTER key.

Figure 3–39

Other Ways

1. Click Styles Dialog Box Launcher (Home tab | Styles group), click desired style in Styles task pane

2. Press CTRL+SHIFT+S, click Style Name arrow in Apply Styles task pane, click desired style in list

CONSIDER THIS

What elements should a business letter contain?

Be sure to include all essential business letter elements, properly spaced, in your letter:

- The **date line**, which consists of the month, day, and year, is positioned two to six lines below the letterhead.

- The **inside address**, placed three to eight lines below the date line, usually contains the addressee's courtesy title plus full name, job title, business affiliation, and full geographical address.

- The **salutation**, if present, begins two lines below the last line of the inside address. If you do not know the recipient's name, avoid using the salutation "To whom it may concern" — it is impersonal. Instead, use the recipient's title in the salutation, e.g., Dear Personnel Director. In a business letter, use a colon (:) at the end of the salutation; in a personal letter, use a comma.

- The body of the letter, the **message**, begins two lines below the salutation. Within the message, paragraphs are single-spaced with one blank line between paragraphs.

- Two lines below the last line of the message, the **complimentary close** is displayed. Capitalize only the first word in a complimentary close.

- Type the **signature block** at least four blank lines below the complimentary close, allowing room for the author to sign his or her name.

CONSIDER THIS

What are the common styles of business letters?

Three common business letter styles are the block, the modified block, and the modified semi-block. Each style specifies different alignments and indentations.

- In the block letter style, all components of the letter begin flush with the left margin.

- In the modified block letter style, the date, complimentary close, and signature block are positioned approximately one-half inch to the right of center or at the right margin. All other components of the letter begin flush with the left margin.

- In the modified semi-block letter style, the date, complimentary close, and signature block are centered, positioned approximately one-half inch to the right of center or at the right margin. The first line of each paragraph in the body of the letter is indented one-half to one inch from the left margin. All other components of the letter begin flush with the left margin.

The business letter in this project follows the modified block style.

Using Tab Stops to Align Text

A **tab stop** is a location on the horizontal ruler that tells Word where to position the insertion point when you press the TAB key on the keyboard. Word, by default, places a tab stop at every one-half inch mark on the ruler. You also can set your own custom tab stops. Tab settings are a paragraph format. Thus, each time you press the ENTER key, any custom tab stops are carried forward to the next paragraph.

To move the insertion point from one tab stop to another, press the TAB key on the keyboard. When you press the TAB key, a **tab character** formatting mark appears in the empty space between the tab stops.

When you set a custom tab stop, you specify how the text will align at a tab stop. The tab marker on the ruler reflects the alignment of the characters at the location of the tab stop. Table 3–3 shows types of tab stop alignments in Word and their corresponding tab markers.

Table 3–3 Types of Tab Stop Alignments

Tab Stop Alignment	Tab Marker	Result of Pressing TAB Key	Example
Left Tab	⌞	Left-aligns text at the location of the tab stop	toolbar ruler
Center Tab	⊥	Centers text at the location of the tab stop	toolbar ruler
Right Tab	⌟	Right-aligns text at the location of the tab stop	toolbar ruler
Decimal Tab	⊥	Aligns text on decimal point at the location of the tab stop	45.72 223.75
Bar Tab	I	Aligns text at a bar character at the location of the tab stop	toolbar ruler

To Display the Ruler

One way to set custom tab stops is by using the horizontal ruler. Thus, the following steps display the ruler in the document window.

1 If the rulers are not showing, display the View tab.

2 Click the View Ruler check box (View tab | Show group) to place a check mark in the check box and display the horizontal and vertical rulers on the screen (shown in Figure 3–40).

1 CREATE & FORMAT LETTERHEAD WITH GRAPHICS | **2 SPECIFY LETTER FORMATS**
3 INSERT TABLE | 4 FORMAT TABLE | 5 INSERT BULLETED LIST | 6 ADDRESS ENVELOPE

To Set Custom Tab Stops

The first required element of the business letter is the date line, which in this letter is positioned two lines below the letterhead. The date line contains the month, day, and year, and begins four inches from the left margin. ***Why?*** *Business letter guidelines specify to begin the date line approximately one-half inch to the right of center. Thus, you should set a custom tab stop at the 4" mark on the ruler.* The following steps set a left-aligned tab stop.

● With the insertion point on the paragraph mark below the border (shown in Figure 3–39), press the ENTER key so that a blank line appears above the insertion point.

● If necessary, click the tab selector at the left edge of the horizontal ruler until it displays the type of tab you wish to use, which is the Left Tab icon in this case.

● Position the pointer on the 4" mark on the ruler, which is the location of the desired custom tab stop (Figure 3–40).

Q&A What is the purpose of the tab selector?
Before using the ruler to set a tab stop, ensure the correct tab stop icon appears in the tab selector. Each time you click the tab selector, its icon changes. The Left Tab icon is the default. For a list of the types of tab stops, see Table 3–3.

Figure 3–40

● Click the 4" mark on the ruler to place a tab marker at that location (Figure 3–41).

Q&A What if I click the wrong location on the ruler?
You can move a custom tab stop by dragging the tab marker to the desired location on the ruler. Or, you can remove an existing custom tab stop by pointing to the tab marker on the ruler and then dragging the tab marker down and out of the ruler.

What if I am using a touch screen?
Display the Home tab, tap the Paragraph Settings Dialog Box Launcher (Home tab | Paragraph group), tap the Tabs button (Paragraph dialog box), type **4** in the Tab stop position box (Tabs dialog box), tap the Set button, and then tap the OK button to set a custom tab stop and place a corresponding tab marker on the ruler.

Figure 3–41

Other Ways

1. Click Paragraph Dialog Box Launcher (Home tab or Layout tab | Paragraph group), click Tabs button (Paragraph dialog box), type tab stop position (Tabs dialog box), click Set button, click OK button

To Insert the Current Date in a Document

The next step is to enter the current date at the 4" tab stop in the document. *Why? The date in this letter will be positioned according to the guidelines for a modified block style letter.* In Word, you can insert a computer's system date in a document. The following steps insert the current date in the letter.

1

- Press the TAB key to position the insertion point at the location of the tab stop in the current paragraph.

- Display the Insert tab.

- Click the 'Insert Date and Time' button (Insert tab | Text group) to display the Date and Time dialog box.

- Select the desired format (Date and Time dialog box), in this case October 2, 2017.

- If the Update automatically check box is selected, click the check box to remove the check mark (Figure 3–42).

Q&A | Why should the Update automatically check box not be selected?
In this project, the date at the top of the letter always should show today's date (for example, October 2, 2017). If, however, you wanted the date always to change to reflect the current computer date (for example, showing the date you open or print the letter), then you would place a check mark in this check box.

Figure 3–42

2

- Click the OK button to insert the current date at the location of the insertion point (Figure 3–43).

Figure 3–43

To Enter the Inside Address and Salutation

The next step in composing the business letter is to type the inside address and salutation. The following steps enter this text.

1 With the insertion point at the end of the date (shown in Figure 3–43), press the ENTER key three times.

2 Type **Ms. Tamara Lee** and then press the ENTER key.

3 Type **Tam's Artistic Designs** and then press the ENTER key.

4 Type **1587 Willow Road** and then press the ENTER key.

5 Type **Juniper, MT 33522** and then press the ENTER key twice.

6 Type **Dear Ms. Lee:** to complete the inside address and salutation entries. Scroll up, if necessary (Figure 3–44).

Figure 3–44

To Create a Building Block

1 CREATE & FORMAT LETTERHEAD WITH GRAPHICS | 2 SPECIFY LETTER FORMATS
3 INSERT TABLE | 4 FORMAT TABLE | 5 INSERT BULLETED LIST | 6 ADDRESS ENVELOPE

If you use the same text or graphic frequently, you can store the text or graphic as a **building block** and then insert the stored building block entry in the open document, as well as in future documents. That is, you can create the entry once as a building block and then insert the building block when you need it. In this way, you avoid entering text or graphics inconsistently or incorrectly in different locations throughout the same or multiple documents.

The following steps create a building block for the vendor business name, Tam's Artistic Designs. *Why?* *Later, you will insert the building block in the document instead of typing the vendor business name again.*

1

• Select the text to be a building block, in this case Tam's Artistic Designs. Do not select the paragraph mark at the end of the text because you do not want the paragraph to be part of the building block.

Q&A Why is the paragraph mark not part of the building block?
Select the paragraph mark only if you want to store paragraph formatting, such as indentation and line spacing, as part of the building block.

- Click the 'Explore Quick Parts' button (Insert tab | Text group) to display the Explore Quick Parts gallery (Figure 3–45).

Figure 3–45

- Click 'Save Selection to Quick Part Gallery' in the Explore Quick Parts gallery to display the Create New Building Block dialog box.
- Type **tad** in the Name text box (Create New Building Block dialog box) to replace the proposed building block name (Tam's Artistic, in this case) with a shorter building block name (Figure 3–46).

- Click the OK button to store the building block entry and close the dialog box.
- If Word displays another dialog box, click the Yes button to save changes to the building blocks.

Figure 3–46

Q&A Will this building block be available in future documents?
When you exit Word, a dialog box may appear asking if you want to save changes to the building blocks. Click the Save button if you want to use the new building block in future documents.

1 CREATE & FORMAT LETTERHEAD WITH GRAPHICS | 2 SPECIFY LETTER FORMATS
3 INSERT TABLE | 4 FORMAT TABLE | 5 INSERT BULLETED LIST | 6 ADDRESS ENVELOPE

To Modify a Building Block

When you save a building block in the Explore Quick Parts gallery, the building block is displayed at the top of the Explore Quick Parts gallery. When you point to the building block in the Explore Quick Parts gallery, a ScreenTip displays the building block name. If you want to display more information when the user points to the building block, you can include a description in the ScreenTip.

The following steps modify a building block to include a description and change its category to AutoText. **Why?** *Because you want to reuse this text, you place it in the AutoText gallery, which also is accessible through the Explore Quick Parts gallery.*

1

- Click the 'Explore Quick Parts' button (Insert tab | Text group) to display the Explore Quick Parts gallery.

- Right-click the Tam's Artistic Design building block to display a shortcut menu (Figure 3–47).

Figure 3–47

2

- Click Edit Properties on the shortcut menu to display the Modify Building Block dialog box, filled in with information related to the selected building block.

- Click the Gallery arrow (Modify Building Block dialog box) and then click AutoText to change the gallery in which the building block will be placed.

- Type **Event Vendor** in the Description text box (Figure 3–48).

3

- Click the OK button to store the building block entry and close the dialog box.

- Click the Yes button when asked if you want to redefine the building block entry.

Figure 3–48

To Insert a Building Block

1 CREATE & FORMAT LETTERHEAD WITH GRAPHICS | 2 SPECIFY LETTER FORMATS
3 INSERT TABLE | 4 FORMAT TABLE | 5 INSERT BULLETED LIST | 6 ADDRESS ENVELOPE

The vendor business name, Tam's Artistic Designs, appears in the first sentence in the body of the letter. You will type the building block name, tad, and then instruct Word to replace this building block name with the stored building block entry, Tam's Artistic Designs. The following steps insert a building block. *Why? Instead of typing the name, you will insert the stored building block.*

1

- Click to the right of the colon in the salutation and then press the ENTER key twice to position the insertion point one blank line below the salutation.

- Type the beginning of the first sentence as follows, entering the building block name as shown: **The park district board has approved the vendor application for your business, tad** (Figure 3–49).

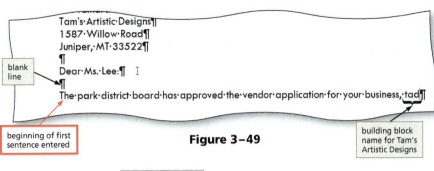

blank line

beginning of first sentence entered

building block name for Tam's Artistic Designs

Figure 3–49

2

- Press the F3 key to instruct Word to replace the building block name (tad) with the stored building block entry (Tam's Artistic Designs).

- Press the PERIOD key (Figure 3–50).

stored building block entry inserted in document

insertion point

Figure 3–50

Other Ways

1. Click 'Explore Quick Parts' button (Insert tab | Text group), if necessary point to AutoText, select desired building block

2. Click 'Explore Quick Parts' button (Insert tab | Text group), click Building Blocks Organizer, select desired building block, click Insert button

Building Blocks versus AutoCorrect

In Module 2, you learned how to use the AutoCorrect feature, which enables you to insert and create AutoCorrect entries, similarly to how you created and inserted building blocks in this module. The difference between an AutoCorrect entry and a building block entry is that the AutoCorrect feature makes corrections for you automatically as soon as you press the SPACEBAR or type a punctuation mark, whereas you must instruct Word to insert a building block. That is, you enter the building block name and then press the F3 key, or click the Explore Quick Parts button and select the building block from one of the galleries or the Building Blocks Organizer.

To Insert a Nonbreaking Space

1 CREATE & FORMAT LETTERHEAD WITH GRAPHICS | 2 SPECIFY LETTER FORMATS

3 INSERT TABLE | 4 FORMAT TABLE | 5 INSERT BULLETED LIST | 6 ADDRESS ENVELOPE

Some compound words, such as proper nouns, dates, units of time and measure, abbreviations, and geographic destinations, should not be divided at the end of a line. These words either should fit as a unit at the end of a line or be wrapped together to the next line.

Word provides two special characters to assist with this task: the nonbreaking space and the nonbreaking hyphen. A **nonbreaking space** is a special space character that prevents two words from splitting if the first word falls at the end of a line. Similarly, a **nonbreaking hyphen** is a special type of hyphen that prevents two words separated by a hyphen from splitting at the end of a line.

The following steps insert a nonbreaking space between the two words, Fall Festival. ***Why?*** *You want these two words to appear on the same physical line.*

- With the insertion point at the end of the first sentence in the body of the letter (as shown in Figure 3–50), press the SPACEBAR.

- Type **Your check for $150 for a 10 x 20 booth has been deposited, and we are excited that you will be participating in our Fall** and then press CTRL+SHIFT+SPACEBAR to insert a nonbreaking space after the entered word (Figure 3–51).

Figure 3–51

- Type **Festival** and then press PERIOD key (Figure 3–52).

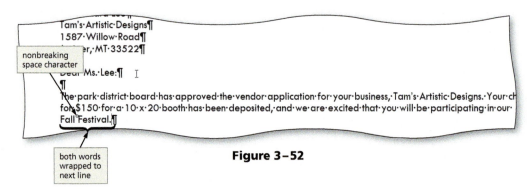

Figure 3–52

Other Ways

1. Click 'Insert a Symbol' button (Insert tab | Symbols group), click More Symbols, click Special Characters tab (Symbol dialog box), click Nonbreaking Space in Character list, click Insert button, click Close button

BTW

Nonbreaking Hyphen

If you wanted to insert a nonbreaking hyphen, you would press CTRL+SHIFT+HYPHEN.

To Enter Text

The next step in creating the letter is to enter the rest of the text in the first paragraph. The following steps enter this text.

1 Press the SPACEBAR.

2 Type this sentence: **The table below outlines the timetable for vendors:**

3 Press the ENTER key twice to place a blank line between paragraphs (shown in Figure 3–53).

Q&A Why does my document wrap on different words?
Differences in wordwrap may relate to the printer connected to your computer. Thus, it is possible that the same document could wordwrap differently if associated with a different printer.

4 Save the letterhead again on the same storage location with the same file name.

Break Point: If you wish to take a break, this is a good place to do so. You can exit Word now. To resume at a later time, run Word, open the file called Lee Vendor Letter, and continue following the steps from this location forward.

Tables

The next step in composing the business letter is to place a table listing the vendor timetable (shown in Figure 3–1). A Word **table** is a collection of rows and columns. The intersection of a row and a column is called a **cell**, and cells are filled with data.

The first step in creating a table is to insert an empty table in the document. When inserting a table, you must specify the total number of rows and columns required, which is called the **dimension** of the table. The table in this project has three columns. You often do not know the total number of rows in a table. Thus, many Word users create one row initially and then add more rows as needed. In Word, the first number in a dimension is the number of columns, and the second is the number of rows. For example, in Word, a 3 × 1 (pronounced "three by one") table consists of three columns and one row.

To Insert an Empty Table

1 CREATE & FORMAT LETTERHEAD WITH GRAPHICS | 2 SPECIFY LETTER FORMATS

3 INSERT TABLE | 4 FORMAT TABLE | 5 INSERT BULLETED LIST | 6 ADDRESS ENVELOPE

The next step is to insert an empty table in the letter. The following steps insert a table with three columns and one row at the location of the insertion point. *Why? The first column will identify the activity, the second will identify the event dates, and the third will identify the activity times. You will start with one row and add them as needed.*

- Scroll the document so that you will be able to see the table in the document window.

- Display the Insert tab.

- With the insertion point positioned as shown in Figure 3–53, click the 'Add a Table' button (Insert tab | Tables group) to display the Add a Table gallery (Figure 3–53).

Experiment

- Point to various cells on the grid to see a preview of various table dimensions in the document window.

Figure 3–53

- Position the pointer on the cell in the first row and third column of the grid to preview the desired table dimension in the document (Figure 3–54).

Figure 3–54

- Click the cell in the first row and third column of the grid to insert an empty table with one row and three columns in the document.

- If necessary, scroll the document so that the table is visible (Figure 3–55).

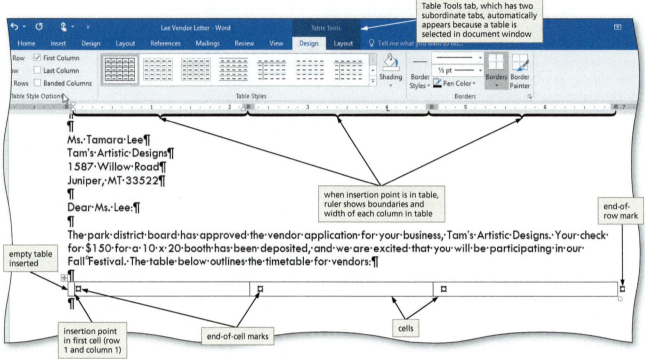

Figure 3–55

What are the small circles in the table cells?

Each table cell has an **end-of-cell mark**, which is a formatting mark that assists you with selecting and formatting cells. Similarly, each row has an **end-of-row mark**, which you can use to add columns to the right of a table. Recall that formatting marks do not print on a hard copy. The end-of-cell marks currently are left-aligned, that is, positioned at the left edge of each cell.

Other Ways

1. Click 'Add a Table' button (Insert tab | Tables group), click Insert Table in Add a Table gallery, enter number of columns and rows (Insert Table dialog box), click OK button

To Enter Data in a Table

The next step is to enter data in the cells of the empty table. The data you enter in a cell wordwraps just as text wordwraps between the margins of a document. To place data in a cell, you click the cell and then type.

To advance rightward from one cell to the next, press the TAB key. When you are at the rightmost cell in a row, press the TAB key to move to the first cell in the next row; do not press the ENTER key. *Why? The ENTER key is used to begin a new paragraph within a cell.* One way to add new rows to a table is to press the TAB key when the insertion point is positioned in the bottom-right corner cell of the table. The following step enters data in the first row of the table and then inserts a blank second row.

- With the insertion point in the left cell of the table, type **Activity** and then press the TAB key to advance the insertion point to the next cell.

- Type **Event Dates** and then press the TAB key to advance the insertion point to the next cell.
- Type **Times** and then press the TAB key to add a second row at the end of the table and position the insertion point in the first column of the new row (Figure 3–56).

Figure 3–56

Q&A How do I edit cell contents if I make a mistake?
Click in the cell and then correct the entry.

To Enter More Data in a Table

The following steps enter the remaining data in the table.

1 Type **Booth Setup** and then press the TAB key to advance the insertion point to the next cell. Type **Friday, October 27** and then press the TAB key to advance the insertion point to the next cell. Type **5:00 to 9:00 p.m.** and then press the TAB key to add a row at the end of the table and position the insertion point in the first column of the new row.

2 In the third row, type **Booth Sales** in the first column, **Saturday, October 28** in the second column, and **9:00 a.m. to 6:00 p.m.** in the third column. Press the TAB key to position the insertion point in the first column of a new row.

3 In the fourth row, type **Booth Sales** in the first column, **Sunday, October 29** in the second column, and **9:00 a.m. to 3:00 p.m.** in the third column. Press the TAB key.

4 In the fifth row, type **Booth Takedown** in the first column, **Sunday, October 29** in the second column, and **3:00 to 7:00 p.m.** in the third column (Figure 3–57).

BTW

Tables
For simple tables, such as the one just created, Word users often select the table dimension in the Add a Table gallery to create the table. For a more complex table, such as one with a varying number of columns per row, Word has a Draw Table feature that allows users to draw a table in the document using a pencil pointer. To use this feature, click the 'Add a Table' button (Insert tab | Tables group) and then click Draw Table on the Add a Table menu.

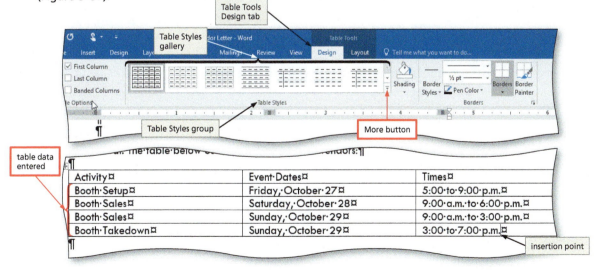

Figure 3–57

To Apply a Table Style

Word provides a gallery of more than 90 table styles, which include a variety of colors and shading. *Why? Table styles allow you to change the basic table format to a more visually appealing style.* The following steps apply a table style to the table in the letter.

- If the First Column check box in the Table Style Options group (Table Tools Design tab) contains a check mark, click the check box to remove the check mark because you do not want the first column in the table formatted differently from the rest of the table. Be sure the remaining check marks match those in the Table Style Options group (Table Tools Design tab) as shown in Figure 3–58.

Q&A

What if the Table Tools Design tab no longer is the active tab?
Click in the table and then display the Table Tools Design tab.

What do the options in the Table Style Options group mean?
When you apply table styles, if you want the top row of the table (header row), a row containing totals (total row), first column, or last column to be formatted differently, select those check boxes. If you want the rows or columns to alternate with colors, select Banded Rows or Banded Columns, respectively.

- With the insertion point in the table, click the More button in the Table Styles gallery (Table Tools Design tab | Table Styles group), shown in Figure 3–57, to expand the gallery.

- Scroll and then point to 'Grid Table 6 Colorful - Accent 3' in the Table Styles gallery to display a live preview of that style applied to the table in the document (Figure 3–58).

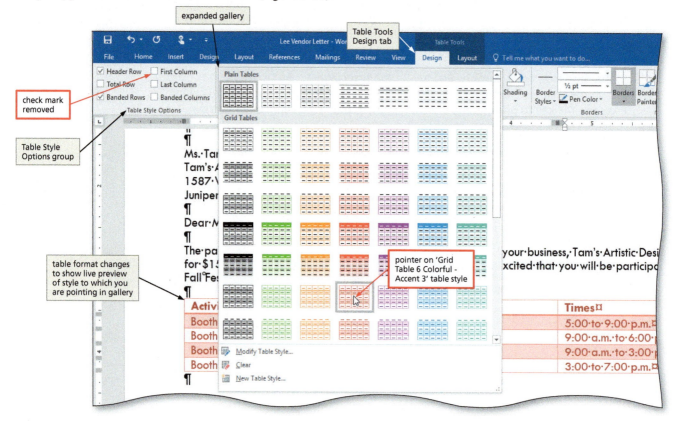

Figure 3–58

Experiment

- Point to various styles in the Table Styles gallery and watch the format of the table change in the document window.

③

- Click 'Grid Table 6 Colorful - Accent 3' in the Table Styles gallery to apply the selected style to the table. Scroll up, if necessary (Figure 3–59).

🔎 **Experiment**

- Select and remove check marks from various check boxes in the Table Style Options group and watch the format of the table change in the document window. When finished experimenting, be sure the check marks match those shown in Figure 3–58.

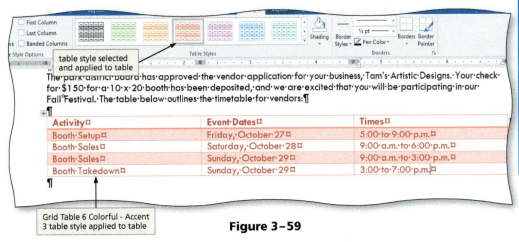

Figure 3–59

To Resize Table Columns to Fit Table Contents

1 CREATE & FORMAT LETTERHEAD WITH GRAPHICS | 2 SPECIFY LETTER FORMATS
3 INSERT TABLE | 4 FORMAT TABLE | 5 INSERT BULLETED LIST | 6 ADDRESS ENVELOPE

The table in this project currently extends from the left margin to the right margin of the document. The following steps instruct Word to fit the width of the columns to the contents of the table automatically. *Why? You want each column to be only as wide as the longest entry in the table. That is, the first column must be wide enough to accommodate the words, Booth Takedown, and the second column should be only as wide as the words, Saturday, October 28, and so on.*

①

- With the insertion point in the table, display the Table Tools Layout tab.

- Click the AutoFit button (Table Tools Layout tab | Cell Size group) to display the AutoFit menu (Figure 3–60).

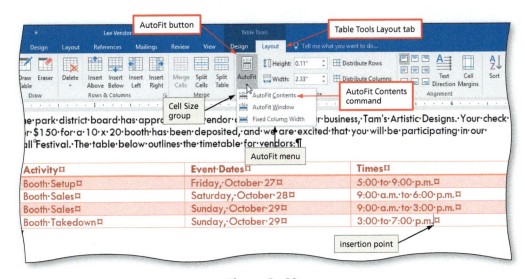

Figure 3–60

②

- Click AutoFit Contents on the AutoFit menu, so that Word automatically adjusts the widths of the columns based on the text in the table (Figure 3–61).

Figure 3–61

Can I resize columns manually?

Yes, you can drag a **column boundary**, the border to the right of a column, until the column is the desired width. Similarly, you can resize a row by dragging the **row boundary**, the border at the bottom of a row, until the row is the desired height. You also can resize the entire table by dragging the **table resize handle**, which is a small square that appears when you point to a corner of the table.

What causes the table move handle and table resize handle to appear and disappear from the table?

They appear whenever you position the pointer in the table.

Other Ways

1. Double-click column boundary

To Select a Column

1 CREATE & FORMAT LETTERHEAD WITH GRAPHICS | 2 SPECIFY LETTER FORMATS
3 INSERT TABLE | **4 FORMAT TABLE** | **5 INSERT BULLETED LIST** | **6 ADDRESS ENVELOPE**

The next task is to change the alignment of the data in cells in the third column of the table. To do this, you first must select the column. *Why? If you want to format the contents of a single cell, simply position the insertion point in the cell. To format a series of cells, you first must select them.* The following step selects a column.

1

- Position the pointer at the boundary above the column to be selected, the third column in this case, so that the pointer changes to a downward pointing arrow and then click to select the column (Figure 3–62).

 What if I am using a touch screen?

Position the insertion point in the third column, tap the Select Table button (Table Tools Layout tab | Table group), and then tap Select Column on the Select Table menu.

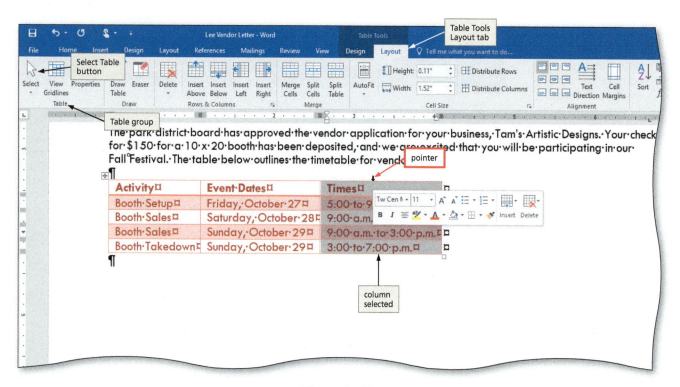

Figure 3–62

Other Ways

1. Click Select Table button (Table Tools Layout tab | Table group), click Select Column in Select Table gallery

Selecting Table Contents

When working with tables, you may need to select the contents of cells, rows, columns, or the entire table. Table 3–4 identifies ways to select various items in a table.

Table 3–4 Selecting Items in a Table	
Item to Select	**Action**
Cell	Point to left edge of cell and then click when the pointer changes to a small solid upward angled pointing arrow. Or Position insertion point in cell, click Select Table button (Table Tools Layout tab | Table group), and then click Select Cell on the Select Table menu.
Column	Point to border at top of column and then click when the pointer changes to a small solid downward-pointing arrow. Or Position insertion point in column, click Select Table button (Table Tools Layout tab | Table group), and then click Select Column on the Select Table menu.
Row	Point to the left of the row and then click when pointer changes to a right-pointing block arrow. Or Position insertion point in row, click Select Table button (Table Tools Layout tab | Table group), and then click Select Row on the Select Table menu.
Multiple cells, rows, or columns adjacent to one another	Drag through cells, rows, or columns.
Multiple cells, rows, or columns not adjacent to one another	Select first cell, row, or column (as described above) and then hold down CTRL key while selecting next cell, row, or column.
Next cell	Press TAB key.
Previous cell	Press SHIFT+TAB
Table	Point somewhere in table and then click table move handle that appears in upper-left corner of table (shown in Figure 3-63). Or Position insertion point in table, click Select Table button (Table Tools Layout tab | Table group), and then click Select Table on the Select Table menu.

BTW

Word Help

At any time while using Word, you can find answers to questions and display information about various topics through Word Help. Used properly, this form of assistance can increase your productivity and reduce your frustrations by minimizing the time you spend learning how to use Word. For instructions about Word Help and exercises that will help you gain confidence in using it, read the Office and Windows module at the beginning of this book.

1 CREATE & FORMAT LETTERHEAD WITH GRAPHICS | 2 SPECIFY LETTER FORMATS
3 INSERT TABLE | **4 FORMAT TABLE** | 5 INSERT BULLETED LIST | 6 ADDRESS ENVELOPE

To Align Data in Cells

The next step is to change the alignment of the data in cells in the third column of the table. In addition to aligning text horizontally in a cell (left, center, or right), you can align it vertically within a cell (top, center, bottom). When the height of the cell is close to the same height as the text, however, differences in vertical alignment are not readily apparent, which is the case for this table. The following step centers data in cells. *Why?* *The column containing the times would look better if its contents are centered.*

1

- With the cells (column) selected, as shown in Figure 3–62, click the desired alignment, in this case the 'Align Top Center' button (Table Tools Layout tab | Alignment group) to center the contents of the selected cells (Figure 3–63).

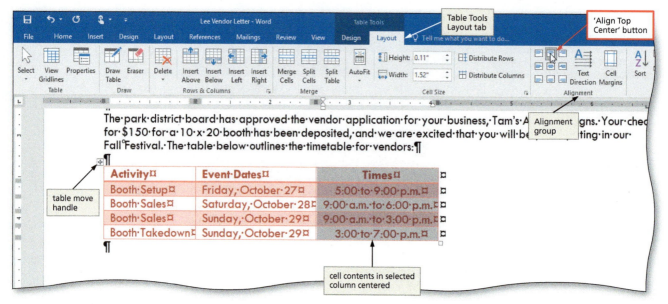

Figure 3–63

To Center a Table

1 CREATE & FORMAT LETTERHEAD WITH GRAPHICS | 2 SPECIFY LETTER FORMATS
3 INSERT TABLE | 4 FORMAT TABLE | 5 INSERT BULLETED LIST | 6 ADDRESS ENVELOPE

When you first create a table, it is left-aligned; that is, it is flush with the left margin. In this letter, the entire table should be centered between the margins of the page. To center a table, you first select the entire table. The following steps select and center a table using the mini toolbar. *Why? Recall that you can use buttons and boxes on the mini toolbar instead of those on the ribbon.*

1

- Position the pointer in the table so that the table move handle appears (shown in Figure 3–63).

Q&A What if the table move handle does not appear?
You also can select a table by clicking the Select Table button (Table Tools Layout tab | Table group) and then clicking Select Table on the menu.

2

- Click the table move handle to select the entire table (Figure 3–64).

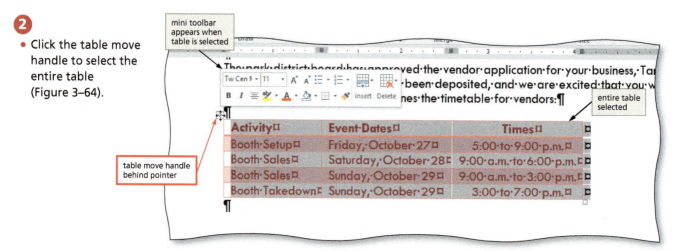

Figure 3–64

What if I am using a touch screen?

Tap the Select Table button (Table Tools Layout tab | Table group) and then tap Select Table on the Select Table menu to select the table.

3

- Click the Center button on the mini toolbar to center the selected table between the left and right page margins (Figure 3–65).

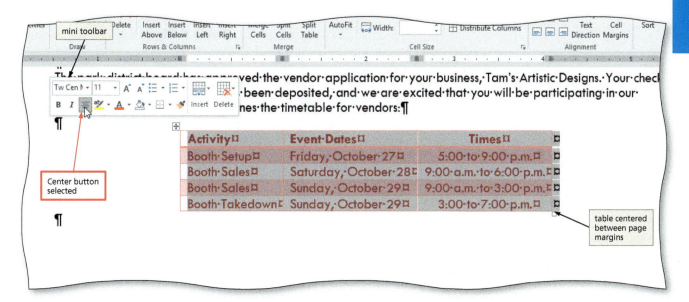

Figure 3–65

Could I have clicked the Center button on the Home tab?

Yes. If the command you want to use is not on the currently displayed tab on the ribbon and it is available on the mini toolbar, use the mini toolbar instead of switching to a different tab. This technique minimizes mouse movement.

What if I am using a touch screen?

Display the Home tab and then tap the Center button (Home tab | Paragraph group) to center the table.

To Insert a Row in a Table

1 CREATE & FORMAT LETTERHEAD WITH GRAPHICS | 2 SPECIFY LETTER FORMATS

3 INSERT TABLE | 4 FORMAT TABLE | 5 INSERT BULLETED LIST | 6 ADDRESS ENVELOPE

The next step is to insert a row at the top of the table. *Why? You want to place a title on the table.* As discussed earlier, you can insert a row at the end of a table by positioning the insertion point in the bottom-right corner cell and then pressing the TAB key. You cannot use the TAB key to insert a row at the beginning or middle of a table. Instead, you use the 'Insert Rows Above' or 'Insert Rows Below' command (Table Tools Layout tab | Rows & Columns group) or the Insert Control (shown in Figure 3–70). The following steps insert a row at the top of a table.

• Position the insertion point somewhere in the first row of the table because you want to insert a row above this row (Figure 3–66).

Figure 3–66

• Click the 'Insert Rows Above' button (Table Tools Layout tab | Rows & Columns group) to insert a row above the row containing the insertion point and then select the newly inserted row (Figure 3–67).

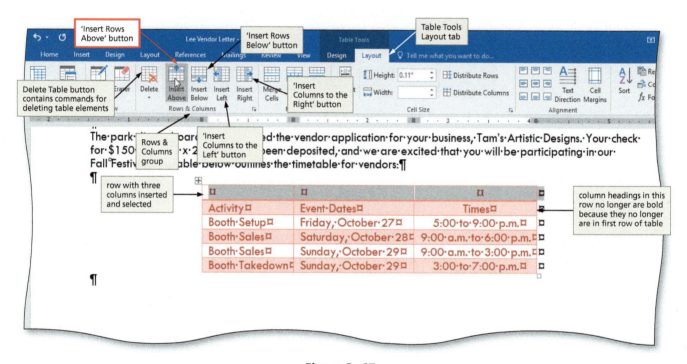

Figure 3–67

Q&A

Do I have to insert rows above the row containing the insertion point?

No. You can insert below the row containing the insertion point by clicking the 'Insert Rows Below' button (Table Tools Layout tab | Rows & Columns group).

Why did the colors in the second row change?

The table style specifies to format the header row differently, which is the first row.

Other Ways

1. Point to the left of the table and click the desired Insert Control

2. Right-click row, point to Insert on shortcut menu (or, if using touch, tap Insert Table button on mini toolbar), click desired option on Insert submenu

BTW

Resizing Table Columns and Rows
To change the width of a column or height of a row to an exact measurement, hold down the ALT key while dragging markers on the ruler. Or, enter values in the 'Table Column Width' or 'Table Row Height' boxes (Table Tools Layout tab | Cell Size group).

TO INSERT A COLUMN IN A TABLE

If you wanted to insert a column in a table, instead of inserting rows, you would perform the following steps.

1. Point above the table and then click the desired Insert Control.

or

1. Position the insertion point in the column to the left or right of where you want to insert the column.

2. Click the 'Insert Columns to the Left' button (Table Tools Layout tab | Rows & Columns group) to insert a column to the left of the current column, or click the 'Insert Columns to the Right' button (Table Tools Layout tab | Rows & Columns group) to insert a column to the right of the current column.

or

1. Right-click the table, point to Insert on the shortcut menu (or, if using touch, tap Insert Table button on the mini toolbar), and then click 'Insert Columns to the Left' or 'Insert Columns to the Right' on the Insert submenu (or, if using touch, tap Insert Left or Insert Right).

To Merge Cells

1 CREATE & FORMAT LETTERHEAD WITH GRAPHICS | 2 SPECIFY LETTER FORMATS
3 INSERT TABLE | 4 FORMAT TABLE | 5 INSERT BULLETED LIST | 6 ADDRESS ENVELOPE

The row just inserted has one cell for each column, in this case, three cells (shown in Figure 3–67). The top row of the table, however, is to be a single cell that spans all rows. *Why?* *The top row contains the table title, which should be centered above the columns of the table.* Thus, the following steps merge the three cells into a single cell.

- With the cells to merge selected (as shown in Figure 3–67), click the Merge Cells button (Table Tools Layout tab | Merge group) to merge the selected cells into a single cell (Figure 3–68).

Figure 3–68

2

- Position the insertion point in the first row and then type **Vendor Timetable** as the table title (Figure 3–69).

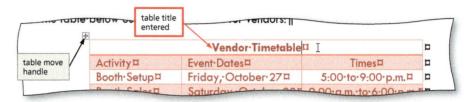

Figure 3–69

Other Ways

1. Right-click selected cells (or, if using touch, tap 'Show Context Menu' button on mini toolbar), click Merge Cells on shortcut menu

---

BTW

Moving Tables

If you wanted to move a table to a new location, you would point to the upper-left corner of the table until the table move handle appears (shown in Figure 3–69), point to the table move handle, and then drag it to move the entire table to a new location.

TO SPLIT TABLE CELLS

Instead of merging multiple cells into a single cell, sometimes you want to split a single cell into multiple cells. If you wanted to split cells, you would perform the following steps.

1. Position the insertion point in the cell to split.
2. Click the Split Cells button (Table Tools Layout tab | Merge group) (or, if using touch, tap 'Show Context Menu' button on mini toolbar), or right-click the cell and then click Split Cells on the shortcut menu, to display the Split Cells dialog box.
3. Enter the number of columns and rows into which you want the cell split (Split Cells dialog box).
4. Click the OK button.

BTW

Tab Character in Tables

In a table, the TAB key advances the insertion point from one cell to the next. To insert a tab character in a cell, you must press CTRL+TAB.

TO SPLIT A TABLE

Instead of splitting table cells into multiple cells, sometimes you want to split a single table into multiple cells. If you wanted to split a table, you would perform the following steps.

1. Position the insertion point in the cell where you want the table to be split.
2. Click the Split Table button (Table Tools Layout tab | Merge group) to split the table into two tables at the location of the insertion point.

To Change the Font of Text in a Table Row

When you added a row to the top of the table for the title, Word moved the bold format from the column headings (which originally were in the first row of the table) to the title row (which now is the first row). Because you would like the columns headings bold also, the following steps select a table row and bold its contents.

1 Select the row containing the column headings (Figure 3–70).

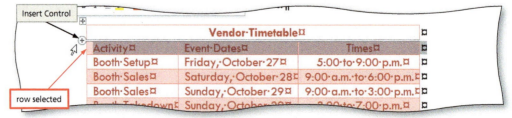

Figure 3–70

2 With the text selected, click the Bold button (Home tab | Font group) to bold the selected text.

What is the symbol that appeared to the left of the table?

When you select a row or column in a table, Word displays an Insert Control. You can click the **Insert Control** to add a row or column to the table at that location.

Deleting Table Data

If you want to delete row(s) or delete column(s) from a table, position the insertion point in the row(s) or column(s) to delete, click the Delete Table button (Table Tools Layout tab | Rows & Columns group), and then click Delete Rows or Delete Columns on the Delete Table menu. Or, select the row or column to delete, right-click the selection, and then click Delete Rows or Delete Columns on the mini toolbar or shortcut menu.

To delete the contents of a cell, select the cell contents and then press the DELETE or BACKSPACE key. You also can drag and drop or cut and paste the contents of cells. To delete an entire table, select the table, click the Delete Table button (Table Tools Layout tab | Rows & Columns group), and then click Delete Table on the Delete Table menu. To delete the contents of a table and leave an empty table, you would select the table and then press the DELETE key.

To Add More Text

The table now is complete. The next step is to enter text below the table. The following steps enter text.

1 Position the insertion point on the paragraph mark below the table and then press the ENTER key.

2 Type **Please note the following vendor guidelines:** and then press the ENTER key (shown in Figure 3–71).

To Bullet a List as You Type

1 CREATE & FORMAT LETTERHEAD WITH GRAPHICS | 2 SPECIFY LETTER FORMATS
3 INSERT TABLE | 4 FORMAT TABLE | **5 INSERT BULLETED LIST** | 6 ADDRESS ENVELOPE

In Module 1, you learned how to apply bullets to existing paragraphs. If you know before you type that a list should be bulleted, you can use Word's AutoFormat As You Type feature to bullet the paragraphs as you type them (see Table 3–2 shown earlier in this module). *Why? The AutoFormat As You Type feature saves you time because it applies formats automatically.* The following steps add bullets to a list as you type.

1
• Press the ASTERISK key (*) as the first character on the line (Figure 3–71).

2
• Press the SPACEBAR to convert the asterisk to a bullet character.

Figure 3–71

Q&A What if I did not want the asterisk converted to a bullet character?

You could undo the AutoFormat by clicking the Undo button; pressing CTRL+Z; clicking the AutoCorrect Options button that appears to the left of the bullet character as soon as you press the SPACEBAR and then clicking Undo Automatic Bullets on the AutoCorrect Options menu; or clicking the Bullets button (Home tab | Paragraph group).

3

- Type **Vendors must bring their own tables and chairs.** as the first bulleted item.
- Press the ENTER key to place another bullet character at the beginning of the next line (Figure 3–72).

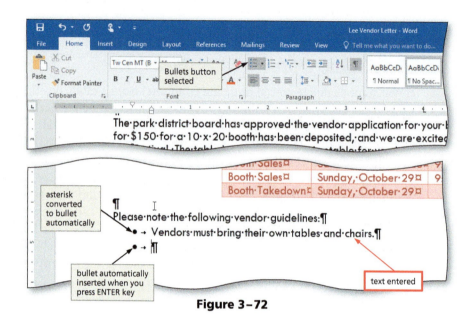

Figure 3–72

4

- Type **Vendors must supply their own electrical cords.** and then press the ENTER key.
- Type **Vendors shall comply with fire, safety, and health regulations.** and then press the ENTER key.
- Press the ENTER key to turn off automatic bullets as you type (Figure 3–73).

Q&A Why did automatic bullets stop?

When you press the ENTER key without entering any text after the automatic bullet character, Word turns off the automatic bullets feature.

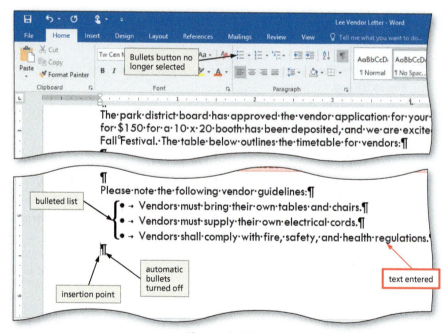

Figure 3–73

Other Ways

1. Click Bullets arrow (Home tab | Paragraph group), click desired bullet style

2. Right-click paragraph to be bulleted, click Bullets button on mini toolbar, click desired bullet style, if necessary

To Enter More Text and then Save and Print the Letter

The following steps enter the remainder of text in the letter.

1 With the insertion point positioned on the paragraph below the bulleted list, press the ENTER key and then type the paragraph shown in Figure 3–74, making certain you use the building block name, tad, to insert the organization name.

2 Press the ENTER key twice. Press the TAB key to position the insertion point at the tab stop set at the 4" mark on the ruler. Type **Sincerely,** and then press the ENTER key four times.

3 Press the TAB key to position the insertion point at the tab stop set at the 4" mark on the ruler. Type **Camden Ackerman** and then press the ENTER key.

If requested by your instructor, enter your name instead of the name stated above.

4 Press the TAB key to position the insertion point at the tab stop set at the 4" mark on the ruler. Type **Park District Events Coordinator** to finish the letter. Scroll up, if necessary (Figure 3–74).

5 Save the letter again on the same storage location with the same file name.

6 If requested by your instructor, print the letter.

BTW

Conserving Ink and Toner

If you want to conserve ink or toner, you can instruct Word to print draft quality documents by clicking File on the ribbon to open the Backstage view, clicking the Options tab in the Backstage view to display the Word Options dialog box, clicking Advanced in the left pane (Word Options dialog box), scrolling to the Print area in the right pane, placing a check mark in the 'Use draft quality' check box, and then clicking the OK button. Then, use the Backstage view to print the document as usual.

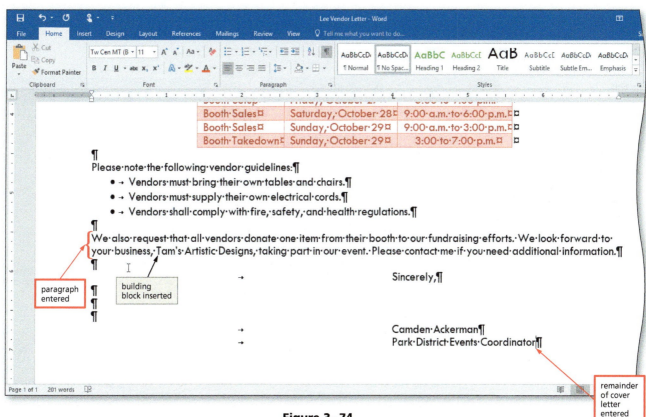

Figure 3–74

Addressing and Printing Envelopes and Mailing Labels

With Word, you can print mailing address information on an envelope or on a mailing label. Computer-printed addresses look more professional than handwritten ones.

To Address and Print an Envelope

1 CREATE & FORMAT LETTERHEAD WITH GRAPHICS | 2 SPECIFY LETTER FORMATS
3 INSERT TABLE | 4 FORMAT TABLE | 5 INSERT BULLETED LIST | **6 ADDRESS ENVELOPE**

The following steps address and print an envelope. If you are in a lab environment, check with your instructor before performing these steps. *Why? Some printers may not accommodate printing envelopes; others may stop printing until an envelope is inserted.*

- Scroll through the letter to display the inside address in the document window.
- Drag through the inside address to select it (Figure 3–75).

Figure 3–75

2
- Display the Mailings tab.
- Click the Create Envelopes button (Mailings tab | Create group) to display the Envelopes and Labels dialog box.
- If necessary, click the Envelopes tab (Envelopes and Labels dialog box), which automatically displays the selected delivery address in the dialog box.
- Type the return address as shown in Figure 3–76.

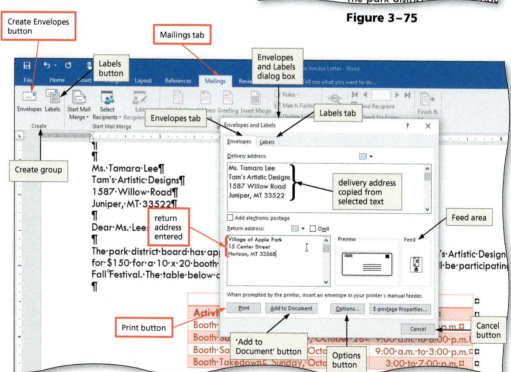

Figure 3–76

3
- Insert an envelope in your printer, as shown in the Feed area of the dialog box (your Feed area may be different depending on your printer).
- If your printer can print envelopes, click the Print button (Envelopes and Labels dialog box) to print the envelope; otherwise, click the Cancel button to close the dialog box.
- Because the project now is complete, you can exit Word.

Envelopes and Labels

Instead of printing the envelope immediately, you can add it to the document by clicking the 'Add to Document' button (Envelopes and Labels dialog box) (shown in Figure 3–76). To specify a different envelope or label type (identified by a number on the box of envelopes or labels), click the Options button (Envelopes and Labels dialog box) (shown in Figure 3–76).

Instead of printing an envelope, you can print a mailing label. To do this, click the Labels button (Mailings tab | Create group) (shown in Figure 3–76) and then type the delivery address in the Delivery address box. To print the same address on all labels on the page, select the 'Full page of the same label' option button in the Print area. Click the Print button (Envelopes and Labels dialog box) to print the label(s).

Summary

In this module, you have learned how to use Word to change margins, insert and format a shape, change text wrapping, insert and format a picture, move and copy graphics, insert symbols, add a border, clear formatting, convert a hyperlink to regular text, set and use tab stops, insert the current date, create and insert building blocks, insert and format tables, and address and print envelopes and mailing labels.

CONSIDER THIS: PLAN AHEAD

What decisions will you need to make when creating your next business letter?

Use these guidelines as you complete the assignments in this module and create your own business letters outside of this class.

1. Create a letterhead.
   a) Ensure that the letterhead contains a complete legal name, mailing address, phone number, and if applicable, fax number, email address, web address, logo, or other image.
   b) Place elements in the letterhead in a visually appealing location.
   c) Format the letterhead with appropriate fonts, font sizes, font styles, and color.
2. Compose an effective business letter.
   a) Include a date line, inside address, message, and signature block.
   b) Use proper spacing and formats for letter contents.
   c) Follow the alignment and spacing guidelines based on the letter style used (i.e., block, modified block, or modified semi-block).
   d) Ensure the message is well written, properly formatted, and logically organized.

Apply Your Knowledge

Reinforce the skills and apply the concepts you learned in this module.

Working with Tabs and a Table

Note: To complete this assignment, you will be required to use the Data Files. Please contact your instructor for information about accessing the Data Files.

Instructions: Run Word. Open the document called Apply 3–1 Fall Semester Schedule Draft located on the Data Files. The document is a Word table that you are to edit and format. The revised table is shown in Figure 3–77.

Fall Semester Schedule

Class/Activity	Monday	Tuesday	Wednesday	Thursday	Friday	Saturday
ENG 101	9:30-11:00 a.m.		9:30-11:00 a.m.			
COM 110		12:30-2:00 p.m.		12:30-2:00 p.m.		
MAT 120	1:00-2:00 p.m.		1:00-2:00 p.m.		1:00-2:00 p.m.	
CHM 102	3:30-5:00 p.m.		3:30-5:00 p.m.		3:00-5:00 p.m.	
MUS 152		9:30-11:00 a.m.		9:30-11:00 a.m.		
Yoga	6:00-7:00 p.m.			3:00-4:00 p.m.		8:00-9:00 a.m.
Work		4:00-8:00 p.m.			8:00-11:00 a.m.	1:00-4:00 p.m.

Figure 3–77

Perform the following tasks:

1. Change the document theme to Organic.

2. In the line containing the table title, Fall Semester Schedule, remove the tab stop at the 1" mark on the ruler.

3. Set a centered tab at the 3" mark on the ruler. Move the centered tab stop to the 3.5" mark on the ruler.

4. Bold the characters in the title. Use the 'Increase Font Size' button to increase their font size to 14. Change their color to Red, Accent 4, Darker 25%.

5. In the table, delete the row containing the HIS 107 class.

6. In the table, delete the Sunday column.

7. Insert a column between the Monday and Wednesday columns. Fill in the column as follows:

Column Title – Tuesday

COM 110 – 12:30-2:00 p.m.

MUS 152 – 9:30-11:00 a.m.

If the column heading, Tuesday, is not bold, apply the bold format to the text in this cell.

8. Insert a new row at the bottom of the table. In the first cell of the new row, enter the word, Work, in the cell. If this cell's contents are bold, remove the bold format. Fill in the cells in the remainder of the row as follows:

Tuesday – 4:00-8:00 p.m.

Friday – 8:00-11:00 a.m.

Saturday – 1:00-4:00 p.m.

9. In the Table Style Options group (Table Tools Design tab), ensure that these check boxes have check marks: Header Row, Banded Rows, and First Column. The Total Row, Last Column, and Banded Columns check boxes should not have check marks.

10. Apply the Grid Table 5 Dark - Accent 4 style to the table.

11. Select the entire table. Click the 'Decrease Font Size' button once to decrease the font size of all characters in the table to 10 point.

12. Make all columns as wide as their contents (AutoFit Contents). Note that you may need to perform this step a couple of times to achieve the desired results.

13. Align center left all cells in the first column.

14. Align center the column headings containing the weekday names.

15. Align center right all cells containing times.

16. Center the table between the left and right margins of the page.

17. If requested by your instructor, enter your name on the line below the table.

18. Save the document using the file name, Apply 3–1 Fall Semester Schedule Modified, and submit the document (shown in Figure 3–77) in the format specified by your instructor.

19. ✳ If you wanted to add a row to the middle of the table, how would you add the row?

Extend Your Knowledge

Extend the skills you learned in this module and experiment with new skills. You may need to use Help to complete the assignment.

Working with Formulas, Graphics, Sorting, Picture Bullets, and Mailing Labels

Note: To complete this assignment, you will be required to use the Data Files. Please contact your instructor for information about accessing the Data Files.

Instructions: Run Word. Open the document called Extend 3–1 Donation Letter Draft located on the Data Files. You will use the Format Picture task pane, group objects, enter formulas in the table, change the table style, sort paragraphs, use picture bullets, move tabs, and print mailing labels.

Perform the following tasks:
1. Use Help to learn about grouping objects, entering formulas, sorting, picture bullets, and printing mailing labels.

Continued >

Extend Your Knowledge *continued*

2. Select the graphic of the globe in the hand, click the Format Shape Dialog Box Launcher (Picture Tools Format tab | Picture Styles group) to display the Format Picture task pane, and then click the Picture button in the task pane (Figure 3–78). Experiment with all the buttons in the task pane and modify the look of the graphic to your preferences.

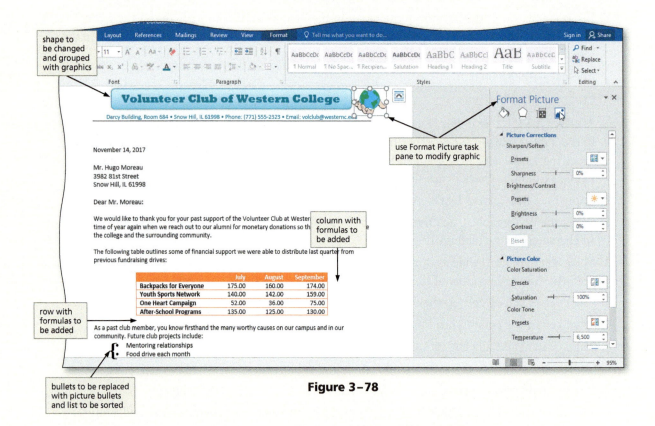

Figure 3–78

3. Select the shape around the Volunteer Club of Western College title and then use the Edit Shape button (Drawing Tools Format tab | Insert Shapes group) to change the shape to your preference. Position the globe in the hand graphic in the desired location to the right of the shape.

4. Copy and paste the modified globe in the hand graphic, flip it horizontally, and then position it on the opposite site of the shape. Group the two globe in hand graphics with the shape at the top of the letterhead. Change the text wrapping of the grouped shape to Top and Bottom.

5. Add a row to the bottom of the table. Insert the word, Total, in the first column of the new row. In the cell to contain the total for September, use the Formula dialog box to insert a formula that adds the cells in the column so that the total amount is displayed; in the dialog box, select a number format so that the total displays with dollar signs. *Hint:* Click the Formula button (Table Tools Format tab | Data group). Repeat this process for the August and July totals. Which formula did you use? Which number format?

6. Add a column to the right of the table. Insert the word, Total, as the column heading for the new column. Use the Formula dialog box to insert a formula that adds the cells each row so that the total amount is displayed. Use the same number format as you used in the previous step. Which formula did you use? What is the grand total for the quarter?

7. Position the insertion point in the table and one at a time, select and deselect each check box in the Table Style Options group. What are the functions of each check box: Header Row, Total Row, Banded Rows, First Column, Last Column, and Banded Columns? Select the check boxes you prefer for the table.

8. Sort the paragraphs in the bulleted list.

9. Change the bullets in the bulleted list to picture bullets.

10. Set a tab stop for the date line at the 4" mark on the ruler. Move the tab stops in the complimentary close and signature block from the 3.5" mark to the 4" mark on the ruler.

11. If requested by your instructor, change the name in the signature block to your name.

12. Save the revised document using the file name, Extend 3–1 Donation Letter Modified, and then submit it in the format specified by your instructor.

13. If requested by your instructor, print a single mailing label for the letter and then a full page of mailing labels, each containing the address shown in Figure 3–78.

14. ✺ Answer the questions posed in #5, #6, and #7. Why would you group objects? Which picture bullet did you use and why?

Expand Your World

Create a solution that uses cloud or web technologies by learning and investigating on your own from general guidance.

Using Google Docs to Upload and Edit Files

Notes:

- To complete this assignment, you will be required to use the Data Files. Please contact your instructor for information about accessing the Data Files.

- To complete this assignment, you will use a Google account, which you can create at no cost. If you do not have a Google account and do not want to create one, read this assignment without performing the instructions.

Instructions: You have created a letter in Word at your office and want to proofread and edit it at home. The problem is that you do not have Word at home. You do, however, have an Internet connection at home. Because you have a Google account, you upload your Word document to Google Drive so that you can view and edit it later from a computer that does not have Word installed.

Perform the following tasks:

1. In Word, open the document, Expand 3–1 Inquiry Letter in Word, from the Data Files. Look through the letter so that you are familiar with its contents and formats. If desired, print the letter so that you easily can compare it to the Google Docs converted file. Close the document.

2. Run a browser. Search for the text, google docs, using a search engine. Visit several websites to learn about Google Docs and Google Drive. Navigate to the Google website. Read about how to create files in Google Docs and upload files to Google Drive. If you do not have a Google account and you want to create one, follow the instructions to create an account. If you do not have a Google account and you do not want to create one, read the remaining instructions without performing them. If you have a Google account, sign in to your account.

3. If necessary, display Google Drive. Upload the file, Expand 3–1 Inquiry Letter in Word, to Google Drive.

Continued >

Expand Your World *continued*

4. Rename the file on Google Drive to Expand 3–1 Inquiry Letter in Google. Open the file in Google Docs (Figure 3–79). What differences do you see between the Word document and the Google Docs converted document?

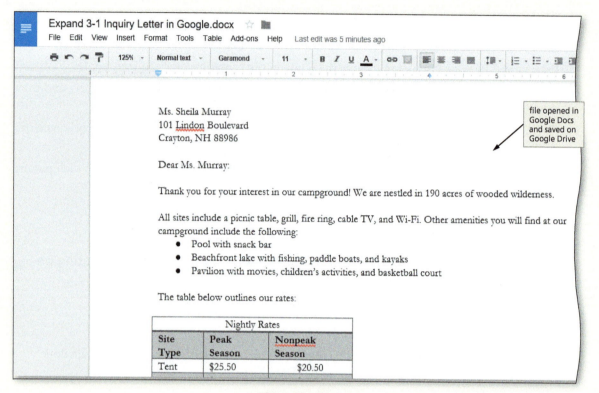

Figure 3–79

5. Fix the document in Google Docs so that it looks appealing, based on the concepts and techniques learned in this module. Add another item to the bulleted list: Fully-stocked camp store with attached laundry facilities. Add a row to the table: Pavilion, $20.00, $40.00. Insert a horizontal line below the line containing the mailing address.

6. If requested by your instructor, change the name in the signature block to your name.

7. Download the revised document to your local storage media, changing its format to Microsoft Word. Submit the document in the format requested by your instructor.

8. ✺ What is Google Drive? What is Google Docs? Answer the question posed in #4. Do you prefer using Google Docs or Word? Why?

In the Labs

Design, create, modify, and/or use a document following the guidelines, concepts, and skills presented in this module. Labs 1 and 2, which increase in difficulty, require you to create solutions based on what you learned in the module; Lab 3 requires you to apply your creative thinking and problem-solving skills to design and implement a solution.

Lab 1: **Creating a Letter with a Letterhead**

Problem: As a junior at your school, you are seeking a summer internship. One letter you prepare is shown in Figure 3–80.

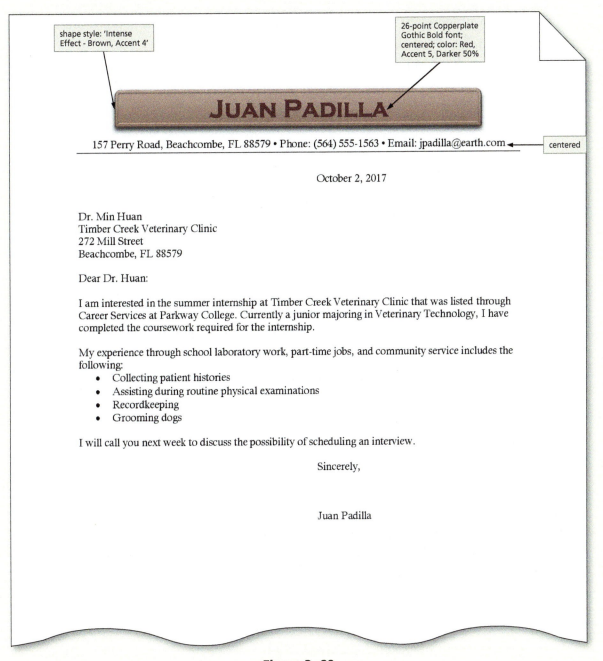

shape style: 'Intense Effect - Brown, Accent 4'

26-point Copperplate Gothic Bold font; centered; color: Red, Accent 5, Darker 50%

JUAN PADILLA

157 Perry Road, Beachcombe, FL 88579 • Phone: (564) 555-1563 • Email: jpadilla@earth.com

centered

October 2, 2017

Dr. Min Huan
Timber Creek Veterinary Clinic
272 Mill Street
Beachcombe, FL 88579

Dear Dr. Huan:

I am interested in the summer internship at Timber Creek Veterinary Clinic that was listed through Career Services at Parkway College. Currently a junior majoring in Veterinary Technology, I have completed the coursework required for the internship.

My experience through school laboratory work, part-time jobs, and community service includes the following:
- Collecting patient histories
- Assisting during routine physical examinations
- Recordkeeping
- Grooming dogs

I will call you next week to discuss the possibility of scheduling an interview.

Sincerely,

Juan Padilla

Figure 3–80

Perform the following tasks:

1. Run Word. Create a new blank document. Change the theme to Slate.

2. Create the letterhead shown at the top of Figure 3–80, following these guidelines:

    a. Insert the Rounded Same Side Corner Rectangle shape at an approximate height of 0.53" and width of 5.4". Change position of the shape to 'Position in Top Center with Square Text

Continued >

In the Labs *continued*

Wrapping'. Change the text wrapping for the shape to Top and Bottom. Add the student name, Juan Padilla, to the shape. Format the shape and its text as indicated in the figure.

b. Insert the dot symbols as shown in the contact information. Remove the hyperlink format from the email address. If necessary, clear formatting after entering the bottom border.

c. Save the letterhead with the file name, Lab 3–1 Padilla Letterhead.

3. Create the letter shown in Figure 3–80 using the modified block letter style, following these guidelines:

a. Apply the No Spacing Quick Style to the document text (below the letterhead).

b. Set a left-aligned tab stop at the 3.5" mark on the ruler for the date line, complimentary close, and signature block. Insert the current date.

c. Bullet the list as you type it.

d. If requested by your instructor, change the name in the shape and the signature block to your name.

e. Check the spelling of the letter. Save the letter with Lab 3–1 Internship Letter as the file name and then submit it in the format specified by your instructor.

4. If your instructor permits, address and print an envelope or a mailing label for the letter.

5. ✳ The letter in this assignment uses the modified block letter style. If you wanted to use the modified semi-block letter style, what changes would you make to this letter?

Lab 2: Creating a Letter with a Letterhead and Table

Note: To complete this assignment, you may be required to use the Data Files. Please contact your instructor for information about accessing the Data Files.

Problem: As the community education class coordinator, you are responsible for sending class registration confirmation letters. You prepare the letter shown in Figure 3–81.

Perform the following tasks:

1. Run Word. Create a new blank document. Change the theme to Berlin. Change the margins to 1" top and bottom and .75" left and right (Moderate).

2. Create the letterhead shown at the top of Figure 3–81, following these guidelines:

a. Insert the Horizontal Scroll shape at an approximate height of 0.74" and width of 6.32". Change the position of the shape to 'Position in Top Center with Square Text Wrapping'. Change the text wrapping for the shape to Top and Bottom. Add the name to the shape. Format the shape and its text as indicated in the figure.

b. Insert a picture of a rose, similar to the one shown in the figure (the exact figure, if required, is located in the Data Files). Resize the picture, change its text wrapping to In Front of Text, and move it to the left on the shape. Change its color tone to Temperature: 4700K. Copy the picture and move the copy of the image to the right on the shape, as shown in the figure. Flip the copied image horizontally.

c. Insert the small open diamond symbols as shown in the contact information. Remove the hyperlink format from the email address. If necessary, clear formatting after entering the bottom border.

d. Save the letterhead with the file name, Lab 3–2 Rosewood Letterhead.

3. Create the letter shown in Figure 3–81, following these guidelines:

   a. Apply the No Spacing Quick Style to the document text (below the letterhead).

   b. Set a left-aligned tab stop at the 4" mark on the ruler for the date line, complimentary close, and signature block. Insert the current date.

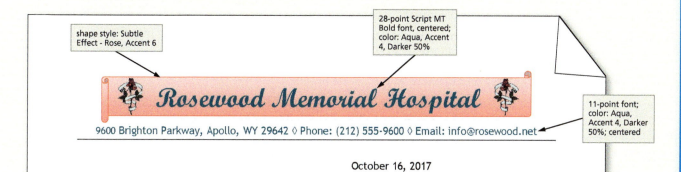

shape style: Subtle
Effect - Rose, Accent 6

28-point Script MT
Bold font, centered;
color: Aqua, Accent
4, Darker 50%

11-point font;
color: Aqua,
Accent 4, Darker
50%; centered

9600 Brighton Parkway, Apollo, WY 29642 ◊ Phone: (212) 555-9600 ◊ Email: info@rosewood.net

October 16, 2017

Ms. Natalia Zajak
88 Sycamore Street
Apollo, WY 29642

Dear Ms. Zajak:

Thank you for your interest in our community education classes. We look forward to seeing you! The table below confirms the classes in which you are registered during November:

table style: Grid
Table 5 Dark -
Accent 4; table style
options: Header Row
and Banded Rows

bold text

November Class Registration Confirmation			
Class	**Date**	**Time**	**Location**
Diabetes Risk Assessment	November 6	5:00 to 6:00 p.m.	Suite 101
First Aid and CPR	November 11	9:00 a.m. to 3:00 p.m.	Suite 220
Healthy Cooking	November 14	4:00 to 5:00 p.m.	Suite 203
Basics of Meditation	November 17	11:00 a.m. to 12:30 p.m.	Suite 124

Please note the following:
- Arrive 10 minutes early for all classes.
- No outside food or drink allowed in classrooms.
- Kindly give 48-hour cancellation notice.

If you have any questions, please contact me via email at jgreen@rosewood.net or phone at 212-555-9612.

Sincerely,

Jerome Green
Community Education Class Coordinator

Figure 3–81

Continued >

In the Labs *continued*

c. If requested by your instructor, change the name in the inside address and salutation to your name.

d. Insert and center the table. Format the table as specified in the figure. Make all columns as wide as their contents (AutoFit Contents). Left-align the Class, Date, and Location columns. Center the Time column.

e. Bullet the list as you type it.

f. Convert the email address to regular text.

g. Use nonbreaking hyphens in the phone number.

h. Check the spelling of the letter. Save the letter with Lab 3–2 Confirmation Letter as the file name and then submit it in the format specified by your instructor.

4. If your instructor permits, address and print an envelope or a mailing label for the letter.

5. ✳ What is the purpose of the nonbreaking hyphens in this letter? Why do you think the picture in this letter used a text wrapping of In Front of Text? If the table used banded columns instead of banded rows, how would its appearance change?

Lab 3: **Consider This: Your Turn**

Create a Letter to a Potential Employer

Note: To complete this assignment, you may be required to use the Data Files. Please contact your instructor for information about accessing the Data Files.

Problem: As an intern in the career development office at your school, your boss has asked you to prepare a sample letter to a potential employer. Students seeking employment will use this letter as a reference document when creating their own letters.

Perform the following tasks:

Part 1: Using your name, mailing address, phone number, and email address, create a letterhead for the letter. Once the letterhead is designed, write the letter to this potential employer: Ms. Latisha Adams, Personnel Director, Cedar Plank Hotels, 85 College Grove Lane, P.O. Box 582, Gartner, TX 74812.

The draft wording for the letter is as follows:

First paragraph:
I am responding to your advertisement in the Texas Post for the Assistant Manager position. I have the credentials you are seeking and believe I can be a valuable asset to Cedar Plank Hotels.

Second paragraph:
In May, I will be earning my bachelor's degree in Hospitality Management from Greenville College. My relevant coursework includes the following:

Below the second paragraph, insert the following table:

Restaurant management	18 hours
Nutrition	15 hours
Tourism management	12 hours
Hotel management	12 hours

Third paragraph:

In addition to my college coursework, I have the following experience:

Below the third paragraph, insert the following items as a bulleted list:

Assistant to school cafeteria director; Volunteer in Hope Mission kitchen; Developed website and Facebook page for local cafe.

Last paragraph:

I look forward to hearing from you to schedule an interview and to discuss my career opportunities at Cedar Plank Hotels.

The letter should contain a letterhead that uses a shape and picture(s); a table with an appropriate table title, column headings, and table style applied (unformatted table shown above); and a bulleted list (to present the experience). Insert nonbreaking spaces in the company name. Create a building block for the company name, edit the building block so that it has a ScreenTip, and insert the building block whenever you have to enter the company name.

Use the concepts and techniques presented in this module to create and format a letter according to a letter style, creating appropriate paragraph breaks and rewording the draft as necessary. The unformatted paragraphs in the letter are in a file called Lab 3–1 Letter Paragraphs, which is located on the Data Files. If you prefer, you can copy and paste this text into your letter instead of typing the paragraphs yourself. Use your name in the signature line in the letter. Be sure to check the spelling and grammar of the finished letter. Submit your assignment in the format specified by your instructor.

Part 2:   ✳ You made several decisions while creating the letter in this assignment: where to position elements in the letterhead, how to format elements in the letterhead, which graphics to use in the letterhead, which theme to use in the letter, which font size to use for the letter text, which table style to use, and which letter style to use. What was the rationale behind each of these decisions?

4 | Creating a Document with a Title Page, Lists, Tables, and a Watermark

Objectives

You will have mastered the material in this module when you can:

- Border a paragraph
- Change paragraph indentation
- Insert and format a SmartArt graphic
- Apply character effects
- Insert a section break
- Insert a Word document in an open document
- Insert formatted headers and footers

- Sort paragraphs and tables
- Use the format painter
- Add picture bullets to a list
- Create a multilevel list
- Modify and format Word tables
- Sum columns in a table
- Create a watermark
- Change theme fonts

Introduction

During the course of your business and personal endeavors, you may want or need to provide a recommendation to a person or group of people for their consideration. You might suggest they purchase a product, such as a vehicle or books, or contract a service, such as designing their webpage or remodeling their house. Or, you might try to convince an audience to take an action, such as signing a petition, joining a club, visiting an establishment, or donating to a cause. You may be asked to request funds for a new program or activity or to promote an idea, such as a benefits package to company employees or a budget plan to upper management. To present these types of recommendations, you may find yourself writing a proposal.

A proposal generally is one of three types: sales, research, or planning. A **sales proposal** sells an idea, a product, or a service. A **research proposal** usually requests funding for a research project. A **planning proposal** offers solutions to a problem or improvement to a situation.

Project — Sales Proposal

Sales proposals describe the features and value of products and services being offered, with the intent of eliciting a positive response from the reader. Desired outcomes include the reader accepting ideas, purchasing products, contracting services, volunteering time, contributing to a cause, or taking an action. A well-written proposal can be the key to obtaining the desired results.

The project in this module follows generally accepted guidelines for writing short sales proposals and uses Word to create the sales proposal shown in Figure 4–1. The sales proposal in this module is designed to persuade readers to patronize an animal clinic. The proposal has a colorful title page to attract readers' attention. To add impact, the sales proposal has a watermark consisting of animal paw prints, positioned behind the content on each page. It also uses lists and tables to summarize and highlight important data.

In this module, you will learn how to create the sales proposal shown in Figure 4–1. The following roadmap identifies general activities you will perform as you progress through this module:

1. **CREATE** a **TITLE PAGE** for the proposal.
2. **INSERT** an **EXISTING** Word **DOCUMENT** in the proposal.
3. **CREATE** a **HEADER AND FOOTER** in the proposal.
4. **EDIT AND FORMAT LISTS** in the proposal.
5. **EDIT AND FORMAT TABLES** in the proposal.
6. **CREATE** a **WATERMARK** in the proposal.

To Run Word and Change Word Settings

If you are using a computer to step through the project in this module and you want your screens to match the figures in this book, you should change your screen's resolution to 1366 × 768.

The following steps run Word, display formatting marks, and change the zoom to page width.

1 Run Word and create a blank document in the Word window. If necessary, maximize the Word window.

2 If the Print Layout button on the status bar is not selected (shown in Figure 4–2), click it so that your screen is in Print Layout view.

3 If the 'Show/Hide ¶' button (Home tab | Paragraph group) is not selected already, click it to display formatting marks on the screen.

4 To display the page the same width as the document window, if necessary, click the Page Width button (View tab | Zoom group).

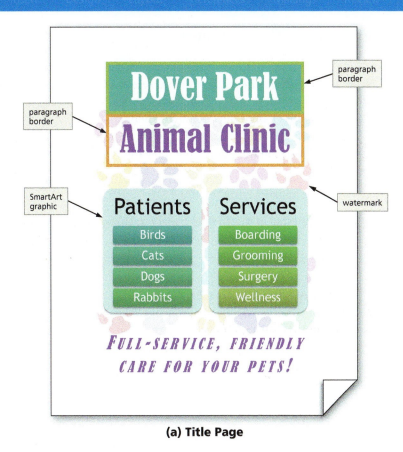

paragraph border

paragraph border

SmartArt graphic

watermark

(a) Title Page

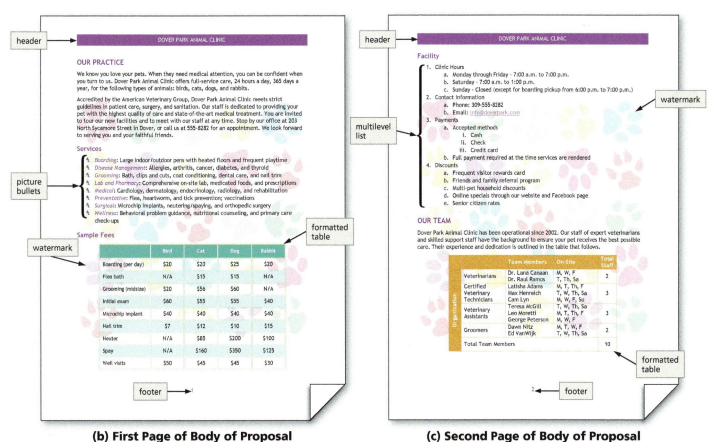

header

OUR PRACTICE

Services

picture bullets

watermark

formatted table

footer

(b) First Page of Body of Proposal

header

multilevel list

watermark

OUR TEAM

formatted table

footer

(c) Second Page of Body of Proposal

Figure 4–1

To Change Theme Colors

Recall that Word provides document themes, which contain a variety of color schemes and other effects. You should select a theme that includes colors that reflect the goals of a sales proposal. This proposal uses the Celestial document theme. The following steps change the document theme.

1 Click Design on the ribbon to display the Design tab.

2 Click the Themes button (Design tab | Document Formatting group) to display the Themes gallery.

3 Click Celestial in the Themes gallery to change the document theme to the selected theme.

Creating a Title Page

A **title page** is a separate cover page that contains, at a minimum, the title of a document. For a sales proposal, the title page usually is the first page of the document. Solicited proposals often have a specific format for the title page. Guidelines for the title page of a solicited proposal may stipulate the margins, spacing, layout, and required contents, such as title, sponsor name, author name, date, etc. With an unsolicited proposal, by contrast, you can design the title page in a way that best presents its message.

CONSIDER THIS

How do you design an eye-catching title page?
The title page is the first section a reader sees on a sales proposal. Thus, it is important that the title page appropriately reflects the goal of the sales proposal. When designing the title page, consider its text and graphics.

• **Use concise, descriptive text.** The title page should contain a short, descriptive title that accurately reflects the message of the sales proposal. The title page also may include a theme or slogan. Do not place a page number on the title page.

• **Identify appropriate fonts, font sizes, and colors for the text.** Use fonts that are easy to read. Avoid using more than three different fonts because too many fonts can make the title page visually confusing. Use larger font sizes to add impact to the title page. To give the title more emphasis, its font size should be larger than any other text on the title page. Use colors that complement one another and convey the meaning of the proposal.

• **Use graphics to reinforce the goal.** Select simple graphics that clearly communicate the fundamental nature of the proposal. Possible graphics include shapes, pictures, and logos.

• **Use colors that complement text colors.** Be aware that too many graphics and colors can be distracting. Arrange graphics with the text so that the title page is attractive and uncluttered.

The title page of the sales proposal in this module (shown in Figure 4–1a) contains a colorful title that is surrounded by a border with some shading, an artistic graphic with text, a colorful slogan, and the faded paw prints image in the background. The steps in the next several sections create this title page. The faded image of the paw prints is added to all pages at the end of this module.

To Format Characters

The title in the sales proposal should use a large font size and an easy-to-read font, and should be the focal point on the page. *Why? To give the title more emphasis, its font size should be larger than any other text on the title page.* The following steps enter the title, Dover Park Animal Clinic, with the first two words centered on the first line and the second two words centered on the second line.

1 Click Home on the ribbon to display the Home tab.

2 Click the Center button (Home tab | Paragraph group) to center the paragraph that will contain the title.

3 Click the Font arrow (Home tab | Font group). Scroll to and then click 'Bernard MT Condensed' (or a similar font) in the Font gallery, so that the text you type will use the selected font.

4 Click the Font Size arrow (Home tab | Font group) and then click 72 in the Font Size gallery, so that the text you type will use the selected font size.

5 Type **Dover Park** and then press the ENTER key to enter the first line of the title.

6 Click the Font Color arrow (Home tab | Font group) and then click 'Purple, Accent 1' (fifth color, first row) in the Font Color gallery, so that the text you type will use the selected font color.

7 Type **Animal Clinic** as the second line of the title (shown in Figure 4–2).

BTW

The Ribbon and Screen Resolution
Word may change how the groups and buttons within the groups appear on the ribbon, depending on the computer or mobile device's screen resolution. Thus, your ribbon may look different from the ones in this book if you are using a screen resolution other than 1366 × 768.

To Border a Paragraph

1 CREATE TITLE PAGE | 2 INSERT EXISTING DOCUMENT | 3 CREATE HEADER & FOOTER
4 EDIT & FORMAT LISTS | 5 EDIT & FORMAT TABLES | 6 CREATE WATERMARK

If you click the Borders button (Home tab | Paragraph group), Word applies the most recently defined border, or, if one has not been defined, it applies the default border to the current paragraph. To specify a border different from the most recently defined border, you click the Borders arrow (Home tab | Paragraph group).

In this project, the first line of the title in the sales proposal (Dover Park) has a 6-point olive green border around it. *Why? You want the title to stand out more than the rest of the text on the title page.* The following steps add a border to all edges of a paragraph.

1
- Position the insertion point in the paragraph to border, in this case, the first line of the document.
- Click the Borders arrow (Home tab | Paragraph group) to display the Borders gallery (Figure 4–2).

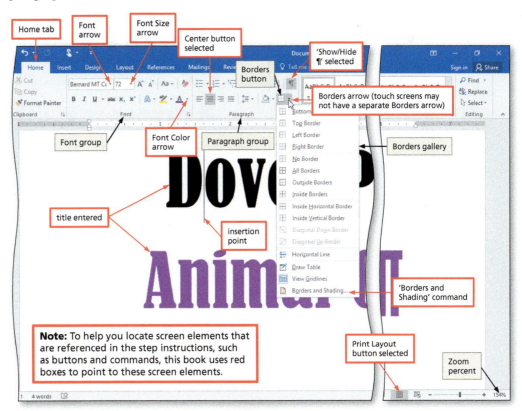

Note: To help you locate screen elements that are referenced in the step instructions, such as buttons and commands, this book uses red boxes to point to these screen elements.

Figure 4–2

2

- Click Borders and Shading in the Borders gallery to display the Borders and Shading dialog box.
- Click Box in the Setting area (Borders and Shading dialog box), which will place a border on each edge of the current paragraph.
- Click the Color arrow and then click 'Olive Green, Accent 4' (eighth color, first row) in the Color palette to specify the border color.
- Click the Width arrow and then click 6 pt to specify the thickness of the border (Figure 4–3).

Q&A For what purpose are the buttons in the Preview area used?
They are toggles that display and remove the top, bottom, left, and right borders from the diagram in the Preview area.

Figure 4–3

3

- Click the OK button (Borders and Shading dialog box) to place the border shown in the preview area of the dialog box around the current paragraph in the document (Figure 4–4).

Q&A How would I remove an existing border from a paragraph?
Click the Borders arrow (Home tab | Paragraph group) and then click the border in the Borders gallery that identifies the border you wish to remove, or click No Border to remove all borders.

Figure 4–4

Other Ways

1. Click 'Borders and Shading' button (Design tab | Page Background group), click Borders tab (Borders and Shading dialog box), select desired border, click OK button

To Shade a Paragraph and Change Font Color

To make the first line of the title of the sales proposal more eye-catching, it is shaded in teal. When you shade a paragraph, Word shades the rectangular area behind any text or graphics in the paragraph from the left margin of the paragraph to the right margin. If the paragraph is surrounded by a border, Word shades inside the border. The following steps shade a paragraph and change font color.

1 With the insertion point in the paragraph to shade, the first line in this case (shown in Figure 4–4), click the Shading arrow (Home tab | Paragraph group) to display the Shading gallery.

2 Click 'Teal, Accent 3' (seventh color, first row) in the Shading gallery to shade the current paragraph (shown in Figure 4–5).

3 Drag through the words, Dover Park, in the first line of the title to select the text.

4 Click the Font Color arrow (Home tab | Font group) to display the Font Color gallery and then click 'White, Background 1' (first color, first row) to change the color of the selected text (shown in Figure 4–5).

To Border Another Paragraph

To make the second line of the title of the sales proposal (Animal Clinic) more eye-catching, it has a 6-point gold border around it. The following steps add a border to all edges of a paragraph.

1 Position the insertion point in the paragraph to border (in this case, the second paragraph containing the text, Animal Clinic).

2 Click the Borders arrow (Home tab | Paragraph group) to display the Borders gallery and then click 'Borders and Shading' in the Border gallery to display the Borders and Shading dialog box.

3 Click Box in the Setting area (Borders and Shading dialog box), which will place a border on each edge of the current paragraph.

4 Click the Color arrow and then click 'Gold, Accent 5' (ninth color, first row) in the Color palette to specify the border color.

5 If necessary, click the Width arrow and then click 6 pt to specify the thickness of the border.

6 Click the OK button to place the defined border shown around the current paragraph in the document (Figure 4–5).

BTW
Touch Screen Differences
The Office and Windows interfaces may vary if you are using a touch screen. For this reason, you might notice that the function or appearance of your touch screen differs slightly from this module's presentation.

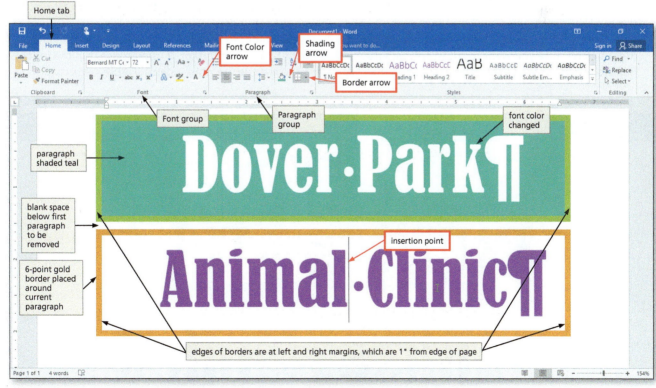

Figure 4–5

To Change Spacing after a Paragraph

Currently, a small amount of blank space exists between the two paragraph borders because Word automatically places 8 points of blank space below paragraphs (shown in Figure 4–5). The following steps remove the blank space below the first paragraph.

1 Position the insertion point in the paragraph to be adjusted (in this case, the paragraph containing the text, Dover Park).

2 Display the Layout tab. Click the Spacing After down arrow (Layout tab | Paragraph group) as many times as necessary until 0 pt is displayed in the Spacing After box to remove the space below the current paragraph (shown in Figure 4–6).

Q&A What if I am using a touch screen?
Tap the Spacing After box (Layout tab | Paragraph group) and then type 0 to change the spacing below the paragraph.

To Change Left and Right Paragraph Indent

1 CREATE TITLE PAGE | 2 INSERT EXISTING DOCUMENT | 3 CREATE HEADER & FOOTER | 4 EDIT & FORMAT LISTS | 5 EDIT & FORMAT TABLES | 6 CREATE WATERMARK

The borders around the first and second paragraphs and the shading in the first paragraph currently extend from the left margin to the right margin (shown in Figure 4–5). In this project, the edges of the border and shading are closer to the text in the title. **Why?** *You do not want such a large gap between the edge of the text and the border.* If you want the border and shading to start and end at a location different from the margin, you change the left and right paragraph indent.

The Increase Indent and Decrease Indent buttons (Home tab | Paragraph group) change the left indent by ½-inch, respectively. In this case, however, you cannot use these buttons because you want to change both the left and right indent. The following steps change the left and right paragraph indent.

1

- Be sure the insertion point is positioned in the paragraph to indent (the first paragraph, in this case). Click the Indent Left up arrow (Layout tab | Paragraph group) five times so that 0.5" is displayed in the Indent Left box because you want to adjust the paragraph left indent by this amount (or, if using touch, tap the Indent Left box (Layout tab | Paragraph group) and then type **0.5** to change the left indent).
- Click the Indent Right up arrow (Layout tab | Paragraph group) five times so that 0.5" is displayed in the Indent Right box because you want to adjust the paragraph right indent by this amount (or, if using touch, tap the Indent Right box (Layout tab | Paragraph group) and then type **0.5** to change the right indent) (Figure 4–6).

Figure 4–6

⌕ Experiment

- Repeatedly click the Indent Right and Indent Left up and down arrows (Layout tab | Paragraph group) and watch the left and right edges of the current paragraph change in the document window. When you have finished experimenting, set the left and right indent each to 0.5".

2

- Repeat Step 1 for the second paragraph, so that the paragraph containing the words, Animal Clinic, also has a left and right indent of 0.5" (shown in Figure 4–7).

Other Ways

1. Drag Left Indent and Right Indent markers on ruler	2. Click Paragraph Settings Dialog Box Launcher (Home tab | Paragraph group), click Indents and Spacing tab (Paragraph dialog box), set indentation values, click OK button	3. Right-click paragraph (or, if using touch, tap 'Show Context Menu' button on mini toolbar), click Paragraph on shortcut menu, click Indents and Spacing tab (Paragraph dialog box), set indentation values, click OK button

To Clear Formatting

The title is finished. When you press the ENTER key to advance the insertion point from the end of the second line to the beginning of the third line on the title page, the border will be carried forward to line 3, and any text you type will be a 72-point Bernard MT Condensed Purple, Accent 1 font. The paragraphs and characters on line 3 should not have the same paragraph and character formatting as line 2. Instead, they should be formatted using the Normal style. The following steps clear formatting, which applies the Normal style formats to the location of the insertion point.

1 If necessary, press the END key to position the insertion point at the end of line 2, that is, after the c in Clinic.

2 Press the ENTER key.

3 Display the Home tab. Click the 'Clear All Formatting' button (Home tab | Font group) to apply the Normal style to the location of the insertion point (Figure 4–7).

Q&A Could I have clicked Normal in the Styles gallery instead of the Clear All Formatting button?
Yes.

Figure 4–7

4 Save the title page on your hard drive, OneDrive, or other storage location using the file name, Animal Clinic Title Page.

Q&A Why should I save the title page at this time?
You have performed many tasks while creating this title page and do not want to risk losing work completed thus far.

SmartArt Graphics

Microsoft Office 2016 includes **SmartArt graphics**, which are visual representations of information. Many different types of SmartArt graphics are available, allowing you to choose one that illustrates your message best. Table 4–1 identifies the purpose of some of the more popular types of SmartArt graphics. Within each type, Office provides numerous layouts. For example, you can select from 40 different layouts of the list type.

Table 4–1 SmartArt Graphic Types

Type	Purpose
List	Shows nonsequential or grouped blocks of information.
Process	Shows progression, timeline, or sequential steps in a process or workflow.
Cycle	Shows continuous sequence of steps or events.
Hierarchy	Illustrates organization charts, decision trees, and hierarchical relationships.
Relationship	Compares or contrasts connections between concepts.
Matrix	Shows relationships of parts to a whole.
Picture	Uses images to present a message.
Pyramid	Shows proportional or interconnected relationships with the largest component at the top or bottom.

SmartArt graphics contain shapes. You can add text or pictures to shapes, add more shapes, or delete shapes. You also can modify the appearance of a SmartArt graphic by applying styles and changing its colors. The next several sections demonstrate the following general tasks to create the SmartArt graphic on the title page in this project:

1. Insert a SmartArt graphic.
2. Delete unneeded shapes from the SmartArt graphic.
3. Add shapes to the SmartArt graphic.
4. Add text to the shapes in the SmartArt graphic.
5. Change colors of the SmartArt graphic.
6. Apply a style to the SmartArt graphic.

BTW

Resetting Graphics
If you want to remove all formats from a SmartArt graphic and start over, you would click the Reset Graphic button (SmartArt Tools Design tab | Reset group), which is shown in Figure 4–15.

To Insert a SmartArt Graphic

Below the title on the title page is a grouped list SmartArt graphic. *Why? The Grouped List SmartArt graphic allows you to place multiple lists side by side on the document, which works well for the content on this title page.* The following steps insert a SmartArt graphic centered below the title on the title page.

1

- With the insertion point on the blank paragraph below the title (shown in Figure 4–7), click the Center button (Home tab | Paragraph group) so that the inserted SmartArt graphic will be centered below the title.
- Display the Insert tab.
- Click the 'Insert a SmartArt Graphic' button (Insert tab | Illustrations group) to display the Choose a SmartArt Graphic dialog box (Figure 4–8).

Figure 4–8

🔍 **Experiment**

- Click various SmartArt graphic types in the left pane of the dialog box and watch the related layout choices appear in the middle pane.

- Click various layouts in the list of layouts in the middle pane to see the preview and description of the layout appear in the right pane of the dialog box.

2

- Click List in the left pane (Choose a SmartArt Graphic dialog box) to display the layout choices related to the selected SmartArt graphic type.
- Click Grouped List in the middle pane, which displays a preview and description of the selected layout in the right pane (Figure 4–9).

Figure 4–9

3

- Click the OK button to insert the selected SmartArt graphic in the document at the location of the insertion point (Figure 4–10).

Q&A

What if the Text Pane appears next to the SmartArt graphic?

Close the Text Pane by clicking its Close button or clicking the Text Pane button (SmartArt Tools Design tab | Create Graphic group).

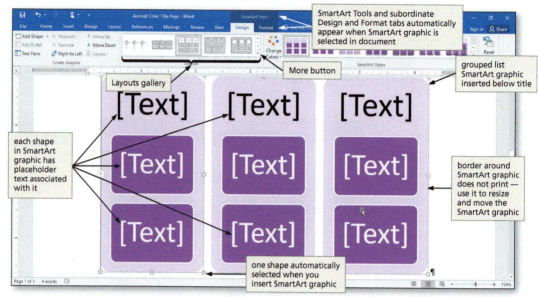

Figure 4–10

Can I change the layout of the inserted SmartArt graphic?
Yes. Click the More button in the Layouts gallery (SmartArt Tools Design tab | Layouts group) to display the list of layouts and then select the desired layout.

To Delete Shapes from a SmartArt Graphic

1 CREATE TITLE PAGE | 2 INSERT EXISTING DOCUMENT | 3 CREATE HEADER & FOOTER
4 EDIT & FORMAT LISTS | 5 EDIT & FORMAT TABLES | 6 CREATE WATERMARK

The Grouped List SmartArt graphic initially has three outer groups that consist of nine different shapes (shown in Figure 4–10). Notice that each shape in the SmartArt graphic initially shows **placeholder text**, which indicates where text can be typed in a shape. The next step in this project is to delete one entire group. *Why? The SmartArt graphic in this project consists of only two major groups (Patients and Services).* The following steps delete one entire group, or three shapes, in the SmartArt graphic.

1

- Click one of the shapes in the rightmost group in the SmartArt graphic and then press the DELETE key to delete the selected shape from the graphic (or, if using touch, tap the Cut button (Home tab | Clipboard group)).

2

- Repeat Step 1 to delete the next shape in the rightmost group.

3

- Repeat Step 1 to delete the rightmost group and notice the other shapes resize and relocate in the graphic (Figure 4–11).

Figure 4–11

Other Ways

1. Click Cut button (Home tab | Clipboard group)   2. Right-click selected shape, click Cut on shortcut menu

To Add Text to Shapes in a SmartArt Graphic

The placeholder text in a shape indicates where text can be typed in the shape. The following steps add text to the three shapes in the first group via their placeholder text. *Why? After entering the text in these three shapes, you will need to add two more shapes to finish the content in the group.*

1

- Click the top-left shape to select it and then type **Patients** to replace the placeholder text, [Text], with the entered text.

 How do I edit placeholder text if I make a mistake?
Click the placeholder text to select it and then correct the entry.

What if my typed text is longer than the shape?
The font size of the text may be adjusted or the text may wordwrap within the shape.

2

- Click the middle-left shape to select it and then type **Birds** as the new text.

- Click the lower-left shape to select it and then type **Cats** as the new text (Figure 4–12).

Figure 4–12

Other Ways

1. Click Text Pane control, enter text in Text Pane, close Text Pane

2. Click Text Pane button (SmartArt Tools Design tab | Create Graphic group), enter text in Text Pane, click Text Pane button again

3. Right-click shape (or, if using touch, tap Edit Text button on mini toolbar), click Exit Edit Text on shortcut menu, enter text

To Add Shapes to a SmartArt Graphic

The following steps add shapes to the SmartArt graphic. *Why? Each group in this project has four subordinate items, which means two shapes need to be added to each group.*

1

- Click the Add Shape button (SmartArt Tools Design tab | Create Graphic group) to add a shape to the SmartArt graphic (or, if using touch, tap the Add Shape button (SmartArt Tools Design tab | Create Graphic group) and then tap 'Add Shape After').

2

- Repeat Step 1 to add the final shape to the group.

- Click a subordinate shape on the right (one of the purple shapes) to select it.
- Repeat Steps 1 and 2 so that the same number of shapes appear on the right and left sides of the SmartArt graphic.

4

- Enter the text in the shapes as shown in Figure 4–13.

Figure 4–13

Other Ways

1. Click Add Shape arrow (SmartArt Tools Design tab), click desired shape position

2. Right-click paragraph (or, if using touch, tap 'Show Context Menu' button on mini toolbar), point to Add Shape on shortcut menu, click desired shape position

To Change Colors of a SmartArt Graphic

1 CREATE TITLE PAGE | 2 INSERT EXISTING DOCUMENT | 3 CREATE HEADER & FOOTER
4 EDIT & FORMAT LISTS | 5 EDIT & FORMAT TABLES | 6 CREATE WATERMARK

Word provides a variety of colors for a SmartArt graphic and the shapes in the graphic. In this project, the inside shapes are green, instead of purple. *Why? The current dark purple color competes with the title, so you want a softer color for the shapes.* The following steps change the colors of a SmartArt graphic.

- With the SmartArt graphic selected (shown in Figure 4–13), click the Change Colors button (SmartArt Tools Design tab | SmartArt Styles group) to display the Change Colors gallery.

Q&A What if the SmartArt graphic is not selected?
Click the SmartArt graphic to select it.

- Point to 'Colorful Range - Accent Colors 3 to 4' in the Change Colors gallery to display a live preview of the selected color applied to the SmartArt graphic in the document (Figure 4–14).

 Experiment

- Point to various colors in the Change Colors gallery and watch the colors of the graphic change in the document window.

Figure 4–14

- Click 'Colorful Range - Accent Colors 3 to 4' in the Change Colors gallery to apply the selected color to the SmartArt graphic.

To Apply a SmartArt Style

1 CREATE TITLE PAGE | 2 INSERT EXISTING DOCUMENT | 3 CREATE HEADER & FOOTER
4 EDIT & FORMAT LISTS | 5 EDIT & FORMAT TABLES | 6 CREATE WATERMARK

The next step is to apply a SmartArt style to the SmartArt graphic. **Why?** *Word provides a SmartArt Styles gallery, allowing you to change the SmartArt graphic's format to a more visually appealing style.* The following steps apply a SmartArt style to a SmartArt graphic.

- With the SmartArt graphic still selected, click the More button in the SmartArt Styles gallery (shown in Figure 4–14) to expand the SmartArt Styles gallery.

- Point to Moderate Effect in the SmartArt Styles gallery to display a live preview of that style applied to the graphic in the document (Figure 4–15).

 Experiment

- Point to various SmartArt styles in the SmartArt Styles gallery and watch the style of the graphic change in the document window.

- Click Moderate Effect in the SmartArt Styles gallery to apply the selected style to the SmartArt graphic.

Figure 4–15

To Modify Character Spacing and Format Characters Using the Font Dialog Box

In this project, the next step is to enter and format the text at the bottom of the title page. This text is the theme of the proposal and is formatted so that it is noticeable. Its characters are a 36-point, italic, purple Bernard MT Condensed font. Each letter in this text is formatted in **small caps**, which are letters that look like capital letters but are not as tall as a typical capital letter. Also, you want extra space between each character so that the text spans the width of the page.

Thus, the next steps apply all of the formats mentioned above using the Font dialog box. *Why? Although you could use buttons on the Home tab to apply some of these formats, the small caps effect and expanded spacing are applied using the Font dialog box. Thus, you apply all the formats using the Font dialog box.*

- Position the insertion point on the paragraph mark to the right of the SmartArt graphic and then press the ENTER key to position the insertion point centered below the SmartArt graphic.

- Type **Full-service, friendly care for your pets!**

- Select the sentence you just typed and then click the Font Dialog Box Launcher (Home tab | Font group) to display the Font dialog box. If necessary, click the Font tab in the dialog box to display the Font sheet.

- Scroll to and then click 'Bernard MT Condensed' in the Font list (Font dialog box) to change the font of the selected text.

- Click Italic in the Font style list to italicize the selected text.

- Scroll through the Size list and then click 36 to change the font size of the selected text.

- Click the Font color arrow and then click 'Purple, Accent 1' (fifth color, first row) in the Font color palette to change the color of the selected text.

- Click the Small caps check box in the Effects area so that each character is displayed as a small capital letter (Figure 4–16).

Figure 4–16

- Click the Advanced tab (Font dialog box) to display the Advanced sheet in the Font dialog box.
- Click the Spacing arrow and then click Expanded to increase the amount of space between characters by 1 pt, which is the default.
- Double-click the value in the Spacing By box to select it and then type 7 because you want this amount of blank space to be displayed between each character.
- Click in any box in the dialog box for the change to take effect and display a preview of the entered value in the Preview area (Figure 4–17).

Figure 4–17

Q&A Can I click the Spacing By arrows instead of typing a value in the box? Yes.

- Click the OK button to apply font changes to the selected text. If necessary, scroll so that the selected text is displayed completely in the document window.
- Click to remove the selection from the text (Figure 4–18).

36-point italic purple Bernard MT Condensed font in small caps and expanded

Figure 4–18

Other Ways

1. Right-click selected text (or, if using touch, tap 'Show Context Menu' button on mini toolbar), click Font on shortcut menu, select formats (Font dialog box), click OK button

2. Press CTRL+D, select formats (Font dialog box), click OK button

To Zoom One Page, Change Spacing before and after a Paragraph, and Set Zoom Level

The final step in creating the title page is to adjust spacing above and below the SmartArt graphic. You want to see the entire page while adjusting the spacing. Thus, the following steps zoom one page, increase spacing before and after the paragraph containing the SmartArt graphic, and then set the zoom level back to page width because you will be finished with the title page.

1 Display the View tab. Click the One Page button (View tab | Zoom group) to display the entire page as large as possible centered in the document window.

2 Position the insertion point in the paragraph to adjust, in this case, on the paragraph mark to the right of the SmartArt graphic.

3 Display the Layout tab. Click the Spacing Before up arrow (Layout tab | Paragraph group) as many times as necessary until 42 pt is displayed in the Spacing Before box because you want to increase the space above the graphic (or, if using touch, tap the Spacing After box (Layout tab | Paragraph group) and then type **42** to change the spacing below the paragraph).

4 Click the Spacing After up arrow (Layout tab | Paragraph group) as many times as necessary until 30 pt is displayed in the Spacing After box because you want to increase the space below the graphic (or, if using touch, tap the Spacing After box (Layout tab | Paragraph group) and then type **30** to change the spacing below the paragraph) (Figure 4–19).

Figure 4–19

Q&A What if the document spills to two pages?
Decrease the spacing above or below the SmartArt graphic until the title page contents fit on a single page.

5 Display the View tab. Click the Page Width button (View tab | Zoom group) to change the zoom to page width.

6 Save the title page again on the same storage location with the same file name.

Break Point: If you wish to take a break, this is a good place to do so. You can exit Word now. To resume at a later time, run Word, open the file called Animal Clinic Title Page, and continue following the steps from this location forward.

Inserting an Existing Document in an Open Document

Assume you already have prepared a draft of the body of the proposal and saved it with the file name, Animal Clinic Draft. You would like the draft to be displayed on a separate page following the title page.

In the following sections, you will insert the draft of the proposal below the title page and then edit the draft by deleting a page break and applying styles.

To Save an Open Document with a New File Name

The current file name on the title bar is Animal Clinic Title Page, yet the document you will work on from this point forward in the module will contain both the title page and the body of the sales proposal. To keep the title page as a separate document called Animal Clinic Title Page, you should save the open document with a new file name. If you save the open document by using the Save button on the Quick Access Toolbar, Word will assign it the current file name. You want the open document to have a new file name. The following step saves the open document with a new file name.

 Save the title page on your hard drive, OneDrive, or other storage location using the file name, Animal Clinic Sales Proposal.

Sections

All Word documents have at least one section. A Word document can be divided into any number of sections. During the course of creating a document, you will create a new **section** if you need to change the top margin, bottom margin, page alignment, paper size, page orientation, page number position, or contents or position of headers, footers, or footnotes in just a portion of the document.

The pages in the body of the sales proposal require page formatting different from that of the title page. The title page will not have a header or footer; the next two pages will have a header and footer. When you want to change page formatting for a portion of a document, you create a new section in the document. Each section then may be formatted differently from the others. Thus, the title page formatted with no header or footer will be in one section, and the next two pages of the proposal, which will have a header and footer, will be in another section.

To Insert a Next Page Section Break

1 CREATE TITLE PAGE | 2 INSERT EXISTING DOCUMENT | 3 CREATE HEADER & FOOTER
4 EDIT & FORMAT LISTS | 5 EDIT & FORMAT TABLES | 6 CREATE WATERMARK

When you insert a section break, you specify whether the new section should begin on a new page. *Why? Sometimes you want a page break to occur with a section break, as in this project. Other times, you do not want a page break to occur with a section break (which will be illustrated in a later module).* In this project, the title page is separate from the next two pages. Thus, the section break should contain a page break. The following steps insert a next page section break, which instructs Word to begin the new section on a new page in the document.

- Position the insertion point at the end of the title page (following the exclamation point), which is the location where you want to insert the next page section break.

BTW

Inserting Documents
When you insert a Word document in another Word document, the entire inserted document is placed at the location of the insertion point. If the insertion point is positioned in the middle of the open document when you insert another Word document, the open document continues after the last character of the inserted document; therefore, pay close attention to where the insertion point is positioned before inserting a document.

BTW

Section Numbers
If you want to display the current section number on the status bar, right-click the status bar to display the Customize Status Bar menu and then click Section on the Customize Status Bar menu. The section number appears at the left edge of the status bar. To remove the section number from the status bar, perform the same steps.

• Display the Layout tab. Click the 'Insert Page and Section Breaks' button (Layout tab | Page Setup group) to display the Insert Page and Section Breaks gallery (Figure 4–20).

Figure 4–20

2

• Click Next Page in the Section Breaks area of the Insert Page and Section Breaks gallery to insert a next page section break in the document at the location of the insertion point. If necessary, scroll so that your screen matches Figure 4–21.

Figure 4–21

To Delete a Section Break

Word stores all section formatting in the section break. If you wanted to delete a section break and all associated section formatting, you would perform the following tasks.

1. Select the section break notation by dragging through it.
2. Right-click the selection to display a mini toolbar or shortcut menu and then click Cut on the mini toolbar or shortcut menu to delete the selection.

or

1. Position the insertion point immediately to the left or right of the section break notation.
2. Press the DELETE key to delete a section break to the right of the insertion point or press the BACKSPACE key to delete a section break to the left of the insertion point.

To Clear Formatting

When you create a section break, Word carries forward any formatting at the location of the insertion point to the next section. Thus, the current paragraph is formatted the same as the last line of the title page. In this project, the paragraphs and characters on the second page should be returned to the Normal style. Thus, the following step clears formatting.

1 Display the Home tab. With the insertion point positioned on the paragraph mark on the second page, click the 'Clear All Formatting' button (Home tab | Font group) to apply the Normal style to the location of the insertion point (shown in Figure 4–22).

To Insert a Word Document in an Open Document

1 CREATE TITLE PAGE | **2 INSERT EXISTING DOCUMENT** | 3 CREATE HEADER & FOOTER
4 EDIT & FORMAT LISTS | 5 EDIT & FORMAT TABLES | 6 CREATE WATERMARK

The next step is to insert the draft of the sales proposal at the top of the second page of the document. *Why? You will modify a draft of the body of the proposal, which is located on the Data Files. Please contact your instructor for information about accessing the Data Files.* The following steps insert an existing Word document in an open document.

1

- Be sure the insertion point is positioned on the paragraph mark at the top of page 2, which is the location where you want to insert the contents of the Word document.

- Display the Insert tab.

- Click the Object arrow (Insert tab | Text group) to display the Object menu (Figure 4–22).

 What if I click the Object button by mistake?
Click the Cancel button (Object dialog box) and then repeat this step.

Figure 4–22

BTW

Sections
To see the formatting associated with a section, double-click the section break notation, or click the Page Setup Dialog Box Launcher (Layout tab | Page Setup group) to display the Page Setup dialog box. You can change margin settings and page orientation for a section in the Margins sheet. To change paper sizes for a section, click the Paper tab (Page Setup dialog box). The Layout tab (Page Setup dialog box) allows you to change header and footer specifications and vertical alignment for the section. To add a border to a section, click the Borders button in the Layout sheet.

- Click 'Text from File' on the Object menu to display the Insert File dialog box.

- Navigate to the location of the file to be inserted (in this case, the Module 04 folder in the Data Files folder in the Word folder).

- Click Animal Clinic Draft to select the file name (Figure 4–23).

Figure 4–23

- Click the Insert button (Insert File dialog box) to insert the file, Animal Clinic Draft, in the open document at the location of the insertion point.

Q&A Where is the insertion point now?
When you insert a file in an open document, Word positions the insertion point at the end of the inserted document.

- Press SHIFT+F5 to position the insertion point on line 1 of page 2, which was its location prior to inserting the new Word document (Figure 4–24).

Q&A What is the purpose of SHIFT+F5?
The keyboard shortcut, SHIFT+F5, positions the insertion point at your last editing location. Word remembers your last three editing locations, which means you can press this keyboard shortcut repeatedly to return to one of your three most recent editing locations.

What if my keyboard does not have function keys?
Scroll to display the top of page 2 in the document window.

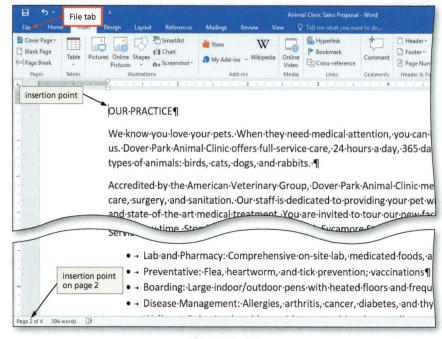

Figure 4–24

Other Ways

1. Click Object button (Insert tab | Text group), click 'Create from File' tab (Object dialog box), click Browse button, locate file, click Insert button (Browse dialog box), click OK button (Object dialog box)

To Print Specific Pages in a Document

The title page is the first page of the proposal. The body of the proposal spans the second and third pages. The following steps print a hard copy of only the body of the proposal, that is, pages 2 and 3. *Why? You would like to see the contents of the body of the proposal before you begin modifying it.*

- Click File on the ribbon to open the Backstage view and then click the Print tab in the Backstage view to display the Print gallery.
- Verify that the printer listed on the Printer Status button will print a hard copy of the document. If necessary, click the Printer Status button to display a list of available printer options and then click the desired printer to change the selected printer.
- Type **2-3** in the Pages text box in the Settings area of the Print gallery (Figure 4–25).

Figure 4–25

- Click the Print button to print the inserted draft of the sales proposal (Figure 4–26).

Q&A   How would I print pages from a certain point to the end of a document?
You would enter the page number followed by a dash in the Pages text box. For example, 5- will print from page 5 to the end of the document. To print up to a certain page, put the dash first (e.g., -5 will print pages 1 through 5).

Why does my document wrap on different words than Figure 4–26?
Differences in wordwrap may be related to the printer used by your computer.

Why does my screen show the document has four pages?
You may have an extra blank page at the end of the document. This blank page will be deleted later in the module.

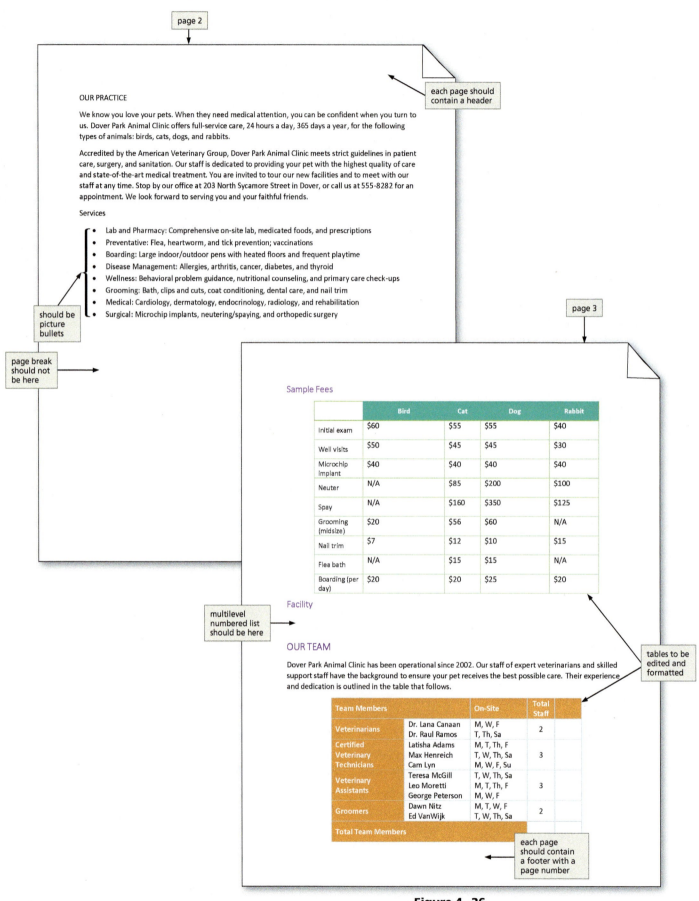

page 2

each page should contain a header

OUR PRACTICE

We know you love your pets. When they need medical attention, you can be confident when you turn to us. Dover Park Animal Clinic offers full-service care, 24 hours a day, 365 days a year, for the following types of animals: birds, cats, dogs, and rabbits.

Accredited by the American Veterinary Group, Dover Park Animal Clinic meets strict guidelines in patient care, surgery, and sanitation. Our staff is dedicated to providing your pet with the highest quality of care and state-of-the-art medical treatment. You are invited to tour our new facilities and to meet with our staff at any time. Stop by our office at 203 North Sycamore Street in Dover, or call us at 555-8282 for an appointment. We look forward to serving you and your faithful friends.

Services

- Lab and Pharmacy: Comprehensive on-site lab, medicated foods, and prescriptions
- Preventative: Flea, heartworm, and tick prevention; vaccinations
- Boarding: Large indoor/outdoor pens with heated floors and frequent playtime
- Disease Management: Allergies, arthritis, cancer, diabetes, and thyroid
- Wellness: Behavioral problem guidance, nutritional counseling, and primary care check-ups
- Grooming: Bath, clips and cuts, coat conditioning, dental care, and nail trim
- Medical: Cardiology, dermatology, endocrinology, radiology, and rehabilitation
- Surgical: Microchip implants, neutering/spaying, and orthopedic surgery

should be picture bullets

page break should not be here

page 3

Sample Fees

	Bird	Cat	Dog	Rabbit
Initial exam	$60	$55	$55	$40
Well visits	$50	$45	$45	$30
Microchip implant	$40	$40	$40	$40
Neuter	N/A	$85	$200	$100
Spay	N/A	$160	$350	$125
Grooming (midsize)	$20	$56	$60	N/A
Nail trim	$7	$12	$10	$15
Flea bath	N/A	$15	$15	N/A
Boarding (per day)	$20	$20	$25	$20

Facility

multilevel numbered list should be here

OUR TEAM

Dover Park Animal Clinic has been operational since 2002. Our staff of expert veterinarians and skilled support staff have the background to ensure your pet receives the best possible care. Their experience and dedication is outlined in the table that follows.

tables to be edited and formatted

Team Members		On-Site	Total Staff
Veterinarians	Dr. Lana Canaan Dr. Raul Ramos	M, W, F T, Th, Sa	2
Certified Veterinary Technicians	Latisha Adams Max Henreich Cam Lyn	M, T, Th, F T, W, Th, Sa M, W, F, Su	3
Veterinary Assistants	Teresa McGill Leo Moretti George Peterson	T, W, Th, Sa M, T, Th, F M, W, F	3
Groomers	Dawn Nitz Ed VanWijk	M, T, W, F T, W, Th, Sa	2
Total Team Members			

each page should contain a footer with a page number

Figure 4–26

Other Ways

1. Press CTRL+P; press ENTER

What elements should the body of a sales proposal contain?

Be sure to include basic elements in your sales proposals:

- **Include an introduction, body, and conclusion.** The introduction could contain the subject, purpose, statement of problem, need, background, or scope. The body may include costs, benefits, supporting documentation, available or required facilities, feasibility, methods, timetable, materials, or equipment. The conclusion summarizes key points or requests an action.

- **Use headers and footers.** Headers and footers help to identify every page. A page number should be in either the header or footer. If the sales proposal should become disassembled, the reader can use the page numbers in the headers or footers to determine the order and pieces of your proposal.

To Delete a Page Break

1 CREATE TITLE PAGE | 2 INSERT EXISTING DOCUMENT | 3 CREATE HEADER & FOOTER
4 EDIT & FORMAT LISTS | 5 EDIT & FORMAT TABLES | 6 CREATE WATERMARK

After reviewing the draft in Figure 4–26, you notice it contains a page break below the bulleted list. The following steps delete a page break. *Why? This page break below the bulleted list should not be in the proposal.*

- Scroll to display the page break notation.
- To select the page break notation, double-click it (Figure 4–27).

- Press the DELETE key to remove the page break from the document.

Figure 4–27

Other Ways

1. With page break notation selected, click Cut button (Home tab | Clipboard group)
2. With page break notation selected, right-click selection and then click Cut on mini toolbar or shortcut menu
3. With the insertion point to the left or right of the page break notation, press DELETE or BACKSPACE, respectively

To Apply Heading Styles

Word has many built-in, or predefined, styles that you can use to format text. Three of the Styles shown in the Styles gallery in Figure 4–28 are for headings: Heading 1 for the major headings and Heading 2 and Heading 3 for minor headings. In the Animal Clinic Draft, all headings except for the first two were formatted using heading styles.

The following steps apply the Heading 1 style to the paragraph containing the text, OUR PRACTICE, and the Heading 2 style to the paragraph containing the text, Services.

1 Position the insertion point in the paragraph to be formatted to the Heading 1 style, in this case, the first line on the second page with the text, OUR PRACTICE.

2 Click Heading 1 in the Style gallery (Home tab | Styles group) to apply the selected style to the paragraph containing the insertion point.

Q&A Why did a square appear on the screen near the left edge of the paragraph formatted with the Heading 1 style?
The square is a nonprinting character, like the paragraph mark, that indicates text to its right has a special paragraph format applied to it.

3 Position the insertion point in the paragraph to be formatted to the Heading 2 style, in this case, the line above the bulleted list with the text, Services.

4 Click Heading 2 in the Style gallery (Home tab | Styles group) to apply the selected style to the paragraph containing the insertion point (Figure 4–28).

Figure 4–28

To Change Spacing before and after a Paragraph

The next step is to adjust spacing above and below the current paragraph, that is, the heading above the bulleted list. This paragraph is formatted using the Heading 2 style, which places no space above the paragraph and 8 points below the paragraph. You would like this paragraph, and all other paragraphs formatted using the Heading 2 style, to have 12 points of space above them and 6 points of space below them. Thus, the following steps adjust the spacing before and after a paragraph.

1 Display the Layout tab. Position the insertion point as shown in Figure 4–29. Click the Spacing Before up arrow (Layout tab | Paragraph group) as many times as necessary so that 12 pt is displayed in the Spacing Before box (or, if using touch, tap the Spacing Before box (Layout tab | Paragraph group) and then type **12** to change the spacing above the paragraph).

2 If necessary, click the Spacing After up arrow (Layout tab | Paragraph group) so that 6 pt is displayed in the Spacing After box (or, if using touch, tap the Spacing After box (Layout tab | Paragraph group) and then type **6** to change the spacing below the paragraph).

To Update a Style to Match a Selection

You want all paragraphs formatted in the Heading 2 style in the proposal to use this adjusted spacing. Thus, the following steps update the Heading 2 style so that this adjusted spacing is applied to all Heading 2 paragraphs in the document.

1 If necessary, position the insertion point in the paragraph containing the style to be updated.

2 Display the Home tab. Right-click Heading 2 in the Styles gallery (Home tab | Styles group) to display a shortcut menu (Figure 4–29).

3 Click 'Update Heading 2 to Match Selection' on the shortcut menu to update the Heading 2 style to reflect the settings at the location of the insertion point.

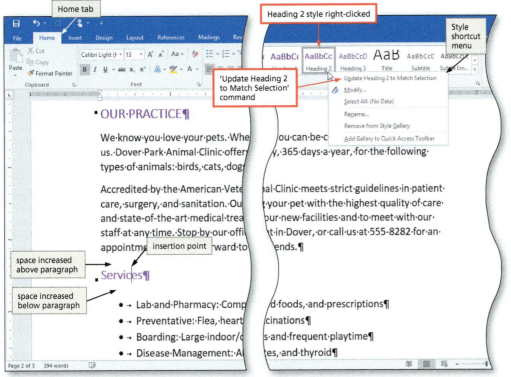

Figure 4–29

Creating Headers and Footers

A header is text that prints at the top of each page in the document. A footer is text that prints at the bottom of each page. In this proposal, you want the header and footer to appear on each page after the title page; that is, you do not want the header and footer on the title page. Recall that the title page is in a separate section from the rest of the sales proposal. Thus, the header and footer should not be in section 1, but they should be in section 2. The steps in the following sections explain how to create a header and footer in section 2 only.

To Insert a Formatted Header Different from the Previous Header

1 CREATE TITLE PAGE | 2 INSERT EXISTING DOCUMENT | **3 CREATE HEADER & FOOTER**
4 EDIT & FORMAT LISTS | 5 EDIT & FORMAT TABLES | 6 CREATE WATERMARK

Word provides several built-in preformatted header designs for you to insert in documents. The following steps insert a formatted header in section 2 of the sales proposal that is different from the previous header. *Why? You do not want the header to appear on the title page, so you will instruct Word to not place the header in the previous section. Recall that the title page is in section 1 and the body of the proposal is in section 2.*

1

- Display the Insert tab. Click the 'Add a Header' button (Insert tab | Header & Footer group) and then click Edit Header in the Header gallery to switch to the header for section 2.
- If the 'Link to Previous' button (Header & Footer Tools Design tab | Navigation group) is selected, click it to deselect the button because you do not want the header in this section to be copied to the previous section (that is, the header should not be on the title page).

BTW

Headers and Footers
If a portion of a header or footer does not print, it may be in a nonprintable area. Check the printer user instructions to see how close the printer can print to the edge of the paper. Then, click the Page Setup Dialog Box Launcher (Layout tab | Page Setup group), click the Layout tab (Page Setup dialog box), adjust the From edge text box to a value that is larger than the printer's minimum margin setting, click the OK button, and then print the document again.

- Click the 'Add a Header' button (Header & Footer Tools Design tab | Header & Footer group) to display the Add a Header gallery (Figure 4–30).

 Experiment

- Scroll through the list of built-in headers to see the variety of available formatted header designs.

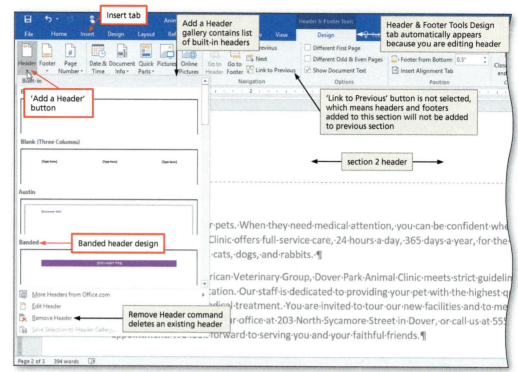

Figure 4–30

2

- If necessary, scroll to and then click the Banded header design in the Add a Header gallery to insert the formatted header in the header of section 2, which contains a content control (Figure 4–31).

Figure 4–31

 What is a content control?

A **content control** is an object that contains sample text or instructions for filling in text and graphics.

3

- Click the content control, [DOCUMENT TITLE], to select it and then type **Dover Park Animal Clinic** in the content control (Figure 4–32).

Figure 4–32

If requested by your instructor, enter your name instead of the clinic name shown in Figure 4–32.

Q&A
How would I delete a header?
You would click Remove Header in the Header gallery.

Other Ways

1. Click 'Add a Header' button (Insert tab | Header & Footer group), select desired header in list

2. Click 'Explore Quick Parts' button (Insert tab | Text group), click 'Building Blocks Organizer' on Quick Parts menu, select desired header (Building Blocks Organizer dialog box), click Insert button

To Insert a Formatted Footer

The next step is to insert the footer. Word provides the same built-in preformatted footer designs as header designs. The footer design that corresponds to the header just inserted contains a centered page number. The following steps insert a formatted footer in section 2 of the sales proposal that corresponds to the header just inserted.

1 Click the 'Go to Footer' button (shown in Figure 4–32) (Header & Footer Tools Design tab | Navigation group) to display the footer for section 2.

2 If the 'Link to Previous' button (Header & Footer Tools Design tab | Navigation group) is selected, click it to deselect the button because you do not want the footer in this section to be copied to the previous section (that is, the footer should not be on the title page).

3 Click the 'Add a Footer' button (shown in Figure 4–32) (Header & Footer Tools Design tab | Header & Footer group) to display the Add a Footer gallery.

4 Click the Banded footer design to insert the formatted footer in the footer of section 2 (shown in Figure 4–33).

Q&A
Why is the page number a 2?
The page number is 2 because, by default, Word begins numbering pages from the beginning of the document.

BTW

Page Numbers
If Word displays {PAGE} instead of the actual page number, press ALT+F9 to turn off field codes. If Word prints {PAGE} instead of the page number, open the Backstage view, click the Options tab to display the Word Options dialog box, click Advanced in the left pane (Word Options dialog box), scroll to the Print area, remove the check mark from the 'Print field codes instead of their values' check box, and then click the OK button.

To Format Page Numbers to Start at a Different Number

1 CREATE TITLE PAGE | 2 INSERT EXISTING DOCUMENT | **3 CREATE HEADER & FOOTER**
4 EDIT & FORMAT LISTS | 5 EDIT & FORMAT TABLES | 6 CREATE WATERMARK

On the page after the title page in the proposal, you want to begin numbering with a number 1, instead of a 2 as shown in Figure 4–33. *Why? Word begins numbering pages from the beginning of the document, and you want it to begin numbering from the first page of the body of the proposal. Thus, you need to instruct Word to begin numbering the pages in section 2 with the number 1.* The following steps format the page numbers so that they start at a different number.

1

- Click the 'Add Page Numbers' button (Header & Footer Tools Design tab | Header & Footer group) to display the Add Page Numbers menu (Figure 4–33).

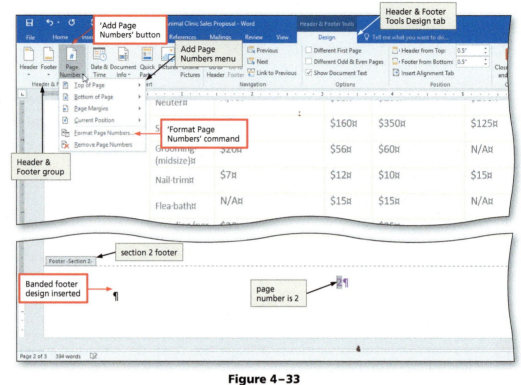

Figure 4–33

2

- Click 'Format Page Numbers' on the Add Page Numbers menu to display the Page Number Format dialog box.

- Click Start at in the Page numbering area (Page Number Format dialog box), which displays a 1 by default as the starting page number (Figure 4–34).

Q&A Can I also change the look of the page number?
Yes. Click the Number format arrow (Page Number Format dialog box) for a list of page number variations.

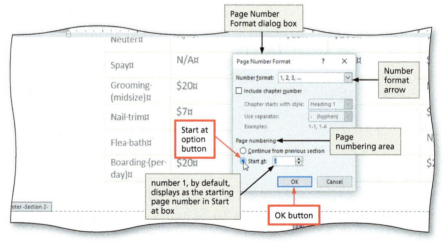

Figure 4–34

3

- Click the OK button to change the starting page number for section 2 to the number 1 (Figure 4–35).

- Click the 'Close Header and Footer' button (Header & Footer Tools Design tab | Close group) to close the header and footer.

Figure 4–35

Other Ways

1. Click 'Add Page Numbers' button (Insert tab | Header & Footer group), click 'Format Page Numbers' on Add Page Numbers menu, set page formats (Page Number Format dialog box), click OK button

Editing and Formatting Lists

The finished sales proposal in this module has two lists: a bulleted list and a numbered list (shown in Figures 4–1b and 4–1c at the beginning of this module). The bulleted list is in alphabetical (sorted) order, the first word of each list item is emphasized, and the bullets are graphical instead of simple round dots. The numbered list has multiple levels for each numbered item. The following sections illustrate steps used to edit and format the lists in the proposal:

1. Sort a list of paragraphs.
2. Format text in the first list item and then copy the format to text in each of the remaining list items.
3. Customize bullets in a list of paragraphs.
4. Create a multilevel numbered list.

To Sort Paragraphs

1 CREATE TITLE PAGE | 2 INSERT EXISTING DOCUMENT | 3 CREATE HEADER & FOOTER
4 EDIT & FORMAT LISTS | 5 EDIT & FORMAT TABLES | 6 CREATE WATERMARK

The next step is to alphabetize the paragraphs in the bulleted list. *Why? It is easier for readers to locate information in lists that are in alphabetical order.* In Word, you can arrange paragraphs in alphabetic, numeric, or date order based on the first character in each paragraph. Ordering characters in this manner is called **sorting**. The following steps sort paragraphs.

- If necessary, scroll to display the paragraphs to be sorted.
- Drag through the paragraphs to be sorted, in this case, the bulleted list.
- Click the Sort button (Home tab | Paragraph group) to display the Sort Text dialog box (Figure 4–36).

Q&A
What does ascending mean?
Ascending means to sort in alphabetic, numeric, or earliest-to-latest date order.

Figure 4–36

- Click the OK button (Sort Text dialog box) to instruct Word to alphabetize the selected paragraphs (shown in Figure 4–37).
- Click anywhere to remove the selection from the text.

To Apply a Style Using the Mini Toolbar

The text up to the colon in each list item is to be formatted in italic with the color purple. Although you could apply formatting using buttons in the Font group on the ribbon, it is more efficient to use the Intense Emphasis style. If you use a style and decide at a later time that you want to modify the formatting, you simply modify the style and Word will apply the changes to all text formatted with that style. Thus, the following steps format text using a style.

1 Select the text to be formatted (in this case, the text, Boarding, in the first list item).

2 Click the Styles button on the mini toolbar to display the Styles gallery (Figure 4–37).

3 Click Intense Emphasis in the Styles gallery to apply the selected style to the selected text.

Q&A Could I use the Styles gallery on the Home tab instead of the mini toolbar?
Yes.

BTW

Format Painter

If you also want to copy paragraph formatting, such as alignment and line spacing, select the paragraph mark at the end of the paragraph prior to clicking the Format Painter button (Home tab | Clipboard group). If you want to copy only character formatting, such as fonts and font sizes, do not include the paragraph mark in your selected text.

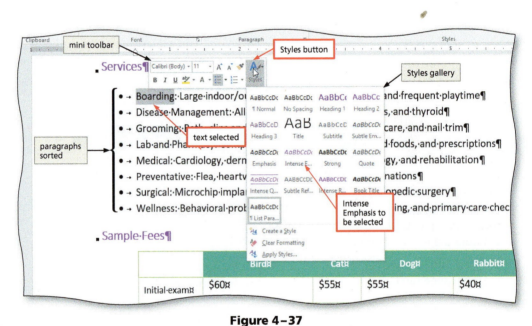

Figure 4–37

To Use the Format Painter Button

1 CREATE TITLE PAGE | 2 INSERT EXISTING DOCUMENT | 3 CREATE HEADER & FOOTER
4 EDIT & FORMAT LISTS | 5 EDIT & FORMAT TABLES | 6 CREATE WATERMARK

The first words in each of the remaining list items is to be formatted the same as the first words in the first list item. **Why?** *You would like the lists to be formatted consistently.* Instead of selecting the text in each list item one at a time and then formatting it, you will copy the format from the first word to the remaining words. The following steps copy formatting.

1
- Position the insertion point in the text that contains the formatting you wish to copy (the text, Boarding, in this case).
- Double-click the Format Painter button (Home tab | Clipboard group) to turn on the format painter.

Q&A Why double-click the Format Painter button?
To copy formats to only one other location, click the Format Painter button (Home tab | Clipboard group) once. If you want to copy formatting to multiple locations, however, double-click the Format Painter button so that the format painter remains active until you turn it off.

- Move the pointer to where you want to copy the formatting (the text, Disease Management, in this case) and notice that the format painter is active (Figure 4–38).

How can I tell if the format painter is active?

The pointer has a paintbrush attached to it when the format painter is active.

- Select the text in the next list item (the text, Disease Management, in this case) to paste the copied format to the selected text.

What if the Format Painter button no longer is selected?

Repeat Step 1.

Figure 4–38

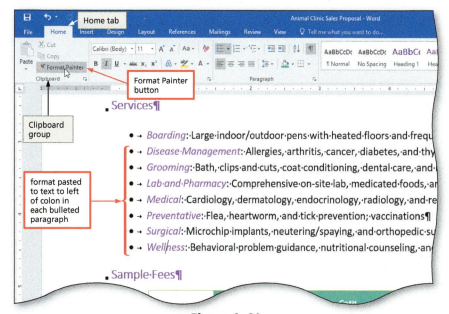

- Repeat Step 2 for the remaining the list items, selecting text up to the colon in Grooming, Lab and Pharmacy, Medical, Preventative, Surgical, and Wellness.
- Click the Format Painter button (Home tab | Clipboard group) to turn off the format painter (Figure 4–39).

Figure 4–39

To Customize Bullets in a List

1 CREATE TITLE PAGE | 2 INSERT EXISTING DOCUMENT | 3 CREATE HEADER & FOOTER
4 EDIT & FORMAT LISTS | 5 EDIT & FORMAT TABLES | 6 CREATE WATERMARK

The bulleted list in the sales proposal draft uses default bullet characters, that is, the dot symbol. The following steps change the bullets in a list from the default to picture bullets. ***Why?*** *You want to use a more visually appealing bullet that looks like a veterinary caduceus. Word refers to graphical bullets as picture bullets.*

1

- Select all the paragraphs in the bulleted list.

- Click the Bullets arrow (Home tab | Paragraph group) to display the Bullets gallery (Figure 4–40).

Can I select any of the bullet characters in the Bullet Library area of the Bullets gallery?
Yes, but if you prefer a different bullet character, follow the rest of these steps.

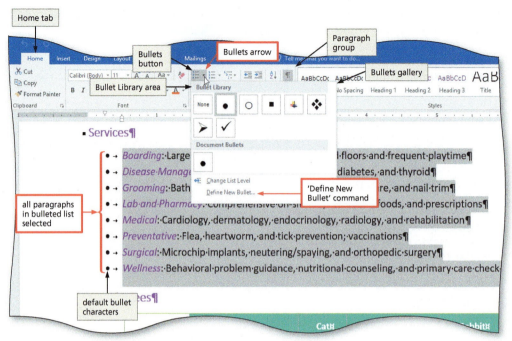

Figure 4–40

2

- Click 'Define New Bullet' in the Bullets gallery to display the Define New Bullet dialog box.

- Click the Picture button (Define New Bullet dialog box) to display the Insert Pictures dialog box.

- Type **veterinary caduceus** in the search box (Insert Pictures dialog box) and then click the Search button to display a list of pictures that matches the entered search text.

- Scroll through the list of pictures to locate the one shown in Figure 4–41, or a similar image. (If necessary, click the 'Show all web results' button to display more images that match the search text.)

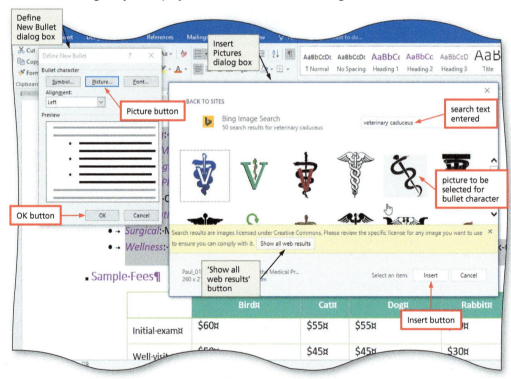

Figure 4–41

What if I cannot locate the image in Figure 4-41, and I would like to use that exact image?
The image is located on the Data Files. You can click the Cancel button, click the 'Browse from a file' link in the Insert Pictures dialog box, navigate to the file called aesculab-stab-2400px.png in the Data Files, select the file, and then click the Insert button (Insert Picture dialog box) to show a preview of the selected picture bullet in the Define New Bullet dialog box. Proceed to Step 4.

- Click the desired picture to select it.

- Click the Insert button (Insert Pictures dialog box) to download the image, close the dialog box, and show a preview of the selected picture bullet in the Define New Bullet dialog box.

- Click the OK button (Define New Bullet dialog box) to change the bullets in the selected list to picture bullets.

- When the Word window is visible again, click in the selected list to remove the selection (Figure 4–42).

Figure 4–42

To Create a Multilevel Numbered List

1 CREATE TITLE PAGE | 2 INSERT EXISTING DOCUMENT | 3 CREATE HEADER & FOOTER
4 EDIT & FORMAT LISTS | 5 EDIT & FORMAT TABLES | 6 CREATE WATERMARK

The next step is to create a multilevel numbered list below the Facility heading on the last page of the sales proposal in this module (shown in Figure 4–1c at the beginning of this module). *Why? You would like to list the team members and their hours at the clinic.*

A **multilevel list** is a list that contains several levels of list items, with each lower level displaying a different numeric, alphabetic, or bullet character. In a multilevel list, the first level is displayed at the left edge of the list and subsequent levels are indented; that is, the second level is indented below the first, the third level is indented below the second level, and so on. The list is referred to as a numbered list if the first level contains numbers or letters and is referred to as a bulleted list if the first level contains a character other than a number or letter.

For the list in this project, the first level uses numbers (i.e., 1., 2., 3.), the second level uses lowercase letters (a., b., c.), and the third level uses lowercase Roman numerals (for example, i., ii., iii.). The following steps create a multilevel numbered list.

- Position the insertion point at the location for the multilevel numbered list, which in this case is the blank line below the Facility heading on the last page of the sales proposal.

- Click the Multilevel List button (Home tab | Paragraph group) to display the Multilevel List gallery (Figure 4–43).

Figure 4–43

• Click the Current List format in the Multilevel List gallery to display the current paragraph as a multilevel list item using the current number format, which in this case is an indented 1 followed by a period.

Q&A
What if I wanted a different number format?
You would click the Multilevel List button (Home tab | Paragraph group) and then select the desired format in the Multilevel List gallery, or click Define New Multilevel List in the Multilevel List gallery (shown in Figure 4-43) to define your own format.

• Type **Clinic Hours** as a first-level list item and then press the ENTER key, which automatically places the next sequential number for the current level at the beginning of the next line (in this case, 2.) (Figure 4-44).

Figure 4-44

• Press the TAB key to demote the current list item (the 2.) to the next lower level, which is indented below the higher-level list item (in this case, converting 2. to a.).

• Type the text for list item 1-a as shown in Figure 4-45 and then press the ENTER key, which

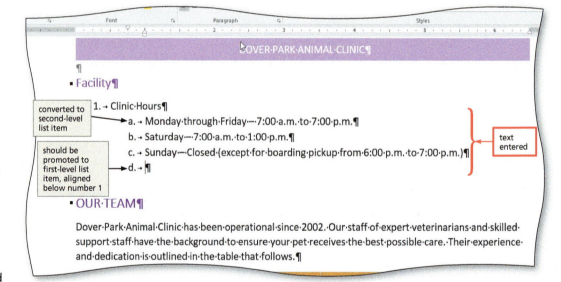

Figure 4-45

automatically places the next sequential list item for the current level on the next line (in this case, b.).

• Type the text for list item 1-b as shown in Figure 4-45 and then press the ENTER key, which automatically places the next sequential list item on the next line (in this case, c.).

• Type the text for list item 1-c as shown in Figure 4-45 and then press the ENTER key, which automatically places the next sequential list item on the next line (Figure 4-45).

• Press SHIFT+TAB to promote the current-level list item to a higher-level list item (in this case, converting d. to 2.).

Q&A
Can I use buttons on the ribbon instead of pressing TAB or SHIFT+TAB to promote and demote list items?
Yes. With the insertion point in the item to adjust, you can click the Increase Indent or Decrease Indent button (Home tab | Paragraph group) or right-click the list item and then click the desired command on the shortcut menu.

6

- Type **Contact Information** as a first-level list item and then press the ENTER key.

- Press the TAB key to demote the current level list item to a lower-level list item (in this case, converting 3. to a.).

- Type **Phone: 309-555-8282** and then press the ENTER key.

- Type **Email: info@ doverpark.com** and then press the ENTER key.

- Press SHIFT+TAB to promote the current-level list item to a higher-level list item (in this case, converting c. to 3.).

- Type **Payments** as a first-level list item, press the ENTER key, and then press the TAB key to demote the current-level list item to a lower-level list item (in this case, converting 4. to a.).

- Type **Accepted methods** and then press the ENTER key (Figure 4-46).

Figure 4-46

7

- Press the TAB key to demote the current-level list item to a lower-level list item (in this case, converting b. to i.).

- Type **Cash** and then press the ENTER key.

- Type **Check** and then press the ENTER key.

- Type **Credit card** and then press the ENTER key.

- Press SHIFT+TAB to promote the current-level list item to a higher-level list item (in this case, converting iii. to b.).

- Type the text for list item 3-b as shown in Figure 4-47 and then press the ENTER key.

- Press SHIFT+TAB to promote the current-level list item to a higher-level list item (in this case, converting c. to 4.).

- Finish entering the list as shown in Figure 4-47.

Figure 4-47

- Save the proposal again on the same storage location with the same file name.

Other Ways

1. Type **1.,** press SPACEBAR, type numbered list, pressing ENTER key at end of each item in list

Break Point: If you wish to take a break, this is a good place to do so. You can exit Word now. To resume at a later time, run Word, open the file called Animal Clinic Sales Proposal, and continue following the steps from this location forward.

Editing and Formatting Tables

The sales proposal draft contains two Word tables: the sample fees table and the team members table (shown earlier in the module in Figure 4–26). The sample fees table shows the sample fees for a variety of patient types, and the team members table shows details about various staff members at the clinic. In this section, you will make several modifications to these two tables so that they appear as shown in Figure 4–1 at the beginning of this module.

The following pages explain how to modify the tables in the sales proposal draft:

1. Sample fees table
   a. Change the column width for the column containing the type of services.
   b. Change row heights so that they are not so tall.
   c. Shade table cells.
   d. Sort the table contents by service type.
   e. Change cell spacing.
   f. Change the column width of columns containing costs.
2. Team members table
   a. Delete the extra column on the right edge of the table.
   b. Split table cells so that the heading, Team Members, is above the second column.
   c. Display text in a cell vertically to the left of the table.
   d. Remove cell shading from the table.
   e. Add borders to the table.
   f. Sum columns in the table.

BTW

Table Wrapping
If you want text to wrap around a table, instead of displaying above and below the table, do the following: either right-click the table and then click Table Properties on the shortcut menu, or click the Table Properties button (Table Tools Layout tab | Table group), click the Table tab (Table Properties dialog box), click Around in the Text wrapping area, and then click the OK button.

CONSIDER THIS

Why should you include visuals in a sales proposal?

Studies have shown that most people are visually oriented, preferring images to text. Use tables to clarify ideas and illustrate points. Be aware, however, that too many visuals can clutter a document.

To Show Gridlines

1 CREATE TITLE PAGE | 2 INSERT EXISTING DOCUMENT | 3 CREATE HEADER & FOOTER
4 EDIT & FORMAT LISTS | **5 EDIT & FORMAT TABLES** | **6 CREATE WATERMARK**

When a table contains no borders or light borders, it may be difficult to see the individual cells in the table. Thus, the following step shows gridlines. *Why? To help identify the location of cells, you can display gridlines, which show cell outlines on the screen.* **Gridlines** are formatting marks, which means the gridlines do not print.

- Display the table to be edited in the document window (in this case, the sample fees table).
- Position the insertion point in any cell in the table.
- Display the Table Tools Layout tab.

- If gridlines are not displayed on the screen, click the 'View Table Gridlines' button (Table Tools Layout tab | Table group) to show gridlines in the table (Figure 4–48).

Q&A

How do I turn off table gridlines?
Click the 'View Table Gridlines' button again.

Figure 4–48

To Change Column Width

1 CREATE TITLE PAGE | 2 INSERT EXISTING DOCUMENT | 3 CREATE HEADER & FOOTER
4 EDIT & FORMAT LISTS | 5 EDIT & FORMAT TABLES | 6 CREATE WATERMARK

Notice in Figure 4–48 that the leftmost column containing the types of services is not wide enough to fit the contents; that is, some of the services wrap in the cells. Thus, you will change the column width of just this single column. **Why?** *In this proposal, the services should appear on a single line that is just wide enough to accommodate the types of services.*

You can change a column width by entering a specific value on the ribbon or in a dialog box, or by using a marker on the ruler or the column boundary. The following steps change column width by using a column's boundary.

1

- Position the pointer on the column boundary to the right of the column to adjust (in this case, to the right of the first column) so that the pointer changes to a double-headed arrow split by two vertical bars (Figure 4–49).

Figure 4–49

• Double-click the column boundary so that Word adjusts the column width according to the column contents. (If all of the contents in the column still are not displayed on a single line, double-click the column boundary again so that all contents are displayed on a single line) (Figure 4–50).

Q&A What if I am using a touch screen?
Position the insertion point in the column to adjust, tap the AutoFit button (Table Tools Layout tab | Cell Size group), and then tap AutoFit Contents on the AutoFit menu.

Figure 4–50

Experiment

• Practice changing this column's width using other techniques: drag the 'Move Table Column' marker on the horizontal ruler to the right and then to the left. Click the 'Table Column Width' box up and down arrows (Table Tools Layout tab | Cell Size group). When you have finished experimenting, type 1.34 in the 'Table Column Width' box (Table Tools Layout tab | Cell Size group).

Other Ways

1. Drag 'Move Table Column' marker on horizontal ruler to desired width

2. Enter desired value in 'Table Column Width' box (Table Tools Layout tab | Cell Size group)

3. Click Table Properties button (Table Tools Layout tab | Table group), click Column tab (Table Properties dialog box), enter width, click OK button

---

To Change Row Height

1 CREATE TITLE PAGE | 2 INSERT EXISTING DOCUMENT | 3 CREATE HEADER & FOOTER
4 EDIT & FORMAT LISTS | 5 EDIT & FORMAT TABLES | 6 CREATE WATERMARK

The next step in this project is to narrow the height of the rows containing the services and fees. *Why? This table extends close to the bottom of the page, and you want to ensure that it does not spill onto the next page. (Note that it already may spill onto a second page.)*

You change row height in the same ways you change column width. That is, you can change row height by entering a specific value on the ribbon or in a dialog box, or by using a marker on the ruler or the row boundary. The latter two methods, however, work only for a single row at a time. The following steps change row height by entering a value on the ribbon.

• Select the rows to change (in this case, all the rows below the first row).

Q&A How do I select rows?
Point to the left of the first row and then drag downward when the pointer changes to a right-pointing arrow (or, if using touch, drag through the rows).

2

- Click the 'Table Row Height' box up or down arrows (Table Tools Layout tab | Cell Size group) as many times as necessary until the box displays 0.3" to change the row height to this value (or, if using touch, enter **0.3** in the 'Table Row Height' box (Table Tools Layout tab | Cell Size group) (Figure 4–51).

- Click anywhere to remove the selection from the table.

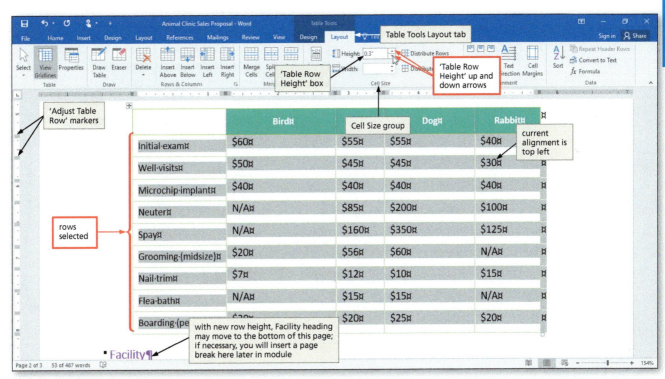

Figure 4–51

Other Ways

1. Click Table Properties button (Table Tools Layout tab | Table group), click Row tab (Table Properties dialog box), enter row height, click OK button

2. Right-click selected row (or, if using touch, tap 'Show Context Menu' button on mini toolbar), click Table Properties on shortcut menu, click Row tab, enter row height (Table Properties dialog box), click OK button

3. For a single row, drag row boundary (horizontal gridline at bottom of row in table) to desired height

4. Drag 'Adjust Table Row' marker on vertical ruler to desired height

To Align Data in Cells

The next step is to change the alignment of the data in cells that contain the dollar amounts. Recall that, in addition to aligning text horizontally in a cell (left, center, or right), you can align it vertically within a cell (top, center, or bottom). Currently, the dollar amounts have a top left alignment (shown in Figure 4–51). In this project, they should be aligned center so that they are more centered within the row height and width. The following steps change the alignment of data in cells.

1 Select the cells containing dollar amounts, as shown in Figure 4–52.

Q&A How do I select a series of cells?
Drag through the cells.

BTW

Page Breaks and Tables

If you do not want a page break to occur in the middle of a table, position the insertion point in the table, click the Table Properties button (Table Tools Layout tab | Table group), click the Row tab (Table Properties dialog box), remove the check mark from the 'Allow row to break across pages' check box, and then click the OK button. To force a table to break across pages at a particular row, click in the row that you want to appear on the next page and then press CTRL+ENTER.

2 Click the Align Center button (Table Tools Layout tab | Alignment group) to center the contents of the selected cells (Figure 4–52).

3 Click anywhere to remove the selection from the table.

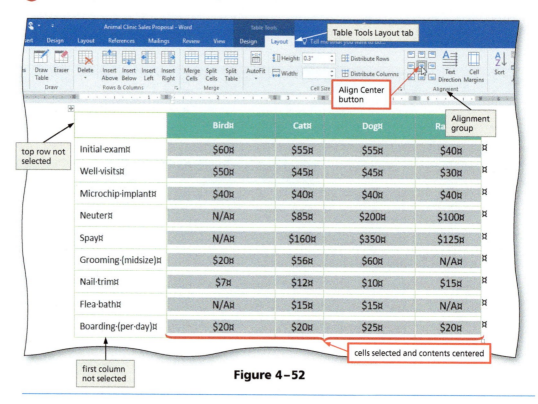

Figure 4–52

To Shade a Table Cell

In this table, the cell in the upper-left corner of the table is to be shaded teal. *Why? You want all cells in the top row shaded the same color.* The following steps shade a cell.

1
- Position the insertion point in the cell to shade (in this case, the cell in the upper-left corner of the table).
- Display the Table Tools Design tab.
- Click the Shading arrow (Table Tools Design tab | Table Styles group) to display the Shading gallery (Figure 4–53).

Figure 4–53

 Experiment

- Point to various colors in the Shading gallery and watch the shading color of the current cell change.

②

• Click 'Teal, Accent 3' (seventh color, first row) in the Shading gallery to apply the selected shading color to the current cell (shown in Figure 4-54).

◄ | How do I remove shading from a cell?

◦ʊ | Click the Shading arrow (Table Tools Design tab | Table Styles group) and then click No Color in the Shading gallery.

To Sort a Table

1 CREATE TITLE PAGE | 2 INSERT EXISTING DOCUMENT | 3 CREATE HEADER & FOOTER
4 EDIT & FORMAT LISTS | 5 EDIT & FORMAT TABLES | 6 CREATE WATERMARK

The next task is to sort rows in the table. **Why?** *The services should be listed in alphabetical order.* The following steps sort rows in a table.

①

• Select the rows to be sorted (in this case, all the rows below the first row).

◄ | What if I want to sort all rows in the table?

◦ʊ | Place the insertion point anywhere in the table instead of selecting the rows.

• Display the Table Tools Layout tab.
• Click the Sort button (Table Tools Layout tab | Data group) to display the Sort dialog box (Figure 4–54).

◄ | What is the purpose of the Then by area (Sort dialog box)?

◦ʊ | If you have multiple values for a particular column, you can sort by columns within columns. For example, if the table had a city column and a last name column, you could sort by last names within cities.

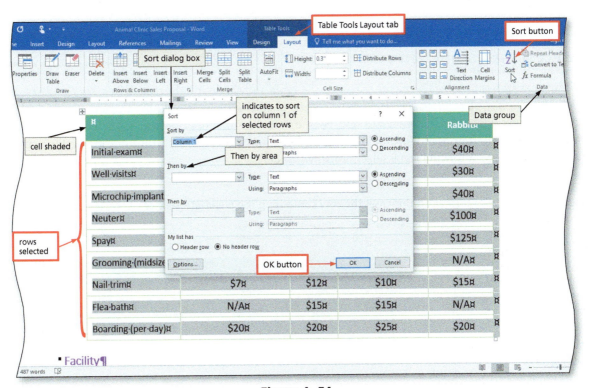

Figure 4–54

2

- Click the OK button (Sort dialog box) to instruct Word to alphabetize the selected rows.
- Click anywhere to remove the selection from the text (Figure 4–55).

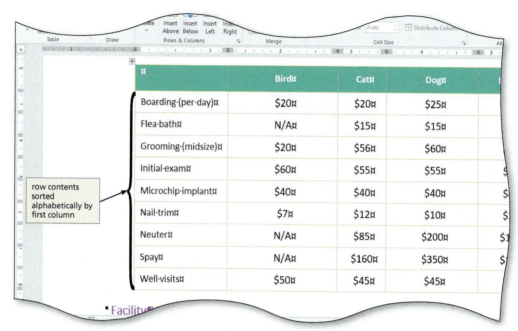

Figure 4–55

To Select Nonadjacent Items

1 CREATE TITLE PAGE | 2 INSERT EXISTING DOCUMENT | 3 CREATE HEADER & FOOTER
4 EDIT & FORMAT LISTS | **5 EDIT & FORMAT TABLES** | 6 CREATE WATERMARK

The next step is to select every other row in the table and shade it light teal. **Why?** *You feel that using shading on alternating rows will make it easier to read across individual rows.* Word provides a method of selecting nonadjacent items, which are items such as text, cells, or graphics that are not next to each other, that is, not to the immediate right, left, top, or bottom. When you select nonadjacent items, you can format all occurrences of the items at once. The following steps select nonadjacent cells.

1

- Select the first row to format (in this case, the row containing the Flea bath service).

2

- While holding down the CTRL key, select the next row to format (in this case, the row containing the Initial exam service) to select the nonadjacent row.

- While holding down the CTRL key, select the remaining nonadjacent rows (that is, the rows containing the Nail trim and Spay services), as shown in Figure 4–56.

Figure 4–56

Do I follow the same procedure to select any nonadjacent item?
Yes. Select the first item and then hold down the CTRL key while selecting the remaining items.

What if my keyboard does not have a CTRL key?
You will need to format each row individually, one at a time.

To Shade Selected Cells

With the alternating rows selected, the next step is to shade them light teal. The following steps shade selected cells.

1 Display the Table Tools Design tab.

2 With the rows selected, click the Shading arrow (Table Tools Design tab | Table Styles group) to display the Shading gallery and then click 'Teal, Accent 3, Lighter 80%' (seventh color, second row) in the Shading gallery to shade the selected rows with the selected color.

3 Click anywhere to remove the selection from the table (Figure 4–57).

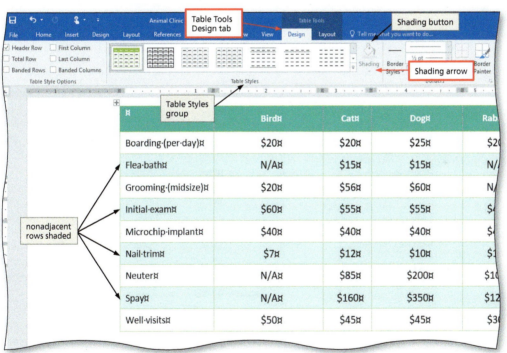

Figure 4–57

BTW

Table Headings
If a table continues on the next page, you can instruct Word to repeat the table headings at the top of the subsequent page(s) containing the table. To do this, select the first row in the table and then click the 'Repeat Header Rows' button (Table Tools Layout tab | Data group).

1 CREATE TITLE PAGE | 2 INSERT EXISTING DOCUMENT | 3 CREATE HEADER & FOOTER
4 EDIT & FORMAT LISTS | 5 EDIT & FORMAT TABLES | 6 CREATE WATERMARK

To Change Cell Spacing

The next step in formatting the sample fees table is to place a small amount of white space between every cell in the table. *Why? You feel the table would be easier to read with shite space surrounding each cell.* The following steps change spacing between cells.

- Display the Table Tools Layout tab.
- Position the insertion point somewhere in the table and then click the Cell Margins button (Table Tools Layout tab | Alignment group) to display the Table Options dialog box.

- Place a check mark in the 'Allow spacing between cells' check box and then click the up arrow once so that 0.02" is displayed in this box, because you want to increase space between cells by this value (Figure 4–58).

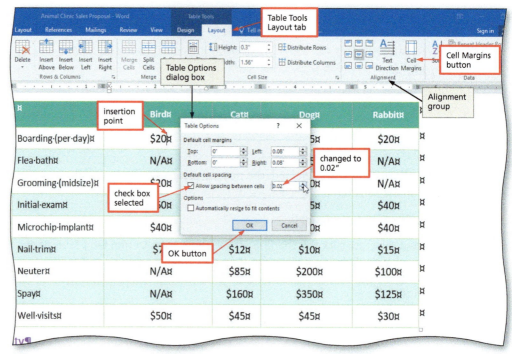

Figure 4–58

2

- Click the OK button (Table Options dialog box) to apply the cell spacing changes to the current table (Figure 4–59).

Q&A

Why are the column dividers in the first row wavy?
Gridlines are still showing, which causes a wavy appearance of the lines. When you hide gridlines later in the project, the wavy lines will disappear.

Figure 4–59

Other Ways

1. Click Table Properties button (Table Tools Layout tab | Table group), click Table tab (Table Properties dialog box), click Options button, select desired options (Table Options dialog box), click OK button in each dialog box

2. Right-click table (or, if using touch, tap 'Show Context Menu' button on mini toolbar), click Table Properties on shortcut menu, click Table tab (Table Properties dialog box), click Options button, select desired options (Table Options dialog box), click OK button in each dialog box

To Change Column Width

In reviewing the sample fees table, you notice that the columns containing the fees are different widths. Thus, the final step in formatting the sample fees table is to change the column widths because you want the columns containing the rates to all be the same width, specifically .95". The following steps change column widths by specifying a value on the ribbon.

1 Select the columns to be resized, in this case, all columns except the first.

2 Click the 'Table Column Width' box (Table Tools Layout tab | Cell Size group) to select it.

3 Type .95 in the 'Table Column Width' box and then press the ENTER key to change the width of the selected table columns (Figure 4–60).

4 Click anywhere to remove the selection from the table.

Figure 4–60

BTW

Table Columns
If you hold down the ALT key while dragging a column marker on the ruler or a column boundary in the table, the width measurements of all columns appear on the ruler as you drag the column marker or boundary.

To Page Break Manually

If the Facility heading appears at the bottom of the page below the sample fees table, insert a page break immediately to its left so that this heading appears at the top of the last page of the proposal (as shown in Figure 4–1 at the beginning of this module). The following steps insert a manual page break, if necessary.

1 If the Facility heading is not on the last page of the proposal, position the insertion point immediately to the left of the F in Facility.

2 Display the Insert tab.

3 Click the 'Insert a Page Break' button (Insert tab | Pages group) to insert a manual page break at the location of the insertion point, which will move the Facility heading to the last page of the proposal.

To Delete a Column

1 CREATE TITLE PAGE | 2 INSERT EXISTING DOCUMENT | 3 CREATE HEADER & FOOTER
4 EDIT & FORMAT LISTS | 5 EDIT & FORMAT TABLES | 6 CREATE WATERMARK

With the service fees table finished, the next task is to format the team members table. The following steps delete a column from a table. *Why? The table in the draft of the proposal contains a blank column that should be deleted.*

- Scroll to display the team members table in the document window.
- Position the insertion point in the column to be deleted (in this case, the rightmost column).

- Click the Delete Table button (Table Tools Layout tab | Rows & Columns group) to display the Delete Table menu (Figure 4–61).

- Click Delete Columns on the Delete Table menu to delete the column containing the insertion point (shown in Figure 4–62).

Figure 4–61

Other Ways

1. Right-click column to delete, click Delete Cells on shortcut menu, click 'Delete entire column' (Delete Cells dialog box), click OK button

2. Select column, right-click selection, click Delete Columns on shortcut menu

3. If using touch, press and hold column to delete, tap Delete Table button on mini toolbar, tap Delete Columns

TO DELETE A ROW

If you wanted to delete a row, you would perform the following tasks.

1. Position the insertion point in the row to be deleted; click the Delete Table button (Table Tools Layout tab | Rows & Columns group) and then click Delete Rows on the Delete Table menu.

or

2. If using touch, press and hold row to delete, tap Delete Table button on mini toolbar, tap Delete Rows.

or

3. Right-click the row to delete, click Delete Cells on the shortcut menu, click 'Delete entire row' (Delete Cells dialog box), and then click the OK button.

or

4. Select the row to be deleted, right-click the selected row, and then click Delete Rows on the shortcut menu.

To Split Cells

1 CREATE TITLE PAGE | 2 INSERT EXISTING DOCUMENT | 3 CREATE HEADER & FOOTER
4 EDIT & FORMAT LISTS | 5 EDIT & FORMAT TABLES | 6 CREATE WATERMARK

The top, left cell of the table contains the text, Team Members. In the draft of the sales proposal, this row is above the first two columns in the table (the job titles and employee name). This heading, Team Members, should be above the descriptions of the employee names, that is, above the second column. Thus, you will split the cell into two cells. *Why? With the cell split, you can reposition the heading, Team Members, above the second column.* The following steps split a single cell into two separate cells.

- Position the insertion point in the cell to split, in this case the top left cell as shown in Figure 4–62.
- Click the Split Cells button (Table Tools Layout tab | Merge group) to display the Split Cells dialog box (Figure 4–62).

Figure 4–62

②
- Verify the number of columns and rows into which you want the cell split, in this case, 2 columns and 1 row.
- Click the OK button (Split Cells dialog box) to split the one cell into two columns (Figure 4–63).

Figure 4–63

Other Ways

1. Right-click cell, click Split Cells on shortcut menu (or, if using touch, tap 'Show Context Menu' button on mini toolbar)

To Move Cell Contents

When you split a cell into two cells, Word places the contents of the original cell in the leftmost cell after the split. In this case, the contents (Team Members) should be in the right cell. Thus, the following steps move cell contents.

① Select the cell contents to be moved (in this case, Team Members).

② Drag the cell contents to the desired location (in this case, the second cell in the first row) (shown in Figure 4–64).

Q&A What if I cannot drag the cell contents properly?
Use the Cut and Paste commands.

BTW

Moving Tables
If you wanted to move a table to a new location, you would click in the table to display the table move handle in the upper-left corner of the table (shown in Figure 4–63) and then drag the table move handle to move the entire table to a new location.

To Move a Cell Boundary

1 CREATE TITLE PAGE | 2 INSERT EXISTING DOCUMENT | 3 CREATE HEADER & FOOTER
4 EDIT & FORMAT LISTS | 5 EDIT & FORMAT TABLES | 6 CREATE WATERMARK

Notice in Figure 4–64 that the cell boundary to the left of the Team Members label does not line up with the boundary to the right of the job titles. *Why not? This is because when you split a cell, Word divides the cell into evenly sized cells.* If you want the boundary to line up with other column boundaries, drag it to the desired location. The following steps move a cell boundary.

- Position the pointer on the cell boundary you wish to move so that the pointer changes to a double-headed arrow split by two vertical bars (Figure 4–64).

Q&A What if I cannot see the cell boundary?
Be sure that table gridlines are showing: View Table Gridlines button (Table Tools Layout tab | Table group).

Figure 4–64

- Drag the cell boundary to the desired new location, in this case, to line up with the column boundary to its right, as shown in Figure 4–65.

Q&A What if I am using a touch screen?
Position the insertion point in the upper-left cell, tap the Table Properties button (Table Tools Layout tab | Table group), tap the Cell tab (Table Properties dialog box), type 1.27 in the Preferred width box, and then tap the OK button.

Figure 4–65

Other Ways

1. Drag 'Move Table Column' marker on horizontal ruler to desired width

To Distribute Columns

1 CREATE TITLE PAGE | 2 INSERT EXISTING DOCUMENT | 3 CREATE HEADER & FOOTER
4 EDIT & FORMAT LISTS | 5 EDIT & FORMAT TABLES | 6 CREATE WATERMARK

The next step in formatting the team members table is to make the width of the first three columns uniform, that is, the same width. The following step distributes selected columns. *Why? Instead of checking and adjusting the width of each column individually, you can make all columns uniform at the same time.*

- Select the columns to format, in this case, the three leftmost columns.
- Click the Distribute Columns button (Table Tools Layout tab | Cell Size group) to make the width of the selected columns uniform (Figure 4–66).

Q&A How would I make all columns in the table uniform?
Simply place the insertion point somewhere in the table before clicking the Distribute Columns button.

Figure 4–66

Other Ways

1. Right-click selected columns, click 'Distribute Columns Evenly' on shortcut menu (or, if using touch, tap 'Show Context Menu' button on mini toolbar)

TO DISTRIBUTE ROWS

If you wanted to make rows the same height, you would perform the following tasks.

1. Select the rows to format.
2. Click the Distribute Rows button (Table Tools Layout tab | Cell Size group) (shown in Figure 4-66) to make the width of the selected rows uniform.

or

1. Right-click selected columns and then click 'Distribute Rows Evenly' on the shortcut menu (or, if using touch, tap the 'Show Context Menu' button on the mini toolbar).

To Insert a Column

In this project, the left edge of the team members table has a column that displays the label, Organization. Thus, the following steps insert a column at the left edge of the table.

1 Position the insertion point somewhere in the first column of the table.

2 Click the 'Insert Columns to the Left' button (Table Tools Layout tab | Rows & Columns group) to insert a column to the left of the column containing the insertion point (Figure 4–67).

3 Click anywhere in the table to remove the selection.

BTW

Draw Table

If you want to draw the boundary, rows, and columns of a table, click the 'Add a Table' button (Insert tab | Tables group) and then click Draw Table in the Add a Table gallery. Use the pencil-shaped pointer to draw the perimeter of the table and the inside rows and columns. Use the Table Eraser button (Table Tools Design tab | Draw group) to erase lines in the table. To continue drawing, click the Draw Table button (Table Tools Design tab | Draw group).

Figure 4–67

To Merge Cells and Enter Text

The label, Organization, is to be displayed vertically to the left of the bottom five rows in the table. To display this text, the five cells should be merged into a single cell. The following steps merge cells and then enter text in the merged cell.

1 Select the cells to merge, in this case, the bottom five cells in the first column of the table.

2 Click the Merge Cells button (Table Tools Layout tab | Merge group) to merge the five selected cells into one cell.

3 Type **Organization** in the merged cell.

4 If necessary, center the entered text (Figure 4–68).

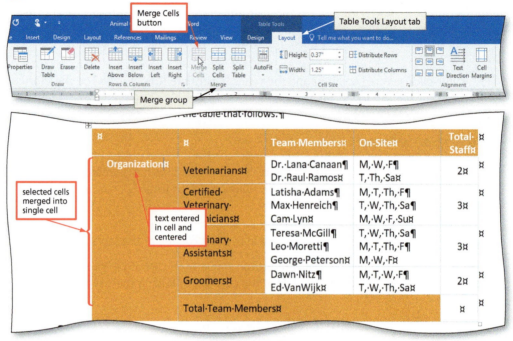

Figure 4–68

To Display Text in a Cell Vertically

1 CREATE TITLE PAGE | 2 INSERT EXISTING DOCUMENT | 3 CREATE HEADER & FOOTER
4 EDIT & FORMAT LISTS | 5 EDIT & FORMAT TABLES | 6 CREATE WATERMARK

The data you enter in cells is displayed horizontally by default. You can rotate the text so that it is displayed vertically. Changing the direction of text adds variety to your tables. The following step displays text vertically in a cell. **Why?** *The label, Organization, is displayed vertically at the left edge of the table.*

1

- Position the insertion point in the cell that contains the text to rotate (in this case, Organization).

- Click the Text Direction button twice (Table Tools Layout tab | Alignment group) so that the text reads from bottom to top in the cell (Figure 4–69).

Q&A | Why click the Text Direction button twice?
The first time you click the Text Direction button (Table Tools Layout tab | Alignment group), the text in the cell reads from top to bottom. The second time you click it, the text is displayed so that it reads from bottom to top (Figure 4–69). If you were to click the button a third time, the text would be displayed horizontally again.

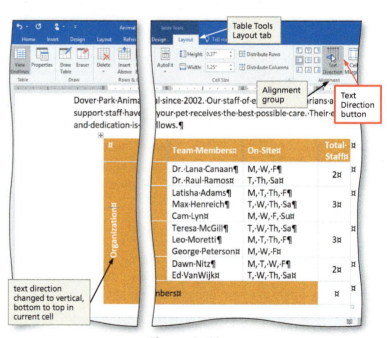

Figure 4–69

To Change Column Width

The cell containing the vertical text is too wide. Thus, the next step is to change the width of that column. The following step changes column width using the ruler.

1 Drag the column's boundary inward, as shown in Figure 4–70, to resize the column.

Q&A What if I am using a touch screen?

Position the insertion point in the column to adjust. Tap the 'Table Column Width' box (Table Tools Layout tab | Cell Size group), type `.35` as the column width, and then press the ENTER key.

Figure 4–70

To Remove Cell Shading

In this table, only the first row and first column should have shading. Thus, the following steps remove shading from table cells.

1 Select the cells that should not contain shading (in this case, all of the cells below the first row and to the right of the first column).

2 Display the Table Tools Design tab. Click the Shading arrow (Table Tools Design tab | Table Styles group) to display the Shading gallery (Figure 4–71).

Figure 4–71

③ Click No Color in the Shading gallery to remove the shading from the selected cells (shown in Figure 4–72).

④ Click anywhere in the table to remove the selection.

To Hide Gridlines

You no longer need to see the gridlines in the table. Thus, you can hide the gridlines. The following steps hide gridlines.

① If necessary, position the insertion point in a table cell.

② Display the Table Tools Layout tab.

③ Click the 'View Table Gridlines' button (Table Tools Layout tab | Table group) to hide gridlines in the table on the screen.

To Border a Table

1 CREATE TITLE PAGE | 2 INSERT EXISTING DOCUMENT | 3 CREATE HEADER & FOOTER
4 EDIT & FORMAT LISTS | 5 EDIT & FORMAT TABLES | 6 CREATE WATERMARK

The table in this project has a ½-point, gold border around all cells. The following steps change the border color in a table using the Borders and Shading dialog box. *Why? Earlier in this module when you created the title page, the border line weight was changed to 6 point. Because the table border should be ½ point, you will use the Borders and Shading dialog box to change the line weight before adding the border to the table.*

①

- Position the insertion point somewhere in the table.

- Display the Table Tools Design tab. Click the Borders arrow (Table Tools Design tab | Table Styles group) to display the Borders gallery.

- Click Borders and Shading in the Borders gallery to display the Borders and Shading dialog box.

- Click All in the Setting area (Borders and Shading dialog box), which will place a border on every cell in the table.

- Click the Color arrow and then click 'Gold, Accent 5' (ninth color, first row) in the Color palette to specify the border color (Figure 4–72).

②

- Click the OK button to place the border shown in the preview area of the dialog box around the table cells in the document (shown in Figure 4–73).

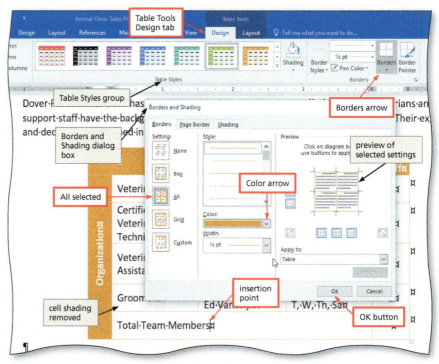

Figure 4–72

To Sum Columns in a Table

Word can calculate the totals of rows and columns. You also can specify the format for how the totals will be displayed. The following steps sum a column in the table. *Why? In this project, the last row should display the sum (total) of the values in the last column: Total Staff.*

1

- Position the insertion point in the cell to contain the sum (last row, Total Staff column).

2

- Display the Table Tools Layout tab.

- Click the Formula button (Table Tools Layout tab | Data group) to display the Formula dialog box (Figure 4–73).

Q&A What is the formula that shows in the Formula box, and can I change it?
Word places a default formula in the Formula box, depending on the location of the

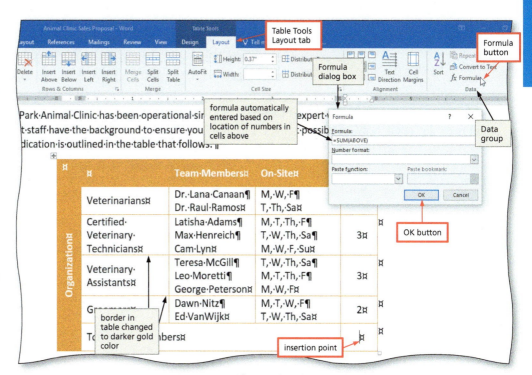

Figure 4–73

numbers in surrounding cells. In this case, because numbers are above the current cell, Word displays a formula that will add the numbers above the current cell. You can change the formula that Word proposes, or type a different formula. For example, instead of summing numbers you can multiply them.

3

- Click the Number format arrow (Formula dialog box) and then click the desired format for the result of the computation, in this case, the format with the numeral 0 (Figure 4–74).

Q&A Why select the format with the numeral 0?
You want the result to be displayed as a whole number, so you select the numeral 0. If you

Figure 4–74

wanted the result to display with cents, you would select the format #,##0.00 (the # symbol means to display a blank if the number has a value of zero).

4

- Click the OK button (Formula dialog box) to place the sum of the numbers using the specified format in the current cell (Figure 4–75).

Q&A Can I sum a row instead of a column?
Yes. You would position the insertion point in an empty cell at the right edge of the row before clicking the Formula button.

If I make a change to a number in a table, does Word automatically recalculate the sum?
No. You will need to update the field by right-clicking it and then clicking Update Field on the shortcut menu or by selecting the field and then pressing the F9 key.

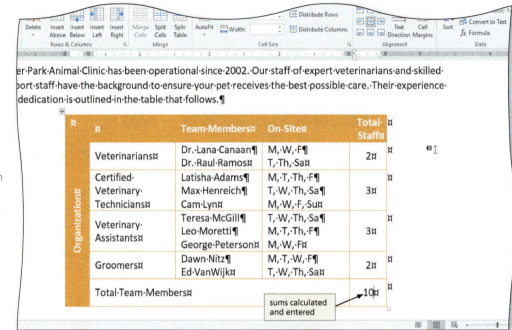

Figure 4–75

To Delete a Blank Paragraph

If you notice an extra paragraph mark below the team member table that it is causing an extra blank page in the document, you should delete the blank paragraph. If necessary, the following steps delete a blank paragraph.

1 Press CTRL+END to position the insertion point at the end of the document.

2 If necessary, press the BACKSPACE key to remove the extra blank paragraph and delete the blank page.

3 If text spills onto a fourth page, remove space above paragraphs in the sales proposal until the entire proposal fits on three pages, as shown in Figure 4–1.

BTW
Distributing a Document
Instead of printing and distributing a hard copy of a document, you can distribute the document electronically. Options include sending the document via email; posting it on cloud storage (such as OneDrive) and sharing the file with others; posting it on social media, a blog, or other website; and sharing a link associated with an online location of the document. You also can create and share a PDF or XPS image of the document, so that users can view the file in Acrobat Reader or XPS Viewer instead of in Word.

Creating a Watermark

The final task in this module is to create a watermark for the pages of the sales proposal. A **watermark** is text or a graphic that is displayed on top of or behind the text in a document. For example, a catalog may print the words, Sold Out, on top of sold-out items. The first draft of a five-year-plan may have the word, Draft, printed behind the text of the document. Some companies use their logos or other graphics as watermarks to add visual appeal to their documents.

To Zoom Multiple Pages

The following steps display multiple pages in their entirety in the document window as large as possible, so that you can see the position of the watermark as you create it.

 Press CTRL+HOME to position the insertion point at the beginning of the document.

 Display the View tab. Click the Multiple Pages button (View tab | Zoom group) to display all three pages in the document window as large as possible.

To Create a Watermark

1 CREATE TITLE PAGE | 2 INSERT EXISTING DOCUMENT | 3 CREATE HEADER & FOOTER
4 EDIT & FORMAT LISTS | 5 EDIT & FORMAT TABLES | **6 CREATE WATERMARK**

In this project, the image of paw prints is displayed behind all content in the proposal as a watermark. *Why? The graphic adds visual appeal to the document, enticing readers to look at its contents.* The following steps create a watermark.

- Display the Design tab.

- Click the Watermark button (Design tab | Page Background group) to display the Watermark gallery (Figure 4–76).

Figure 4–76

- Click Custom Watermark in the Watermark gallery to display the Printed Watermark dialog box.

- Click the Picture watermark option button to select it (Printed Watermark dialog box), which enables you to select an image for the watermark.

- Click the Select Picture button to display the Insert Pictures dialog box.

- Type **paw prints** in the Search box and then click the Search button. Click the paw prints image shown in Figure 4–1, or a similar image, and then click the Insert button to download the image and close the dialog box. (Or, you can click the 'Browse from a file' link in the Insert Pictures dialog box, navigate to the file called Colorful-Paw-Prints-Pattern-Background-2400px.png in the Data Files, select the file, and then click the Insert button (Insert Picture dialog box)).

- Click the Apply button to show a preview of the watermark on the pages in the document window (Figure 4–77).

Figure 4–77

- Click the Close button (Printed Watermark dialog box) to close the dialog box.

Q&A

How do I remove a watermark from a document?
Click the Watermark button (Design tab | Page Background group) and then click Remove Watermark in the Watermark gallery (shown in Figure 4-76).

How do I create a text watermark?
Click Text watermark in the Printed Watermark dialog box (shown in Figure 4–77), select or type the text for the watermark, select format options, and then click the OK button.

Other Ways

1. Click 'Explore Quick Parts' button (Insert tab | Text group), click 'Building Blocks Organizer' on Explore Quick Parts menu, select desired watermark (Building Blocks Organizer dialog box), click Insert button

To Change Theme Fonts

1 CREATE TITLE PAGE | 2 INSERT EXISTING DOCUMENT | 3 CREATE HEADER & FOOTER
4 EDIT & FORMAT LISTS | 5 EDIT & FORMAT TABLES | 6 CREATE WATERMARK

The final step in formatting this project is to change the fonts used for text in the document. *Why? With the watermark, some of the text is difficult to read. You would prefer a bolder font.* If text is entered using the headings and body text fonts, you easily can change the font in the entire document by changing the theme fonts, or font set. A **font set** defines one font for headings and another for body text. The default font set is Office, which uses the Cambria font for headings and the Calibri font for body text. In Word, you can select from more than 20 predefined, coordinated font sets to give the document's text a new look.

If you previously changed a font using buttons on the ribbon or mini toolbar, Word will not alter those when you change the font set because changes to the font set are not applied to individually changed fonts. This means the font of the title on the title page will remain as Bernard MT Condensed if you change the font set. The following steps change the theme fonts to TrebuchetMs for headings and for body text.

1

- Click the Theme Fonts button (Design tab | Document Formatting group) to display the Theme Fonts gallery (Figure 4–78).

Experiment

- Point to various font sets in the Theme Fonts gallery and watch the fonts of text in the document change.

2

- Scroll through the Theme Fonts gallery and then click TrebuchetMs in the Fonts gallery to set the document theme fonts to the selected font (shown in Figure 4-1 at the beginning of this module).

Q&A

What if I want to return to the default font set?

You would click the Theme Fonts button and then click Office in the Fonts gallery.

- If necessary, insert a page break before the Facility heading. Make any additional adjustments to spacing, table column widths, etc., so that your document looks like Figure 4–1 shown at the beginning of this module.

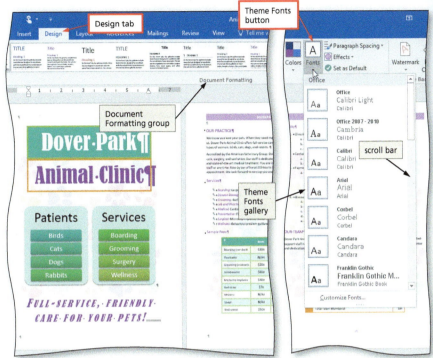

Figure 4–78

To Check Spelling, Save, Print, and Exit Word

The following steps check the spelling of the document, save and print the document, and then exit Word.

1 Display the Review tab. Click the 'Spelling & Grammar' button (Review tab | Proofing group) to begin the spelling and grammar check. Correct any misspelled words.

2 Save the sales proposal again with the same file name.

3 If requested by your instructor, print the sales proposal (shown in Figure 4–1 at the beginning of this module).

4 Exit Word.

BTW

Conserving Ink and Toner

If you want to conserve ink or toner, you can instruct Word to print draft quality documents by clicking File on the ribbon to open the Backstage view, clicking the Options tab in the Backstage view to display the Word Options dialog box, clicking Advanced in the left pane (Word Options dialog box), scrolling to the Print area in the right pane, placing a check mark in the 'Use draft quality' check box, and then clicking the OK button. Then, use the Backstage view to print the document as usual.

Summary

In this module, you learned how to add a border to a paragraph, change paragraph indentation, insert and format a SmartArt graphic, apply character effects, insert a section break, insert a Word document in an open document, change theme fonts, insert formatted headers and footers, sort lists and tables, modify and format existing Word tables, sum columns in a table, insert a watermark, and change theme fonts.

What decisions will you need to make when creating your next proposal?

Use these guidelines as you complete the assignments in this module and create your own proposals outside of this class.

1. Identify the nature of the proposal.

    a) If someone else requests that you develop the proposal, it is solicited. Be sure to include all requested information in a **solicited proposal**.

    b) When you write a proposal because you recognize a need, the proposal is unsolicited. With an **unsolicited proposal**, you must gather information you believe will be relevant and of interest to the intended audience.

2. Design an eye-catching title page.

    a) The title page should convey the overall message of the sales proposal.

    b) Use text, graphics, formats, and colors that reflect the goals of the sales proposal.

    c) Be sure to include a title.

3. Compose the text of the sales proposal.

    a) Sales proposals vary in length, style, and formality, but all should be designed to elicit acceptance from the reader.

    b) The sales proposal should have a neat, organized appearance.

    c) A successful sales proposal uses succinct wording and includes lists for textual messages.

    d) Write text using active voice, instead of passive voice.

    e) Assume that readers of unsolicited sales proposals have no previous knowledge about the topic.

    f) Be sure the goal of the proposal is clear.

    g) Establish a theme and carry it throughout the proposal.

4. Enhance the sales proposal with appropriate visuals.

    a) Use visuals to add interest, clarify ideas, and illustrate points.

    b) Visuals include tables, charts, and graphical images (i.e., photos, etc.).

5. Proofread and edit the proposal.

    a) Carefully review the sales proposal to be sure it contains no spelling, grammar, mathematical, or other errors.

    b) Check that transitions between sentences and paragraphs are smooth. Ensure that the purpose of the proposal is stated clearly.

    c) Ask others to review the proposal and give you suggestions for improvements.

Apply Your Knowledge

Reinforce the skills and apply the concepts you learned in this module.

Working with a Table

Note: To complete this assignment, you will be required to use the Data Files. Please contact your instructor for information about accessing the Data Files.

Instructions: Run Word. Open the document called Apply 4–1 Projected College Expenses Draft located on the Data Files. The document contains a Word table that you are to modify. The modified table is shown in Figure 4–79.

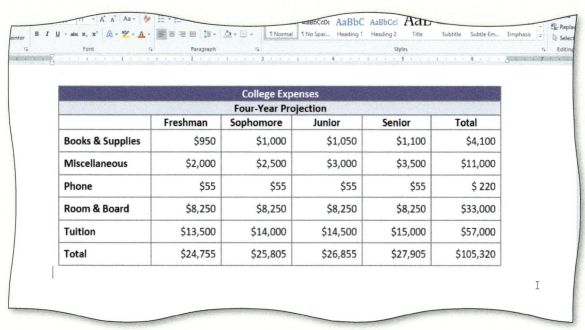

College Expenses					
Four-Year Projection					
	Freshman	Sophomore	Junior	Senior	Total
Books & Supplies	$950	$1,000	$1,050	$1,100	$4,100
Miscellaneous	$2,000	$2,500	$3,000	$3,500	$11,000
Phone	$55	$55	$55	$55	$ 220
Room & Board	$8,250	$8,250	$8,250	$8,250	$33,000
Tuition	$13,500	$14,000	$14,500	$15,000	$57,000
Total	$24,755	$25,805	$26,855	$27,905	$105,320

Figure 4–79

Perform the following tasks:

1. Show gridlines.

2. Delete the blank column between the Junior and Senior columns.

3. Use the Distribute Rows command to evenly space all the rows in the table.

4. Use the Distribute Columns command to make the Freshman, Sophomore, Junior, Senior, and Total columns evenly spaced.

5. Change the width of the Freshman, Sophomore, Junior, Senior, and Total columns to 1".

6. Use the Formula button (Table Tools Layout tab | Data group) to place totals in the bottom row for the Freshman, Sophomore, Junior, and Senior columns. The totals should be formatted to display dollar signs (no cents). *Hint*: You will need to edit the formula and remove the .00 from the end of it.

7. Use the Formula button (Table Tools Layout tab | Data group) to place totals in the right column, also formatted to display dollar signs (no cents). Start in the bottom-right cell and work your way up the column.

8. Add a row to the top of the table. Merge all cells in the first row into a single cell. Enter the title, College Expenses, as the table title. Change the alignment to Align Top Center.

9. Split the cell in the first row into two rows (one column). In the new cell below the title, enter the text, Four-Year Projection, as the subtitle.

10. Shade the first row Purple, Accent 4, Darker 25%. Change the font color of text in the first row to White, Background 1. Shade the second row Purple, Accent 4, Lighter 80%.

11. Add a 1 pt, White, Background 1, Darker 50% border to all cells in the table.

12. Hide gridlines.

13. Change the height of the row containing the year-in-college headings (row 3) to 0.1". Change the alignment of these headings to Align Top Center.

Continued >

Apply Your Knowledge *continued*

14. Change the height of all expense rows and the total row (rows 4 through 9) to 0.3".

15. Change the alignment of the cells in the first column to Align Center Left.

16. Change the alignment of the cells containing dollar amounts to Align Center Right.

17. Center the entire table across the width of the page.

18. Sort the rows containing the expenses.

19. If requested by your instructor, add your last name to the first row of the table before the words, College Expenses.

20. Save the modified file with the file name, Apply 4–1 Projected College Expenses Modified, and submit it (shown in Figure 4–79) in the format specified by your instructor.

21. ✳ Which number format did you use in the Formula dialog box in #6 in this exercise? Why do some totals have a space after the dollar sign and others do not? Which formula appeared in #7?

Extend Your Knowledge

Extend the skills you learned in this module and experiment with new skills. You may need to use Help to complete the assignment.

Using Word's Draw Table Feature

Instructions: Run Word. You will use Word's Draw Table feature to draw a table.

Perform the following tasks:

1. Use Help to learn about Draw Table and text watermarks.

2. Draw the table shown in Figure 4–80. That is, use the Draw Table button to create the blank table.

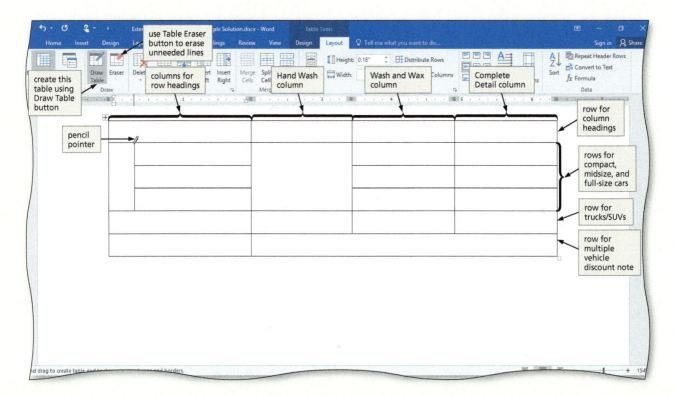

Figure 4–80

3. In the top row, enter these headings in the columns: Type of Vehicle, Hand Wash, Wash and Wax, and Complete Detail.

4. In the leftmost column of the table, enter the text, Car, so that it displays vertically in the cell.

5. In the second column of the table, enter these labels in the second, third, and fourth rows (to the right of the vertical text, Car): Compact, Midsize, and Full-size. Enter these labels in the bottom two leftmost rows: Truck/SUV and Multiple vehicle discount.

6. For the Hand Wash column, enter $50 in the cell to the right of the Compact, Midsize, and Full-size rows.

7. For the Wash and Wax column, use this data for the table: Compact – $100, Midsize - $115, Full-size - $120, and Truck/SUV - $150.

8. For the Complete Detail column, use this data for the table: Compact – $225, Midsize - $250, Full-size - $300, and Truck/SUV - $375.

9. Enter the text, $20 savings per vehicle serviced in a single month!, in the rightmost bottom row.

10. Align and shade table cells, along with any other relevant enhancements, as you deem appropriate (alignment, shading, etc.).

11. If requested by your instructor, enter your name below the table.

12. Save the revised document using the file name, Extend 4–1 Car Wash Table, and then submit it in the format specified by your instructor.

13. ❋ Which alignment and shading for the table cells did you choose and why?

Expand Your World

Create a solution that uses cloud or web technologies by learning and investigating on your own from general guidance.

Using Word Online to Create a Table

Instructions: You are using a mobile device or computer at school that does not have Word but has Internet access. To make use of time between classes, you use Word Online to create a table showing your volunteer service (Figure 4–81).

Perform the following tasks:

1. Run a browser. Search for the text, Word Online, using a search engine. Visit several websites to learn about Word Online. Navigate to the Office Online website. You will need to sign in to your OneDrive account.

2. Create a new blank Word document using Word Online. Name the document Expand 4–1 Volunteer Services. Change the zoom to page width.

3. Enter and format the table, as shown in Figure 4–81.

4. Apply a table style to the table (any style).

5. Change colors of the table to a color other than blue.

6. Remove the First Column shading (Table Tools Layout tab | Table Style Options group).

Continued >

Expand Your World *continued*

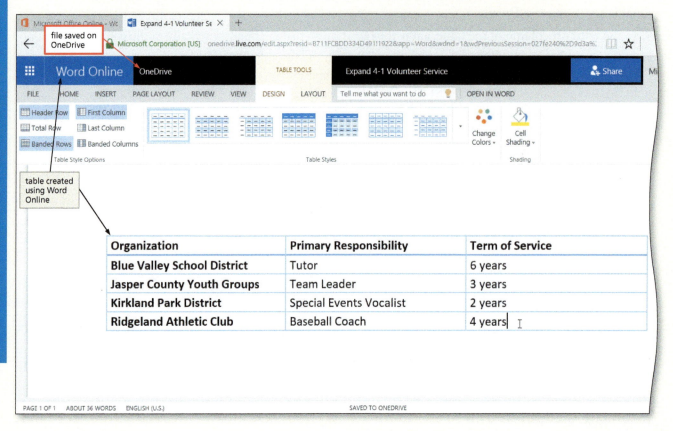

Figure 4–81

7. Narrow the width of the last column to fit the contents better and then change the cell alignment in this column to Align Top Center. How did you adjust the column width?

8. Add a row to the bottom of the table that identifies volunteer service you have performed.

9. Save the document again.

10. Submit the Expand 4–1 Volunteer Service document in the format requested by your instructor. Sign out of your OneDrive account.

11. ✹ Which table features that are covered in the module are not available in Word Online? Answer the question posed in #7.

In the Labs

Design, create, modify, and/or use a document following the guidelines, concepts, and skills presented in this module. Labs 1 and 2, which increase in difficulty, require you to create solutions based on what you learned in the module; Lab 3 requires you to apply your creative thinking and problem-solving skills to design and implement a solution.

Lab 1: **Creating a Proposal with a SmartArt Graphic, a Bulleted List, and a Table**

Note: To complete this assignment, you will be required to use the Data Files. Please contact your instructor for information about accessing the Data Files.

Problem: The owner of Java Junction has hired you to prepare a sales proposal for her coffee shop (Figure 4–82).

Perform the following tasks:

1. Change the document theme to Retrospect.

2. Change the theme fonts to the Tw Cen MT-Rockwell font set.

3. Create the title page as shown in Figure 4–82a. Be sure to do the following:

   a. Insert the SmartArt graphic, add text to it, and bold the text. Change the colors and style of the SmartArt graphic as shown. Change the spacing above the SmartArt graphic to 42 points and the spacing after the graphic to 54 points.

   b. Change the fonts, font sizes, and font colors as specified in the figure. Add the paragraph border. Indent the left and right edges of the title paragraph by 0.25 inches and the left and right edges of the paragraph below the SmartArt graphic by 0.5 inches. Expand the characters in the sentence at the bottom of the page by 7 points.

4. At the bottom of the title page, insert a next page section break. Clear formatting.

5. Create the second page of the proposal as shown in Figure 4–82b.

   a. Format the Heading 1 style as shown and update the Heading 1 style accordingly.

   b. Enter the multilevel list as shown.

   c. Create the table as shown. Border the table as specified. Distribute rows so that they are all the same height. Change the row height to 0.21 inches. Center the table between the margins. Change the first column's alignment to Align Top Left the text, and all other text in the table to Align Top Center. Shade the table cells as specified. Change cell spacing to 0.04 inches between cells.

   d. Insert the formatted footer using the Blank (Three Columns) design. The footer should appear only on the second page (section) of the proposal. Enter the footer text as shown.

   e. If requested by your instructor, change the phone number in the footer to your phone number.

6. Add a picture watermark of the coffee beans. The picture is located on the Data Files. Scale the picture to 50% in the Printed Watermark dialog box.

7. Adjust the spacing above and below paragraphs as necessary to fit all content as shown in the figure.

8. Check the spelling. Save the document with Lab 4–1 Coffee House Proposal as the file name.

9. ✹ This proposal contains a multilevel numbered list. How would you change the font size of the numbers and letters at the beginning of each list item?

Continued >

In the Labs *continued*

Figure 4–82 (a)

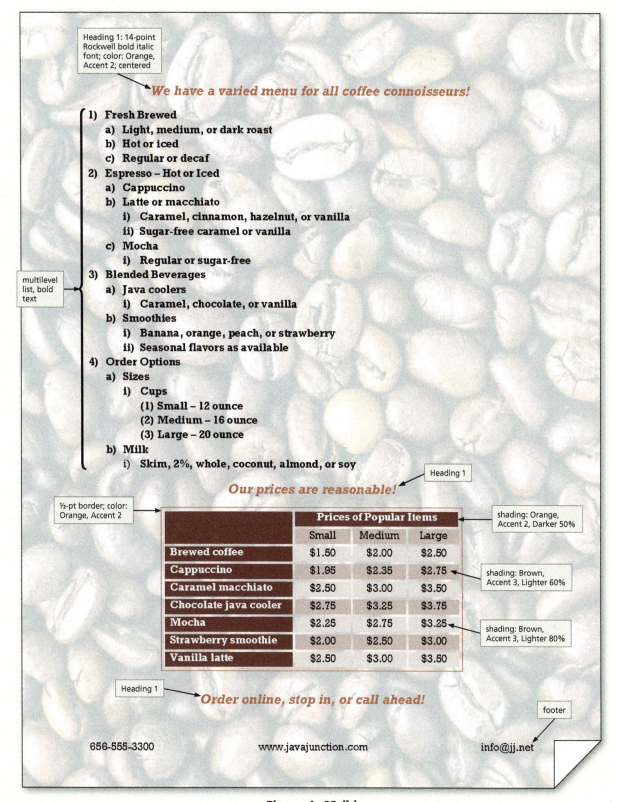

Heading 1: 14-point Rockwell bold italic font; color: Orange, Accent 2; centered

We have a varied menu for all coffee connoisseurs!

multilevel list, bold text

1) **Fresh Brewed**
   a) **Light, medium, or dark roast**
   b) **Hot or iced**
   c) **Regular or decaf**
2) **Espresso – Hot or Iced**
   a) **Cappuccino**
   b) **Latte or macchiato**
      i) **Caramel, cinnamon, hazelnut, or vanilla**
      ii) **Sugar-free caramel or vanilla**
   c) **Mocha**
      i) **Regular or sugar-free**
3) **Blended Beverages**
   a) **Java coolers**
      i) **Caramel, chocolate, or vanilla**
   b) **Smoothies**
      i) **Banana, orange, peach, or strawberry**
      ii) **Seasonal flavors as available**
4) **Order Options**
   a) **Sizes**
      i) **Cups**
         (1) **Small – 12 ounce**
         (2) **Medium – 16 ounce**
         (3) **Large – 20 ounce**
   b) **Milk**
      i) **Skim, 2%, whole, coconut, almond, or soy**

Heading 1

Our prices are reasonable!

½-pt border; color: Orange, Accent 2

shading: Orange, Accent 2, Darker 50%

shading: Brown, Accent 3, Lighter 60%

shading: Brown, Accent 3, Lighter 80%

	Prices of Popular Items		
	Small	Medium	Large
Brewed coffee	$1.50	$2.00	$2.50
Cappuccino	$1.95	$2.35	$2.75
Caramel macchiato	$2.50	$3.00	$3.50
Chocolate java cooler	$2.75	$3.25	$3.75
Mocha	$2.25	$2.75	$3.25
Strawberry smoothie	$2.00	$2.50	$3.00
Vanilla latte	$2.50	$3.00	$3.50

Heading 1

Order online, stop in, or call ahead!

footer

656-555-3300   www.javajunction.com   info@jj.net

Figure 4–82 (b)

Continued >

In the Labs *continued*

Lab 2: **Creating a Proposal with a SmartArt Graphic, a Complex Table, Picture Bullets, and a Numbered List**

Problem: The owner of the A-Plus Tutoring has hired you to prepare a sales proposal that describes the center (Figure 4–83).

Perform the following tasks:

1. Change the document theme to the Facet theme.

2. Change the theme fonts to the Franklin Gothic font set.

3. Create the title page as shown in Figure 4–83a. Be sure to do the following:

   a. Insert the Vertical Equation SmartArt graphic, located in the Relationship category.

   b. Change the fonts, font sizes, font colors, and shading as indicated in the figure. Indent the left and right edges of the title paragraph by 0.5 inches. Expand the characters in the sentence at the bottom of the page by 7 points.

4. At the bottom of the title page, insert a next page section break. Clear formatting.

5. Create the second page of the proposal as shown in Figure 4–83b.

   a. Insert the formatted header using the Banded design. The header should appear only on the second page of the proposal. Enter the header text as shown.

   b. If requested by your instructor, add your name to the header.

   c. Format the headings using the heading styles specified. Adjust spacing before the Heading 1 style to 18 point and after to 6 point, and before the Heading 2 style to 12 point and after to 6 point. Update both heading styles.

   d. Create the bulleted list using the picture bullets shown (search for the keyword, star, or use the image on the Data Files).

   e. Create the multilevel numbered list as shown.

   f. Create the table as shown. Distribute rows so that they are all the same height (about 0.29"). Align center all text except the row headings, which should be set to Align Center Left. Center the table. Change the direction of the Weekdays heading as shown. Shade the table cells as indicated in the figure.

6. Create a text watermark of 10 occurrences of the text, A+, with each occurrence separated by a space. In the Printed Watermark dialog box, change the watermark to 48-point Verdana with a semitransparent color of Blue-Gray, Text 2, Lighter 60%. The layout should be diagonal.

7. If necessary, adjust spacing above and below paragraphs to fit all content as shown in the figure. Check the spelling of the proposal. Save the document with Lab 4–2 Tutoring Center Proposal as the file name and then submit it in the format specified by your instructor.

8. ✳ This proposal contains a text watermark, which is semitransparent by default. For what type of text would you want to remove the check mark from the semitransparent check box?

72-point Rockwell Extra Bold font; color: Yellow

72-point Rockwell Extra Bold font; color: White, Background 1

shading color and 6-point box border color: Orange, Accent 4

72-point Rockwell Extra Bold font; color: Orange, Accent 4

SmartArt graphic – Type: Relationship Layout: Vertical Equation Colors: Colored Fill - Accent 2 Style: Intense Effect

13-point Franklin Gothic Book font

30-point Franklin Gothic Book font

36-point Rockwell bold italic font; color: Orange, Accent 4

text watermark

Figure 4–83 (a)

Continued >

In the Labs *continued*

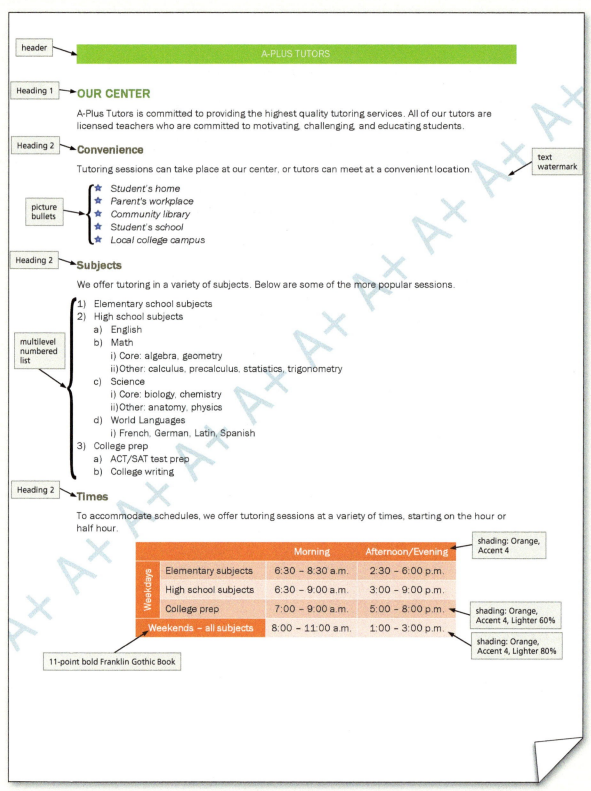

Figure 4–83 (b)

Lab 3: **Consider This: Your Turn**

Create a Proposal for a Small Business

Note: To complete this assignment, you will be required to use the Data Files. Please contact your instructor for information about accessing the Data Files.

Problem: As a part-time employee at a local deli, you have been asked to design a multipage sales proposal that can be distributed in the community.

Part 1:   The proposal should contain a title page, followed by a page of information about the deli. The title page is to contain the deli name, Deli Delicious, formatted with a border and shading. Include an appropriate SmartArt graphic that contains these words, at a minimum: fresh ingredients, reasonable prices, fast service, and dine in or carry out. Include this text on the title page: Stop by, call ahead, or order online!

The source content for the second page of the proposal is in a file called Lab 4–3 Consider This Your Turn Deli Draft. Use the concepts and techniques presented in this module to create and format the sales proposal. Include an appropriate watermark. Be sure to check the spelling and grammar of the finished document. Submit your assignment in the format specified by your instructor.

Part 2:   ✷ You made several decisions while creating the sales proposal in this assignment: how to organize and format the title page (fonts, font sizes, colors, shading, styles, etc.), which SmartArt graphic to use on the title page, and how to organize and format the tables and lists. What was the rationale behind each of these decisions? When you proofread the document, what further revisions did you make and why?

5 Using a Template to Create a Resume and Sharing a Finished Document

Objectives

You will have mastered the material in this module when you can:

- Use a template to create a document
- Change document margins
- Personalize a document template
- Indent a paragraph
- Customize theme fonts
- Create and modify a style
- Insert a building block
- Save a Word document as a PDF file and edit a PDF file

- Run the compatibility checker
- Enable others to access a document on OneDrive
- Send a Word document using email
- Save a Word document as a webpage
- Format text as a hyperlink
- Change a style set

Introduction

Some people prefer to use their own creative skills to design and compose Word documents. Using Word, for example, you can develop the content and decide the location of each item in a document. On occasion, however, you may have difficulty composing a particular type of document. To assist with the task of creating certain types of documents, such as resumes and letters, Word provides templates. A **template** is similar to a form with prewritten text; that is, Word prepares the requested document with text and/or formatting common to all documents of this nature. After Word creates a document from a template, you fill in the blanks or replace prewritten words in the document.

Once you have created a document, such as a resume, you often share it with others electronically via email, webpages, or links.

Project — Resume

At some time, you will prepare a resume to send to prospective employers. In addition to some personal information, a **resume** usually contains the applicant's educational background and job experience. Employers review many resumes for each vacant position. Thus, you should design your resume carefully so that it presents you as the best candidate for the job.

The project in this module follows generally accepted guidelines for creating resumes and uses Word to create the resume shown in Figure 5–1. The resume for Nina Tamaya Yazzie, an upcoming graduate of a journalism program, uses a Word template to present relevant information to a potential employer.

2640 Bartlett Street
Ponrolet, MI 66589
872-555-1547 (cell)
nyazzie@world.net

NINA TAMAYA YAZZIE

OBJECTIVE To obtain a full-time reporter position with a broadcasting station in the Midwest.

EDUCATION **B.A. JOURNALISM – HARTFORD COLLEGE**
December 2017, GPA 3.92/4.00

- Dean's List, every semester
- Student Publications Award, May 2017
- *Civics Journal*, 1st Place, political perspective article
- Areas of concentration:
  Broadcast reporting
  Intercultural communications
  Mass media
  Newswriting

A.A. TECHNICAL WRITING – WHEATON COMMUNITY COLLEGE
December 2015, GPA 3.94/4.00

EXPERIENCE **ASSISTANT COORDINATOR – PONROLET COMMUNITY CENTER**
August 2016 – Present

Assist in developing programs designed to increase literacy and reading skills; conduct reading programs for children; compose, proofread, and edit monthly newsletter.

MEMBERSHIPS Alpha Kappa Omega National Honor Society

Literacy Council, Ponrolet Village Board

Student Government Association, Secretary

COMMUNITY SERVICE **READING BUDDY – PONROLET PARK DISTRICT**
October 2016 – Present

Volunteer eight hours a week at the local community center in the district's Reading Buddy program, which works to develop reading skills of children in elementary school.

Figure 5–1

In this module, you will learn how to create the resume shown in Figure 5–1. The following roadmap identifies general activities you will perform as you progress through this module:

1. CREATE a new resume DOCUMENT FROM a Word TEMPLATE.

2. MODIFY AND FORMAT the resume TEMPLATE.

3. SAVE the resume DOCUMENT IN OTHER FORMATS so that you can share it with others.

4. MAKE the resume DOCUMENT AVAILABLE ONLINE so that others can access it.

5. CREATE a WEBPAGE FROM the resume WORD DOCUMENT.

6. FORMAT the resume WEBPAGE.

To Run Word and Change Word Settings

If you are using a computer to step through the project in this module and you want your screens to match the figures in this book, you should change your screen's resolution to 1366 × 768. The following steps run Word, display formatting marks, and change the zoom to page width.

1 Run Word and create a blank document in the Word window. If necessary, maximize the Word window.

2 If the Print Layout button on the status bar is not selected (shown in Figure 5–4), click it so that your screen is in Print Layout view.

3 If the 'Show/Hide ¶' button (Home tab | Paragraph group) is not selected already, click it to display formatting marks on the screen.

4 To display the page the same width as the document window, if necessary, click the Page Width button (View tab | Zoom group).

BTW

Touch Screen Differences
The Office and Windows interfaces may vary if you are using a touch screen. For this reason, you might notice that the function or appearance of your touch screen differs slightly from this module's presentation.

Using a Template to Create a Resume

Although you could compose a resume in a blank document window, this module shows how to use a template instead, where Word formats the resume with appropriate headings and spacing. You then customize the resume that the template generated by filling in blanks and by selecting and replacing text.

To Create a New Document from an Online Template

1 CREATE DOCUMENT FROM TEMPLATE | 2 MODIFY & FORMAT TEMPLATE | 3 SAVE DOCUMENT IN OTHER FORMATS
4 MAKE DOCUMENT AVAILABLE ONLINE | 5 CREATE WEBPAGE FROM WORD DOCUMENT | 6 FORMAT WEBPAGE

Word has a variety of templates available online to assist you with creating documents. Available online templates include agendas, award certificates, calendars, expense reports, greeting cards, invitations, invoices, letters, meeting minutes, memos, resumes, and statements. When you select an online template, Word downloads (or copies) it from the Office.com website to your computer or mobile device. Many of the templates use the same design or style. *Why? If you create related documents, such as a resume and a cover letter, you can use the same template design or style so that the documents complement one another.* The following steps create a resume using the Basic resume (Timeless design) template.

● Click File on the ribbon to open the Backstage view and then click the New tab in the Backstage view to display the New gallery, which initially lists several featured templates.

● Type **resume** in the 'Search for online templates' box and then click the Start searching button to display a list of online resume templates.

● If necessary, scroll through the list of templates to display the Basic resume (Timeless design) thumbnail (Figure 5–2).

Can I select a template from the Word start screen that appears when I initially run Word? Yes, instead of selecting Blank document from the Word start screen, you can select any of the available templates.

Figure 5–2

● Click the 'Basic resume (Timeless design)' thumbnail to select the template and display it in a preview window (Figure 5–3).

🔍 **Experiment**

● Click the Back and Forward buttons on the sides of the preview window to view previews of other templates. When finished, display the 'Basic resume (Timeless design)' thumbnail in the preview window.

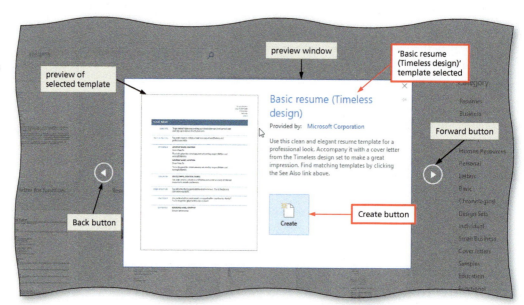

Figure 5–3

What if I cannot locate the Basic resume (Timeless design) template? Exit the Backstage view and then proceed to the steps called To Open a Document Created from a Template that are shaded yellow and immediately follow these steps.

3

- Click the Create button to create a new document based on the selected template (Figure 5–4).

- If the resume template displays your name instead of the text, YOUR NAME, as shown in Figure 5–4, click the Undo button on the Quick Access Toolbar to reset the content control (content controls are discussed in the next section).

Figure 5–4

4

- If requested by your instructor, print the resume template so that you can see the entire resume created by the resume template using the Basic resume (Timeless design) (Figure 5–5).

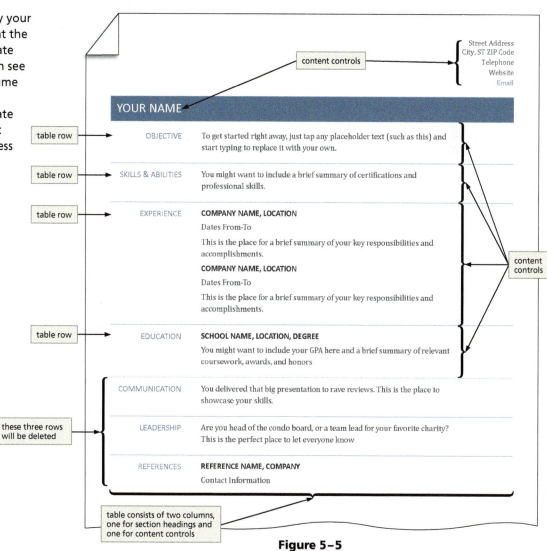

Figure 5–5

To Open a Document Created from a Template

If you are unable to locate the Basic resume (Timeless design) template in the previous steps or the template you located differs from Figure 5–5, you can open it from the Data Files. Please contact your instructor for information about accessing the Data Files. The following step opens a document. NOTE: PERFORM THE STEP IN THIS YELLOW BOX ONLY IF YOU WERE UNABLE TO LOCATE THE BASIC RESUME (TIMELESS DESIGN) TEMPLATE IN THE PREVIOUS STEPS OR THE TEMPLATE YOU LOCATED DIFFERS FROM FIGURE 5–5.

 Open the file named Basic resume (Timeless design), located on the Data Files, from your hard drive, OneDrive, or other storage location.

CONSIDER THIS

How do you craft a successful resume?

Two types of resumes are the chronological resume and the functional resume. A chronological resume sequences information by time, with the most recent listed first. This type of resume highlights a job seeker's job continuity and growth. A functional resume groups information by skills and accomplishments. This resume emphasizes a job seeker's experience and qualifications in specialized areas. Some resumes use a combination of the two formats. For an entry-level job search, experts recommend a chronological resume or a combination of the two types of resumes.

When creating a resume, be sure to include necessary information and present it appropriately. Keep descriptions concise, using action words and bulleted lists.

- **Include necessary information.** Your resume should include contact information, a clearly written objective, educational background, and experience. Use your legal name and mailing address, along with your phone number and email address, if you have one. Other sections you might consider including are memberships, skills, recognitions and awards, and/or community service. Do not include your Social Security number, marital status, age, height, weight, gender, physical appearance, health, citizenship, previous pay rates, reasons for leaving a prior job, current date, high-school information (if you are a college graduate), and references. Employers assume you will provide references, if asked, and this information simply clutters a resume.

- **Present your resume appropriately.** For printed resumes, use a high-quality ink-jet or laser printer to print your resume on standard letter-sized white or ivory paper. Consider using paper that contains cotton fibers for a professional look.

BTW

Conserving Ink and Toner

If you want to conserve ink or toner, you can instruct Word to print draft quality documents by clicking File on the ribbon to open the Backstage view, clicking the Options tab in the Backstage view to display the Word Options dialog box, clicking Advanced in the left pane (Word Options dialog box), scrolling to the Print area in the right pane, placing a check mark in the 'Use draft quality' check box, and then clicking the OK button. Then, use the Backstage view to print the document as usual.

Resume Template

The resume created from the template, shown in Figure 5–5, contains several content controls and a table. A **content control** is an object that contains instructions for filling in text and graphics. To select a content control, you click it. As soon as you begin typing in the selected content control, your typing replaces the instructions in the control. Thus, you do not need to delete the selected instructions before you begin typing.

The table below the name in the document consists of seven rows and two columns. Each resume section is contained in one row (i.e., Objective, Skills & Abilities, Experience, etc.) The section headings are in the first column, followed by the second column that contains the content controls.

The following pages personalize the resume created by the resume template using these general steps:

1. Change the name at the top of the resume.
2. Fill in the contact information at the top of the resume.
3. Fill in the Objective section.
4. Move the Education and Experience sections above the Skills & Abilities section.

5. Fill in the Education and Experience sections.

6. Change the Skills & Abilities heading to Memberships and fill in this section.

7. Add a row for the Community Service section and fill in this section.

8. Delete the last three unused rows.

To Change Theme Colors

Recall that Word provides document themes, which contain a variety of color schemes and other effects. This resume uses the Aspect theme colors. The following steps change the theme colors.

① Click Design on the ribbon to display the Design tab.

② Click the Themes Colors button (Design tab | Document Formatting group) to display the Theme Colors gallery.

③ Scroll to and then click Aspect in the Theme Colors gallery to change the theme colors to the selected theme.

BTW

The Ribbon and Screen Resolution
Word may change how the groups and buttons within the groups appear on the ribbon, depending on the computer or mobile device's screen resolution. Thus, your ribbon may look different from the ones in this book if you are using a screen resolution other than 1366 x 768.

To Set Custom Margins

1 CREATE DOCUMENT FROM TEMPLATE | 2 MODIFY & FORMAT TEMPLATE | 3 SAVE DOCUMENT IN OTHER FORMATS
4 MAKE DOCUMENT AVAILABLE ONLINE | 5 CREATE WEBPAGE FROM WORD DOCUMENT | 6 FORMAT WEBPAGE

The resume template selected in this project uses .75-inch top, bottom, left, and right margins. You prefer slightly wider margins for the top, left, and right edges of the resume and a smaller bottom margin. *Why? You do not want the text to run so close to the top edge and sides of the page and do not want the resume to spill to a second page.* In earlier modules, you changed the margins by selecting predefined settings in the Margins gallery. The margins you will use for the resume in this module, however, are not predefined. Thus, the next steps set custom margins.

①
- Display the Layout tab.

- Click the Adjust Margins button (Layout tab | Page Setup group) to display the Margins gallery (Figure 5–6).

Q&A What is the difference between the Custom Margins setting and the Custom Margins command?
The Custom Margins setting applies the most recent custom margins to the current document, whereas the Custom Margins command displays the Custom Margins dialog box so that you can specify new margin settings.

Figure 5–6

• Click Custom Margins in the Margins gallery to display the Page Setup dialog box. If necessary, click the Margins tab (Page Setup dialog box) to display the Margins sheet.

• Type **1** in the Top box to change the top margin setting and then press the TAB key to position the insertion point in the Bottom box.

• Type **.5** in the Bottom box to change the bottom margin setting and then press the TAB key to position the insertion point in the Left box.

• Type **1** in the Left box to change the left margin setting and then press the TAB key to position the insertion point in the Right box.

• Type **1** in the Right box to change the right margin setting (Figure 5–7).

Figure 5–7

• Click the OK button to set the custom margins for this document.

Other Ways

1. Drag margin boundaries on ruler

To View Gridlines

When tables contain no borders, such as those in this resume, it can be difficult to see the individual cells in the table. To help identify the location of cells, you can display gridlines, which show cell outlines on the screen. The following steps show gridlines.

1 Scroll the document up, if desired. Position the insertion point in any table cell (in this case, the cell containing the Objective heading).

2 Display the Table Tools Layout tab.

3 If it is not selected already, click the 'View Table Gridlines' button (Table Tools Layout tab | Table group) to show gridlines in the table (Figure 5–8).

Figure 5–8

To Modify a Content Control and Replace Its Placeholder Text

The next step is to select the Your Name content control that the template inserted in the resume, increase its font size slightly, and replace its placeholder text with the job seeker's name. Word uses **placeholder text** to indicate where text can be typed. To replace placeholder text in a content control, you select the content control and then type.

The Your Name content control on your resume may already contain your name. *Why? Word copies the user name from the Word Options dialog box and places it in the Your Name content control. Note that if your name appears instead of the text, YOUR NAME, the following steps may execute differently.* The next steps modify a content control and replace its placeholder text.

- Click the content control to be modified (in this case, the Your Name content control) to select it.

Q&A How can I tell if a content control is selected?
The appearance of selected content controls varies. When you select some content controls, they are surrounded by a rectangle. Selected content controls also may have a name that is attached to the top, and/or a tag that is attached to its upper-left corner. You can drag a tag to move a content control from one location to another. With other content controls, the text inside the content control appears selected as shown in Figure 5–9.

- If necessary, click the content control name (in this case, the words Your Name) to select the contents of the content control (Figure 5–9).

Figure 5–9

②

- Click the 'Increase Font Size' button (Home tab | Font group) to increase the font size of the text in the selected content control to the next font size (Figure 5–10).

Q&A What if my font size does not change?
You may need to modify the style: right-click the Name style in the Styles gallery, click Modify on the shortcut menu, change the font size to 18 (Modify Style dialog box), and then click the OK button.

Figure 5–10

- Type **Nina Tamaya Yazzie** to replace the content control with the job seeker's name (Figure 5–11).

  If requested by your instructor, enter your name instead of the job seeker's name shown in Figure 5–11.

Q&A

Why does the text appear in uppercase letters even though I type in lowercase letters?
This content control includes formatting that displays the text in uppercase letters.

Figure 5–11

To Replace Placeholder Text in More Content Controls

The next step is to select the Contact Info, Telephone, and Email content controls in the upper-right corner of the resume and replace their placeholder text with personal information. Because you do not have a website, you will leave the website contact control as is and delete it in later steps. The following steps replace the placeholder text in content controls.

1. Click the Contact Info content control to select it (Figure 5–12).

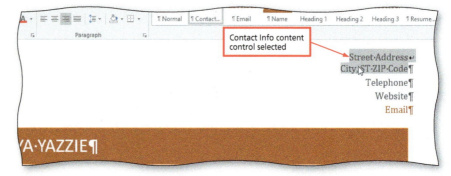

Figure 5–12

BTW

Selecting Rows
To move table rows (discussed in the next section), you must select them first. To do this, point to the left of the first row to select and then drag downward or upward when the pointer changes to a right-pointing block arrow. If you are using a touch screen, drag the selection handles to select the rows.

2. Type **2640 Bartlett Street** as the street address, press the ENTER key, and then type **Ponrolet, MI 66589** as the city, state, and ZIP code.

3. Click the Telephone content control to select it and then type **872-555-1547 (cell)** as the cell phone number.

4. Click the Email content control to select it and then type **nyazzie@world.net** as the email address.

To Delete a Content Control

1 CREATE DOCUMENT FROM TEMPLATE | **2 MODIFY & FORMAT TEMPLATE** | 3 SAVE DOCUMENT IN OTHER FORMATS
4 MAKE DOCUMENT AVAILABLE ONLINE | 5 CREATE WEBPAGE FROM WORD DOCUMENT | 6 FORMAT WEBPAGE

The following steps delete the Website content control. *Why? You do not have a website.*

- Click the Website content control to select it.

- Right-click the selected content control to display a shortcut menu (Figure 5–13).

Figure 5–13

- Click 'Remove Content Control' on the shortcut menu to delete the selected content control, which also deletes the placeholder text contained in the content control.

- Press the DELETE key to remove the blank line between the phone number and the email address (Figure 5–14).

- Save the title page on your hard drive, OneDrive, or other storage location using the file name, Yazzie Resume.

Figure 5–14

Q&A | Why should I save the resume at this time?
You have performed many tasks while creating this resume and do not want to risk losing work completed thus far.

Other Ways

1. With content control selected, click Cut button (Home tab | Clipboard group)   2. With content control selected, press CTRL+X or DELETE or BACKSPACE

To Move Table Rows

1 CREATE DOCUMENT FROM TEMPLATE | 2 MODIFY & FORMAT TEMPLATE | 3 SAVE DOCUMENT IN OTHER FORMATS
4 MAKE DOCUMENT AVAILABLE ONLINE | 5 CREATE WEBPAGE FROM WORD DOCUMENT | 6 FORMAT WEBPAGE

In the resume, you would like the Education and Experience sections immediately below the Objective section, in that order. ***Why?*** *You want to emphasize your educational background and experience.* Thus, the next step is to move rows in the resume. Each row contains a separate section in the resume. You will move the row containing the Education section below the row containing the Objective section. Then, you will move the row containing the Experience section so that it is below the moved row containing the Education section.

You use the same procedure to move table rows as to move text. That is, select the rows to move and then drag them to the desired location. The following steps use drag-and-drop editing to move table rows.

- Display the View tab. Click the 100% button (View tab | Zoom group) to display the resume at 100 percent zoom in the document window.

- Scroll so that the Objective, Experience, and Education sections appear in the document window at the same time.

2

- Select the row to be moved, in this case, the row containing the Education section.

- Position the pointer in the selected row, press and hold down the mouse button and then drag the insertion point to the location where the selected row is to be moved (Figure 5–15).

Figure 5–15

3

- Release the mouse button to move the selected row to the location of the insertion point (Figure 5–16).

What if I accidentally drag text to the wrong location?
Click the Undo button on the Quick Access Toolbar and try again.

What if I am using a touch screen?
If you have a stylus, you can follow Steps 1 through 3 using the stylus. If you are using your finger, you will need to use the cut-and-paste technique: tap to position the insertion point in the row to be moved, tap the Select Table button (Table Tools Layout tab | Table group), and then tap Select Row; press the selection to display the mini toolbar and then tap the Cut button on the mini toolbar to remove the row; tap to position the insertion point at the location where you want to move the row; display the Home tab and then tap the Paste button (Home tab | Clipboard group) to place the row at the location of the insertion point.

Figure 5–16

Repeat Steps 2 and 3 to move the row containing the Experience section so that it is positioned below the row containing the Education section (Figure 5–17).

- Click anywhere to remove the selection.

- Change the zoom to page width.

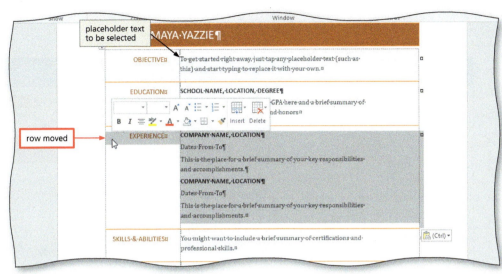

Figure 5–17

Other Ways

1. Click Cut button (Home tab | Clipboard group), click where text or object is to be pasted, click Paste button (Home tab | Clipboard group)

2. Right-click selected text, click Cut on shortcut menu or mini toolbar, right-click where text or object is to be pasted, click 'Keep Source Formatting' on shortcut menu (or, if using touch, tap Paste on mini toolbar)

3. Press CTRL+X, position insertion point where text or object is to be pasted, press CTRL+V

To Modify Text in a Content Control

The following steps select the Objective content control in the resume and then replace its placeholder text with personal information.

1. If necessary, scroll to display the Objective section of the resume in the document window.

2. In the Objective section of the resume, click the placeholder text that begins, 'To get started…', in the Objective content control (shown in Figure 5–17) to select it.

3. Type the objective: **To obtain a full-time reporter position with a broadcasting station in the Midwest.**

BTW

Insert Controls
The content controls in some templates contain an Insert Control, which allows you to duplicate text in the control. Because the template used in the module does not contain an Insert Control, you copy and paste items to duplicate them. Lab 2 in the student assignments at the end of this module uses a template that contains an Insert Control.

To Copy and Paste Items in a Table Cell

1 CREATE DOCUMENT FROM TEMPLATE | **2 MODIFY & FORMAT TEMPLATE** | 3 SAVE DOCUMENT IN OTHER FORMATS
4 MAKE DOCUMENT AVAILABLE ONLINE | 5 CREATE WEBPAGE FROM WORD DOCUMENT | 6 FORMAT WEBPAGE

In the resume, you copy the school name information in the Education section so that it appears twice in the table cell containing the Education content control. ***Why?*** *You would like to add two degrees to the resume.* The following steps copy and paste text in a cell.

- Select the text to be copied (in this case, all of the text in the Education content control).

- Display the Home tab.

- Click the Copy button (Home tab | Clipboard group) to copy the selected item in the table cell to the Office Clipboard (Figure 5–18).

Figure 5–18

2

- Position the insertion point at the end of the text in the Education content control (that is, after the s in honors) and then press the ENTER key to place the insertion point at the location where the copied item should be pasted.

- Click the Paste button (Home tab | Clipboard group) to paste the copied item in the document at the location of the insertion point (Figure 5–19).

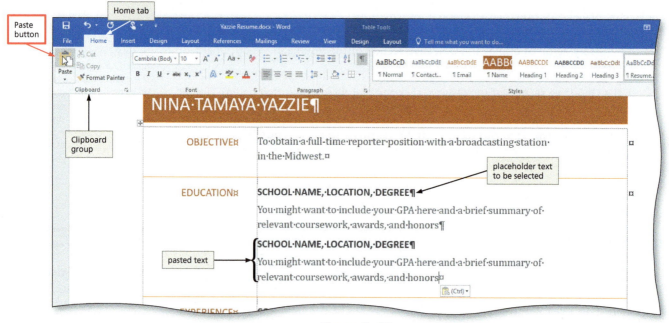

Figure 5–19

Q&A What if I click the Paste arrow by mistake?
Click the Paste arrow again to remove the Paste menu and repeat Step 2.

Other Ways

1. Click Copy on shortcut menu (or, if using touch, tap Copy on mini toolbar), right-click where item is to be pasted, click 'Keep Source Formatting' in Paste Options area on shortcut menu (or, if using touch, tap Paste on mini toolbar)

2. Select item, press CTRL+C, position insertion point at paste location, press CTRL+V

To Replace Placeholder Text in a Content Control

The next step is to begin to enter text in the Education section of the resume. The following step replaces placeholder text.

 In the Education section of the resume, select the placeholder text, SCHOOL NAME, LOCATION, DEGREE, in the first content control (shown in Figure 5–19) and then type **B.A. JOURNALISM - HARTFORD COLLEGE** as the degree and school name (shown in Figure 5–20).

To Use AutoComplete

1 CREATE DOCUMENT FROM TEMPLATE | 2 MODIFY & FORMAT TEMPLATE | 3 SAVE DOCUMENT IN OTHER FORMATS
4 MAKE DOCUMENT AVAILABLE ONLINE | 5 CREATE WEBPAGE FROM WORD DOCUMENT | 6 FORMAT WEBPAGE

As you begin typing, Word may display a ScreenTip that presents a suggestion for the rest of the word or phrase you are typing. ***Why?*** *With its **AutoComplete** feature, Word predicts the word or phrase you are typing and displays its prediction in a ScreenTip.* If the AutoComplete prediction is correct, you can instruct Word to finish your typing with its prediction, or you can ignore Word's prediction. Word draws its AutoComplete suggestions from its dictionary and from AutoText entries you create and save in the Normal template.

The following steps use the AutoComplete feature as you type the graduation date in the Education section of the resume.

1

- In the Education section of the resume, click the placeholder text that begins, 'You might want to…', in the first content control and then type **Dece** and notice the AutoComplete ScreenTip that appears on the screen (Figure 5–20).

Figure 5–20

Why would my screen not display the AutoComplete ScreenTip?
Depending on previous Word entries, you may need to type more characters in order for Word to predict a particular word or phrase accurately. Or, you may need to turn on AutoComplete by clicking File on the ribbon to open the Backstage view, clicking the Options tab in the Backstage view to display the Word Options dialog box, clicking Advanced in the left pane (Word Options dialog box), placing a check mark in the 'Show AutoComplete suggestions' check box, and then clicking the OK button.

2

- Press the ENTER key to instruct Word to finish your typing with the word or phrase that appeared in the AutoComplete ScreenTip.

What if I do not want to use the text proposed in the AutoComplete ScreenTip?
Simply continue typing and the AutoComplete ScreenTip will disappear from the screen.

3

- Press the SPACEBAR. Type **2017, GPA 3.92/4.00** and then press the ENTER key (Figure 5–21).

Figure 5–21

To Enter More Text

The following steps continue entering text in the Education section of the resume.

1 Type **Dean's List, every semester** and then press the ENTER key.

2 Type **Student Publications Award, May 2017** and then press the ENTER key.

3 Type **Civics Journal, 1st Place, political perspective article** and then italicize the journal title.

4 Bullet the three paragraphs just entered (Figure 5–22).

BTW
AutoFormat
Word automatically formats quotation marks, dashes, lists, fractions, ordinals, and other items, depending on your typing and settings. To check if an AutoFormat option is enabled, click File on the ribbon to open the Backstage view, click the Options tab in the Backstage view, click Proofing in the left pane (Word Options dialog box), click the AutoCorrect Options button, click the 'AutoFormat As You Type' tab (AutoCorrect dialog box), select the appropriate check boxes, and then click the OK button in each open dialog box.

Figure 5–22

To Enter a Line Break

1 CREATE DOCUMENT FROM TEMPLATE | 2 MODIFY & FORMAT TEMPLATE | 3 SAVE DOCUMENT IN OTHER FORMATS
4 MAKE DOCUMENT AVAILABLE ONLINE | 5 CREATE WEBPAGE FROM WORD DOCUMENT | 6 FORMAT WEBPAGE

The next step in personalizing the resume is to enter the areas of concentration in the Education section. You want only the first line, which says, Areas of concentration:, to begin with a bullet. If you press the ENTER key on subsequent lines, Word automatically will carry forward the paragraph formatting, which includes the bullet. Thus, you will not press the ENTER key between each line. Instead, you will create a line break. *Why? A line break advances the insertion point to the beginning of the next physical line, ignoring any paragraph formatting.* The following steps enter the areas of concentration using a line break, instead of a paragraph break, between each line.

1

• With the insertion point positioned as shown in Figure 5–22, press the ENTER key.

• If necessary, turn off italics. Type **Areas of concentration:** and then press SHIFT+ENTER to insert a line break character and move the insertion point to the beginning of the next physical line (Figure 5–23).

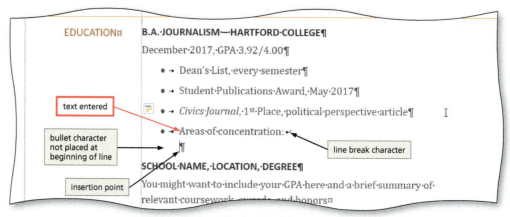

Figure 5–23

2

- Type **Broadcast reporting** and then press SHIFT+ENTER.

- Type **Intercultural communications** and then press SHIFT+ENTER.

- Type **Mass media** and then press SHIFT+ENTER.

- Type **Newswriting** as the last entry. Do not press SHIFT+ENTER at the end of this line (Figure 5–24).

Figure 5–24

To Replace Placeholder Text in Content Controls

The next step is to enter the information for the second degree in the Education section of the resume. The following steps replace placeholder text.

1 In the Education section of the resume, select the placeholder text, SCHOOL NAME, LOCATION, DEGREE, in the second content control (shown in Figure 5–24) and then type **A.A. TECHNICAL WRITING – WHEATON COMMUNITY COLLEGE** as the degree and school name.

2 Select the placeholder text that begins, 'You might want to…', in the second content control and then type **December 2015, GPA 3.94/4.00** (Figure 5–25).

BTW

Line Break Characters
A line break character is a formatting mark that indicates a line break at the end of the line. Like paragraph marks, tab characters, and other formatting marks, line break characters do not print.

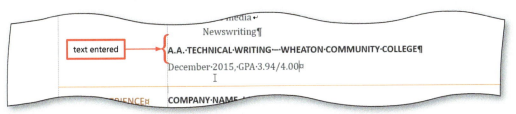

Figure 5–25

To Delete Text

The following steps delete text from the Experience content control. **Why?** *You have only one job experience entry for the resume.*

1 Select the text to delete (in this case, the entire second job experience entry in the Experience section) (Figure 5–26).

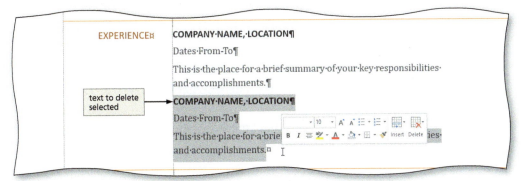

Figure 5–26

② Press the DELETE key to delete the second job experience entry from the content control.

③ Press the BACKSPACE key to remove the blank line below the remaining item in the content control (shown in Figure 5–27).

To Replace Placeholder Text in Content Controls

The next step is to enter the job information for the Experience section of the resume. The following steps replace placeholder text.

① In the Experience section of the resume, select the placeholder text, COMPANY NAME, LOCATION, in the content control and then type **ASSISTANT COORDINATOR – PONROLET COMMUNITY CENTER** as the job title and company name.

② Select the placeholder text that begins 'Dates From…' in the content control and then type **August 2016 – Present** as the dates. Press the SPACEBAR so that the hyphen changes to an en dash.

③ Select the placeholder text that begins 'This is the place…' in the content control and then type this text (Figure 5–27): **Assist in developing programs designed to increase literacy and reading skills; conduct reading programs for children; compose, proofread, and edit monthly newsletter.**

Figure 5–27

To Indent a Paragraph

1 CREATE DOCUMENT FROM TEMPLATE | **2 MODIFY & FORMAT TEMPLATE** | 3 SAVE DOCUMENT IN OTHER FORMATS
4 MAKE DOCUMENT AVAILABLE ONLINE | 5 CREATE WEBPAGE FROM WORD DOCUMENT | 6 FORMAT WEBPAGE

In the resume, the lines below the job start date and end date that contain the job responsibilities are to be indented. **Why?** *You believe the responsibilities would be easier to read if they are indented.* The following step indents the left and right edges of a paragraph.

- With the insertion point in the paragraph to indent (shown in Figure 5–27), display the Layout tab.
- Click the Indent Left up arrow (Layout tab | Paragraph group) until the Indent Left box displays 0.5" to indent the left margin of the current paragraph one-half inch.
- Click the Indent Right down arrow (Layout tab | Paragraph group) until the Indent Right box displays 0.5" to indent the right margin of the current paragraph one-half inch (Figure 5–28).

Figure 5–28

Other Ways

1. Drag Left Indent/Right Indent marker on horizontal ruler

2. For left margin, click Increase Indent button (Home tab | Paragraph group)

3. Click Paragraph Dialog Box Launcher (Home tab | Paragraph group), click Indents and Spacing tab (Paragraph dialog box), set indentation in Left/Right boxes, click OK button

4. Right-click text (or, if using touch, tap 'Show Context Menu' button on mini toolbar), click Paragraph on shortcut menu, click Indents and Spacing tab (Paragraph dialog box), set indentation in Left/Right boxes, click OK button

5. For left margin, press CTRL+M

To Replace Placeholder Text in Content Controls

The next step is to enter the membership information. You will replace the text in the Skills & Abilities section with membership information. The following steps replace placeholder text.

① Select the text, SKILLS & ABILITIES, and then type **MEMBERSHIPS** as the new section heading.

② In the Memberships section, select the placeholder text that begins, 'You might want...', in the content control and then type **Alpha Kappa Omega National Honor Society** and then press the ENTER key.

③ Type **Literacy Council, Ponrolet Village Board** and then press the ENTER key.

④ Type **Student Government Association, Secretary** as the final item in this section (shown in Figure 5–29).

To Copy and Paste a Table Item

1 CREATE DOCUMENT FROM TEMPLATE | 2 MODIFY & FORMAT TEMPLATE | 3 SAVE DOCUMENT IN OTHER FORMATS
4 MAKE DOCUMENT AVAILABLE ONLINE | 5 CREATE WEBPAGE FROM WORD DOCUMENT | 6 FORMAT WEBPAGE

The next section of the resume in this module is the Community Service section, which is organized exactly like the Experience section. Thus, you copy the Experience section and paste it below the Memberships section. *Why? It will be easier to edit the Experience section rather than format the Community Service section from scratch.*

You use the same procedure to copy table rows that you use to copy text. That is, select the rows to copy and then paste them at the desired location. The following steps copy table rows.

- Display the View tab. Click the 100% button (View tab | Zoom group) to display the resume at 100 percent zoom in the document window.

- If necessary, scroll so that the Experience and Memberships sections appear in the document window at the same time.

- Select the row to be copied, in this case, the row containing the Experience section in the resume.

- Display the Home tab.

- Click the Copy button (Home tab | Clipboard group) to copy the selected row in the document to the Office Clipboard (Figure 5–29).

Figure 5–29

- Position the insertion point at the location where the copied row should be pasted, in this case, to the left of the M in the Memberships heading.

- Click the Paste arrow (Home tab | Clipboard group) to display the Paste gallery.

Q&A What if I click the Paste button by mistake?

Click the Undo button on the Quick Access Toolbar and then try again.

- Point to the 'Insert as New Rows' button in the Paste gallery to display a live preview of that paste option applied to the row in the table (Figure 5–30).

Figure 5–30

 Experiment

- Point to the four options in the Paste gallery and watch the format of the pasted row change in the document window.

3

- Click the 'Insert as New Rows' button in the Paste gallery to apply the selected option to the pasted table row because you want the pasted row to use the same formatting as the copied row.

- Change the zoom to page width.

Other Ways

1. Right-click selected item, click Copy on mini toolbar or shortcut menu, right-click where item is to be pasted, click desired option in Paste Options area on shortcut menu

2. Select item, press CTRL+C, position insertion point at paste location, press CTRL+V

To Delete Rows and Edit Text

Because you will not be using the last three rows of the resume template, the next step is to delete them and then enter the remainder of the text in the resume, that is, the Community Service section. The following steps delete rows and edit text.

1 If necessary, display the Table Tools Layout tab.

2 Select the last three rows of the table (Communication, Leadership, and References), which might appear on a second page, click the Delete Table button (Table Tools Layout tab | Rows & Columns group), and then click Delete Rows on the Delete Table menu.

3 Below the Memberships heading, select the text, EXPERIENCE, and then type **COMMUNITY SERVICE** as the new section heading.

4 In the Community Service section of the resume, select the text, ASSISTANT COORDINATOR, and then type **READING BUDDY** to replace the text.

5 Select the text, COMMUNITY CENTER, and then type **PARK DISTRICT** to replace the text.

6 Select the text, August, and then type **October** to replace the month.

7 Select the indented paragraph of text and then type this text (Figure 5–31):
Volunteer eight hours a week at the local community center in the district's Reading Buddy program, which works to develop reading skills of children in elementary school.

8 Save the resume again on the same storage location with the same file name.

last section of resume entered

last three rows deleted

Figure 5–31

To Customize Theme Fonts

Recall that a font set defines one font for headings in a document and another font for body text. This resume currently uses the Calibri-Cambria font set, which specifies the Calibri font for the headings and the Cambria font for body text. The resume in this module creates a customized font set (theme font). *Why?* *You want the headings to use the Berlin Sans FB Demi font and the body text to use the Bookman Old Style font.* The following steps create a customized theme font set with the name, Resume Text.

- Display the Design tab.

- Click the Theme Fonts button (Design tab | Document Formatting group) to display the Theme Fonts gallery (Figure 5–32).

Figure 5–32

- Click Customize Fonts in the Theme Fonts gallery to display the Create New Theme Fonts dialog box.

- Click the Heading font arrow (Create New Theme Fonts dialog box); scroll to and then click 'Berlin Sans FB Demi' (or a similar font).

- Click the Body font arrow; scroll to and then click 'Bookman Old Style' (or a similar font).

- Type **Resume Text** in the Name text box as the name for the new theme font (Figure 5–33).

Figure 5–33

- Click the Save button (Create New Theme Fonts dialog box) to create the customized theme font with the entered name (Resume Text, in this case) and apply the new heading fonts to the current document (Figure 5–34).

Figure 5–34

To Create a Style

1 CREATE DOCUMENT FROM TEMPLATE | 2 MODIFY & FORMAT TEMPLATE | 3 SAVE DOCUMENT IN OTHER FORMATS
4 MAKE DOCUMENT AVAILABLE ONLINE | 5 CREATE WEBPAGE FROM WORD DOCUMENT | 6 FORMAT WEBPAGE

Recall that a style is a predefined set of formats that appears in the Styles gallery. You have used styles in the Styles gallery to apply formats to text and have updated existing styles. You also can create your own styles.

The next task in this project is to create a style for the section headings in the resume. *Why? To illustrate creating a style, you will increase the font size of a section heading and save the new format as a style. Then, you will apply the newly defined style to the remaining section headings.* The following steps format text and then create a style based on the formats in the selected paragraph.

- Position the insertion point in the Memberships heading, display the Home tab, and then click the 'Increase Font Size' button (Home tab | Font group) to increase the font size of the heading.

- Click the More button (shown in Figure 5–36) in the Styles gallery (Home tab | Styles group) to expand the gallery (Figure 5–35).

Figure 5–35

- Click 'Create a Style' in the Styles gallery to display the Create New Style from Formatting dialog box.

- Type **Resume Headings** in the Name text box (Create New Style from Formatting dialog box) (Figure 5–36).

Figure 5–36

3

- Click the OK button to create the new style and add it to the Styles gallery (shown in Figure 5–37).

How can I see the style just created?

If the style name does not appear in the in-ribbon Styles gallery, click the More button in the Styles gallery (Home tab | Styles group) to display the expanded Styles gallery.

To Apply a Style

The next step is to apply the style just created to the other section headings in the resume. The following step applies a style.

1

One at a time, position the insertion point in the remaining section headings (Objective, Education, Experience, and Community Service) and then click Resume Headings in the Styles gallery to apply the selected style to each heading.

To Reveal Formatting

1 CREATE DOCUMENT FROM TEMPLATE | 2 MODIFY & FORMAT TEMPLATE | 3 SAVE DOCUMENT IN OTHER FORMATS
4 MAKE DOCUMENT AVAILABLE ONLINE | 5 CREATE WEBPAGE FROM WORD DOCUMENT | 6 FORMAT WEBPAGE

Sometimes, you want to know what formats were applied to certain text items in a document. *Why? For example, you may wonder which font, font size, font color, and other effects were applied to the degree and job titles in the resume.* To display formatting applied to text, use the Reveal Formatting task pane. The following steps open and then close the Reveal Formatting task pane.

1

- Position the insertion point in the text for which you want to reveal formatting (in this case, the degree name in the Education section).

- Press SHIFT+F1 to open the Reveal Formatting task pane, which shows formatting applied to the location of the insertion point in (Figure 5–37).

Experiment

- Click the Font collapse button to hide the Font formats. Click the Font expand button to redisplay the Font formats.

Figure 5–37

Why do some of the formats in the Reveal Formatting task pane appear as links?

Clicking a link in the Reveal Formatting task pane displays an associated dialog box, allowing you to change the format of the current text. For example, clicking the Font link in the Reveal Formatting task pane would display the Font dialog box. If you made changes in the Font dialog box and then clicked the OK button, Word would change the format of the current text.

2

- Close the Reveal Formatting task pane by clicking its Close button.

To Modify a Style Using the Styles Dialog Box

The next step is to modify the Heading 2 style. ***Why?*** *The degree and job names in the resume currently have a different font than the other text in the resume. You prefer that all text in the resume use the same font.* Thus, the following steps modify a style.

- Right-click the style name to modify in the Styles gallery (Heading 2 in this case) (Home tab | Styles group) to display a shortcut menu (Figure 5–38).

Figure 5–38

- Click Modify on the shortcut menu to display the Modify Style dialog box.

- Click the Font arrow (Modify Style dialog box) and then click Bookman Old Style in the Font gallery to change the font of the current style.

- Place a check mark in the Automatically update check box so that any future changes you make to the style in the document will update the current style automatically (Figure 5–39).

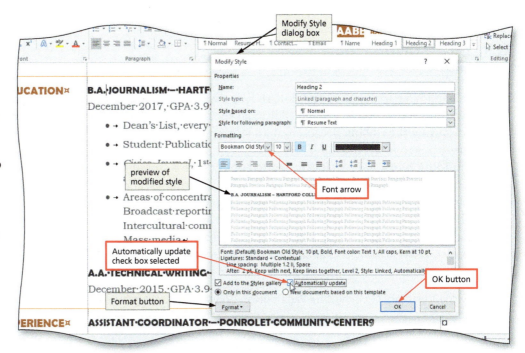

Figure 5–39

Q&A   What is the purpose of the Format button in the Modify Style dialog box?

If the formatting you wish to change for the style is not available in the Modify Style dialog box, you can click the Format button and then select the desired command after you click the Format button to display a dialog box that contains additional formatting options.

- Click the OK button to close the dialog box and apply the style changes to the paragraphs in the document (Figure 5–40).

- Save the resume again on the same storage location with the same file name.

- If requested by your instructor, print the finished resume (shown in Figure 5–1).

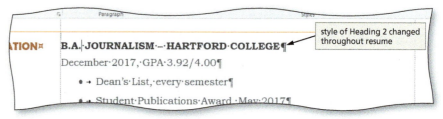

Figure 5–40

Other Ways

1. Click Styles Dialog Box Launcher (Home tab | Styles group), click arrow to right of style to modify, click Modify on menu, change settings (Modify Style dialog box), click OK button

2. Click Styles Dialog Box Launcher, click Manage Styles button, scroll to style and then select it (Manage Styles dialog box), click Modify button, change settings (Modify Style dialog box), click OK button in each dialog box

Break Point: If you wish to take a break, this is a good place to do so. You can exit Word now. To resume at a later time, run Word, open the file called Yazzie Resume, and continue following the steps from this location forward.

Sharing a Document with Others

You may want to share Word documents with others electronically, such as via email, USB flash drive, or cloud storage. To ensure that others can read and/or open the files successfully, Word provides a variety of formats and tools to assist with sharing documents. This section uses the Yazzie Resume created in this module to present a variety of these formats and tools.

To Insert a Building Block Using the Building Blocks Organizer

1 CREATE DOCUMENT FROM TEMPLATE | 2 MODIFY & FORMAT TEMPLATE | **3 SAVE DOCUMENT IN OTHER FORMATS**
4 MAKE DOCUMENT AVAILABLE ONLINE | 5 CREATE WEBPAGE FROM WORD DOCUMENT | 6 FORMAT WEBPAGE

You would like to place the text, DRAFT, as a watermark on the resume before you share it, so that others are aware you might be making additional changes to the document. In an earlier module, you inserted a watermark using the ribbon. Because watermarks are a type of building block, you also can use the Building Blocks Organizer to insert them.

A **building block** is a reusable formatted object that is stored in a gallery. Examples of building blocks include cover pages, headers, footers, page numbers, watermarks, and text boxes. You can see a list of every available building block in the **Building Blocks Organizer**. From the Building Blocks Organizer, you can sort building blocks, change their properties, or insert them in a document.

The next steps sort the Building Blocks Organizer by gallery and then insert the Draft 1 building block in the document. **Why?** *Sorting the building blocks by gallery makes it easier to locate them.*

- Display the View tab. Click the One Page button (View tab | Zoom group) to display the resume in its entirety in the document window.

- Display the Insert tab.

- Click the 'Explore Quick Parts' button (Insert tab | Text group) to display the Explore Quick Parts menu (Figure 5–41).

Figure 5–41

2

- Click 'Building Blocks Organizer' on the Explore Quick Parts menu to display the Building Blocks Organizer dialog box.

Experiment

- Drag the scroll bars in the Building Blocks Organizer so that you can look at all the columns and rows in the dialog box.

- Click the Gallery heading (Building Blocks Organizer dialog box) in the building blocks list to sort the building blocks by gallery (Figure 5–42).

Experiment

- Click various names in the building blocks list and notice that a preview of the selected building block appears in the dialog box.

Figure 5–42

3

- Scroll through the building blocks list to the Watermarks group in the Gallery column and then click DRAFT 1 to select this building block (Figure 5–43).

Figure 5–43

4

- Click the Insert button to insert the selected building block in the document (Figure 5–44).

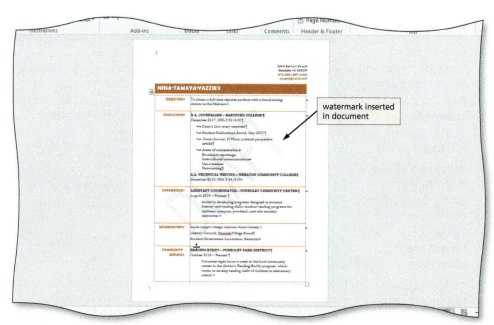

watermark inserted in document

Figure 5–44

TO EDIT PROPERTIES OF BUILDING BLOCK ELEMENTS

Properties of a building block include its name, gallery, category, description, location where it is saved, and how it is inserted in the document. If you wanted to change any of these building block properties for a particular building block, you would perform these steps.

1. Click the 'Explore Quick Parts' button (Insert tab | Text group) to display the Explore Quick Parts menu.
2. Click 'Building Blocks Organizer' on the Explore Quick Parts menu to display the Building Blocks Organizer dialog box.
3. Select the building block you wish to edit (Building Blocks Organizer dialog box).
4. Click the Edit Properties button (shown in Figure 5–43) to display the Modify Building Block dialog box.
5. Edit any property (Modify Building Block dialog box) and then click the OK button. Close the Building Blocks Organizer dialog box.

CONSIDER THIS

Will a document look the same on another computer when you share it electronically?

When sharing a Word document with others, you cannot be certain that it will look or print the same on their computers or mobile devices as on your computer or mobile device. For example, the document may wordwrap text differently on others' computers and mobile devices. If others do not need to edit the document (that is, if they need only to view and/or print the document), you could save the file in a format that allows others to view the document as you see it. Two popular such formats are PDF and XPS.

To Save a Word Document as a PDF File and View the PDF File in Adobe Reader

1 CREATE DOCUMENT FROM TEMPLATE | 2 MODIFY & FORMAT TEMPLATE | **3 SAVE DOCUMENT IN OTHER FORMATS**
4 MAKE DOCUMENT AVAILABLE ONLINE | 5 CREATE WEBPAGE FROM WORD DOCUMENT | 6 FORMAT WEBPAGE

PDF, which stands for Portable Document Format, is a file format created by Adobe Systems that shows all elements of a printed document as an electronic image. Users can view a PDF file without the software that created the original document. Thus, the PDF format enables users to share documents with others easily. To view, navigate, and print a PDF file, you use an application called **Adobe Reader**, which can be downloaded free from Adobe's website.

When you save a Word document as a PDF file, the original Word document remains intact; that is, Word creates a copy of the file in the PDF format. The following steps save the Yazzie Resume Word document as a PDF file and then open the Yazzie Resume PDF file in Adobe Reader. *Why? You want to share the resume with others but want to ensure it looks the same on their computer or mobile device as it does on yours.*

1

- Open the Backstage view and then click the Export tab in the Backstage view to display the Export gallery.

- If necessary, click 'Create PDF/XPS Document' in the left pane of the Export gallery to display information about creating PDF/XPS documents in the right pane (Figure 5–45).

Q&A Why does the left pane of my Export gallery have an additional command related to creating an Adobe PDF?
Depending on your installation settings in Adobe, you may have an additional tab on your ribbon and/or additional commands in galleries, etc., related to Adobe functionality.

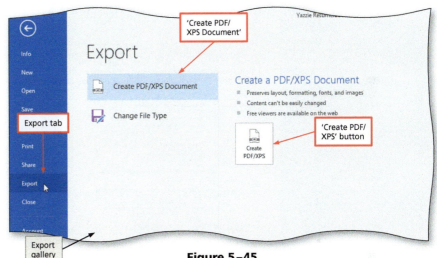

Figure 5–45

2

- Click the 'Create PDF/XPS' button in the right pane to display the Publish as PDF or XPS dialog box.

- Navigate to the desired save location (Publish as PDF or XPS dialog box).

Q&A Can the file name be the same for the Word document and the PDF file?
Yes. The file names can be the same because the file types are different: one is a Word document and the other is a PDF file.

- If necessary, click the 'Save as type' arrow and then click PDF.

- If necessary, place a check mark in the 'Open file after publishing' check box so that Word will display the resulting PDF file in Adobe Reader (Figure 5–46).

Figure 5–46

Why is my 'Open file after publishing' check box dimmed?

You do not have Adobe Reader installed on your computer. Use a search engine, such as Google, to search for the text, get adobe reader. Then, click the link in the search results to download Adobe Reader and follow the on-screen instructions to install the program. After installing Adobe Reader, repeat these steps.

3

- Click the Publish button to create the PDF file from the Word document and then, because the check box was selected, open the resulting PDF file in Adobe Reader.

- If necessary, click the Maximize button in the Adobe Reader window to maximize the window (Figure 5–47).

Figure 5–47

 Do I have to display the resulting PDF file in Adobe Reader?

No. If you do not want to display the document in Adobe Reader, you would not place a check mark in the 'Open file after publishing' check box in the Publish as PDF or XPS dialog box (shown in Figure 5–46).

Is the Yazzie Resume Word document still open?

Yes. Word still is running with the Yazzie Resume document opened.

What if a blank screen appears instead of Adobe Reader or if the document appears in a different program?

You may not have Adobe Reader installed. Press the Start key on the keyboard to redisplay the Start screen and then navigate back to Word, or close the program in which the document opened.

4

- Click the Close button on the Adobe Reader title bar to close the Yazzie Resume.pdf file and exit Adobe Reader.

Can I edit documents in Adobe Reader?

No, you need Adobe Acrobat or some other program that enables editing of PDF files.

Other Ways

1. Press F12, click 'Save as type' box arrow (Save As dialog box), select PDF in list, click Save button

To Open a PDF File from Word

When you use Word to open a PDF file, Word converts it to an editable document. ***Why?*** *You may want to change the contents of a PDF file.* The editable PDF file that Word creates from the PDF file may appear slightly different from the PDF due to the conversion process. To illustrate this feature, the next steps open the PDF file just saved.

1

- Open the Backstage view and then click the Open tab in the Backstage view to display the Open gallery.

- Click OneDrive, This PC, or another location in the left pane that references the location of the saved PDF file, click the Browse button, and then navigate to the location of the PDF file to be opened.

- If necessary, click the File Types arrow to display a list of file types that can be opened by Word (Figure 5–48).

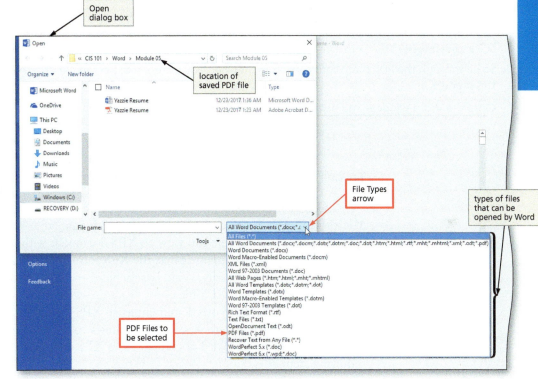

Figure 5–48

Q&A Why does the PDF file already appear in my list?
If the file type is All Word Documents, Word displays all file types that it can open in the file list.

2

- Click PDF Files in the File Types list, so that Word displays PDF file names in the dialog box.

- Click Yazzie Resume to select the PDF file to be opened (Figure 5–49).

Figure 5–49

- Click the Open button (Open dialog box) to open the selected file and display the opened document in the Word window.
- If Word displays a dialog box indicating it will begin converting the document, click its OK button.

- If necessary, click the Print Layout button on the status bar to switch to Print Layout view.

🔎 Experiment

- Scroll through the PDF that Word converted, noticing any differences between it and the original resume created in this module.
- Close the Word window and do not save this converted PDF file.

To Save a Word Document as an XPS Document

XPS, which stands for XML Paper Specification, is a file format created by Microsoft that shows all elements of a printed document as an electronic image. As with the PDF format, users can view an XPS document without the software that created the original document. Thus, the XPS format also enables users to share documents with others easily. Windows includes an XPS Viewer, which enables you to view, navigate, and print XPS files.

When you save a Word document as an XPS document, the original Word document remains intact; that is, Word creates a copy of the file in the XPS format. If you wanted to save a Word document as an XPS document, you would perform the following steps.

1. Open the Backstage view and then click the Export tab in the Backstage view to display the Export gallery.
2. Click 'Create PDF/XPS Document' in the left pane of the Export gallery to display information about PDF/XPS documents in the right pane and then click the 'Create PDF/XPS' button to display the Publish as PDF or XPS dialog box.
3. If necessary, navigate to the desired save location.
4. If necessary, click the 'Save as type' arrow and then click XPS Document.
5. Click the Publish or Save button to create the XPS document from the Word document and then, if the 'Open file after publishing' check box was selected, open the resulting XPS document in the XPS Viewer.

or

1. Press F12 to display the Save As dialog box.
2. If necessary, navigate to the desired save location.
3. If necessary, click the 'Save as type' arrow and then click XPS Document.
4. Click the Publish or Save button to create the XPS document from the Word document and then, if the 'Open file after publishing' check box was selected, open the resulting XPS document in the XPS Viewer.

Q&A What if I do not have an XPS Viewer?
The document will open in a browser window.

5. If necessary, exit the XPS Viewer.

BTW

Distributing a Document
Instead of printing and distributing a hard copy of a document, you can distribute the document electronically. Options include sending the document via email; posting it on cloud storage (such as OneDrive) and sharing the file with others; posting it on social media, a blog, or other website; and sharing a link associated with an online location of the document. You also can create and share a PDF or XPS image of the document, so that users can view the file in Adobe Reader or XPS Viewer instead of in Word.

To Run the Compatibility Checker

Word 2016 enables you to determine if a document is compatible (will work with) with earlier versions of Microsoft Word. *Why? If you would like to save a document, such as your resume, in the Word 97-2003 format so that it can be opened by users with earlier versions of Microsoft Word, you want to ensure that all of its elements (such as building blocks, content controls, and graphics) are compatible with earlier versions of Word.* The following steps run the compatibility checker.

- Open the Backstage view and then, if necessary, click the Info tab in the Backstage view to display the Info gallery.

- Click the 'Check for Issues' button in the Info gallery to display the Check for Issues menu (Figure 5–50).

Figure 5–50

- Click Check Compatibility on the Check for Issues menu to display the Microsoft Word Compatibility Checker dialog box, which shows any content that may not be supported by earlier versions of Word (Figure 5–51).

- Click the OK button (Microsoft Word Compatibility Checker dialog box) to close the dialog box.

Figure 5–51

To Save a Word 2016 Document in an Earlier Word Format

If you send a document created in Word 2016 to users who have a version of Word earlier than Word 2007, they will not be able to open the Word 2016 document. *Why? Word 2016 saves documents in a format that is not backward compatible with versions earlier than Word 2007. Word 2016 documents have a file type of .docx, and versions prior to Word 2007 have a .doc file type.* To ensure that all Word users can open your Word 2016 document, you should save the document in a Word 97-2003 format. The following steps save the Word 2016 format of the Yazzie Resume document in the Word 97-2003 format.

- Open the Backstage view and then click the Export tab in the Backstage view to display the Export gallery.
- Click 'Change File Type' in the left pane of the Export gallery to display information in the right pane about various Word file types.
- Click 'Word 97-2003' in the right pane to specify the new file type (Figure 5–52).

Figure 5–52

- Click the Save As button in the right pane to display the Save As dialog box.
- If necessary, navigate to the desired save location (Save As dialog box) (Figure 5–53).

Figure 5–53

Can the file name be the same for the Word 2016 document and the Word 97-2003 document?
Yes. The file names can be the same because the file types are different: one is a Word document with a .docx extension, and the other is a Word document with a .doc extension. The next section discusses file types and extensions.

3

- Click the Save button, which may display the Microsoft Word Compatibility Checker dialog box before saving the document (Figure 5–54).

 My screen did not display the Microsoft Word Compatibility Checker dialog box. Why not?
If the 'Check compatibility when saving documents' check box is not selected (as shown in Figure 5–51), Word will not check compatibility when saving a document.

Figure 5–54

4

- If the Microsoft Word Compatibility Checker dialog box is displayed, click its Continue button to save the document on the selected drive with the current file name in the specified format (Figure 5–55).

 Is the Word 2016 format of the Yazzie Resume document still open?
No. Word closed the original document (the Word 2016 format of the Yazzie Resume).

Can I use Word 2016 to open a document created in an earlier version of Word?
Yes, but you may notice that the appearance of the document differs when opened in Word 2016.

Figure 5–55

- Because you are finished with the Word 97-2003 format of the Yazzie Resume, close the document.

Other Ways

1. Press F12, click 'Save as type' arrow (Save As dialog box), select 'Word 97-2003 Document' in list, click Save button

File Types

When saving documents in Word, you can select from a variety of file types that can be opened in Word using the Export gallery in the Backstage view (shown in Figure 5–52) or by clicking the 'Save as type' arrow in the Save As dialog box. To save in these varied formats (Table 5–1), you follow the same basic steps as just illustrated.

Table 5–1 File Types

File Type	File Extension	File Explorer Image	Description
OpenDocument Text	.odt		Format used by other word processing programs, such as Google Docs and OpenOffice.org
PDF	.pdf		Portable Document Format, which can be opened in Adobe Reader
Plain Text	.txt		Format where all or most formatting is removed from the document
Rich Text Format	.rtf		Format designed to ensure file can be opened and read in many programs; some formatting may be lost to ensure compatibility
Single File Web Page	.mht		HTML (Hypertext Markup Language) format that can be opened in a browser; all elements of the webpage are saved in a single file
Web Page	.htm		HTML format that can be opened in a browser; various elements of the webpage, such as graphics, saved in separate files and folders
Word 97-2003 Document	.doc		Format used for documents created in versions of Word from Word 97 to Word 2003
Word 97-2003 Template	.dot		Format used for templates created in versions of Word from Word 97 and Word 2003
Word Document	.docx		Format used for Word 2016, Word 2013, Word 2010, or Word 2007 documents
Word Template	.dotx		Format used for Word 2016, Word 2013, Word 2010, or Word 2007 templates
XPS	.xps		XML (Extensible Markup Language) Paper Specification, which can be opened in the XPS Viewer

To Save a Word 2016 Document as a Different File Type

To save a Word 2016 document as a different file type, you would follow these steps.

1. Open the Backstage view and then click the Export tab in the Backstage view to display the Export gallery.
2. Click 'Change File Type' in the Export gallery to display information in the right pane about various file types that can be opened in Word.
3. Click the desired file type in the right pane and then click the Save As button to display the Save As dialog box.
4. Navigate to the desired save location (Save As dialog box) and then click the Save button in the dialog box.
5. If the Microsoft Word Compatibility Checker dialog box appears and you agree with the changes that will be made to the document, click the Continue button (Microsoft Word Compatibility Checker dialog box) to save the document on the selected drive with the current file name in the specified format.

To Invite Others to View or Edit a Document

If you have a OneDrive account, you can share a Word document saved on OneDrive with others through email message invitations. *Why? Invited users can click a link in an email message that displays a webpage enabling them to view or edit the document on OneDrive.* The following steps invite a user to view the Yazzie Resume document. If you do not have a Microsoft account or an Internet connection, read these steps without performing them.

- If necessary, run Word. Open the Word 2016 format of the Yazzie Resume and then save the Yazzie Resume on OneDrive.

- Click the Share button in the upper-right corner of the ribbon to open the Share pane (Figure 5–56).

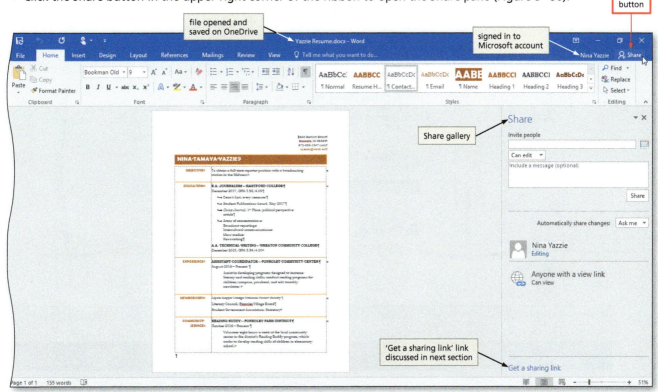

Figure 5–56

Why does my screen display a 'Save to Cloud' button in the Share pane?
The document has not been saved on OneDrive and/or you are not signed in to your Microsoft account.

- In the Share pane, type the email address(es) of the person(s) with whom you want to share the document, click the box arrow so that you can specify Can edit, if necessary, and then type a message to the recipient(s) (Figure 5–57).

Figure 5–57

3

- Click the Share button in the Share pane to send the message along with a link to the document on OneDrive to the listed recipient(s).

Other Ways

1. Open Backstage view, click Share tab, click 'Share with People' in left pane in Share gallery, enter email address and message in Share pane, click Share button in Share pane

CONSIDER THIS

How does a recipient access the shared document?

The recipient receives an email message that indicates it contains a link to a shared document (Figure 5–58). When the recipient clicks the link in the email message, the document opens in Word Online on OneDrive (Figure 5–59).

Figure 5–58

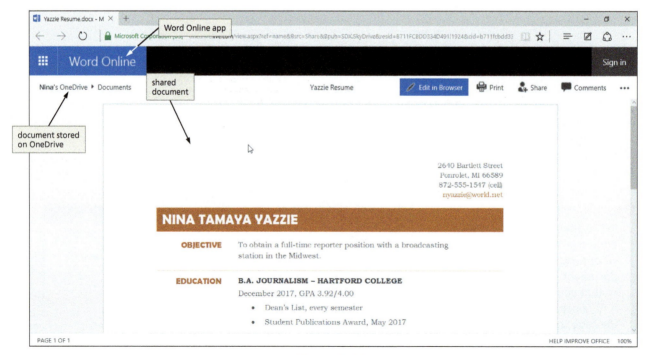

Figure 5–59

To Get a Sharing Link

Why share a link? Instead of inviting people to view or edit a document, you can create a link to the document's location on OneDrive and then send others the link via an email message or text message, post it on a website or online social network, or communicate it via some other means. The following steps get a sharing link. If you do not have a Microsoft account or an Internet connection, read these steps without performing them.

- If necessary, click Share button in the upper-right corner of the ribbon to open the Share pane and then click 'Get a sharing link' at the bottom of the Share pane (shown in Figure 5–56) to display options for obtaining a link to a document on OneDrive in the right pane (Figure 5–60).

Q&A Why does my screen display a 'Save to Cloud' button in the right pane?

The document has not been saved on OneDrive and/or you are not signed in to your Microsoft account.

Figure 5–60

- Click the 'Create a view-only link' button in the Share pane to create the link associated with the file on OneDrive (Figure 5–61).

Q&A What do I do with the link?

You can copy and paste the link in an email or text message, on a webpage, or some other location.

What is the difference between a view link and an edit link?

A view link enables others to read the document but not modify it, while an edit link enables others to both view and edit the document.

Figure 5–61

- Click the Close button in the upper-right corner of the Share pane to close the pane.

Other Ways
1. Open Backstage view, click Share tab, click 'Share with People' in right pane in Share gallery, enter email address and message in Share pane, click 'Get a sharing link' in Share pane

To Remove a Watermark

The following steps remove the DRAFT watermark from the resume in the document window, if it was saved with the document, because you now consider the document final and would like to distribute it to potential employers.

1 If necessary, open the Yazzie Resume (Word 2016 format).

2 Display the Design tab.

3 Click the Watermark button (Design tab | Page Background group) to display the Watermark gallery.

4 Click Remove Watermark in the Watermark gallery to remove the watermark.

5 Save the resume again with the same file name.

What file type should you use when emailing documents?

If you email a document, such as your resume, consider that the recipient, such as a potential employer, may not have the same software you used to create the resume and, thus, may not be able to open the file. As an alternative, you could save the file in a format, such as a PDF or XPS, that can be viewed with a reader program. Many job seekers also post their resumes on the web.

To Send a Document Using Email

1 CREATE DOCUMENT FROM TEMPLATE | 2 MODIFY & FORMAT TEMPLATE | 3 SAVE DOCUMENT IN OTHER FORMATS
4 MAKE DOCUMENT AVAILABLE ONLINE | 5 CREATE WEBPAGE FROM WORD DOCUMENT | 6 FORMAT WEBPAGE

In Word, you can include the current document as an attachment to an email message. An attachment is a file included with an email message. The following steps send the Yazzie Resume as an email attachment, assuming you use Outlook as your default email program. *Why? When you attach an email document from within Word, it automatically uses the default email program, which is Outlook in this case.*

1

- Open the Backstage view and then click the Share tab in the Backstage view to display the Share gallery.

- If necessary, click Email in the left pane of the Share gallery to display information in the right pane about various ways to send a document via email from within Word (Figure 5–62).

Figure 5–62

Why is my list of share options in the Share gallery shorter?
You have not saved the document previously on OneDrive.

What are the purpose of the 'Send as PDF' and 'Send as XPS' buttons?
Depending on which button you click, Word converts the current document either to the PDF or XPS format and then attaches the PDF or XPS document to the email message.

Why is my 'Send a Link' button dimmed?
You have not saved the document previously on OneDrive.

- Click the 'Send as Attachment' button to run your default email program (Outlook, in this case), which automatically attaches the active Word document to the email message.

- Fill in the To text box with the recipient's email address.

- Fill in the message text (Figure 5–63).

- Click the Send button to send the email message along with its attachment to the recipient named in the To text box and then close the email window.

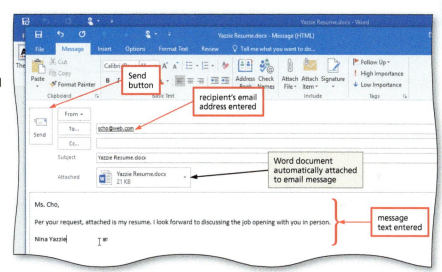

Figure 5–63

- Because you are finished working with the Yazzie Resume on OneDrive, you can sign out of your Microsoft Account, if you wish to do so.

To Use the Document Inspector

Word includes a Document Inspector that checks a document for content you might not want to share with others, such as personal information. Before sharing a document with others, you may want to check for this type of content. If you wanted to use the Document Inspector, you would do the following:

1. Open the Backstage view and, if necessary, click the Info tab in the Backstage view to display the Info gallery.

2. Click the 'Check for Issues' button in the Info gallery to display the Check for Issues menu.

3. Click Inspect Document on the Check for Issues menu to display the Document Inspector dialog box.

4. Click the Inspect button (Document Inspector dialog box) to instruct Word to inspect the document.

5. Review the results (Document Inspector dialog box) and then click the Remove All button(s) for any item that you do not want to be saved with the document.

6. When finished removing information, click the Close button to close the dialog box.

To Customize How Word Opens Email Attachments

When a user sends you an email message that contains a Word document as an attachment, Word may display the document in Read mode. This view is designed to

BTW

Internet Fax
If you do not have a stand-alone fax machine, you can send and receive faxes in Word by clicking the 'Send as Internet Fax' button in the Backstage view (shown in Figure 5–62). To send or receive faxes using Word, you first must sign up with a fax service provider by clicking the OK button in the Microsoft Office dialog box that appears the first time you click the 'Send as Internet Fax' button, which displays an Available Fax Services webpage. You also may need to install either the Windows Fax printer driver or Windows Fax Services component on your computer. When sending a fax, Word converts the document to an image file and attaches it to an email message where you enter the recipient's fax number, name, subject, and message for the cover sheet, and then click a Send button to deliver the fax.

increase the readability and legibility of an on-screen document. Read mode, however, does not represent how the document will look when it is printed. For this reason, many users prefer working in Print Layout view to read documents. To exit Read mode, press the ESC key.

If you wanted to customize how Word opens email attachments, you would do the following.

1. Open the Backstage view and then click the Options tab in the Backstage view to display the Word Options dialog box.

2. If necessary, click General in the left pane (Word Options dialog box).

3. If you want email attachments to open in Read mode, place a check mark in the 'Open e-mail attachments and other uneditable files in reading view' check box; otherwise, remove the check mark to open email attachments in Print Layout view.

4. Click the OK button to close the dialog box.

Creating a Webpage from a Word Document

If you have created a document, such as a resume, using Word, you can save it in a format that can be opened by a browser, such as Internet Explorer. When you save a file as a webpage, Word converts the contents of the document into **HTML** (Hypertext Markup Language), which is a set of codes that browsers can interpret. Some of Word's formatting features are not supported by webpages. Thus, your webpage may look slightly different from the original Word document.

When saving a document as a webpage, Word provides you with three choices:

- The **single file web page format** saves all of the components of the webpage in a single file that has a **.mht** extension. This format is particularly useful for sending documents via email in HTML format.

- The **web page format** saves some of the components of the webpage in a folder, separate from the webpage. This format is useful if you need access to the individual components, such as images, that make up the webpage.

- The **filtered web page format** saves the file in webpage format and then reduces the size of the file by removing specific Microsoft Office formats. This format is useful if you want to speed up the time it takes to download a webpage that contains graphics, video, audio, or animations.

The webpage created in this section uses the single file web page format.

BTW

Saving as a Webpage
Because you might not have access to OneDrive or a web server, the webpage you create in this module is saved in your class folder rather than on OneDrive or a web server.

To Save a Word Document as a Webpage

1 CREATE DOCUMENT FROM TEMPLATE | 2 MODIFY & FORMAT TEMPLATE | 3 SAVE DOCUMENT IN OTHER FORMATS
4 MAKE DOCUMENT AVAILABLE ONLINE | **5 CREATE WEBPAGE FROM WORD DOCUMENT** | 6 FORMAT WEBPAGE

The following steps save the Yazzie Resume created earlier in this module as a webpage. *Why? You intend to post your resume online.*

- If necessary, open the Word 2016 format of the resume file. Open the Backstage view and then click the Export tab in the Backstage view to display the Export gallery.

- Click 'Change File Type' in the left pane of the Export gallery to display information in the right pane about various file types that are supported by Word.

- Click 'Single File Web Page' in the right pane to specify a new file type (Figure 5–64).

Q&A

What if I wanted to save the document as a web page instead of a single file web page?
You would click 'Save as Another File Type' in the Change File Type area, click the Save As button, click the 'Save as type' arrow in the Save As dialog box, and then click Web Page in the Save as type list.

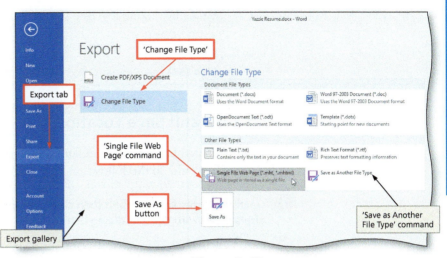

Figure 5–64

2

- Click the Save As button in the right pane to display the Save As dialog box.

- If necessary, navigate to the desired save location (Save As dialog box).

- If necessary, type **Yazzie Resume** in the File name box to change the file name.

- Click the Change Title button to display the Enter Text dialog box.

- Type **Yazzie Resume** in the Page title text box (Enter Text dialog box) (Figure 5–65).

Figure 5–65

3

- Click the OK button (Enter Text dialog box) to close the dialog box.

- Click the Save button (Save As dialog box) to save the resume as a webpage and then display it in the document window in Web Layout view.

- If necessary, change the zoom to 100% (Figure 5–66).

- If the Microsoft Word Compatibility Checker dialog box appears, click its Continue button.

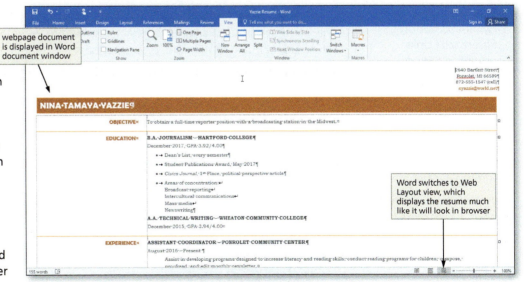

Figure 5–66

To Set a Default Save Location

If you wanted to change the default location that Word uses when it saves a document, you would do the following.

 1 Open the Backstage view and then click the Options tab in the Backstage view to display the Word Options dialog box.

2 Click Save in the left pane (Word Options dialog box) to display options for saving documents in the right pane.

3 In the 'Default file location' text box, type the new desired save location.

4 Click the OK button to close the dialog box.

To Format Text as a Hyperlink

1 CREATE DOCUMENT FROM TEMPLATE | 2 MODIFY & FORMAT TEMPLATE | 3 SAVE DOCUMENT IN OTHER FORMATS
4 MAKE DOCUMENT AVAILABLE ONLINE | 5 CREATE WEBPAGE FROM WORD DOCUMENT | **6 FORMAT WEBPAGE**

The email address in the resume webpage should be formatted as a hyperlink. ***Why?*** *When webpage visitors click the hyperlink-formatted email address, you want their email program to run automatically and open an email window with the email address already filled in.* The following steps format the email address as a hyperlink.

1

- Select the email address in the resume webpage (nyazzie@world.net, in this case).

- Display the Insert tab.

- Click the 'Add a Hyperlink' button (Insert tab | Links group) to display the Insert Hyperlink dialog box (Figure 5–67).

Figure 5–67

2

- Click E-mail Address in the Link to bar (Insert Hyperlink dialog box) so that the dialog box displays email address settings instead of webpage settings.

- In the E-mail address text box, type **nyazzie@world.net** to specify the email address that the browser uses when a user clicks the hyperlink.

- If the email address in the 'Text to display' text box is preceded by the text, mailto:, delete this leading text because you want only the email address to appear in the document.

- Click the ScreenTip button to display the Set Hyperlink ScreenTip dialog box.

• Type **Send email message to Nina Yazzie.** in the 'ScreenTip text' text box (Set Hyperlink ScreenTip dialog box) to specify the text that will be displayed when a user points to the hyperlink (Figure 5–68).

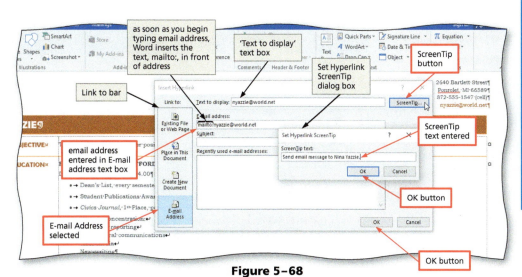

Figure 5–68

❸

• Click the OK button in each dialog box to format the email address as a hyperlink (Figure 5–69).

Q&A How do I know if the hyperlink works?
In Word, you can test the hyperlink by holding down the CTRL key while clicking the hyperlink. In this case, CTRL+clicking the email address should open an email window.

Figure 5–69

Other Ways

1. Right-click selected text, click Hyperlink on shortcut menu

2. Select text, press CTRL+K

TO EDIT A HYPERLINK

If you needed to edit a hyperlink, for example, to change its ScreenTip or its link, you would follow these steps.

1. Position the insertion point in the hyperlink.

2. Click the 'Add a Hyperlink' button (Insert tab | Links group) or press CTRL+K to display the Edit Hyperlink dialog box.

   or

1. Right-click the hyperlink to display a shortcut menu.

2. Click Edit Hyperlink on the shortcut menu to display the Edit Hyperlink dialog box.

To Change the Style Set

1 CREATE DOCUMENT FROM TEMPLATE | 2 MODIFY & FORMAT TEMPLATE | 3 SAVE DOCUMENT IN OTHER FORMATS
4 MAKE DOCUMENT AVAILABLE ONLINE | 5 CREATE WEBPAGE FROM WORD DOCUMENT | 6 FORMAT WEBPAGE

Word provides several built-in style sets to help you quickly change the look of an entire document. *Why? A style set contains formats for fonts and paragraphs.* The following steps change the style set to the Shaded style set.

• Display the Design tab.

• Click the More button (Design tab | Document Formatting group) (shown in Figure 5–71) to display the expanded Style Set gallery (Figure 5–70).

Experiment

- Point to various style sets in the Style Set gallery and watch the font and paragraph formatting change in the document window.

Figure 5–70

2

- Click Shaded to change the style set to the selected style set (Figure 5–71).

Q&A Can I create my own style sets?

Yes. Modify the fonts and other formats as desired, click 'Save as a New Style Set' in the expanded Style Set gallery (shown in Figure 5–70), enter the name for the style set (Save as a New Style Set dialog box), and then click the Save button to create the custom style set. You then can access the custom style set through the Style Set gallery.

Figure 5–71

- Save the resume webpage again on the same storage location with the same file name and then exit Word.

To Test a Webpage in a Browser

1 CREATE DOCUMENT FROM TEMPLATE | 2 MODIFY & FORMAT TEMPLATE | 3 SAVE DOCUMENT IN OTHER FORMATS
4 MAKE DOCUMENT AVAILABLE ONLINE | 5 CREATE WEBPAGE FROM WORD DOCUMENT | 6 FORMAT WEBPAGE

After creating and saving a webpage, you should test it in at least one browser. *Why? You want to be sure it looks and works the way you intended.* The following steps use File Explorer to display the resume webpage in the Microsoft Edge browser.

1

- Click the File Explorer button on the Windows taskbar to open the File Explorer window.

- Navigate to the location of the saved resume webpage file (Figure 5–72).

Figure 5–72

2

- Double-click the webpage file name, Yazzie Resume, to run Microsoft Edge and display the webpage file in the browser window (Figure 5–73).

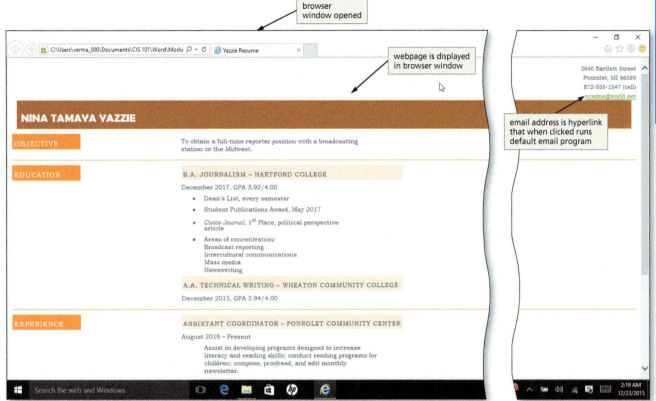

Figure 5–73

3

- With the webpage document displayed in the browser, click the email address link to run the email program with the email address displayed in the email window (Figure 5–74).

- If Microsoft Edge displays a security dialog box, click its Allow button.

Figure 5–74

4

- Exit all running apps.

CONSIDER THIS

How do you publish a webpage?

Once you have created a webpage, you can publish it. **Publishing** is the process of making a webpage available to others on a network, such as the Internet or a company's intranet. Many Internet service providers (ISPs) offer storage space on their web servers at no cost to their subscribers.

Summary

In this module, you learned how to use a Word template to create a document, set custom margins, personalize a document template, indent a paragraph, customize theme fonts, create a style, modify a style, insert building blocks, save a Word document in a variety of formats, share a document online via OneDrive, insert a hyperlink, and change the style set.

CONSIDER THIS: PLAN AHEAD

What decisions will you need to make when creating your next resume?

Use these guidelines as you complete the assignments in this module and create your own resumes outside of this class.

1. Craft a successful resume.

    a) Include necessary information (at a minimum, your contact information, objective, educational background, and work experience).

    b) Honestly present all your positive points.

    c) Organize information appropriately.

    d) Ensure the resume is error free.

2. For electronic distribution, ensure the document is in the proper format.

    a) Save the resume in a format that can be shared with others.

    b) Ensure that others will be able to open the resume using software on their computers or mobile devices and that the look of the resume will remain intact when recipients open the resume.

3. If desired, create a resume webpage from your resume Word document.

    a) Improve the usability of the resume webpage by making your email address a link to an email program.

    b) Enhance the look of the webpage by adding, for example, a background color.

    c) Test your finished webpage document in at least one browser to be sure it looks and works as intended.

    d) Publish your resume webpage.

Apply Your Knowledge

Reinforce the skills and apply the concepts you learned in this module.

Saving a Word Document in a Variety of Formats

Note: To complete this assignment, you will be required to use the Data Files. Please contact your instructor for information about accessing the Data Files.

Instructions: Run Word. Open the document, Apply 5 – 1 Protect Your Hearing, from the Data Files. You are to save the document as a single file web page (Figure 5 – 75), a PDF document, an XPS document, and in the Word 97-2003 format.

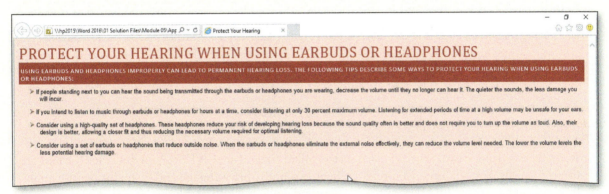

Figure 5 – 75

Perform the following tasks:

1. Save the document as a single file web page using the file name, Apply 5 – 1 Protect Your Hearing Webpage. In the Save As dialog box, click the Change Title button and change the webpage title to Protect Your Hearing. If necessary, increase the zoom percentage so that the document is readable on your screen.

2. If requested by your instructor, add another bullet point with a personal suggestion about protecting hearing when using earbuds or headphones followed by your name in parentheses.

3. Add the background color Orange, Accent 2, Lighter 80% to the webpage document.

4. Change the style set to Shaded. Save the file again.

5. Use Microsoft Edge or another browser to view the webpage (shown in Figure 5 – 75). If requested by your instructor, print the webpage. What differences do you notice between the Word document format and the single file web page format? Exit the browser and then close the webpage document in Word.

6. Open the original Apply 5 – 1 Protect Your Hearing document. If requested by your instructor, perform Step 2 again. Save the document as a PDF document and then view the PDF document in Adobe Reader. Submit the document as specified by your instructor. Exit Adobe Reader. In Word, open the PDF document just created. What differences do you notice between the Word document format and the PDF format? Close the converted PDF document without saving it.

7. If necessary, open the original Apply 5 – 1 Protect Your Hearing document. If requested by your instructor, perform Step 2 again. Save the document as an XPS Document and then view the XPS document in the XPS Viewer. Submit the document as specified by your instructor. What differences do you notice between the Word document format and the XPS format? Exit the XPS Viewer.

Continued >

Apply Your Knowledge *continued*

8. If necessary, open the original Apply 5–1 Protect Your Hearing document. Run the compatibility checker. What issue(s) were identified by the compatibility checker? Save the document in the Word 97-2003 format. Submit the document as specified by your instructor.

9. If your instructor allows, email the document saved in #8 to his or her email account.

10. ✳ Answer the questions posed in #5, #6, #7, and #8. If you wanted to email this document to others, which format would you choose and why?

Extend Your Knowledge

Extend the skills you learned in this module and experiment with new skills. You may need to use Help to complete the assignment.

Creating a Multi-File Webpage, Applying a Fill Effect and Highlights, and Inserting Screen Shots

Note: To complete this assignment, you will be required to use the Data Files. Please contact your instructor for information about accessing the Data Files.

Instructions: Run Word. Open the document called Extend 5–1 NFC Chips and Tags located on the Data Files. You will save a Word document as a multi-file webpage and format it by inserting links, adding a pattern fill effect as the background, and applying highlights to text. Then, you will create a new document that contains screen shots of the webpage and files created for the webpage.

Perform the following tasks:

1. Use Help to learn about saving as a webpage (not a single file web page), hyperlinks, pattern fill effects, text highlight color, and screen shots.

2. If requested by your instructor, add your name on a separate line at the end of the document.

3. Save the Extend 5–1 NFC Chips and Tags file in the web page format (not as a single file web page) using the file name, Extend 5–1 NFC Chips and Tags Webpage.

4. Using a browser, search for a website that lists phones with NFC technology. At the end of the document, type a line of text that directs the reader to that web address for a list of phones with NFC technology. Format the web address in the document as a hyperlink so that when a user clicks the web address, the associated webpage is displayed in the browser window.

5. Add a page color of your choice to the document. Add a pattern fill effect of your choice to the page color.

6. Apply a text highlight color of your choice to at least five words in the document.

7. Save the document again. Test the webpage by double-clicking its file name in File Explorer. Test the web address link on the webpage. Leave this window open so that you can include its screen shot in the next step.

8. Redisplay the Word window. Create a new Word document. Use Word to insert a screen shot of the webpage displaying in the File Explorer window. Below the screen shot of the webpage, insert a screen shot(s) of File Explorer that shows all the files and folders created by saving the document as a webpage. Insert callout shapes with text that points to and identifies the files and folders created by saving the document as a webpage (Figure 5–76). Save the document with the file name, Extend 5–1 NFC Chips and Tags Screen Shots.

Figure 5–76

9. Close all open windows. Submit the files in the format specified by your instructor.

10. ✳ Why would you add a pattern fill effect to a background?

Expand Your World

Create a solution that uses cloud or web technologies by learning and investigating on your own from general guidance.

Sharing a Resume Online

Notes:

- You will use OneDrive and a job sharing website account, which you can create at no cost, to complete this assignment. If you do not have these accounts and do not want to create them, read this assignment without performing the instructions.

- To complete this assignment, you will be required to use the Data Files. Please contact your instructor for information about accessing the Data Files.

Instructions: You are a marketing management graduate from Mockingbird College. You have prepared a resume and are ready to share it with potential employers. You will save it on your OneDrive account, invite others to view it, get a sharing link, send it via email, and post it on a job sharing website (Figure 5–77).

Perform the following tasks:

1. In Word, open the document, Expand 5–1 Cucci Resume, from the Data Files. Look through the resume so that you are familiar with its contents and formats.

2. If requested by your instructor, change the name at the top of the resume to your name.

3. Save the resume on your OneDrive account.

Continued >

Expand Your World *continued*

4. In Word, invite at least one of your classmates to view your resume document. If requested, include your instructor in the invitation.

5. In Word, get a sharing link for the resume. Email the sharing link to at least one of your classmates. Submit the link in the format requested by your instructor.

6. Save the resume as a PDF file. Search for the text, post resume online, using a search engine. Visit several of the job search websites and determine on which one you would like to post a resume. If requested, create an account or profile, fill in the requested information, and then upload the PDF format of the resume (Figure 5–77). Submit the posting in the format requested by your instructor. Delete the posted resume from the job search website.

7. ✺ Which job search websites did you evaluate? Which one did you select to use and why? What would cause the file size of your resume to be too large to upload (post)? How can you reduce the file size?

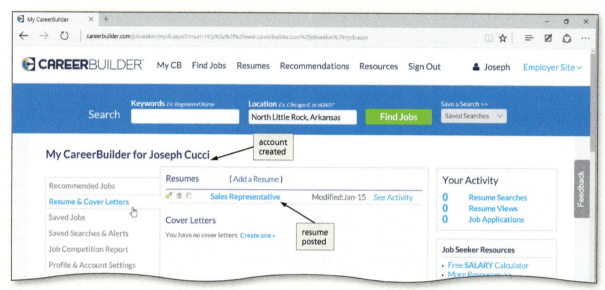

Figure 5–77

In the Labs

Design, create, modify, and/or use a document following the guidelines, concepts, and skills presented in this module. Labs 1 and 2, which increase in difficulty, require you to create solutions based on what you learned in the module; Lab 3 requires you to apply your creative thinking and problem-solving skills to design and implement a solution.

Lab 1: Creating a Resume from a Template (same template as in this module's project)

Problem: You are psychology student at Olympia State College. As graduation quickly is approaching, you prepare the resume shown in Figure 5–78 using one of Word's resume templates.

Perform the following tasks:

1. Use the Basic resume (Timeless design) template to create a resume. If you cannot locate this template or if the template you locate differs from Figure 5–5 shown at the beginning of this module, open the file called Basic resume (Timeless design) from the Data Files.

2. Change the document theme to Headlines.

18 point

30 Fifth Avenue
Branch Center, WA 98472
503-555-1147 (cell)
boskovich@link.com

JOVAN MARKO BOSKOVICH

OBJECTIVE   To obtain a counselor position with a local elementary or high school.

EDUCATION   **B.A. PSYCHOLOGY – OLYMPIA STATE COLLEGE**
May 2017, GPA 3.89/4.00

- Dean's List, every semester
- Gavin Perkins Fellowship, May 2015
- *Social Psychology Journal*, 1st Place, cognition and learning article
- Areas of concentration:
Behavior disorders
Cognitive science
Psychology of personality
Youth and child psychology

A.A. HEALTH SCIENCES – OLYMPIA STATE COLLEGE
December 2015, GPA 3.92/4.00

EXPERIENCE   **CRISIS ADVOCATE – COMMUNITY CARES CENTER**
February 2016 – Present

left and right margins indented

Work 15 hours a week at the crisis call center or hospital offering emotional support, information, education, option identification, safety planning, and intervention to callers and clients.

MEMBERSHIPS   Psychology Club, secretary

Sigma Delta Pi National Honor Society

Student Government Association

COMMUNITY SERVICE   **ADVISORY BOARD MEMBER – BRANCH CENTER SENIOR CARE**
October 2016 – Present

left and right margins indented

Volunteer on the advisory board for the senior center; responsible for planning senior networking, public relations, education, and community outreach.

Figure 5–78

3. Personalize the resume as shown in Figure 5–78. Following are some guidelines for some sections of the resume:

a. Change the margins to 1" on the top, left, and right, and .5" on the bottom.

b. If requested by your instructor, use your own name and contact information in the content controls. Delete the line containing the Website content control.

c. Move the Education and Experience rows so that they appear as shown in Figure 5–78. Insert line breaks in the areas of concentration section of the education information.

Continued >

In the Labs *continued*

  d. Copy and paste the text in the table cell containing the Education content control so that you can enter both degrees.

  e. Delete the second item from the Experience content control because the resume lists only one job.

  f. In the Experience section, indent the left and right margins of the job responsibilities paragraphs one-half inch.

  g. Change the heading, Skill & Abilities, to Memberships.

  h. Copy the Experience section to below the Memberships section. Change the added row to show the community service information.

  i. Customize the theme fonts so that the headings are Arial Black and the body text is Verdana. Name the customized font Lab 1 Resume.

  j. Modify the Heading 2 style to the Verdana font.

  k. Delete any unused rows in the resume.

4. The entire resume should fit on a single page. If it flows to two pages, decrease spacing before and after paragraphs until the entire resume text fits on a single page.

5. Check the spelling of the resume. Save the resume with Lab 5 – 1 Boskovich Resume as the file name, and submit it in the format specified by your instructor.

6. ✸ Look through the other resume templates available. Which would work best for your resume? Why?

Lab 2: Creating a Resume from a Template (different template from this module's project)

Problem: You are a business student at Eureka Falls College. As graduation is approaching quickly, you prepare the resume shown in Figure 5 – 79 using one of Word's resume templates.

Perform the following tasks:

1. Use the Resume (color) template to create a resume. If you cannot locate this template, open the file called Resume (color) from the Data Files.

2. Change the document theme to slate. Personalize, modify, format the resume as shown in Figure 5 – 79. If requested by your instructor, use your personal information in the contact information content controls at the top of the resume. Insert and remove other content controls, as necessary, and modify placeholder in the resume as shown in the figure. Following are some guidelines for some sections of the resume:

  a. After entering text in the contact information content controls at the top of the resume template, remove the content controls (right-click the content control and then click 'Remove Content Control' on the shortcut menu so that your text remains but the content control is deleted). When you selected the contact information content controls, they appeared on the screen different from the template used in this module. How did they differ?

  b. To add the third job in the Experience section, click the bottom job experience control to select it and then click the Insert Control at the bottom right edge of the selected control. After entering the text in the content control, remove the content control so that text remains but the content control is deleted. Note that the resume template in this module's project did not contain an Insert Control. Describe the appearance of the Insert Control.

  c. Create a customized theme font set that uses Rockwell for headings and Arial for body text. Save the theme font with the name, Lab 2 Resume.

Figure 5–79

d. Modify the Section style to contain paragraph shading of Gray 80%, Text 2, Lighter 90%. Update the style so that it applies to the entire resume.

e. Increase the font size of the name to 28 point and the street address control to 10 point. Create a style called Contact Info using the format in the street address. Apply the Contact Info style to the city, state, ZIP code, phone number, and email address (the vertical bars before and after the phone number should remain at 9 point).

Continued >

In the Labs *continued*

3. The entire resume should fit on a single page. If it flows to two pages, decrease spacing before and after paragraphs until the entire resume text fits on a single page.

4. Check the spelling of the resume. Save the resume with Lab 5 – 2 Washington Resume as the file name, and submit it in the format specified by your instructor.

5. ✳ Answer the questions posed in #2a and 2b. Look through the templates available besides resumes. Which ones might you find useful? Why?

Lab 3: Consider This: Your Turn

Create a Calendar and an Invitation Using Templates

Problem: To help organize your appointments and important dates, you use a calendar template. While filling in the calendar, you decide to schedule a retirement party for your dad for which you will need to send out invitations.

Part 1: Browse through Word's online templates and download appropriate calendar and invitation templates and then use the text in the next two paragraphs for content. Use the concepts and techniques presented in this module to create and format the invitation and calendar. Be sure to check the spelling and grammar of the finished documents. When finished with the two documents, save them in a form suitable for electronic distribution. Decide which document would be best to create as a webpage; then, create the webpage from that document and format the webpage. Submit your assignment documents in the format specified by your instructor.

Calendar information: November 1 – Send out retirement party invitations, November 2 – Student Council meeting at 1:00 p.m. in Room 103 in Pace Hall, November 7 – Vote! It's Election Day, November 8 – Marianne's birthday, November 10 – Job Fair from noon to 4:00 p.m. in Bard Hall, November 11 – Volunteer at VFW's pancake breakfast for Veteran's Day, November 14 – My birthday!, November 15 – Grandma's birthday, November 17 – Dentist appointment at 9:00 a.m. and Photography Club luncheon at Jack's Pizza from 11:30 a.m. to 2:00 p.m., November 18 – Thanksgiving break starts, November 20 – Eye doctor appointment at 1:00 p.m., November 23 – Thanksgiving Day, November 25 – Dad's retirement party from 2:00 to 6:00 p.m. at Reimer's Restaurant, November 26 – Thanksgiving break ends, November 27 – Corporate Law term paper due by 11:59 p.m., November 28 – internship presentation at 10:00 a.m., and November 30 – capstone project due.

If the template requires, insert appropriate clip art or an image of your own. If requested by your instructor, insert a personal event in the calendar.

Invitation information: Congratulations Jeremy Winters!; Retirement Party!; Saturday, November 26, 2:00 to 6:00 p.m.; Reimer's Restaurant, 10 Chestnut Street, Mitcheltown, DE 19722; Come hungry!; Send a photo of you and Jeremy to mwinters@earth.link by November 20 for the slide show!; Hope you can join us!

If the template requires, insert appropriate clip art or an image of your own. If requested by your instructor, use your name and contact information instead of the information listed here.

Part 2: ✳ You made several decisions while creating the calendar and invitation in this assignment: which template to use, where to position elements, how to format elements, which graphic(s) to use, in which format to save the documents for electronic distribution, which document to create as a webpage, and how to format the webpage. What was the rationale behind each of these decisions?

6 Generating Form Letters, Mailing Labels, and a Directory

Objectives

You will have mastered the material in this module when you can:

- Explain the merge process
- Use the Mail Merge task pane and the Mailings tab on the ribbon
- Use a letter template as the main document for a mail merge
- Create and edit a data source
- Insert merge fields in a main document
- Use an IF field in a main document
- Merge form letters
- Select records to merge
- Sort data records
- Address and print mailing labels and envelopes
- Change page orientation
- Merge all data records to a directory
- Convert text to a table

Introduction

People are more likely to open and read a personalized letter than a letter addressed as Dear Sir, Dear Madam, or To Whom It May Concern. Creating individual personalized letters, though, can be a time-consuming task. Thus, Word provides the capability of creating a form letter, which is an easy way to generate mass mailings of personalized letters. The basic content of a group of form letters is similar. Items such as name and address, however, vary from one letter to the next. With Word, you easily can address and print mailing labels or envelopes for the form letters.

Project — Form Letters, Mailing Labels, and a Directory

Both businesses and individuals regularly use form letters to communicate with groups of people via the postal service or email. Types of form letter correspondence include announcements of sales to customers, notices of benefits to employees, invitations to the public to participate in a sweepstakes giveaway, and job application letters to potential employers.

The project in this module follows generally accepted guidelines for writing form letters and uses Word to create the form letters shown in Figure 6–1. The form letters inform potential employers of your interest in a job opening at their organization. Each form letter states the potential employer's name and address, available job position, and whether the job is at a radio or television station.

To generate form letters, such as the ones shown in Figure 6–1, you create a main document for the form letter (Figure 6–1a), create or specify a data source (Figure 6–1b), and then **merge**, or blend, the main document with the data source to generate a series of individual letters (Figure 6–1c). In Figure 6–1a, the main document represents the portion of the form letter that is repeated from one merged letter to the next. In Figure 6–1b, the data source contains the individual's and organization's name and address, available position, and type of broadcast station for various potential employers. To personalize each letter, you merge the potential employer data in the data source with the main document for the form letter, which generates or prints an individual letter for each potential employer listed in the data source.

Word provides two methods of merging documents: the Mail Merge task pane and the Mailings tab on the ribbon. The Mail Merge task pane displays a wizard, which is a step-by-step progression that guides you through the merging process. The Mailings tab provides buttons and boxes you use to merge documents. This module illustrates both techniques.

In this module, you will learn how to create the form letters shown in Figure 6–1. The following roadmap identifies general activities you will perform as you progress through this module:

1. IDENTIFY the MAIN DOCUMENT for the form letters.

2. CREATE a DATA SOURCE.

3. COMPOSE the MAIN DOCUMENT for the form letters.

4. MERGE the DATA SOURCE with the main document.

5. ADDRESS the MAILING LABELS.

6. MERGE all data records TO a DIRECTORY.

To Run Word and Change Word Settings

If you are using a computer to step through the project in this module and you want your screens to match the figures in this book, you should change your screen's resolution to 1366 × 768. The following steps run Word, display formatting marks, and change the zoom to page width.

1 Run Word and create a blank document in the Word window. If necessary, maximize the Word window.

2 If the Print Layout button on the status bar is not selected, click it so that your screen is in Print Layout view.

(a) Main Document for the Form Letter

(b) Data Source

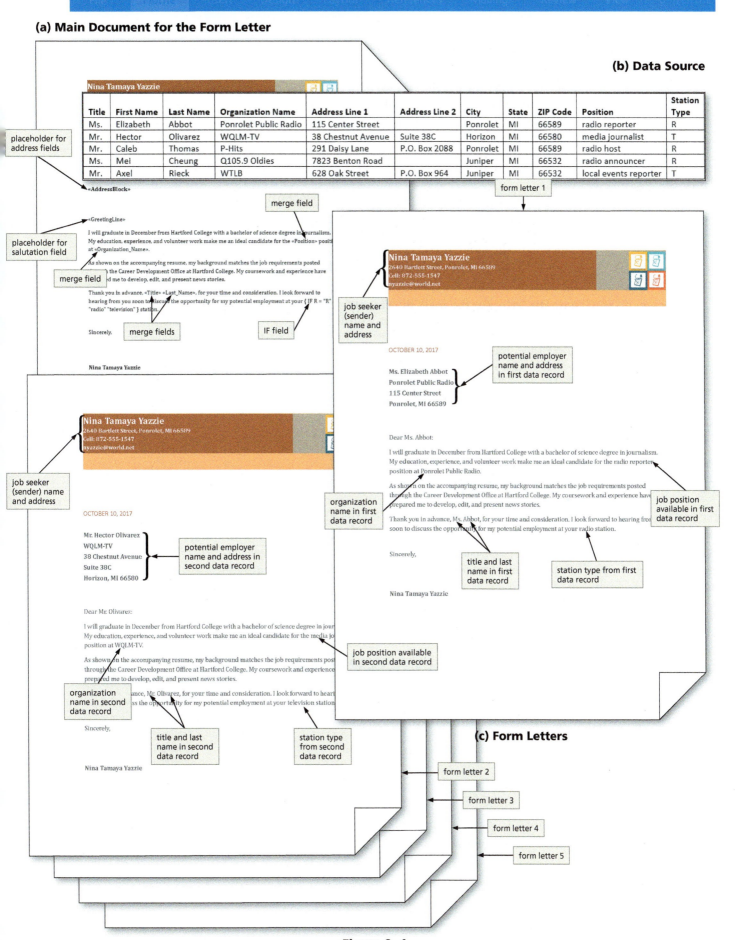

placeholder for address fields

Title	First Name	Last Name	Organization Name	Address Line 1	Address Line 2	City	State	ZIP Code	Position	Station Type
Ms.	Elizabeth	Abbot	Ponrolet Public Radio	115 Center Street		Ponrolet	MI	66589	radio reporter	R
Mr.	Hector	Olivarez	WQLM-TV	38 Chestnut Avenue	Suite 38C	Horizon	MI	66580	media journalist	T
Mr.	Caleb	Thomas	P-Hits	291 Daisy Lane	P.O. Box 2088	Ponrolet	MI	66589	radio host	R
Ms.	Mei	Cheung	Q105.9 Oldies	7823 Benton Road		Juniper	MI	66532	radio announcer	R
Mr.	Axel	Rieck	WTLB	628 Oak Street	P.O. Box 964	Juniper	MI	66532	local events reporter	T

form letter 1

«AddressBlock»

merge field

placeholder for salutation field

«GreetingLine»

merge field

I will graduate in December from Hartford College with a bachelor of science degree in journalism. My education, experience, and volunteer work make me an ideal candidate for the «Position» position at «Organization_Name».

As shown on the accompanying resume, my background matches the job requirements posted through the Career Development Office at Hartford College. My coursework and experience have prepared me to develop, edit, and present news stories.

Thank you in advance, «Title» «Last_Name», for your time and consideration. I look forward to hearing from you soon to discuss the opportunity for my potential employment at your { IF R = "R" "radio" "television" } station.

merge fields

IF field

job seeker (sender) name and address

Sincerely,

Nina Tamaya Yazzie

Nina Tamaya Yazzie
2640 Bartlett Street, Ponrolet, MI 66589
Cell: 872-555-1547
nyazzie@world.net

OCTOBER 10, 2017

potential employer name and address in first data record

Ms. Elizabeth Abbot
Ponrolet Public Radio
115 Center Street
Ponrolet, MI 66589

job seeker (sender) name and address

Nina Tamaya Yazzie
2640 Bartlett Street, Ponrolet, MI 66589
Cell: 872-555-1547
nyazzie@world.net

OCTOBER 10, 2017

Mr. Hector Olivarez
WQLM-TV
38 Chestnut Avenue
Suite 38C
Horizon, MI 66580

potential employer name and address in second data record

Dear Ms. Abbot:

I will graduate in December from Hartford College with a bachelor of science degree in journalism. My education, experience, and volunteer work make me an ideal candidate for the radio reporter position at Ponrolet Public Radio.

As shown on the accompanying resume, my background matches the job requirements posted through the Career Development Office at Hartford College. My coursework and experience have prepared me to develop, edit, and present news stories.

organization name in first data record

Thank you in advance, Ms. Abbot, for your time and consideration. I look forward to hearing from soon to discuss the opportunity for my potential employment at your radio station.

job position available in first data record

Sincerely,

title and last name in first data record

station type from first data record

Nina Tamaya Yazzie

Dear Mr. Olivarez:

I will graduate in December from Hartford College with a bachelor of science degree in journalism. My education, experience, and volunteer work make me an ideal candidate for the media journalist position at WQLM-TV.

As shown on the accompanying resume, my background matches the job requirements posted through the Career Development Office at Hartford College. My coursework and experience have prepared me to develop, edit, and present news stories.

job position available in second data record

organization name in second data record

Thank you in advance, Mr. Olivarez, for your time and consideration. I look forward to hearing discuss the opportunity for my potential employment at your television station.

Sincerely,

title and last name in second data record

station type from second data record

(c) Form Letters

Nina Tamaya Yazzie

form letter 2

form letter 3

form letter 4

form letter 5

Figure 6–1

3 If the 'Show/Hide ¶' button (Home tab | Paragraph group) is not selected already, click it to display formatting marks on the screen.

4 To display the page the same width as the document window, if necessary, click the Page Width button (View tab | Zoom group).

Identifying the Main Document for Form Letters

The first step in the mail merge process is to identify the type of document you are creating for the main document. Typical installations of Word support five types of main documents: letters, email messages, envelopes, labels, and a directory. In this section of the module, you create letters as the main document. Later in this module, you will specify labels and a directory as the main document.

CONSIDER THIS

How should you create the letter for the main document?

When creating form letters, you either can type the letter for the main document from scratch in a blank document window or use a letter template. If you enter the contents of the main document from scratch, you can compose it according to the block, modified block, or semi-block letter style, formatted appropriately with business letter spacing. Alternatively, you can use a letter template to save time because Word prepares a letter with text and/or formatting common to all letters. Then, you customize the resulting letter by selecting and replacing prewritten text.

To Identify the Main Document for the Form Letter Using the Mail Merge Task Pane

1 IDENTIFY MAIN DOCUMENT | **2 CREATE DATA SOURCE** | **3 COMPOSE MAIN DOCUMENT**
4 MERGE DATA SOURCE | **5 ADDRESS MAILING LABELS** | **6 MERGE TO DIRECTORY**

This module uses a template for the main document for the form letter, where you select predefined content controls and placeholder text and replace them with personalized content, adjusting formats as necessary. *Why? You use the same style that you used with the resume in the previous module so that the two documents complement one another.* The following steps use the Mail Merge task pane to identify the Timeless letter template as the main document for a form letter.

1

- Click Mailings on the ribbon to display the Mailings tab.

- Click the 'Start Mail Merge' button (Mailings tab | Start Mail Merge group) to display the Start Mail Merge menu (Figure 6–2).

 Q&A
What is the function of the E-mail Messages command?
Instead of sending individual letters, you can send individual email messages using email addresses in the data source or using a Microsoft Outlook Contacts list.

Figure 6–2

2

- Click 'Step-by-Step Mail Merge Wizard' on the Start Mail Merge menu to display Step 1 of the Mail Merge wizard in the Mail Merge task pane (Figure 6–3).

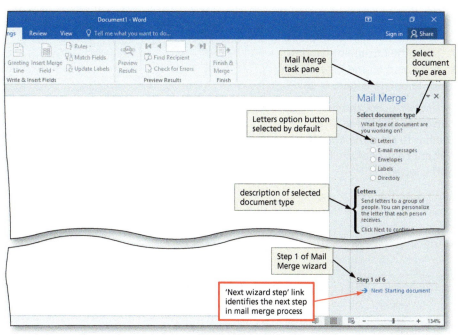

Figure 6–3

3

- Click the 'Next wizard step' link at the bottom of the Mail Merge task pane to display Step 2 of the Mail Merge wizard, which requests you select a starting document.

- Click 'Start from a template' in the Select starting document area and then click the 'Select mail merge template' link to display the Select Template dialog box.

Q&A Why does the link name in the step differ from the name displayed in the Mail Merge task pane?

As with buttons and boxes, the text that appears on the screen may vary, depending on your screen resolution. The name that appears in the ScreenTip (when you point to the link), however, never changes. For this reason, this book uses the name that appears in the ScreenTip to identify links, buttons, boxes, and other on-screen elements.

- Click the Letters tab (Select Template dialog box) to display the Letters sheet and then click Timeless letter, which shows a preview of the selected template in the Preview area (Figure 6–4).

Figure 6–4

 Experiment

- Click various Letter templates in the Letters sheet and watch the preview change in the right pane of the dialog box. When you are finished experimenting, click the Timeless letter template to select it.

Q&A What if I cannot locate the Timeless letter template?

Skip the remainder of these steps and proceed to the steps called To Start a Mail Merge from an Existing Document that are shaded yellow, which immediately follow this set of steps.

4

- Click the OK button to display a letter in the document window that is based on the Timeless letter template (Figure 6–5).

- If necessary, click the Undo button on the Quick Access Toolbar to reset the Your Name content control at the bottom of the letter.

Q&A
Can I close the Mail Merge task pane?

Yes, you can close the Mail Merge task pane at any time by clicking its Close button. When you want to continue with the merge process, you repeat these steps and Word will resume the merge process at the correct step in the Mail Merge wizard.

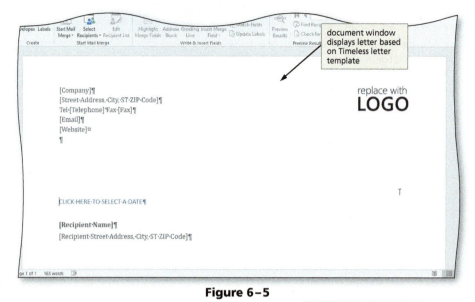

Figure 6–5

5

- Print the document shown on the screen so that you easily can see the entire letter contents (Figure 6–6).

Q&A
What are the content controls in the document?

Recall that a content control contains placeholder text and instructions for filling in areas of the document. To select a content control, click it. Later in this module, you will personalize the placeholder text and content controls. You also will remove the content controls as you are finished adding text to them.

Figure 6–6

To Start a Mail Merge from an Existing Document

If you are unable to locate the Timeless letter template in the previous steps or if your template differs from the one shown in Figure 6–6, you can open the template from the Data Files. Please contact your instructor for information about accessing the Data Files. The following steps open a document. NOTE: PERFORM THE STEPS IN THIS YELLOW BOX ONLY IF YOU WERE UNABLE TO LOCATE THE TIMELESS LETTER TEMPLATE IN THE PREVIOUS STEPS.

1 Click the 'Start from existing document' option button in the Mail Merge task pane to display options for opening a document in the task pane.

2 Click the Open button that appears in the Mail Merge task pane to display the Open dialog box.

3 Navigate to the location of the Timeless letter file to be opened. Click the Timeless letter file to select it.

4 Click the Open button (Open dialog box) to open the selected file.

To Change the User Name and Initials

If you wanted to change the user name and initials associated with your copy of Microsoft Word, you would perform the following steps.

1. Open the Backstage view and then click the Options tab to display the Word Options dialog box.
2. If necessary, click General in the left pane (Word Options dialog box).
3. Enter your name in the User name text box.
4. Enter your initials in the Initials text box.
5. Click the OK button.

BTW

Touch Screen Differences
The Office and Windows interfaces may vary if you are using a touch screen. For this reason, you might notice that the function or appearance of your touch screen differs slightly from this module's presentation.

To Change Theme Colors

Recall that Word provides document themes, which contain a variety of color schemes and other effects. This cover letter uses the Aspect theme colors to match the theme colors used in the resume. The following steps change the theme colors.

1 Click Design on the ribbon to display the Design tab.

2 Click the Theme Colors button (Design tab | Document Formatting group) to display the Theme Colors gallery.

3 Scroll to and then click Aspect in the Theme Colors gallery to change the theme colors to the selected theme.

To Enter and Format the Sender Information

The next step is to enter the sender's contact information at the top of the letter. You will use the [Company] placeholder text for the sender's name. You will delete the [Fax] and [Website] placeholder text because this sender does not have a fax or website.

Then, you will change the font size of the text. The following steps enter and format the sender information.

1 Select the placeholder text, [Company], and then type **Nina Tamaya Yazzie** as the sender name.

If requested by your instructor, enter your name instead of the job seeker's name.

2 Select the placeholder text, [Street Address, City, ST ZIP Code], and then type **2640 Bartlett Street, Ponrolet, MI 66589** as the sender's address.

3 Select the text, Tel, and then type **Cell:** as the label. Select the placeholder text, [Telephone], and then type **872-555-1547** as the sender's cell phone number.

4 Delete the Fax label and [Fax] placeholder text.

5 Select the placeholder text, [Email], and then type **nyazzie@world.net** as the sender's email address.

6 Delete the [Website] placeholder text and then press the BACKSPACE key to delete the blank line.

7 Increase the font size of the name to 14 point, and decrease the font size of the street address, cell phone, and email address to 9 point.

8 Select the name and all contact information. Bold the text (shown in Figure 6–7).

To Change a Picture and Format It

The current picture in the letter contains the text, replace with LOGO, which is a placeholder for a picture. The following steps change a picture.

1 Right-click the picture to be changed (in this case, the picture placeholder with the text, replace with LOGO) to display a shortcut menu (Figure 6–7).

Figure 6–7

2 Click Change Picture on the shortcut menu to display the Insert Pictures dialog box.

Q&A Can I use the Change Picture button (Picture Tools Format tab | Adjust group) instead of the shortcut menu to display the Insert Pictures dialog box?
Yes.

3 Type **notepad** in the Search box (Insert Pictures dialog box) and then click the Search button to display a list of images that matches the entered search text.

4 Scroll through the list of images to locate the one shown in Figure 6–8 (or a similar image), click the image to select it, and then click the Insert button (Insert Picture dialog box) to download the image, close the dialog box, and replace the selected placeholder with the new picture file (shown in Figure 6–8).

Q&A What if I cannot locate the same image?
Click the Cancel button and then click the From File button (Insert tab | Illustrations group), navigate to the Notepad-Icons-2400px.png file on the Data Files, and then click the Insert button (Insert Picture dialog box) to insert the picture.

5 Use the Shape Height and Shape Width boxes (Picture Tools Format tab | Size group) to change the picture height to approximately .8″ and width to .79″.

To Shade Cells and a Shape

In the letter in this module, the left and right cells of the table containing the contact information and picture are shaded different colors. These two cells are contained in a rectangular shape, which extends below these two cells. By shading the cells in the table and the rectangular shape each a separate color, you create a letterhead with three different colors. The following steps shade table cells and a shape.

1 Position the insertion point in the contact information (upper-left cell of table). Display the Table Tools Layout tab and then, if necessary, click the 'View Table Gridlines' button (Table Tools Layout tab | Table group) to show table gridlines.

Q&A Why show table gridlines?
With table gridlines showing, the cells are easier to see.

2 Display the Table Tools Design tab. With the insertion point in the left cell, click the Shading arrow (Table Tools Design tab | Table Styles group) and then click 'Orange, Accent 1, Darker 25%' (fifth color, fifth row) to shade the current cell with the selected color.

3 Select the contact information in the left cell and change its font color to 'White, Background 1' (first color, first row).

4 Position the insertion point in the cell with the picture, click the Shading arrow (Table Tools Design tab | Table Styles group) and then click 'Tan, Background 2, Darker 25%' (third color, third row) to shade the current cell with the selected color.

5 Position the insertion point on the paragraph mark below the shaded cell to select the rectangle drawing object. Display the Drawing Tools Format tab. Click the Shape Fill arrow (Drawing Tools Format tab | Shape Styles group) to display the Shape Fill gallery (Figure 6–8) and then click 'Orange, Accent 1, Lighter 40%' (fifth color, fourth row) to shade the selected shape with the selected color.

6 Hide table gridlines.

Figure 6–8

To Change Margin Settings

The Timeless letter template uses 1.9-inch top and .75-inch bottom, left, and right margins. You want the form letter to use 1-inch top and bottom margins and 1.25-inch left and right margins. The following steps change the margin settings.

1 Click the Date content control to deselect the drawing object.

2 Display the Layout tab. Click the Adjust Margins button (Layout tab | Page Setup group) to display the Margins gallery and then click Custom Margins at the bottom of the gallery to display the Page Setup dialog box.

3 Change the values in the Top, Bottom, Left, and Right boxes (Page Setup dialog box) to 1", 1", 1.25", and 1.25", respectively (Figure 6–9).

Figure 6–9

4 Click the OK button to change the margin values.

Q&A Why is the top margin unchanged?
The template specifies that the rectangle shape be positioned a certain distance from the top of the page, regardless of margin settings. The next steps change the position of the shape.

To Specify the Position of a Graphic

1 IDENTIFY MAIN DOCUMENT | 2 CREATE DATA SOURCE | 3 COMPOSE MAIN DOCUMENT
4 MERGE DATA SOURCE | 5 ADDRESS MAILING LABELS | 6 MERGE TO DIRECTORY

The next step is to change the distance between the shape and the top of the page. *Why? You want a one-inch space above the shape.* The following steps specify the position of a graphic.

- Click the rectangle shape to select it.

- Click the Layout Options button attached to the shape to display the Layout Options gallery (Figure 6–10).

Figure 6–10

- Click the See more link (Layout Options gallery) to display the Position tab in the Layout dialog box.

- Click Absolute position in the Vertical area (Layout dialog box), select the value in the Absolute position box, and then type **1** to specify the distance in inches from the top of the page.

- If necessary, click the below arrow and select Page (Figure 6–11).

Q&A What is the difference between the specifications in the Horizontal and Vertical areas?
Horizontal settings specify the graphic's position left to right on the page, whereas vertical settings specify the graphic's position top to bottom on the page.

Figure 6–11

- Click the OK button to change the position of the selected graphic (Figure 6–12).

Figure 6–12

To Create a Folder while Saving

1 IDENTIFY MAIN DOCUMENT | 2 CREATE DATA SOURCE | 3 COMPOSE MAIN DOCUMENT
4 MERGE DATA SOURCE | 5 ADDRESS MAILING LABELS | 6 MERGE TO DIRECTORY

You have performed several tasks while creating this project and, thus, should save it. The following steps assume you already have created folders for storing files, for example, a CIS 101 folder (for your class) that contains a Word folder and module folders. You want to save this and all other documents created in this module in a folder called Job Hunting folder in the Word folder. The following steps create a folder during the process of saving a document. *Why? This folder does not exist, so you must create it. Rather than creating the folder in Windows, you can create folders in Word.*

- Display the Save As dialog box associated with your desired save location, type **Yazzie Cover Letter** as the file name, and navigate to the desired save location for the new folder.

- Click the 'Create a new folder' button to display a new folder icon with the name, New folder, selected in the dialog box (Figure 6–13).

Figure 6–13

2

- Type **Job Hunting** as the new folder name and then press the ENTER key to create the new folder.

- Click the Open button to open the selected folder, in this case, the Job Hunting folder (Figure 6–14).

3

- Click the Save button (Save As dialog box) to save the current document in the selected folder on the selected drive.

Q&A Can I create a folder in any other dialog box?
Yes. Any dialog box that displays a File list, such as the Open and Insert File dialog boxes, also has the 'Create a new folder' button, allowing you to create a new folder in Word instead of using Windows for this task.

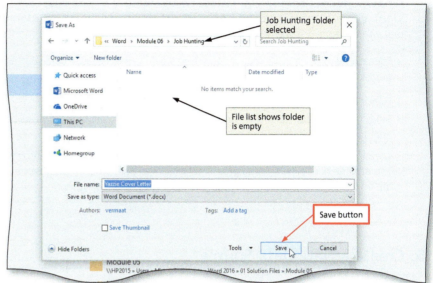

Figure 6–14

Creating a Data Source

The **data source** is a file that contains the variable, or changing, values from one merged document to the next. A data source can be an Access database table, an Outlook contacts list, or an Excel worksheet. If the necessary and properly organized data already exists in one of these Office programs, you can instruct Word to use the existing file as the data source for the mail merge. Otherwise, you can create a new data source using one of these programs.

As shown in Figure 6–15, a data source often is shown as a table that consists of a series of rows and columns. Each row is called a **record**. The first row of a data source is called the **header record** because it identifies the name of each column. Each row below the header row is called a data record. A **data record** contains the text that varies in each occurrence of the merged document. The data source for the project in this module contains five data records. In this project, each data record identifies a different potential employer. Thus, five form letters will be generated from this data source.

Each column in the data source is called a **data field**. A data field represents a group of similar data. Each data field must be identified uniquely with a name, called a **field name**. For example, Position is the name of the data field (column) that contains the available job position. In this module, the data source contains 11 data fields with the following field names: Title, First Name, Last Name, Organization Name, Address Line 1, Address Line 2, City, State, ZIP Code, Position, and Station Type.

BTW

Fields and Records
Field and record are terms that originate from the software development field. Do not be intimidated by these terms. A field is simply a column in a table, and a record is a row. Instead of as a field, some software developers identify a column of data as a variable or an attribute. All three terms (field, variable, and attribute) have the same meaning.

Figure 6–15

What guidelines should you follow when creating a data source?

When you create a data source, you will need to determine the fields it should contain. That is, you will need to identify the data that will vary from one merged document to the next. Following are a few important points about fields:

- For each field, you may be required to create a field name. Because data sources often contain the same fields, some programs create a list of commonly used field names that you may use.

- Field names must be unique; that is, no two field names may be the same.

- Fields may be listed in any order in the data source. That is, the order of fields has no effect on the order in which they will print in the main document.

- Organize fields so that they are flexible. For example, separate the name into individual fields: title, first name, and last name. This arrangement allows you to print a person's title, first name, and last name (e.g., Ms. Elizabeth Abbot) in the inside address but only the title and last name in the salutation (Dear Ms. Abbot).

To Create a New Data Source

1 IDENTIFY MAIN DOCUMENT | **2 CREATE DATA SOURCE** | 3 COMPOSE MAIN DOCUMENT
4 MERGE DATA SOURCE | 5 ADDRESS MAILING LABELS | 6 MERGE TO DIRECTORY

Word provides a list of 13 commonly used field names. This project uses 9 of the 13 field names supplied by Word: Title, First Name, Last Name, Company Name, Address Line 1, Address Line 2, City, State, and ZIP Code. This project does not use the other four field names supplied by Word: Country or Region, Home Phone, Work Phone, and E-mail Address. Thus, you will delete these four field names. Then, you will change the Company Name field name to Organization Name. *Why? The term, organization, better describes the potential employers in this project.* You also will add two new field names (Position and Station Type) to the data source. *Why? You want to reference the available position, as well as the station type, in the form letter.* The next steps create a new data source for a mail merge.

1

- Click the 'Next wizard step' link at the bottom of the Mail Merge task pane (shown in Figure 6–12) to display Step 3 of the Mail Merge wizard, which requests you select recipients.

- Click 'Type a new list' in the Select recipients area, which displays the Type a new list area.

- Click the 'Create new recipient list' link to display the New Address List dialog box (Figure 6–16).

Q&A

When would I use the other two option buttons in the Select recipients area?

If a data source already was created, you would use the first option: Use an existing list. If you wanted to use your Outlook contacts list as the data source, you would choose the second option.

Figure 6–16

- Click the Customize Columns button (New Address List dialog box) to display the Customize Address List dialog box (Figure 6–17).

Figure 6–17

- Click 'Country or Region' in the Field Names list (Customize Address List dialog box) to select the field to be deleted and then click the Delete button to display a dialog box asking if you are sure you want to delete the selected field (Figure 6–18).

Figure 6–18

4

- Click the Yes button (Microsoft Word dialog box) to delete the field.
- Click Home Phone in the Field Names list to select the field. Click the Delete button (Customize Address List dialog box) and then click the Yes button (Microsoft Word dialog box) to delete the field.
- Use this same procedure to delete the Work Phone and E-mail Address fields.

5

- Click Company Name in the Field Names list to select the field to be renamed.
- Click the Rename button to display the Rename Field dialog box.
- Type **Organization Name** in the To text box (Rename Field dialog box) (Figure 6–19).

Figure 6–19

6

- Click the OK button to close the Rename Field dialog box and rename the selected field.

7

- Click the Add button to display the Add Field dialog box.

- Type **Position** in the 'Type a name for your field' text box (Add Field dialog box) (Figure 6–20).

Figure 6–20

8

- Click the OK button to close the Add Field dialog box and add the Position field name to the Field Names list immediately below the selected field (Figure 6–21).

Q&A Can I change the order of the field names in the Field Names list?

Yes. Select the field name and then click the Move Up or Move Down button (Customize Address List dialog box) to move the selected field in the direction of the button name.

Figure 6–21

9

- With the Position field selected, click the Move Down button five times to position the selected field at the end of the Field Names list.

- Click the Add button to display the Add Field dialog box.

- Type **Station Type** (Add Field dialog box) in the 'Type a name for your field' text box and then click the OK button to close the Add Field dialog box and add the Station Type field name to the bottom of the Field Names list (Figure 6–22).

Q&A Could I add more field names to the list?

Yes. You would click the Add button for each field name you want to add.

Figure 6–22

- Click the OK button to close the Customize Address List dialog box, which positions the insertion point in the Title text box for the first record (row) in the New Address List dialog box (Figure 6–23).

Figure 6–23

- Type **Ms.** and then press the TAB key to enter the title for the first data record.

- Type **Elizabeth** and then press the TAB key to enter the first name.

- Type **Abbot** and then press the TAB key to enter the last name.

- Type **Ponrolet Public Radio** and then press the TAB key to enter the organization name.

- Type **115 Center Street** to enter the first address line (Figure 6–24).

Figure 6–24

Q&A What if I notice an error in an entry?

Click the entry and then correct the error as you would in the document window.

What happened to the rest of the Organization Name entry?

It is stored in the field, but you cannot see the entire entry because it is longer than the display area.

- Press the TAB key twice to leave the second address line empty.

- Type **Ponrolet** and then press the TAB key to enter the city.

- Type **MI** and then press the TAB key to enter the state code.

- Type **66589** and then press the TAB key to enter the ZIP code.

- Type **radio reporter** and then press the TAB key to enter the position.

- Type **R** to enter the code for the station type (Figure 6–25).

Figure 6–25

Q&A What does the R mean in the station type?

You decide to enter R for radio station and T for television station to minimize the amount of redundant typing for these records.

13

- Press the TAB key to add a new blank record and position the insertion point in the Title field of the new record (Figure 6–26).

Figure 6–26

Other Ways

1. Click Select Recipients button (Mailings tab | Start Mail Merge group)

To Enter More Records

The following steps enter the remaining four records in the New Address List dialog box.

1 Type **Mr.** and then press the TAB key. Type **Hector** and then press the TAB key. Type **Olivarez** and then press the TAB key. Type **WQLM-TV** and then press the TAB key.

2 Type **38 Chestnut Avenue** and then press the TAB key. Type **Suite 38C** and then press the TAB key.

3 Type **Horizon** and then press the TAB key. Type **MI** and then press the TAB key. Type **66580** and then press the TAB key.

4 Type **media journalist** and then press the TAB key. Type **T** and then press the TAB key.

Q&A Instead of pressing the TAB key, can I click the New Entry button at the end of one row to add a new blank record?
Yes. Clicking the New Entry button at the end of a row has the same effect as pressing the TAB key.

5 Type **Mr.** and then press the TAB key. Type **Caleb** and then press the TAB key. Type **Thomas** and then press the TAB key. Type **P-Hits** and then press the TAB key.

6 Type **291 Daisy Lane** and then press the TAB key. Type **P.O. Box 2088** and then press the TAB key.

7 Type **Ponrolet** and then press the TAB key. Type **MI** and then press the TAB key. Type **66589** and then press the TAB key.

8 Type **radio host** and then press the TAB key. Type **R** and then press the TAB key.

9 Type **Ms.** and then press the TAB key. Type **Mei** and then press the TAB key. Type **Cheung** and then press the TAB key. Type **Q105.9 Oldies** and then press the TAB key.

10 Type **7823 Benton Road** and then press the TAB key twice. Type **Juniper** and then press the TAB key. Type **MI** and then press the TAB key. Type **66532** and then press the TAB key.

11 Type **radio announcer** and then press the TAB key. Type **R** and then press the TAB key.

BTW

Saving Data Sources
Word, by default, saves a data source in the My Data Sources folder on your computer or mobile device's default storage location. Likewise, when you open a data source, Word initially looks in the My Data Sources folder for the file. Because the data source files you create in Word are saved as Microsoft Access database file types, you can open and view these files in Access if you are familiar with Microsoft Access.

⑫ Type **Mr.** and then press the TAB key. Type **Axel** and then press the TAB key. Type **Rieck** and then press the TAB key. Type **WTLB** and then press the TAB key.

⑬ Type **628 Oak Street** and then press the TAB key. Type **P.O. Box 694** and then press the TAB key.

⑭ Type **Juniper** and then press the TAB key. Type **MI** and then press the TAB key. Type **66532** and then press the TAB key.

⑮ Type **local events reporter** and then press the TAB key. Type **T** and then click the OK button (shown in Figure 6–26), which displays the Save Address List dialog box (shown in Figure 6–27).

To Save a Data Source when Prompted by Word

1 IDENTIFY MAIN DOCUMENT | **2 CREATE DATA SOURCE** | 3 COMPOSE MAIN DOCUMENT
4 MERGE DATA SOURCE | 5 ADDRESS MAILING LABELS | 6 MERGE TO DIRECTORY

When you click the OK button in the New Address List dialog box, Word displays the Save Address List dialog box. *Why? You immediately save the data source so that you do not lose any entered information.* By default, the save location is the My Data Sources folder on your computer's hard drive. In this module, you save the data source to the Job Hunting folder created earlier in this module. The following steps save the data source.

 1

- Type **Yazzie Prospective Employers** in the File name box (Save Address List dialog box) as the name for the data source. Do not press the ENTER key after typing the file name because you do not want to close the dialog box at this time.

- Navigate to the desired save location for the data source (for example, the Job Hunting folder) (Figure 6–27).

Q&A What is a Microsoft Office Address Lists file type?

It is a Microsoft Access database file. If you are familiar with Microsoft Access, you can open the Yazzie Prospective Employers file in Access. You do not have to be familiar with Access or have

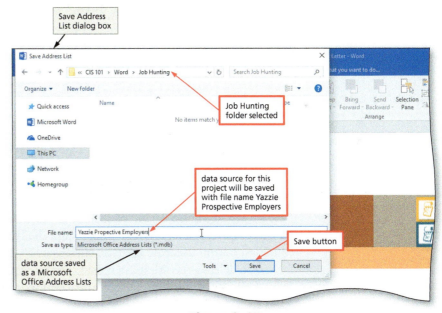

Figure 6–27

Access installed on your computer, however, to continue with this mail merge process. Word simply stores a data source as an Access table because it is an efficient method of storing a data source.

2

- Click the Save button (Save Address List dialog box) to save the data source in the selected folder using the entered file name and then display the Mail Merge Recipients dialog box (Figure 6–28).

Q&A What if the fields in my Mail Merge Recipients list are in a different order?

The order of fields in the Mail Merge Recipients list has no effect on the mail merge process. If Word rearranges the order, you can leave them in the revised order.

 3

- Click the OK button to close the Mail Merge Recipients dialog box.

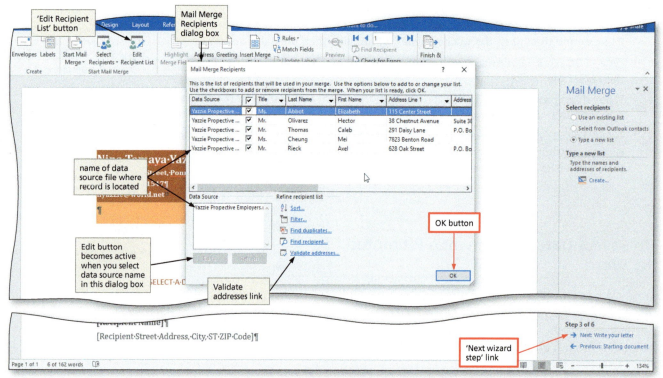

Figure 6–28

BTW

Validating Addresses
If you have installed address validation software, you can click the Validate addresses link (shown in Figure 6–28) in the Mail Merge Recipients dialog box to validate your recipients' addresses. If you have not yet installed address validation software and would like information about doing so, click the Validate addresses link in the Mail Merge Recipients dialog box and then click the Yes button in the Microsoft Word dialog box to display a related Microsoft Office webpage.

Editing Records in the Data Source

All of the data records have been entered in the data source and saved with the file name, Yazzie Prospective Employers. To add or edit data records in the data source, you would click the 'Edit Recipient List' button (Mailings tab | Start Mail Merge group) to display the Mail Merge Recipients dialog box (shown in Figure 6–28). Click the data source name in the Data Source list and then click the Edit button (Mail Merge Recipients dialog box) to display the data records in a dialog box similar to the one shown in Figure 6–26. Then, add or edit records as described in the previous steps. If you want to edit a particular record and the list of data records is long, you can click the Find button to locate an item, such as a last name, quickly in the list.

To delete a record, select it using the same procedure described in the previous paragraph. Then, click the Delete Entry button in the dialog box (shown in Figure 6–26).

Using an Existing Data Source

Instead of creating a new data source, you can use an existing Microsoft Outlook Contacts list, an Access database table, or an Excel table as a data source in a mail merge. To use an existing data source, select the appropriate option in the Select recipients area in the Mail Merge task pane or click the Select Recipients button (Mailings tab | Start Mail Merge group) and then click the desired option on the Select Recipients menu.

For a Microsoft Outlook Contacts list, click 'Select from Outlook contacts' in the Mail Merge task pane or 'Choose from Outlook Contacts' on the Select Recipients menu to display the Select Contacts dialog box. Next, select the contact folder you wish to import (Select Contacts dialog box) and then click the OK button.

For other existing data source types, such as an Access database table or an Excel worksheet, click 'Use an existing list' in the Mail Merge task pane or on the Select Recipients menu to display the Select Data Source dialog box. Next, select the file name of the data source you wish to use and then click the Open button (Select Data Source dialog box).

With Access, you can use any field in the database in the main document. (Later in this module you use an existing Access database table as the data source.) For the merge to work correctly with an Excel table, you must ensure data is arranged properly and that the table is the only element in the file. The first row of the table should contain unique field names, and the table cannot contain any blank rows.

Composing the Main Document for the Form Letters

The next step in this project is to enter and format the text and fields in the main document for the form letters (shown in Figure 6–1a at the beginning of this module). A **main document** contains the constant, or unchanging, text, punctuation, spaces, and graphics, as well as references to the data in the data source. You will follow these steps to compose the main document for the form letter.

1. Enter the date.
2. Enter the address block.
3. Enter the greeting line (salutation).
4. Enter text and insert a merge field.
5. Enter additional text and merge fields.
6. Insert an IF field.
7. Enter the remainder of the letter.
8. Merge the letters.

CONSIDER THIS

What guidelines should you follow when composing the main document for a form letter?
The finished main document letter should look like a symmetrically framed picture with evenly spaced margins, all balanced below an attractive letterhead or return address. The content of the main document for the form letter should contain proper grammar, correct spelling, logically constructed sentences, flowing paragraphs, and sound ideas; it also should reference the data in the data source properly.

Be sure the main document for the form letter includes all essential business letter elements. All business letters should contain a date line, inside address, message, and signature block. Many business letters contain additional items, such as a special mailing notation(s), an attention line, a salutation, a subject line, a complimentary close, reference initials, and an enclosure notation. When finished, proofread your letter carefully.

To Display the Next Step in the Mail Merge Wizard

The following step displays the next step in the Mail Merge wizard, which is to write the letter.

 Click the 'Next wizard step' link at the bottom of the Mail Merge task pane (shown in Figure 6–28) to display Step 4 of the Mail Merge wizard in the Mail Merge task pane (shown in Figure 6–29).

To Enter the Date

The next step is to enter the date in the letter. ***Why?*** *All business letters should contain a date, which usually is positioned below the letterhead or return address.* You can click the date content control and type the correct date, or you can click the arrow and select the date from a calendar. The following steps use the calendar to select the date.

- Click the Date content control to select it and then click its arrow to display a calendar.

- Scroll through the calendar months until the desired month appears, October 2017, in this case (Figure 6–29).

- Click 10 in the calendar to display the selected month, day, and year in the date line of the form letter (shown in Figure 6–30).

- Click outside the content control to deselect it.

- Right-click the date to display a shortcut menu and then click 'Remove Content Control' on the shortcut menu so that your text (the selected date) remains but the content control is deleted.

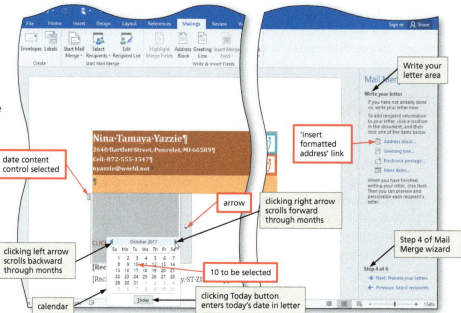

Figure 6–29

Q&A Why delete the content control?
You no longer need the content control because you already selected the date.

Other Ways
1. Type date in Date content control   2. Click 'Insert Date & Time' button (Insert tab | Text group)

Merge Fields

In this form letter, the inside address appears below the date line, and the salutation is placed below the inside address. The contents of the inside address and salutation are located in the data source. To link the data source to the main document, you insert the field names from the data source in the main document.

In the main document, field names linked to the data source are called **merge fields** because they merge, or combine, the main document with the contents of the data source. When a merge field is inserted in the main document, Word surrounds the field name with **merge field characters**, which are chevrons (« ») that mark the beginning and ending of a merge field. Merge field characters are not on the keyboard; therefore, you cannot type them directly in the document. Word automatically displays them when a merge field is inserted in the main document.

Most letters contain an address and salutation. For this reason, Word provides an AddressBlock merge field and a GreetingLine merge field. The **AddressBlock merge field** contains several fields related to an address: Title, First Name, Middle Name, Last Name, Suffix, Company, Street Address 1, Street Address 2, City, State, and ZIP Code. When Word uses the AddressBlock merge field, it automatically looks for any fields in the associated data source that are related to an address and then formats the address block properly when you merge the data source with the main document. For example, if your inside address does not use a middle name, suffix, or company, Word omits these items from the inside address and adjusts the spacing so that the address prints correctly.

To Insert the AddressBlock Merge Field

1 IDENTIFY MAIN DOCUMENT | 2 CREATE DATA SOURCE | 3 COMPOSE MAIN DOCUMENT
4 MERGE DATA SOURCE | 5 ADDRESS MAILING LABELS | 6 MERGE TO DIRECTORY

The default format for the AddressBlock merge field is the first name and last name on one line, followed by the street address on the next line, and then the city, state, and postal code on the next line. In this letter, you want the potential employer's title (i.e., Ms.) to appear to the left of the first name. *Why? You want to address the potential employers formally.* You also want the organization name to appear above the street address, if it does not already. The following steps insert the AddressBlock merge field in this format.

- Delete the content control that contains placeholder text for the recipient's address and then press the DELETE key to delete the blank paragraph.

- Delete the [Recipient Name] placeholder text but leave the paragraph mark; position the insertion point to the left of the paragraph mark because you will insert the AddressBlock merge field in that location.

- Click the 'Insert formatted address' link in the Mail Merge task pane (shown in Figure 6–29) to display the Insert Address Block dialog box.

- Scroll through the list of recipient name formats (Insert Address Block dialog box) and then click the format 'Mr. Joshua Randall Jr.' in this list, because that format places the title to the left of the first name and last name.

🔎 Experiment

- Click various recipient name formats and watch the preview change in the dialog box. When finished experimenting, click 'Mr. Joshua Randall Jr.' for the format.

Q&A Why is the 'Insert company name' check box dimmed?
The data source does not have a match to the Company Name in the AddressBlock merge field so this check box will be dimmed. Recall that earlier in this project the Company Name field was renamed as Organization Name, which causes the fields to be unmatched. The next step shows how to match the fields. If the Organization Name already appears in your AddressBlock merge field, proceed to Step 4.

- Click the Match Fields button (Insert Address Block dialog box) to display the Match Fields dialog box (Figure 6–30).

Figure 6–30

- Click the Company arrow (Match Fields dialog box) to display a list of fields in the data source and then click Organization Name to place that selected field as the match field (Figure 6–31).

- Click the OK button (Match Fields dialog box) to close the dialog box, and notice the 'Insert company name' check box no longer is dimmed (Insert Address Block dialog box) because the Company field now has a matched field in the data source.

Figure 6–31

4

- Click the OK button (Insert Address Block dialog box) to insert the AddressBlock merge field at the location of the insertion point (Figure 6–32).

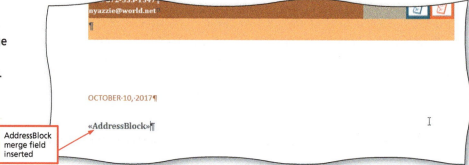

Figure 6–32

To Edit the AddressBlock Merge Field

If you wanted to change the format of or match fields in the AddressBlock merge field, you would perform the following steps.

1. Right-click the AddressBlock merge field to display a shortcut menu.

2. Click 'Edit Address Block' on the shortcut menu to display the Modify Address Block dialog box.

3. Make necessary changes and then click the OK button (Modify Address Block dialog box).

1 IDENTIFY MAIN DOCUMENT | 2 CREATE DATA SOURCE | 3 COMPOSE MAIN DOCUMENT
4 MERGE DATA SOURCE | 5 ADDRESS MAILING LABELS | 6 MERGE TO DIRECTORY

To View Merged Data in the Main Document

Instead of displaying merge fields, you can display merged data. *Why? One way to see how fields, such as the AddressBlock fields, will look in the merged letter, is to view merged data.* The following step views merged data.

- Click the 'View Merged Data' button (Mailings tab | Preview Results group) to display the values in the current data record, instead of the merge fields.

- Scroll up, if necessary, to view the address fields (Figure 6–33).

Q&A How can I tell which record is showing?
The current record number is displayed in the Preview Results group.

Why is the spacing in my address different from Figure 6–33?
You may have inserted the AddressBlock field on the line in the template that contained the recipient's address, instead of the line that contained the recipient's name. To fix the address spacing, select the entire address and then change the spacing before and after to 2 pt (Layout tab | Paragraph group).

Figure 6–33

1 IDENTIFY MAIN DOCUMENT | 2 CREATE DATA SOURCE | 3 COMPOSE MAIN DOCUMENT
4 MERGE DATA SOURCE | 5 ADDRESS MAILING LABELS | 6 MERGE TO DIRECTORY

To Insert the GreetingLine Merge Field

The **GreetingLine merge field** contains text and fields related to a salutation. The default greeting for the salutation is in the format, Dear Elizabeth, followed by a comma. In this letter, you want the salutation to be followed by a colon. *Why? Business letters use a more formal salutation (Dear Ms. Abbot:) in the cover letter.* The following steps insert the GreetingLine merge field.

- Delete the word, Dear, the [Recipient] placeholder text, and the comma in the salutation but leave the paragraph mark; position the insertion point to the left of the paragraph mark because you will insert the GreetingLine merge field in that location.

- Click the 'Insert formatted salutation' link in the Mail Merge task pane to display the Insert Greeting Line dialog box.

- If necessary, click the middle arrow in the Greeting line format area (Insert Greeting Line dialog box); scroll to and then click the format, Mr. Randall, in this list because you want the title followed by the last name format.

- If necessary, click the rightmost arrow in the Greeting line format area and then click the colon (:) in the list (Figure 6–34).

Figure 6–34

2

- Click the OK button (Insert Greeting Line dialog box) to insert the GreetingLine merge field at the location of the insertion point (Figure 6–35).

Q&A

Why are the values for the title and last name displayed instead of the merge field names?
With the 'View Merged Data' button (Mailings tab | Preview Results group) still selected, the field values are displayed instead of the field names.

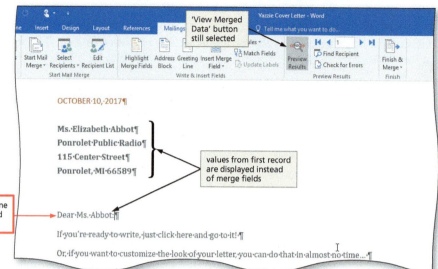

Figure 6–35

TO EDIT THE GREETINGLINE MERGE FIELD

If you wanted to change the format of or match fields in the GreetingLine merge field, you would perform the following steps.

1. Right-click the GreetingLine merge field to display a shortcut menu.
2. Click 'Edit Greeting Line' on the shortcut menu to display the Modify Greeting Line dialog box.
3. Make the necessary changes and then click the OK button (Modify Greeting Line dialog box).

To View Merge Fields in the Main Document

Because you will be entering merge fields in the document next, you wish to display the merge fields instead of the merged data. The following step views merge fields instead of merged data.

1 Click the 'View Merged Data' button (Mailings tab | Preview Results group) to display the merge fields instead of the values in the current data record (shown in Figure 6–36).

To Begin Typing the Body of the Form Letter

The next step is to begin typing the message, or body of the letter, which is located at the content control that begins with the placeholder text, If you're ready to write…, below the GreetingLine merge field. The following steps begin typing the letter at the location of the content control.

1 Click the body of the letter to select the content control (Figure 6–36).

2 With the content control selected, type `I will graduate in December from Hartford College with a bachelor of science degree in journalism. My education, experience, and volunteer work make me an ideal candidate for the` and then press the SPACEBAR (shown in Figure 6–37).

Q&A Why is the text, bachelor of science, in all lowercase letters?

This book uses the *Chicago Manual of Style* for grammar and punctuation rules, which specifies that degree names should be written in all lowercase letters.

Figure 6–36

BTW

'Insert Merge Field' Button

If you click the 'Insert Merge Field' button instead of the 'Insert Merge Field' arrow (Figure 6–37), Word displays the Insert Merge Field dialog box instead of the Insert Merge Field menu. To insert fields from the dialog box, click the field name and then click the Insert button. The dialog box remains open so that you can insert multiple fields, if necessary. When you have finished inserting fields, click the Close button in the dialog box.

To Insert a Merge Field in the Main Document

1 IDENTIFY MAIN DOCUMENT | 2 CREATE DATA SOURCE | **3 COMPOSE MAIN DOCUMENT**
4 MERGE DATA SOURCE | 5 ADDRESS MAILING LABELS | 6 MERGE TO DIRECTORY

The next step is to insert the Position merge field into the main document. *Why? The first sentence in the first paragraph of the letter identifies the advertised job position, which is a merge field.* To instruct Word to use data fields from the data source, you insert merge fields in the main document for the form letter. The following steps insert a merge field at the location of the insertion point.

1

- Click the 'Insert Merge Field' arrow (Mailings tab | Write & Insert Fields group) to display the Insert Merge Field menu (Figure 6–37).

Q&A What if I accidentally click the 'Insert Merge Field' button instead of the arrow?

Click the Cancel button in the Insert Merge Field dialog box and repeat Step 1.

Why is the underscore character in some of the field names?

Word places an underscore character in place of the space in merge fields.

Figure 6–37

• Click Position on the Insert Merge Field menu to insert the selected merge field in the document at the location of the insertion point (Figure 6–38).

Q&A Will the word, Position, and the chevron characters print when I merge the form letters?

No. When you merge the data source with the main document, the value in the Position field (e.g., radio reporter) will print at the location of the merge field, Position.

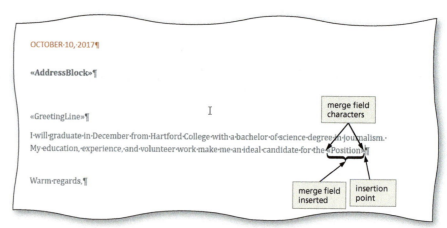

Figure 6–38

Other Ways

1. Click 'Insert Merge Field' button (Mailings tab | Write & Insert fields group), click desired field (Insert Merge Field dialog box), click Insert button, click Close button

---

To Enter More Text and Merge Fields in the Main Document

The following steps enter more text and merge fields into the form letter.

1 With the insertion point at the location shown in Figure 6–38, press the SPACEBAR, type **position at** and then press the SPACEBAR again.

2 Click the 'Insert Merge Field' arrow (Mailings tab | Write & Insert Fields group) and then click Organization_Name on the Insert Merge Field menu to insert the selected merge field in the document. Press the PERIOD key.

3 Press the ENTER key. Type **As shown on the accompanying resume, my background matches the job requirements posted through the Career Development Office at Hartford College. My coursework and experience have prepared me to develop, edit, and present news stories.** and then press the ENTER key.

4 Type **Thank you in advance,** and then press the SPACEBAR. Insert the Title merge field, press the SPACEBAR, and then insert the Last Name merge field. Type **, for your time and consideration. I look forward to hearing from you soon to discuss the opportunity for my potential employment at your** and then press the SPACEBAR (shown in Figure 6–39).

IF Fields

In addition to merge fields, you can insert Word fields that are designed specifically for a mail merge. An **IF field** is an example of a Word field. One form of the IF field is called an **If...Then**: If a condition is true, then perform an action. For example, if Mary owns a house, then send her information about homeowner's insurance. Another form of the IF field is called an **If...Then...Else**: if a condition is true, then perform an action; else perform a different action. For example, if John has an email address, then send him an email message; else send him the message via the postal service.

In this project, the form letter checks the station type and displays text associated with the station type. If the station type is R, then the form letter should print the text, radio; else if the station type is T, then the form letter should print the text, television. Thus, you will use an If...Then...Else: IF the Station_Type is equal to R, then insert radio; else insert television.

The phrase that appears after the word If is called a rule, or condition. A **condition** consists of an expression, followed by a comparison operator, followed by a final expression.

Expression   The expression in a condition can be a merge field, a number, a series of characters, or a mathematical formula. Word surrounds a series of characters with quotation marks ("). To indicate an empty, or null, expression, Word places two quotation marks together ("").

Comparison Operator   The comparison operator in a condition must be one of six characters: = (equal to or matches the text), <> (not equal to or does not match text), < (less than), <= (less than or equal to), > (greater than), or >= (greater than or equal to).

If the result of a condition is true, then Word evaluates the **true text**. If the result of the condition is false, Word evaluates the **false text** if it exists. In this project, the first expression in the condition is a merge field (Station_Type); the comparison operator is equal to (=); and the second expression is the text "R". The true text is "radio". The false text is "television". The complete IF field is as follows:

IF Station_Type = "R"	"radio"	"television"
condition	true text	false text

BTW

IF Fields
The phrase, IF field, originates from computer programming. Do not be intimidated by the terminology. An IF field simply specifies a decision. Some software developers refer to it as an IF statement. Complex IF statements include one or more nested IF fields. A nested IF field is a second IF field inside the true or false text of the first IF field.

To Insert an IF Field in the Main Document

1 IDENTIFY MAIN DOCUMENT | 2 CREATE DATA SOURCE | **3 COMPOSE MAIN DOCUMENT**
4 MERGE DATA SOURCE | 5 ADDRESS MAILING LABELS | 6 MERGE TO DIRECTORY

The next step is to insert an IF field in the main document. ***Why?*** *You want to print the station type in the letter.* The following steps insert this IF field in the form letter: If the Station_Type is equal to R, then insert radio, else insert television.

- With the insertion point positioned as shown in Figure 6–39, click the Rules button (Mailings tab | Write & Insert Fields group) to display the Rules menu (Figure 6–39).

Figure 6–39

2

- Click 'If…Then…Else…' on the Rules menu to display the Insert Word Field: IF dialog box, which is where you enter the components of the IF field (Figure 6–40).

Figure 6–40

3

- Click the Field name arrow (Insert Word Field: IF dialog box) to display the list of fields in the data source.

- Scroll through the list of fields in the Field name list and then click Station_Type to select the field.

- Position the insertion point in the Compare to text box and then type **R** as the comparison text.

- Press the TAB key and then type **radio** as the true text.

- Press the TAB key and then type **television** as the false text (Figure 6–41).

Q&A Does the capitalization matter in the comparison text?
Yes. The text, R, is different from the text, r, in a comparison. Be sure to enter the text exactly as you entered it in the data source.

Figure 6–41

4

- Click the OK button (Insert Word Field: IF dialog box) to insert the IF field at the location of the insertion point (Figure 6–42).

Q&A Why does the main document display the text, radio, instead of the IF field instructions?
The text, radio, is displayed because the first record in the data source has a station type equal to R. Word, by default, evaluates the IF field using the current record and displays the results, called the **field results**, in the main document instead of displaying the IF field instructions. Later in the module, you will view the IF field instructions.

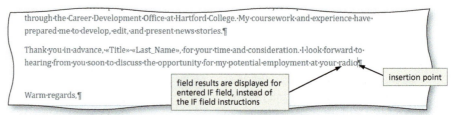

Figure 6–42

To Enter the Remaining Text in the Main Document

The following steps enter the remainder of the text into the form letter.

1 Press the SPACEBAR. Type **station** and then press the PERIOD key.

2 Change the closing to the word, Sincerely.

3 Change the placeholder text in the Your Name content control to Nina Tamaya Yazzie. If necessary, delete the content control so that the name remains but the content control is deleted.

If requested by your instructor, enter your name instead of the job seeker's name.

4 Delete the Your Title content control (Figure 6–43).

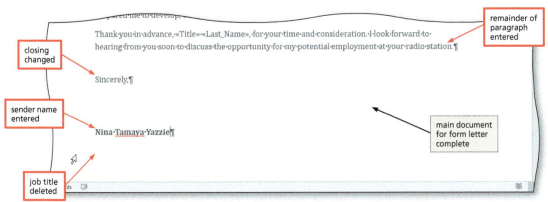

Figure 6–43

5 Make any additional adjustments to spacing, formats, etc., so that your main document looks like Figure 5–1 shown at the beginning of this module.

TO HIGHLIGHT MERGE FIELDS

If you wanted to highlight all the merge fields in a document so that you could identify them quickly, you would perform the following steps.

1. Click the 'Highlight Merge Fields' button (Mailings tab | Write & Insert Fields group) to highlight the merge fields in the document.

2. When finished viewing merge fields, click the 'Highlight Merge Fields' button (Mailings tab | Write & Insert Fields group) again to remove the highlight from the merge fields in the document.

BTW

Word Fields
In addition to the IF field, Word provides other fields that may be used in form letters. For example, the ASK and FILLIN fields prompt the user to enter data for each record in the data source. The SKIP RECORD IF field instructs the mail merge not to generate a form letter for a data record if a specific condition is met.

To Display a Field Code

1 IDENTIFY MAIN DOCUMENT | 2 CREATE DATA SOURCE | 3 COMPOSE MAIN DOCUMENT
4 MERGE DATA SOURCE | 5 ADDRESS MAILING LABELS | 6 MERGE TO DIRECTORY

The instructions in the IF field are not displayed in the document; instead, the field results are displayed for the current record (shown in Figure 6–42). The instructions of an IF field are called **field codes**, and the default for Word is for field codes not to be displayed. Thus, field codes do not print or show on the screen unless you turn them on. You use one procedure to show field codes on the screen and a different procedure to print them on a hard copy.

The following steps show a field code on the screen. *Why? You might want to turn on a field code to verify its accuracy or to modify it. Field codes tend to clutter the screen. Thus, most Word users turn them off after viewing them.*

1

- If necessary, scroll to display the last paragraph of the letter in the document window.

- Right-click the field results showing the text, radio, to display a shortcut menu (Figure 6–44).

Figure 6–44

• Click 'Toggle Field Codes' on the shortcut menu to display the field codes instead of the field results for the IF field (Figure 6–45).

Q&A

Will displaying field codes affect the merged documents?
No. Displaying field codes has no effect on the merge process.

What if I wanted to display all field codes in a document?
You would press ALT+F9. Then, to hide all the field codes, press ALT+F9 again.

Why does the IF field turn gray?
Word, by default, shades a field in gray when the field is selected. The shading displays on the screen to help you identify fields; the shading does not print on a hard copy.

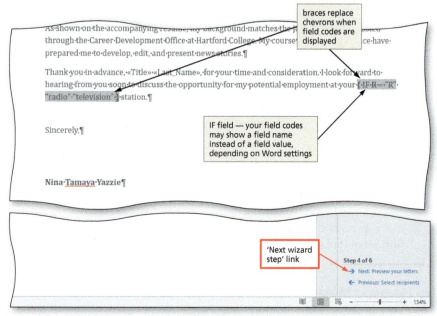

Figure 6–45

• Save the main document for the form letter again on the same storage location with the same file name.

Other Ways

1. With insertion point in field, press SHIFT+F9

BTW

Locking Fields
If you wanted to lock a field so that its field results cannot be changed, click the field and then press CTRL+F11. To subsequently unlock a field so that it may be updated, click the field and then press CTRL+SHIFT+F11.

TO PRINT FIELD CODES IN THE MAIN DOCUMENT

When you merge or print a document, Word automatically converts field codes that show on the screen to field results. You may want to print the field codes version of the form letter, however, so that you have a hard copy of the field codes for future reference. When you print field codes, you must remember to turn off the field codes option so that merged documents print field results instead of field codes. If you wanted to print the field codes in the main document, you would perform the following steps.

1. Open the Backstage view and then click the Options tab to display the Word Options dialog box.

2. Click Advanced in the left pane (Word Options dialog box) to display advanced options in the right pane and then scroll to the Print area in the right pane of the dialog box.

3. Place a check mark in the 'Print field codes instead of their values' check box.

4. Click the OK button to instruct Word to show field codes when the document prints.

5. Open the Backstage view, click the Print tab, and then click the Print button to print the document with all field codes showing.

6. Open the Backstage view and then click the Options tab to display the Word Options dialog box.

7. Click Advanced in the left pane (Word Options dialog box) to display advanced options in the right pane and then scroll to the Print area in the right pane of the dialog box.

8. Remove the check mark from the 'Print field codes instead of their values' check box.

9. Click the OK button to instruct Word to show field results the next time you print the document.

Opening a Main Document

You open a main document the same as you open any other Word document (i.e., clicking Open in the Backstage view). If Word displays a dialog box indicating it will run an SQL command, click the Yes button (Figure 6–46).

Figure 6–46

When you open a main document, Word attempts to open the associated data source file, too. If the data source is not in exactly the same location (i.e., drive and folder) as when it originally was saved, Word displays a dialog box indicating that it could not find the data source (Figure 6–47). When this occurs, click the 'Find Data Source' button to display the Open Data Source dialog box, which allows you to locate the data source file. (Word may display several dialog boxes requiring you to click an OK (or similar) button until the one shown in Figure 6–47 appears.)

Figure 6–47

Break Point: If you wish to take a break, this is a good place to do so. You can exit Word now. To resume at a later time, run Word, open the file called Yazzie Cover Letter, and continue following the steps from this location forward.

Merging the Data Source with the Main Document to Generate Form Letters

The next step in this project is to merge the data source with the main document to generate the form letters (shown in Figure 6–1c at the beginning of this module). **Merging** is the process of combining the contents of a data source with a main document.

You can merge the form letters to a new document, which you can edit, or merge them directly to a printer. You also have the option of merging all data in a data source or merging just a portion of it. The following sections discuss various ways to merge.

To Preview the Merged Letters Using the Mail Merge Task Pane

1 IDENTIFY MAIN DOCUMENT | 2 CREATE DATA SOURCE | 3 COMPOSE MAIN DOCUMENT
4 MERGE DATA SOURCE | 5 ADDRESS MAILING LABELS | 6 MERGE TO DIRECTORY

Earlier in this module, you previewed the data in the letters using a button on the ribbon. The following step uses the Mail Merge wizard to preview the letters. *Why? The next wizard step previews the letters so that you can verify the content is accurate before performing the merge.*

1

• Click the 'Next wizard step' link at the bottom of the Mail Merge task pane (shown in Figure 6–45) to display Step 5 of the Mail Merge wizard in the Mail Merge task pane (Figure 6–48).

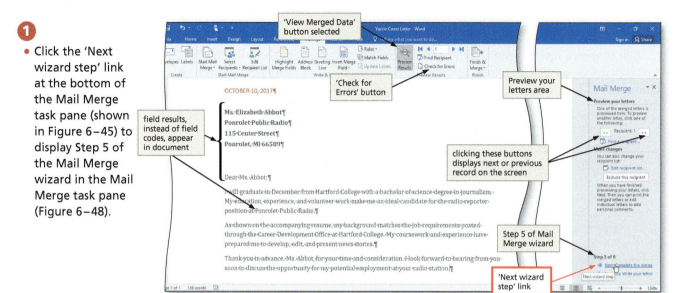

Figure 6–48

TO CHECK FOR ERRORS

Before merging documents, you can instruct Word to check for errors that might occur during the merge process. If you wanted to check for errors, you would perform the following steps.

1. Click the 'Check for Errors' button (Mailings tab | Preview Results group) (shown in Figure 6–48) or press ALT+SHIFT+K to display the Checking and Reporting Errors dialog box.

2. Select the desired option and then click the OK button.

To Merge the Form Letters to a New Document Using the Mail Merge Task Pane

1 IDENTIFY MAIN DOCUMENT | 2 CREATE DATA SOURCE | 3 COMPOSE MAIN DOCUMENT
4 MERGE DATA SOURCE | 5 ADDRESS MAILING LABELS | 6 MERGE TO DIRECTORY

With the data source and main document for the form letter complete, the next step is to merge them to generate the individual form letters. You can merge the letters to the printer or to a new document. *Why? If you merge the documents to a new document, you can save the merged documents in a file and then print them later, review the merged documents for accuracy and edit them as needed, or you can add personal messages to individual merged letters.* The following steps merge the form letters to a new document.

1

• Click the 'Next wizard step' link at the bottom of the Mail Merge task pane (shown in Figure 6–48) to display Step 6 of the Mail Merge wizard in the Mail Merge task pane.

• Click the 'Merge to new document' link in the Mail Merge task pane to display the Merge to New Document dialog box (Figure 6–49).

Q&A

What if I wanted to print the merged letters immediately instead of reviewing them first in a new document window?

You would click the 'Merge to printer' link instead of the 'Merge to new document' link.

Figure 6–49

2

- If necessary, click All (Merge to New Document dialog box) so that all records in the data source are merged.

Q&A Do I have to merge all records?
No. Through this dialog box, you can merge the current record or a range of record numbers.

- Click the OK button to merge the letters to a new document, in this case, five individual letters — one for each potential employer in the data source. (If Word displays a dialog box containing a message about locked fields, click its OK button.)

3

- Display the View tab and then click the Multiple Pages button (View tab | Zoom group) so that you can see miniature versions of all five letters in the document window at once (Figure 6–50).

Figure 6–50

4

- Change the zoom back to page width.

Experiment

- Scroll through the merged documents so that you can read all five letters.

Q&A Why does my screen show an extra blank page at the end?
You might have a blank record in the data source, or the spacing may cause an overflow to a blank page.

Can I edit the merged letters?
Yes, you can edit the letters as you edit any other Word document. Always proofread the merged letters for accuracy before distributing them.

- Save the merged letters in the Job Hunting folder on your hard drive, OneDrive, or other storage location using the file name, Yazzie Merged Cover Letters. If requested by your instructor, print the merged letters. Close the document window containing the merged letters.

Q&A Do I have to save the document containing the merged letters?
No. You can close the document without saving it.

- Click the Close button on the Mail Merge task pane title bar (shown in Figure 6–49) because you are finished with the Mail Merge wizard.

- If necessary, click the 'View Merged Data' button to show field codes instead of merged data.

Other Ways

1. Click 'Finish & Merge' button (Mailings tab | Finish group), click 'Edit Individual Documents'

Correcting Merge Field Errors in Merged Documents

If the wrong field results appear, Word may be mapping the fields incorrectly. To view fields, click the Match Fields button (Mailings tab | Write & Insert Fields group) (shown in Figure 6–49). Then, review the fields in the list. For example, Last Name should map to the Last Name field in the data source. If it does not, click the arrow to change the name of the data source field.

If the fields are mapped incorrectly, the data in the data source may be incorrect. For a discussion about editing records in the data source, refer to that section earlier in this module.

BTW

Conserving Ink and Toner

If you want to conserve ink or toner, you can instruct Word to print draft quality documents by clicking File on the ribbon to open the Backstage view, clicking the Options tab in the Backstage view to display the Word Options dialog box, clicking Advanced in the left pane (Word Options dialog box), scrolling to the Print area in the right pane, placing a check mark in the 'Use draft quality' check box, and then clicking the OK button. Then, use the Backstage view to print the document as usual.

To Merge the Form Letters to a Printer

If you are certain the contents of the merged letters will be correct and do not need individual editing, you can perform the following steps to merge the form letters directly to the printer.

1. If necessary, display the Mailings tab.

2. Click the 'Finish & Merge' button (Mailings tab | Finish group) and then click Print Documents on the Finish & Merge menu, or click the 'Merge to printer' link (Mail Merge task pane), to display the Merge to Printer dialog box.

3. If necessary, click All (Merge to Printer dialog box) and then click the OK button to display the Print dialog box.

4. Select desired printer settings. Click the OK button (Print dialog box) to print five separate letters, one for each potential employer in the data source, as shown in Figure 6–1c at the beginning of this module. (If Word displays a message about locked fields, click its OK button.)

To Select Records to Merge

1 IDENTIFY MAIN DOCUMENT | 2 CREATE DATA SOURCE | 3 COMPOSE MAIN DOCUMENT
4 MERGE DATA SOURCE | 5 ADDRESS MAILING LABELS | 6 MERGE TO DIRECTORY

Instead of merging all of the records in the data source, you can choose which records to merge, based on a condition you specify. The dialog box in Figure 6–49 allows you to specify by record number which records to merge. Often, though, you want to merge based on the contents of a specific field. The following steps select records for a merge. **Why?** *You want to merge just those potential employers who are television stations.*

- Click the 'Edit Recipient List' button (Mailings tab | Start Mail Merge group) to display the Mail Merge Recipients dialog box (Figure 6–51).

Figure 6–51

2

- Drag the scroll box to the right edge of the scroll bar (Mail Merge Recipients dialog box) so that the Station Type field appears in the dialog box.

- Click the arrow to the right of the field name, Station Type, to display sort and filter criteria for the selected field (Figure 6–52).

Q&A

What are the filter criteria in the parentheses?

The (All) option clears any previously set filter criteria. The (Blanks) option selects records that contain blanks in that field, and the (Nonblanks) option selects records that do not contain blanks in that field. The (Advanced) option displays the Filter and Sort dialog box, which allows you to perform more advanced record selection operations.

Figure 6–52

3

- Click T to reduce the number of data records displayed (Mail Merge Recipients dialog box) to two, because two potential employers are television stations (Figure 6–53).

Q&A

What happened to the other three records that did not meet the criteria?

They still are part of the data source; they just are not appearing in the Mail Merge Recipients dialog box. When you clear the filter, all records will reappear.

4

- Click the OK button to close the Mail Merge Recipients dialog box.

Figure 6–53

Other Ways

1. Click Filter link (Mail Merge Recipients dialog box), click Filter Records tab (Sort and Filter dialog box), enter filter criteria, click OK button

To Merge the Form Letters to a New Document Using the Ribbon

1 IDENTIFY MAIN DOCUMENT | 2 CREATE DATA SOURCE | 3 COMPOSE MAIN DOCUMENT
4 MERGE DATA SOURCE | 5 ADDRESS MAILING LABELS | 6 MERGE TO DIRECTORY

The next step is to merge the selected records. To do this, you follow the same steps described earlier. The difference is that Word will merge only those records that meet the criteria specified, that is, just those with a station type equal to T (for television). The following steps merge the filtered records to a new document using the ribbon.

- Click the 'Finish & Merge' button (Mailings tab | Finish group) to display the Finish & Merge menu (Figure 6–54).

Figure 6–54

- Click 'Edit Individual Documents' on the Finish & Merge menu to display the Merge to New Document dialog box. If necessary, click All in the dialog box.

- Click the OK button (Merge to New Document dialog box) to display the merged documents in a new document window.

- Change the zoom so that both documents, one for each potential employer whose station type field equals T, appear in the document window at the same time (Figure 6–55). (If Word displays a message about locked fields, click its OK button.)

- Close the window. Do not save the merged documents.

Figure 6-55

To Remove a Merge Condition

1 IDENTIFY MAIN DOCUMENT | 2 CREATE DATA SOURCE | 3 COMPOSE MAIN DOCUMENT
4 MERGE DATA SOURCE | 5 ADDRESS MAILING LABELS | 6 MERGE TO DIRECTORY

The next step is to remove the merge condition. *Why? You do not want future merges be restricted to potential employers with a station type equal to T.* The following steps remove a merge condition.

1
- Click the 'Edit Recipient List' button (Mailings tab | Start Mail Merge group) to display the Mail Merge Recipients dialog box.

2
- Click the Filter link (Mail Merge Recipients dialog box) to display the Filter and Sort dialog box.

- If necessary, click the Filter Records tab to display the Filter Records sheet (Figure 6–56).

Figure 6–56

Q&A
Can I specify a merge condition in this dialog box instead of using the box arrow in the Mail Merge Recipients dialog box?
Yes.

3
- Click the Clear All button (Filter and Sort dialog box) to remove the merge condition from the dialog box.
- Click the OK button in each of the two open dialog boxes to close the dialog boxes.

To Sort the Data Records in a Data Source

The following steps sort the data records by ZIP code. *Why? You may want the form letters printed in a certain order. For example, if you mail the form letters using the U.S. Postal Service's bulk rate mailing service, the post office requires that you sort and group the form letters by ZIP code.*

- Click the 'Edit Recipient List' button (Mailings tab | Start Mail Merge group) to display the Mail Merge Recipients dialog box.

- Scroll to the right until the ZIP Code field shows in the dialog box.

- Click the arrow to the right of the field name, ZIP Code, to display a menu of sort and filter criteria (Figure 6–57).

Figure 6–57

- Click Sort Ascending on the menu to sort the data source records in ascending (smallest to largest) order by ZIP Code (Figure 6–58).

- Click the OK button to close the Mail Merge Recipients dialog box.

Q&A In what order would the form letters print if I merged them again now?

Word would merge them in ZIP code order; that is, the records with ZIP code 66532 would appear first, and the records with ZIP code 66589 would appear last.

Figure 6–58

Other Ways

1. Click Sort link (Mail Merge Recipients dialog box), enter sort criteria (Sort and Filter dialog box), click OK button

To Find and Display Data

Why? *If you wanted to find a particular record in the data source and display that record's data in the main document on the screen, you can search for a field value.* The following steps find Cheung, which is a last name in the data source, and display that record's values in the form letter currently displaying on the screen.

- If necessary, click the 'View Merged Data' button (Mailings tab | Preview Results group) to show field results instead of merged fields on the screen.

- Click the Find Recipient button (Mailings tab | Preview Results group) to display the Find Entry dialog box.

- Type **Cheung** in the Find text box (Find Entry dialog box) as the search text.

- Click the Find Next button to display the record containing the entered text (Figure 6–59).

- Click the Cancel button (Find Entry dialog box) to close the dialog box.

- Close the open document. If a Microsoft Word dialog box is displayed, click the Save button to save the changes.

Figure 6–59

Displaying Data Source Records in the Main Document

When you are viewing merged data in the main document (shown in Figure 6–59) — that is, the 'View Merged Data' button (Mailings tab | Preview Results group) is selected — you can click buttons and boxes in the Preview Results group on the Mailings tab to display different results and values. For example, click the Last Record button to display the values from the last record in the data source, the First Record button to display the values in record one, the Next Record button to display the values in the next consecutive record number, or the Previous Record button to display the values from the previous record number. You also can display a specific record by clicking the 'Go to Record' text box, typing the record number you would like to be displayed in the main document, and then pressing the ENTER key.

Addressing Mailing Labels and Envelopes

Now that you have merged and printed the form letters, the next step is to print addresses on mailing labels to be affixed to envelopes for the form letters. The mailing labels will use the same data source as the form letter, Yazzie Prospective Employers. The format and content of the mailing labels will be exactly the same as the inside address in the main document for the form letter. That is, the first line will contain the title and first name followed by the last name. The second line will contain the organization name, and so on. Thus, you will use the AddressBlock merge field in the mailing labels.

You follow the same basic steps to create the main document for the mailing labels as you did to create the main document for the form letters. That is, determine the appropriate data source, create the label main document, and then merge the main document with the data source to generate the mailing labels and envelopes. The major difference here is that the data source already exists because you created it earlier in this module.

To Address and Print Mailing Labels Using an Existing Data Source

1 IDENTIFY MAIN DOCUMENT | 2 CREATE DATA SOURCE | 3 COMPOSE MAIN DOCUMENT
4 MERGE DATA SOURCE | **5 ADDRESS MAILING LABELS** | 6 MERGE TO DIRECTORY

To address mailing labels, you specify the type of labels you intend to use. Word will request the label information, including the label vendor and product number. You can obtain this information from the box of labels. For illustration purposes in addressing these labels, the label vendor is Avery and the product number is J8158. The following steps address and print mailing labels using an existing data source. *Why? You already created the data source earlier in this module, so you will use that data source.*

Note: If your printer does not have the capability of printing mailing labels, read these steps without performing them. If you are in a laboratory environment, ask your instructor if you should perform these steps or read them without performing them.

- Open the Backstage view. Click the New tab in the Backstage view to display the New gallery. Click the Blank document thumbnail to open a new blank document window.

- If necessary, change the zoom to page width.

- Display the Mailings tab. Click the 'Start Mail Merge' button (Mailings tab | Start Mail Merge group) and then click 'Step-by-Step Mail Merge Wizard' on the Start Mail Merge menu to display Step 1 of the Mail Merge wizard in the Mail Merge task pane.

- Click Labels in the Select document type area to specify labels as the main document type (Figure 6–60).

Figure 6–60

2

- Click the 'Next wizard step' link at the bottom of the Mail Merge task pane to display Step 2 of the Mail Merge wizard.

- In the Mail Merge task pane, click the 'Select label size' link to display the Label Options dialog box.

- Select the label vendor and product number (in this case, Avery A4/A5 and J8158), as shown in Figure 6–61.

Figure 6–61

3

- Click the OK button (Label Options dialog box) to display the selected label layout as the main document (Figure 6–62).

- If gridlines are not displayed, click the 'View Table Gridlines' button (Table Tools Layout tab | Table group) to show gridlines.

Figure 6–62

- Click the 'Next wizard step' link at the bottom of the Mail Merge task pane to display Step 3 of the Mail Merge wizard, which allows you to select the data source.

- If necessary, click 'Use an existing list' in the Select recipients area. Click the 'Select recipient list file' link to display the Select Data Source dialog box.

- If necessary, navigate to the location of the data source (in this case, the Job Hunting folder).

- Click the file name, Yazzie Prospective Employers, to select the data source you created earlier in the module (Figure 6–63).

Figure 6–63

Q&A What is the folder initially displayed in the Select Data Source dialog box?

It is the default folder for storing data source files. Word looks in that folder, by default, for an existing data source.

- Click the Open button (Select Data Source dialog box) to display the Mail Merge Recipients dialog box (Figure 6–64).

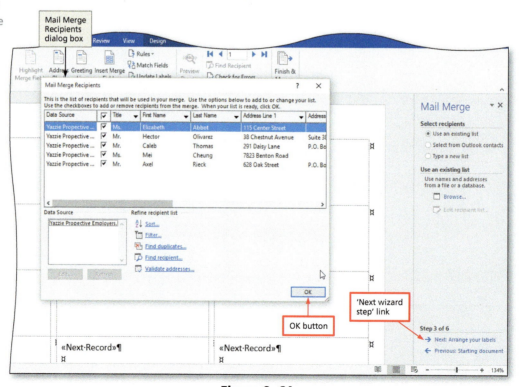

Figure 6–64

6

- Click the OK button (Mail Merge Recipients dialog box) to close the dialog box.

- At the bottom of the Mail Merge task pane, click the 'Next wizard step' link to display Step 4 of the Mail Merge wizard in the Mail Merge task pane.

- In the Mail Merge task pane, click the 'Insert formatted address' link to display the Insert Address Block dialog box (Figure 6–65).

- If necessary, match the company name to the Organization Name field by clicking the Match Fields button (Insert Address Block dialog box), clicking the Company box arrow (Match Fields dialog box), clicking Organization Name in the list, and then clicking the OK button (Match Fields dialog box).

Figure 6–65

7

- Click the OK button to close the dialog box and insert the AddressBlock merge field in the first label of the main document (Figure 6–66).

Q&A

Do I have to use the AddressBlock merge field?

No. You can click the Insert Merge Field button (Mailings tab | Write & Insert Fields group) and then select the preferred fields for the mailing labels, organizing the fields as desired.

Figure 6–66

8

- Click the 'Update all labels' button (shown in Figure 6–66) in the Mail Merge task pane to copy the layout of the first label to the remaining label layouts in the main document (Figure 6–67).

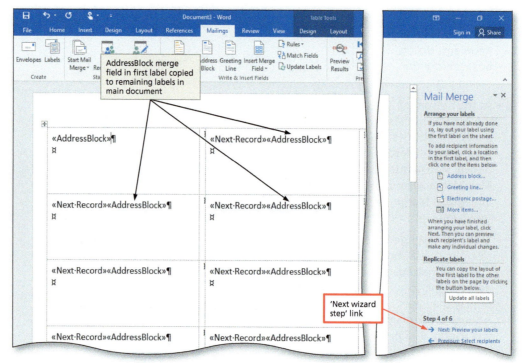

Figure 6–67

9

- Click the 'Next wizard step' link at the bottom of the Mail Merge task pane to display Step 5 of the Mail Merge wizard, which shows a preview of the mailing labels in the document window.

- Because you do not want a blank space between each line in the printed mailing address, select the table containing the label layout (that is, click the table move handle in the upper-left corner of the table), display the Layout tab, change the Spacing Before and After boxes to 0 pt, and then click anywhere to remove the selection (Figure 6–68).

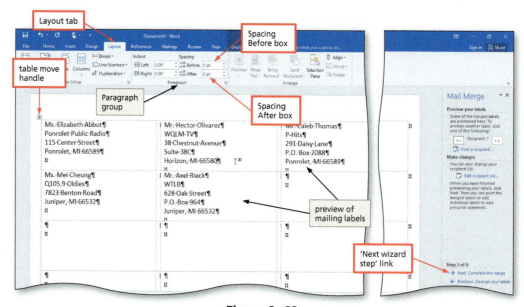

Figure 6–68

Q&A What if the spacing does not change?

Drag through the labels and try changing the Spacing Before and After boxes to 0 again.

- Click the 'Next wizard step' link at the bottom of the Mail Merge task pane to display Step 6 of the Mail Merge wizard.

- Click the 'Merge to a new document' link to display the Merge to New Document dialog box.

- If necessary, click All (Merge to New Document dialog box) so that all records in the data source will be included in the merge (Figure 6–69).

Figure 6–69

- If necessary, insert a sheet of blank mailing labels in the printer.

- Click the OK button (Merge to New Document dialog box) to merge the mailing labels to a new document.

- Save the merged mailing labels in the Job Hunting folder on your hard drive, OneDrive, or other storage location using the file name, Yazzie Merged Mailing Labels. If requested by your instructor, print the merged labels (Figure 6–70).

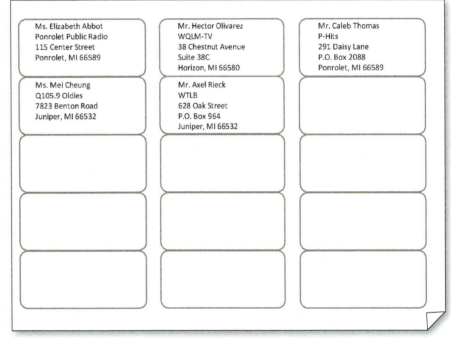

Figure 6–70

⓬

- Close the document window containing the merged labels.

- Click the Close button at the right edge of the Mail Merge task pane.

- Click the 'View Merged Data' button to show field codes instead of merged data on the labels.

- Save the mailing label main document in the Job Hunting folder on your hard drive, OneDrive, or other storage location using the file name, Yazzie Mailing Labels.

- Close the mailing label main document.

How should you position addresses on an envelope?

An envelope should contain the sender's full name and address in the upper-left corner of the envelope. It also should contain the addressee's full name and address, positioned approximately in the vertical and horizontal center of the envelope. The address can be printed directly on the envelope or on a mailing label that is affixed to the envelope.

CONSIDER THIS

TO ADDRESS AND PRINT ENVELOPES

Instead of addressing mailing labels to affix to envelopes, your printer may have the capability of printing directly on envelopes. If you wanted to print address information directly on envelopes, you would perform the following steps to merge the envelopes directly to the printer.

1. Open the Backstage view. Click the New tab in the Backstage view to display the New gallery. Click the Blank document thumbnail to open a new blank document window.

2. Display the Mailings tab. Click the 'Start Mail Merge' button (Mailings tab | Start Mail Merge group) and then click 'Step-by-Step Mail Merge Wizard' on the Start Mail Merge menu to display Step 1 of the Mail Merge wizard in the Mail Merge task pane. Specify envelopes as the main document type by clicking Envelopes in the Select document type area.

3. Click the 'Next wizard step' link at the bottom of the Mail Merge task pane to display Step 2 of the Mail Merge wizard. In the Mail Merge task pane, click the 'Set Envelope Options' link to display the Envelope Options dialog box.

4. Select the envelope size and then click the OK button (Envelope Options dialog box), which displays the selected envelope layout as the main document.

5. If your envelope does not have a preprinted return address, position the insertion point in the upper-left corner of the envelope layout and then type a return address.

6. Click the 'Next wizard step' link at the bottom of the Mail Merge task pane to display Step 3 of the Mail Merge wizard, which allows you to select the data source. Select an existing data source or create a new one. At the bottom of the Mail Merge task pane, click the 'Next wizard step' link to display Step 4 of the Mail Merge wizard in the Mail Merge task pane.

7. Position the insertion point in the middle of the envelope. In the Mail Merge task pane, click the 'Insert formatted address' link to display the Insert Address Block dialog box. Select desired settings and then click the OK button to close the dialog box and insert the AddressBlock merge field in the envelope layout of the main document. If necessary, match fields so that the Company is matched to the Organization_Name field.

8. Click the 'Next wizard step' link at the bottom of the Mail Merge task pane to display Step 5 of the Mail Merge wizard, which shows a preview of an envelope in the document window.

9. Click the 'Next wizard step' link at the bottom of the Mail Merge task pane to display Step 6 of the Mail Merge wizard. In the Mail Merge task pane, click the 'Merge to printer' link to display the Merge to Printer dialog box. If necessary, click All (Merge to Printer dialog box) so that all records in the data source will be included in the merge.

10. If necessary, insert blank envelopes in the printer. Click the OK button to display the Print dialog box. Click the OK button (Print dialog box) to print the addresses on the envelopes. Close the Mail Merge task pane.

Merging All Data Records to a Directory

You may want to print the data records in the data source. Recall that the data source is saved as a Microsoft Access database table. Thus, you cannot open the data source in Word. To view the data source, you click the 'Edit Recipient List' button

(Mailings tab | Start Mail Merge group), which displays the Mail Merge Recipients dialog box. This dialog box, however, does not have a Print button.

One way to print the contents of the data source is to merge all data records in the data source into a single document, called a directory. A **directory** is a listing from the contents of the data source. A directory does not merge each data record to a separate document; instead, a directory lists all records together in a single document. When you merge to a directory, the default organization of a directory places each record one after the next, similar to the look of entries in a telephone book.

To create a directory, follow the same process as for the form letters. That is, determine the appropriate data source, create the directory main document, and then merge the main document with the data source to create the directory.

The directory in this module is more organized with the rows and columns divided and field names placed above each column (shown in Figure 6–83). To accomplish this look, the following steps are required:

1. Change the page orientation from portrait to landscape, so that each record fits on a single row.

2. Create a directory layout, placing a separating character between each merge field.

3. Merge the directory to a new document, which creates a list of all records in the data source.

4. Convert the directory to a table, using the separator character as the identifier for each new column.

5. Format the table containing the directory.

6. Sort the table by organization name within city, so that it is easy to locate a particular record.

BTW

Converting Main Document Files

If you wanted to convert a mail merge main document to a regular Word document, you would open the main document, click the 'Start Mail Merge' button (Mailings tab | Start Mail Merge group), and then click 'Normal Word Document' on the Start Mail Merge menu (shown in Figure 6–72).

1 IDENTIFY MAIN DOCUMENT | 2 CREATE DATA SOURCE | 3 COMPOSE MAIN DOCUMENT
4 MERGE DATA SOURCE | 5 ADDRESS MAILING LABELS | **6 MERGE TO DIRECTORY**

To Change Page Orientation

When a document is in **portrait orientation**, the short edge of the paper is the top of the document. You can instruct Word to lay out a document in **landscape orientation**, so that the long edge of the paper is the top of the document. The following steps change the orientation of the document from portrait to landscape. *Why? You want an entire record to fit on a single line in the directory.*

1

● If necessary, create a new blank document in the Word window and change the zoom to page width.

● Display the Layout tab.

● Click the 'Change Page Orientation' button (Layout tab | Page Setup group) to display the Change Page Orientation gallery (Figure 6–71).

Figure 6–71

2

● Click Landscape in the Change Page Orientation gallery to change the page orientation to landscape.

● If necessary, change the zoom to page width again so that both the left and right edges of the page are visible in the document window.

To Merge to a Directory

The next steps merge the data records in the data source to a directory. *Why? You would like a listing of all records in the data source.* For illustration purposes, the following steps use the buttons on the Mailings tab rather than using the Mail Merge task pane to merge to a directory.

1

- Display the Mailings tab.

- Click the 'Start Mail Merge' button (Mailings tab | Start Mail Merge group) to display the Start Mail Merge menu (Figure 6–72).

Figure 6–72

2

- Click Directory on the Start Mail Merge menu to select the main document type.

3

- Click the Select Recipients button (Mailings tab | Start Mail Merge group) to display the Select Recipients menu (Figure 6–73).

Figure 6–73

4

- Click 'Use an Existing List' on the Select Recipients menu to display the Select Data Source dialog box.

- If necessary, navigate to the location of the data source (in this case, the Job Hunting folder).

- Click the file name, Yazzie Prospective Employers, to select the data source you created earlier in the module (Figure 6–74).

Figure 6–74

5

- Click the Open button (Select Data Source dialog box) to associate the selected data source with the current main document.

6

- Click the 'Insert Merge Field' arrow (Mailings tab | Write & Insert Fields group) to display the Insert Merge Field menu (Figure 6–75).

Figure 6–75

7

- Click Title on the Insert Merge Field menu to insert the selected merge field in the document.

- Press the COMMA (,) key to place a comma after the inserted merge field.

Q&A Why insert a comma after the merge field?

In the next steps, you will convert the entered merge fields to a table format with the records in rows and the fields in columns. To do this, Word divides the columns based on a character separating each field. In this case, you use the comma to separate the merge fields.

8

- Repeat Steps 6 and 7 for the First_Name, Last_Name, Organization_Name, Address_Line_1, Address_Line_2, City, State, and ZIP_Code fields on the Insert Merge Field menu, so that these fields in the data source appear in the main document separated by a comma, except do not type a comma after the last field (ZIP_Code).

- Press the ENTER key (Figure 6–76).

Figure 6–76

Q&A Why press the ENTER key after entering the merge fields names?

This will place the first field in each record at the beginning of a new line.

Why are the Position and Station_Type fields not included in the directory?

You just want the directory listing to show the contact information for each potential employer.

9

- Save the directory main document in the Job Hunting folder on your hard drive, OneDrive, or other storage location using the file name, Yazzie Potential Employer Directory.

To Merge to a New Document

The next step is to merge the data source and the directory main document to a new document, so that you can edit the resulting document. The following steps merge to a new document.

1 Click the 'Finish & Merge' button (Mailings tab | Finish group) to display the Finish & Merge menu.

2 Click 'Edit Individual Documents' on the Finish & Merge menu to display the Merge to New Document dialog box.

3 If necessary, click All (Merge to New Document dialog box).

4 Click the OK button to merge the data records to a directory in a new document window (Figure 6–77).

Figure 6–77

To Convert Text to a Table

1 IDENTIFY MAIN DOCUMENT | 2 CREATE DATA SOURCE | 3 COMPOSE MAIN DOCUMENT
4 MERGE DATA SOURCE | 5 ADDRESS MAILING LABELS | 6 MERGE TO DIRECTORY

You want each data record to be in a single row and each merge field to be in a column. *Why? The directory will be easier to read if it is in table form.* The following steps convert the text containing the merge fields to a table.

• Press CTRL+A to select the entire document, because you want all document contents to be converted to a table.

• Display the Insert tab.

• Click the 'Add a Table' button (Insert tab | Tables group) to display the Add a Table gallery (Figure 6–78).

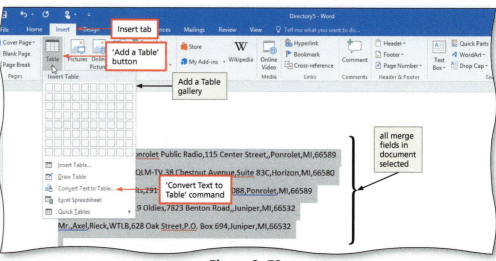

Figure 6–78

2

- Click 'Convert Text to Table' in the Add a Table gallery to display the Convert Text to Table dialog box.

- If necessary, type   9   in the 'Number of columns' box (Convert Text to Table dialog box) to specify the number of columns for the resulting table.

- Click 'AutoFit to window', which instructs Word to fit the table and its contents to the width of the window.

- If necessary, click Commas to specify the character that separates the merge fields in the document (Figure 6–79).

Figure 6–79

3

- Click the OK button to convert the selected text to a table and then, if necessary, click to remove the selection from the table (Figure 6–80).

Q&A Can I format the table?
Yes. You can use any of the commands on the Table Tools Design and Table Tools Layout tabs to change the look of the table.

Ms.¤	Elizabeth¤	Abbot¤	Ponrolet·Public·Radio¤	115·Center·Street¤	¤	Ponrolet¤	MI¤	66589¤	¤
Mr.¤	Hector¤	Olivarez¤	WQLM-TV¤	38·Chestnut·Avenue¤	Suite·38C¤	Horizon¤	MI¤	66580¤	¤
Mr.¤	Caleb¤	Thomas¤	P-Hits¤	291·Daisy·Lane¤	P.O.·Box·2088¤	Ponrolet¤	MI¤	66589¤	¤
Ms.¤	Mei¤	Cheung¤	Q105.9·Oldies¤	7823·Benton·Road¤	¤	Juniper¤	MI¤	66532¤	¤
Mr.¤	Axel¤	Rieck¤	WTLB¤	628·Oak·Street¤	P.O.·Box·964¤	Juniper¤	MI¤	66532¤	¤

Figure 6–80

To Modify and Format a Table

The table would be more descriptive if the field names were displayed in a row above the actual data. The following steps add a row to the top of a table and format the data in the new row.

1 Add a row to the top of the table by positioning the insertion point in the first row of the table and then clicking the 'Insert Rows Above' button (Table Tools Layout tab | Rows & Columns group).

2 Click in the first (leftmost) cell of the new row. Type **Title** and then press the TAB key. Type **First Name** and then press the TAB key. Type **Last Name** and then press the TAB key. Type **Organization Name** and then press the TAB key. Type **Address Line 1** and then press the TAB key. Type **Address Line 2** and then press the TAB key. Type **City** and then press the TAB key. Type **State** and then press the TAB key. Type **ZIP Code** as the last entry in the row.

3 Bold the contents of the first row.

4 Use the AutoFit Contents command on the ribbon or the shortcut menu to make all columns as wide as their contents. If necessary, adjust individual column widths so that the table looks like Figure 6–81.

5 Center the table between the margins (Figure 6–81).

header row added and bold

Title¤	First·Name¤	Last·Name¤	Organization·Name¤	Address·Line·1¤	Address·Line·2¤	City¤	State¤	ZIP·Code¤	¤
Ms.¤	Elizabeth¤	Abbot¤	Ponrolet·Public·Radio¤	115·Center·Street¤	¤	Ponrolet¤	MI¤	66589¤	¤
Mr.¤	Hector¤	Olivarez¤	WQLM-TV¤	38·Chestnut·Avenue¤	Suite·38C¤	Horizon¤	MI¤	66580¤	¤
Mr.¤	Caleb¤	Thomas¤	P-Hits¤	291·Daisy·Lane¤	P.O.·Box·2088¤	Ponrolet¤	MI¤	66589¤	¤
Ms.¤	Mei¤	Cheung¤	Q105.9·Oldies¤	7823·Benton·Road¤	¤	Juniper¤	MI¤	66532¤	¤
Mr.¤	Axel¤	Rieck¤	WTLB¤	628·Oak·Street¤	P.O.·Box·964¤	Juniper¤	MI¤	66532¤	¤

Figure 6–81

TO REPEAT HEADER ROWS

If you had a table that exceeded a page in length and you wanted the header row (the first row) to appear at the top of the table on each continued page, you would perform the following steps.

1. Position the insertion point in the header row.

2. Click the 'Repeat Header Rows' button (Table Tools Layout tab | Data group) (shown in Figure 6–82) to repeat the row containing the insertion point at the top of every page on which the table continues.

To Sort a Table by Multiple Columns

1 IDENTIFY MAIN DOCUMENT | 2 CREATE DATA SOURCE | 3 COMPOSE MAIN DOCUMENT
4 MERGE DATA SOURCE | 5 ADDRESS MAILING LABELS | 6 MERGE TO DIRECTORY

The next step is to sort the table. *Why? In this project, the table records are displayed by organization name within city.* The following steps sort a table by multiple columns.

1

• With the table selected or the insertion point in the table, click the Sort button (Table Tools Layout tab | Data group) to display the Sort dialog box.

• Click the Sort by arrow (Sort dialog box); scroll to and then click City in the list.

• Click the first Then by arrow and then click Organization Name in the list.

• If necessary, click Header row so that the first row remains in its current location when the table is sorted (Figure 6–82).

Figure 6–82

2

- Click the OK button to sort the records in the table in ascending Organization Name order within ascending City order (Figure 6–83).

- If necessary, click to deselect the table.

- Save the merged directory in the Job Hunting folder on your hard drive, OneDrive, or other storage location using the file name, Yazzie Merged Potential Employer Directory.

- If requested by your instructor, print the merged directory.

Q&A | If Microsoft Access is installed on my computer, can I use that to print the data source?
As an alternative to merging to a directory and printing the results, if you are familiar with Microsoft Access and it is installed on your computer, you can open and print the data source in Access.

- Exit Word.

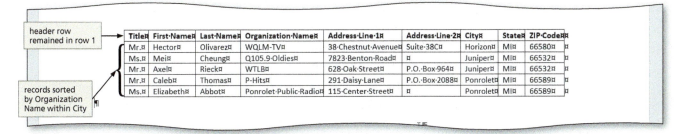

Figure 6–83

Summary

In this module, you learned how to create and print form letters, work with merge fields and an IF field, open a main document, create and edit a data source, address mailing labels and envelopes from a data source, change page orientation, merge to a directory, and convert text to a table.

What decisions will you need to make when creating your next form letter?

Use these guidelines as you complete the assignments in this module and create your own form letters outside of this class.

1. Identify the main document for the form letter.

   a) Determine whether to type the letter from scratch in a blank document window or use a letter template.

2. Create or specify the data source.

   a) Determine if the data exists already in an Access database table, an Outlook contacts list, or an Excel worksheet.

   b) If you cannot use an existing data source, create a new one using appropriate field names.

3. Compose the main document for the form letter.

   a) Ensure the letter contains all essential business letter elements and is visually appealing.

   b) Be sure the letter contains proper grammar, correct spelling, logically constructed sentences, flowing paragraphs, and sound ideas.

   c) Properly reference the data in the data source.

4. Merge the main document with the data source to create the form letters.

   a) Determine the destination for the merge (i.e., a new document, the printer, etc.).

   b) Determine which records to merge (all of them or a portion of them).

5. Determine whether to generate mailing labels or envelopes.

   a) Create or specify the data source.

   b) Ensure the mailing label or envelope contains all necessary information.

6. Create a directory of the data source.

   a) Create or specify the data source.

   b) If necessary, format the directory appropriately.

Apply Your Knowledge

Reinforce the skills and apply the concepts you learned in this module.

Editing, Printing, and Merging a Form Letter and Its Data Source

Note: To complete this assignment, you will be required to use the Data Files. Please contact your instructor for information about accessing the Data Files.

Instructions: Run Word. Open the document, Apply 6–1 Oil Change Letter Draft, from the Data Files. When you open the main document, if Word displays a dialog box about an SQL command, click the Yes button. If Word prompts for the name of the data source, select Apply 6–1 Customer List on the Data Files.

The document is a main document for a form letter for Auto Express (Figure 6–84). You are to edit the date content control and GreetingLine merge field, add a merge field, print the form letter, add a record to the data source, and merge the form letters to a file.

Perform the following tasks:

1. Edit the date content control so that it contains the date 10/30/2017.

2. Edit the GreetingLine merge field so that the salutation ends with a comma (,).

3. At the end of the last paragraph of the letter, insert the Vehicle_Type merge field between the word, your, and the exclamation point (shown in Figure 6–84).

4. Save the modified main document for the form letter with the file name, Apply 6–1 Oil Change Letter Modified.

5. Highlight the merge fields in the document. How many were highlighted? Remove the highlight from the merge fields.

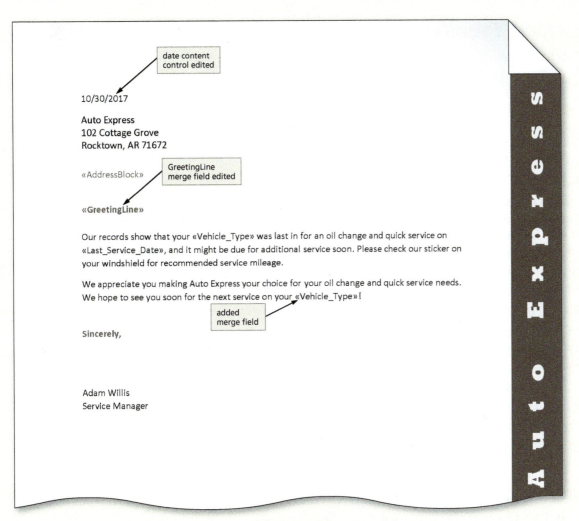

date content
control edited

10/30/2017

Auto Express
102 Cottage Grove
Rocktown, AR 71672

«AddressBlock»

GreetingLine
merge field edited

«GreetingLine»

Our records show that your «Vehicle_Type» was last in for an oil change and quick service on «Last_Service_Date», and it might be due for additional service soon. Please check our sticker on your windshield for recommended service mileage.

We appreciate you making Auto Express your choice for your oil change and quick service needs. We hope to see you soon for the next service on your «Vehicle_Type»!

added
merge field

Sincerely,

Adam Willis
Service Manager

Figure 6–84

6. View merged data in the document. Use the navigation buttons in the Preview Results group to display merged data from various records in the data source. What is the last name shown in the first record? The third record? The fifth record? View merge fields (that is, turn off the view merged data).

7. Print the main document for the form letter (shown in Figure 6–84). If requested by your instructor, save the main document as a PDF.

8. If requested by your instructor, add a record to the data source that contains your personal information. Type **7/14/2016** in the Last_Service_Date field, and add the type of vehicle you own (or would like to own) in the Vehicle_Type field.

9. In the data source, change Kimberly Johnson's last name to Holloway.

10. Sort the data source by the Last Name field.

11. Save the main document for the form letter again.

12. Merge the form letters to a new document. Save the new document with the file name, Apply 6–1 Oil Change Merged Letters.

13. If requested by your instructor, merge the form letters directly to the printer.

14. Submit the saved documents in the format specified by your instructor.

15. ✸ Answer the questions posed in #5 and #6. The form letter used in this assignment was based on one of Word's online mail merge letter templates called Adjacency letter. What other online mail merge letter templates are available through Word? Which template do you like best and why?

Extend Your Knowledge

Extend the skills you learned in this module and experiment with new skills. You may need to use Help to complete the assignment.

Editing an IF Field, Inserting a Fill-In Field, and Merging Using Outlook and Access

Note: To complete this assignment, you will be required to use the Data Files. Please contact your instructor for information about accessing the Data Files.

Instructions: Run Word. Open the document called Extend 6–1 Donation Letter Draft located on the Data Files. When you open the main document, if Word displays a dialog box about an SQL command, click the Yes button. If Word prompts for the name of the data source, select Extend 6–1 Donor List on the Data Files.

The document is a main document for a form letter thanking and inviting a donor to a pancake breakfast (Figure 6–85). You will modify an IF field, and add a Fill-in field, print field codes, create envelopes for records in the data source, use an Access database file as a data source, and merge to email addresses.

Perform the following tasks:

1. Use Help to learn about mail merge, IF fields, Fill-in fields, and merging to email addresses.
2. The IF field in the draft file has the true and false text reversed. Edit the IF field so that donations greater than or equal to $25 may bring two guests and all others may bring one guest. *Hint:* Use the 'Toggle Field Codes' command on the shortcut menu (right-click the IF field code in the document window) and edit the IF field directly in the document.
3. Above the GreetingLine merge field (shown in Figure 6–85), insert a Fill-in field that asks this question: What date will you be mailing these letters? Select the Ask once check box so that the question is asked only once, instead of for each letter. When merging the letters, use a date in October of 2017. What is the purpose of the Fill-in field?
4. If requested by your instructor, add a record to the data source that contains your personal information and a donation amount of 25.
5. Save the modified letter with the file name, Extend 6–1 Donation Letter Modified.
6. Merge the letters to a new document. Save the merged letters using the file name, Extend 6–1 Donation Merged Letters. On the letter with the donation of $100, add an extra sentence of thanks at the end of the first paragraph.
7. Print the main document for the form letter. If requested by your instructor, save the main document as a PDF.
8. Print the form letter with field codes showing; that is, print it with the 'Print field codes instead of their values' check box selected in the Word Options dialog box. Be sure to deselect this check box after printing the field codes version of the letter. How does this printout differ from the one printed in #7?
9. Submit the main document and merged letters in the format specified by your instructor.
10. If your instructor requests, create envelopes for each letter in the data source. Submit the merged envelopes in the format specified by your instructor.
11. If Access is installed on your computer or mobile device, and if you are familiar with Access and your instructor requests it, create the data source included with the assignment in Access and then open the main document with the Access database file as the data source.
12. If your instructor requests, display your personal record on the screen and merge the form letter to an email message, specifying that only the current receives the message. Submit the merged email message in the format specified by your instructor.
13. ✳ Answer the questions posed in #3 and #8. If you choose to merge to email addresses, what is the purpose of the various email formats?

Figure 6–85

Expand Your World

Create a solution that uses cloud or web technologies by learning and investigating on your own from general guidance.

Exploring Add-Ins for Office Apps

Instructions: You regularly use apps on your phone and tablet to look up a variety of information. In Office apps, you can use add-ins, which essentially are apps that work with Word and the other Office apps. You would like to investigate some of the add-ins available for Word to determine which ones would be helpful for you to use.

Note: You will be required to use your Microsoft account to complete this assignment. If you do not have a Microsoft account and do not want to create one, read this assignment without performing the instructions.

Perform the following tasks:

1. Use Help to learn about Office add-ins. If necessary, sign in to your Windows account.

2. If you are not signed in already, sign in to your Microsoft Account in Word.

3. Display the Insert tab and then click the 'Insert an Add-in' button (Insert tab | Add-ins group) to display the Office Add-ins dialog box. (If a menu is displayed, click the See All link to display the Office Add-ins dialog box.) Click the Office Store button or the STORE tab (Office Add-ins dialog box) to visit the online Office Store.

4. Scroll through add-ins in the various categories (Figure 6–86). Locate a free add-in that you feel would be helpful to you while you use Word, click the Add button, and then follow the instructions to add the add-in to Word.

5. In Word, click the 'Insert an Add-in' button again to display the Office Add-ins dialog box. Click the add-in you added and then click the Insert button to use the add-in. Click the 'Insert an Add-in' arrow to see the added add-in in the list.

6. Practice using the add-in. Does the add-in work as you intended? Would you recommend the add-in to others?

7. ✻ Which add-ins, if any, were already on your computer or mobile device? Which add-in did you download and why? Answer the questions in #6.

Figure 6–86

In the Labs

Design, create, modify, and/or use a document following the guidelines, concepts, and skills presented in this module. Labs 1 and 2, which increase in difficulty, require you to create solutions based on what you learned in the module; Lab 3 requires you to apply your creative thinking and problem-solving skills to design and implement a solution.

Lab 1: Creating a Form Letter Using a Template, a Data Source, Mailing Labels, and a Directory

Problem: You are graduating this May and have prepared your resume (shown in Figure 5–78 in Module 5). You decide to create a cover letter for your resume as a form letter that you will send to potential employers. The main document for the form letter is shown in Figure 6–87a.

Perform the following tasks:

1. Use the Timeless letter template to begin creating the main document for the form letter. If you cannot locate this template, open the file called Timeless letter from the Data Files. If necessary, change the document theme to Headlines (or a similar theme). Customize the theme fonts to match the resume (that is, headings Arial Black and body text Verdana). Save the main document for the form letter with the file name, Lab 6–1 Boskovich Cover Letter.

2. Type a new data source using the data shown in Figure 6–87b. Delete the field names not used and add one field name: Position. Rename the Company_Name field to Organization_Name. If requested by your instructor, add a record to the data source that contains your personal information. Save the data source with the file name, Lab 6–1 Boskovich Potential Employers.

3. Save the main document for the form letter again. Enter the text, image, merge fields, and formats as shown in the figure. Insert the AddressBlock and GreetingLine merge fields according to the sample formats shown in the figure. (Be sure to match the Company Name to the Organization_Name field so that the organization name appears in the AddressBlock field. *Hint:* Use the Insert Address Block dialog box, or click the Match Fields button (Mailings tab | Write & Insert Fields group). Change the top and bottom margins to 1 inch and the left and right margins to 1.25 inches. Specify the position of the rectangle graphic to 1 inch from the top of the page. Reduce the space above the paragraph containing the date to 36 point. If requested by your instructor, save the main document as a PDF.

4. Merge the form letters to a new document. Save the merged letters in a file called Lab 6–1 Boskovich Merged Letters.

5. In a new document window, address mailing labels using the same data source you used for the form letters. Be sure to match the Company Name to the Organization_Name field so that the organization name appears in the AddressBlock field. Select the table containing the mailing labels and change the Spacing Before and Spacing After to 0 point to remove the blank space between each line in the printed mailing label. Save the mailing label layout with the file name, Lab 6–1 Boskovich Mailing Label Layout. Merge the mailing labels to a new document. Save the merged mailing labels in a file called Lab 6–1 Boskovich Merged Mailing Labels. If requested by your instructor, merge the mailing labels to the printer.

6. In a new document window, specify the main document type as a directory. Change the page layout to landscape orientation. Change the margins to narrow. Insert all merge fields in the document, separating each with a comma. Save the directory layout with the file name, Lab 6–1 Boskovich Directory Layout. Merge the directory layout to a new document window. Convert the list of fields to a Word table (the table will have 10 columns). Add a row to the top of the table and insert field names in the empty cells. Change the font size of all text in the table to 9 point. Apply the List Table 3 - Accent 3 table style (remove formatting from the first column).

Resize the table columns so that the table looks like Figure 6–87b. Center the table. Sort the table in the directory listing by the Last Name field. Save the merged directory with the file name, Lab 6–1 Boskovich Merged Sorted Directory Listing.

7. Submit all documents in the format specified by your instructor.

8. ✺ If you did not want to use the AddressBlock and Greeting Line fields, how would you enter the address and salutation so that the letters printed the correct fields from each record?

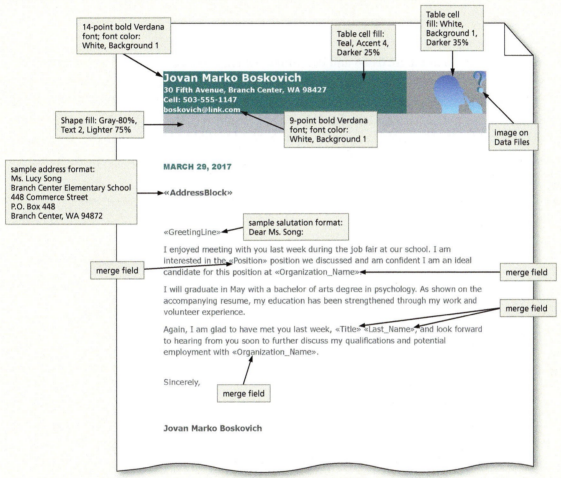

(a) Main Document for Form Letter

Figure 6–87

Title	First Name	Last Name	Organization Name	Address Line 1
Ms.	Lucy	Song	Branch Center Elementary School	448 Commerce Street
Mr.	Miguel	Arroyo	Johnston Elementary	829 Placid Boulevard
Mr.	Dashuan	Titus	Delman High School	17 South Street
Ms.	LaToya	Carrothers	Harrust High School	85 Windmill Lane
Mr.	Matthew	Mason	Squire Elementary	200 Eaton Parkway

Address Line 2	City	State	ZIP Code	Position
P.O. Box 448	Branch Center	WA	98472	counselor
	Sandfly	WA	98420	school counselor
P.O Box 17	Delman	WA	98404	high school counselor
	Harrust	WA	98496	student services counselor
	Mitcheltown	WA	98461	school counselor

(b) Data Source

Figure 6–87

Continued >

In the Labs *continued*

Lab 2: Designing a Data Source, Form Letter, and Directory from Sample Letters

Problem: You are graduating this May and have prepared your resume (shown in Figure 5–79 in Module 5). You decide to create a cover letter for your resume as a form letter that you will send to potential employers. Sample drafted letters for the cover letter are shown in Figure 6–88a and Figure 6–88b.

Perform the following tasks:

1. Review the letters in Figure 6–88 and determine the fields that should be in the data source. Write the field names on a piece of paper.

2. Do not use a template to create this form letter. In Word, create a main document for the letters using the block letter style. Create the letterhead as shown in Figure 6–88a. Apply the No Spacing style to all paragraphs. Save the main document for the form letter with the file name, Lab 6–2 Washington Cover Letter. If requested by your instructor, save the cover letter main document as a PDF.

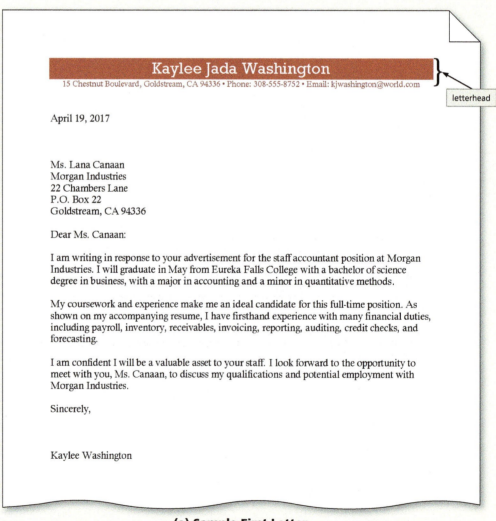

(a) Sample First Letter

Figure 6–88

3. Create a data source containing five records, consisting of data from the two letters shown in Figure 6–88 and then add three more records with your own data. If requested by your instructor, add a record to the data source that contains your personal information. Save the data source with the file name, Lab 6–2 Washington Potential Employers.

4. Enter the text and merge fields into the letter. The letter requires one IF field that displays the text, full-time, if the available job position is for a full-time employee; otherwise, it displays the words, part-time, if the available job position is for a part-time employee. Merge the form letters to a new document. Save the merged letters with the file name, Lab 6–2 Washington Merged Letters. Submit the merged letters in the format specified by your instructor.

5. Merge the data source to a directory. Convert it to a Word table. Add an attractive border to the table and apply any other formatting you feel necessary. Submit the directory in the format specified by your instructor.

6. ✸ Which fields did you use in your data source?

Kaylee Jada Washington

15 Chestnut Boulevard, Goldstream, CA 94336 • Phone: 308-555-8752 • Email: kjwashington@world.com

April 19, 2017

Mr. Raul Ramos
Bartlett Insurance
104 Michigan Street
P.O. Box 104
Goldstream, CA 94336

Dear Mr. Ramos:

I am writing in response to your advertisement for the accounting analyst position at Bartlett Insurance. I will graduate in May from Eureka Falls College with a bachelor of science degree in business, with a major in accounting and a minor in quantitative methods.

My coursework and experience make me an ideal candidate for this part-time position. As shown on my accompanying resume, I have firsthand experience with many financial duties, including payroll, inventory, receivables, invoicing, reporting, auditing, credit checks, and forecasting.

I am confident I will be a valuable asset to your staff. I look forward to the opportunity to meet with you, Mr. Ramos, to discuss my qualifications and potential employment with Bartlett Insurance.

Sincerely,

Kaylee Washington

(b) Sample Second Letter

Figure 6–88

Continued >

STUDENT ASSIGNMENTS

In the Labs *continued*

Lab 3: **Consider This: Your Turn**

Create Thank You Form Letters

Problem: As owner of Pine Valley Campground, you would like to send form letters to recent guests, thanking them for their stay.

Part 1: Pine Valley Campground is located at 8754 Wilderness Lane, Harpville, KY 42194; website is www.pinevalley.com; email address is info@pinevalley.com. In the form letters, thank guests for their recent stay — identifying the starting date of their stay, the type of campsite in which they stayed, and the length of their stay. Mention you hope they enjoyed their stay and look forward to seeing them again. Also mention that they will receive a 10 percent discount on any future stays this season if they bring this letter to check-in.

Use the concepts and techniques presented in this module to create and format this form letter. Use your name and phone number in the sender information in the main document. The merge fields for the data source are shown in Table 6–1. All merge fields in the data source should be used at least once in the form letter. Merge all records and use a filter to merge just those guests who stayed at tent sites. Be sure to check the spelling and grammar of the finished documents. Create a directory of the data source records. Address and print accompanying labels or envelopes for the form letters. Submit your assignment in the format specified by your instructor.

Table 6–1

Title	First Name	Last Name	Address Line 1	Address Line 2	City	State	ZIP Code	Site Type	Reservation Date	Length of Stay
Mr.	Jonah	Weinberg	35009 Clark Street	Apt. D3	Harpville	KY	42194	tent	September 8	two nights
Ms.	Shannon	O'Malley	13292 Cherry Street		Hill City	KY	42002	full hookup	September 12	four nights
Mr.	Tyrone	Davis	908 Wilson Court	P.O. Box 77	Harpville	KY	42194	water and electric	September 7	three nights
Ms.	Louella	Drake	172 East Park Street	Apt. 132	Blackburg	KY	42392	full hookup	September 8	two nights
Ms.	Roberta	Jeffries	201 Timmons Place	Unit 20C	Horizon	KY	42509	tent	September 10	two nights

Part 2: ✳ You made several decisions while creating the form letter, data source, and directory in this assignment: whether to use a template or create the letter from scratch, wording to use, where to position text and merge fields in the letter, how to format elements, how to set up the data source, and how to format the directory. What was the rationale behind each of these decisions?

7 Creating a Newsletter with a Pull-Quote and Graphics

Objectives

You will have mastered the material in this module when you can:

- Insert and format WordArt
- Set custom tab stops
- Crop a graphic
- Rotate a graphic
- Format a document in multiple columns
- Justify a paragraph
- Hyphenate a document
- Format a character as a drop cap

- Insert a column break
- Insert and format a text box
- Copy and paste using a split window
- Balance columns
- Modify and format a SmartArt graphic
- Copy and paste using the Office Clipboard
- Add an art page border

Introduction

Professional-looking documents, such as newsletters and brochures, often are created using desktop publishing software. With desktop publishing software, you can divide a document in multiple columns, wrap text around diagrams and other graphical images, change fonts and font sizes, add color and lines, and so on, to create an attention-grabbing document. Desktop publishing software, such as Microsoft Publisher, Adobe PageMaker, or QuarkXpress, enables you to open an existing word processing document and enhance it through formatting tools not provided in your word processing software. Word, however, provides many of the formatting features that you would find in a desktop publishing program. Thus, you can use Word to create eye-catching newsletters and brochures.

Project — Newsletter

A newsletter is a publication geared for a specific audience that is created on a recurring basis, such as weekly, monthly, or quarterly. The audience may be subscribers, club members, employees, customers, patrons, students, etc.

The project in this module uses Word to produce the two-page newsletter shown in Figure 7–1. The newsletter is a monthly publication called *Security Trends*. Each issue of *Security Trends* contains a feature article and announcements. This month's feature article discusses biometrics. The feature article spans the first two columns of the first page of the newsletter and then continues on the second page. The announcements, which are located in the third column of the first page, inform subscribers about discounts and an upcoming webinar and announce the topic of the next issue's feature article.

The *Security Trends* newsletter in this module incorporates the desktop publishing features of Word. The body of each page of the newsletter is divided in three columns. A variety of fonts, font sizes, and colors add visual appeal to the document. The first page has text wrapped around a pull-quote, and the second page has text wrapped around a graphic. Horizontal and vertical lines separate distinct areas of the newsletter, including a page border around the perimeter of each page.

The project in this module involves several steps requiring you to drag and drop. If you drag to the wrong location, you may want to cancel an action. Remember that you always can click the Undo button on the Quick Access Toolbar or press CTRL+Z to cancel your most recent action.

In this module, you will learn how to create the newsletter shown in Figure 7–1. The following roadmap identifies general activities you will perform as you progress through this module:

1. CREATE the NAMEPLATE FOR the FIRST PAGE of the newsletter.
2. FORMAT the FIRST PAGE of the body of the newsletter.
3. CREATE a PULL-QUOTE on the first page of the newsletter.
4. CREATE the NAMEPLATE FOR the SECOND PAGE of the newsletter.
5. FORMAT the SECOND PAGE of the body of the newsletter.
6. ADD a PAGE BORDER to the newsletter.

Desktop Publishing Terminology

As you create professional-looking newsletters and brochures, you should be familiar with several desktop publishing terms. Figure 7–1 identifies these terms:

- A **nameplate**, or **banner**, is the portion of a newsletter that contains the title of the newsletter and usually an issue information line.
- The **issue information line** identifies the specific publication.
- A **ruling line**, usually identified by its direction as a **horizontal rule** or **vertical rule**, is a line that separates areas of the newsletter.
- A **subhead** is a heading within the body of the newsletter.
- A **pull-quote** is text that is *pulled*, or copied, from the text of the document and given graphical emphasis.

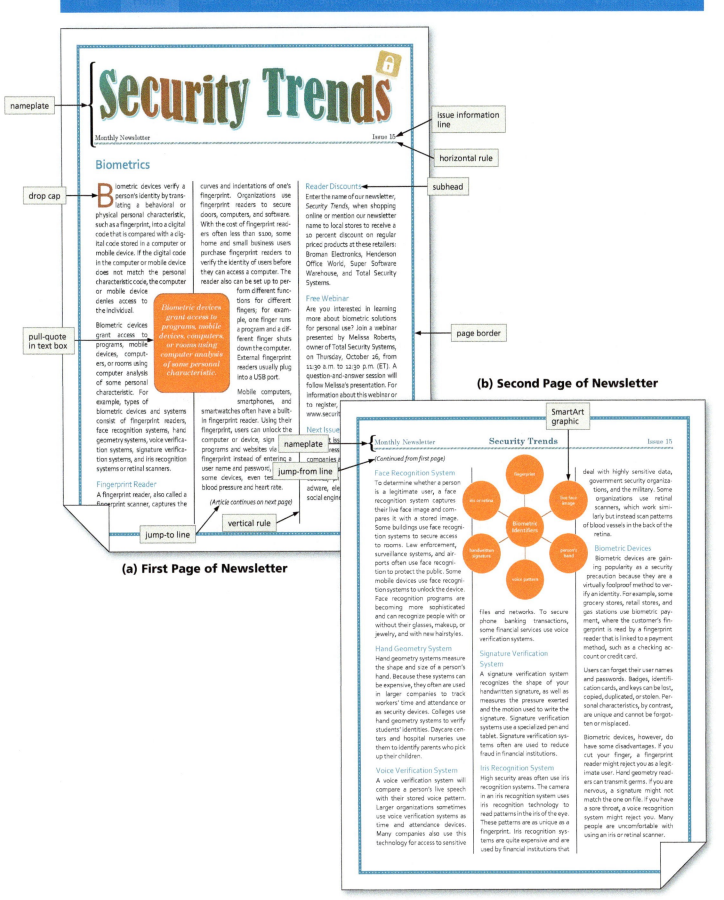

Figure 7-1

To Run Word and Change Word Settings

If you are using a computer to step through the project in this module and you want your screens to match the figures in this book, you should change your screen's resolution to 1366 × 768. The following steps run Word, display formatting marks, and change the zoom to page width.

BTW
The Ribbon and Screen Resolution
Word may change how the groups and buttons within the groups appear on the ribbon, depending on the computer or mobile device's screen resolution. Thus, your ribbon may look different from the ones in this book if you are using a screen resolution other than 1366 × 768.

1 Run Word and create a blank document in the Word window. If necessary, maximize the Word window.

2 If the Print Layout button on the status bar is not selected, click it so that your screen is in Print Layout view.

3 If the 'Show/Hide ¶' button (Home tab | Paragraph group) is not selected already, click it to display formatting marks on the screen.

4 To display the page the same width as the document window, if necessary, click the Page Width button (View tab | Zoom group).

To Change Spacing above and below Paragraphs and Margin Settings

Recall that Word is preset to use standard 8.5-by-11-inch paper, with 1-inch top, bottom, left, and right margins. In earlier modules, you changed the margins by selecting predefined settings in the Margins gallery. For the newsletter in this module, all margins (left, right, top, and bottom) are .75 inches, which is not a predefined setting in the Margins gallery. Thus, the following steps set custom margins.

1 Display the Layout tab.

2 Click the Adjust Margins button (Layout tab | Page Setup group) to display the Margins gallery and then click Custom Margins at the bottom of the Margins gallery to display the Page Setup dialog box.

3 Change each value in the Top, Bottom, Left, and Right boxes (Page Setup dialog box) to .75 (Figure 7–2).

4 Click the OK button to change the margin values.

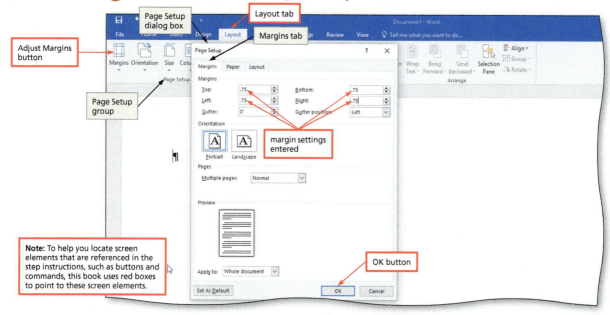

Figure 7–2

To Change Theme Colors

The newsletter in this module uses the Frame theme. The following steps change the theme to Frame.

1 Display the Design tab.

2 Click the Themes button (Design tab | Document Formatting group) and then click Frame in the Themes gallery to change the document theme.

BTW

Touch Screen Differences
The Office and Windows interfaces may vary if you are using a touch screen. For this reason, you might notice that the function or appearance of your touch screen differs slightly from this module's presentation.

Creating the Nameplate

The nameplate on the first page of this newsletter consists of the information above the multiple columns (shown in Figure 7–1a at the beginning of this module). In this project, the nameplate includes the newsletter title, Security Trends, an image of a lock, and the issue information line.

The following sections use the steps outlined below to create the nameplate for the first page of the newsletter in this module.

1. Enter and format the newsletter title using WordArt.
2. Set custom tab stops for the issue information line.
3. Enter text in the issue information line.
4. Add a horizontal rule below the issue information line.
5. Insert and format the image.

CONSIDER THIS

How should you design a nameplate?
A nameplate visually identifies a newsletter. It should catch the attention of readers, enticing them to read a newsletter. Usually, the nameplate is positioned horizontally across the top of the newsletter, although some nameplates are vertical. The nameplate typically consists of the title of the newsletter and the issue information line. Some also include a subtitle, a slogan, and a graphical image or logo.

Guidelines for the newsletter title and other elements in the nameplate are as follows:

• Compose a title that is short, yet conveys the contents of the newsletter. In the newsletter title, eliminate unnecessary words such as these: the, newsletter. Use a decorative font in as large a font size as possible so that the title stands out on the page.

• Other elements on the nameplate should not compete in size with the title. Use colors that complement the title. Select easy-to-read fonts.

• Arrange the elements of the nameplate so that it does not have a cluttered appearance. If necessary, use ruling lines to visually separate areas of the nameplate.

To Insert WordArt

1 CREATE NAMEPLATE FOR FIRST PAGE | 2 FORMAT FIRST PAGE | 3 CREATE PULL-QUOTE
4 CREATE NAMEPLATE FOR SECOND PAGE | 5 FORMAT SECOND PAGE | 6 ADD PAGE BORDER

In Module 3, you inserted a shape drawing object in a document. Recall that a drawing object is a graphic you create using Word. Another type of drawing object, called **WordArt**, enables you to create text with special effects, such as shadowed, rotated, stretched, skewed, and wavy effects.

This project uses WordArt for the newsletter title, Security Trends. *Why? A title created with WordArt is likely to draw the reader's attention.* The following steps insert WordArt.

- Display the Insert tab.

- Click the Insert WordArt button (Insert tab | Text group) to display the Insert WordArt gallery (Figure 7–3).

Q&A Once I select a WordArt style, can I customize its appearance?
Yes. The next steps customize the WordArt style selected here.

Figure 7–3

- Click 'Fill - Teal, Accent 1, Outline - Background 1, Hard Shadow - Accent 1' in the WordArt gallery (third WordArt style in last row) to insert a drawing object in the document that is formatted according to the selected WordArt style, which contains the placeholder text, Your text here (Figure 7–4).

- Type **Security Trends** to replace the selected placeholder text in the WordArt drawing object (shown in Figure 7–5).

Q&A What if my placeholder text no longer is selected?
Drag through it to select it.

How do I correct a mistake in the WordArt text?
You correct WordArt text using the same techniques you use to correct document text.

Figure 7–4

To Resize WordArt

You resize WordArt the same way you resize any other graphic. That is, you can drag its sizing handles or enter values in the Shape Height and Shape Width boxes. The next steps resize the WordArt drawing object.

1. With the WordArt drawing object selected, if necessary, display the Drawing Tools Format tab.

2. Change the value in the Shape Height box to 1.44 and the value in the Shape Width box to 7 (Figure 7–5).

Figure 7-5

To Change the Font and Font Size of WordArt Text

You change the font and font size of WordArt text the same way you change the font and font size of any other text. That is, you select the text and then change its font and font size. The following steps change the font and font size of WordArt text.

1 Select the WordArt text, in this case, Security Trends.

2 Change the font of the selected text to Bernard MT Condensed (or a similar font).

3 Change the font size of the selected text to 72 point (shown in Figure 7–6).

BTW
Deleting WordArt
If you want to delete a WordArt drawing object, right-click it and then click Cut on the shortcut menu, or select the WordArt drawing object and then click the Cut button (Home tab | Clipboard group).

To Change an Object's Text Wrapping

When you insert a drawing object in a Word document, the default text wrapping is Square, which means text will wrap around the object in the shape of a square. Because you want the nameplate above the rest of the newsletter, you change the text wrapping for the drawing object to Top and Bottom. The following steps change a drawing object's text wrapping.

1 With the WordArt drawing object selected, click the Layout Options button that is attached to the WordArt drawing object to display the Layout Options gallery.

2 Click 'Top and Bottom' in the Layout Options gallery so that the WordArt drawing object will not cover the document text; in this case, the paragraph mark moves below the WordArt drawing object (Figure 7–6).

3 Close the Layout Options gallery.

Figure 7–6

To Change the WordArt Fill Color

The next step is to change the color of the WordArt text so that it displays a teal and orange gradient fill color. **Gradient** means the colors blend into one another. Word includes several built-in gradient fill colors, or you can customize one for use in drawing objects. The following steps change the fill color of the WordArt drawing object to a built-in gradient fill color and then customize the selected fill color. *Why? Using a gradient fill color will add interest to the title.*

1

- With the WordArt drawing object selected, click the Text Fill arrow (Drawing Tools Format tab | WordArt Styles group) to display the Text Fill gallery.

Q&A

The Text Fill gallery did not appear. Why not?
Be sure you click the Text Fill arrow, which is to the right of the Text Fill button. If you mistakenly click the Text Fill button, Word places a default fill in the selected WordArt instead of displaying the Text Fill gallery.

2

- Point to Gradient in the Text Fill gallery to display the Gradient gallery (Figure 7–7).

Figure 7–7

③
- Click More Gradients in the Gradient gallery to open the Format Shape task pane. If necessary, click the Text Options tab in the Format Shape task pane and then, if necessary, click the 'Text Fill & Outline' button. If necessary, expand the Text Fill section.

- Click Gradient fill in the Text Fill section to display options related to gradient colors in the task pane (Figure 7–8).

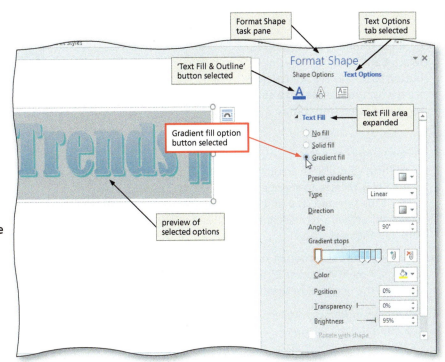

Figure 7–8

④
- Click the Preset gradients button in the Format Shape task pane to display a palette of built-in gradient fill colors (Figure 7–9).

Figure 7–9

⑤
- Click 'Radial Gradient - Accent 5' (bottom row, fifth column) in the Preset gradients palette to select the built-in gradient color, which shows a preview in the Gradient stops area (Figure 7–10).

Q&A | What is a gradient stop?
A gradient stop is the location where two colors blend. You can change the color of a stop so that Word changes the color of the blend. You also can add or delete stops, with a minimum of two stops and a maximum of ten stops per gradient fill color.

Figure 7–10

- Click the second gradient stop to select it and then click the Color button to display a Color palette, from which you can select a color for the selected stop (Figure 7–11).

- Click 'Orange, Accent 4, Darker 25%' (fifth row, eighth column) in the Color palette to change the color of the selected stop and the gradient between the selected stop and the next stop.

Figure 7–11

- Click the rightmost gradient stop to select it and then click the Color button to display a Color palette. Click 'Orange, Accent 4, Darker 25%' (fifth row, eighth column) in the Color palette to change the color of the selected stop and the gradient between the selected stop and the previous stop.

Can I move a gradient stop?

Yes. You can drag a stop to any location along the color bar. You also can adjust the position, brightness, and transparency of any selected stop.

- Click the Direction button to display a gallery that shows a variety of directions for the gradient colors (Figure 7–12).

Figure 7–12

- Click 'From Top Left Corner' (rightmost direction) in the Direction gallery to specify the direction to blend the colors.
- Click the Close button in the task pane.
- Click the paragraph mark below the WordArt drawing object to deselect the text so that you can see its gradient fill colors (Figure 7–13).

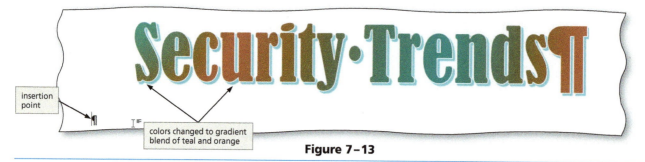

Figure 7–13

1 CREATE NAMEPLATE FOR FIRST PAGE | **2 FORMAT FIRST PAGE** | **3 CREATE PULL-QUOTE**

4 CREATE NAMEPLATE FOR SECOND PAGE | **5 FORMAT SECOND PAGE** | **6 ADD PAGE BORDER**

To Change the WordArt Shape

Word provides a variety of shapes to make your WordArt more interesting. The following steps change the WordArt shape. ***Why?*** *The WordArt in this newsletter has a wavy appearance.*

- Click the WordArt drawing object to select it.

- If necessary, display the Drawing Tools Format tab.

- Click the Text Effects button (Drawing Tools Format tab | WordArt Styles group) to display the Text Effects gallery.

- Point to Transform in the Text Effects gallery to display the Transform gallery.

- Point to 'Double Wave 1' (third effect, fifth row in Warp area) in the Transform gallery to display a live preview of the selected transform effect applied to the selected drawing object (Figure 7–14).

 Experiment

- Point to various text effects in the Transform gallery and watch the selected drawing object conform to that transform effect.

Figure 7–14

- Click 'Double Wave 1' in the Transform gallery to change the shape of the WordArt drawing object.

To Set Custom Tab Stops Using the Tabs Dialog Box

1 CREATE NAMEPLATE FOR FIRST PAGE | **2 FORMAT FIRST PAGE** | **3 CREATE PULL-QUOTE**

4 CREATE NAMEPLATE FOR SECOND PAGE | **5 FORMAT SECOND PAGE** | **6 ADD PAGE BORDER**

The issue information line in this newsletter contains the text, Monthly Newsletter, at the left margin and the issue number at the right margin (shown in Figure 7–1a at the beginning of this module). In Word, a paragraph cannot be both left-aligned and right-aligned. ***Why?*** *If you click the 'Align Text Right' button (Home tab | Paragraph group), for example, all text will be right-aligned.* To place text at the right margin of a left-aligned paragraph, you set a tab stop at the right margin.

One method of setting custom tab stops is to click the ruler at the desired location of the tab stop, which you learned in an earlier module. You cannot click, however, at the right margin location. Thus, the following steps use the Tabs dialog box to set a custom tab stop.

- If necessary, display the Home tab.

- Position the insertion point on the paragraph mark below the WordArt drawing object, which is the paragraph to be formatted with the custom tab stops.

- Click the Paragraph Settings Dialog Box Launcher to display the Paragraph dialog box (Figure 7–15).

Figure 7–15

- Click the Tabs button (Paragraph dialog box) to display the Tabs dialog box.

- Type 7 in the 'Tab stop position' text box (Tabs dialog box).

- Click Right in the Alignment area to specify alignment for text at the tab stop (Figure 7–16).

- Click the Set button (Tabs dialog box) to set a right-aligned custom tab stop at the specified position.

- Click the OK button to set the defined tab stops.

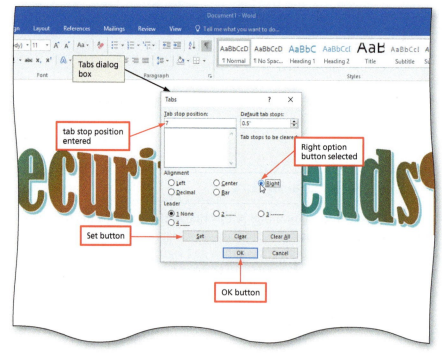

Figure 7–16

Other Ways

1. Click desired tab stop on ruler

2. Right-click paragraph (or, if using touch, tap 'Show Context Menu' button on mini toolbar), click Paragraph on shortcut menu, click Tabs button (Paragraph dialog box), enter desired settings, click OK button

To Enter Text

The following steps enter the issue information line text.

1 With the insertion point on the paragraph below the WordArt, change the font to Century Schoolbook (or a similar font) and the font size to 10 point.

2 Type **Monthly Newsletter** on line 2 of the newsletter.

If requested by your instructor, enter your name instead of the word, Monthly.

3 Press the TAB key and then type **Issue 15** to complete the issue information line (Figure 7–17).

Figure 7–17

Q&A

The nameplate does not appear to extend to the right margin. Why not?

If you have formatting marks displaying, the paragraph mark consumes space at the right margin. To see how the nameplate will print, turn off formatting marks.

1 CREATE NAMEPLATE FOR FIRST PAGE | 2 FORMAT FIRST PAGE | 3 CREATE PULL-QUOTE
4 CREATE NAMEPLATE FOR SECOND PAGE | 5 FORMAT SECOND PAGE | 6 ADD PAGE BORDER

To Border One Edge of a Paragraph

In Word, you use borders to create ruling lines. As discussed in previous modules, Word can place borders on any edge of a paragraph; that is, Word can place a border on the top, bottom, left, and right edges of a paragraph.

One method of bordering paragraphs is by clicking the desired border in the Borders gallery, which you learned in an earlier module. If you want to specify a particular border, for example, one with color, you use the Borders and Shading dialog box. The following steps use the Borders and Shading dialog box to place a border below a paragraph. **Why?** *In this newsletter, the issue information line has a 3-point diagonally striped teal border below it.*

1

- Click the Borders arrow (Home tab | Paragraph group) to display the Borders gallery (Figure 7–18).

Figure 7–18

● Click 'Borders and Shading' in the Borders gallery to display the Borders and Shading dialog box.

● Click Custom in the Setting area (Borders and Shading dialog box) because you are setting just a bottom border.

● Scroll through the Style list and click the style shown in Figure 7–19, which is a diagonally striped line for the border.

● Click the Color button and then click 'Teal, Accent 5, Darker 50%' (ninth column, bottom row) in the Color gallery.

● Click the Bottom Border button in the Preview area of the dialog box to show a preview of the selected border style (Figure 7–19).

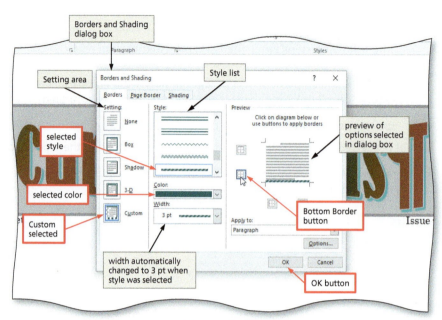

Figure 7–19

Q&A What is the purpose of the buttons in the Preview area?
They are toggles that display and remove the top, bottom, left, and right borders from the diagram in the Preview area.

● Click the OK button to place the defined border on the paragraph containing the insertion point (Figure 7–20).

Figure 7–20

Q&A How would I change an existing border?
You first remove the existing border by clicking the Borders arrow (Home tab | Paragraph group) and then clicking the border in the Borders gallery that identifies the border you wish to remove. Then, add a new border as described in these steps.

Other Ways

1. Click 'Borders and Shading' button (Design tab | Page Background group), click Borders tab (Borders and Shading dialog box), select desired border, click OK button

To Insert a Picture

The next steps insert an image of locks in the nameplate.

1 Display the Insert tab.

2 Click the Online Pictures button (Insert tab | Illustrations group) to display the Insert Pictures dialog box.

③ Type **locks** in the Search box (Insert Pictures dialog box) to specify the search text and then click the Search button to display a list of images that match the entered search text.

④ Scroll through the list of images to locate the one shown in Figure 7–21 (or a similar image), click the image to select it, and then click the Insert button (Insert Picture dialog box) to download the image, close the dialog box, and insert the selected image at the location of the insertion point in the document.

Q&A What if I cannot locate the same image as in Figure 7–21?
Click the Cancel button to close the dialog box and then click the From File button (Insert tab | Illustrations group) to display the Insert Picture dialog box, navigate to and select the 1383900176-2400px.png file on the Data Files, and then click the Insert button (Insert Picture dialog box) to insert the picture.

What if my inserted image is not in the same location as in Figure 7–21?
The image may be in a different location, depending on the position of the insertion point when you inserted the image. In a later section, you will move the image to a different location.

To Change the Color of a Graphic

The following steps change the color of the graphic (the locks) to a shade of gold.

① With the graphic still selected, click the Color button (Picture Tools Format tab | Adjust group) to display the Color gallery (Figure 7–21).

② Click 'Gold, Accent color 2 Light' (third color, bottom row) in the Recolor area in the Color gallery to change the color of the selected graphic.

Figure 7–21

To Crop a Graphic

The next step is to format the image just inserted. You would like to remove the rightmost lock from the image. *Why? You want just one lock to appear in the newsletter.* Word allows you to **crop**, or remove edges from, a graphic. The following steps crop a graphic.

- With the graphic selected, click the Crop button (Picture Tools Format tab | Size group), which places cropping handles on the image in the document.

Q&A What if I mistakenly click the Crop arrow?
Click the Crop button.

- Position the pointer on the right-middle cropping handle so that it looks like a sideways letter T (Figure 7–22).

Figure 7–22

- Drag the right-middle cropping handle inward to the location shown in Figure 7–23 to crop the rightmost lock from the image.

3

- Click the Crop button (Picture Tools Format tab | Size group) to deactivate the cropping tool, which removes the cropping handles from the selected image.

Figure 7–23

Other Ways

1. Right-click graphic, click Crop button on mini toolbar, drag cropping handles, click Crop button

To Change an Object's Text Wrapping and Size

When you insert an object (image) in a Word document, the default text wrapping is In Line with Text, which means the object is part of the current paragraph. Because you want the lock image behind the newsletter title, you change the text wrapping for the image to Behind Text. The next steps change a drawing object's text wrapping and also change its size.

1 With the lock graphic selected, click the Layout Options button attached to the graphic to display the Layout Options gallery.

2 Click Behind Text in the Layout Options gallery so that the image is positioned behind text in the document.

3 Close the Layout Options gallery.

4 Change the values in the Shape Height and Shape Width boxes (Picture Tools Format tab | Size group) to .6" and .51", respectively.

To Move a Graphic

The clip art image needs to be moved up so that the bottom of the lock is on the s in the word, Trends, in the newsletter title. The following steps move a graphic.

1 Hide formatting marks so that you can see exactly where the letter s ends.

2 Drag the graphic to the location shown in Figure 7–24.

Figure 7–24

1 CREATE NAMEPLATE FOR FIRST PAGE | 2 FORMAT FIRST PAGE | 3 CREATE PULL-QUOTE

4 CREATE NAMEPLATE FOR SECOND PAGE | 5 FORMAT SECOND PAGE | 6 ADD PAGE BORDER

To Use the Selection Task Pane

The next step is to rotate the lock image, but because it is positioned behind the text, it may be difficult to select it. The following step opens the Selection task pane. *Why? The Selection task pane enables you easily to select items on the screen that are layered behind other objects.*

1

- If necessary, click in the graphic to display the Picture Tools Format tab.

- Click the 'Display the Selection Pane' button (Picture Tools Format tab | Arrange group) to open the Selection task pane (Figure 7–25).

Figure 7–25

Experiment

- Click Text Box 1 in the Selection task pane to select the WordArt drawing object. Click Picture 2 in the Selection task pane to select the lock image.

Q&A | What are the displayed names in the Selection task pane?
Word assigns names to each object in the document. The names displayed on your screen may differ.

To Rotate a Graphic

1 CREATE NAMEPLATE FOR FIRST PAGE | 2 FORMAT FIRST PAGE | 3 CREATE PULL-QUOTE
4 CREATE NAMEPLATE FOR SECOND PAGE | 5 FORMAT SECOND PAGE | 6 ADD PAGE BORDER

The following steps rotate a graphic. **Why?** *You would like the lock image angled inward a bit more.*

1

- If necessary, click Picture 2 in the Selection task pane to select the lock image.

- Position the pointer on the graphic's rotate handle (Figure 7–26).

Figure 7–26

2

- Drag the rotate handle rightward and outward to rotate the graphic slightly as shown in Figure 7–27. (You may need to rotate the graphic a few times to position it in the desired location.)

Q&A | Can I drag the rotate handle in any direction?
You can drag the rotate handle clockwise or counterclockwise.

What if I am using a touch screen?
Because the rotate handle is not available on a touch screen, you enter the degree of rotation in the Size dialog box. Tap the Rotate Objects button (Picture Tools Format tab | Arrange group) to display the Rotate Objects menu, tap 'More Rotation Options' on the Rotate Objects menu to display the Size sheet in the Layout dialog box, change the Rotation value to 14, and then tap the OK button.

Figure 7–27

3

- Click the Close button on the Selection task pane to close the task pane.

- Click somewhere in the issue information line to deselect the graphic.

- Save the title page on your hard drive, OneDrive, or other storage location using the file name, Security Trends Newsletter.

Break Point: If you wish to take a break, this is a good place to do so. You can exit Word now. To resume at a later time, run Word, open the file called Security Trends Newsletter, and continue following the steps from this location forward.

Formatting the First Page of the Body of the Newsletter

The next step is to format the first page of the body of the newsletter. The body of the newsletter in this module is divided in three columns (shown in Figure 7–1a at the beginning of this module). The first two columns contain the feature article, and the third column contains announcements. The characters in the paragraphs are aligned on both the right and left edges — similar to newspaper columns. The first letter in the first paragraph is much larger than the rest of the characters in the paragraph. A vertical rule separates the columns. The steps in the following sections format the first page of the body of the newsletter using these desktop publishing features.

What guidelines should you follow when creating the body of a newsletter?
While content and subject matter of newsletters may vary, the procedures used to create newsletters are similar:

- **Write the body copy.** Newsletters should contain articles of interest and relevance to readers. Some share information, while others promote a product or service. Use active voice in body copy, which is more engaging than passive voice. Proofread the body copy to be sure it is error free. Check all facts for accuracy.

- **Organize body copy in columns.** Most newsletters arrange body copy in columns. The body copy in columns, often called **snaking columns** or newspaper-style columns, flows from the bottom of one column to the top of the next column.

- **Format the body copy.** Begin the feature article on the first page of the newsletter. If the article spans multiple pages, use a continuation line, called a jump or jump line, to guide the reader to the remainder of the article. The message at the end of the article on the first page of the newsletter is called a **jump-to line**, and a **jump-from line** marks the beginning of the continuation, which is usually on a subsequent page.

- **Maintain consistency.** Be consistent with placement of body copy elements in newsletter editions. If the newsletter contains announcements, for example, position them in the same location in each edition so that readers easily can find them.

- **Maximize white space.** Allow plenty of space between lines, paragraphs, and columns. Tightly packed text is difficult to read. Separate the text adequately from graphics, borders, and headings.

- **Incorporate color.** Use colors that complement those in the nameplate. Be careful not to overuse color. Restrict color below the nameplate to drop caps, subheads, graphics, and ruling lines. If you do not have a color printer, still change the colors because the colors will print in shades of black and gray, which add variety to the newsletter.

- **Select and format subheads.** Develop subheads with as few words as possible. Readers should be able to identify content of the next topic by glancing at a subhead. Subheads should be emphasized in the newsletter but should not compete with text in the nameplate. Use a larger, bold, or otherwise contrasting font for subheads so that they stand apart from the body copy. Use this same format for all subheads for consistency. Leave a space above subheads to visually separate their content from the previous topic. Be consistent with spacing above and below subheads throughout the newsletter.

- **Divide sections with vertical rules.** Use vertical rules to guide the reader through the newsletter.

- **Enhance the document with visuals.** Add energy to the newsletter and emphasis to important points with graphics, pull-quotes, and other visuals, such as drop caps, to mark beginning of an article. Use these elements sparingly, however, so that the newsletter does not have a crowded appearance. Fewer, large visuals are more effective than several smaller ones. If you use a graphic that you did not create, be sure to obtain permission to use it in the newsletter and give necessary credit to the creator of the graphic.

To Clear Formatting

The next step is to enter the title of the feature article below the horizontal rule. To do this, position the insertion point at the end of the issue information line (after the 5 in Issue 15) and then press the ENTER key. Recall that the issue information line has a bottom border. When you press the ENTER key in a bordered paragraph, Word carries forward any borders to the next paragraph. Thus, after you press the ENTER key, you should clear formatting to format the new paragraph as the Normal style. The following steps clear formatting.

1 Click at the end of line 2 (the issue information line) so that the insertion point is immediately after the 5 in Issue 15. Press the ENTER key to advance the insertion point to the next line, which also moves the border down one line.

2 If necessary, display the Home tab. Click the 'Clear All Formatting' button (Home tab | Font group) to apply the Normal style to the location of the insertion point, which in this case moves the new paragraph below the border on the issue information line.

To Format Text as a Heading Style, Modify a Heading Style, and Adjust Spacing before and after the Paragraph

Below the bottom border in the nameplate is the title of the feature article, Biometrics. The following steps apply the Heading 1 style to this paragraph, modify the style, and adjust the paragraph spacing.

1 If necessary, display formatting marks.

2 With the insertion point on the paragraph mark below the border, click Heading 1 (Home tab | Styles group) to apply the Heading 1 style to the paragraph containing the insertion point.

3 Increase the font size 20 point. Bold the paragraph. Update the Heading 1 style to reflect these changes.

4 Type **Biometrics** as the title of the feature article.

5 Display the Layout tab. Change the Spacing Before box to 18 pt and the Spacing After box to 12 pt (Figure 7–28).

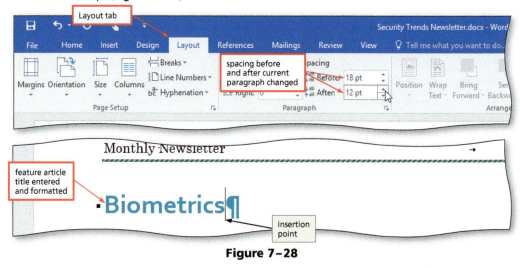

Figure 7–28

Columns

When you begin a document in Word, it has one column. You can divide a portion of a document or the entire document in multiple columns. Within each column, you can type, modify, or format text.

To divide a portion of a document in multiple columns, you use section breaks. Word requires that a new section be created each time you alter the number of columns in a document. Thus, if a document has a nameplate (one column) followed by an article of three columns followed by an article of two columns, the document would be divided in three separate sections.

CONSIDER THIS

How should you organize the body copy in columns?

Be consistent from page to page with the number of columns. Narrow columns generally are easier to read than wide ones. Columns, however, can be too narrow. A two- or three-column layout generally is appealing and offers a flexible design. Try to have between five and fifteen words per line. To do this, you may need to adjust the column width, the font size, or the leading (line spacing). Font size of text in columns should be no larger than 12 point but not so small that readers must strain to read the text.

1 CREATE NAMEPLATE FOR FIRST PAGE | 2 FORMAT FIRST PAGE | 3 CREATE PULL-QUOTE
4 CREATE NAMEPLATE FOR SECOND PAGE | 5 FORMAT SECOND PAGE | 6 ADD PAGE BORDER

To Insert a Continuous Section Break

The next step is to insert a continuous section break below the nameplate. *Why? In this module, the nameplate is one column and the body of the newsletter is three columns.* The term, continuous, means the new section should be on the same page as the previous section, which, in this case, means that the three columns of body copy will be positioned directly below the nameplate on the first page of the newsletter. The following steps insert a continuous section break.

1

- With the insertion point at the end of the feature article title (shown in Figure 7–28), press the ENTER key to position the insertion point below the article title.

- Click the 'Insert Page and Section Breaks' button (Layout tab | Page Setup group) to display the Insert Page and Section Breaks gallery (Figure 7–29).

Figure 7–29

2

- Click Continuous in the Insert Page and Section Breaks gallery to insert a continuous section break above the insertion point (Figure 7–30).

Figure 7–30

1 CREATE NAMEPLATE FOR FIRST PAGE | 2 FORMAT FIRST PAGE | 3 CREATE PULL-QUOTE
4 CREATE NAMEPLATE FOR SECOND PAGE | 5 FORMAT SECOND PAGE | 6 ADD PAGE BORDER

To Change the Number of Columns

The document now has two sections. The nameplate is in the first section, and the insertion point is in the second section. The second section should be formatted to three columns. *Why? The feature article and announcements appear in three columns that snake across the page.* Thus, the following steps format the second section in the document as three columns.

①

- Click the 'Add or Remove Columns' button (Layout tab | Page Setup group) to display the Add or Remove Columns gallery (Figure 7–31).

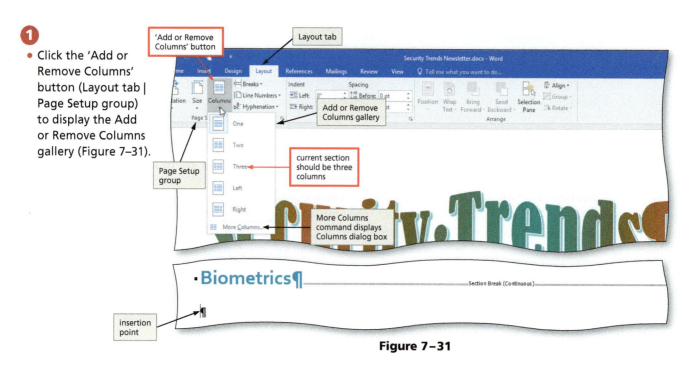

Figure 7–31

②

- Click Three in the Add or Remove Columns gallery to divide the section containing the insertion point in three evenly sized and spaced columns

- Display the View tab and then, if necessary, click the View Ruler check box so that the rulers appear on the screen (Figure 7–32).

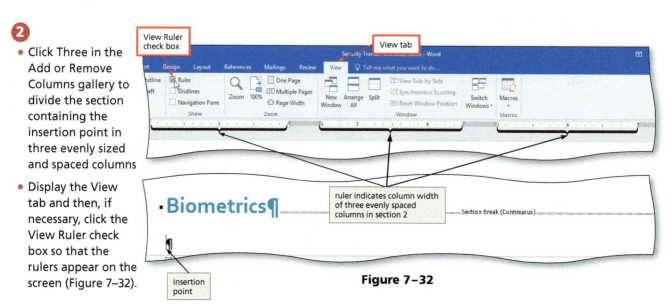

Figure 7–32

Q&A

Why display the rulers?

You want to see the column widths on the ruler.

What if I want columns of different widths?

You would click More Columns in the Add or Remove Columns gallery, which displays the Columns dialog box. In this dialog box, you can specify varying column widths and spacing.

1 CREATE NAMEPLATE FOR FIRST PAGE | **2 FORMAT FIRST PAGE** | 3 CREATE PULL-QUOTE
4 CREATE NAMEPLATE FOR SECOND PAGE | 5 FORMAT SECOND PAGE | 6 ADD PAGE BORDER

To Justify a Paragraph

The following step enters the first paragraph of the feature article using justified alignment. **Why?** *The text in the paragraphs of the body of the newsletter is **justified**, which means that the left and right margins are aligned, like the edges of newspaper columns.*

- Display the Home tab.

- Click the Justify button (Home tab | Paragraph group) so that Word aligns both the left and right margins of typed text.

- Type the first paragraph of the feature article (Figure 7–33): `Biometric devices verify a person's identity by translating a behavioral or physical personal characteristic, such as a fingerprint, into a digital code that is compared with a digital code stored in a computer or mobile device. If the digital code in the computer or mobile device does not match the personal characteristic code, the computer or mobile device denies access to the individual.` and then press the ENTER key.

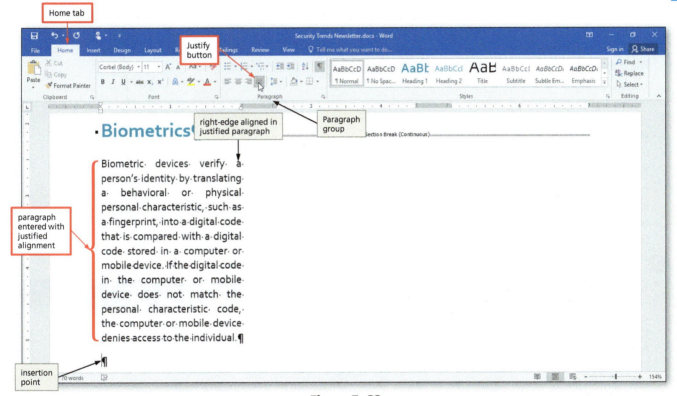

Figure 7–33

Q&A

Why do some words have extra space between them?

When a paragraph is formatted to justified alignment, Word places extra space between words so that the left and right edges of the paragraph are aligned. To remedy big gaps, sometimes called rivers, you can add or rearrange words, change the column width, change the font size, and so on.

Other Ways

1. Right-click paragraph (or, if using touch, tap 'Show Context Menu' button on mini toolbar), click Paragraph on shortcut menu, click 'Indents and Spacing' tab (Paragraph dialog box), click Alignment arrow, click Justified, click OK button

2. Click Paragraph Settings Dialog Box Launcher (Home tab or Layout tab | Paragraph group), click Indents and Spacing tab (Paragraph dialog box), click Alignment arrow, click Justified, click OK button

3. Press CTRL+J

To Insert a File in a Column of the Newsletter

1 CREATE NAMEPLATE FOR FIRST PAGE | 2 FORMAT FIRST PAGE | 3 CREATE PULL-QUOTE | 4 CREATE NAMEPLATE FOR SECOND PAGE | 5 FORMAT SECOND PAGE | 6 ADD PAGE BORDER

The next step is to insert a file named Biometrics Article in the newsletter. *Why? To save you time typing, the rest of the feature article is located on the Data Files.* Please contact your instructor for information about accessing the Data Files. The following steps insert the Biometrics Article file in a column of the newsletter.

1

- Display the Insert tab.

- With the insertion point positioned in the left column as shown in Figure 7–33, click the Object arrow (Insert tab | Text group) to display the Object menu.

- Click 'Text from File' on the Object menu to display the Insert File dialog box.

- Navigate to the location of the file to be inserted (in this case, the Module 07 files in the Data Files folder).

- Click the file named Biometrics Article to select the file (Figure 7–34).

Figure 7–34

2

- Click the Insert button (Insert File dialog box) to insert the file, Biometrics Article, in the current document at the location of the insertion point.

- So that you can see the entire inserted article, display multiple pages on the screen by clicking the Multiple Pages button (View tab | Zoom group) (Figure 7–35).

3

- When you are finished viewing the document, change the zoom to page width so that the newsletter content is larger on the screen.

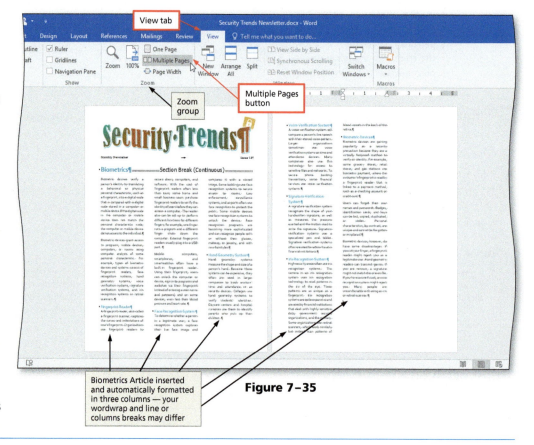

Figure 7–35

Biometrics Article inserted and automatically formatted in three columns — your wordwrap and line or columns breaks may differ

To Increase Column Width and Place a Vertical Rule between Columns

The columns in the newsletter currently contain many rivers. *Why? The justified alignment in the narrow column width often causes large gaps between words.* To eliminate some of the rivers, you increase the size of the columns slightly in this newsletter. In newsletters, you often see a vertical rule separating columns. Through the Columns dialog box, you can change column width and add vertical rules. The following steps increase column widths and add vertical rules between columns.

1
- Position the insertion point somewhere in the feature article text.
- Display the Layout tab.
- Click the 'Add or Remove Columns' button (Layout tab | Page Setup group) to display the Add or Remove Columns gallery (Figure 7–36).

Figure 7–36

2
- Click More Columns in the Add or Remove Columns gallery to display the Columns dialog box.
- If necessary, in the Width and spacing area (Columns dialog box), click the Width up arrow until the Width box reads 2.1".

Q&A

How would I make the columns different widths?
You would remove the check mark from the 'Equal column width' check box and then set the individual column widths in the dialog box.

- Place a check mark in the Line between check box to select the check box (Figure 7–37).

Figure 7–37

- Click the OK button to make the columns slightly wider and place a line (vertical rule) between each column in the document (Figure 7–38).

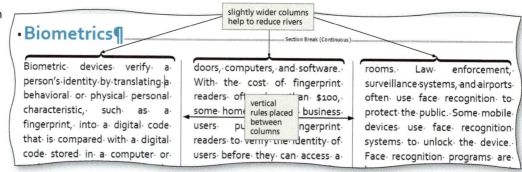

Figure 7–38

Other Ways

1. Double-click shaded space between columns on ruler, enter settings (Columns dialog box), click OK button

2. To adjust column widths, drag column boundaries on ruler

3. To insert single rule, click Borders arrow (Home tab | Paragraph group)

To Hyphenate a Document

1 CREATE NAMEPLATE FOR FIRST PAGE | 2 FORMAT FIRST PAGE | 3 CREATE PULL-QUOTE
4 CREATE NAMEPLATE FOR SECOND PAGE | 5 FORMAT SECOND PAGE | 6 ADD PAGE BORDER

The following steps turn on the hyphenation feature. *Why?* *To further eliminate some of the rivers in the columns of the newsletter, you turn on Word's hyphenation feature so that words with multiple syllables are hyphenated at the end of lines instead of wrapped in their entirety to the next line.*

- Click the Change Hyphenation button (Layout tab | Page Setup group) to display the Change Hyphenation gallery (Figure 7–39).

Q&A What is the difference between Automatic and Manual hyphenation?

Automatic hyphenation places hyphens wherever words can break at a syllable in the document. With manual hyphenation, Word displays a dialog box for each word it could hyphenate, enabling you to accept or reject the proposed hyphenation.

Figure 7–39

- Click Automatic in the Change Hyphenation gallery to hyphenate the document (Figure 7–40).

Q&A What if I do not want a particular word hyphenated?

You can reword text, and Word will redo the hyphenation automatically.

Biometric devices verify a person's identity by translating a behavioral or physical personal characteristic, such as a fingerprint, into a digital code that is compared with a digital code stored in a computer or mobile device. If the digital code in the computer or mobile device does not match the personal characteristic code, the computer or mobile device denies access to the individual.¶

With the cost of fingerprint readers often *several words hyphenated in document* 100, some home ar ness users purchase fingerprint readers to verify the identity of users before they can access a computer. The reader also can be set up to perform different functions for different fingers; for example, one finger runs a program and a different finger shuts down the computer. External fingerprint readers usually plug into a USB port.¶

and airports o nition to prot mobile devic tion systems Face recogni becoming m and can recog without their jewelry, and v

▪ Hand Geo

Hand geomet the shape an hand. Because

Figure 7–40

To Format a Character as a Drop Cap

The first character in the feature article in this newsletter; that is, the capital letter B, is formatted as a drop cap. **Why?** *To add interest to an article, you often see a **drop cap**, which is a capital letter whose font size is larger than the rest of the characters in the paragraph.* In Word, the drop cap can sink into the first few lines of text, or it can extend into the left margin, which often is called a stick-up cap. In this newsletter, the paragraph text wraps around the drop cap.

The following steps create a drop cap in the first paragraph of the feature article in the newsletter.

- Position the insertion point somewhere in the first paragraph of the feature article.

- Display the Insert tab.

- Click the 'Add a Drop Cap' button (Insert tab | Text group) to display the Add a Drop Cap gallery (Figure 7–41).

Experiment

- Point to various commands in the Add a Drop Cap gallery to see a live preview of the drop cap formats in the document.

Figure 7–41

- Click Dropped in the Add a Drop Cap gallery to format the first letter in the paragraph containing the insertion point (the B in Biometric, in this case) as a drop cap and wrap subsequent text in the paragraph around the drop cap (Figure 7–42).

Q&A What is the outline around the drop cap in the document? When you format a letter as a drop cap, Word places a frame around it. A **frame** is a container for text that allows you to position the text anywhere on the page. Word formats a frame for the drop cap so that text wraps around it. The frame also contains a paragraph mark nonprinting character to the right of the drop cap, which may or may not be visible on your screen.

Figure 7–42

To Format the Drop Cap

The following step changes the font color of the drop cap.

① With the drop cap selected, display the Home tab and then change the font color of the drop cap to 'Orange, Accent 4, Darker 25%' (eighth color, fifth row) in Font Color gallery (shown in Figure 7–1a at the beginning of this module).

Q&A What if my frame no longer is displayed?
Click the drop cap to select it. Then, click the blue selection rectangle to display the frame.

To Insert a Next Page Section Break

1 CREATE NAMEPLATE FOR FIRST PAGE | **2 FORMAT FIRST PAGE** | 3 CREATE PULL-QUOTE
4 CREATE NAMEPLATE FOR SECOND PAGE | 5 FORMAT SECOND PAGE | 6 ADD PAGE BORDER

The third column on the first page of the newsletter is not a continuation of the feature article. *Why not? The third column, instead, contains several reader announcements. The feature article continues on the second page of the newsletter (shown in Figure 7–1b at the beginning of this module).* Thus, you must insert a next page section break, which is a section break that also contains a page break, at the bottom of the second column so that the remainder of the feature article moves to the second page. The following steps insert a next page section break in the second column.

- Position the insertion point at the location for the section break, in this case, to the left of the F in the Face Recognition System heading.

- Display the Layout tab.

- Click the 'Insert Page and Section Breaks' button (Layout tab | Page Setup group) to display the Insert Page and Section Breaks gallery (Figure 7–43).

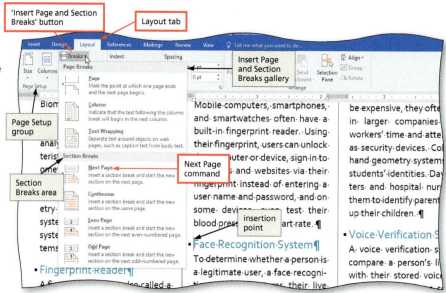

Figure 7–43

②

- In the Section Breaks area in the gallery, click Next Page to insert a next page section break, which positions the insertion point on the next page.

- If necessary, scroll to the bottom of the first page so that you can see the moved text (Figure 7–44).

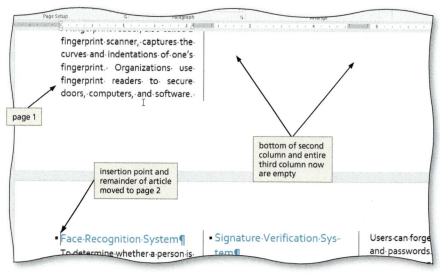

Figure 7–44

To Enter Text

The next step is to insert a jump-to line at the end of the second column, informing the reader where to look for the rest of the feature article. The following steps insert a jump-to line at the end of the text in the second column on the first page of the newsletter.

1 Scroll to display the end of the text in the second column of the first page of the newsletter and then position the insertion point to the left the paragraph mark that is to the left of the section break notation.

2 Press the ENTER key twice to insert a blank line for the jump-to text above the section break notation.

3 Press the UP ARROW key to position the insertion point on the blank line. If the blank line is formatted in the Heading 1 style, click the 'Clear All Formatting' button (Home tab | Font group) so that the entered text follows the Normal style.

4 Press CTRL+R to right align the paragraph mark. Press CTRL+I to turn on the italic format. Type **(Article continues on next page)** as the jump-to text and then press CTRL+I again to turn off the italic format.

To Insert a Column Break

1 CREATE NAMEPLATE FOR FIRST PAGE | 2 FORMAT FIRST PAGE | 3 CREATE PULL-QUOTE
4 CREATE NAMEPLATE FOR SECOND PAGE | 5 FORMAT SECOND PAGE | 6 ADD PAGE BORDER

In the *Security Trends* newsletters, for consistency, the reader announcements always begin at the top of the third column. If you insert the Security Trends Announcements at the current location of the insertion point, however, they will begin at the bottom of the second column. **Why?** *The insertion point currently is at the bottom of the second column.*

For the reader announcements to be displayed in the third column, you insert a **column break** at the bottom of the second column, which places the insertion point at the top of the next column. Thus, the following steps insert a column break at the bottom of the second column.

1

- Position the insertion point to the left of the paragraph mark on the line containing the next page section break, which is the location where the column break should be inserted.

- If necessary, display the Layout tab.

- Click the 'Insert Page and Section Breaks' button (Layout tab | Page Setup group) to display the Insert Page and Section Breaks gallery (Figure 7–45).

Figure 7–45

2

- Click Column in the Insert Page and Section Breaks gallery to insert a column break at the location of the insertion point and move the insertion point to the top of the next column (Figure 7–46).

Figure 7–46

What if I wanted to remove a column break?

You would double-click it to select it and then click the Cut button (Home tab | Clipboard group) or press the DELETE key.

Other Ways

1. Press CTRL+SHIFT+ENTER

To Insert a File in a Column of the Newsletter

So that you do not have to enter the entire third column of announcements in the newsletter, the next step in the project is to insert the file named Security Trends Announcements in the third column of the newsletter. This file contains the three announcements: the first about reader discounts, the second about an upcoming webinar, and the third about the topic of the next newsletter issue.

The Security Trends Announcements file is located on the Data Files. Please contact your instructor for information about accessing the Data Files. The following steps insert a file in a column of the newsletter.

1 With the insertion point at the top of the third column, display the Insert tab.

2 Click the Object arrow (Insert tab | Text group) to display the Object menu and then click 'Text from File' on the Object menu to display the Insert File dialog box.

3 Navigate to the location of the file to be inserted (in this case, the Data Files folder).

4 Click Security Trends Announcements to select the file.

5 Click the Insert button (Insert File dialog box) to insert the file, Security Trends Announcements, in the document at the location of the insertion point.

Q&A What if text from the announcements column spills onto the second page of the newsletter?

You will format text in the announcements column so that all of its text fits in the third column of the first page.

6 Press SHIFT+F5 to return the insertion point to the last editing location, in this case, the top of the third column on the first page of the newsletter (Figure 7–47).

7 Save the newsletter again on the same storage location with the same file name.

Figure 7–47

Creating a Pull-Quote

A pull-quote is text pulled, or copied, from the text of the document and given graphical emphasis so that it stands apart and commands the reader's attention. The newsletter in this project copies text from the first page of the newsletter and places it in a pull-quote, also on the first page between the first and second columns (shown in Figure 7–1a at the beginning of this module).

What guidelines should you follow when using pull-quotes?

Because of their bold emphasis, pull-quotes should be used sparingly in a newsletter. Pull-quotes are useful for breaking the monotony of long columns of text. Typically, quotation marks are used only if you are quoting someone directly. If you use quotation marks, use curly (or smart) quotation marks instead of straight quotation marks.

To create the pull-quote in this newsletter, follow this general procedure:

1. Create a **text box**, which is a container for text that allows you to position the text anywhere on the page.

2. Copy the text from the existing document to the Office Clipboard and then paste the text from the Office Clipboard to the text box.

3. Resize and format the text box.

4. Move the text box to the desired location.

To Insert a Text Box

1 CREATE NAMEPLATE FOR FIRST PAGE | 2 FORMAT FIRST PAGE | 3 CREATE PULL-QUOTE
4 CREATE NAMEPLATE FOR SECOND PAGE | 5 FORMAT SECOND PAGE | 6 ADD PAGE BORDER

The first step in creating the pull-quote is to insert a text box. A text box is like a frame; the difference is that a text box has more graphical formatting options than does a frame. The following steps insert a built-in text box. **Why?** *Word provides a variety of built-in text boxes, saving you the time of formatting the text box.*

- Click the 'Choose a Text Box' button (Insert tab | Text group) to display the Choose a Text Box gallery.

Experiment

- Scroll through the Choose a Text Box gallery to see the variety of available text box styles.

- Scroll to display Simple Quote in the Choose a Text Box gallery (Figure 7–48).

Figure 7–48

- Click Simple Quote in the Choose a Text Box gallery to insert that style of text box in the document.

- If necessary, drag the text box to the approximate location shown in Figure 7–49.

Figure 7–49

Does my text box need to be in the exact same location as in Figure 7–49?

No. You will move the text box later.

The layout of the first page is not correct because of the text box. What do I do?

You will enter text in the text box and then position it in the correct location. At that time, the layout of the first page will be fixed.

Other Ways

1. Click 'Explore Quick Parts' button (Insert tab | Text group), click 'Building Blocks Organizer' on Explore Quick Parts menu, select desired text box name in Building blocks list, click Insert button

To Split the Window

1 CREATE NAMEPLATE FOR FIRST PAGE | 2 FORMAT FIRST PAGE | **3 CREATE PULL-QUOTE**
4 CREATE NAMEPLATE FOR SECOND PAGE | 5 FORMAT SECOND PAGE | 6 ADD PAGE BORDER

The text that you will copy for the pull-quote is in the middle of the first page on the newsletter and the pull-quote (text box) is near the top of the first page of the newsletter. Thus, the next step is to copy the pull-quote text from the middle of the first page and then paste it in the pull-quote at the top of the first page. You would like to view the pull-quote and the text to be copied on the screen at the same time. *Why? Viewing both simultaneously will simplify the copying and pasting process.*

Word allows you to split the window in two separate panes, each containing the current document and having its own scroll bar. This enables you to scroll to and view two different portions of the same document at the same time. The following step splits the Word window.

- Display the View tab.

- Click the Split Window button (View tab | Window group) to divide the document window in two separate panes — both the upper and lower panes display the current document (Figure 7–50).

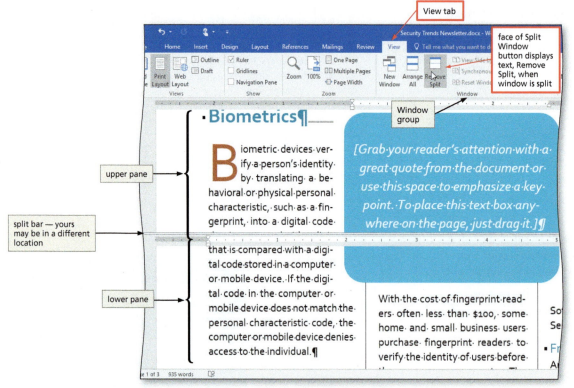

Figure 7–50

Other Ways

1. Press ALT+CTRL+S

TO ARRANGE ALL OPEN WORD DOCUMENTS ON THE SCREEN

If you have multiple Word documents open and want to view all of them at the same time on the screen, you can instruct Word to arrange all the open documents on the screen from top to bottom. If you wanted to arrange all open Word documents on the same screen, you would perform the following steps.

1. Click the Arrange All button (View tab | Window group) to display each open Word document on the screen.

2. To make one of the arranged documents fill the entire screen again, maximize the window by clicking its Maximize button or double-clicking its title bar.

To Copy and Paste Using Split Windows

1 CREATE NAMEPLATE FOR FIRST PAGE | 2 FORMAT FIRST PAGE | 3 CREATE PULL-QUOTE
4 CREATE NAMEPLATE FOR SECOND PAGE | 5 FORMAT SECOND PAGE | 6 ADD PAGE BORDER

The following steps copy text from the middle of the first page of the newsletter to the Clipboard (the source) and then paste the text into the text box (the destination) at the top of the newsletter. *Why?* *The item being copied is called the* **source**. *The location to which you are pasting is called the* **destination**.

- In the upper pane, scroll so that all placeholder text in the text box is visible, as shown in Figure 7–51.

- In the lower pane, scroll to display the text to be copied, as shown in Figure 7–51, and then select the text to be copied: Biometric devices grant access to programs, mobile devices, computers, or rooms using computer analysis of some personal characteristic.

- Display the Home tab.

- Click the Copy button (Home tab | Clipboard group) to copy the selected text to the Clipboard (Figure 7–51).

Figure 7–51

- In the upper pane, if necessary, scroll to display the text in the text box. Click the text in the text box to select it.

- Click the Paste arrow (Home tab | Clipboard group) to display the Paste menu.

Q&A What if I click the Paste button by mistake?
Click the Paste Options button to the right of the pasted text in the text box to display the Paste Options menu.

- Point to the Merge Formatting button on the Paste menu and notice the text box shows a live preview of the selected paste option (Figure 7–52).

Figure 7–52

Q&A Why select the Merge Formatting button on the Paste menu?
You want the pasted text to use the formats that were in the text box (the destination) instead of the formats of the copied text (the source).

- Click the Merge Formatting button on the Paste menu to paste the copied text into the text box.

Q&A Why does a hyphen appear in the source?
Word may have hyphenated the word automatically. You will format the pull-quote text next.

Other Ways

1. Click copy on shortcut menu (or, if using touch, tap Copy on mini toolbar), right-click where item is to be pasted, click 'Keep Source Formatting' in Paste Options area on shortcut menu (or, if using touch, tap Paste on mini toolbar)

2. Select text to copy, press CTRL+C; select destination for pasted text, press CTRL+V

To Remove a Split Window

The next step is to remove the split window so that you can position the pull-quote. The following step removes a split window.

1. Double-click the split bar (shown in Figure 7–52), or click the Split Window button again (View tab | Window group), or press ALT+SHIFT+C, to remove the split window and return to a single Word window on the screen.

To Format Text in the Text Box

The next steps format text in the pull-quote.

1. If necessary, scroll to display the text box in the document window.

2. Select all the text in the text box, change its font to Century Schoolbook (or a similar font), bold the text, and change its font size to 11 point. If necessary, center this paragraph.

3. Click in the text box to deselect the text, but leave the text box selected (shown in Figure 7–53).

BTW
Rotating Text Box Text
To rotate text in a text box, select the text box, click the Text Direction button (Drawing Tools Format tab | Text group), and then click the desired direction on the Text Direction menu.

To Resize a Text Box

The next step in formatting the pull-quote is to resize the text box. You resize a text box the same way as any other object. That is, you drag its sizing handles or enter values in the height and width boxes through the Size button (Drawing Tools Format tab | Size group). The following steps resize the text box and insert line break characters.

1. Drag the sizing handles so that the pull-quote looks about the same size as Figure 7–53.

2. Verify the pull-quote dimensions in the Shape Height and Shape Width boxes (Drawing Tools Format tab | Size group) and, if necessary, change the value in the Shape Height box to 1.75 and the Shape Width box to 2.08.

Q&A What if some of the words in the text box are hyphenated?
Insert line break characters to eliminate any hyphenated words in the text box; that is, position the insertion point to the left of the first letter in the hyphenated word and then press SHIFT+ENTER to insert a line break character, which places the entire word on the next line and removes the hyphen.

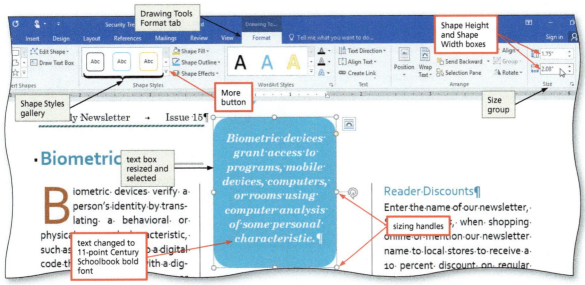

Figure 7–53

To Apply a Shape Style to a Text Box

The next step in formatting the pull-quote is to apply a shape style to the text box to coordinate its colors with the rest of the newsletter. The following steps apply a shape style to a text box.

① With the text box still selected, click the More button (shown in Figure 7–53) in the Shape Styles gallery (Drawing Tools Format tab | Shape Styles group) to expand the gallery.

② Point to 'Colored Fill - Orange, Accent 4' (fifth style, second row) in the Shape Styles gallery to display a live preview of that style applied to the text box (Figure 7–54).

③ Click 'Colored Fill - Orange, Accent 4' in the Shape Styles gallery to apply the selected style to the shape.

BTW

Text Box Styles
Like other drawing objects or pictures, text boxes can be formatted or have styles applied. You can change the fill in a text box by clicking the Shape Fill button or arrow (Drawing Tools Format tab | Shape Styles group), add an outline to a text box by clicking the Shape Outline button or arrow (Drawing Tools Format tab | Shape Styles group), and apply an effect, such as shadow or 3-D effects, by clicking the Shape Effects button (Drawing Tools Format tab | Shape Styles group).

Figure 7–54

To Position a Text Box

The following steps move the text box to the desired location in the newsletter.

① With the text box still selected, drag the text box to its new location (Figure 7–55). You may need to drag and/or resize the text box a couple of times so that it looks similar to this figure.

BTW
Moving Text Boxes
To move a text box using the keyboard, select the text box and then press the arrow keys on the keyboard. For example, each time you press the down arrow key, the selected text box moves down one line.

Figure 7–55

2 Click outside the text box to remove the selection.

Q&A Why does my text wrap differently around the text box?
Differences in wordwrap often relate to the printer used by your computer. Thus, your document may wordwrap around the text box differently.

3 If the jump-to line, which is supposed to appear at the bottom of the second column (shown in Figure 7–56), moved to the top of the third column, position the insertion point in the article title (Biometrics) and decrease the spacing before and after (Layout tab) until the jump-to line moves back to the bottom of the second column.

4 Save the newsletter again on the same storage location with the same file name.

Break Point: If you wish to take a break, this is a good place to do so. You can exit Word now. To resume at a later time, run Word, open the file called Security Trends Newsletter, and continue following the steps from this location forward.

Formatting the Second Page of the Newsletter

The second page of the newsletter (shown in Figure 7–1b at the beginning of this module) continues the feature article that began in the first two columns on the first page. The nameplate on the second page is less elaborate than the one on the first page of the newsletter. In addition to the text in the feature article, page two contains a graphic. The following sections format the second page of the newsletter in this project.

CONSIDER THIS

How do you create a nameplate for inner pages of a newsletter?
The top of the inner pages of a newsletter may or may not have a nameplate. If you choose to create one for your inner pages, it should not be the same as, or compete with, the one on the first page. Inner page nameplates usually contain only a portion of the nameplate from the first page of a newsletter.

To Change Column Formatting

1 CREATE NAMEPLATE FOR FIRST PAGE | 2 FORMAT FIRST PAGE | 3 CREATE PULL-QUOTE
4 CREATE NAMEPLATE FOR SECOND PAGE | 5 FORMAT SECOND PAGE | 6 ADD PAGE BORDER

The document currently is formatted in three columns. The nameplate at the top of the second page, however, should be in a single column. **Why?** *The nameplate should span across the top of the three columns below it.* The next step, then, is to change the number of columns at the top of the second page from three to one.

As discussed earlier in this project, Word requires a new section each time you change the number of columns in a document. Thus, you first must insert a continuous section break and then format the section to one column so that the nameplate can be entered on the second page of the newsletter. The following steps insert a continuous section break and then change the column format.

1

- If you have a blank page between the first and second pages of the newsletter, position the insertion point to the left of the paragraph mark at the end of the third column on the first page of the newsletter and then press the DELETE key as many times as necessary to delete the blank line causing the overflow.

- Position the insertion point at the upper-left corner of the second page of the newsletter (to the left of F in Face).

- Display the Layout tab.

- Click the 'Insert Page and Section Breaks' button (Layout tab | Page Setup group) to display the Insert Page and Section Breaks gallery (Figure 7–56).

Figure 7–56

2

- Click Continuous in the Insert Page and Section Breaks gallery to insert a continuous section break above the insertion point.

- Press the UP ARROW key to position the insertion point to the left of the continuous section break just inserted.

- Click the 'Add or Remove Columns' button (Layout tab | Page Setup group) to display the Add or Remove Columns gallery (Figure 7–57).

Figure 7–57

3

- Click One in the Add or Remove Columns gallery to format the current section to one column, which now is ready for the second page nameplate.

- If necessary, scroll to display the bottom of the first page and the top of the second page, so that you can see the varying columns in the newsletter (Figure 7–58).

Q&A Can I change the column format of existing text?

Yes. If you already have typed text and would like it to be formatted in a different number of columns, select the text, click the 'Add or Remove Columns' button (Layout tab | Page Setup group), and then click the number of columns desired in the Add or Remove Columns gallery. Word automatically creates a new section for the newly formatted columns.

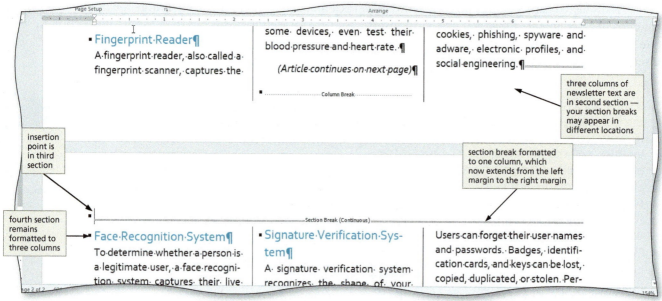

- Fingerprint·Reader¶

A·fingerprint·reader,·also·called·a·fingerprint·scanner,·captures·the·

some· devices,· even· test· their· blood·pressure·and·heart·rate.·¶

(Article·continues·on·next·page)¶

Column Break

cookies,· phishing,· spyware· and· adware,· electronic· profiles,· and· social·engineering.·¶

three columns of newsletter text are in second section — your section breaks may appear in different locations

insertion point is in third section

section break formatted to one column, which now extends from the left margin to the right margin

fourth section remains formatted to three columns

Section Break (Continuous)

Face·Recognition·System¶

To·determine·whether·a·person·is·a·legitimate·user,·a·face·recogni-tion·system·captures·their·live·

- Signature·Verification·Sys-tem¶

A· signature· verification· system· recognizes· the· shape· of· your·

Users·can·forget·their·user·names· and· passwords.· Badges,· identifi-cation·cards,·and·keys·can·be·lost,· copied,·duplicated,·or·stolen.·Per-

Figure 7–58

To Set Custom Tab Stops Using the Tabs Dialog Box

The nameplate on the second page of the newsletter contains the text, Monthly Newsletter, at the left margin, the newsletter title in the center, and the issue number at the right margin (shown in Figure 7–1a at the beginning of this module). To properly align the text in the center and at the right margin, you will set custom tab stops at these locations. The following steps set custom tab stops.

1 Press the ENTER key twice and then position the insertion point on the first line of the second page of the newsletter, which is the paragraph to be formatted with the custom tab stops.

2 Display the Home tab and then click the 'Clear All Formatting' button (Home tab | Font group) to apply the Normal style to the first line on the second page of the newsletter.

3 Click the Paragraph Settings Dialog Box Launcher (Home tab | Paragraph group) to display the Paragraph dialog box and then click the Tabs button (Paragraph dialog box) to display the Tabs dialog box.

4 Type 3.5 in the Tab stop position text box (Tabs dialog box), click Center in the Alignment area to specify the tab stop alignment, and then click the Set button to set the custom tab stop.

5 Type 7 in the Tab stop position text box (Tabs dialog box), click Right in the Alignment area to specify the tab stop alignment, and then click the Set button to set the custom tab stop (Figure 7–59).

6 Click the OK button to set custom tab stops using the specified alignments.

Figure 7–59

To Format and Enter Text and Add a Border

BTW
Leader Characters
Leader characters, such as a series of dots, often are used in a table of contents to precede page numbers. Four types of leader characters, which Word places in the space occupied by a tab character, are available in the Leader area of the Tabs dialog box (shown in Figure 7–59).

The following steps enter the newsletter title at the top of the second page in the third section.

1 With the insertion point on the first line of the second page of the newsletter, click the Font Color arrow and then change the font color of the current text to 'Teal, Accent 5, Darker 50%' (ninth column, bottom row). Change the font to Century Schoolbook (or a similar font) and then type **Monthly Newsletter** at the left margin.

If requested by your instructor, enter your name instead of the word, Monthly.

2 Press the TAB key to advance the insertion point to the centered tab stop. Increase the font size to 14 point and then click the Bold button (Home tab | Font group) to bold the text. Type **Security Trends** at the centered tab stop.

3 Press the TAB key to advance the insertion point to the right-aligned tab stop. Reduce the font size to 11 point and then click the Bold button (Home tab | Font group) to turn off the bold format. Type **Issue 15** at the right-aligned tab stop.

4 Click the Borders button (Home tab | Paragraph group) to add a bottom border (shown in Figure 7–60).

Q&A Why is the border formatted already?
When you define a custom border, Word uses that custom border the next time you click the Borders button in the Borders gallery.

To Enter Text

The second page of the feature article on the second page of this newsletter begins with a jump-from line (the continued message) immediately below the nameplate. The next steps enter the jump-from line.

1 Position the insertion point on the blank line above the heading, Face Recognition System, to the left of the paragraph mark.

2 Click the 'Clear All Formatting' button (Home tab | Font group) to apply the Normal style to the location of the insertion point.

3 Press CTRL+I to turn on the italic format.

4 Type **(Continued from first page)** and then press CTRL+I to turn off the italic format (Figure 7–60).

Figure 7–60

To Balance Columns

Currently, the text on the second page of the newsletter completely fills up the first and second columns and almost fills the third column. The text in the three columns should consume the same amount of vertical space. **Why?** *Typically, the text in columns of a newsletter is balanced.* To balance columns, you insert a continuous section break at the end of the text. The following steps balance columns.

- Scroll to the bottom of the text in the third column on the second page of the newsletter and then position the insertion point at the end of the text.

- If an extra paragraph mark is below the last line of text, press the DELETE key to remove the extra paragraph mark.

- Display the Layout tab.

- Click the 'Insert Page and Section Breaks' button (Layout tab | Page Setup group) to display the Insert Page and Section Breaks gallery (Figure 7–61).

Figure 7–61

- Click Continuous in the Insert Page and Section Breaks gallery to insert a continuous section break, which balances the columns on the second page of the newsletter (Figure 7–62).

- Save the newsletter again on the same storage location with the same file name.

Figure 7–62

Modifying and Formatting a SmartArt Graphic

Recall from Module 4 that Microsoft Office includes **SmartArt graphics**, which are visual representations of ideas. Many different types of SmartArt graphics are available, allowing you to choose one that illustrates your message best.

In this newsletter, a SmartArt graphic is positioned on the second page, at the top of the second column. Because the columns are small in the newsletter, it is best to work with a SmartArt graphic in a separate document window so that you easily can see all of its components. When finished editing the graphic, you can copy and paste it in the newsletter. You will follow these steps for the SmartArt graphic in this newsletter:

1. Open the document that contains the SmartArt graphic for the newsletter.
2. Modify the layout of the graphic.
3. Add a shape and text to the graphic.
4. Format a shape and the graphic.
5. Copy and paste the graphic in the newsletter.
6. Resize the graphic and position it in the desired location.

To Open a Document from Word

The first draft of the SmartArt graphic is in a file called Biometrics Diagram on the Data Files. Please contact your instructor for information about accessing the Data Files. The following steps open the Biometrics Diagram file.

1 Navigate to the location of the Data Files on your hard drive, OneDrive, or other storage location.

2 Open the file named Biometrics Diagram on the Data Files.

3 Click the graphic to select it and display the SmartArt Tools Design and Format tabs (Figure 7–63).

Q&A Is the *Security Trends* Newsletter file still open?
Yes. Leave it open because you will copy the modified diagram to the second page of the newsletter.

Figure 7–63

To Change the Layout of a SmartArt Graphic

The following step changes the layout of an existing SmartArt graphic. *Why? The SmartArt graphic currently uses the Radial Cycle layout, and this newsletter uses the Basic Radial layout.*

1

- If necessary, display the SmartArt Tools Design tab.

- Scroll through the layouts in the Layouts gallery until Basic Radial appears, if necessary, and then click Basic Radial to change the layout of the SmartArt graphic (Figure 7–64).

Figure 7–64

Other Ways

1. Right-click the selected graphic, click Layout button on mini toolbar and select desired layout, or click Change Layout on shortcut menu, select desired layout, click OK button

To Add a Shape to a SmartArt Graphic

The current SmartArt graphic has five perimeter shapes. This newsletter has a sixth shape. The following step adds a shape to a SmartArt graphic.

Figure 7–65

1 With the diagram selected, click the Add Shape button (SmartArt Tools Design tab | Create Graphic group) to add a shape to the SmartArt graphic (Figure 7–65).

Q&A Why did my screen display a menu instead of adding a shape?
You clicked the Add Shape arrow instead of the Add Shape button. Clicking the Add Shape button adds the shape automatically; clicking the Add Shape arrow displays a menu allowing you to specify the location of the shape.

How do I delete a shape?
Select the shape by clicking it and then press the DELETE key, or right-click the shape and then click Cut on the mini toolbar or shortcut menu.

To Add Text to a SmartArt Graphic through the Text Pane

1 CREATE NAMEPLATE FOR FIRST PAGE | 2 FORMAT FIRST PAGE | 3 CREATE PULL-QUOTE
4 CREATE NAMEPLATE FOR SECOND PAGE | 5 FORMAT SECOND PAGE | 6 ADD PAGE BORDER

In Module 4, you added text directly to the shapes in a SmartArt graphic. In this project, you enter the text through the Text Pane. **Why?** *Some users prefer to enter text in the Text Pane instead of in the shape.* The following steps use the Text Pane to add text to a shape.

1
- Click the Text Pane control, which is on the left side of the SmartArt graphic, to display the Text Pane to the left of the SmartArt graphic.

2
- In the Text Pane, if necessary, position the insertion point to the right of the bullet that has no text to its right.
- Type **iris or retina** as the text for the shape (Figure 7–66).

3
- Click the Close button in the Text Pane to close the Text Pane.

Figure 7–66

Q&A Can I instead close the Text Pane by clicking the Text Pane button (SmartArt Tools Design tab | Create Graphic group)? Yes.

- Save the file containing the SmartArt graphic with a new file name on your hard drive, OneDrive, or other storage location using Biometrics Diagram Modified as the file name.

Other Ways

1. Click Text Pane button (SmartArt Tools Design tab | Create Graphic group)

To Format SmartArt Graphic Text

To format text in an entire SmartArt graphic, select the graphic and then apply the format. The following steps bold the text in the SmartArt graphic.

1 If necessary, click the shape just added to select it.

2 Display the Home tab. Click the Bold button (Home tab | Font group) to bold the text in the SmartArt graphic (shown in Figure 7–67).

TO MODIFY THEME EFFECTS

If you wanted to change the look of graphics, such as SmartArt graphics, you would perform the following steps to change the theme effects.

1. Click the Theme Effects button (Design tab | Document Formatting group).

2. Click the desired effect in the Theme Effects gallery.

TO SAVE CUSTOMIZED THEMES

When you modify the theme effects, theme colors, or theme fonts, you can save the modified theme for future use. If you wanted to save a customized theme, you would perform the following steps.

1. Click the Themes button (Design tab | Document Formatting group) to display the Themes gallery.

BTW

Demoting Text Pane Text
Instead of pressing the TAB key in the Text Pane, you could click the Demote Selection button (SmartArt Tools Design tab | Create Graphic group) to increase (or move to the right) the indent for a bulleted item. You also can click the Promote Selection button (SmartArt Tools Design tab | Create Graphic group) to decrease (or move to the left) the indent for a bulleted item.

BTW

Clipboard Task Pane and Icon
You can control when the Clipboard task pane appears on the Word screen and the Office Clipboard icon appears in the notification area on the taskbar. To do this, first display the Clipboard task pane by clicking the Clipboard Dialog Box Launcher on the Home tab. Next, click the Options button at the bottom of the Clipboard task pane and then click the desired option on the menu. For example, if you want to be able to open the Clipboard task pane by clicking the Office Clipboard icon on the Windows taskbar, click 'Show Office Clipboard Icon on Taskbar' on the Options menu.

2. Click 'Save Current Theme' in the Themes gallery.

3. Enter a theme name in the File name box (Save Current Theme dialog box).

4. Click the Save button to add the saved theme to the Themes gallery.

Copying and Pasting

The next step is to copy the SmartArt graphic from this document window and then paste it in the newsletter. To copy from one document and paste into another, you can use the Office Clipboard. Through the Office Clipboard, you can copy multiple items from any Office document and then paste them into the same or another Office document by following these general guidelines:

1. Items are copied *from* a **source document**. If the source document is not the active document, display it in the document window.

2. Open the Office Clipboard task pane and then copy items from the source document to the Office Clipboard.

3. Items are copied *to* a **destination document**. If the destination document is not the active document, display the destination document in the document window.

4. Paste items from the Office Clipboard to the destination document.

To Copy a SmartArt Graphic Using the Office Clipboard

1 CREATE NAMEPLATE FOR FIRST PAGE | 2 FORMAT FIRST PAGE | 3 CREATE PULL-QUOTE
4 CREATE NAMEPLATE FOR SECOND PAGE | 5 FORMAT SECOND PAGE | 6 ADD PAGE BORDER

The following step copies the SmartArt graphic to the Office Clipboard. *Why? Sometimes you want to copy multiple items to the Office Clipboard through the Clipboard task pane and then paste them later.*

- Click the Clipboard Dialog Box Launcher (Home tab | Clipboard group) to open the Clipboard task pane.

- If the Office Clipboard in the Clipboard task pane is not empty, click the Clear All button in the Clipboard task pane.

- With the SmartArt graphic selected in the document window, click the Copy button (Home tab | Clipboard group) to copy the selected text to the Clipboard (Figure 7–67).

Figure 7–67

Other Ways

1. With Clipboard task pane open, right-click selected item, click Copy on mini toolbar or shortcut menu

2. With Clipboard task pane open and item to copy selected, press CTRL+C

To Switch from One Open Document to Another

1 CREATE NAMEPLATE FOR FIRST PAGE | 2 FORMAT FIRST PAGE | 3 CREATE PULL-QUOTE
4 CREATE NAMEPLATE FOR SECOND PAGE | 5 FORMAT SECOND PAGE | 6 ADD PAGE BORDER

The following steps switch from the open Biometrics Diagram Modified document (the source document) to the open Security Trends Newsletter document (the destination document). *Why? You want to paste the copied diagram into the newsletter document.*

1

- Point to the Word app button on the taskbar to display a live preview of the open documents or window titles of the open documents, depending on your computer's configuration (Figure 7–68).

Figure 7–68

2

- Click the live preview of the Security Trends Newsletter on the Windows taskbar to display the selected document in the document window (shown in Figure 7–69).

Other Ways

1. Click Switch Windows button (View tab | Window group), click document name

2. Press ALT+TAB

To Paste from the Office Clipboard

1 CREATE NAMEPLATE FOR FIRST PAGE | 2 FORMAT FIRST PAGE | 3 CREATE PULL-QUOTE
4 CREATE NAMEPLATE FOR SECOND PAGE | 5 FORMAT SECOND PAGE | 6 ADD PAGE BORDER

The following steps paste from the Office Clipboard. **Why?** *You want to paste the copied SmartArt graphic into the destination document, in this case, the newsletter document.*

1

- Position the insertion point at the end of the first paragraph at the top of the second column on the second page of the newsletter.

- If the Clipboard task pane is not open on the screen, display the Home tab and then click the Clipboard Dialog Box Launcher (Home tab | Clipboard group) to open the Clipboard task pane.

- Click the SmartArt graphic entry in the Office Clipboard to paste it in the document at the location of the insertion point (Figure 7–69).

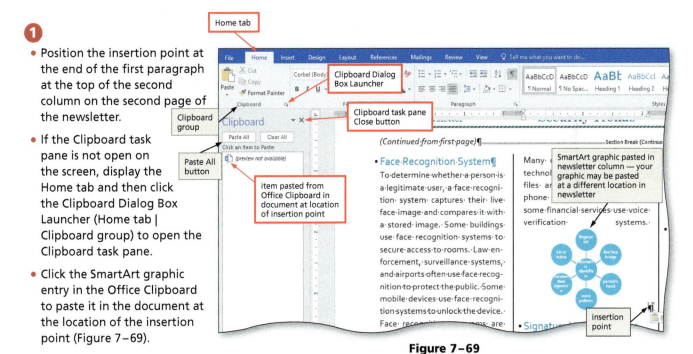

Figure 7–69

Q&A

What if my pasted graphic is in a different location?
The location of your graphic may differ. You will move the graphic in the next steps.

Does the destination document have to be a different document?
No. The source and destination documents can be the same document.

What is the function of the Paste All button?
If you have multiple items on the Office Clipboard, it pastes all items in a row, without any characters between them, at the location of the insertion point or selection.

- Click the Close button in the Clipboard task pane.

Other Ways

1. With Clipboard task pane open, right-click selected item, click Paste on shortcut menu
2. With Clipboard task pane open, press CTRL+V

To Format a Graphic as Floating

The text in the newsletter should wrap tightly around the graphic; that is, the text should conform to the graphic's shape. Thus, the next step is to change the graphic from inline to floating with a wrapping style of tight. The following steps format the graphic as floating with tight wrapping.

1 Click the SmartArt graphic to select it.

2 With the SmartArt graphic selected, click the Layout Options button that is attached to the graphic to display the Layout Options gallery.

3 Click Tight in the Layout Options gallery to change the graphic from inline to floating with tight wrapping.

4 Close the Layout Options gallery.

To Format and Position the SmartArt Graphic

The next tasks are to change the color of the graphic, increase its size, and then position it at the top of the second column on the second page. The following steps format and then position the graphic.

1 With the graphic selected, click the Change Colors button (SmartArt Design tab | SmartArt Styles group) and then click 'Colored Fill - Accent 4'.

2 Drag the sizing handles outward until the graphic is approximately the same size as shown in Figure 7–70, which has a height of 3.32" and a width of 4.25". (Verify the dimensions of the graphic in the Height and Width boxes (SmartArt Tools Format tab | Size group)).

3 Drag the edge of the graphic to the location shown in Figure 7–70. You may have to drag the graphic a couple of times to position it similarly to the figure.

4 If the newsletter spills onto a third page, reduce the size of the SmartArt graphic. You may need to delete an extra paragraph mark at the end of the document, as well.

TO LAYER THE SMARTART GRAPHIC IN FRONT OF TEXT

In Word, you can layer objects on top of or behind other objects. If you wanted to layer the SmartArt graphic on top of all text, you would perform the following steps.

1. Click the SmartArt graphic to select it. Click the Bring Forward arrow (SmartArt Tools Format tab | Arrange group) to display the Bring Forward menu.

2. Click 'Bring in Front of Text' on the Bring Forward menu to position the selected object on top of all text.

To Edit Wrap Points in an Object

In Word, you can change how text wraps around an object, called editing wrap points. The following steps edit the wrap points in the SmartArt diagram at the top of the second page of the newsletter. *Why? You want to ensure that text starts on a complete line below the bottom of the graphic.*

1

- If necessary, click the SmartArt graphic to select it. Click the Wrap Text button (SmartArt Tools Format tab | Arrange group) to display the Wrap Text menu (Figure 7–70).

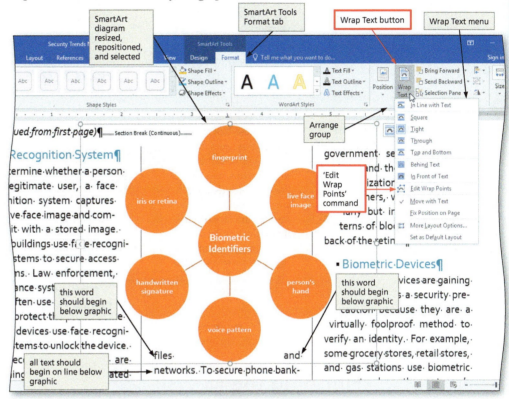

Figure 7–70

2

- Click 'Edit Wrap Points' on the Wrap Text menu to display wrap points around the graphic.

- Position the pointer on the black wrap point to the lower-left of the shape in the diagram containing the text, voice pattern, as shown in Figure 7–71, so that the pointer changes to a four-headed dot.

Figure 7–71

- Drag the black wrap point to the lower-left of the graphic as shown in Figure 7–72, so that the text (the word, files, in this case) will appear on a complete line below the shape.

Figure 7–72

- Drag the black wrap point to the lower-right of the graphic as shown in Figure 7–73, so that the text begins on a complete line below the graphic.

- Click outside the graphic so that it no longer is selected.

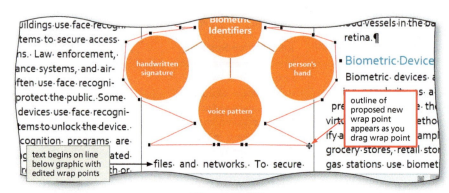

Figure 7–73

Finishing the Newsletter

With the text and graphics in the newsletter entered and formatted, the next step is to view the newsletter as a whole and determine if it looks finished in its current state. To give the newsletter a finished appearance, you will add a border to its edges.

BTW

Distributing a Document

Instead of printing and distributing a hard copy of a document, you can distribute the document electronically. Options include sending the document via email; posting it on cloud storage (such as OneDrive) and sharing the file with others; posting it on social media, a blog, or other website; and sharing a link associated with an online location of the document. You also can create and share a PDF or XPS image of the document, so that users can view the file in Adobe Reader or XPS Viewer instead of in Word.

To Adjust Headings, Turn Off Formatting Marks, and Zoom Multiple Pages

The last step in formatting the newsletter is to place a border around its edges. First, you remove a hyphen from a heading by adding a line break. Then, you turn off formatting marks to remove the clutter from the screen, and you place both pages in the document window at once so that you can see all the page borders applied. The following steps add a line break, turn off formatting marks, and zoom multiple pages.

1. If necessary, scroll below the SmartArt graphic to display the Signature Verification System heading. To remove the hyphen in the word, System, place the insertion point to the left of the S and then press SHIFT+ENTER to create a line break and move the entire word, System, to the next line (shown in Figure 7–74).

2. If necessary, display the Home tab and then turn off formatting marks.

3. Display the View tab and then display multiple pages on the screen. You may need to increase the zoom slightly so that the borders in the nameplates appear.

1 CREATE NAMEPLATE FOR FIRST PAGE | 2 FORMAT FIRST PAGE | 3 CREATE PULL-QUOTE
4 CREATE NAMEPLATE FOR SECOND PAGE | 5 FORMAT SECOND PAGE | 6 ADD PAGE BORDER

To Add an Art Page Border

The following steps add a page border around the pages of the newsletter. *Why? This newsletter has a teal art border around the perimeter of each page.*

 1

- Display the Design tab.

- Click the 'Borders and Shading' button (Design tab | Page Background group) to display the Borders and Shading dialog box. If necessary, click the Page Border tab.

Q&A

What if I cannot select the 'Borders and Shading' button because it is dimmed?
Click somewhere in the newsletter to make the newsletter the active document and then repeat Step 1.

 2

- Click Box in the Setting area (Borders and Shading dialog box) to specify a border on all four sides of the page.

- Click the Art arrow, scroll to and then click the art border shown in Figure 7–74.

- Click the Color arrow and then click 'Teal, Accent 5, Darker 50%' (bottom row, ninth column) on the palette (Figure 7–74).

Figure 7–74

3

- Click the OK button to place the defined border on each page of the newsletter (Figure 7–75).

Figure 7–75

BTW

Conserving Ink and Toner

If you want to conserve ink or toner, you can instruct Word to print draft quality documents by clicking File on the ribbon to open the Backstage view, clicking the Options tab in the Backstage view to display the Word Options dialog box, clicking Advanced in the left pane (Word Options dialog box), scrolling to the Print area in the right pane, placing a check mark in the 'Use draft quality' check box, and then clicking the OK button. Then, use the Backstage view to print the document as usual.

To Save, Print, and Exit Word

The newsletter now is complete. You should save the document, print it, and then exit Word.

1 Save the newsletter again on the same storage location with the same file name.

2 If desired, print the newsletter (shown in Figure 7–1 at the beginning of this module).

Q&A

What if an error message appears about margins?
Depending on the printer you are using, you may need to set the margins differently for this project.

What if one or more of the borders do not print?
Click the 'Borders and Shading' button (Design tab | Page Background group), click the Options button (Borders and Shading dialog box), click the Measure from arrow and click Text, change the four text boxes to 15 pt, and then click the OK button in each dialog box. Try printing the document again. If the borders still do not print, adjust the text boxes in the dialog box to a number smaller than 15 pt.

3 Exit Word, closing all open documents.

Summary

In this module, you have learned how to create a professional-looking newsletter using Word's desktop publishing features such as the following: inserting and modifying WordArt, organizing a document in columns, adding horizontal and vertical rules, inserting and formatting pull-quotes, inserting and formatting graphics, and adding an art page border.

CONSIDER THIS: PLAN AHEAD

What decisions will you need to make when creating your next newsletter?
Use these guidelines as you complete the assignments in this module and create your own newsletters outside of this class.

1. Create the nameplate.

   a) Determine the location of the nameplate.

   b) Determine content, formats, and arrangement of text and graphics.

   c) If appropriate, use ruling lines.

2. Determine content for the body of the newsletter.

   a) Write the body copy.

   b) Organize the body copy in columns.

   c) Format the body copy and subheads.

   d) Incorporate color.

   e) Divide sections with vertical rules.

   f) Enhance with visuals.

3. Bind and distribute the newsletter.

   a) Determine if newsletters should be printed, posted on bulletin boards, sent as an email message, or posted on websites.

   b) For multipage newsletters that will be printed, determine the appropriate method of binding the pages.

   c) For online newsletters, select a format that most users will be able to open.

Apply Your Knowledge

Reinforce the skills and apply the concepts you learned in this module.

Working with Desktop Publishing Elements of a Newsletter

Note: To complete this assignment, you will be required to use the Data Files. Please contact your instructor for information about accessing the Data Files.

Instructions: Run Word. Open the document named Apply 7–1 Energy Saver Newsletter Draft from the Data Files. The document contains a newsletter that you are to modify so that it appears as shown in Figure 7–76.

Perform the following tasks:

1. Change the WordArt shape to Chevron Down.

2. Turn on automatic hyphenation.

3. Change the column width of the columns in the body of the newsletter to 1.9".

4. Add a vertical rule (line) between each column.

5. Change the style of the pull-quote (text box) to 'Light 1 Outline, Colored Fill - Dark Green, Accent 3' (Drawing Tools Format tab | Shape Styles group).

6. Format the first paragraph with a drop cap.

7. Change the alignment of the paragraph containing the drop cap from left-aligned to justified.

8. Change the layout of the SmartArt graphic to Converging Radial.

9. Use the Text Pane to add the text, Building Automation, to the empty shape in the SmartArt graphic. Verify that the font size of text in the top and bottom shapes is 14 point and 11 point, respectively.

10. If necessary, move the SmartArt graphic and the pull-quote so that they are positioned similarly to the ones in Figure 7–76.

11. Change the color of the page border to Orange, Accent 5, Lighter 40%.

12. If requested by your instructor, add your name to the left of the text, Weekly Newsletter, in the issue information line.

13. If the newsletter flows to two pages, reduce the size of elements such as WordArt or pull-quote, or adjust spacing above or below paragraphs so that the newsletter fits on a single page. Make any other necessary adjustments to the newsletter.

14. Save the modified file with the file name, Apply 7–1 Energy Saver Newsletter Modified.

15. Submit the revised newsletter in the format specified by your instructor.

16. ✳ When you use hyphenation to divide words at the end of a line, what are the accepted guidelines for dividing the words? *Hint:* Use a search engine to search the text, end of line hyphenation.

Figure 7–76

Extend Your Knowledge

Extend the skills you learned in this module and experiment with new skills. You may need to use Help to complete the assignment.

Adding Equations to a Newsletter and Enhancing a Nameplate

Note: To complete this assignment, you will be required to use the Data Files. Please contact your instructor for information about accessing the Data Files.

Instructions: Run Word. Open the document, Extend 7–1 Frosh Tips Newsletter Draft, from the Data Files. You will add equations to the newsletter, change the format of the WordArt, format the drop cap, adjust the hyphenation rules, move the page border closer to the text, clear tabs, and insert leader characters.

Perform the following tasks:

1. Use Help to learn about equations, WordArt options, borders, hyphenation, and tabs.

2. Insert the equations shown in Figure 7–77 in the newsletter in their appropriate locations. *Hint:* Use the 'Insert an Equation' arrow or 'Insert an Equation' button (Insert tab | Symbols group).

3. Change the WordArt by adding at least two WordArt style text effects. Change the color of the WordArt text outline. Change the color of the WordArt text fill color.

4. Add a shape fill color to the text box surrounding the WordArt.

5. Add a drop cap to the first paragraph in the body of the newsletter. Change the number of lines to drop from three to four lines. Change the distance from the text to 0.1".

6. Change the hyphenation rules to limit consecutive hyphens to two.

7. Change the page border so that the border is closer to the text.

8. If the newsletter flows to two pages, reduce the size of elements, such as WordArt or the pull-quote or the table, or adjust spacing above or below paragraphs so that the newsletter fits on a single page. Make any other necessary adjustments to the newsletter.

9. Clear the tabs in the issue information line in the nameplate. Use the Tabs dialog box to insert a right-aligned tab stop at the 7" mark. Fill the tab space with a leader character of your choice.

10. If requested by your instructor, change the word, Freshman, in the issue information line to your last name.

11. Submit the revised newsletter in the format specified by your instructor.

12. ✳ Which equations are predefined in Word? Which structures are available on the Equation Tools Design tab? How do you change the alignment of an equation?

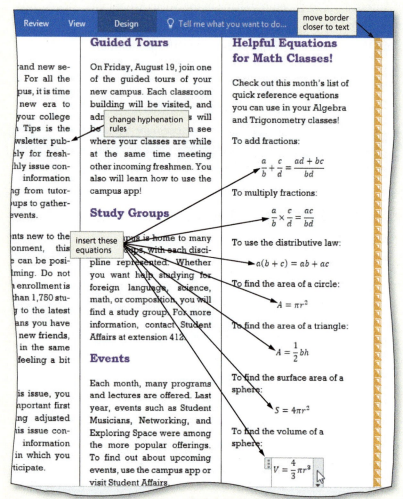

Figure 7–77

Expand Your World

Create a solution that uses cloud or web technologies by learning and investigating on your own from general guidance.

Using Windows Essentials

Instructions: You have heard that Windows Essentials includes some useful programs, so you decide to learn about it, download it, and use its programs.

Note: You may be required to use your Microsoft account to complete this assignment. If you do not have a Microsoft account and do not want to create one, read the assignment without performing the instructions.

Perform the following tasks:

1. Run a browser. Search for the text, Windows Essentials, using a search engine. Click a link to learn about Windows Essentials.

2. Navigate to the website to download Windows Essentials (Figure 7–78) and then follow the instructions to download Windows Essentials.

3. One at a time, run each program included with Windows Essentials. Browse through the features and functions of each program.

4. ✳ What programs are included with Windows Essentials? What is the purpose of each program? Which programs will you use and why?

Figure 7–78

In the Labs

Design, create, modify, and/or use a document following the guidelines, concepts, and skills presented in this module. Labs 1 and 2, which increase in difficulty, require you to create solutions based on what you learned in the module; Lab 3 requires you to apply your creative thinking and problem-solving skills to design and implement a solution.

Lab 1: Creating a Newsletter with a Pull-Quote (Text Box) and an Article on File

Note: To complete this assignment, you will be required to use the Data Files. Please contact your instructor for information about accessing the Data Files.

Problem: You are an editor of the newsletter, *Vintage Living.* The next edition is due out in one week (Figure 7–79). The text for the articles in the newsletter is in a file on the Data Files. You need to create the nameplate and the text box for the pull-quote.

Perform the following tasks:

1. Change all margins to .75 inches. Depending on your printer, you may need different margin settings. Change the theme to Retrospect.

2. Create the nameplate using the formats identified in Figure 7–79. Create the title using WordArt. Set the WordArt wrapping to 'Top and Bottom'. If necessary, drag the bottom of the WordArt up to shorten the image. Dimensions of WordArt should be approximately 1.41" x 7.06". Set a right-aligned custom tab stop at the right margin.

Continued >

In the Labs *continued*

3. Below the nameplate, enter the heading, Purchasing an Old House: Part 1, as shown in the figure. Format the heading using the Heading 1 style. Change the spacing above this paragraph to 24 pt and the spacing after to 12 pt.

4. Create a continuous section break below the heading, Purchasing an Old House: Part 1.

5. Format section 2 to three columns.

6. Insert the Lab 7–1 Purchasing an Old House - Part 1 Article file, which is located on the Data Files, in section 2 below the nameplate.

7. Format the newsletter according to Figure 7–79. Insert a column break before the heading, Brick and Stone. Columns should have a width of 2.1" with spacing of 0.35". Place a vertical rule between the columns.

8. If necessary, insert a continuous section break at the end of the document to balance the columns.

9. Format the subheads using the Heading 2 style.

10. Insert a text box using the Retrospect Quote built-in text box. The text for the pull-quote is in the Paint section of the article. Split the window. Use the split window to copy the text and then paste it in the text box. Remove the split window. Change the fill color (shape fill) of the text box to Brown, Accent 4. Change the font to 12-point Bookman Old Style. Resize the text box so that it is similar in size to Figure 7–79. Position the text box as shown in Figure 7–79.

11. Add the page border as shown in the figure.

12. If the document does not fit on a single page, adjust spacing above and below paragraphs.

13. If requested by your instructor, change the word, Weekly, in the issue information line to your name.

14. Save the document with Lab 7–1 Vintage Living Newsletter as the file name and then submit it in the format specified by your instructor.

15. ✳ This newsletter used a pull-quote. What other text in the newsletter could appear in the pull-quote?

WordArt:
- style – Fill - Tan, Accent 1, Outline - Background 1, Hard Shadow - Accent 1;
- font – 72-point bold Harrington
- text outline – Orange, Accent 1
- text fill – gradient preset – Radial Gradient - Accent 1; second and fourth stop color – Tan, Accent 5, Darker 50%; direction – From Center
- text effect shape (transform) - square

Vintage Living

Weekly Newsletter   Issue 36

Purchasing an Old House: Part 1   [heading]

[subhead]

When purchasing an old house with the intent of saving money, you must be aware of several potential hidden costs. Many ... unchecked, can lead ... expected costs after you have closed a sale. Once you have located a potential house for purchase, therefore, you should inspect (or hire a professional to inspect) all areas of the home.

[Tan, Accent 5, Darker 50%]

Part 1 of the Purchasing an Old House article in this issue of *Vintage Living* discusses some checks for the exterior. Three common home ... ... and stone.

[pull-quote]

Paint
If the house is painted, look for peeling, checking, and chalking.

Peeling is when the paint has lifted from the wall (like orange peels). Peeling usually is caused from old paint or poor insulation.

When a house is poorly insulated, heat escapes and moisture develops.

If the paint is older than seven years, peeling is natural. When a house is insulated poorly, heat escapes and moisture develops. The moisture saturates the wood while trying to escape. In these cases, the house has to be reinsulated by removing the outside or inside walls to make the paint stick.

Checking is when the paint has little cracks on its surface with a rough-looking finish. Checking is caused by insufficient drying time between coats or poor-quality paint. To correct a checking problem, you have to remove the paint by stripping or sandblasting it and then repaint.

Chalking is when the paint surface is dull and powdery. It is caused from the use of oil-based paints. To correct chalking, simply wash the wall surface. Be aware, though, that each time the surface is washed, the paint becomes thinner.

Brick and Stone
If the house has brick ... if it is a solid brick w... brick. Solid brick v... have a header brace every third or fourth row with full bricks in the wall. A header brace is full bricks laid the opposite direction. Veneer brick, the most common today, is an outside layer of brick attached to an existing studded wall, giving the appearance of an all-brick home. Although veneer brick can look fine, check for these potential problems: moisture in the wood, termites, and poor insulation.

Stone houses are a lot like veneer brick houses in their construction and potential problems. The major difference is stone houses are much more expensive because of construction methods.

Next Issue – Part 2
Next week's issue, which is the second of a four-part article about items to look for when purchasing an old house, covers these areas of the house: foundation, crawl space, and roof.

[31-point Orange, Accent 1, Darker 50% double bottom border]

[31-point Orange, Accent 1, art page border]

Figure 7–79

Lab 2: **Creating a Newsletter with a SmartArt Graphic and an Article on File**

Note: To complete this assignment, you will be required to use the Data Files. Please contact your instructor for information about accessing the Data Files.

Problem: You are responsible for the monthly preparation of the newsletter called *Health Check*. The next edition discusses technology-related repetitive strain injuries (Figure 7–80). This article already has been prepared and is on the Data Files. You need to create the nameplate, the SmartArt graphic, and the section at the bottom of the newsletter.

Perform the following tasks:

1. Change all margins to .75 inches. Depending on your printer, you may need different margin settings. Change the document theme to Droplet.

2. Create the nameplate using the formats identified in Figure 7–80. Create the title using WordArt. Set a right-aligned custom tab stop at the right margin. Set the WordArt wrapping to Top and Bottom. If necessary, drag the bottom of the Word Art up to shorten the image. Search for and insert an image of a check mark, similar to the one shown in the figure (the exact image is located on the Data Files). Resize and rotate the image as shown in the figure. Format the image as Behind Text and position the image as shown.

3. Below the nameplate, enter the heading, Technology-Related Repetitive Strain Injuries, as shown in the figure.

4. Create a continuous section break below the heading.

5. Format section 2 to two columns.

6. Insert the Lab 7–2 Health Risks for Technology Users Article file, which is located on the Data Files, in section 2 below the nameplate.

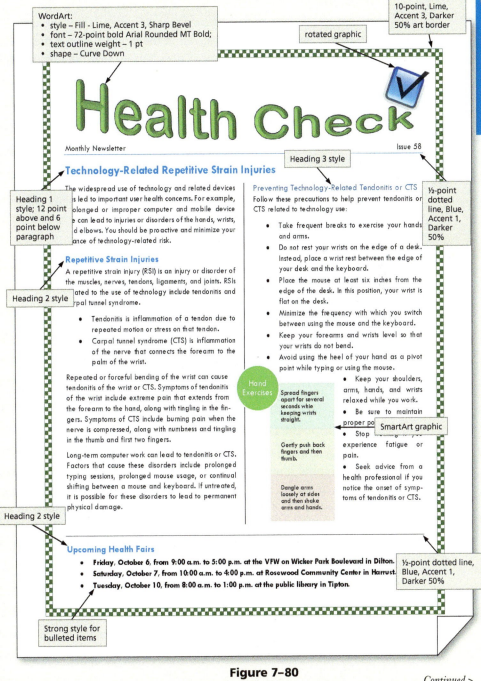

Figure 7–80

Continued >

In the Labs *continued*

7. Format the newsletter according to Figure 7–80. Columns should have a width of 3.33" with spacing of 0.35". Place a vertical rule between the columns.

8. Use Word's automatic hyphenation feature to hyphenate the document.

9. Insert a continuous section break at the end of the last bulleted item in the second column to balance the columns.

10. In the next section, change the number of columns from two to one. Enter the text shown at the bottom of the newsletter.

11. Add the page border as shown in the figure.

12. Open a new document window and create the SmartArt graphic shown in Figure 7–80. Use the Stacked List layout. Because this newsletter has only one list, delete the shapes for the second list. Add the text shown in the figure (you will need to add shapes to this list). Resize the border of the SmartArt graphic to the edges of the list shapes. Use the Office Clipboard to copy and paste the SmartArt graphic from the current window to the newsletter. Change the wrapping to tight. Resize the pasted graphic as shown in the figure. Change the colors to Colorful Range - Accent Colors 3 to 4. Edit wrap points as necessary so that the text wrapping is similar to the figure. Note that your graphic may look slightly different from the figure due to variations in the shape size.

13. If the document does not fit on a single page, adjust spacing above and below paragraphs.

14. If requested by your instructor, change the community center name from Rosewood to your last name.

15. Save the newsletter using Lab 7–2 Health Check Newsletter as the file name and submit it in the format specified by your instructor.

16. ✳ How many sections are in this newsletter? How many columns are in each section? If you wanted to add a second page to this newsletter, what type of section break would appear at the end of the first page?

Lab 3: Consider This: Your Turn

Create a Newsletter about ATM Safety

Note: To complete this assignment, you will be required to use the Data Files. Please contact your instructor for information about accessing the Data Files.

Problem: As a part-time employee at a local bank, you have been assigned the task of creating a newsletter called *Bank News*, which will be available to all patrons. The article in Issue 28 of the *Bank News* newsletter covers ATM safety. The text for the article is in a file called Lab 7–3 ATM Safety Article on the Data Files.

Part 1: The newsletter should contain at least two of these graphical elements: an image, a SmartArt graphic, a pull-quote, or a table. Enhance the newsletter with a drop cap, WordArt, color, ruling lines, and a page border. Be sure to use appropriate desktop publishing elements, including a nameplate, columns of text, balanced columns, and a variety of font sizes, font colors, and shading. Use the concepts and techniques presented in this module to create and format the newsletter. Be sure to check spelling and grammar of the finished newsletter. Submit your assignment in the format specified by your instructor.

Part 2: ✳ You made several decisions while creating the newsletter in this assignment: how to organize and format the nameplate (location, content, formats, arrangement of text and graphics, ruling lines, etc.), which two graphics to use (image, SmartArt graphic, text box, or table), and how to organize and format the body copy (columns, formats, headings and subheads, color, vertical rules, etc.). What was the rationale behind each of these decisions? When you proofread the document, what further revisions did you make and why?

Index

Note: **Boldfaced** page numbers indicate key terms

A

accounts
 signing in to Windows 10, OFF 6–7
 signing out from Microsoft, OFF 36
actions, undoing and redoing, WD 22–23
active tab, **OFF 16**
adding
 text in tables, WD 169
 text to shape, WD 129–130
add-in software, **PA-10**
additions to documents, WD 43
address bar, **OFF 27**
AddressBlock merge field, **WD 334**
 editing, WD 336
 inserting, WD 335–336
addressing envelope, WD 172
Adobe Reader, **WD 285**
American Psychological Association (APA), **WD 58**
animation emphasis effects, **PA-8**
app(s)
 exiting Office, OFF 51
 exiting Office, with one document open, OFF 40
 Microsoft Office 2016, OFF 7–8
 obtaining Help while working, OFF 57–58
 Office Mix, PA-12
 opening Help Window, OFF 54
 running from File Explorer, OFF 49–50
 running using Search box, OFF 44
 running using Start menu, OFF 9–11
 switching from one to another, OFF 29–30
Augmented reality with Office Mix, teaching, PA-13
AutoComplete, **WD 271**
AutoCorrect
 building block *vs.*, WD 155
 creating entry, WD 75–76
 definition, **WD 74**
 dialog box, WD 77
 entering more text, WD 77–78

AutoCorrect Options button, WD 75
AutoFormat As You Type options, WD 145
automatically updated properties, **WD 42**
automatic page breaks
 definition, **WD 91**
 editing sources, WD 93–94
 entering text, WD 94
 inserting citation placeholder, WD 91
 white space, hiding and showing, WD 92–93

B

background repagination, **WD 91**
Backstage view
 closing file, OFF 47–48
 creating new document from, OFF 45–46
 opening recent file using, OFF 48
banner, **WD 378**
bibliographical list, **WD 96**
 creating, WD 96–98
bibliography, **WD 95**
bibliography style, changing, WD 78–79
blank document, creating, OFF 9–11
blank line, inserting, WD 5–6
blank paragraph, WD 240
body copy, **WD 10**
body of letter, WD 338–339
bold, **WD 27**
border, **WD 143**
 in paragraphs, WD 143–144
border color, changing, WD 137
bordering
 another paragraphs, title page, WD 191
 paragraphs, title page, WD 189–190
 tables, WD 238
brightness, in graphics, WD 136
browser, testing webpages, WD 302–303
building block, **WD 282**
 AutoCorrect *vs.*, WD 155
 creating, WD 152–153
 definition, **WD 152**
 editing properties, WD 284

inserting, WD 154–155, WD 282–284
 modifying, WD 153–154
Building Blocks Organizer, **WD 282**
bulleted list
 definition, **WD 21**
 paragraph, WD 21–22
bullet symbol, WD 141
business letter, WD 121–123
 common styles, WD 148
 creating, WD 147
 elements, WD 148
 printing, WD 171
 saving, WD 171

C

card, **PA-6**
cell(s)
 definition, **WD 157**
 merge, WD 167–168
 splitting table, WD 168
centering
 another paragraph in pictures, WD 31
 page contents vertically, WD 41–42
 paragraph, WD 13
 table contents, WD 164–165
character(s)
 bold, WD 27
 formatting, **WD 11**
 formatting single *vs.* multiple, WD 14
 formatting, title page, WD 188–189
 keyboard shortcuts, WD 71
citation
 bibliography style, changing, WD 78–79
 creating its sources, WD 79–81
 description, WD 78
 entering more text, WD 81–82
 inserting, WD 79–81
 placeholder, inserting, WD 83–84
clear formatting, WD 144–145
Click and Type feature, WD 70
clip, **PA-11**
closing file, Backstage view, OFF 47–48
color
 border, changing, WD 137
 changing theme, WD 29

creating documents for, WD 29
text, WD 24
transparent, setting, WD 135–136
using, **WD 12**
color scheme, WD 29
column(s)
deleting in tables, WD 231–232
distributing in tables, WD 234
inserting in tables, WD 235
summing in tables, WD 239–240
columns
inserting in table, WD 167
resizing in tables, WD 161–162
selecting table, WD 162
column width, tables, WD
223–224, WD 230–231, WD
237
command, **OFF 9**
comparison operator, WD 341
complimentary close, **WD 148**
condition, **WD 341**
content control, **WD 262**
deleting, WD 266–267
modifying, WD 265–266
modifying text in, WD 269
replacing placeholder text, WD
265–266, WD 271, WD 275
copying, **WD 101**, WD 102
folder to OneDrive, OFF 40–42
graphics, WD 138–139
copying and pasting table items,
resume template, WD 275–277
Cortana, **PA-14**
in Microsoft Edge, PA-14–16
count words, WD 90–91
creating
AutoCorrect entry, WD 75–76
bibliographical list, WD 96–98
blank document from File
Explorer, OFF 48–49
blank document, Office 2016,
OFF 9–11
building block, WD 152–153
business letter, WD 147
citation sources, WD 79–81
data sources, WD 326–330
documents, color, WD 29
folders, OFF 26–27
folder within folder, OFF 28
footer, WD 211–214
header, WD 211–214
letterhead, WD 124–125

multilevel numbered lists, WD
219–221
new document from Backstage
view, OFF 45–46
webpage from Microsoft Word
2016, WD 298–303
Creative Commons license, **PA-7**
current date, inserting, 151
custom dictionary
setting default, WD 108
viewing and modifying, WD 108
customizing bullets, lists, WD
217–219
custom tab stop, WD 149–150
cutting, **WD 101**

D

data field, **WD 325**
data record, **WD 325**
data source
addressing and printing, mailing
labels, WD 354–359
creating new, WD 326–330
definition, **WD 325**
editing records, WD 332
entering records, WD 330–331
finding and displaying data, WD
353
guidelines, WD 326
saving, WD 331–332
sorting data records, WD 352
using existing, WD 332–333
date line, **WD 148**
deleting
blank paragraph, tables, WD 240
bullet list, WD 169–170
column, tables, WD 231–232
content control, WD 266–267
data tables, WD 169–171
file, OFF 53
page break, WD 209
rows, resume template, WD 277
rows, tables, WD 232
section break, WD 205
shapes from SmartArt graphics,
WD 196
text, WD 44
text, resume template, WD
273–274
deletions to documents, WD 43
destination document, **WD 420**

dialog boxes, navigating, OFF
33–36
Dialog Box Launcher, **OFF 14**
dictionaries, main and custom, WD
107–111
dimension of table, **WD 157**
directory, **WD 361**
changing page orientation, WD
361
converting text to table, WD
364–365
merging to, WD 362–363
merging to new document, WD
364
modifying and formatting table,
WD 366
sorting table by multiple columns,
WD 366–367
displaying
data source records, main
document, WD 353
field codes, WD 343
formatting marks, WD 5
Paste Options menu, WD 103
rulers, 72
rulers, tab stop, WD 149
distributing
columns, WD 234
rows, WD 235
Docs.com, Microsoft, **PA-8**
Document Inspector, WD 297
document properties, **OFF 22**
documents
automatically updated properties,
WD 42
centering page contents vertically,
WD 41–42
color creation for, WD 29
creating new document from
Backstage view, OFF 45–46
deleting text, WD 44
distributing, OFF 23
entering text, OFF 21, OFF 47,
OFF 50
formatting marks, WD 5
graphic file location, WD 31
inserting blank line, WD 5–6
inserting current date, 151
inserting shapes, WD 125–126
left-aligned, **WD 12**
moving text, WD 44–45
navigating, WD 10–11
opening, WD 43

printing, OFF 23–24, WD 45–46, WD 111
revising, WD 42
saving, WD 42, WD 45–46, WD 111
Spelling and Grammar Check icon, WD 8–10
standard properties, WD 42
switching read mode, WD 46
switching to print layout view, WD 46–47
text inserting in existing document, WD 43–44
types of changes, WD 43
wordwrap, WD 7
zooming, WD 33–34
document settings, changing, WD 60–64
document theme, **WD 131**
document window, **OFF 12**
double-space, **WD 62**
download, **WD 31**
drawing canvas, **PA-3**
drawing object, **WD 125**
drop cap, **WD 403**
  formatting, WD 404
  formatting characters, WD 403

E

editing
  AddressBlock merge field, WD 336
  citations, WD 88–89
  hyperlinks, Microsoft Word 2016, WD 301
  lists, WD 215–221
  records, data source, WD 332
  sources, WD 86–88, WD 93–94
  text, resume template, WD 277
endnote, **WD 82**
  working with, WD 89–91
enhancing pages, WD 38–42
envelope
  addressing, WD 172
  labels and, WD 173
  printing, WD 172
envelopes
  addressing, WD 360
  printing, WD 360
error, correcting, WD 42
exiting
  Office apps, OFF 51

Office apps, with one document open, OFF 40
Word, WD 42
expression, WD 341

F

false text, WD 341
field codes, **WD 343**
  displaying, WD 343
  printing in main document, WD 344
field name, **WD 325**
file(s)
  closing in Backstage view, OFF 47–48
  definition, **OFF 7**
  deleting, OFF 53
  moving, OFF 52
  opening existing, OFF 45
  organizing, OFF 25–27
  renaming, OFF 51–52
  saving existing file with same file name, OFF 50
  saving in folder, OFF 47
  saving in folders, OFF 30–33
  saving with new file name, OFF 50–51
File Explorer
  creating new blank document, OFF 48–49
  running app from, OFF 49–50
File Explorer window, OFF 27
file management, **OFF 51**
file name, **OFF 23**
file types, WD 291–292
filtered web page format, **WD 298**
finding
  synonym, WD 105–106
  text, WD 103–104
Find Next button, WD 105
first-line indent, **WD 72**
'First Line Indent' marker, **WD 72**
First-Line Indent paragraphs, WD 72–74
fitting table contents, WD 161–162
flipping graphics, WD 140
floating object, **WD 127**
flyer. See also documents
  adding page borders, WD 39–40
  decisions for next, WD 47
  described, WD 1–3

format usage, WD 12
  text in, WD 10
folder(s), **OFF 9**
  copying to OneDrive, OFF 40–42
  creating, OFF 26–27
  organizing, OFF 25–27
  saving file in, OFF 30–33, OFF 47
folder window, **OFF 27**
  collapsing folder, OFF 28–29
  creating folder within folder, OFF 28
  expanding folder, OFF 28–29
  scroll through folder contents, OFF 28–29
font
  changing selected text, WD 16–17
  definition, **WD 12**
  WordArt text, WD 383
font color, changing title page, WD 190–191
font set, **WD 242**
font size
  changing selected text, WD 15, WD 20–21
  definition, **WD 12**
  WordArt text, WD 383
footer, **WD 64**
  creating, WD 211–214
  inserting formatted, WD 213
footnote
  definition, **WD 82**
  entering text, WD 83
  inserting citation placeholder, WD 83–84
  inserting footnote reference mark, WD 82–83
  working with, WD 89–91
Footnote Text style
  editing citations, WD 88–89
  editing sources, WD 86–88
  modifying style using shortcut menu, WD 84–86
formatted footer, WD 213
formatted header, WD 211–213
formatting
  character, **WD 11**
  characters in title page, WD 188–189
  clear, WD 144–145
  clearing in title page, WD 193–194
  definition, **WD 11**
  letters, WD 319–320

lists, WD 215–221
paragraph, **WD 11**
paragraphs with hanging indent, WD 98
single *vs.* multiple characters, WD 14
single *vs.* multiple paragraphs, WD 14
text using keyboard shortcuts, WD 71
usage in flyer, WD 12
using mini toolbar, WD 25–26
formatting marks
definition, **WD 5**
displaying, WD 5
free-response quiz, **PA-12**
Full Screen mode, **OFF 17**

G

gallery, **OFF 14**
gesture
definition, **OFF 3**
touch screen, OFF 3
gradient, **WD 384**
graphics
border color changing, WD 137
brightness adjusting, WD 136
changing color of, WD 134–135
contrast of, WD 136
copying, WD 138–139
file location, documents, WD 31
flipping, WD 140
moving, WD 138–140
resizing, WD 34–35, WD 133–134
setting transparent color, WD 135–136
using Paste Options, WD 139
zooming, WD 34–35
green computing, **OFF 23**
GreetingLine merge field, **WD 337**
editing, WD 338
gridlines, **WD 222**
hiding, tables, WD 238
showing in tables, WD 222–223
viewing, resume template, WD 264
group, **OFF 14**

H

hanging indent, **WD 98**
Hanging Indent marker, **WD 98**

hard copy, **OFF 23**
hard page break, **WD 95**
header
closing, WD 68
creating, WD 64–68, WD 211–214
definition, **WD 64**
entering text, WD 66
inserting formatted, WD 211–213
inserting page number, WD 66–67
switching to, WD 65
header record, **WD 325**
headline, **WD 10**
Help window
opening in apps, OFF 54
using Search text box, OFF 56–57
horizontal rule, **WD 378**
horizontal ruler, **WD 72**
HTML (Hypertext Markup Language), **WD 298**
Hub, **PA-14**
hyperlink(s)
converting to text, WD 146
editing, Microsoft Word 2016, WD 301
formatting text, Microsoft Word 2016, WD 300–301
Hypertext Markup Language (HTML), **WD 298**

I

IF field, **WD 340**
If...Then, **WD 340**
If...Then...Else, **WD 340**
'Increase Font Size' button, WD 130
Inked handwriting, **PA-3**
Inking toolbar, **PA-15**
Ink to Math tool, **PA-3**
Ink to Text tool, **PA-3**
inline object, **WD 127**
inserting
AddressBlock merge field, WD 335–336
blank line, WD 5–6
building block, WD 154–155, WD 282–284
citation placeholder, footnotes, WD 83–84
citations, WD 79–81

column break, newsletter, WD 405
columns in table, WD 167
columns, tables, WD 235
continuous section break, newsletter, WD 397
current date, 151
empty table, WD 157–158
existing document in open document, WD 203
file in columns, newsletter, WD 399–400, WD 406
footnote reference mark, WD 82–83
formatted footer, WD 213
formatted header, WD 211–213
next page section break, WD 203–204
next page section break, newsletter, WD 404
nonbreaking space, WD 155–156
Online Picture, WD 131–133
page number, WD 66–67
pictures, WD 31–33
pictures in nameplate, WD 390–391
rows in table, WD 165–166
shapes, WD 125–126
SmartArt graphics, WD 195–196
symbols from Symbol dialog box, WD 141–142
symbols from Symbol gallery, WD 142–143
synonym, WD 105–106
text box, pull-quote, WD 407
text in existing document, WD 43–44
WordArt, WD 381–382
inside address, **WD 148**
business letter, WD 152
issue information line, **WD 378**
italic text, **WD 23**

K

keyboard shortcuts, **OFF 5, WD 71**
KeyTips, **OFF 15**

L

labels, envelope and, WD 173
landscape orientation, **WD 361**

lecture in OneNote, recording, PA-4
left-aligned document, **WD 12**
Left Indent marker, **WD 72**
letterhead
  business letter, WD 121–123
  contents of, WD 124–125
  creating, WD 124–125
  definition, **WD 124**
  placement and appearance, WD 125
letters
  changing pictures, WD 320–321
  changing user name and initials, WD 319
  creating folder while saving, WD 324–325
  identifying document, using Mail Merge task pane, WD 316–318
  margin settings, WD 322
  sender information, entering and formatting, WD 319–320
  shading cells, WD 321–322
  specifying position of graphics, WD 323–324
  starting Mail Merge from existing document, WD 319
  theme colors, changing, WD 319
line break, resume template, WD 272–273
lines
  insering blank, WD 5–6
  multiple selection, WD 20
  selecting, WD 14
line spacing
  changing, WD 62–63
  definition, **WD 62**
list(s)
  applying style using mini toolbar, WD 216
  creating multilevel numbered, WD 219–221
  customizing bullets, WD 217–219
  editing, WD 215–221
  formatting, WD 215–221
  sorting paragraphs, WD 215
  using Format Painter button, WD 216–217
live preview, **OFF 14**
lock screen, **OFF 5**
looking up information, WD 108–109

M

mailing labels, addressing and printing, WD 354–359
Mail Merge task pane
  merged letters to new document, WD 346–347
  previewing merged letters, WD 345–346
main document, **WD 333**
  displaying data source records, WD 353
  displays next step, Mail Merge wizard, WD 333
  entering date, WD 334
  entering more text, WD 340
  entering remaining text, WD 342–343
  guidelines for form letter, WD 333
  inserting IF field, WD 341–342
  inserting merge field, WD 339–340
  opening, WD 345
  printing field codes, WD 344
  viewing merged data, WD 337–338
manual page break, **WD 95**
margin settings, changing, WD 123–124
maximize
  definition, **OFF 11**
  Word window, OFF 11–12
merge cells, WD 167–168
merge field, **WD 334**
  correcting errors, merged documents, WD 348
  editing AddressBlock merge field, WD 336
  highlighting, WD 343
  inserting AddressBlock merge field, WD 335–336
  inserting in main document, WD 339–340
merge field characters, **WD 334**
merge/merging, **WD 314, WD 345**
  cells in tables, WD 235–236
  directory, WD 362–363
  form letters to new document using ribbon, WD 350–351
  form letters to printer, WD 348
  removing merge condition, WD 351
  selecting records, WD 348–349

message, **WD 148**
.mht extension, **WD 298**
Microsoft Access 2016, **OFF 8**
Microsoft Account Area, **OFF 15**
Microsoft account, signing out, OFF 36
Microsoft Edge, PA-14
  annotating webpages, PA-15
  browsing web with, PA-14
  inking with, PA-16
  locating information with Cortana, PA-14–15
  tools, PA-14
  using Cortana in, PA-16
Microsoft Excel 2016, **OFF 8**
Microsoft Office 365, **OFF 8**
Microsoft Office 2016
  apps, OFF 7–8
  creating blank document, OFF 9–11
  definition, **OFF 7**
  printing, saving, and organizing files, OFF 23–36
  renaming, moving, deleting files, OFF 51–53
  running and using, OFF 9–21
  running app using Start menu, OFF 9–11
  suites, OFF 8
Microsoft Office Online, **OFF 8**
Microsoft OneNote 2016, **OFF 8**
Microsoft OneNote Mobile app, **PA-2**
Microsoft Outlook 2016, **OFF 8**
Microsoft PowerPoint 2016, **OFF 8**
Microsoft Publisher 2016, **OFF 8**
Microsoft Word 2016, **OFF 7**
  changing style sets, WD 301–302
  creating webpage, WD 298–303
  customizing email attachments, WD 297–298
  Document Inspector, WD 297
  editing hyperlink, WD 301
  file types, WD 291–292
  formatting text as hyperlink, WD 300–301
  getting sharing link, WD 295
  inviting others to view/edit, WD 293–294
  opening PDF file from, WD 287–288
  removing watermark, WD 296

running Compatibility Checker, WD 289
saving as webpage, WD 298–299
saving in earlier word format, WD 289–291
saving word as PDF, WD 285–286
sending document using email, WD 296–298
setting default save location, WD 300
testing webpage in browser, WD 302–303
viewing PDF, Adobe Reader, WD 285–286
minimized window, **OFF 33**
mini toolbar
  formatting text using, WD 25–26
  ribbon, **OFF 14**
Modern Language Association of America (MLA), **WD 58**
  documentation style, WD 58–60
  parenthetical references, WD 58
  works cited, WD 60
modifying
  building block, WD 153–154
  content control, WD 265–266
  custom dictionary, WD 108
  directory, WD 366
  to documents, WD 43
  style, WD 61–62
mouse, Windows 10, OFF 3–4
moving
  file, OFF 52
  graphics, WD 138–140
  text, WD 44–45
  windows, OFF 54–55
multilevel lists, **WD 219**
  creating, WD 219–221

N

nameplate, **WD 378**
  changing color of graphic, WD 391
  crop of graphic, WD 392
  designing, WD 381
  inserting pictures, WD 390–391
  inserting WordArt, WD 381–382
  moving graphic, WD 393
  object's text wrapping and size, WD 393
  rotating graphic, WD 394
  Selection task pane, WD 393–394

setting custom tab stops, using Tabs dialog box, WD 387–388
navigating
  definition, **OFF 33**
  dialog boxes, OFF 33–36
  documents, WD 10–11
navigation pane, **OFF 28**
newsletter, formatting first page
  adding art page border, WD 425
  adjusting spacing before and after paragraph, WD 396
  changing number of columns, WD 397–398
  clear formatting, WD 395–396
  drop cap, WD 403–404
  finishing, WD 424–426
  formatting text as heading style, WD 396
  guidelines, WD 395
  hyphenation features, WD 402
  increasing column width, WD 400–401
  inserting column break, WD 405
  inserting continuous section break, WD 397
  inserting file in column, WD 399–400, WD 406
  inserting next page section break, WD 404
  justifying paragraph, WD 398–399
  modifying heading style, WD 396
  saving, printing and exit word, WD 426
  turning off formatting marks, WD 424
  zooming multiple pages, WD 424
newsletter, formatting second page
  adding border, WD 415
  balance columns, WD 416
  changing colum formatting, WD 412–414
  entering text, WD 415
  formatting text, WD 415
  setting custom tab stops using Tabs dialog box, WD 414
nonbreaking space
  definition, **WD 155**
  inserting, WD 155–156
Normal style, **WD 60**
note, PA-2
note reference mark, **WD 82**
note text, **WD 82**

O

object's position, changing, WD 127–128
object's text wrapping, changing, WD 128, WD 137–138
Office 365, **OFF 8**
Office apps. *See* app(s)
Office Clipboard, **WD 101**
Office Mix, PA-10
  adding to PowerPoint, PA-10
  capturing video clips, PA-11
  inserting quizzes, live webpages, and apps, PA-12
  marketing travel destination with, PA-13
  for OneNote, PA-13
  sharing presentation, PA-12
  teaching augmented reality with, PA-13
OneDrive
  copying folder to, OFF 40–42
  definition, **OFF 8**
  saving file on, OFF 34–35
  unlinking account, OFF 42–43
OneNote 2016
  converting handwriting to text, PA-13–14
  creating notebook, PA-2
  creating Office Mix for, PA-13
  organizing research paper, PA-5
  recording lecture, PA-4
  syncing notebook to cloud, PA-2–3
  taking notes, PA-3
Online Picture, inserting, WD 131–133
Online Sway Newsletter, creating, PA-9
open document
  inserting existing document in, WD 203
  inserting word document, WD 205–206
  printing specific pages, WD 207–208
  saving with new file name, WD 203
opening
  existing file, OFF 45
  Help Window in apps, OFF 54
  recent file using Backstage view, OFF 48
operating system (OS), **OFF 2**
OS (operating system), **OFF 2**

P

page(s)
  adding borders, WD 39–40
  centering contents vertically, WD 41–42
  enhancing, WD 38–42
  zooming, WD 28, WD 40
  zooming multiple, WD 109–110
page break, inserting manually, WD 95
page number, inserting, WD 66–67
page width, zooming, WD 30
paragraph(s)
  bordering another, title page, WD 191
  bordering, title page, WD 189–190
  bottom border, WD 143–144
  bulleted list, WD 21–22
  centering, WD 13
  centering another, WD 13
  centering another, in pictures, WD 31
  changing spacing before and after, WD 40–41
  First-Line Indent, WD 72–74
  formatting, **WD 11**
  formatting single *vs.* multiple, WD 14
  formatting with hanging indent, WD 98
  indent changing, left/right, WD 192–193
  indenting, resume template, WD 274–275
  keyboard shortcuts, WD 71
  removing space after, WD 63–64
  right-aligning, WD 66
  shading, WD 19
  shading, title page, WD 190–191
  sorting, lists, WD 215
  spacing, **WD 62**
  spacing after, title page, WD 192
parenthetical references, **WD 58**
password, **OFF 5**
Paste Options menu, displaying, WD 103
pasting, **WD 101,** WD 102
path, **OFF 25**
PDF (Portable Document Format), **WD 285**
picture(s)
  applying effects, WD 37–38

applying style, WD 36–37
  centering another paragraph, WD 31
  inserting, WD 31–33
  inserting and formatting in documents, WD 31–38
  inserting in nameplate, WD 390–391
  in letters, WD 320–321
  resizing, WD 34–35
placeholder, inserting citation, WD 83–84
planning proposal, **WD 185**
point, **WD 12**
Portable Document Format (PDF), **WD 285**
portrait orientation, **WD 361**
PowerPoint, adding to Office Mix, PA-10
presentation (PowerPoint)
  creating Sway, PA-6–7
  sharing Office Mix, PA-12
previewing, merged letters, WD 345–346
Previous Locations arrow, **OFF 27**
printing
  business letter, WD 171
  documents, OFF 23–24, WD 45–46, WD 111
  envelope, WD 172
  envelopes, WD 360
  field codes, main document, WD 344
  mailing labels, using data source, WD 354–359
  specific pages in document, WD 207–208
Print Layout view, **OFF 12**
printout, **OFF 23**
proofreading, **WD 98**
  Go to page, WD 101
  modifying source, WD 99
  updating field, WD 99–100
publishing, **WD 304**
pull-quote, **WD 378,** WD 406
  adding shape style, text box, WD 411
  copy and paste using split windows, WD 409–410
  formatting text, text box, WD 410
  guidelines, WD 407
  inserting text box, WD 407
  positioning text box, WD 411–412
  removing split windows, WD 410

resizing, text box, WD 410–411
  split window, WD 408–409

Q

Quick access area, **OFF 28**
Quick Access Toolbar
  customizing, OFF 20–21
  ribbon, **OFF 15**
  using shortcut menu to relocate, OFF 19–20

R

Reading view, **PA-14**
  viewing online news with, PA-16
read mode
  changing, WD 110–111
  definition, **WD 46**
  switching, **WD 46**
record, **WD 325**
Recycle Bin, **OFF 7**
Redo button, actions, WD 22–23
Refresh button, **OFF 27**
relocating, Quick Access Toolbar, OFF 19–20
removing
  space after a paragraph, WD 63–64
  watermark, Word 2016, WD 296
renaming file, OFF 51–52
Replace All button, WD 105
replacing text, WD 104–105
research paper
  Click and Type feature, WD 70
  definition, **WD 57**
  name and course information, WD 69
research proposal, **WD 185**
resizing, **WD 34**
  graphics, WD 133–134
  table columns, WD 161–162
  text box, WD 410–411
  windows, OFF 55
responsive design, **PA-6**
Restart command, OFF 6
restoring window, OFF 33–34
resume, **WD 257**
  crafting successful, WD 262
resume template
  applying style, WD 280
  changing theme colors, WD 263
  content control, WD 262

content control, replacing placeholder text, WD 265–266, WD 271, WD 273, WD 275
copying and pasting items, table cell, WD 269–270
copying and pasting table items, WD 275–277
creating style, WD 279–280
customizing theme fonts, WD 278–279
deleting content control, WD 266–267
deleting rows, WD 277
deleting text, WD 273–274
editing text, WD 277
entering line break, WD 272–273
entering more text, WD 272
general steps, WD 262–263
indenting paragraph, WD 274–275
modifying content control, WD 265–266
modifying text, content control, WD 269
modify style using Style dialog box, WD 281–282
moving table rows, WD 267–269
reveal formatting, WD 280
setting custom margins, WD 263–264
using AutoComplete, WD 271
viewing gridlines, WD 264
revising documents, WD 42
ribbon, **OFF 28**
collapsing and expanding, OFF 17–19
dispalying different tab, OFF 16–17
folder windows, OFF 28
Full Screen mode, OFF 17–19
KeyTips, OFF 15
mini toolbar, OFF 14
Quick Access Toolbar, OFF 15
Tell Me box, OFF 14
Word window, OFF 12–15
right-aligning, **WD 66**
paragraph, WD 66
row(s)
changing height, tables, WD 224–225
changing text font in tables, WD 168–169
deleting, resume template, WD 277

deleting, tables, WD 232
distributing, tables, WD 235
inserting in table, WD 165–166
rulers, WD 72
displaying in tab stop, WD 149
ruling line, **WD 378**

S

sales proposal, **WD 185**
project details, WD 186–188
salutation, **WD 148**
business letter, WD 152
sandbox, PA-15
saving
business letter, WD 171
data source, WD 331–332
document as different file type, WD 292
document in earlier word format, WD 289–291
documents, WD 42, WD 45–46, WD 111
document with new file name, WD 147
existing file with same file name, OFF 50
file in folders, OFF 30–33, OFF 47
file on OneDrive, OFF 34–35
file with new file name, OFF 50–51
open document with new file name, WD 203
webpage, Microsoft Word 2016, WD 298–299
word document as PDF, WD 285–286
word document as XPS document, WD 288
screen clipping, PA-15
screen recording, **PA-11**
screen resolution
changing, OFF 38–39
definition, **OFF 37**
ScreenTip, **OFF 14**
scroll, **WD 10**
scroll arrows, **OFF 4**
scroll bar, **OFF 4**
Word window, OFF 12
scroll box, **OFF 4**
Search box, **OFF 27**
running using apps, OFF 44
using Windows, OFF 59

Search text box, obtaining Help window using, OFF 56–57
section
applying heading styles, WD 209–210
clear formatting, WD 205
definition, **WD 203**
deleting page break, WD 209
deleting section break, WD 205
inserting next page section break, WD 203–204
inserting word document in open document, WD 205–206
spacing before and after paragraph, WD 210
updating style for matching selection, WD 210–211
section tab, **PA-2**
selecting
groups of words, WD 26
lines, WD 14
multiple lines, WD 20
table columns, WD 162
table contents, WD 163–169
text, techniques, WD 30
shade, **WD 19**
shading
cells, tables, WD 226–227
paragraph, WD 19
removing cell, tables, WD 237–238
selected cells, tables, WD 229
title page, paragraphs, WD 190–191
shape(s)
adding, SmartArt graphics, WD 197–198
adding text, WD 129–130
adding text to, SmartArt graphics, WD 197
applying style, WD 129
deleting, SmartArt graphics, WD 196
inserting, WD 125–126
shortcut menu, **OFF 19**
modifying Footnote Text style using, WD 84–86
Shut down command, OFF 6
signature block, **WD 148**
signature line, **WD 10**
signing in, to Windows 10 accounts, OFF 6–7
signing out, Microsoft account, OFF 36

sign-in screen, **OFF 5**

single file web page format, **WD 298**

Sleep command, OFF 6

Slide Notes, **PA-11**

slide recording, **PA-11**

small caps, **WD 200**

SmartArt graphics, **WD 194**
 adding shapes, WD 197–198
 adding shape to, WD 418
 adding text through Text pane, WD 419
 adding text to shapes, WD 197
 applying SmartArt style, WD 199
 changing colors of, WD 198–199
 changing layout of, WD 417–418
 copying, using Office Clipboard, WD 420
 deleting shapes from, WD 196
 editing wrap points, WD 423–424
 format characters, Font dialog box, WD 200–201
 formatting, WD 422
 formatting graphic as floating, WD 422
 formatting text, WD 419–420
 inserting, WD 195–196
 modifying character spacing, Font dialog box, WD 200–201
 one page zooming, WD 201–202
 open document from word, WD 417
 pasting from Office Clipboard, WD 421
 positioning, WD 422
 setting zoom level, WD 201–202
 switching documents, WD 420–421
 types, WD 194

SmartArt style, WD 199

soft page breaks, **WD 91**

sorting
 data records, data source, WD 352
 paragraphs, lists, WD 215
 table by multiple columns, directory, WD 366–367
 tables, WD 227–228

source document, **WD 420**

spacing paragraph, title page, WD 192

Spelling and Grammar Check icon, WD 8–10

splitting cells, tables, WD 232–233

splitting table, WD 168

splitting table cells, WD 168

standard properties, **WD 42**

Start button, **OFF 9**

starting Windows 10, OFF 5–7

Start menu, **OFF 9**

status bar
 Spelling and Grammar Check icon, WD 8
 Word window, **OFF 12**

Storyline, **PA-6**

style
 applying, WD 147–148
 applying in tables, WD 160–161
 applying picture, WD 36–37
 business letter, WD 148
 definition, **WD 36, WD 60**
 modifying, WD 61–62
 Normal, WD 60
 updating to match selection, WD 64

subhead, **WD 378**

suite, **OFF 8**

Sway
 adding content to build story, PA-7
 creating presentation, PA-6–7
 creating Sway resume, PA-9
 designing, PA-8
 presentation, PA-9
 publishing, PA-8
 sharing, PA-8

Sway site, **PA-6**

switching
 to header, WD 65
 from one to another apps, OFF 29–30
 to print layout view, WD 46–47
 read mode, **WD 46**

Symbol dialog box, inserting symbols, WD 141–142

symbols
 bullet, WD 141
 inserting from Symbol dialog box, WD 141–142
 inserting from Symbol gallery, WD 142–143

sync, **PA-2**

synonym
 definition, **WD 105**
 finding, WD 105–106
 inserting, WD 105–106

T

tab
 active, OFF 16
 definition, **OFF 14**
 tool, OFF 14

tab character, **WD 149**

table(s)
 adding text, WD 169
 aligning data in cells, WD 225–226
 applying style, WD 160–161
 bordering, WD 238
 changing cell spacing, WD 229–230
 changing column width, WD 223–224, WD 230–231, WD 237
 changing row height, WD 224–225
 changing text font in rows, WD 168–169
 definition, **WD 157**
 deleting blank paragraph, WD 240
 deleting column, WD 231–232
 deleting data, WD 169–171
 deleting rows, WD 232
 dimension, **WD 157**
 displaying text in vertically, WD 236
 distributing columns, WD 234
 distributing rows, WD 235
 entering data, WD 158–159
 hiding gridlines, WD 238
 inserting columns, WD 235
 inserting empty, WD 157–158
 inserting rows, WD 165–166
 merging cells, WD 235–236
 moving cell boundaries, WD 233–234
 moving cell contents, WD 233
 page breaking manually, WD 231
 removing cell shading, WD 237–238
 resizing columns, WD 161–162
 sales proposal draft, WD 222
 selecting columns, WD 162
 selecting nonadjacent items, WD 228–229
 shading cells, WD 226–227
 shading selected cells, WD 229
 showing gridlines, WD 222–223
 sorting, WD 227–228

splitting, WD 168
splitting cells, WD 232–233
summing columns, WD 239–240
table contents
  centering, WD 164–165
  data alignment in cells, WD 163–164
  fitting, WD 161–162
  selecting, WD 163–169
tab stop, **WD 149**
  alignments, WD 149
  displaying rulers, WD 149
  setting custom, WD 149–150
task pane, **OFF 14**
Tell Me box, **OFF 14**, OFF 58
template(s), PA-2, **WD 257**. *See also* resume template
  creating new document from online, WD 259–261
  opening document created from, WD 262
text. *See also* documents; paragraph
  adding in tables, WD 169
  applying text effect to selected, WD 18
  AutoCorrect, WD 77–78
  bold, WD 27–28
  bold selected, WD 131
  changing case of selected, WD 17
  changing font for selected, WD 16–17
  changing font size for selected, WD 20–21
  citations in, WD 81–82
  color, WD 24
  deleting, WD 44
  deleting, resume template, WD 273–274
  editing, resume template, WD 277
  entering, WD 3–11
  entering in document, OFF 47, OFF 50
  finding, WD 103–104
  in flyer, WD 10
  formatting and entering, WD 140
  formatting single *vs.* multiple paragraphs and characters, WD 14
  formatting using mini toolbar, WD 25–26
  format using keyboard shortcuts, WD 71

inserting in existing document, WD 43–44
  italicize, WD 23
  moving, WD 44–45
  replacing, WD 104–105
  selecting multiple lines, WD 20
  selecting, techniques, WD 30
  shade, WD 19
  typing, WD 4
  underlining, WD 27
  wordwrap, WD 7
  wrapping options, WD 127
  zooming page, WD 28
  zoom page width, WD 6, WD 30
text box
  adding shape style, WD 411
  formatting text, WD 410
  inserting, WD 407
  positioning, WD 411–412
  resizing, WD 410–411
theme, **WD 12**
  changing color, WD 29
theme colors
  letters, WD 319
theme colors, resume template, WD 263
theme fonts, resume template, WD 278–279
thesaurus, **WD 105**
title page
  bordering another paragraph, WD 191
  bordering paragraphs, WD 189–190
  changing font color, WD 190–191
  clearing formats, WD 193–194
  definition, **WD 188**
  designing, WD 188
  formatting characters, WD 188–189
  indent changing, left/right paragraphs, WD 192–193
  shading paragraphs, WD 190–191
  spacing after paragraph, WD 192
To Do tag, PA-2
tool tabs, **OFF 14**
touch keyboard, WD 5
touch screen, WD 5
  gestures, OFF 3
  Windows 10, OFF 3–4
transparent color, graphics, WD 135–136
true text, WD 341
typing text, WD 4

U
underlining text, WD 27
Undo button, actions, WD 22–23
unlinking OneDrive account, OFF 42–43
user account, **OFF 5**
user icon, **OFF 5**
user name, **OFF 5**

V
vertical rule, **WD 378**
vertical ruler, **WD 72**
viewing
  custom dictionary, WD 108
  gridlines, resume template, WD 264
  merged data, main document, WD 337–338
  PDF, Adobe Reader, WD 285–286
  Print Layout, Word, OFF 12
virus, **WD 31**

W
watermark, **WD 240**
  changing theme fonts, WD 242–243
  creating, WD 241–242
  removing, Word 2016, WD 296
Web Note, **PA-15**
webpage(s)
  saving as, Microsoft Word 2016, WD 298–299
  testing in browser, WD 302–303
web page format, **WD 298**
white space, hiding and showing, WD 92–93
windows
  minimized, OFF 33–34
  moving by dragging, OFF 54–55
  resizing by dragging, OFF 55
  restoring, OFF 33–34
Windows 10
  introduction to, OFF 2–7
  keyboard shortcut, **OFF 5**
  operating system, OFF 2
  roadmap, OFF1–2
  scrolling, OFF 4
  signing in to accounts, OFF 6–7
  starting, OFF 5–7

using touch screen and mouse,
OFF 3–4
Windows desktop 10, OFF 7
Windows search box, OFF 59
Word. *See also* documents
creating blank document, OFF
9–11
entering text in document,
OFF 21
exiting, WD 42, WD 111
roadmap, OFF1–2
running, WD 43, WD 60
running app using Start menu,
OFF 9–11
WordArt, **WD 381**
bordering one edge of paragraph,
WD 389–390
changing fill color, WD 384–386
changing object's text wrapping,
WD 383–384
entering text, WD 389

inserting, WD 381–382
resizing, WD 382–383
setting custom tab stops, using
Tabs dialog box, WD 387–388
shape, WD 387
Word window
document window, **OFF 12**
maximize, OFF 11–12
Print Layout view, **OFF 12**
ribbon, OFF 12–15
scroll bar, OFF 12
status bar, OFF 12
wordwrap, **WD 7**
works cited, **WD 60**
works cited page
applying style, WD 96
centered text, WD 96
creating bibliographical list, WD
96–98
definition, **WD 95**
page break manually, WD 96

X
XML Paper Specification (XPS),
WD 288
XPS (XML Paper Specification),
WD 288

Z
zooming
100%, WD 35–36
document, WD 33–34
graphic, WD 34–35
multiple pages, WD 109–110,
WD 241
multiple pages, newsletter, WD
424
one page, WD 28, WD 40
one page, SmartArt graphics, WD
201–202
page width, WD 30
setting zoom level, WD 201–202